ESSENTIALS OF INVESTMENTS

ESSENTIALS OF INVESTMENTS

Zvi Bodie
Boston University

Alex Kane
University of California, San Diego

Alan J. Marcus
Boston College

IRWIN

Homewood, IL 60430
Boston, MA 02116

This symbol indicates that the paper in this book is made from recycled paper. Its fiber content exceeds the recommended minimum of 50% waste paper fibers as specified by the EPA.

3 2280 00475 3182

© RICHARD D. IRWIN, INC., 1992

Sponsoring editor:	Michael W. Junior
Developmental editor:	Thomas G. Sharpe
Project editor:	Waivah Clement
Production manager:	Bob Lange
Art manager:	Kim Meriwether
Art:	Caliber
Compositor:	Weimer Typesetting Co., Inc.
Typeface:	10/12 Times Roman
Printer:	Von Hoffmann Press

Library of Congress Cataloging-in-Publication Data

Bodie, Zvi.
  Essentials of investments / Zvi Bodie, Alex Kane, Alan J. Marcus.
    p.   cm.
  ISBN 0-256-09815-8
    1. Investments. I. Kane, Alex,   II. Marcus, Alan J.   III. Title.
HG4521.B563   1992
332.6—dc20   91–27711

Printed in the United States of America
1 2 3 4 5 6 7 8 9 0 VH 8 7 6 5 4 3 2 1

To our families with love and gratitude.

About the Authors

Zvi Bodie
Boston University

Zvi Bodie is professor of finance and economics at the Boston University School of Management. He is the former director of Boston University's Chartered Financial Analysts Examination Review Program and has served as a consultant to many private and governmental organizations. Professor Bodie is a research associate of the National Bureau of Economic Research, where he was director of the NBER Project on Financial Aspects of the U.S. Pension System, and he is a member of the Pension Research Council of The Wharton School. He is also currently a member of the Financial Accounting Standards Board Task Force on Interest Methods. Professor Bodie is widely published in leading professional journals, and his previous books include *Pensions in the U.S. Economy, Issues in Pension Economics, Financial Aspects of the U.S. Pension System*, and most recently *Pensions and the Economy: Sources, Uses and Limitations of Data.*

Alex Kane
University of California, San Diego

Alex Kane is a professor of finance and economics at the Graduate School of International Relations and Pacific Studies at the University of California, San Diego, and is a research associate of the National Bureau of Economic Research in the Financial Markets and Monetary Economics Group. The author of many articles published in finance and management journals, Professor Kane's research is mainly in the areas of portfolio management, capital markets, and corporate finance. With a newly designed experimental laboratory which serves as a training center for decision makers, Professor Kane has been studying the formation of price expectations and the structure of equilibrium asset prices. Professor Kane has been named the Yamaichi Visiting Professor of Finance at the University of Tokyo for 1991.

Alan J. Marcus
Boston College

Alan Marcus is associate professor of finance in the Wallace E. Carroll School of Management at Boston College and a research fellow at the National Bureau of Economic Research, where he participates in the Financial Markets and Economics Group. He received his Ph.D. in Economics from MIT in 1981. His main research interests are futures and options markets. He has published widely in these and related fields. Professor Marcus's consulting work has ranged from new product development to provision of expert testimony in utility rate proceedings. He recently spent two years at the Federal Home Loan Mortgage Corporation (Freddie Mac) where he developed models of mortgage pricing and credit risk.

Preface

In no other field, perhaps, is the transfer of theory to real-world practice as rapid as it is now in the financial industry. New securities and trading strategies derived from financial theory emerge continually. As a result, the line between finance practitioners and theorists has become increasingly fuzzy. A solid grounding in principles is required for all those who participate in the markets and work with the instruments now commonly traded.

Essentials of Investments is intended as a textbook on investment analysis. Our goal has been to present this material in a framework organized around a central core of consistent fundamental principles. These principles are crucial to understanding the securities already traded in financial markets and in understanding new securities that will be introduced in the future. We have eliminated unnecessary mathematical detail and concentrated on the intuition and insights that will be useful to practitioners throughout their careers as new ideas and challenges emerge from the financial marketplace.

Our goal has been to convey insights of practical value. We believe—and hope you will agree—that many of the topics in this book also are of considerable intellectual interest. To us, this is one of the most pleasing features of finance as an academic field. The centerpieces of modern finance have been intellectually important subjects of inquiry and, indeed, have affected much of the broader field of economics. Still, they remain of immense practical importance for the sophisticated investor.

We also have attempted to make our approach to investments consistent with that of the **Institute of Chartered Financial Analysts, (ICFA)** a subsidiary of the **Association of Investment Management and Research (AIMR).** In addition to fostering research in finance, the AIMR and ICFA administer an education and certification program to candidates for the title of **Chartered Financial Analyst (CFA).** The CFA curriculum represents the consensus of a committee of distinguished scholars and practitioners regarding the core of knowledge required by the investment professional. You will see from the end-of-chapter problem sets that the material in this text is consistent with and relevant to the CFA curriculum. Moreover, Chapters 2 and 3, which present an overview of the investment process and strategies, are modeled after the ICFA outline.

What Is Special about This Text?

The exposition in this book is special in several ways. First, this book is thematic, meaning we never offer rules of thumb without reference to the central tenets of the modern approach to finance. Rather than present a mass of loosely connected material, we instead treat all topics within a common framework holding that security markets are nearly efficient, meaning most securities are usually priced appropriately given their risk and return attributes. There are few free lunches found in markets as competitive as the financial market. This simple observation is, nevertheless, remarkably powerful in its implications for the design of investment strategies, and our discussions of strategy are always guided by the implications of the market efficiency hypothesis. While the degree of market efficiency is, and will always be, a matter of debate, we hope our discussions throughout the book will convey a good dose of healthy criticism concerning much conventional wisdom.

Second, this text places greater emphasis on asset allocation than most of its competitors do. Asset allocation refers to an investor's choice among broad asset classes, such as stock versus bond markets, rather than the choice of specific securities within an asset class. We prefer this emphasis for two important reasons. First, it corresponds to the procedure that most individuals actually follow. Typically, one starts with all of one's money in a bank account, only then considering how much to invest in something riskier that might offer a higher expected return. The logical step at this point is to consider other risky asset classes, such as stock, bonds, or real estate. This is an asset allocation decision. Second, in most cases the asset allocation choice is far more important in determining overall investment performance than is the set of security selection decisions. Asset allocation is the primary determinant of the risk-return profile of the investment portfolio, and so it deserves primary attention in a study of investment policy.

Third, this text has a much broader and deeper treatment of futures, options, and other derivative security markets than most of its competitors have. These markets have become crucial and integral to the financial universe and are the major sources of innovation in that universe. One has no choice but to become conversant in these markets if one is to be a finance professional, or simply a sophisticated individual investor.

Organization and Content

The text is composed of six sections that are fairly independent and may be studied in a variety of sequences. Since there is enough material in the book for two one-semester courses, clearly a one-semester course will require the instructor to decide which parts to include and which to exclude. The Instructor's Manual that accompanies the text offers several alternative syllabi for a one- or a two-course sequence in investments.

Part I is introductory and contains some interesting institutional material. Chapters 1 and 2 lay out the general framework of the investment process. This part of the book should be of special interest to students participating in the CFA program. Chapter 3 is a description of the financial environment that contains useful background information for the student of investments.

Chapter 4 is an overview of the types of securities traded in financial markets: fixed-income, equities, options, and futures contracts. It presents a complete list of security types, describes their main features, and explains how to read security listings in the financial pages of the newspaper. The emphasis throughout the chapter is on understanding the essential features of the financial instruments without getting bogged down in unnecessary detail.

Chapter 5 explains how and where securities are traded. It starts from the issuance of new securities in the primary market, explains the securities exchanges and the over-the-counter market and how they operate, and then gives a thorough but not overly detailed presentation of the mechanics of trading. It goes through the types of orders an investor might give and explains the meaning and mechanics of buying and short-selling. It also discusses the costs of trading, how to choose a broker, and the use of mutual funds and other investment companies by the individual investor.

The material presented in Chapters 4 and 5 should make it possible for the instructor to assign term projects early in the course. These projects might require the students to analyze in detail a particular security or group of securities. Many instructors like to involve their students in some sort of invetment game, which gets them to simulate the process of real-world investing. The material in these two chapters is intended to facilitate this.

Part II contains the core of modern portfolio theory. Chapter 6 introduces the fundamental concepts of expected return, risk, risk aversion, and diversification. Chapter 7 develops the model of portfolio optimization with a risk-free asset and a single risky asset, and Chapter 8 generalizes it to encompass many risky assets.

The level of analysis in this part of the book is as nontechnical as possible without being operationally useless. The computer software diskette provided free to adopters of the book contains a portfolio optimization program that is quite easy to use.

Chapter 9 discusses the equilibrium structure of expected rates of return on risky assets. Topics covered include the capital asset pricing model and the arbitrage pricing theory.

Chapter 10 treats the efficient markets hypothesis. It gives rigorous definitions of the alternative forms of the hypothesis, explains the rationale behind it, and summarizes in some detail the evidence for and against it.

Chapter 11 addresses the evaluation of portfolio performance. It develops the theory behind some of the popularly used risk-adjusted performance measures and explains the methods of evaluating whether a portfolio manager has superior market timing or security selection ability.

Part III, which focuses on the analysis and valuation of fixed-income securities, is the first of three parts devoted to security valuation. The other two deal with equity securities and derivative securities. For a course emphasizing security analysis and excluding portfolio theory, one may proceed directly from Part I to Part III with no loss in continuity.

Chapter 12 introduces the fundamentals of bond pricing and yield calculations and the term structure of interest rates. Chapter 13 deals with fixed-income investment strategies, including the concepts of duration and immunization.

Part IV is devoted to equity securities. Chapter 14 treats the broad macroeconomic environment in which all firms operate.

Chapter 15 presents the theory of equity valuation, primarily discounted dividend models of progressively greater degrees of complexity and realism. It attempts to reach the level of sophistication at which professional security analysts employ these models. Chapter 16 is devoted to fundamental analysis, including the analysis of financial statements, the preparation of earnings forecasts, and other applied techniques used in trying to identify mispriced common stocks. Chapter 17 is an overview of technical analysis.

Part V covers derivative assets, such as options, futures contracts, and convertible securities. It contains two chapters on options and one on futures. Chapter 18, the first of two chapters on options, is a general introduction to options markets and securities with optionlike features. Chapter 19 contains material on the theory of option valuation.

Chapter 20 is an introduction to futures contracts. It explains the kinds of contracts traded, their uses in hedging and in speculating, and the equilibrium relationships between spot and futures prices. It takes a closer look at several selected futures contracts.

Part VI presents extensions of previous material. Chapter 21 is a treatment of portfolio strategy and market equilibrium that accounts for international assets and nontraditional assets. Chapter 22 develops the theory of active portfolio management. It attempts to integrate the material on security analysis in Parts IV through V with the material on portfolio selection in Part II by addressing the question of how to combine securities that you believe are mispriced into an efficiently diversified overall portfolio. To the best of our knowledge, the material in this chapter has never before appeared in a textbook.

Pedagogical Features and Ancillary Materials

This book contains several features designed to make it easy for the student to understand, absorb, and apply the concepts and techniques presented. Each chapter begins with an overview, which states the objectives of the chapter and describes the material to be covered, and ends with a detailed summary, which recapitulates the main ideas presented.

Learning investments is in many ways like learning a new language. Before one can communicate, one must learn the basic vocabulary. To facilitate this process, all new terms are presented in **boldface** type the first time we use them, and at the end of each chapter a **Key Terms** section lists the most important new terms introduced in that chapter. A **Running Glossary** of all of the terms used appears in the margins of each chapter.

Boxes containing short articles from business periodicals are included throughout the book. We think they enliven the text discussion with examples from the world of current events. The article in the Prologue from *The Wall Street Journal* on the recent Nobel prizewinners in financial economics is an example. We chose the boxed material on the basis of relevance, clarity of presentation, and consistency with good sense.

A unique feature of this book is the inclusion of **Concept Checks** in the body of the text. These self-test questions and problems enable the student to determine whether he or she has understood the preceding material and to reinforce that understanding. Detailed solutions to all these questions are provided at the end of the book.

These Concept Checks may be approached in a variety of ways. They may be skipped altogether in a first reading of the chapter with no loss in continuity. They can then be answered with any degree of diligence and application upon the second reading. Finally, they can serve as models for solving the end of-chapter problems assigned by the instructor.

Each chapter also contains a list of **Selected Readings** annotated to guide the student toward useful sources of additional information in specific subject areas.

The **end-of-chapter problems** progress from the simple to the complex. We strongly believe that practice in solving problems is a critical part of learning investments, so we have provided lots of problems. Many are taken from CFA examinations and therefore represent the kinds of questions that professionals in the field believe are relevant to the "real world." These problems are identified by an icon in the text margin.

Software is available for use with the text. *The Innovative Investor,* Version 2A, prepared by David Shinko, consists of a set of LOTUS 1-2-3® templates designed to provide undergraduate business students quick access to difficult financial calculations: stocks, bonds, callables and convertibles, options, futures, asset allocation, portfolio performance evaluation and more! All spreadsheets come complete with comprehensive "What-if" analysis, and automatic graphing and printing capabilities. These user-friendly capsules are designed to solve many problems a student of investments might encounter, beginning with chapter problems in the textbook, but continuing to other real-world problems encountered in a career as a financial analyst or as a sophisticated individual investor. Together with the text, the software enables students not only to process calculations, but to ask questions of the software and build upon the intuition established in the text.

The **Instructor's Manual,** prepared by Joe Walker, that accompanies this text provides instructors with an annotated lecture note outline of each chapter. This manual has been structured with utility in mind. Outlines are formatted so that instructors may add their own notes, and pages have been perforated so that they may be removed and organized in any arrangement. Incorporated in the outlines are perspectives that offer the instructor alternative approaches to teaching particular topics, alert them to areas where students typically have problems in understanding concepts, and suggest solutions to these problems. In addition, the outlines direct instructors to optimal places where specific overhead acetates may be integrated into lectures. Detailed solutions have been provided for all of the end-of-chapter questions and problems in the text.

The **Test Bank,** prepared by Elias Raad and David Peters, contains over 750 multiple-choice questions that test students on the topics and concepts covered in the 22 chapters of the text. Approximately 25 percent of these questions are based on questions found on past CFA examinations. A key feature is the five or ten questions in every chapter that may be converted to a problem-solving format by removing the distractors.

Acknowledgments

We received help from many quarters as we prepared this book. An insightful group of reviewers read and commented on the first draft of the text, and another group reviewed the second draft. Their comments and suggestions improved the exposition of the material considerably. These reviewers all deserve special thanks for their contributions.

Randall S. Billingsley
*Virginia Polytechnic
Institute and State
University*

Paul J. Bolster
Northeastern University

David C. Distad
*University of California
at Berkeley*

Peter D. Ekman
Kansas State University

Steven V. Mann
*University of South
Carolina*

Robert J. Martel
Bentley College

Elias A. Raad
Ithaca College

George S. Swales
*Southwest Missouri
State University*

Joe Walker
*University of Alabama
at Birmingham*

Andrew L. Whitaker
North Central College

Thomas J. Zwirlein
*University of Colorado
at Colorado Springs*

For granting us permission to include many of their examination questions in the text, we are grateful to Peggy Slaughter and the Institute of Chartered Financial Analysts.

Much credit also is due to the development and production team: our special thanks go to Mike Junior, sponsoring editor; Tom Sharpe, developmental editor; Waivah Clement, project editor; Bob Lange, production manager; and John Rokusek and Heidi Baughman, designers.

We also thank Lise LePage and Joyce O'Connor for heroic assistance in manuscript preparation.

Finally, once again, our most important debts are to Judy, Hava, and Sheryl for their unflagging support.

Zvi Bodie
Alex Kane
Alan J. Marcus

A Note to the Student

"Knowledge comes by taking things apart, but wisdom comes from putting things together."

We have written this book for you if you want to become a *wise*:

- Investment professional or
- Individual investor.

In either case, your goal should be to gain a clear understanding of financial markets, valuation principles (how to determine the value of a stock, bond, or other financial assets), and the relationship between risk and return. You will learn about a wide range of markets where various financial assets are traded.

As you read the assigned chapters you will encounter various important principles and concepts. We have taken great pains to ensure that the concepts included are all useable and that these practical principles can guide you as you manage your own investments or those of your clients.

After studying this book you will have a command of many of the most important valuation and risk management tools commonly used in the money management industry and of a framework that will enable you to confront new types of securities and problems in a consistent and logical manner. Essentially, you will have the ability to put these together to solve *new* problems. This, we hope, will serve you long into your careers.

We wish you the best as you study from ESSENTIALS OF INVESTMENTS and we hope the text will help you gain an appreciation for this dynamic, exciting field and the rewards it can yield.

Z. B.
A. K.
A. J. M.

List of Boxes

Contents in Brief

Contents

Part One
Elements of Investments

■ ■

Prologue

Investments: What's It All About?

Investment portfolio
Set of securities
chosen by an investor.

Security analysis
Determining the cor-
rect value of a security
in the marketplace.

Portfolio management
Process of combining
securities in a portfolio
tailored to the inves-
tor's preferences and
needs, monitoring that
portfolio, and evaluat-
ing its performance.

This is a book about investing in securities such as stocks, bonds, options, and futures contracts. It is intended to provide an understanding of how to analyze these securities, how to determine whether they are appropriate for inclusion in your **investment portfolio** (the set of securities you choose to hold), and how to buy and sell them.

We can usefully divide the process of investing, both in theory and in practice, into two parts: security analysis and portfolio management. **Security analysis** is the attempt to determine whether an individual security is correctly valued in the marketplace; it is the search for mispriced securities. **Portfolio management** is the process of combining securities into a portfolio tailored to the investor's preferences and needs, monitoring that portfolio, and evaluating its performance. We provide a thorough treatment of both parts of the investment process.

This book is designed first and foremost to impart knowledge of practical value to anyone interested in becoming an investment professional or a sophisticated private investor. It provides a lot of institutional detail, but it also contains a lot of theory. It is impossible to be a sophisticated investor or investment professional today without a sound basis in valuation theory, modern portfolio theory, and option pricing theory.

Like any profession, investment professionals use lingo that is sprinkled with jargon. While one is advised not to overuse buzzwords and jargon, a novice needs to understand this jargon. For this reason, we use jargon often, sometimes adding the lingo in parenthesis. It should be tolerated on these grounds.

Current understanding of the learning process attributes value to repetition and rote exercises. On that premise, we shamelessly repeat the major principles of investments wherever we can without affecting the flow.

Legend has it that a student once approached a renowned conservative scholar and requested that he teach him the Bible while he is standing on one foot. The angry scholar kicked the fresh would-be student right out the door. The student was relentless, and so he approached the best-known liberal scholar with the same query. "This is quite simple," the wise man told the boy. "Thou shalt love thy neighbor as thyself." "Is that all?" gasped the fellow in disbelief. "Oh yes," said the old man with patience. "All the rest is explanations."

In that spirit, here are some of the basic questions that motivate the study of investments, with the short answers. The explanations can be found in the chapters that follow.

The Risk-Return Trade-Off

Is there a perfectly safe investment asset to be found?

No! A perfectly safe asset guarantees future payments that will translate to a fixed amount of purchasing power. First, we require that the promised amount will be paid up, that is, a zero probability of default. A bond that is backed by a credible government that owns the mint is as close as we may get to safety in terms of default. At this stage, we have a nominally risk-free asset.

Second, investors are interested in nominal dollars only for the purchasing power they provide. Purchasing power is measured in units of a specific basket of goods. In sum, a perfectly safe asset would have to pay default-free interest and principal, in amounts linked to the price index of the exact consumption basket of the investor. Such a bond would be a real, risk-free asset.

The safety of assets is relative. A savings account with a U.S. bank that is insured by the Federal Deposit Insurance Corporation (FDIC) is nominally risk free. Junk bonds are IOUs of companies that issued so much debt the probability of bankruptcy is significant. These are risky assets, riskier than many stocks; although, in general, stocks are riskier than bonds.

Why would anyone invest in a risky asset?

This question is relevant because we assume investors are risk averse. Some do engage in gambling, but except for compulsive gamblers, this activity is really part of recreation. When it comes to investing household savings, investors prefer low-risk assets.

The demand for safety will cause prices of safe assets to rise and prices of risky assets to fall, until equilibrium is reached and every asset is sufficiently attractive to be owned by somebody. In the end, a more risk-averse investor will hold safer assets than a more risk-tolerant investor. But the first can *expect* a lower average rate of return than the latter. The *actual* rate of return is unknown at the time the asset is bought—which is the essence of risk.

How do we measure the risk of an investment asset?

It is difficult! (And if the short answer overwhelms you, don't worry. The "explanations" in Chapter 6 and Part Two will make the subject clearer.) The future rate of return on an asset can take on many values, with probabilities that can only be subjectively assessed. It is, in general, impossible to convey a complete description of a future risky rate of return by a single number, or even a short set of statistics. Applying analysis to the return history of an asset is like using a résumé and references to determine the fit of a new hire to an organization. It is helpful, but the agony of making a chancy decision remains.

The actual measurement of the riskiness of an asset derives from three principles:

Expected rate of return The mean or expected value of the rate of return.

1. We identify the reward from holding an asset as its **expected rate of return.** This is the rate we would average if we held the asset over the long run. Technically, it is the weighted average of all possible rates of return, each weighted by its probability.

2. The risk element in the rate of return is the surprise component, that is, the amount of deviation from the expectation. The magnitude and probability of these deviations are used to form various measures of risk. The **variance** is the most widely used. To compute the variance, we take the expected value of the *squared* deviations from the expected rate of return. That is, we compute the weighted average of the squares of all possible surprises, using the probabilities as weights. Usually the variance is used after it has been reduced to the original units (percents) by taking the square root. This measure is called **standard deviation.**

Variance of the dispersion of a random variable.

Standard deviation Square root of the variance.

3. Risk must be viewed in a portfolio context. Investors are primarily interested in the bottom line of their total investments. It follows that investors are interested in the risk (standard deviation) of the rate of return on the entire portfolio, and they will question whether the risk is commensurate with the expected return on the portfolio. To judge an individual asset, we need to know its contribution to the standard deviation of the overall portfolio. That contribution is derived from the *covariance* of the asset rate of return with the portfolio rate of return, which measures the extent to which the rates of return on the asset and the portfolio move in tandem.

In sum, the risk-return trade-off can be conceptualized, quantified (at least approximately), and operationalized by comparing portfolios on the basis of the combination of expected return/standard deviation that they offer. For individual assets, we assess the expected return in relation to the covariance of the asset with the total portfolio.

What is the practical value of investment theory?

We have a full-blown investment theory that explains and anticipates risk-return trade-offs. It carries intuitive appeal that improves our insight into capital market phenomena. But, as in any science, its ultimate value derives from empirical content.

We also have overwhelming documented evidence from historical rates of return on investment assets showing that the degree of risk is correlated with average returns. This implies prices of investment assets adjust to the risk of future returns.

Splicing implications from investment theory with statistical analysis of market data can contribute enormously to improved investment decisions. (To be certified as a chartered financial analyst (CFA) one has to demonstrate knowledge of investment theory and analysis of market data.)

What is the major strategic implication of portfolio theory?

Diversification. Wise men have been advising investors not to put all their eggs in one basket since the dawn of humanity, but it took Nobel laureate Harry

Markowitz, armed with post–World War II mathematical programming, to hatch more efficient diversification strategies. Minimizing portfolio risk for any level of expected rate of return is portfolio theory in a nutshell.

Active versus Passive Management of Investments

What are the essential elements of investment management?

Rebalance the portfolio
Realign the proportions of assets in a portfolio as needed.

The bottom line of the investment process is the purchase of securities until your investment budget is exhausted. These securities make up the investment portfolio. Once established, a portfolio is maintained by: (1) selling existing securities and using the proceeds to buy new securities so as to **rebalance the portfolio** in line with reassessments of asset returns, and (2) increasing or decreasing the investment in the portfolio (by buying or selling an additional proportion of the set of all the securities in the portfolio) to accommodate the net inflow (or outflow) to the investment budget.

Asset allocation
Choosing among broad asset classes such as stocks vs. bonds.

Investment assets can be categorized into asset classes such as stocks, bonds, precious metals, real estate, and so on. Conceptually, a shift from one asset class to another, say from stocks to precious metals, is a higher hierarchy decision than a shift from ABC stock to XYZ stock. Accordingly, you find that investment management is divided into **asset allocation** (deciding how much to invest in each asset class) and **security selection** (deciding on individual securities within each asset class).

Security selection
Choosing the particular securities to include in a portfolio.

How does active investment management differ from passive?

Passive management
Buying a well-diversified portfolio without attempting to search out mispriced securities.

Passive management is a strategy of holding a well-diversified portfolio without attempting to outperform other investors through superior market forecasting or superior ability to find mispriced securities. Passive strategies may be quite sophisticated and surprisingly effective, creating a challenging benchmark for active managers.

Active management
Attempts to achieve portfolio returns more than commensurate with risk, either by forecasting broad market trends or by identifying particular mispriced securities.

Active management can take two forms: market timing and security selection. Active market timing is a particular kind of active asset allocation. The most popular is trying to time the stock market, increasing one's commitment to stocks when one is "bullish" (when one thinks the market will do relatively well) and moving out of stocks when one is "bearish." But active market timing is potentially just as profitable in the market for fixed-income securities, where the name of the game is forecasting interest rates. Successful market timing, whatever the asset class, requires superior forecasting ability.

Security selection is the attempt to find mispriced securities and to improve one's risk-return trade-off by concentrating on such securities. Successful security selection requires sacrificing some diversification. Active management in general is costly in that it requires highly skilled manpower and generates transaction and monitoring costs.

Efficient market hypothesis *The prices of securities fully reflect available information.*

How effective is passive management?

A large body of empirical evidence supports a theory called the **efficient market hypothesis (EMH),** which says that active management of both types should not be expected to work for very long. The basic reasoning behind the hypothesis is that, in a competitive financial environment, successful trading strategies tend to self-destruct. Bargains may exist for brief periods, but with so many talented, highly paid analysts scouring the markets for them, by the time you or I discover them, they are no longer bargains.

There are some extremely successful investors, but according to the EMH, one can account for some or all of them on the basis of luck rather than skill. And even if their success in the past derived from skill at finding some extraordinary bargains, the EMH would say their chances to continue to find more in the future are slight. Even the legendary Benjamin Graham,[1] the father of modern security analysis and the teacher of some of today's investment giants, has said the job of finding true bargains has become difficult if not impossible in today's competitive environment. In part, this situation is testimony to the success Graham and his followers have had teaching the principles of fundamental analysis.

Investment theory does not subscribe to the EMH literally. It holds that markets can achieve only near-efficiency. Otherwise, only fools (or snake-oil merchants with foolish clients) would be actively managing investments. If that were the case, then prices would no longer track fundamental values, thus recreating incentives for experts to move in. Therefore, even in this competitive environment, profit opportunities may exist for especially diligent and creative investors. This idea motivates our treatment of active portfolio management in Chapter 22.

Equilibrium Pricing Relationships

What are the essential implications of investment theory to asset prices?

A fascinating feature of financial markets, and one that is not apparent to the untrained observer, is that prices of securities must have a specific relationship to each other. If the relationships are violated, market forces will restore them. For this reason financial economists refer to them as *equilibrium pricing relationships,* and in this text we explain them in detail.

Perhaps the best-known equilibrium pricing relationships are the following:

1. The security market line (expected return-beta relationship).
2. The put-call parity relationship.
3. The Black-Scholes option pricing model.
4. The spot-futures parity relationship.
5. The international interest rate parity relationship.

These relationships are more than just intellectually pleasing theoretical constructs. In most cases, if they are violated, the first investors to discover the violation have opportunities for large profits with little or no risk. For example, program trading is primarily a systematic method of profiting from violations of equilibrium pricing relationships.

A well-trained investment professional not only must be aware of these equilibrium relationships, but also must understand why they exist and how to profit from any violation of them. We have tried to provide the basis for this knowledge

---

[1]We will have more to say about Graham and his ideas about investing in Part Four.

throughout the book, as well as in the specific chapters in which these relationship are presented and explained.

Are all equilibrium pricing relationships the same?

Equilibrium pricing relationships are of two types. Both require that no asset (or portfolio of assets) dominate another, so that investors will not be compelled to purchase the dominant asset, sell the dominated asset, and thus induce a new equilibrium.

The first and most powerful type of equilibrium pricing relationship is the "*no arbitrage*" requirement, which is an extension of the law of one price. It says that if two portfolios can be constructed (in the simplest case each containing one asset) so that they provide *identical future cash flows under any circumstances,* they must sell for the same price. If two such portfolios sell for different prices, then an **arbitrage opportunity** arises: investors can simultaneously buy the less expensive portfolio and sell the more expensive portfolio. The price difference is a riskless profit, and the opportunity will exist until trade pressures equalize the prices.

Arbitrage opportunity A set of prices that allows for riskless economic profit.

As long as arbitrage opportunities exist, equilibrium cannot prevail, because any investor who bec`  `es aware of them will execute arbitrage trades to the largest possible scale. Thus, it takes only a few informed investors to restore equilibrium where prices leave no arbitrage opportunities. Examples of no-arbitrage conditions are the parity relationships referred to above that provide conditions that must be satisfied by prices on assets in spot and futures markets.

The second type of equilibrium pricing relationships arises from **dominance.** If the price of an asset goes up, then, other things equal, the rate of return from holding the asset must go down and the asset will become less attractive to any investor, and vice versa. If the expected return and risk characteristics make an asset a better buy than other assets, we say it dominates the other assets. Dominance does not guarantee the dominant asset will produce a higher rate of return, only a higher *expected* return per unit of risk. Informed investors will buy more of such an asset, pushing its price up until it no longer dominates other assets.

Dominance   When one portfolio is preferred to another by its risk-return characteristics.

The reason dominance pricing relationships are less powerful than no-arbitrage pricing relationships is that the first do not provide a risk-free profit. As compelling as a dominance trade may be, because it is still risky, each investor will trade only at a limited scale. Hence, the power of this type of relationship to force prices to an equilibrium where no asset dominates another depends on the cumulative effect of a multitude of investors that become informed and take advantage of the opportunity. Nevertheless, the growth and global integration of financial markets, the improved technology of processing and disseminating information, and the proliferation of investment expertise combine to make dominance-driven equilibrium pricing relationships extremely powerful. An example of a dominance relationship is the expected return-beta relationship referred to above, which predicts the relationship between the risk of an asset and its expected rate of return.

What feature best represents the nature of contemporary investments?

In today's securities markets, sophisticated investors have a variety of ways to tailor the set of possible investment outcomes to their specific knowledge or preferences regarding security returns. The emergence of markets for so-called derivative securities such as options and futures contracts has made it possible to implement strategies unheard of only a few years ago.

One of them is portfolio insurance, which has come under fire in the wake of the 1987 stock market crash. An investor can combine stocks and/or bonds with derivative securities in many ways to eliminate the possibility of loss of principal while preserving much of the upside potential of an investment in the stock market. While the portfolio insurance industry has never fully recovered from the October 1987 crash, sophisticated hedging vehicles and strategies are here to stay. The investment professional must understand and master them if he or she is to avoid technological obsolescence.

In our chapters on derivative securities, we explain in some detail and with a minimum of mathematics the use of options and futures in implementing some of the more controversial policies such as program trading, portfolio insurance, and index arbitrage.

The Text and Its Organization

How difficult is the subject matter in this text?

The conceptual difficulty of a subject is often confused with mathematical complexity of the subject matter. But they are different sides of the same coin.

One important difference is that mathematical complexity discriminates against people who could otherwise be valuable, creative experts. Mathematicians would be the first to require that one should strip an argument of any and all unnecessary math. We have done just that.

Investment is not an easy subject matter, however, which is not all bad, or else there would be little challenge in pursuing it. In many instances, oversimplification has left textbooks with slogans, rules of thumb, and inexplicable formulas. We spared no effort to explain the difficult issues as clearly as possible, remaining loyal to the spirit of modern finance.

What are the essential features of the text organization?

The text has six parts, which are fairly independent and may be studied in a variety of sequences. Part One is introductory and contains much institutional detail. The material in this part can be self-taught as an independent assignment.

Part Two contains the core of modern portfolio theory as it relates to optimal portfolio selection and to the equilibrium structure of expected rates of returns on risky assets, that is, equilibrium pricing relationships. Part Three applies economics and investment theory to bond pricing and presents the principles of managing fixed-income investments.

The next two parts are devoted to security analysis and valuation. Part Four is devoted to the analysis of equity securities, and Part Five covers derivative assets such as options, futures contracts, and convertible securities.

Part Six extends the investment framework to international diversification and other types of investments. It also expands on practical issues of active management: market timing and security analysis.

The Investment Field and Career Opportunities

Is academic research relevant to the investments industry?

As with any other field of scientific inquiry, the theory of investments is constantly changing and, we believe, advancing. In that sense, we too are always learning something new. What makes it especially exciting is that the lag between discovery and application in investments is extraordinarily short. For example, the Black-Scholes option pricing formula and the dynamic hedging strategy that is its mainspring were developed in 1973. Just a few years later, practitioners were busy applying it on the Chicago Board Options Exchange.

Can one make a living as an investment professional?

Far from being an exception, the example of the Black-Scholes formula has become the paradigm for the relationship between the academic and applied worlds in investments. Fischer Black and Myron Scholes are examples of this development. Fischer Black has moved from a professorship at Massachusetts Institute of Technology's Sloan School of Management to a full partnership in the investment banking firm of Goldman Sachs, and Myron Scholes, a professor at Stanford's Graduate School of Business, is active at the investment banking, brokerage, and security trading house of Salomon Brothers.

We believe the field of investments offers great opportunities for careers that are both fascinating and lucrative, but the competition is fierce. A mastery of the material in this text will, we hope, give you a competitive advantage.

Key Terms

active management, 6
arbitrage
    opportunity, 8
asset allocation, 6
dominance, 8
efficient market
    hypothesis (EMH), 6

expected rate of
    return, 5
investment portfolio, 3
passive management, 6
portfolio
    management, 3

rebalance the
    portfolio, 6
security analysis, 3
security selection, 6
standard deviation, 5
variance, 5

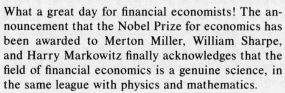

En-Nobeling Financial Economics

What a great day for financial economists! The announcement that the Nobel Prize for economics has been awarded to Merton Miller, William Sharpe, and Harry Markowitz finally acknowledges that the field of financial economics is a genuine science, in the same league with physics and mathematics.

Largely thanks to these three fathers of finance, academics who study corporate finance, investment management and financial markets can walk a little taller around their campuses. Finance has been instrumental in defining the contributions of other Nobel-winning economists, such as James Tobin, Paul Samuelson, and Franco Modigliani. But, finance was not the central subject for these men and their contributions to the field of finance were not responsible for their awards. Messrs. Miller, Markowitz, and Sharpe are pureblood financial economists and their prize-winning contributions are strictly on the subject of finance. What are these contributions to financial knowledge?

Historically, portfolio theory focused on picking "winners." All sorts of ad hoc ideas about security pricing, many found in the still-popular book "Security Analysis" by Benjamin Graham and David Dodd, supported the central investment goal of attempting to pick undervalued stocks to beat the market. Harry Markowitz, a mathematician by training and an expert on statistical theory, began thinking about the statistical properties of security returns around 40 years ago. He published an article called "Portfolio Selection" in the *Journal of Finance* in 1952 and a book by the same title the same year.

Portfolio Risk

Mr. Markowitz defined the risk to owning securities as variance, a familiar statistical concept, and rigorously developed the principles governing how portfolio variance, or risk, is affected by adding and subtracting individual securities from a portfolio, which is simply a combination of securities. The major lesson implied by this math is that portfolios offer far superior returns for given risk (variance) than do individual securities. This insight flew in the face of the conventional practice of emphasizing individual securities in an effort to pick winners. Mr. Markowitz showed that eschewing diversification was enormously risky and could only be justified economically as a general approach if financial markets were unbelievably inefficient.

William Sharpe was the most notable of several financial economists, including names like Treynor, Lintner, Mossin, and Black, who extended Mr. Markowitz's powerful insights and created the revolutionary theories of asset pricing based on Mr. Markowitz's mathematical treatment of security returns and variances. Specifically, William Sharpe, in his 1964 *Journal of Finance* article, "Capital Asset Prices: A Theory of Market Equilibrium under Conditions of Risk," assumed that all investors looked at security risk and return as did Mr. Markowitz. Under these assumptions, Mr. Sharpe developed a model of market equilibrium that showed how the risk of individual securities would be priced in a "Markowitz world."

The main insight here was that only the so-called systematic risk of individual securities (the famous beta risk) would be priced in such a market. The holding of unsystematic risk, which is variance in returns to individual securities that could be eliminated through diversification, would earn no additional return. So, in such a market, diversification was imperative to sensible and successful investing. Refusing to diversify exposed one to additional risk with no market-based prospect for reward.

These contributions were the genesis of a revolution in finance, leading to an explosion of theoretical and empirical advances that has yet to run its course. The emphasis on diversification and portfolio management is at the heart of practical investment management today. Indeed, even program trading, which is really another innovation developed to heighten the efficiency of portfolio management, is a direct descendant of the theoretical innovations of Messrs. Markowitz and Sharpe. Benjamin Graham, the co-author of "Security Analysis"—often called the bible of Wall Street—reportedly repudiated the stock-picking principles underlying his book in a 1974 interview in reaction to the compelling new thinking on efficient capital markets generated by the Markowitz-and-Sharpe revolution of finance.

Merton Miller won his share of the Nobel prize for his contributions to the field of corporate finance, which is mainly the study of corporations' debt and dividend payout policies. Mr. Miller's seminal contribution came in an article co-authored with Franco Modigliani, entitled "The Cost of Cap-

continued

ital, Corporation Finance, and the Theory of Investment," that appeared in the *American Economic Review* in June 1958.

Corporate finance before Mr. Miller was in very sad shape. The study of corporate debt and dividend policies amounted to a series of rules of thumb that simply described widespread practice and justified them logically in consistent, normative assertions. Financial economists in academia were treated as second-class citizens at the universities, and their weak, unpromising body of knowledge deserved this treatment. Mr. Miller's article applied the physics principle of conservation of matter to the study of the value and riskiness of the corporate entity. In his theory the corporation was a stream of expected future cash flows, or profits from operations. These were independent of the financial policies and dividend payout policies of the firm.

Rigorous Analysis
This approach allowed Mr. Miller and his followers to apply rigorous mathematical analysis in understanding how increasing long-term debt levels or changing dividend payout rates affected the overall value of the firm. Two revolutionary principles, called irrelevance propositions, emerged from this early work. First, that the value of the firm is independent of the degree of financial leverage employed by the firm (debt levels are irrelevant to firm value). Second, that the value of the firm is independent of the level of dividends chosen by the firm (dividends, too, are irrelevant). These two propositions, derived mathematically, were completely counterintuitive and caused an enormous academic debate.

In hindsight, it was no contest. Mr. Miller, armed with enormous intelligence, humor, energy, and a genius of a co-author, won over the finance profession and started the field on its way to becoming rich with scientifically rigorous theories and statistically sophisticated empirical knowledge. Mr. Miller has not been the retiring father on the sidelines. Far from it. He remains today the king of corporate finance, paving the way to understanding the important role of taxes in corporate policy and how financial markets for securities and derivative instruments operate in arbitrage equilibriums.

The Nobel Committee has sifted through the hundreds of contributors to the field of financial economics and has succeeded in selecting the genuine founding fathers of the theories on which all of this modern knowledge is based. Many others have made enormous contributions, such as Gene Fama, Myron Scholes, and Robert Merton. These people too deserve serious consideration for future Nobel Prizes. But every academic in the field of financial economics will work a little harder and teach with a little more conviction, for the Nobel Committee has just said to the world that our science is legitimate and important. Congratulations to Merton Miller, Harry Markowitz, and William Sharpe and, from all of us, thank you very much indeed.

Source: Gregg A. Jarrell, "En-Nobeling Financial Economics," *The Wall Street Journal*, October 17, 1990, p. A14. Reprinted by permission of *THE WALL STREET JOURNAL*, © 1990 Dow Jones & Company, Inc. All Rights Reserved Worldwide.

Chapter

The Investment Process: Investor Objectives and Constraints

The investment process is a chain of considerations and actions for an individual, from thinking about investing to placing buy/sell orders for investment assets such as stocks and bonds. Likewise, for institutions such as insurance companies and pension funds, the investment process starts with a mission and a budget and ends with a detailed investment portfolio.

Establishing a clear hierarchy of the investment process is useful. The first step is to determine the investor's objectives. The second step is to identify all the constraints, that is, the qualifications and requirements of the resultant portfolio. Finally, the objectives and constraints must be translated into investment policies. These steps are necessary for both individual and institutional investors.

Individuals' objectives and constraints are greatly affected by their household's stage in the life cycle. A young father's goals are very different from a retired widow's. Institutional investors do the lion's share of investing, however. Their constraints are often compounded by legal restrictions and regulation. After reading this chapter you should be able to:

- Specify investment objectives of individual and institutional investors.
- Identify constraints on individual and institutional investors.

1.1 Making Investment Decisions

Translating the aspirations and circumstances of diverse households into desirable investment decisions is a daunting task. Accomplishing the same task for institutions with many stakeholders, which are regulated by various authorities, is equally perplexing. Put simply, the investment process is not easily programmable into an efficient procedure.

A natural place to look for quality investment procedures is in the offices of professional investors. Better yet, we chose to examine the approach of the Association for Investment Management and Research (AIMR), which was established by a merger of the Financial Analysts Federation (FAF) with the Institute of Chartered Financial Analysts (ICFA).

The AIMR administers three examinations for those who wish to be certified as chartered financial analysts (CFAs). To become a CFA, a candidate must pass exams at Levels I, II, and III, and show a satisfactory record of experience. The AIMR helps CFA candidates by organizing classes and compiling reading materials. Our analysis in this chapter is compiled along the lines of the AIMR model.

The basic idea is to subdivide the major steps (objectives, constraints, and policies) into concrete considerations of the various aspects, making the task of organization more tractable. The standard format appears in Table 1.1. In the next sections, we elaborate briefly (there is a lot more to be said than this text will allow) on the construction of the three parts of the investment process, along the lines of Table 1.1.

Objectives

Risk-return trade-off If an investor is willing to take on risk, there is the reward of higher expected returns.

Portfolio objectives center on the **risk-return trade-off** between the expected return the investors want (*return requirements* in the first column of Table 1.1) and how much risk they are willing to assume (*risk tolerance*). Investment managers must know the level of risk that can be tolerated in the pursuit of a better expected rate of return (see box).

Constraints

Both households and institutional investors restrict their choice of investment assets. These restrictions arise from their specific circumstances. Identifying these restrictions/constraints will affect the choice of investment policy. Five common types of constraints are described below.

Liquidity

Liquidity Liquidity refers to the speed and ease with which an asset can be converted to cash.

Liquidity is the ease (speed) at which an asset can be sold and still fetch a fair price. It is a relationship between the time dimension (how long will it take to dispose) and the price dimension (what discount from fair market price) of an investment asset.

Table 1.1 *Determination of Portfolio Policies*

Objectives	Constraints	Policies
Return requirements	Liquidity	Asset allocation
Risk tolerance	Horizon	Diversification
	Regulations	Risk positioning
	Taxes	Tax positioning
	Unique needs	Income generation

When an actual concrete measure of liquidity is necessary, one thinks of the discount when an immediate sale is unavoidable.[1] Cash and money market instruments such as Treasury bills and commercial paper, where the bid-ask spread is a fraction of 1 percent, are the most liquid assets, and real estate is among the least liquid. Office buildings and manufacturing structures can easily be assessed a 50 percent liquidity discount.

Both individual and institutional investors must consider how likely they are to dispose of assets at short notice. From this likelihood, they establish the minimum level of liquid assets they want in the investment portfolio.

Investment Horizon

Investment horizon
The planned liqui-
dation date.

This is the *planned* liquidation date of the investment or part of it. Examples of an individual **investment horizon** could be the time to fund college education or the retirement date for a wage earner. For a university endowment, an investment horizon could relate to the time to fund a major campus construction project. Horizon needs to be considered when investors choose between assets of various maturities, such as bonds, which pay off at specified future dates.

Regulations

Prudent man law
The fiduciary responsi-
bility of a professional
investor.

Only professional and institutional investors are constrained by regulations. First and foremost is the **prudent man law.** That is, professional investors who manage other people's money have a fiduciary responsibility to restrict investment to assets that would have been approved by a prudent investor. The law is purposefully nonspecific. Every professional investor must stand ready to defend an investment policy in a court of law, and interpretation may differ according to the standards of the times.

Also, specific regulations apply to various institutional investors. For instance, U.S. mutual funds (institutions that pool individual investor money under professional management) may not hold more than 5 percent of the shares of any publicly traded corporation. This regulation keeps professional investors from getting involved in the actual management of corporations.

Tax Considerations

Tax consequences are central to investment decisions. The performance of any investment strategy should be measured by how much it yields (jargon for what its rate of return is expected to be) in real (constant purchasing power) after-tax investment returns. For household and institutional investors who face significant tax rates, tax sheltering and deferral of tax obligations may be pivotal in their investment strategy.

Unique Needs

Virtually every investor faces special circumstances. Imagine husband-and-wife aeronautical engineers holding high-paying jobs in the same aerospace corpora-

---

[1] In most cases it is impossible to know the liquidity of an asset with certainty, before it is put up for sale. In dealer markets (described in Chapter 4), however, the liquidity of the traded assets can be observed from the bid-ask spread that is quoted by the dealers, that is, the difference between the "bid" quote (the lower price the dealer will pay the owner), and the "ask" quote (the higher price a buyer would have to pay the dealer).

Merrill Lynch Asks: How Much Risk Can You Take?

When it comes to investing, how much risk can you stomach?

Merrill Lynch & Co. wants to know.

In coming weeks, the nation's biggest brokerage firm will begin asking the individual investors behind its 7.2 million retail accounts to decide for themselves just how aggressive they're really willing to be in buying stocks, bonds, and other investments.

With the new setup, individual investors will be asked to put themselves in one of four risk categories: "conservative for income," "conservative for growth," "moderate risk," and "aggressive risk." Each category will have its own recommended asset allocation, or investment mix.

Merrill Lynch isn't the only securities firm that wants investors to state more explicitly how willing they are to risk losing money in the pursuit of profit. Earlier this year, Kidder, Peabody & Co., General Electric Co.'s brokerage unit, adopted a five-category asset-allocation model. Some other brokerage firms say they're looking at such setups, too.

Getting investors to pigeonhole themselves in this way can be a good thing because it forces them to come to grips with their feelings about risk. And it gives their stock brokers formal written notice about these desires. The customer's choice "goes into the record," says George Grune, managing director of Kidder Peabody's asset management group.

At the same time, getting investors on record about their risk tolerances is likely to make it easier for a brokerage firm to defend itself if it gets hit with lawsuits or arbitration claims by investors who don't like what their brokers are doing.

An investor who picks the "aggressive risk" category, for example, is agreeing to "move aggressively among asset classes" and deal in "speculative and high-risk issues," according to guidelines distributed to Merrill Lynch brokers last week. Such an investor might have a difficult time claiming that his or her broker was *too* aggressive.

Legal issues like that are a growing concern on Wall Street. Over the past year, brokerage firms have been forced to pay increasingly stiff punitive-damage awards in arbitration cases brought by disgruntled investors.

Brokers are required by securities law to make sure customers are put into "suitable" investments. Unsuitability lawsuits are brought when it's alleged that a broker knew, or should have known, that an investment wasn't consistent with a client's investment objectives.

Merrill Lynch officials stress that such legal concerns aren't the main reason for the new system, although they don't deny they are a factor. The officials say they mainly wanted to be more "flexible" with the firm's asset-allocation recommendations, tailoring the research department's advice on the markets to an investor's general profile.

Avoiding customer disputes is "one of the side benefits, but that's not why it was created in the first place," says John Steffens, president of Merrill Lynch's individual-investor operations. "'The Street,' in my view, in general has dealt with this whole asset-allocation subject a little bit too simplistically," he says.

Sam Scott Miller, a New York securities lawyer, says getting investors to segment themselves according to risk preferences is a "sound and prudent approach" to heading off legal disputes, providing

tion. The entire human capital of that household is tied to a single player in a rather cyclical industry. This couple would need to hedge the risk (find investment assets that yield more when the risk materializes, thus partly insuring against the risk) of a deterioration in the economic well-being of the aerospace industry.

An example of a unique need for an institutional investor is a university whose trustees let the administration use only cash income from the endowment fund. This constraint would translate into a preference for high-dividend-paying assets.

the firms monitor the systems well. Not only should it protect the firm in disputes with customers, it might also be an early warning to a securities firm if one of its brokers is pushing customers into unsuitable investments. If a certain broker "brings in all 'aggressive' accounts, they're going to want to take a look at it," he says.

Some of Merrill Lynch's competitors have less-formal ways of tailoring asset-allocation recommendations. Firms including St. Louis-based A. G. Edwards & Sons Inc. and Raymond James & Associates Inc., St. Petersburg, Fla., already have more than one asset-allocation model for different investor profiles. But they don't ask investors to commit formally to one or the other.

"There is a temptation with asset allocation to put the retail client into a profile," says Raymond Worseck, investment strategy coordinator at A. G. Edwards, which has decided not to institute a formal system like Merrill Lynch's. Such a system has "compliance pluses" for brokerage firms, "because it protects them legally from a risk standpoint." But the investor can sometimes be better served with a more personalized approach, he says.

Merrill Lynch emphasizes that getting investors to specify their risk tolerance is only a beginning for grooming an investor's portfolio. Once an investor picks a risk category, the broker uses computer models and other tools to build a portfolio of appropriate stocks and bonds. Investors can switch risk categories, but frequent switching isn't encouraged, Merrill Lynch officials say.

Charles Clough, Merrill Lynch's chief investment strategist, says he realizes there are critics of his firm's plan. "You could say a multitude of asset guidelines just adds to the confusion of the issue,"

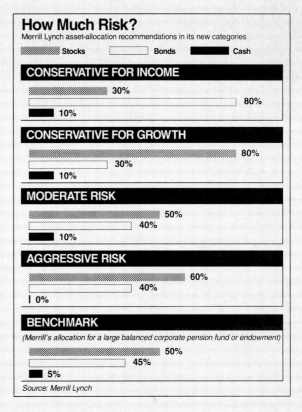

he says. But Mr. Clough adds that having the set categories helps to organize investors whose risk profiles otherwise would be "all over the map."

Source: William Power, "Merrill Lynch Asks: How Much Risk Can You Take?" *The Wall Street Journal*, July 2, 1990. Reprinted by permission of *THE WALL STREET JOURNAL*, © 1990 Dow Jones & Company, Inc. All Rights Reserved Worldwide.

Policies

The policies column in Table 1–1 lists strategies aimed at attaining the expected rate of return requirements, at an acceptable level of risk as expressed by the risk tolerance and without violating any of the applicable constraints. The policies listed in this column—asset allocation, diversification, risk and tax positioning, and income generation from cash distributions (such as dividends and bond coupons)—will underlie many of the later discussions. It is the use of these policies in managing a portfolio that is the theme of investments. Chapter 3 will provide an overview of many policies.

Concept Check

Question 1: Identify the following conditions according to where each fits in the objective-constraints-policies framework.
a. Invest 5 percent in bonds and 95 percent in stocks.
b. Do not invest more than 10 percent of the budget in any one security.
c. Shoot for an average rate of return of 11 percent.
d. Make sure there is $95,000 in cash in the account on December 31, 1998.
e. If the market is bearish,[2] reduce the investment in stocks to 80 percent.
f. As of next year, we will be in a higher tax bracket.
g. Our new president believes pension plans should take no risk whatsoever with the pension fund.
h. Our acquisition plan will require large sums of cash to be available at any time.

1.2   *The Life Cycle and the Risk-Return Trade-Off*

Human Capital and Insurance

The first significant investment decision for most individuals concerns education, building up their human capital. The major asset most people have during their early working years is the earning power that draws on their human capital. In these circumstances, the risk of illness or injury is far greater than the risk associated with their financial wealth.

The most direct way of hedging human capital risk is to purchase insurance. Viewing the combination of your labor income and a disability insurance policy as a portfolio, the rate of return on this portfolio is less risky than the labor income by itself. Life insurance is a hedge against the complete loss of income as a result of death of any of the family's income earners.

Investment in Residence

The first major economic asset many people acquire is their own house. Deciding to buy rather than rent a residence qualifies as an investment decision.

An important consideration in assessing the risk and return aspects of this investment is the value of a house as a hedge against two kinds of risk. The first kind is the risk of increases in rental rates. If you own a house, any increase in rental rates will increase the return on your investment.

The second kind of risk is that the particular house or apartment where you live may not always be available to you. By buying, you guarantee its availability.

Saving for Retirement and the Assumption of Risk

People save and invest money to provide for future consumption and leave an estate. The primary aim of lifetime savings is to allow maintenance of the customary standard of living after retirement. Life expectancy, when one makes it

---

[2]The stock market is called bearish when it is expected to decline, bullish when it is expected to go up.

to retirement at age 65, approaches 85 years, so the average retiree needs to prepare a 20-year nest egg and sufficient savings to cover unexpected health-care costs. Investment income may also increase the welfare of one's heirs, favorable charity, or both.

The leisure that investment income can be expected to produce depends on the degree of risk the household is willing to take with its investment portfolio. Empirical observation summarized in Table 1.2 indicates a person's age and stage in the life cycle affects attitude toward risk.

The evidence in Table 1.2 supports the life-cycle view of investment behavior. Questionnaires suggest that attitudes shift away from risk tolerance and toward risk aversion as investors near retirement age. With age, individuals lose the potential to recover from a disastrous investment performance. When they are young, investors can respond to a loss by working harder and saving more of their income. But as retirement approaches, investors realize there will be less time to recover. Hence the shift to safe assets.

The task of life-cycle financial planning is a formidable one for most people. It is not surprising that a whole industry has sprung up to provide personal financial advice. As the article in the accompanying box points out, the main problem for the client is to differentiate the good from the bad advisor.

Concept Check

Question 2. *a.* Think about the financial circumstances of your closest relative in your parents' generation (preferably your parents' household if you are fortunate to have them around). Write down the objectives and constraints for their investment decisions.
b. Now consider the financial situation of your closest relative who is in his or her 30s. Write down the objectives and constraints that would fit his or her investment decision.
c. How much of the difference between the two statements is due to the age of the investors?

1.3 *Professional and Institutional Investors*

Professional Investors

Professional investors provide investment management services for a fee. Some are employed directly by wealthy individual investors. Most professional investors, however, either pool many individual investor funds and manage them or serve institutional investors.

Table 1.2 *Amount of Risk Investors Said They Were Willing to Take by Age*

	Under 35	**35–54**	**55 and Over**
No risk	54%	57%	71%
A little risk	30	30	21
Some risk	14	18	8
A lot of risk	2	1	1

From Market Facts, Inc., Chicago, Ill.

Time for a Heart-to-Heart with a Planner?

You've been meaning to sit down and put your finances in order, but it takes something drastic to stir you to action. Well, you have it in the great Wall Street wipeout. A calming step might be to see a financial planner—a self-styled financial physician who examines your earnings, assets, and expenses and prescribes strategies to manage them. "Most people come in because they're fed up with saving and investing on an ad hoc basis," says Joel Isaacson at Weber Lipshie, a New York accounting-and-planning firm.

Many insurance companies, brokerage houses, banks, and accounting firms are now establishing "financial advisory" units or will recommend consultants. So will friends, who might be more objective. In any case, there's a critical first question: Is this consultant in your financial class? "You have to match the financial planner to your income level," says Gary Greenbaum, a West Orange (N.J.) planner. Second, determine if you fit his or her clientele. A planner who specializes in, say, self-employed professionals may not be too hot on corporate stock options.

Ask to examine some actual reports the planner has prepared for clients (names will be blanked out, of course). If the reports seem too canned, back off. Most plans have three basic parts: a profile of your current assets, an analysis that projects future income and expenses, and recommendations. A comprehensive plan covering tax, estate, and retirement strategies can range from 30 to 80 pages, but don't assume thicker is better. The proposals should be tailor-made and trim, not padded with boilerplate on medicare and estate-tax rules.

"'Planning by the pound' is one of my pet peeves," says Larry Carroll, chairman of the International Association of Financial Planners.

Pin down the planner's compensation method. Some work on a fee-only basis, charging either an hourly rate or a percentage of total assets, often 1 percent. At Asset Management Group, an Englewood, Colorado, firm that works mainly with senior management executives, clients pay an average of $250 an hour—typically some $15,000 a year.

Your Financial Physician May Not Have a License

Financial planning is an unregulated industry. The International Association for Financial Planning estimates that some 250,000 people now claim to be "financial consultants." Of those, about 30,000 use the titles certified financial planner (CFP) or chartered financial consultant (ChFC). But these designations are educational degrees conferred by industry groups or colleges—unlike a CPA, which signifies a state license. Many planners are also qualified as CPAs, stockbrokers, or insurance agents.

The IAFP (800 241-2148) publishes a directory of independent firms ranging in size from 1 to 100 planners. Those listed have been in practice at least two years and have passed advanced exams. Members maintain their good standing by doing 30 hours of classroom work annually.

Big Commissions

Other planners work on a fee-and-commission basis: They charge a flat sum for the plan and collect

---

Pooling of individual investment funds may take the form of commingled personal trusts managed by banks or mutual funds.

Personal Trusts

Personal trust An interest in an asset held by a trustee for the benefit of another person.

A **personal trust** is established when an individual confers legal title to property to another person or institution, who manages that property for one or more beneficiaries. The holder of the title is called the *trustee*. The trustee is usually a bank, a lawyer, or an investment professional.

Investment of a trust is subject to state trust laws and prudent man rules that limit the types of allowable trust investment (constraints).

The objectives of personal trusts normally are more limited in scope than those of the individual investor. Because of their fiduciary responsibility, per-

commissions for selling financial products. Although some services advertise fees as low as $200, a customized plan usually starts at $1,000. If your income is $75,000 to $200,000, a $5,000 fee would be at the high end.

Fee-and-commission planners' bills often run less than those of their fee-only colleagues. That's because their income derives primarily from the products they sell. "There's no money in just counseling," says David Cohen, a Metairie, Louisiana, planner. But there is in commissions, which can be as much as 8 percent for mutual funds, 10 percent for real estate partnerships, and 130 percent of first-year insurance-policy premiums—and yes, a lot of planners started out in insurance sales.

Multiple Choice

You're under no obligation to invest through the planner. If you are more interested in generic strategies than specific tips, look for a CPA firm that specializes in financial counseling. Since accountants aren't licensed to deal in securities, there's less chance of a conflict of interest. At Weber Lipshie, for example, a typical plan outlines options, such as "intermediate term government bonds" or "a trust generating 7 percent annual income." When diversification is urged, a firm's planner can work with your own accountant, broker, and banker to carry out the proposals.

There are advantages, though, in investing through a financial planner. Often he or she can put you onto private offerings—and can even create deals.

When a planner starts getting specific about investment products, always ask for two or three choices. And if the planner is affiliated with a large broker-dealer, at least one of those options should not be the firm's own product. Some brokerages and insurance companies have the reputation of offering financial planning services as a front to sell their products. Be wary if the planning "service" consists mainly of your filling out a form for a broker or agent: The counseling process should involve several meetings with a full-time planner.

Who doesn't need a financial planner? You're probably in good shape if you already discuss goals and strategies with your broker, accountant, or money manager. "While everyone should have a planning philosophy, not everyone needs a soup-to-nuts plan," says Ken Ziesenheim at Raymond James, a Florida brokerage-and-planning firm. A retiring executive, for example, may just require some ideas on how to invest a lump-sum pension distribution.

Most planners aren't qualified to prepare your taxes, write a will, or set up a trust. So you'll still need an accountant, attorney, and banker. But, says Gary Greenbaum, a planner can be useful in coordinating their efforts, "like a conductor who guides the orchestra into playing together beautifully"—and perhaps profitably.

---

sonal trust managers typically are more risk averse than individual investors. Certain asset classes such as options and futures contracts, for example, and strategies such as short-selling (betting the price of a security will fall) or buying on margin (borrowing up to 50 percent of the purchase price) are ruled out.

Mutual Funds

Mutual fund   A firm pooling and managing funds of investors.

Mutual funds are firms that manage pools of individual investor money. They invest it in various specified ways and issue shares that entitle investors to a pro rata portion of the income generated by the funds.

Mutual funds are analogous to corporations that raise capital by issuing shares that entitle shareholders to a proportion of future dividends and noncash distributions. There are three major differences, however:

1. The charter of mutual funds (prospectus) calls for investing its capital in shares of corporations and other financial assets.
2. The value of the fund shares can be easily computed from the prices of the securities held by the fund. This value is called *net asset value* (NAV). In most mutual funds (those called *open-end funds*), shareholders can redeem their share for the NAV at any time.
3. Shareholders do not have a say in managing the fund through a board of directors. They can effectively vote with their feet by redeeming their shares or buying more of them, according to their assessment of the quality of management.

A small fraction of mutual funds, called *closed-end funds,* do not redeem shares at the NAV, or any other value. These are more like normal corporations, except for the objectives of their investments. A mutual fund's objectives are spelled out in its prospectus. We discuss mutual funds in greater detail in Chapter 3.

Institutional Investors

Institutional investors are professionals who are charged with investing funds that organizations accumulate to finance future liabilities and expenditures. They include pension funds, insurance companies, banks, and endowment funds of various kinds. Institutional investors have different objectives, and they are subject to differing constraints.

Although individual investors are the ultimate beneficiaries of the service performed by these institutional investors, they exercise little, if any, control over them.

Pension Funds

Defined contribution plans *Pension plans in which the corporation is committed to making contributions according to a fixed formula.*

Defined benefit plans *Pension plans in which retirement benefits are set according to a fixed formula.*

Pension fund objectives depend on the type of pension plan. There are two basic types: **defined contribution plans** and **defined benefit plans.** Defined contribution plans are in effect tax-deferred retirement savings accounts established by the firm in trust for its employees. The employee bears all the risk and receives all the return from the plan's assets.

The largest pension funds, however, are defined benefit plans. The pension fund assets serve as collateral for the liabilities the firm sponsoring the plan owes to the plan beneficiaries (the employees). Specifically, the liabilities of the corporation to its employees, as far as retirement benefits go, are life annuities that employees earn during their working years. These annuities come due (begin paying off) when the employees retire. A pension actuary makes an assumption about the rate of return that will be earned on the plan's assets and uses this assumed rate to compute the amount the firm must contribute regularly to fund the plan's liabilities.

For example, if the actuary assumes a rate of return of 10 percent, then the firm must contribute \$385.54 now to fund \$1,000 of pension liabilities that will arise in 10 years, because $\$385.54 \times 1.10^{10} = \$1,000$.

If a pension fund's *actual* rate of return exceeds the actuarial *assumed* rate, then the firm's shareholders reap an unanticipated gain, because the excess return can be used to reduce future contributions. If the plan's actual rate of return falls short of the assumed rate, however, the firm will have to increase future contributions. The sponsoring firm's shareholders bear the risk in a defined benefit pension plan, so a main objective of the plan will be to reward the shareholders for bearing this risk.

Many firms try to match the risk of the pension assets with the risk of their pension liabilities. Often a distinction is made between (1) the firm's liability to already-retired participants, which is a known flow of money, and (2) its liability to active participants (current employees that will retire in the future), which is tied to the employees' final wage or salary under most benefit formulas. The firm can cover its *known* liability to retired workers by investing in fixed-income securities, but it cannot completely hedge (insure coverage of) the pension benefits it owes to active workers because this liability is linked to future wages, which are not known in advance.[3]

Many pension plans view their assumed actuarial rate of return as their target rate of return and have little tolerance for earning less than that.

Life Insurance Companies

Life insurance companies generally invest so as to hedge their liabilities, which are defined by the policies they write. That is, the company's objective is to find assets that will return more in the event the insurance policy coverage becomes more expensive.

For example, if the company writes a policy that pays a death benefit linked to the consumer price index, then the company is subject to inflation risk. It would then be in the market for assets expected to return more when the rate of inflation rises, thus hedging the price-index linkage of the policy.

There are as many objectives as there are distinct types of insurance policies. Until the 1970s, only two types of life insurance policies were available for individuals: whole-life and term.

A *whole-life insurance policy* combines a death benefit with a kind of savings plan that provides for a gradual buildup of cash value that the policyholder can withdraw later in life, usually at age 65.

Term insurance, on the other hand, provides death benefits only, with no buildup of cash value.

The interest rate imbedded in the schedule of cash value accumulation promised under the whole-life policy is a fixed rate. One way life insurance companies try to hedge this liability is by investing in long-term bonds. Often the insured individual has the right to borrow at a prespecified fixed interest rate against the cash value of the policy.

Insurance companies have seen considerable change in policyholder behavior in recent decades. During the inflationary years of the 1970s and early 1980s, many older whole-life policies allowed policyholders to borrow at rates as low as 4 percent or 5 percent per year; some holders borrowed heavily against the cash value to invest in assets paying double-digit yields. Other actual and potential policyholders abandoned whole-life policies and took out term insurance, which accounted for more than half the volume of new sales of individual life policies.

---

[3]This statement is not entirely correct because a pension fund can transfer, for a fee, all of its pension liabilities to a life insurance company. In such a case, the plan is called an insured pension plan.

In response to these developments, the insurance industry came up with two new policy types: variable life and universal life. A variable life policy entitles the insured to a fixed death benefit plus a cash value that can be invested in the policyholder's choice of mutual funds. A universal life policy allows policyholders to increase or reduce either the insurance premium (the annual fee paid on the policy) or the death benefit (the cash amount paid to beneficiaries in the event of death) according to their changing needs. Furthermore, the interest rate on the cash value component changes with market interest rates.

The great advantage of variable and universal life insurance policies is that earnings on the cash value are not taxed until the money is withdrawn. These policies are one of the few tax-advantaged investments left following the Tax Reform Act of 1986.

The life insurance industry also provides two major products for pension plans: insured defined benefit pensions and guaranteed insurance contracts (GICs).

In the case of insured defined benefit pensions, the firm sponsoring the pension plan enters into a contractual agreement where the life insurance company assumes all liability for the benefit accrued under the plan. The insurance company provides this service in return for an annual premium based on the benefit formula and the number and characteristics of the employees covered by the plan.

A GIC promises the pension plan a stated nominal interest rate over some specified period, usually several years. GICs represent, in effect, a *zero-coupon bond* (that is, a bond that pays the entire principal and interest due on maturity) issued by an insurance company. With both types of product, the insurance company usually pursues an investment policy designed to hedge the associated risk.

Life insurance companies may be organized either as mutual companies or stock companies. Theoretically, the organizational form should affect the company's investment objectives: mutual companies are supposed to be run solely for the benefit of their policyholders, while stock companies have as their objective the maximization of shareholder value.

In actuality, it is hard to discern from its investment policies which organizational form a particular insurance company has. Can you differentiate the mutual insurance company Prudential from the stock company Travelers?

Nonlife Insurance Companies

Nonlife insurance companies such as property and casualty insurers have investable funds primarily because they pay claims *after* they collect policy premiums. Typically, they are conservative in their attitude toward risk. As with life insurers, nonlife insurance companies can be either stock companies or mutual companies.

A common thread in the objectives of pension plans and insurance companies is the need to hedge predictable long-term liabilities. Investment strategies typically call for hedging these liabilities with bonds of various maturities.

Banks

Most bank investments (the assets on their balance sheets) are loans to businesses and consumers, and most of their liabilities are accounts of depositors. As investors, banks try to match the risk of assets to liabilities while earning a profitable spread between the lending and borrowing rates. The difference between the interest charged to a borrower and the interest rate that banks pay on their liabilities is called the bank interest rate spread. The bank interest rate spread depends on two elements: the *risk premium* and the *term premium.*

The risk premium is the difference between the interest rate charged on loans and the (virtually) risk-free rate of interest, normally the interest rate on the comparable maturity U.S. Treasury bond, which investors can earn with certainty. Any other borrower is subject to some risk of default, however small, as the default of the state of New York in 1976 taught us.

From the depositor's view, bank deposits are safe because of the deposit insurance by the Federal Deposit Insurance Corporation (FDIC). Therefore, banks can borrow funds at the risk-free interest rate. The bank, when lending money, risks losing its equity capital and its charter. This risk differential justifies charging higher rates to borrowers. While competition or regulation prevents excessive risk premiums, banks will avoid undercharging borrowers in the interest of profitability.

The term premium is the difference between market interest rates on long-term loans and short-term loans. The term premium is in part a form of risk premium because long-term loans are by nature riskier than short-term loans.

A long-term bank loan, therefore, includes a term premium *and* a risk premium to account for the default risk of the particular borrower. Bank profits generally are made up of interest spreads on long-term loans (which include a term premium and a risk premium), spreads on short-term loans (only risk premium), and fee-for-service charges. The proportion of term premiums in bank profits depends on the average maturity of the bank loan portfolio. The more significant this proportion, the higher the expected profits of the bank. At the same time, being locked into the interest rates on the long-term loans exposes the bank to more risk.

Most bank liabilities are checking accounts, time or saving deposits, and certificates of deposit (CDs). Checking account funds may be withdrawn at any time, so they are of the shortest maturity. Time or saving deposits are of various maturities. Some time deposits may extend as long as seven years, but on average, they are of fairly short maturity. CDs are bonds of various maturities that the bank issues to investors. While the range of maturities is from 90 days to 10 years, the average is about one year.

Traditionally, a large part of the banking industry loan portfolio has been in collateralized real estate loans, better known as mortgages. Typically, mortgages are of 15 to 30 years, significantly longer than the maturity of the average liability. Thus, traditionally, bank profits have depended for a large part on the term premium.

Imagine a bank that has just paid out money on a long-term (fixed-rate) mortgage and that the funds were raised from a short-term CD. Suppose the interest rate on the CD is 6 percent while the rate on the mortgage loan is 9 percent. Assume the mortgagee appears safe enough, so it looks as if the bank is sitting pretty on a 3 percentage point interest spread.

But what if the economy heats up, and short-term rates climb to 10 percent? As the original CD matures, the bank needs to borrow at 10 percent to attract funds, but still collects only 9 percent on the loan it is locked into. At this point, the bank faces a negative cash flow that will drive it to insolvency if it has a lot of these long-term loans.

Financial markets responded to this risk by creating mortgage-investment pools that displaced banks as major residential real estate lenders. The loss of this traditional business, combined with some consequences of banking deregulation, squeezed interest rate spreads and required banks to rely more on fee-for-service charges. This trend was a contributing factor in the S&L debacle of the 1980s.

Endowment Funds

Endowment funds

Portfolios operated for the benefit of a nonprofit entity.

Endowment funds are held by organizations chartered to use their money for specific nonprofit purposes. They are financed by gifts from one or more sponsors and are typically managed by educational, cultural, and charitable organizations or by independent foundations established solely to carry out the fund's specific purposes. Generally, the investment objectives of an endowment fund are to produce a steady flow of income subject to only a moderate degree of risk. Trustees of an endowment fund, however, can specify other objectives as circumstances dictate.

Objectives of Various Investors

We are now in a position to compare investors on the basis of their objectives and constraints. The next two tables will show how we can apply the objective/constraint approach to the formation of policies.

Table 1.3 presents a matrix of objectives for various investors. For mutual funds, the return requirement and risk tolerance are said to be variable because mutual funds segment the investor market. Various funds appeal to distinct investor groups and will adopt a return requirement and risk tolerance that fit the representative investor. For example, "high-income" funds cater to the conservative investor, while "high-growth" funds seek out the more risk-tolerant ones. Tax-free bond funds segment the market by tax obligation.

Pension funds must meet the actuarial rate, otherwise the corporation sponsoring the plan will have to come up with additional contributions. Once a pen-

Table 1.3 *Matrix of Objectives*

Type of Investor	Return Requirement	Risk Tolerance
Individual and personal trusts	Life cycle (education, children, retirement)	Life cycle (younger are more risk tolerant)
Mutual funds	Variable	Variable
Pension funds	Assumed actuarial rate	Depends on proximity of payouts
Endowment funds	Determined by current income needs and need for asset growth to maintain real value	Generally conservative
Life insurance companies	Should exceed new money rate by sufficient margin to meet expenses and profit objectives; also actuarial rates important	Conservative
Nonlife insurance companies	No minimum	Conservative
Banks	Interest spread	Variable

sion fund's actuarial rate is set, it establishes the fund return requirement, and additional risk tolerance becomes very low.

Endowment funds are classified "conservative" on risk tolerance on the basis of observation, although institutions can differ in investment policy.

Life insurance companies have obligations to whole-life policyholders that are similar to those of pension funds. These obligations require them to earn a minimum rate (analogous to the actuarial rate), if the company is to meet its liabilities.

Nonlife insurance companies can be looked at as defined contribution pension plans. The sponsor's contribution is analogous to the premiums of the insured, and withdrawals by retirees are analogous to benefits paid out for property damage and casualty claims.

Banks profit by the interest rate spread between loans extended (assets) and deposits and CDs (liabilities), as well as on fees for services. Managing bank assets calls for balancing the loan portfolio with the portfolio of deposits and CDs. A bank can increase the interest rate spread by lending to riskier borrowers and by increasing the proportion of longer-term loans. Both policies threaten bank solvency though, so their deployment must match the risk tolerance of the bank shareholders.

Constraints of Various Investors

Table 1.4 presents a matrix of constraints for various investors. As you would expect, liquidity and tax constraints for individuals are variable because of wealth and age differentials.

A particular constraint for mutual funds arises from investor response to the fund performance. When a mutual fund earns an unsatisfactory rate of return (the value of its portfolio falls), or even when the fund does not appreciate as fast as competing funds do, investors often redeem their shares—they withdraw money from the fund. The mutual fund then contracts. The reverse happens when a mutual fund earns an unusually high return: it can become popular with investors overnight, and its asset base will grow dramatically.

Pension funds are heavily regulated by the Employee Retirement Income Security Act of 1974 (ERISA). This law revolutionized saving for retirement in the United States and remains a major piece of social legislation. Thus, for pension funds, regulatory constraints are relatively important. Also, mature pension funds are required to pay out more than young funds, and hence need more liquidity.

Table 1.4 *Matrix of Constraints*

Type of Investor	Liquidity	Horizon	Regulatory	Taxes
Individuals and personal trusts	Variable	Life cycle	None	Variable
Mutual funds	Low	Short	Little	None
Pension funds	Young, low; mature, high	Long	ERISA	None
Endowment funds	Little	Long	Little	None
Life insurance companies	Low	Long	Complex	Yes
Nonlife insurance companies	High	Short	Little	Yes
Banks	Low	Short	Changing	Yes

Endowment funds, on the other hand, usually do not need to liquidate assets, or even use dividend income, to finance payouts. Contributions are expected to exceed payouts and increase the real value of the endowment fund, so liquidity is not an overriding concern.

Life insurance companies are subject to complex regulation. The corporate tax rate, which is today close to 40 percent, also applies to all insurance company investment income, so taxes are an important concern.

Property and casualty insurance, like term life insurance, is written on a short-term basis. Most policies must be renewed annually, which means property and casualty insurance companies are subject to short-term horizon constraints.

The short horizon constraint for banks comes from the interest rate risk component of the interest rate spread (i.e., the risk of interest rate increases that banks face when financing long-term assets with short-term liabilities).

Concept Check

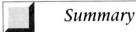

> *Question 3.*   Describe several distinguishing characteristics of endowment funds that differentiate them from pension funds.

Summary

1. The Institute of Certified Financial Analysts (ICFA) developed the industry-standard framework for the translation of investor goals to investment strategy. Its three main parts are: objectives, constraints, and policy.

2. Investor objectives include the return requirement and risk tolerance, articulating the overriding concern of investment with the risk-return trade-off.

3. Investor constraints include liquidity requirements, investment horizon, regulatory concerns, tax obligations, and unique needs of various investors.

4. Investment policies specify the degree of involvement in market timing, asset allocation, and security selection decisions.

5. For individual investors, life-cycle concerns are the most important factor in setting objectives, constraints, and policy.

6. Major institutional investors include pension funds, life insurance companies, nonlife insurance companies, banks, and endowment funds.

Key Terms

defined benefit plans, 22	endowment funds, 26	personal trust, 20
defined contribution plans, 22	investment horizon, 15	prudent man law, 15
	liquidity, 14	risk-return trade-off, 14
	mutual funds, 21	

Selected Readings

For a collection of essays presenting the Institute of Chartered Financial Analysts approach to portfolio management see:
   Maginn, John L., and Donald L. Tuttle, eds. *Managing Investment Portfolios*. Boston: Warren, Gorham, & Lamont, 1990.

A good discussion of asset allocation in practice is:
Brinson, G. P.; J. J. Diermeier; and G. G. Schlarbaum. "A Composite Portfolio Benchmark for Pension Funds." *Financial Analysts Journal,* March–April 1986.

Problem Sets

1. Your client says, "With the unrealized gains in my portfolio, I have almost saved enough money for my daughter to go to college in eight years, but educational costs keep going up." Based on this statement alone, which one of the following appears to be least important to your client's investment policy?
  a. Time horizon.
  b. Purchasing power risk.
  c. Liquidity.
  d. Taxes.

2. The common stock investments of the defined contribution plan of a corporation are being managed by the trust department of a national bank. The risk of investment loss is borne by the
  a. Pension Benefit Guarantee Corporation.
  b. Employees.
  c. Corporation.
  d. Federal Deposit Insurance Corporation.

3. The aspect least likely to be included in the portfolio management process is
  a. Identifying an investor's objectives, constraints, and preferences.
  b. Organizing the management process itself.
  c. Implementing strategies regarding the choice of assets to be used.
  d. Monitoring market conditions, relative values, and investor circumstances.

4. You are a portfolio manager and senior executive vice president of Advisory Securities Selection, Inc. Your firm has been invited to meet with the Trustees of the Wood Museum Endowment Funds. Wood Museum is a privately endowed charitable institution that is dependent on the investment return from a $25 million endowment fund to balance the budget. The treasurer of the museum has recently completed the budget that indicates a need for cash flow of $3 million in 1992, $3.2 million in 1993, and $3.5 million in 1994 from the endowment fund to balance the budget in those years. At the present time, the entire endowment portfolio is invested in Treasury bills and money market funds because the trustees fear a financial crisis. The trustees do not anticipate any further capital contributions to the fund.

   The trustees are all successful businesspeople, and they have been critical of the fund's previous investment advisors because they did not follow a logical decision-making process. In fact, several previous managers have been dismissed because of their inability to communicate with the trustees and their preoccupation with the fund's relative performance rather than the cash flow needs.

   Advisory Securities Selection, Inc., has been contacted by the trustees because of its reputation for understanding and relating to the client's needs. The trustees have asked you, as a prospective portfolio manager for the Wood Museum Endowment Fund, to prepare a written report in response to the following questions. Your report will be circulated to the trustees before the initial interview on June 15, 1992.

   Explain in detail how each of the following relates to the determination of either investor objectives or investor constraints that can be used to determine the portfolio policies for this three-year period for the Wood Museum Endowment Fund.
  a. Liquidity requirements.
  b. Return requirements.

c. Risk tolerance.

d. Time horizon.

e. Tax considerations.

f. Regulatory and legal considerations.

g. Unique needs and circumstances.

5. Mrs. Mary Atkins, age 66, has been your firm's client for five years, since the death of her husband, Dr. Charles Atkins. Dr. Atkins had built a successful newspaper business that he sold two years before his death to Merit Enterprises, a publishing and broadcasting conglomerate, in exchange for Merit common stock. The Atkinses had no children, and their wills provide that upon their deaths the remaining assets shall be used to create a fund for the benefit of Good Samaritan Hospital, to be called the Atkins Endowment Fund.

Good Samaritan is a 180-bed, not-for-profit hospital with an annual operating budget of $12.5 million. In the past, the hospital's operating revenues have often been sufficient to meet operating expenses and occasionally even generate a small surplus. In recent years, however, rising costs and declining occupancy rates have caused Good Samaritan to run a deficit. The operating deficit has averaged $300,000 to $400,000 annually over the last several years. Existing endowment assets (that is, excluding the Atkins' estate) of $7.5 million currently generate approximately $375,000 of annual income, up from less than $200,000 five years ago. This increased income has been the result of somewhat higher interest rates, as well as a shift in asset mix toward more bonds. To offset operating deficits, the Good Samaritan Board of Governors has determined that the endowment's current income should be increased to approximately 6 percent of total assets (up from 5 percent currently). The hospital has not received any significant additions to its endowment assets in the past five years.

Identify and describe an appropriate set of investment objectives and constraints for the Atkins Endowment Fund to be created after Mrs. Atkins's death.

Chapter

2

The Investment Process: Strategy and Policies

Investment strategy for an individual or for an institution involves market timing, asset allocation, and security selection. Investors formulate strategies according to capital market expectations and investor-specific circumstances, such as tax obligations. Investment strategy also calls for portfolio monitoring, performance evaluation, and decisions on portfolio adjustment.

The first aim of this chapter is to describe how the investment industry relates to investor objectives. We present some intuitive arguments that we explain more rigorously in later chapters. Don't be frustrated if at times we skip details. Our intention is to provide some broad perspective on the investment process, with all its spirit, dynamism, and related jargon. If you develop this acquaintance now, you should find our later discussions more productive. After studying this chapter you should be able to:

- Compare and contrast major types of investment strategies.
- Assess capital market expectations underlying investment strategies.

2.1 *Investment Strategy and Policies*

Manage Your Own Portfolio or Rely on Others?

Lots of people have assets such as social security benefits, pension and group insurance plans, and savings components of life insurance policies. Yet they exercise limited control, if any, on the investment decisions of these plans. The funds that secure pension and life insurance plans are managed by institutional investors.

Diversity Is More Than Stocks and Bonds

Every investor has heard about how crucial it is to diversify, but many people—even some with varied stock and bond holdings—probably don't realize how *un*diversified they really are.

"Individuals rarely take an overall view" when it comes to diversification, says Michael Lipper, who heads Lipper Analytical Services. "They think of it in terms of different chunks of money" they have invested in stocks, bonds, cash, and other assets. In reality, "securities are only one part of the total [diversification] picture—and not even the most important one at that."

Take the case of a young Wall Street executive with a mortgaged cooperative apartment in lower Manhattan. A diversified stock portfolio would actually compound, not lessen, such an individual's risk because all those "assets"—job, home, and savings—are heavily exposed to the vagaries of the stock market.

In a similar vein, Lawrence Manchester, head of the private-client group at Standish, Ayer & Wood, says he would advise a client who owns a car agency to avoid long-term bonds, utilities, and insurance stocks. Those investments, just like the car business, are "very interest-rate sensitive," he says. For that client, diversification means "fixing it so that when his company goes in the dumper every four years, he's protected in his portfolio."

The way the professionals see it, diversification for individuals isn't driven by fancy theories about market volatility. Instead, they say, it starts with a basic grasp of personal economic risk.

"I'd always ask myself at the start of the analysis, 'What's the worst that could happen to me? And the next worst?'—and build a portfolio strategy based on that," says Russell Fogler of Aronson + Fogler, a Philadelphia money-management firm. "It's a sequential process."

At different points in an individual's investing lifetime, diversification has two roles to play, the pros say. Initially, its function is to protect the individual from being hit hard by losses in basic "assets," such as job, home, and purchasing power.

"Most people don't think of their job as their No. 1 investment," says Mr. Lipper. "But over their lifetime, it's salary, insurance, and pension benefits that will wind up setting their whole investment picture."

The second purpose of diversification is to protect against the long-term risk of "outliving one's capital" once the job ends, says Mr. Lipper. In this context, says Owen Quattlebaum, head of personal financial services at Brown Brothers Harriman & Co., diversification means "branching out into other, risky assets" such as stocks and bonds. In other words, it becomes "something genuinely defined as a way to make money," he says.

What strategies should the individual use to hedge these risks? The pros offer some advice:

Outside of the "forced savings" plans, however, individuals can manage their own investment portfolios. As the population grows richer, more and more people face this decision.

Managing your own portfolio *appears* to be the lowest-cost solution. Conceptually, there is little difference between managing one's own investments and professional financial planning/investment management.

Against the fees and charges that financial planners and professional investment managers impose, you will want to offset the value of your time and energy expended on diligent portfolio management. People with a suitable background may even look at investment as recreation. Most of all, you must recognize the *potential* difference in investment results.

Besides the need to deliver better-performing investments, professional managers face two added difficulties. First, getting clients to communicate their objectives and constraints requires considerable skill. This is not a one-time task because objectives and constraints are forever changing. Second, the professional needs to articulate the financial plan and keep the client abreast of out-

Job Risk

At the end of a long economic expansion, especially in this age of corporate restructurings and increasing foreign competition, job risk—unemployment and other factors that threaten income and benefits—is relatively high. In such a hazardous environment, individuals should safeguard their option of seeking new opportunity elsewhere.

Depending on how marketable a person's skills are and how vulnerable his or her industry is, everyone should hold between three months' and a year's worth of after-tax salary in short-term cash investments, such as bank deposits and money market funds, the specialists say.

Additionally, says Mr. Lipper, an individual should hedge against the loss of 3 to 12 months of pension and other benefits—a sum usually equal to about a third of pretax salary. That money should be invested in risky assets, such as stocks and long-term bonds. "In this barbell strategy, individuals should be as aggressive as they can stomach on the far end," he says.

House Risk

A mortgaged home is probably the individual's major exposure to "the factors in the local area that will vibrate with the job risk and, in effect, double up the job risk," says Mr. Quattlebaum of Brown Brothers.

The risk of having to meet house payments while searching for a new job would probably be covered by the cash reserves mentioned above. However, says Mr. Lipper, people who think they might have to sell their home and move to find employment in another area should consider protecting themselves against potential losses.

Today's "short-term weakness in housing prices might entail a 10 percent to 20 percent hit to the equity in your house," compared with what it would cost to buy a comparable home in a more-vibrant area, he says. He recommends setting aside money to cover that potential shortage and buying "intermediate bonds of one to five years' maturity and roll them over—so that you get a reasonable interest rate."

In the years ahead, houses—and real-estate assets generally—present another risk: "They will not be as effective a hedge against inflation as in the 1970s because the country is so overbuilt," says Barry Berlin, vice president at First Wachovia Capital Management. Rolled-over positions in intermediate bonds, as well as stocks and foreign securities, could help offset that risk.

comes. Professional management of large portfolios is complicated further by the need to set up an efficient organization where decisions can be decentralized and information properly disseminated.

The box on diversity demonstrates the growing awareness of the need to improve the quality of the household investment decision. Even the popular press is coming closer to professional standards.

A Basic Decomposition: The Risky Portfolio and the Safe Asset

The most important decision an investor makes is: what proportion of the total investment budget should be allocated to *risky* as opposed to *safe* assets. This is another way to state that the trade-off between risk and return dominates investment decisions.

So what is a safe asset? We know that the future value of the money that even the safest bond will deliver is uncertain as of today—the rate of inflation affects purchasing power. So the term *safe asset* is relative. Because short-term forecasts are prone to smaller errors than longer-term forecasts, inflation risk will be least for the shortest-term bond. Therefore, short-term bonds issued by safe (default-free) institutions such as the U.S. government are the safest assets available.

Money markets *Include short-term, highly liquid, and relatively low-risk debt instruments.*

These assets are often called *near money;* and investment professionals refer to them as cash. The markets in which they are traded are called **money markets,** so another name for these safe assets is money market assets, or instruments. Mutual funds that specialize in money market assets are called money market funds, and we often refer to the cash part of a portfolio as the money market fund portfolio. The rate of return on a money market portfolio is referred to as the risk-free rate.

Imagine that you must decide on a risky portfolio without access to information. Your intuitive response would be to choose a "little bit of everything" portfolio, applying the "don't put all your eggs in one basket" principle. Such a theoretical asset can be called the **market portfolio,** as it represents a balanced investment in the entire array of risky assets. It is legitimate to talk about the market portfolio as the risky complement to the money market investment.

Market portfolio *The portfolio which holds each security in proportion to its market value.*

Index funds *A mutual fund holding shares in proportion to their representation in a market index such as the S&P 500.*

This low-cost strategy, which requires no specialized information, has proven to be surprisingly effective. Recognition of its strength has created a demand for **index funds** whose rates of return approximate that of the market portfolio. Financial indexes such as the Dow Jones Industrials or Standard & Poor's 500 measure the average rate of return on a broad set of securities chosen to be representative of the overall market. Index funds actually hold the index assets in their portfolio, so that the returns on the fund mimic the index returns. If the index is broad, as the S&P 500 (but not the DJ Industrials) is, the index portfolio will be a proxy for the conceptual market portfolio.

The most fundamental means of controlling investment risk is determining the amount to invest in risky assets and the amount to keep in safe assets.

Concept Check

Question 1. Suppose a U.S. Treasury bond offers a risk-free rate of return of 7 percent. Investment in a stock index fund represents a risky investment in the market. Assume the return on the stock index fund will be 24 percent with probability of 2/3 and 0 percent with probability of 1/3. Describe to an individual investor who is currently fully invested in the stock index fund how shifting half the investment value to U.S. Treasury bonds will lower risk and expected return.

Market Timing

Market timing *Asset allocation in which the investment in the market is increased if one forecasts that the market will outperform T-bills.*

Market timing refers to changes in how much of the total investment will be allocated to the market portfolio and how much to the safe asset.

Investment managers who pursue an *active* market timing strategy frequently adjust the proportion they invest in the market portfolio, depending on forecasts of future market conditions. The more optimistic the market portfolio rate of return forecast, the more the investment manager will put in it. Obviously, success of a market timing strategy depends on the quality of these forecasts.

A *passive* market timing strategy (which is to say no timing) calls for keeping a basically fixed proportion in the market portfolio while riding out forecasts of temporary changes in market conditions. Even so, occasionally, the market portfolio proportion is adjusted, depending on changing perceptions of the risk and return of the market and the risk tolerance of the investor. Passive timers do not try to time the market with high frequency. They establish market forecasts for a reasonably long horizon and establish the allocation to the market portfolio consistent with overall portfolio strategy.

Active timing requires forecasting expertise. Determining who has what degree of forecasting ability is certainly nontrivial. Pursuing successful market timing requires constant monitoring and performance evaluation.

Benefits of passive timing strategy include freedom from the cost and trouble of forecasting future market conditions. But to arrive at the fixed proportion of investment in the market portfolio, you need to assess its risk and expected return compared to the yield of money market assets. In other words, you need forecasts of future market conditions—a paradox.

Market forecasts for passive timing, however, need not be as frequent and rigorous as those for active timing. For passive timing, the exact moment that you enter or exit the market is less crucial. The focus is on your strategy—not on beating the competition to the punch. Therefore, purchasing forecasts prepared by experts and sold to the public for that purpose is sufficient. Although they are sometimes touted as valuable for active timing as well, the logic of competition implies that publicly available, inexpensive forecasts will not be much use for successful active timing.

Concept Check

Question 2. *a.* What would you say if the investor from question 1 had access to private forecasts that predict the true stock market return with perfect accuracy?
b. Would you revise your advice if the private forecasts are correct only half of the time when predicting either low or high market return?

Asset Allocation

Asset allocation Choosing among broad asset classes such as stocks versus bonds.

Asset allocation refers to deciding how much to invest in each major asset category such as common stocks, bonds, real estate, and so on.

Passive asset allocation is analogous to passive timing, meaning that all asset-class allocations remain largely constant over time. In the case of active asset allocation, the proportion allocated to asset classes (including cash assets) varies in response to forecasts of changing market conditions that will affect the rate of return of the major asset classes.

Major asset classes usually considered are:

1. Money market assets (cash).
2. Fixed-income securities (bonds).
3. Stocks.
4. Real estate.
5. Precious metals.
6. Other, e.g. fine art and collectibles.

The accompanying box demonstrates that the market has responded to the desire for broad asset allocation. The availability of a broad spectrum of mutual

New Funds Broaden Investment Base

Asset Allocation Approach Aims to Spread Risk between Stocks, Bonds, Metals, Others

Talk about market timing.

In 1986 and early 1987, a handful of mutual fund companies introduced funds whose managers were permitted to apportion assets among stocks, bonds, cash, and sometimes precious metals and foreign securities, as market conditions warranted.

Then the stock market collapsed last October. Ever since, some sponsors of these so-called asset allocation funds have advertised them as havens for shell-shocked investors who don't want to be fully invested in stocks at all times, but lack the time or expertise to make market-timing decisions.

What constitutes an asset allocation fund is still being debated in the mutual fund industry, but many fund managers and industry observers agree that such funds come in two basic varieties: flexible and fixed. In the more common flexible funds, the portfolio manager can apportion assets among various investments as he or she sees fit, within broad parameters spelled out in the fund's prospectus. In fixed funds, assets are allocated among stocks, bonds, money market instruments, and other investments in unchanging proportions.

Though asset allocation funds seem similar to old-fashioned balanced funds, there are significant differences. Says Henry Shilling, a vice president with Lipper Analytical Securities Corp., a New York City investment advisory firm: "Balanced funds maintain a specified balance between equities and fixed-income securities—on average, 60 percent equities and 40 percent fixed income. But the managers of some asset allocation funds can place as much as 100 percent of their assets in a single sector."

Fixed asset allocation funds differ from balanced funds in that assets are split among more types of investments than the standard trio of stocks, bonds, and cash.

Are asset allocation funds a worthy investment alternative? It's hard to say because most have only been in business for a year or two. Says Bert Berry, publisher of *NoLoad Fund*X*, a San Francisco-based investment advisory newsletter: "If these guys are smart enough to be in the right sectors at the right time, it's wonderful. But most of these funds haven't been around long enough to prove whether that kind of market timing can be done well."

A Sampling of Asset Allocation Funds (Performance for year ending March 31)

Fund	Year-to-Date Performance
Alliance Balanced Shares	−1.58%
Blanchard Strategic Growth Fund	0.68
Claremont Fund	−2.59
Cornerstone Fund	−5.63
Dreyfus Strategic Investing	4.69
Dreyfus Strategic Aggressive Invest.	65.70
Morison Asset Allocation Fund	−6.14
Oppenheimer Asset Allocation Fund	2.98
Permanent Portfolio	5.01
Primary Trend Fund	5.44
Shearson Lehman Special Equity Portfolios Strategic Investors	−1.85
Strong Total Return Fund	−3.07
Standard & Poor's 500	−11.25

Source: Lipper Analytical Services.

Berry is downright dubious about a fund's chances for long-term success if asset allocations are static. "You're in a self-canceling situation unless most of the sectors are favorable," he says. "If equities are up 50 percent, but bonds are down 50 percent, where have you gone?"

The following descriptions of 15 asset allocation funds [in 1988] illustrate the diversity of their investment philosophies.

• **Alliance Balanced Shares** (sold by brokers; 5.5 percent load; minimum initial and subsequent investments: $250, $50) is the 55-year-old granddaddy of asset allocation funds. No less than 25 percent of the fund's assets must be invested in debt securities, preferred stocks and convertible debt securities. Portfolio manager J. Andrew Richey now has 63 percent in stocks and convertibles, 35 percent in bonds and 2 percent in cash. Says he: "We have a very aggressive portfolio assuming a good stock market and a reasonably solid economy for the next 12 to 18 months. We have no forecast for recession."

• **Blanchard Strategic Growth Fund** (800–922–7771; $125 account startup fee; minimum initial and subsequent investments: $3,000, $500) employs five investment advisors: Four manage investments in U.S. stocks, foreign securities, precious metals, and U.S. and foreign fixed-income securities, and a fifth oversees the investment mix. The fund can invest 5 percent to 35 percent of its assets in fixed-income securities and 10 percent to 50 percent in the other three categories. "We're not market timers," says fund president Michael Freedman. "On average, we make allocation changes every three to four weeks, but we don't make dramatic, radical shifts. We try to read long-term economic trends and make gradual changes." Freedman is now 30 percent in cash, 25 percent in foreign stocks, 18 percent in U.S. stocks, 15 percent in U.S. and foreign fixed-income securities, and 12 percent in precious metals.

Blanchard spawned a clone last year that's sold by brokers: **National Strategic Allocation Fund** (7.75 percent load; minimum initial and subsequent investments: $1,000, $250).

• **The Claremont Fund** (sold by brokers; 4.75 percent load; minimum initial and subsequent investments: $500, $100) gives three investment advisors fairly free rein in allocating assets among stocks, bonds, and cash. According to shareholder services representative Steve Daiken, the fund is now 51 percent in stock, 28 percent in bonds and 21 percent in cash.

• **Cornerstone Fund** (800–531–8000; no load; minimum initial and subsequent investments: $1,000, $100) is managed by USAA Investment Management Co., a Texas firm that started out selling auto and home insurance to military officers. Eighteen to 22 percent of assets is invested in each of five investment groups: U.S. and foreign gold stocks, foreign stocks, U.S. real estate stocks, U.S. government securities, and undervalued U.S. stocks.

• Dreyfus boasts a trio of asset allocation funds: **Strategic Investing, Strategic Aggressive Investing** and **Strategic World Investing** (sold by brokers; 3 percent load; minimum initial and subsequent investments: $2,500, $500). Asset allocations change frequently because fund manager Stanley F. Druckenmiller employs sophisticated trading and hedging techniques, including short-selling. Strategic Investing takes a 6- to 12-month view of the market, while the other two funds shoot for short-term gains. All three can invest in foreign securities, but Strategic World Investing is required to put 65 percent of its assets in securities that aren't traded in the U.S.

• **Morison Asset Allocation Fund** (sold by brokers; 7.25 percent load; minimum initial and subsequent investments: $500, $50) is managed by economist Thomas J. Morison who invests in stocks, government bonds, and cash depending on the availability of securities that meet his investment criteria. Says he: "This isn't market timing. I think that's a low probability." Morison is now 35 percent in stocks, 10 percent in cash, 25 percent in long-term bonds, and 30 percent in bonds with maturities of less than three years.

• **Oppenheimer Asset Allocation Fund** (sold by brokers; 4.7 percent load; minimum initial and subsequent investments: $1,000, $25) is less than a year old. According to executive vice president Bridget Macaskill, the fund is now 45 percent in stocks, 11 percent in foreign securities, 39 percent in bonds, and 5 percent in cash.

• **PaineWebber Asset Allocation Fund** (sold by brokers, 5 percent maximum back-end load; minimum initial and subsequent investments: $1,000, $100) changes its investment mix monthly to reflect shifts in PaineWebber's asset allocation model. According to vice president Ellen Harris, the fund is 36 percent in stocks, 51 percent in bonds, and 13 percent in cash. Performance: Up 4.38 percent.

• **The Permanent Portfolio** (800–531–5142; $35 account startup plus $18 annual maintenance fee; minimum initial and subsequent investments: $1,000, $100) always keeps 20 percent of its assets in gold, 5 percent in silver, 10 percent in Swiss franc assets, 15 percent in U.S. and foreign real estate and natural resource stocks, 15 percent in common stocks and warrants, and 35 percent in U.S. Treasury bills, bonds and other dollar assets.

• **The Primary Trend Fund** (800–443–6544; no load, minimum initial and subsequent investments: $5,000, $100) apportions assets among undervalued stocks, government and corporate bonds and cash. According to fund secretary Roger Stafford, about 50 percent of the fund's assets were in cash during most of last year, but the manager loaded up on equities after the market crash and is now fully invested.

• **Shearson Lehman Special Equity Portfolios Strategic Investors Portfolio** (sold by brokers; 5 percent maximum back-end load; minimum initial and subsequent investments: $500, $200) invests in stocks, bonds, cash and gold securities. Up to 25

continued

New Funds Broaden Investment Base (concluded)

percent of the fund's assets may be invested in gold securities; up to 10 percent may be in foreign stocks and bonds. Currently, the fund is 60 percent in equities, 35 percent in bonds and 5 percent in cash.

• **The Strong Total Return Fund** (sold by brokers; 1 percent load; minimum initial and subsequent investments: $250, $200) has taken a conservative turn: 45 percent of its assets are in cash, 30 percent in stocks and 25 percent in bonds. Says chairman and portfolio manager Richard S. Strong: "The stock market is up five, working on six, years. Relative to history, the financial markets and economy are overextended as far as this economic recovery goes."

Reprinted courtesy of *The Boston Globe*.

funds allows an individual investor to set up an elaborate asset allocation scheme without having to purchase the thousands of individual stocks that would seem to be required.

International Asset Allocation

Investing internationally for improved diversification has become a major concern for institutional investors and is spreading among individual and professional investors.

The fast-paced evolution of an international financial market, one that integrates all the important national financial markets, has made global diversification less costly and more attractive.

The concept of a well-balanced portfolio dictates that foreign country investments be included in the market portfolio. Thus, in an all-out international asset allocation strategy, the risky *world portfolio* would include assets of a growing number of countries.

Internationally diversified investors treat country portfolios as "super class" assets. Allocation of the investment budget occurs in two stages: first, the budget is allocated to the various country portfolios. Only then, each portfolio manager allocates the country portfolio budget to the various asset classes.

The Approved Universe: List of Investable Assets by Class

Individual investors need not concern themselves with organizational efficiency. But professional investors with large amounts to invest must structure asset allocation activities to achieve efficient decentralization.

Suppose the president of Palatial, a U.S. investment company, wants to employ Amy Nakamura as a portfolio manager to run the company's Japanese stock portfolio. She is to make independent investment decisions within the overall objectives and constraints of Palatial.

Common features in an organization like Palatial are the investment committee and the asset universe. The investment committee includes top management officers, senior portfolio managers, and senior security analysts. It determines investment policies and verifies that portfolio managers and security analysts operate within the bounds of Palatial policies.

Asset universe
Approved list of assets for the manager's portfolio.

A major responsibility of the investment committee is to translate the objectives and constraints of the company to an **asset universe:** an approved list of assets for each of the company's portfolios. As part of this activity, Palatial's investment committee will specify a list of Japanese stocks as Amy Nakamura's universe.

An Asset Allocation Decision Procedure
Asset allocation can go something like this:

1. Specify asset classes to be included in the portfolio.
2. Specify capital market expectations. This step calls for using both historical data and economic analysis to determine your expectations of future rates of return on the asset classes to be considered for the portfolio.
3. Identify portfolios (with various combinations of the asset classes) that achieve the maximum rate of return for various levels of risk. This set of candidate portfolios is called the efficient set of portfolios.
4. Find the optimal asset allocation. This step requires you to choose, from the efficient set of portfolios, the one that best meets your risk and return objectives, while satisfying the constraints you face.

Security Selection

Security selection Choosing the particular securities to include in a portfolio.

Passive Security Selection and Bogey Portfolios
Security selection refers to the smallest allocation decision, that is, the choice of specific securities within each asset class.

As part of the asset allocation decision, Amy Nakamura is given a budget to invest in her universe. Amy's job is to determine which assets to include in her portfolio. Without any valuable information, Amy probably would choose to invest a little in everything in her universe.

Bogey portfolio The return an investment manager is compared to, for performance evaluation.

Knowing this, the investment committee has already designated the "little of everything" portfolio as Amy's **bogey portfolio** (benchmark portfolio), to be monitored by Palatial. These portfolios are the benchmarks used to evaluate the performance of both the forecasters behind the asset allocation decision and the portfolio managers.

Successful security analysis requires procurement and processing of valuable information about individual securities. Passive security selection means the bogey portfolio will be held by the manager. This portfolio will remain largely stationary, with occasional updates in response to changing objectives and constraints or to significant changes in the investment environment.

Active Security Selection
Active security selection requires two operational layers: security analysis and portfolio choice. Security analysts specialize in particular industries and companies, and managers of large active portfolios rely on a number of analysts. In large investment organizations, security analysts may be organized in a security analysis unit that serves all portfolio managers.

Portfolio managers sift through many reports from security analysts about assets in their universe. They consult forecasts of market conditions and capital market expectations and then determine the optimal portfolio, starting from the bogey portfolio. Security analysis and considerations of effective diversification are weighed to modify the bogey into the final portfolio.

A company's investment committee uses reports of portfolio managers on the prospects of their active portfolios, in conjunction with capital market expectations, to determine changes in asset allocation.

The Spectrum of Active/Passive Strategies

Figure 2.1 shows a grid that classifies the choice of active/passive strategies with respect to asset allocation and security analysis.

Strategy I is passive on both asset allocation and security selection. That is, the portfolio manager invests in the benchmark portfolio for each asset class. Long-term market forecasts are put together with various objectives and constraints to determine the benchmark asset allocation. The unit in charge of execution (the actual buying and selling of the desired securities) then purchases the securities in quantities dictated by the proportion of each security in the benchmark asset-class portfolio and the proportion allocated to the asset class.

To illustrate, suppose Palatial decides to invest its $1 billion using strategy I. Table 2.1 shows the investment committee universe and the portfolio manager's asset allocation.

For example, the proportion of Exxon in the *total* budget is $.75 \times .45 \times .20 = .0675$. Of a budget of $1 billion, 6.75 percent amounts to $6,750,000. If Exxon is selling for $48 a share, then Palatial's portfolio will include 140,625 shares of Exxon.

With Mitsubishi Chemical there will be one more layer of mathematics, arising from the yen/dollar foreign exchange rate. The portfolio share allocated to Mitsubishi is $.25 \times .40 \times .50 = .05$. The dollar value of the 5 percent allocated to Mitsubishi amounts to $5,000,000. If the exchange rate is ¥154.35/$, this

Figure 2.1
The choice of active
and passive strategies

		Asset Allocation	
		Passive	Active
Security Selection	Passive	I	III
	Active	II	IV

Table 2.1 *Asset Allocation and Universe for Palatial*

Super Class (Country)	Asset Class and Benchmark Weight (Fraction of superclass investment in parentheses)	Benchmark Portfolio for Asset Class (Fraction of asset-class investment in each security in parentheses)
United States (.75)	Cash (.15) ⟶	U.S. 91-day bills (1.0)
	Fixed income (.40) ⟶	U.S. 30-year T-bonds (.60) AT&T 36-year $8^5/_8\%$ coupon bonds (.40)
	Stocks (.45) ⟶	IBM (.45) GM (.35) Exxon (.20)
Japan (.25)	Cash (.60) ⟶	Bank of Japan 1-year notes (1.0)
	Stocks (.40) ⟶	Sumitomo (.50) Mitsubishi Chemical (.50)

amount will be equal to ¥771,750,000. At a price of ¥738 per share, Palatial will hold 1,045,730 shares of Mitsubishi Chemical.

The asset allocation, the associated universe, and the resultant portfolio are shown in the pie chart of Figure 2.2

Suppose Palatial were to shift to strategy II, that is, pursue passive asset allocation with active security selection. Asset allocation would change infrequently, but Palatial portfolio managers would use security analysis. Most of the time they would deviate from the bogey portfolio, attempting to beat its performance.

With active asset allocation and passive security selection, strategy III in Figure 2.1, security analysis is not used. The bogey portfolios of each asset class will remain largely unchanged. At the same time, asset allocation will be updated frequently, according to changes in capital market expectations.

Figure 2.2
From asset allocation to portfolio holdings

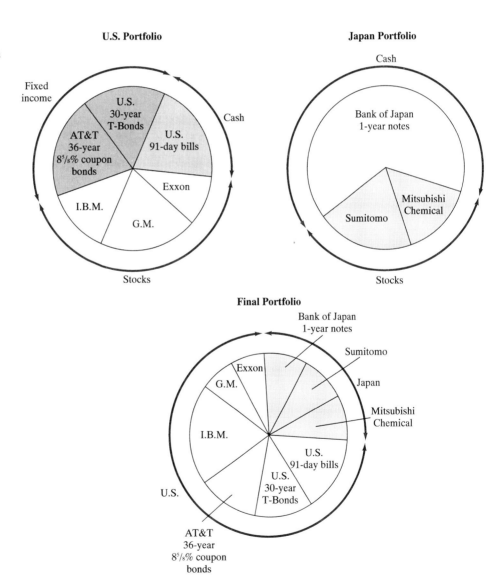

Finally, a truly active strategy (IV in Figure 2.1) requires frequent and harmonious updating of both asset allocation and security selection. Pursuing a fully active strategy is the real challenge of investment management.

Concept Check

> ***Question 3.*** Fill in the dollar amounts invested in each asset in the pie chart of Figure 2.2.

2.2 *Scenario Analysis and Capital Market Expectations*

Holding Periods and Holding-Period Returns

Holding-period return (HPR)   The rate of return over a given period.

Suppose we wish to manage Palatial according to strategy II, and restrict its asset-class universe to cash, bonds, and stocks. To determine asset allocation, we must specify our expectations of the rates of returns on these asset classes over the coming period. The periods between portfolio revisions are called holding periods, and rates of return on assets over this period are called **holding-period returns (HPR).** Holding-period returns are stated on an annualized basis, even if the target holding period is short.

It is customary to revise the asset allocation mix at least every quarter when major economic statistics are published and more often when important information is received.

Sources of Information and Scenario Analysis

Two sources of information are relevant to forming capital market expectations: historical data on capital market rates and economic forecasts. An investment professional must exercise considerable judgment when deciding how much to rely on each of these two sources.

The capital market expectations must be in a form that allows assessment of both expected rates of return and risk. Point forecasts (forecasts of one likely rate of return for each asset) may serve as measures of expected rates of return, but they do not allow assessment of risk. A richer forecast includes a likely rate of return for each asset in a variety of possible scenarios and the likelihood of each scenario.

Suppose economic forecasts derived from careful analysis of all the available information led Palatial to determine the probability distribution (list of possible outcomes and probability of each outcome) of HPRs exhibited in Table 2.2

Scenario analysis A set of possible economic outcomes with probabilities of occurrence, and predicted values for relevant variables.

The table presents a **scenario analysis:** a probabilistic statement of what might happen over the forecast period. The "State of the Economy" defines a distinct scenario for the forecasting period. The second column gives the specified likelihood (a probability estimate) of the occurrence of each scenario. The scenarios are mutually exclusive, and the probabilities add up to 1.0. The remaining columns specify the HPR that is forecast for each asset class in each scenario.

Holding-Period Returns in Various Scenarios

Palatial's assessment of the HPR on bonds comes from consideration of a 30-year U.S. Treasury bond paying a 9 percent interest (or coupon) rate and offering a yield to maturity of 9 percent.

Table 2.2   *Probability Distribution of HPR on Stocks, Bonds, and Cash*

State of Economy	Probability	Holding-Period Return		
		Stocks (%)	Bonds (%)	Cash (%)
Boom with low inflation	.1	74	4	6
Boom with high inflation	.2	20	−10	6
Normal growth	.4	14	9	6
Recession with low inflation	.2	0	35	6
Recession with high inflation	.1	−30	0	6
Expected return, E(r)		14.0	9.0	6
Standard deviation, σ		24.5	14.8	0

Correlation coefficient between stocks and bonds is −.2372.

If there is normal growth, then we expect interest rates to remain at their current level, and we will experience neither capital gains nor losses on holding the bond. Our HPR will simply equal the interest rate of 9 percent.

If there is a boom, then we think interest rates will rise, which means the price of the bond will fall. The amount by which interest rates will rise depends on inflation. At a low rate of inflation, interest rates will rise moderately, causing a capital loss of only 5 percent on the bond, for a net HPR of 4 percent (9 percent coupon minus 5 percent loss). If inflation is high, interest rates will rise considerably, causing a capital loss of 19 percent, for a net HPR of −10 percent on bonds.

If there is a recession, then we think the direction of interest rates will again depend on inflation. With little inflation, interest rates will fall, but if there is high inflation, they will rise despite the recession. In the low-inflation recessionary scenario, bonds will do very well with an HPR of 35 percent. But in the high-inflation recessionary scenario, the bond price will fall by 9 percent, leaving an HPR of 0.

In the case of stocks, the return is expected to be best in an noninflationary boom, worst in an inflationary recession.

Assessment of Expected Returns and Risk in Scenario Analysis

Averaging the holding-period returns of each asset class over the various scenarios (using the probabilities as weights) yields the expected rate of return. This is the HPR we would also forecast with a point forecast.

Scenario analysis allows us to quantify risk. The risk of investing in bonds and stocks can be expressed by the **standard deviation** of the HPR of bonds and stocks, and the correlation between them.

The standard deviation of the HPR measures the average size of the deviation (from the expected HPR) if various scenarios materialize. Obviously, the greater the standard deviation of the stock or bond portfolio, the greater its risk. As we see in Table 2.2, the standard deviation of cash is zero, because its HPR is the same for all scenarios. Stocks have a standard deviation of 24.5 percent, compared to 14.8 percent for bonds, because the stock HPR swings more widely from the expectation of 14 percent than the bond HPR swings from the expectation of 9 percent.

Correlation coefficient
Measures the extent to
which two variables
move in tandem.

The second measure affecting the riskiness of investing in stock and bond portfolios is the correlation between the HPR of bonds and stocks. The **correlation coefficient** expresses how closely the HPRs on the two asset classes move together. The maximum correlation coefficient is 1.0, meaning the HPRs move in unison. The minimum correlation coefficient of -1.0 means the HPRs move in unison, but in the opposite direction. Positive correlation coefficients mean the movement is, on average, in the same direction; negative coefficients mean the movements are in opposite directions. A correlation coefficient of zero means that knowing the direction of one asset's movement will not help us predict the direction of the other's.

The more highly correlated the HPRs are, the less the benefit of diversifying, that is, of holding both stocks and bonds. The virtue of holding a portfolio, rather than a single asset, is that low HPRs of one asset can be offset with high HPRs on the other. A high positive correlation implies that the diversification effect is reduced. In this case, asset HPRs will vary similarly over the different scenarios, and low HPRs may be reinforced rather than offset.

The last line in Table 2.2 gives the correlation coefficient between stocks and bonds that results from the scenario forecasts. Here it is negative, implying that diversification into stocks and bonds will greatly reduce overall risk. This makes a stocks and bonds portfolio less risky than the individual standard deviations might suggest, because some of these risks get offset when combined into a portfolio.

To the extent that the expected returns, standard deviations, or the correlation coefficient resulting from the scenario forecasts differ from what they have been in the past, we can, if we wish, adjust the scenario forecasts so that the resulting estimates of expected returns and risk conform more to historical experience.

Concept Check

> *Question 4.*   Using the data in Table 2.2, estimate the expected rate of return on the U.S. country portfolio of Table 2.1. (Assume the rates of return on the asset-class portfolios will be as predicted by the columns in Table 2.2.)

2.3   *Taxes and Investment Strategy*

Taxes and Asset Allocation

So far, we have ignored income taxes in discussing asset allocation. Of course, to the extent that your investments are tax-exempt, such as pension funds, or if your entire investment portfolio is in a tax-sheltered account, such as an individual retirement account (IRA), taxes are irrelevant to your portfolio decisions.

But say at least some of your investment income is subject to income taxes at the highest rate under current law. You want to know the after-tax HPR on your portfolio. At first glance, it might appear to be a simple matter to figure out after-tax HPRs on stocks, bonds, and cash, if you know what HPRs are before taxes, but there are several complicating factors.

The first is that you can choose between tax-exempt and taxable bonds. You will choose to invest in tax-exempt bonds if your personal tax rate is such that the after-tax rate of interest on taxable bonds is less than the interest rate on tax-exempt bonds.

If you are in the highest tax bracket, you probably will prefer to invest in tax-exempt bonds for both the short maturities (cash) and the long maturities (bonds). This means that cash investments for you will probably be a tax-exempt money market fund.

The second complication is not as easy to deal with. Part of your HPR is in the form of capital gain or loss. Under the current tax system, you pay income taxes on a capital gain only if you *realize* it by selling the asset during the holding period. This applies to bonds as well as stocks and makes the after-tax HPR a function of whether the security will actually be sold by the end of the holding period. Sophisticated investors time the sale of securities, and realization of capital gain or loss, to maximize their tax advantage. This often calls for selling securities that are losing money at the end of the tax year and holding on to those that are making money.

Furthermore, because cash dividends on stocks are fully taxable and capital gains taxes can be deferred by not selling stocks that appreciate in value, the after-tax HPR on stocks will depend on the dividend payout policy of the corporations that issue the stock.

These tax complications make portfolio selection for the taxable investor a lot harder than for the tax-exempt investor. A branch of the money management industry deals with ways to avoid paying taxes through special investment strategies.

Tax-Shelter Options

Four important tax-sheltering options can radically affect optimal asset allocation for individual investors. The first is the tax-deferral option, which arises because you pay tax on a capital gain only when you realize the gain. The second option is tax-deferred retirement plans such as individual retirement accounts. The third is tax-deferred annuities offered by life insurance companies. The last option is investing in tax-exempt instruments.

The next two sections provide numerical examples of the first two options: tax deferral and the tax-deferred retirement plan.

The Tax-Deferral Option
A fundamental feature of the U.S. tax code is that tax on a capital gain on an asset is payable only when the asset is sold.[1] This is the tax-deferral option. The investor can control the timing of the tax payment. From a tax perspective, this option makes stocks in general preferable to fixed-income securities.

To see this, compare IBM stock with an IBM bond. Suppose that both offer an expected total return of 15 percent this year. The stock has a dividend yield of 5 percent with an expected appreciation in price of 10 percent. Dividend yield takes the form of the annual cash dividend as a percent of the current stock price. Dividend yield is the immediately taxable part of the annual rate of return

---

[1]The major exception to this rule occurs in futures investing, where a gain is treated as taxable in the year it occurs regardless of whether the investor closes the position.

on the stock. The bond has an interest rate of 15 percent, and the bond investor must pay tax on the bond's interest in the year it is earned. The IBM stockholder pays tax only on the 5 percent dividend and defers paying tax on the 10 percent capital gain until the stock is sold.

Suppose you invest $5,000 for five years and are in a 28 percent tax bracket. An investment in the bond will earn an after-tax return of 10.8 percent per year: $(1 - \text{tax rate}) \times (\text{rate of return}) = (1.0 - .28).15 = .108$. We assume that the after-tax interest is reinvested in IBM bonds that continue to yield 15 percent before taxes throughout the five years. The yield after taxes at the end of five years is:

$$\$5,000 \times 1.108^5 = \$8,349.66.$$

For the stock, dividend yield after taxes will be 3.6 percent ($.72 \times .05 = .036$), and we assume dividends are reinvested in IBM stock that continues to yield 5 percent in dividends and 10 percent in capital gains throughout the five years. Because no taxes are paid on the capital gain until the fifth year, the return before paying the capital gains tax will be:

$$\$5,000 \times (1 + .036 + .10)^5 = 5,000 \times (1.136)^5 = \$9,459.36.$$

In the fifth year, the capital gain is equal to the full value of the investment less the principal of $5,000 and the reinvested after-tax dividends (at the 3.6 percent rate):

$$\$9,459.36 - 5,000 \times (1.036)^5 = 9459.36 - 5967.18 = \$3,492.18.$$

Taxes due are $.28 \times 3,492.18 = \$977.81$, leaving a net terminal value of $9,459.36 - 977.81 = \$8,481.55$, which is $131.89 more than the bond investment terminal value. Deferral of the capital gains tax allows the investment to compound at a faster rate until the tax is actually paid.

The more an investor's total return is in the form of price appreciation, the greater the value of the tax-deferral option.

Tax-Deferred Retirement Plans and the Value of Tax Deferral

Recent years have seen establishment of a number of tax-deferred retirement plans, where investors can choose how to allocate assets. Individual retirement accounts (IRAs) are one example. In all these plans, contributions and earnings are not subject to federal income tax until the individual withdraws them as benefits.[2]

Consider David who has saved $10,000 from his after-tax wages over the past year. David is in the 28 percent tax bracket and expects that he will stay in the same bracket until he retires in 20 years. For simplicity, we assume that David will withdraw the entire amount on retirement. If he withdraws the retirement funds over a protracted period, then the tax-deferral benefits will be even greater. Assume that the annual, before-tax rate of return on David's savings will be 10 percent until retirement.

---

[2]At this date, tax deferral on contributions to IRAs is severely restricted. (This restriction is often criticized as a damper on the incentive to save.) In the example, we demonstrate the IRA advantage with and without this benefit.

Without any tax sheltering, the terminal value of the $10,000 savings will be:

$$\$10,000 \times [1 + (1 - .28).10]^{20} = \$40,169.43.$$

When the contribution itself is not sheltered, but income on it is tax deferred, the before-tax terminal value will be:

$$\$10,000 \times (1 + .10)^{20} = \$67,275.00,$$

of which all but the original investment of $10,000 is taxable income at 28 percent. The after-tax terminal value in this case will be:

$$\$67,275.00 - .28 \times (67,275.00 - 10,000) = \$51,238.00.$$

The value of the tax deferral of income is $51,238.00 − 40,169.43 = $11,068.57. Another way to look at this is that the deferral of income tax is equivalent to producing an after-tax rate of return of 8.5 percent, compared with 7.2 percent without shelter.

Suppose contributions also are tax deferred, as they still are for some individuals. A contribution of $13,888.89 therefore reduces after-tax income by only $10,000, because $13,888.89 × .72 = $10,000. This means David can actually invest $13,888.89 instead of $10,000 without shelter, which has a before-tax terminal value of:

$$13,888.89 \times (1.1)^{20} = \$93,437.51.$$

This entire amount is subject to taxes, however, because the original contribution was sheltered too. Hence, the after-tax terminal value becomes:

$$\$93,437.51 \times .72 = \$67,275.00.$$

Thus, the net benefit to sheltering the contribution will be:

$$\$67,275.00 - 51,238.00 = \$16,037,$$

and the total value of tax deferral amounts to a hefty $27,105.57.

Another way to express this value is that it is equivalent to an after-tax rate of 10 percent, compared to the 7.2 percent without any shelter.

Investments that Fit Tax-Deferred Plans

Typically, an individual may have some investments in tax-qualified retirement accounts and some in ordinary taxable accounts. The basic investment principle that applies is to hold whatever bonds you want to hold in your retirement account while holding equities in the ordinary account. You maximize the tax advantage of the retirement account by holding in it the security that is the least tax advantaged.

Suppose Eloise has $200,000 of wealth, $100,000 of it in a tax-qualified retirement account. She has decided to invest half of her wealth in bonds and half in stocks, so she allocates half of her retirement account and half of her nonretirement funds to each. By doing this, Eloise is not maximizing her after-tax returns. She could reduce her tax bill with no change in before-tax returns by simply shifting her bonds into the retirement account and holding all her stocks outside the retirement account.

Concept Check

Question 5. *a.* How would the benefits of deferral of income and contributions to an IRA change if David were in the 33 percent tax bracket?
b. How would the benefits change if he were to retire in 20 years?
c. What is Eloise's loss of terminal value in 10 years, if she is in the 28 percent tax bracket? (Assume that both stocks and bonds yield a before-tax rate of 10 percent.)

2.4   *Monitoring Portfolios and Evaluating Performance*

Investment decisions are made under uncertainty. This means good decisions may occasionally lead to bad outcomes, just as bad decision makers may occasionally get lucky. How often such distortion will occur depends on the degree of uncertainty.

The difficulty that uncertainty poses is twofold. It complicates the decision making beforehand; it also makes it difficult to evaluate the quality of the decisions from observed outcomes after the fact.

Internal (Direct) Portfolio Evaluation

Individual investors managing their own portfolios should have the least trouble evaluating their performance. If you know the forecasts and the analytical considerations that went into each decision, presumably you can tell from the results how good the assumptions were.

Now think of portfolio performance. How do you measure the success of a selection from a range of risk-return trade-offs? There is no simple answer. The real advantage for individual investors is that they know the forecasts used as input to the decision, and they can attempt to evaluate their usefulness directly.

In a large investment organization, where decisions are decentralized, however, it is harder to pinpoint various decision inputs to assess the quality of forecasts and the resulting decisions.

External Portfolio Evaluation

The relationship between investors and the professionals who manage their investments is analogous to the relationship between corporate shareholders and corporate management.

Shareholders have no credible access to the input that went into management decisions and often do not even have a way of verifying what decisions were made. An entire industry of accounting and audit exists to provide interested parties outside of corporate management with verified reports on the performance of the firm.

The analogy to investment management is straightforward. Clients and the public get frequent (daily, in many cases) audited reports on the rate of return on the manager's portfolio. Quarterly reports also reveal the exact portfolio positions as of the end of each quarter.

While this represents a lot of data, it still allows clients to evaluate performance only from realized rates of return. As we shall see in Chapter 21, evaluating performance from these data alone is a formidable task that leaves a lot of room for errors and doubt.

2.5 *Investing as a Dynamic Process*

Investment involves a number of discrete but interrelated steps: setting objectives and constraints, devising investment policy on asset allocation and the universe of each asset class, producing capital market expectations, determining asset-class proportions, producing security analysis, and selecting the portfolio. Is the process ever finished and behind us?

By the time we are done with all the steps, the inputs will be out of date. How can we respond to this rate of change? How often must we adjust the various steps in the process? The answer depends on your willingness to spend, as well as on the speed of change in the investment environment.

An important and difficult part of the investment process is to address its dynamism. When to do what is just as important as how to do it. The reality is that the investment environment is changing at a very fast clip, and this may be its most important property.

Summary

1. A basic investment decomposition is into the risky portfolio and the safe asset. A natural benchmark (bogey) for the risky portfolio is the market portfolio. Such a portfolio is well diversified and reflects the "little of everything" approach. The safe asset is a collection of money market assets, which can be viewed as the money market fund part of the investment.

2. Market timing refers to the frequency of and reason for changing the proportion invested in risky versus safe assets. Active timing implies that this proportion responds to forecasts of change in market conditions. Passive timing implies that the proportion of risky assets will be relatively stable, changing mostly in response to changes in objectives and constraints and in long-term market conditions.

3. Major asset classes include: cash (money market assets), fixed-income securities (bonds), stocks, real estate, precious metals, and collectibles. Asset allocation refers to the decision on the investment proportion to be allocated to each asset class. An active asset allocation strategy, analogous to active timing, calls for the production of frequent market forecasts and adjustment of asset allocation according to these forecasts.

4. International asset allocation implies that country portfolios are constructed as "super asset classes." Each country portfolio then includes a further allocation to major asset classes of the country.

5. To invest in an asset class, the investment committee creates a list of investable assets for each class. This list, together with baseline weights for each security in the asset class, serves as a benchmark for evaluating the performance of the actual portfolio chosen by the manager.

6. The asset allocation procedure can be summarized as: (1) specify the relevant asset classes; (2) specify capital market expectations; (3) find the optimal asset allocation.

7. Active security selection requires security analysis and portfolio choice. Analysis of individual securities is required to choose securities making up a coherent portfolio that will outperform the asset-class bogey. The portfolio choice part requires identifying portfolios that achieve the maximum rate of return for various levels of risk.

8. Scenario analysis is a probabilistic statement of the possible economic conditions and the resulting rates of return on various asset classes. The scenario rate of return forecasts with the associated probabilities are used to compute the expected return and risk (measured by standard deviation and correlation between asset classes). These statistics are called capital market expectations and are used to determine asset allocation.

9. Investors have four important tax-sheltering options: tax deferral through the timing of the realization of capital gains and losses, tax-deferred retirement plans, tax-deferred annuities (issued by insurance companies), and tax-exempt securities.

10. Internal (direct) investment performance evaluation requires the recording of forecasts and assessment of their value. This is a nontrivial task. Forecasts have to be quantified and subsequent realizations statistically analyzed.

11. External investment performance evaluation is even more difficult. It requires the clients to evaluate the quality of decisions from realized rates of return. This is a formidable task.

12. Perhaps the most important feature of the investment process is that it is dynamic. The frequency and timing of various decisions are in themselves important decisions. Successful investment management requires management of these dynamic aspects.

Key Terms

asset allocation, 35	holding-period return	market timing, 34
asset universe, 38	(HPR), 42	money market, 34
bogey portfolio, 39	index funds, 34	scenario analysis, 42
correlation	market portfolio, 34	security selection, 39
coefficient, 44		

Problem Sets

1. Several discussion meetings have provided the following information about one of your firm's new advisory clients, a charitable endowment fund recently created by means of a one-time $10 million gift:

Objectives
Return requirement. Planning is based on a minimum total return of 8 percent per year, including an initial current income component of $500,000 (5 percent on beginning capital). Realizing this current income target is the endowment fund's primary return goal. (See "Unique needs" following.)

Constraints
Time horizon. Perpetuity, except for requirement to make an $8,500,000 cash distribution on June 30, 1988. (See "Unique needs.")
Liquidity needs. None of a day-to-day nature until 1998. Income is distributed annually after year-end. (See "Unique needs" below.)

Tax considerations. None; this endowment fund is exempt from taxes.

Legal and regulatory considerations. Minimal, but the prudent man rule applies to all investment actions.

Unique needs, circumstances, and preferences. The endowment fund must pay out to another tax-exempt entity the sum of $8,500,000 in cash on June 30, 1998. The assets remaining after this distribution will be retained by the fund in perpetuity. The endowment fund has adopted a "spending rule" requiring a first-year current income payout of $500,000; thereafter, the annual payout is to rise by 3 percent in real terms. Until 1998, annual income in excess of that required by the spending rule is to be reinvested. After 1998, the spending rate will be reset at 5 percent of the then-existing capital.

With this information and information found in this chapter, do the following:

    a. Formulate an appropriate investment policy statement for the endowment fund.

    b. Identify and briefly explain three major ways in which your firm's initial asset allocation decisions for the endowment fund will be affected by the circumstances of the account.

2. Investors in high marginal tax brackets probably would be least interested in a

    a. Portfolio of diversified stocks.

    b. Tax-free bond fund.

    c. Commodity pool.

    d. High-income bond fund.

3. You have been named as investment advisor to a foundation established by Dr. Walter Jones with an original contribution consisting entirely of the common stock of Jomedco, Inc. Founded by Dr. Jones, Jomedco manufactures and markets medical devices invented by the doctor and collects royalties on other patented innovations.

All of the shares that made up the initial contribution to the foundation were sold at a public offering of Jomedco common stock and the $5 million proceeds will be delivered to the foundation within the next week. At the same time, Mrs. Jones will receive $5 million in proceeds from the sale of her stock in Jomedco.

Dr. Jones's purpose in establishing the Jones Foundation was to "offset the effect of inflation on medical school tuition for the maximum number of worthy students."

You are preparing for a meeting with the foundation trustees to discuss investment policy and asset allocation.

    a. Define and give examples that show the differences between an investment objective, an investment constraint, and investment policy.

    b. Identify and describe an appropriate set of investment objectives and investment constraints for the Jones Foundation.

    c. Based on the investment objectives and investment constraints identified in part *b,* prepare a comprehensive investment policy statement for the Jones Foundation to be recommended for adoption by the trustees.

4. You are P. J. Water, CFA, a managing partner of a prestigious investment counseling firm that specializes in individual rather than institutional accounts. The firm has developed a national reputation for its ability to blend modern portfolio theory and traditional portfolio methods. You have written a number of articles on portfolio management. You are an authority on the subject of establishing investment policies and programs for individual clients, tailored to their particular circumstances and needs.

Dr. and Mrs. A. J. Mason have been referred to your firm and to you in particular. At your first meeting on June 2, 1992, Dr. Mason explained that he is an electrical engineer and long-time professor at the Essex Institute. He is also an investor and, after 30 years of teaching, the rights to one of his patented inventions, the "inverse thermothrocle valve," have just been acquired by a new electronics company, ACS, Inc.

In anticipation of the potential value of his invention, Dr. Mason had followed his accountant's advice and established a private corporation, wholly owned by the Masons, to hold the title to the "inverse thermothrocle valve" patent. It was this corporation that ACS acquired from the Masons for $1 million in cash, payable at the closing on June 7, 1992. In addition, ACS has agreed to pay royalties to Dr. Mason or his heirs, based on its sales of systems that utilize the "inverse thermothrocle valve."

Since ACS has no operating record, it is difficult for either the company or Dr. Mason to forecast future sales and royalties. While all parties are optimistic about prospects for success, they are also mindful of the risks associated with any new firm, especially those exposed to the technological obsolescence of the electronics industry. The management of ACS has indicated to Dr. Mason that he might expect royalties of as much as $100,000 in the first year of production and maximum royalties of as much as $500,000 annually thereafter.

During your counseling meeting, Mrs. Mason expressed concern for the proper investment of the $1,000,000 initial payment. She pointed out that Dr. Mason has invested all of their savings in his inventions. Thus, they will have only their Social Security retirement benefits and a small pension from Essex Institute to provide for their retirement. Dr. Mason will be 65 in 1996. His salary from the Essex Institute is $55,000 per year. Additionally, he expects to continue earning $10,000–$25,000 annually from consulting and speaking engagements.

The Masons have two daughters and a son, all of whom are married and have families of their own. Dr. and Mrs. Mason are interested in helping with the education of their grandchildren and have provided in their wills for their estate to be divided among their children and grandchildren.

In the event that the royalty payments from ACS meet the projections cited above, Mrs. Mason is interested in providing a scholarship fund in the name of Dr. Mason for the benefit of enterprising young engineers attending the Essex Institute. The scholarship fund ranks third behind the provision for the Masons' retirement and for the education of their grandchildren.

In your discussions with Dr. and Mrs. Mason you have stressed the importance of identifying investment objectives and constraints and having an appropriate investment policy. Identify and describe an appropriate set of investment objectives and investment constraints for Dr. and Mrs. Mason, and prepare a comprehensive investment policy statement based on these investment objectives and constraints.

 5. You are being interviewed for a job as a portfolio manager at an investment counseling partnership. As part of the interview, you are asked to demonstrate your ability to develop investment portfolio policy statements for the clients listed below:

a. Pension fund that is described as a mature defined benefit plan; with the work force having an average age of 54; no unfunded pension liabilities; and wage cost increases forecast at 9 percent annually.

b. University endowment fund that is described as conservative; with investment returns being utilized along with gifts and donations received to meet current expenses; the spending rate is 5 percent per year; and inflation in costs is expected at 8 percent annually.

c. Life insurance company that is described as specializing in annuities; policy premium rates are based on a minimum annual accumulation rate of 14 percent in the first year of the policy and a 10 percent minimum annual accumulation rate in the next five years.

List and discuss separately for *each* client described above the objectives and constraints that will determine the portfolio policy you would recommend for that client.

6. A clearly written investment policy statement is critical for
   a. mutual funds.
   b. individuals.
   c. pension funds.
   d. all investors.

7. The investment policy statement of an institution must be concerned with all of the following *except:*
   a. its obligations to its clients.
   b. the level of the market.
   c. legal regulations.
   d. taxation.

Chapter

The Financial System and Institutions

This chapter begins with some preliminaries to understanding the financial system. First, we distinguish between real assets and financial assets. Then, we describe the foundations of the financial system and institutions as evolving responses to private- and public-sector demands. We cite the great savings and loan debacle resulting in part from failures of regulators to recognize the strength of economic incentives.

We end with a discussion of types of financial markets and comment on recent trends in financial market activities. After studying this chapter you should be able to:

- Distinguish among real assets, financial assets, and aggregate wealth.
- Describe the roles of the major institutions in the financial system.
- Identify types of financial markets and recent trends in activity.

3.1 Real Assets versus Financial Assets

Real assets *Assets used to produce goods and services.*

Financial assets *Securities representing claims to the income*

The material wealth of a society is determined ultimately by the productive capacity of its economy, that is, the goods and services its members create. This productive capacity is a function of the **real assets** of the economy: the land, buildings, machines, and knowledge that can be used to produce goods and services.

In contrast to such real assets are **financial assets,** such as stocks or bonds (securities). Shares of stock are no more than sheets of paper, and stock certificates do not contribute directly to the productive capacity of the economy.

generated by real assets or claims on income from the government.

Financial assets contribute to productive capacity *indirectly*. Serving as claims on the cash flow from a company, financial assets allow the owners of the company to step back from active management of the firm and leave it to professionals. This facilitates the transfer of funds from savers to enterprises with attractive investment opportunities, improving the overall efficiency of productive capacity.

Financial assets do contribute to the wealth of the individuals or firms that own them. This is because financial assets are *claims* to the income generated by the real assets or claims on income from the government.

When the real assets used by a firm ultimately generate income, the income is allocated to investors according to their ownership of financial assets, or securities, issued by the firm. Bondholders, for example, who lend money to a firm by buying a bond, are entitled to a flow of income based on the interest rate and par value (face value) of the bond. Equityholders (stockholders) are entitled to any residual income, in the form of dividends, after bondholders and other creditors have been paid. The values of various financial assets depend on the values of the underlying real assets of the firm.

While real assets are income-generating assets, financial assets simply define the allocation of income or wealth among investors. Individuals can choose between consuming their current endowments of wealth today or investing for the future. If they invest for the future, they may choose to hold financial assets; they may buy securities.

When people buy securities, a company uses that money to purchase real assets (plant, equipment, technology, and inventory). Ultimately then, the returns on a security (financial asset) come from the income produced by the real assets that were financed by the issuance of the security. Basically, financial assets are the means by which individuals hold their claims on real assets in well-developed economies. If we cannot own an auto plant, we can buy shares of General Motors or Toyota and thereby share in the income derived from the production of automobiles.

Another way to appreciate the distinction between real and financial assets involves accounting. Real assets appear only on the assets side of the balance sheet. Financial assets, however, always appear on both sides of the balance sheet. Your financial claim on a firm is an asset to you, but to the firm that issued it, the claim is a liability. When we aggregate over all balance sheets—of individuals and firms—financial assets will cancel out, leaving only the sum of real assets as the net wealth of the aggregate economy.

The distinction between real and financial assets is apparent when we compare the composition of national wealth in the United States, presented in Table 3.1, with the financial assets and liabilities of U.S. households shown in Table 3.2. National wealth consists of structures, equipment, inventories of goods, and land (it does not include the value of human capital, the earning potential of the work force). Household wealth includes financial assets such as bank accounts, corporate stock, bonds, and mortgages.

Most people in the United States hold their financial claims in an indirect form. Only about 25 percent of the adult U.S. population holds shares directly. That does not mean they are the only ones with a stake in national production, though. The claims of most individuals are mediated through institutions that hold shares on their behalf: pension funds, insurance companies, mutual funds, and college endowments.

Table 3.1   *National Net Worth*

Assets	$ Billion
Residential structures	$4,604
Plant and equipment	4,811
Inventories	1,063
Consumer durables	2,024
Land	8,740
Gold and SDRs	22
Net claims on foreigners	−695
Total	15,569*

*Column sum may differ from total because of rounding errors.

Source: *Balance Sheets for the United States, 1945–90,* Washington D.C.: Board of the Federal Reserve System, March 1991.

Table 3.2   *Balance Sheet of U.S. Households*

Assets	$ Billion	% Total	Liabilities and Net Worth	$ Billion	% Total
Tangible assets					
Houses	$ 3,420	16.2%	Mortgages	$ 2,641	12.4%
Land	1,316	6.2	Consumer credit	1,028	4.9
Durables	2,024	9.6	Other loans	165	0.8
Other	316	1.5	Other	127	0.6
Total tangibles	7,076	33.5	Total liabilities	3,961	18.7
Financial assets					
Deposits	3,429	16.2			
Life insurance reserves	388	1.8			
Pension reserves	2,945	13.9			
Corporate equity	2,355	11.1			
Equity in noncorporate business	2,634	12.4			
Debt securities	2,073	9.8			
Other	267	1.3			
Total financial assets	14,091	66.5	Net worth	17,206	81.3
Total	21,167	100.0		21,167	100.0

Source: *Balance Sheets for the United States, 1945–90,* Board of the Federal Reserve System, March 1991.

Concept Check

Question 1.   Are the following assets real or financial? *a.* patents, *b.* lease obligations, *c.* customer goodwill, *d.* a college education, *e.* $5 bill.

3.2   *The Financial System Responds to Clientele Demands*

When enough clients demand and are willing to pay for a service, it is likely that a profit-seeking supplier will find a way to provide and charge for that service. This mechanism leads to the diversity of financial markets. Let us consider the market responses to the disparate demands of the various sectors in the economy.

Financial Intermediation

Households want desirable investments for their savings, yet the small (financial) size of most households makes direct investment difficult. A small investor seeking to lend money to businesses that need to finance investments doesn't advertise in the local newspaper. An individual lender would not be able to diversify across borrowers to reduce risk. Finally, an individual lender is not equipped to assess and monitor the credit risk of borrowers.

Financial intermediaries   Institutions that "connect" borrowers and lenders by accepting funds from lenders and loaning funds to borrowers.

For these three reasons, small investors would need to charge more on loans; large investors would outbid them. What happens instead is that **financial intermediaries** evolve to bring lender and borrower together. These financial intermediaries include banks, investment companies, insurance companies, or credit unions. Financial intermediaries sell their own liabilities (issue securities) to raise funds to purchase liabilities (securities) of other corporations.

For example, a bank raises funds by borrowing (taking deposits) and lending that money to (purchasing the liabilities of) other borrowers. The interest spread between the rates paid to depositors and the rates charged to borrowers is the source of the bank's profit. In this way, lenders and borrowers do not need to contact each other directly. Instead, each goes to the bank, which acts as an intermediary between the two. The problem of matching lenders with borrowers is solved when each comes independently to the common intermediary. The convenience and cost savings the bank offers borrowers and lenders allow it to profit from the interest rate spread. In other words, the problem of coordination creates a market niche for the bank as intermediary. Profit opportunities alone dictate that banks will emerge in a trading economy.

Financial intermediaries are distinguished from other businesses in that both their assets and their liabilities are overwhelmingly financial. Table 3.3 shows that the balance sheets of financial institutions include very small amounts of tangible assets. Compare it to the aggregated balance sheet of the nonfinancial corporate sector in Table 3.4. The contrast arises because intermediaries are middlemen, simply moving funds from one sector to another. In fact, this is the primary social function of such intermediaries, to channel household savings to the business sector.

Other examples of financial intermediaries are investment companies, insurance companies, and credit unions. All these firms offer similar advantages in playing a middleman role. First, by pooling the resources of many small investors, they are able to lend considerable sums to large borrowers. Second, by lending to many borrowers, intermediaries achieve significant diversification, so they can accept loans that individually might be too risky given the market interest spread. Third, intermediaries build expertise through the volume of business they do and can use economies of scale and scope to assess and monitor risk.

Investment companies   Firms managing funds for investors. An investment company may manage several mutual funds.

Investment companies, which pool and manage the money of many investors, also arise out of economies of scale. Here, the problem is that most household portfolios are not large enough to be spread among a wide variety of securities. It is very expensive in terms of brokerage fees and research costs to purchase one or two shares of many different firms. This observation reveals a profit opportunity filled by the mutual funds offered by many investment companies. Mu-

Table 3.3   *Balance Sheet of Financial Institutions**

Assets	$ Billion	% Total	Liabilities and Net Worth	$ Billion	% Total
Tangible assets			Liabilities		
Equipment and structures	$ 305	2.7%	Deposits	$ 3,546	31.5%
Land	20	.2	Mutual fund shares	580	5.2
Total tangibles	325	2.9	Life insurance reserves	377	3.4
			Pension reserves	2,695	24.0
			Money market securities	499	4.4
			Bonds and mortgages	531	4.7
			Other	2,360	21.0
			Total liabilities	10,588	94.2
Financial assets					
Deposits and cash	370	3.3			
Government securities	2,478	22.0			
Corporate bonds	1,289	11.5			
Mortgages	2,193	19.5			
Consumer credit	766	6.8			
Other loans	783	7.0			
Corporate equity	1,408	12.5			
Other	1,627	14.5			
Total financial assets	10,914	97.1	Net worth	651	5.8
Total	11,239	100.0		11,239	100.0

*Column sums may differ from total because of rounding error.

Source: *Balance Sheets for the United States, 1945–90,* Board of the Federal Reserve System, March 1991.

Table 3.4   *Balance Sheet of Nonfinancial U.S. Business**

Assets	$ Billion	% Total	Liabilities and Net Worth	$ Billion	% Total
Tangible assets			Liabilities		
Equipment and structures	$ 5,336	46.9%	Bonds and mortgages	$ 2,178	19.1%
Land	2,404	21.1	Bank loans	717	6.3
Inventories	1,082	9.5	Other loans	607	5.3
Total tangibles	8,822	77.5	Trade debt	710	6.2
			Other	628	5.5
			Total liabilities	4,840	42.5
Financial assets					
Deposits and cash	$ 412	3.6%			
Marketable securities	141	1.2			
Consumer credit	43	0.4			
Trade credit	920	8.1			
Other	1,050	9.2			
Total financial assets	2,566	22.5	Net worth	6,548	57.5
Total	11,388	100.0		11,388	100.0

*Column sums may differ from total because of rounding error.

Source: *Balance Sheets for the United States, 1943–90,* Board of the Federal Reserve System, March 1991.

tual funds gain the advantage of large-scale trading and portfolio management, while participating investors are assigned a prorated share of the total funds according to the size of their investment. This system gives small investors advantages they are willing to pay for via a management fee to the mutual fund operator.

Investment companies also can design portfolios specifically for large investors with particular goals. In contrast, mutual funds are sold in the retail market, and their investment philosophies are differentiated mainly by strategies that are likely to attract a large number of clients. Some investment companies manage "commingled funds," in which the monies of different clients with similar goals are merged into a "mini-mutual fund," which is run according to the common preference of those clients.

Economies of scale also explain the proliferation of analytic services available to investors. Newsletters, data bases, and brokerage house research services all engage in research to be sold to a large client base. This setup arises naturally. Investors clearly want information, but with small portfolios to manage, they do not find it economical to personally gather all of it. Hence, a profit opportunity emerges: a firm can perform this service for many clients and charge for it.

Concept Check

Question 2. Tracy Vaughn, a professional investment manager, serves clients in the following way: each client deposits the amount they wish Tracy to manage in a personal account with Merrill Lynch (under the client's name). The account instructions empower Tracy to manage the account independently, buying or selling any security. Does this operation constitute financial intermediation?

Investment Banking

Just as economies of scale and specialization create profit opportunities for financial intermediaries, so too do these economies create niches for firms that perform specialized services for business. Firms raise much of their capital by selling securities such as stocks and bonds to the public. Because these firms do not do so frequently, however, investment banking firms that specialize in such activities offer their services at a cost below that of running an in-house security issuance division.

Investment bankers
Firms specializing in the sale of new securities to the public, typically by underwriting the issue.

Investment bankers such as Goldman Sachs, Merrill Lynch, or Salomon Brothers advise the issuing corporation on the prices it can charge for the securities issued, appropriate interest rates, and so forth. Ultimately, the investment banking firm handles the marketing of the security issue to the public.

Investment bankers also can help firms design securities with special desirable properties. As an example, consider a pharmaceutical company undertaking a risky research and development project for a new drug. It needs to raise money for research costs and, if the research is successful, it will need to build a new manufacturing plant requiring still more financing.

To deal with this contingency, the investment banker might design a bond-with-warrant issue. (A warrant is a security giving its holder the option to purchase stock from the firm at a prespecified price up until the warrant's expiration date.) The bonds and warrants are issued, and the research commences.

Are All Wall Street's New Warrants Really Warranted?

NEW YORK—Like Hollywood, Wall Street likes to clone hits.

Warrants on the Japanese stock market were quick successes this year, so here come warrants on lots of other stock indexes, too.

But after a yearlong dearth of big new-product ideas on Wall Street, efforts to make the most of investors' interest in stock-index warrants are likely to produce lackluster sequels, many market professionals say.

The most popular warrants have all been linked to Japan's Nikkei 225-stock index. These warrants have provided an easy way for big and small U.S. investors to profit from the Tokyo market's slump. The warrants entitle holders to a cash payment that varies with stock indexes' performance after several years.

In total, at least seven Nikkei warrants issues have been publicly underwritten in U.S. markets, and many more have been privately placed here and abroad.

Now, investment bankers are plugging new national markets into their formula. Salomon Brothers Inc. in recent weeks has underwritten two small warrant offerings tied to the London stock market's FT-SE 100 index; it is also looking at Dutch and German issues. And the American Stock Exchange is seeking to list three-year warrants linked to the 20-stock Major Market Index in the United States.

The European and U.S. warrants, however, aren't expected to be nearly as popular with investors. Market professionals point out that U.S. investors already have far more alternatives available if they want to place a long-term bet on the direction of those markets, or hedge their market risk. In the United States, the alternatives include stock-index futures and options, all widely traded.

More broadly, big investors are showing increased skepticism toward Wall Street innovations these days.

"Most new financial products just restructure income streams from existing securities," says Jack Meyer, treasurer of the Rockefeller Foundation. "There's always a haircut built in so that the [Wall Street providers] make a little money. Unless you have a very peculiar risk preference, you're better off doing without."

Without investor support, many of Wall Street's brainstorms aren't making it into the wider world. "Getting the first deal done is a lot tougher than it used to be," says Ron Gallatin, a Shearson Lehman Hutton Inc. managing director in charge of new products. Mr. Gallatin had led Shearson's efforts last year to launch "unbundled stock units," a way of creating three new securities from a single share of common stock; Shearson eventually dropped the idea.

"Institutional buyers are a lot more old-fashioned than people realize," Mr. Gallatin observes. "There's a perception that it's the new things that have caused problems. It's much easier to justify something old and tried, than something new that you can't understand—or do understand, but can't explain to your pension committee."

The Nikkei warrants did well for two reasons. The first was timing; many of the Nikkei warrants

If the research is successful, the stock price will increase, warrant holders will find it advantageous to exercise their option to purchase additional shares, and as they purchase those shares, additional funds will flow to the firm precisely as they are needed to finance the new manufacturing plant. This financing package lets the firm avoid two separate security offerings. The exercise of the warrants provides additional financing at no additional floatation costs. See a discussion of warrants in the box.

Financial Innovation

Our pharmaceutical firm illustrates one source of financial innovation: response of an investment bank to a company's needs. Household objectives, however, are far more diverse. Most firms find it simpler to issue "plain vanilla" securi-

were launched just as the Tokyo stock market began its swoon this past winter. The put warrants, which represented a bet on a market drop, soared 100 percent and more in value. That attracted plenty of interest from U.S. investors large and small.

The Nikkei warrants also had an edge because U.S. investors had long grumbled that the Japanese market was overpriced, but lacked any ready way to put money on that proposition. Although U.S. investors in theory could have sold Japanese stock-index futures, doing so would have required setting up a yen trading account, meeting Japanese margin rules and monitoring their position during Tokyo market hours (nighttime in the U.S.). "That's a little scary," one large U.S. investor said.

In contrast, the Nikkei warrants are dollar denominated and easily traded in the U.S. That appealed to small U.S. investors—as did the quick early profits.

But unless European markets tumble or soar in coming months, it's hard to see how U.S. investors are likely to be drawn to warrants on those markets. Furthermore, underwriters say that the Securities and Exchange Commission is asking plenty of questions about European market disclosure before it is willing to approve U.S.-traded warrants for certain European stock markets.

Investment bankers acknowledge that many of their new products won't catch on, but they regard that as a bearable cost of doing business. A successful product such as the Nikkei warrants has already produced nearly $20 million in underwriting fees alone in the United States and Canada. Since most new products cost $1 million or less to develop, a success ratio of one in 10 can still be profitable for Wall Street's innovators.

Experimentation seems to be the rule at the American Stock Exchange, too, as it seeks to list a three-year warrant on the Major Market Index. (This index closely tracks the Dow Jones Industrial Average.) "Traditionally the Amex has tried to be more flexible and innovative about its new products," says Amex President Ken Liebler. "Some of them are hits and some aren't. If they aren't hits, we move on."

Investment bankers predict that the Major Market Index warrants may have some appeal for those individual investors who prefer the warrants' three-year maturity to the much shorter maturities of most stock-index futures and options. "If you're an institution, you could probably simulate the warrant yourself more cheaply with existing futures and options," says one Wall Street New Product Specialist. "But maybe it will have retail appeal."

And if the Amex's warrants should succeed on any scale at all, expect a sequel to the sequel. "I could see a warrant based on the Standard & Poor's 500-stock index," another new-products specialist says. "There's a tendency to have new issues very similar to one another. People try to capture the halo effect of a success."

George Anders, "Are All Wall Street's New Warrants Really Warranted?" *The Wall Street Journal*, May 3, 1990. Reprinted by permission of *THE WALL STREET JOURNAL*, © 1990 Dow Jones & Company, Inc. All Rights Reserved Worldwide.

ties, leaving exotic variants to specialists. This creates a profit opportunity for innovative security design and repackaging that investment bankers are only too happy to fill.

Pass-through security Pools of loans (such as home mortgage loans) sold in one package. Owners of pass-throughs receive all of the principal and interest payments made by the borrowers.

Consider the astonishing changes in mortgage markets since 1970, when mortgage **pass-through securities** were introduced by the Government National Mortgage Association (GNMA, or Ginnie Mae). These securities aggregate individual home mortgages into relatively homogeneous pools. Each pool acts as backing for a GNMA pass-through security. Investors who buy GNMA securities receive prorated shares of all the principal and interest payments made on the underlying mortgage pool.

For example, the pool might total $100 million of 12 percent, 30-year conventional mortgages. The rights to the cash flows could then be sold as 5,000 units, each worth $20,000. Each unit holder would then receive 1/5,000 of all monthly interest and principal payments made on the pool. The banks that originated the mortgages continue to service them (receiving fee-for-service), but they no longer own the mortgage investment; the investment has been passed through to the GNMA security holders.

Pass-through securities represent a tremendous innovation in mortgage markets. The securitization of mortgages means mortgages can be traded just like other securities in national (internationally integrated) financial markets. Availability of funds no longer depends on local credit conditions and is no longer subject to local banks' potential monopoly powers; with mortgage pass-throughs trading in national markets, mortgage funds can flow from any region (literally worldwide) to wherever demand is greatest.

In short, security demand elicits a market response. The new products developed in the past two decades came about as responses to previously unsatisfied demands for securities with particular risk, return, tax, and timing attributes. As the investment banking system has become ever more sophisticated, security creation and customization have become routine.

A Wall Street joke asks how many investment bankers it takes to sell a light bulb. The answer is 100: one to break the bulb, and 99 to sell the pieces.

Primitive securities, derivative securities A primitive security is an instrument such as a stock or bond for which payments depend only on the financial status of its issuer. A derivative security provides payoffs that depend on the prices of other securities.

This discussion leads to the notion of **primitive securities** versus **derivative securities.** A primitive security offers return based only on the status of the issuer. For example, bondholders get their stipulated interest payments only as long as the issuing firm is solvent. Dividends on stock depend on a board of directors' assessment of the firm's financial position; a firm can decide to omit dividends.

Derivative securities by contrast yield returns that depend on additional factors pertaining to the prices of other assets. For example, a stock option is a derivative security; the payoff to the option depends on the price of the underlying stock. Derivative mortgage-backed securities offer payouts that depend on the original mortgages, which are the primitive securities.

Much of the innovation in security design may be viewed as the continual creation of new types of derivative securities from the available set of primitive securities.

Concept Check

> ***Question 3.*** Identify the following as primitive or derivative securities. For derivative securities, what is the underlying asset?: *a.* 5,000 barrels of oil futures (West Texas crude), *b.* Conrail preferred stock, *c.* AT&T corporate bond, *d.* Digital Equipment Corp. convertible bond, *e.* Mitsubishi shares of common stock held by a U.S. citizen, *f.* option to buy a 767 jet from Boeing, *g.* a car loan.

Response to Taxation and Regulation

Much financial innovation and security creation may be viewed as a natural market response to unmet investor needs. Another driving force behind innovation is political interplay between government and investors on taxation and regulation. Many financial innovations are direct responses to legislation that either regulates or taxes investments of various sorts.

For decades, Regulation Q put a ceiling on the interest rates banks could pay depositors. Before it was repealed by the Depository Institutions Deregulation and Monetary Control Act of 1980, Regulation Q had spawned two financial innovations. One is money market funds. As inflation soared in the 1970s, market interest rates on bonds far exceeded regulated rates offered by banks, which could no longer compete for investor savings. Money market funds simply displaced banks in the pooling of savings into safe short-term bonds, that is, money market assets. Most money market funds even offer checking privileges.

Regulation Q also contributed to the coming of age of the Eurodollar market. Because Regulation Q did not apply to dollar-denominated time deposits in foreign accounts, many U.S. banks and foreign competitors established branches in Western Europe, where they could offer competitive rates outside the jurisdiction of U.S. regulators. The growth of the Eurodollar market was fed by another U.S. regulation: reserve requirements imposed on banks by the Federal Reserve Board. Foreign branches were exempt from such requirements and were thus better able to compete for deposits.

There are plenty of other examples. Financial futures markets were stimulated in the early 1970s by the demise of fixed exchange rates and by new federal regulations that overrode state laws treating some financial futures as gambling arrangements.

The general pattern is consistent. Tax and regulatory pressures often lead to unanticipated financial innovations, as profit-seeking investors make an end run around government restrictions. The constant game of regulatory catch-up sets off another round of innovations.

3.3   *Financial Institutions*

The premier financial institutions are banks, insurance companies, and investment companies, particularly mutual funds. We have already discussed differences in objectives, constraints, and policies of these institutions. Here we elaborate on the nature of the clientele demands they respond to.

Banks and the Need for Liquidity

Goldsmiths and jewelers of medieval Europe had to develop security to guard their valuables. In time, individuals recognized the advantage of pooled or mutual security services and began to go to jewelers for safe storage. While fees for storage of cash imply negative interest rates, the risk of loss and the cost of security for individuals on their own premises presented the possibility of an even greater negative expected return.

Jewelers acting as safekeepers of cash soon discovered that, on average, only a small fraction of the deposits were active at any given time, meaning they could invest a large portion of the deposit to earn a rate of return. The competition among these emerging banks for depositor funds required turning over most of the bank returns as interest to depositors. Competitive equilibrium settled at just enough of an interest rate spread to leave bankers an adequate return on their services.

Depositors were looking for liquidity as well as for safety, however. Enter checking accounts and lines of credit. Providing liquidity has remained the primary role of the banking system, even as other financial institutions came to provide similar pooling and investment services.

A bank pays interest on the entire deposit. At the same time, the bank earns interest only on the amount invested in its loan portfolio. What keeps the bank from lending it all to maximize income is the threat of being unable to provide liquidity to depositors, that is, to pay for a check written on an account.

Individuals approached by a cash-short bank will not agree to lend (i.e., deposit funds) if they suspect the bank will not be able to repay the loan. If the bank must liquidate its loan portfolio, the situation will get worse; illiquid loans are a source of additional losses.

A banker's nightmare is a run on the bank, when worried depositors line up in droves to withdraw all their cash before the bank declares bankruptcy. The possibility of bank runs threatens society's economic health, because they can easily start an economic avalanche. Bank runs and the subsequent collapse of many banks contributed to the onset and depth of the Great Depression of 1929–1933. After that time, the banking industry has been regulated and deregulated. Since then, as well, we have witnessed the great savings and loan debacle in the late 1980s.

Bank Regulation and the Great S&L Debacle

To guard against bank failures and bank runs, regulators have four lines of defense: (1) to protect banks from the vagaries of competition, (2) to mandate bank liquidity and capital adequacy, (3) to regulate the bank's choice of loan portfolio, and (4) to insure depositors against bank failures.

1. Competition leads banks to offer depositors higher rates. This squeeze on the interest-spread profit may pressure banks to make ever riskier loans (at higher interest rates), increasing the probability of default. While protecting bank profit margins, Regulation Q reduced the public incentive to save. In addition, the banking industry had to suffer the consequences of financial innovations that emerged to get around the regulation, and the regulation may have cost banks more profit than it ever secured. In short, Regulation Q and its repeal probably had little to do with the S&L disaster.

2. Banks must satisfy reserve ratio and capital ratio requirements. The reserve ratio, imposed by the Federal Reserve Bank, limits the proportion of deposits that can be invested by the bank. The capital ratio requires the shareholders of the bank to maintain a positive net worth of a minimum proportion of total assets. Shareholders are required to add fresh capital whenever necessary to maintain the capital ratio.

3. To protect against banks making ill-conceived loans, regulators once restricted S&Ls from investment in other than residential mortgages. While residential mortgages are quite risky, commercial and industrial real estate loans may be far riskier. Thus, this regulation was meant to reduce the risk of a typical S&L institution.

4. The most important cog in the machinery to prevent bank runs has been federal deposit insurance. Deposits with S&Ls were guaranteed by the Federal Savings and Loan Insurance Corporation (FSLIC), similar to the Federal Deposit Insurance Corporation (FDIC) for commercial banks, for up to $100,000. Deposit insurance should remove any incentive to run on a bank, regardless of its solvency. The risk of insolvency is shifted to the insuring agency. Note the crucial link: deposit insurance requires regulation. Once depositors have no stake in the safety of the bank loan portfolio, the bank's incentive to assume risk must be checked by regulation.

All this appears foolproof; so what went wrong? Enter the regulators. The U.S. banking industry has always been made of two entities: the commercial banks and the thrift institutions (including the saving and loan associations). Commercial banks specialize in lending to business, while thrifts specialize in mortgages to finance private housing. The safety of commercial banks was regulated by the FDIC while that of thrifts in the 1980s was regulated by the FSLIC.

As it happened, the FSLIC was not up to the task. With deregulation, S&Ls were allowed entry into riskier types of loans, while the deposit insurance was maintained. This incentive to take more risk and profit from a greater interest rate spread was not countered by tighter monitoring of individual S&L practices. Unscrupulous banking entrepreneurs and executives gravitated to the thrift industry, where loose procedures made it relatively easy to maintain or acquire a charter while pursuing policies that exploited high-risk high-spread investments of low-cost (insured) deposits.

The cost of this mismanagement to the taxpayer is still being tallied, but it appears that it will exceed one hundred billion dollars. It appears that, as often happens, economic incentives have been understood but greatly underestimated. Regulators need to appreciate the potential of economic incentives and the importance of compatibility of regulation and enforcement with these incentives.

Concept Check

Question 4. Two S&Ls in Louisiana advertise an interest rate on three-year time deposits. One is a member of the FSLIC and one is not. To stay competitive, which has to offer the higher rate, and what determines the difference?

Insurance and Risk Reduction

Insurance is the most straightforward way of reducing risk. The insurance industry employs about as many people as U.S. agriculture (about 2 percent of the labor force).

Consider a one-year term life insurance policy that pays a death benefit of $200,000. This policy offsets $200,000's worth of the disastrous event "death within a year." If the probability of death over the next year for a healthy person of the insured age group is 0.005 (1/2 of 1 percent), then the expected payoff (calculated below) is $1,000.

The policy as an asset in isolation, however, is risky. As viewed by the underwriter (insurer), the expected payout is:

$$0 \times .995 + (-200,000) \times .005 = -\$1,000.$$

For the insured, the payment is positive, so that the expected value is $1,000. Its risk can be measured by the standard deviation. As explained earlier, the standard deviation is obtained by taking the square root of the variance. The variance, in turn, is the expected value of *squared deviations* from the expected value. Thus, we compute the standard deviation (from the insured's view) as:

$$[(200,000 - 1,000)^2 \times .005 + (0 - 1,000)^2 \times .995]^{1/2} = \$14,107,$$

which is significant, far higher than the expected value. (The standard deviation is always positive.)

To leave the underwriter any profit, the premium on the policy has to exceed the expected value of the payoff to cover cost and ensure an adequate rate of return. (Part of this potential profit is created by the fact that the premium is paid in advance, that is, by the time value of cash flows.) Suppose the insurance company charges $1,300 for the policy and puts up that amount plus $198,700 of equity capital in a reserve account to cover the contingency of a loss of $200,000. (In practice, insurance companies do not fully reserve for maximum possible losses. But let's pursue the example anyway to illustrate some principles.)

The reserve account will not be left idle. Suppose it is invested at the going risk-free rate of 8 percent. The expected end-of-year value of the account (subtracting the expected payout) is thus:

$$1.08 \times \$200,000 - \$1,000 = \$215,000,$$

so the expected rate of return (net cash inflow within the holding period as a percent of the investment) on the *equity capital* is:

$$(215,000 - 198,700)/\$198,700 = .0820,$$

or 8.20 percent. Note how important the portfolio rate of return is to the profitability of the insurance business. Only 0.20 percent (20 basis points) is attributable to the insurance business, and that is gross of selling and administrative expenses. (Insurance companies would love to charge more but are denied by competitive forces and, perhaps, the specter of regulation.)

If the policyholder dies within the year, the rate of return will be:

$$(1.08 \times \$200,000 - \$200,000 - \$198,700)/\$198,700$$
$$= -.9195, \text{ or } -91.95 \text{ percent.}$$

With no benefits paid out, the rate of return will be:

$$(1.08 \times \$200,000 - 198,700)/198,700 = .0871, \text{ or } 8.71 \text{ percent.}$$

The standard deviation of the rate of return of this risky prospect is:

$$[(-91.95 - 8.20)^2 \times .005 + (8.71 - 8.20)^2 \times .995]^{1/2} = 7.10 \text{ percent.}$$

Risk premium *An expected return in excess of that on risk-free securities.*

Risk pooling *Combining many independent sources of risk.*

Insurance principle *The law of averages. The average outcome for many independent trials of an experiment will approach the expected value of the experiment.*

Because the portfolio investment is risk free, the entire risk of the proposition has to be attributed to the insurance side of the business. There being no free lunch, who is carrying that burden? In this case, it is the owners of the insurance company, who must be willing to bear a risk (standard deviation) of 7.1 percent against a reward (expected return *in excess of the risk-free rate,* which we call the **risk premium**) of 20 basis points.

Most people believe the way insurance companies pull this off is by **risk pooling,** that is, by selling many *independent* policies (in the statistical sense, so that the contingency, here the event of death, of the policies will not be correlated and will not "bunch up" to destroy the insurer). With independent risks, losses are offset by gains, and the profit will be relatively safe. The independence of the policies is crucial. This is why the fine print on a policy excludes events that affect many policyholders at once, such as war, riots, plague, and famine. These events have to be insured separately for an additional fee. That extra fee reflects the fact that many insured may die in the event of an outbreak of war, riots, or plague—so there will be no offset. The offset of losses that is expected within a portfolio of independent insurance policies is called the **insurance principle.**

Risk pooling is not the crucial ingredient, however. Proof of this is the existence of relatively small insurers that insure all kinds of risks that cannot be pooled, such as the launch of a commercial satellite. Moreover, risk pooling in the form of selling more policies also raises the ante, the scale of the operation. If you were to insure 1,000 individuals and fully reserve for contingencies, you would have to raise $200 million, and, even though the probability is small, there is a possibility of losing it all. So it is not risk pooling that does the job. The insurance industry is made viable through **risk sharing.**

Risk sharing   Distributing risk among many investors so that each investor's liability is small.

Suppose an entrepreneur discovers that to insure a single individual one must put up $198,700. The entrepreneur approaches nine other people who each have $200,000 to invest. Each of the 10 would-be insurers considers that risking all their money in a single risky venture is not wise. With no alternative venture of reasonable risk, they would rather invest it all risk-free at 8 percent.

So the entrepreneur suggests that each put up 1/10 of the insurance deal (198,700/10 = $19,870) and invest the remainder ($180,130) at 8 percent. Let us examine the prospect. In the event of no loss, the individual's end-of-year portfolio will be worth 1.08 × (200,000/10 + 180,130) = $216,140.40 (a rate of return of 8.07 percent). In the event of a loss, the end-of-year portfolio looks like this:

$$1.08 \times (200,000/10 + 180,130) - 200,000/10 = \$196,140.40$$

(a loss of only 1.93 percent). The expected rate of return is:

$$8.07 \times .995 + (-1.93) \times .005 = 8.02 \text{ percent,}$$

a risk premium of only 0.02 percent (2 basis points). The risk as measured by the standard deviation is also small:

$$[(8.07 - 8.02)^2 \times .995 + (-1.93 - 8.02)^2 \times .005]^{1/2} = .71 \text{ percent,}$$

less than 1 percent.

Our example closely fits the evolution of Lloyd's, the oldest insurance operation. It started at a London pub called Lloyd's, which was frequented by 18th-century ship captains and cargo owners, actively looking for ways to insure their economic survival. The pub patrons began risk sharing, which developed into a concern of independent insurers. When Lloyd's associates agree to underwrite a policy, they turn to other members who then form a concern for the specific policy. Today, however, Lloyd's method of operating is the exception. More often an insurance corporation is set up, with many shareholders, thus obtaining the desired risk sharing.

The idea of risk sharing is appealing from a social welfare standpoint as well. The market for insurance leads to an "all for one" stance, where all share the risk of the individual. Market competitive rates (fair insurance premiums) should lead individuals to use just the right amount of insurance.

Concept Check

Question 5. In the example of the term life insurance policy, suppose the risk-free rate available to the insurer goes up to 10 percent. How would it affect the calculations of the example?

Investment Companies

As we have seen, the investment objective to which investment policies are subordinated is to obtain the best risk-return trade-off. One side of this equation, risk reduction, can be achieved via any and all of three routes: insure against specific risks, reduce the proportion invested in risky assets (in favor of money market assets), and efficiently diversify the risky portfolio.

We have already argued that holding a little bit of everything, or holding the market portfolio, is a legitimate diversification strategy. The large number of assets that need to be included dictates that this task is best left to passive mutual funds, called index funds. Such funds are easy to manage. For example, Vanguard Index Trust Fund holds exactly the S&P 500 index portfolio. Initially, it requires the purchase of 500 different stocks in the appropriate proportions. Once the portfolio is in place, all that remains is to reinvest dividends to maintain the proportions. Thus, index funds are the least expensive diversified investment vehicle.

Many investors believe one should strive to achieve better than the market portfolio's risk-return trade-off. The idea is then to develop information that will identify underpriced and overpriced assets, that is, to engage in security selection. The portfolio should be tilted toward underpriced securities, and away from overpriced assets. The more you tilt the portfolio, the better the expected return. But as you proceed, you must consider that you are losing diversification benefits, thereby increasing risk. The optimal balancing of improved return through research and reduced risk through diversification is what is meant by efficient diversification.

Many mutual funds respond to the demand of individual investors who believe in active management performed by professional investors. The financial pages list over 500 mutual funds to choose from, segmented along lines of asset allocation and security selection. The various specialized strategies are specified in the mutual fund's prospectus and in its promotional materials.

3.4   *Markets and Market Structure*

Just as securities and financial institutions are born and evolve in response to investor demands, financial markets also develop to meet needs for particular trades. Consider what would happen if organized markets did not exist. Any household that wished to invest in some type of financial asset would have to find others that wish to sell.

This is how financial markets evolved. Meeting places established for buyers and sellers of financial assets became a financial market. A pub in old London called Lloyd's launched the maritime insurance industry. A Manhattan curb on Wall Street became synonymous with the financial world.

We can differentiate four types of markets: direct search markets, brokered markets, dealer markets, and auction markets.

Direct Search Markets

A direct search market is the least organized market. Buyers and sellers must seek each other out directly. An example of a transaction in such a market is the sale of a used refrigerator where the seller advertises for buyers in a local newspaper. Such markets are characterized by sporadic participation and low-priced and nonstandard goods. It does not pay most people or firms to seek profits by specializing in such an environment.

Brokered Markets

The next level of organization is a brokered market. In markets where trading in a good is active, brokers find it profitable to offer search services to buyers and sellers. A good example is the real estate market, where economies of scale in searches for available homes and for prospective buyers make it worthwhile for participants to pay brokers to conduct the searches. Brokers in particular markets develop specialized knowledge on valuing assets traded in that market.

Primary market New issues of securities are offered to the public here.

Secondary market Already existing securities are bought and sold on the exchanges or in the OTC market.

An important brokered investment market is the so-called **primary market,** where new issues of securities are offered to the public. In the primary market, investment bankers act as brokers; they seek investors to purchase securities directly from the issuing corporation. By contrast, purchase and sale of existing securities among investors occur in the **secondary market,** which means on established security exchanges (auction markets) or in the over-the-counter (dealer) markets.

Another brokered market is that for large block transactions, in which very large blocks of stock are bought or sold. These blocks are so large (technically more than 10,000 shares but usually much larger) that brokers or "block houses" often are engaged to search directly for other large traders, rather than bring the trade directly to the stock exchange where relatively smaller investors trade.

Dealer Markets

Dealer market A market where traders specializing in particular assets buy and sell for their own accounts.

When trading activity in a particular type of asset increases, **dealer markets** arise. Dealers specialize in various commodities, purchase these assets for their own accounts, and later sell them for a profit from their inventory. Dealers, unlike brokers, trade at a difference between the buy price and the sell price. Dealer markets save traders on search costs because market participants can easily look up the prices at which they can buy from or sell to dealers. A fair amount of market activity is required before dealing in a market is an attractive source of income. The over-the-counter (OTC) market is one example of a dealer market.

Auction Markets

Auction market A market where all traders in a good meet at one place to buy or sell an asset.

The most integrated market is an **auction market,** in which all transactors converge at one place (bids can be transmitted to that one place, saving the trip for the bidder) to bid on or offer a good. The New York Stock Exchange (NYSE) is an example of an auction market. An advantage of auction markets over dealer markets is that one need not search across dealers to find the best price for a good. If all participants converge, they can arrive at mutually agreeable prices and save the bid-ask spread.

Continuous auction markets (as opposed to periodic auctions such as in the antiques world) require very heavy and frequent trading to cover the expense of maintaining the market. For this reason, the NYSE and other exchanges set up listing requirements, which limit the stocks traded on the exchange to those of firms in which sufficient trading interest is likely to exist.

Concept Check

> *Question 6.* Many assets trade in more than one type of market. What types of markets do the following trade in? *a.* used cars, *b.* paintings, *c.* rare coins.

3.5   *Recent Trends*

We have recently seen four trends in the contemporary investment environment: (1) globalization, (2) securitization, (3) credit enhancement, and (4) bundling and unbundling. Each is a logical consequence of the demand and supply forces that give rise to specialized markets and instruments.

Globalization

Globalization
Tendency towards a world-wide investment environment, and the integration of national capital markets.

If a wider array of investment choices can improve welfare, why should we limit ourselves to purely domestic assets? Increasingly efficient communication technology and the dismantling of regulatory constraints have encouraged **globalization** in recent years.

U.S. investors commonly can take advantage of foreign investment opportunities in two ways: (1) purchase of foreign securities using American Depository Receipts (ADRs), which are domestically traded securities, representing claims to shares of foreign stocks, and (2) purchase of foreign securities that are offered in dollars.

Once upon a time, a U.S. investor who wished to hold a French stock had to engage in four transactions: (1) purchase French francs, (2) purchase the stock on the French Bourse, (3) sell the stock in France, and (4) sell the French francs for dollars. Today, the same investor can purchase ADRs of this stock.

Brokers who act as intermediaries for these transactions hold an inventory of stock from which they sell shares, denominated in U.S. dollars. There is no more technical difference between investing in a French or a U.S. stock than there is in holding a Massachusetts-based company compared with a California-based one. Of course, the investment implication may differ: ADRs still expose investors to exchange rate risk.

Many foreign firms are so eager to lure U.S. investors they will save these investors the expense of paying the higher commissions associated with the ADRs. Figure 3.1 shows an example. Cadbury Schweppes is a United Kingdom–based corporation that has marketed its stock directly to U.S. investors in ADRs. Each ADR represents a claim to 10 shares of Cadbury Schweppes stock.

An example of how far globalization has progressed appears in Figure 3.2. Here, Walt Disney is selling debt claims denominated in European currency units (ECUs), an index of a basket of European currency values.

Securitization

Until recently, financial intermediaries channeled funds from national capital markets to smaller local ones. That is, international banks or consortiums of banks channeled funds from savers of one country to borrowers of another.

Figure 3.1
Globalization and American Depository Receipts.

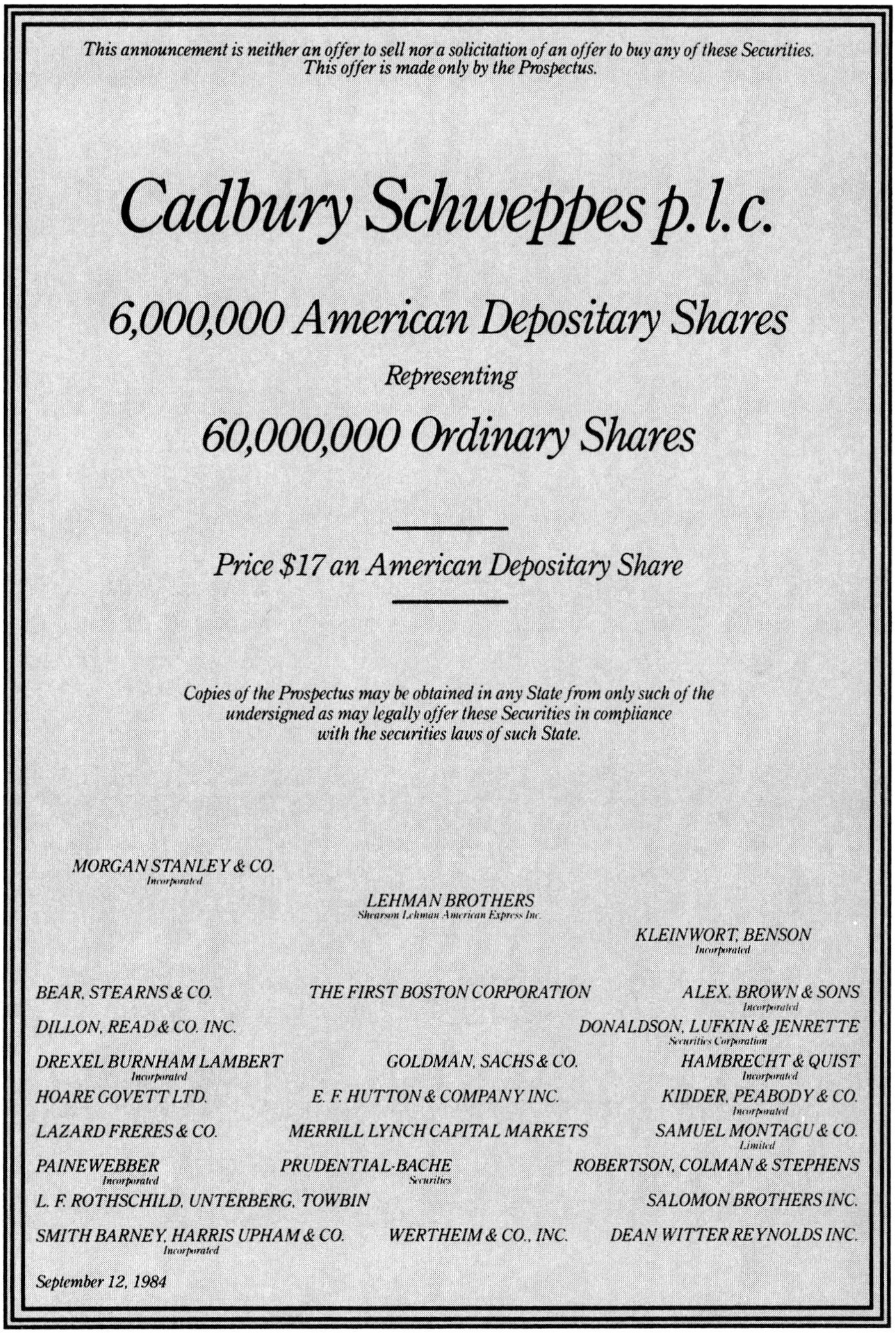

This announcement is neither an offer to sell nor a solicitation of an offer to buy any of these Securities.
This offer is made only by the Prospectus.

Cadbury Schweppes p.l.c.

6,000,000 American Depositary Shares

Representing

60,000,000 Ordinary Shares

———

Price $17 an American Depositary Share

———

Copies of the Prospectus may be obtained in any State from only such of the
undersigned as may legally offer these Securities in compliance
with the securities laws of such State.

MORGAN STANLEY & CO.
Incorporated

LEHMAN BROTHERS
Shearson Lehman American Express Inc.

KLEINWORT, BENSON
Incorporated

BEAR, STEARNS & CO.	THE FIRST BOSTON CORPORATION	ALEX. BROWN & SONS Incorporated
DILLON, READ & CO. INC.		DONALDSON, LUFKIN & JENRETTE Securities Corporation
DREXEL BURNHAM LAMBERT Incorporated	GOLDMAN, SACHS & CO.	HAMBRECHT & QUIST Incorporated
HOARE GOVETT LTD.	E. F. HUTTON & COMPANY INC.	KIDDER, PEABODY & CO. Incorporated
LAZARD FRERES & CO.	MERRILL LYNCH CAPITAL MARKETS	SAMUEL MONTAGU & CO. Limited
PAINEWEBBER Incorporated	PRUDENTIAL-BACHE Securities	ROBERTSON, COLMAN & STEPHENS
L. F. ROTHSCHILD, UNTERBERG, TOWBIN		SALOMON BROTHERS INC.
SMITH BARNEY, HARRIS UPHAM & CO. Incorporated	WERTHEIM & CO., INC.	DEAN WITTER REYNOLDS INC.

September 12, 1984

Figure 3.2
Globalization: a debt
issue denominated in
European currency
units.

This announcement appears as a matter of record only. These Securities have not been
registered under the United States Securities Act of 1933 and may not,
as part of the distribution, be offered, sold or delivered, directly or
indirectly, in the United States or to United States persons.

New Issue December, 1985

ECU 62,500,000

Walt Disney Productions

8¾% Notes Due February 25, 1994

Salomon Brothers International Limited

Crédit Commercial de France   **Kredietbank International Group**

BankAmerica Capital Markets Group	**Banque Bruxelles Lambert S.A.**
Banque Générale du Luxembourg S.A.	**Banque Internationale à Luxembourg S.A.**
Banque Nationale de Paris	**Banque Paribas Capital Markets Limited**
Caisse des Dépôts et Consignations	**Crédit Agricole**
Crédit Lyonnais	**Deutsche Bank Capital Markets Limited**
EBC Amro Bank Limited	**Generale Bank**
Genossenschaftliche Zentralbank AG Vienna	**IBJ International Limited**
Mitsubishi Finance International Limited	**Morgan Guaranty Ltd**
Morgan Stanley International	**Nippon European Bank S.A.**
Nomura International Limited	**Société Génerale**
Swiss Bank Corporation International Limited	**Union Bank of Switzerland (Securities) Limited**
S. G. Warburg & Co. Ltd.	**Westpac Banking Corporation**

Securitization
Pooling loans into standardized securities backed by those loans, which can then be traded like any other security.

Securitization, however, now allows borrowers to enter foreign capital markets directly. In this procedure, pools of loans typically are aggregated into pass-through securities, such as mortgage pass-throughs. Investors then invest in securities backed by those pools. The transformation of these pools into standardized securities enables issuers to deal in a volume large enough that they can bypass intermediaries. We have already discussed this phenomenon in the context of the securitization of the mortgage market.

Another example of securitization is the collateralized automobile receivable (CAR), a pass-through arrangement for car loans. Figure 3.3 shows an example of such a note. The loan originator passes the loan payments through to the holder of the CAR.

Securitization also may represent a way for U.S. banks to unload their portfolios of Third World debt. Many observers believe these loans will be joined into pools, with claims to these pools then sold to outside investors.

Credit Enhancement

In the past, a corporation that was not in the best financial condition could get loans only through commercial banks. The bank's credit department scrutinized each customer. A business shopping around for a loan might be sized up simultaneously by several banks.

Credit enhancement
Purchase of the financial guarantee of an insurance company to enhance the safety of a loan.

Today, the credit-hungry corporation can arrange for **credit enhancement.** It engages an insurance company to put its credit behind the corporation's, for a fee. The firm then floats a bond of "enhanced" credit rating directly to the public.

Figure 3.4 shows an example of credit enhancement in a joint financial venture between the Rockefeller Group and Aetna Casualty and Surety. The Rockefeller Group is a privately held corporation, that is, its stock is not traded on the exchange. Therefore, it is unnecessary to protect investors and hence such corporations are exempt from some typical disclosure rules. Shareholders of a closely held corporation value this privacy, which comes at a cost: They cannot issue publicly traded bonds at reasonable low yields unless they reveal information to the public they wish to keep private. Instead, the firm purchases Aetna's backing. Aetna can perform its own credit analysis, keeping the information confidential.

Bundling and Unbundling

Bundling, unbundling
A trend allowing creation of securities either by combining primitive and derivative securities into one composite hybrid or by separating returns on an asset into classes.

Disparate investor demands are behind a supply of exotic securities. Creative security design often calls for **bundling** primitive and derivative securities into one composite security. One such example appears in Figure 3.5. The Chubb Corporation, with the aid of Goldman, Sachs, has combined three primitive securities—stocks, bonds, and preferred stock—into one hybrid security.

Chubb is issuing preferred stock that is convertible into common stock, at the option of the holder, and exchangeable into convertible bonds at the option of the firm. Hence, this security is a bundling of preferred stock with several options.

Often, creating a security that appears to be attractive requires **unbundling** of an asset. An example is given in Figure 3.6. There, a mortgage pass-through

Figure 3.3
Securitization of
automobile loans.

This announcement is neither an offer to sell nor a solicitation of offers to buy any of these securities.
The offering is made only by the Prospectus and the related Prospectus Supplement.

NEW ISSUE

July 7, 1987

$25,675,000

Asset Backed Securities Corporation

Asset Backed Obligations, Series 3

_____

Collateralized by Automotive Receivables

_____

$15,250,000	$10,425,000
7.40% Class 3-A Notes Due June 15, 1990	7.45% Class 3-B Notes Due June 15, 1992
Price 99.9375%	Price 97.1875%
plus accrued interest at the applicable rate from June 15, 1987	plus accrued interest at the applicable rate from June 15, 1987

_____

*The Notes will be secured by a pool of recently originated retail automotive installment sale contracts (the
"Receivables") purchased from General Electric Credit Corporation (the "Company"), all monies
due thereunder net of servicing and other fees, security interests in the vehicles financed
thereby, the Company's limited guaranty of payments under the Receivables, and
certain other collateral. The Receivables will be secured by new, and used
automobiles and light trucks and will be serviced by the Company.*

*Copies of the Prospectus and the related Prospectus Supplement may be obtained
in any State in which this announcement is circulated where the undersigned
may legally offer these securities in such State.*

The First Boston Corporation

certificate is unbundled into classes. Class 1 receives only principal payments
from the mortgage pool, whereas class 2 receives only interest payments.

Concept Check

Question 7. How can tax motives contribute to the desire for unbundling?

Figure 3.4
Aetna's credit enhancement of the Rockefeller Group's bond.

Offering Circular

$100,000,000

Rockefeller Group International Finance N.V.

13¼% Notes Due 1989

Unconditionally Guaranteed as to Payment of Principal and Interest by

Rockefeller Group, Inc.

and under a Surety Bond Issued by

The Ætna Casualty and Surety Company

Issue Price 99¾%

Principal of, premium, if any, and interest on the Notes will be payable without deduction for, or on account of, United States or Netherlands Antilles withholding taxes, all as set forth herein. Interest will be payable annually on June 21, commencing in 1985.

The Notes will mature on June 21, 1989. The Notes are redeemable (i) as a whole or from time to time in part, on or after June 21, 1987 at a redemption price equal to 101¼% of the principal amount of the Notes if made prior to June 21, 1988 and 100½% of the principal amount of the Notes if made on or after June 21, 1988, plus, in each case, accrued interest to the date fixed for redemption, and (ii) as a whole at any time in the event of certain developments involving United States or Netherlands Antilles withholding taxes, at their principal amount plus accrued interest to the date fixed for redemption. See "Description of the Notes". The Notes may also be redeemed as a whole, at a redemption price equal to their principal amount plus accrued interest to the date fixed for redemption, at the option of The Ætna Casualty and Surety Company ("Ætna") upon the occurrence of certain events. See "Description of the Surety Bond".

The Notes will be unconditionally guaranteed as to the payment of principal, premium, if any, and interest and certain other amounts by Rockefeller Group, Inc. As a private corporation, Rockefeller Group, Inc., does not disclose financial information to the public. Accordingly, arrangements have been made for payments of principal of, premium, if any, and interest on, and certain other amounts with respect to, the Notes to be guaranteed under a Surety Bond issued by Ætna. See "Description of the Notes" and "Description of the Surety Bond".

Application has been made to list the Notes on the Luxembourg Stock Exchange.

The Notes have not been registered under the United States Securities Act of 1933 and may not be offered or sold, directly or indirectly, in the United States of America, or its territories or possessions or to citizens, nationals or residents thereof, except as set forth herein. See "Underwriting".

A temporary global Note without interest coupons in the amount of $100,000,000 will be delivered to a depositary in London for the account of participants in Euro-clear and CEDEL S.A. on or about June 21, 1984 and will be exchangeable for definitive Notes not earlier than 90 days after the completion of the distribution upon certification that such Notes are not beneficially owned by United States citizens, nationals or residents, as set forth herein. Interest on the Notes will not be payable until issuance of the definitive Notes. See "Description of the Notes—Denominaton and Transfer".

Morgan Guaranty Ltd

Amro International Limited	**Chase Manhattan Limited**
Credit Suisse First Boston Limited	**Deutsche Bank Aktiengesellschaft**
Dresdner Bank Aktiengesellschaft	**Enskilda Securities** SKANDINAVISKA ENSKILDA LIMITED
Lehman Brothers International SHEARSON LEHMAN/AMERICAN EXPRESS INC	**Samuel Montagu & Co. Limited**
Orion Royal Bank Limited	**Société Générale**
Société Générale de Banque S.A.	**Swiss Bank Corporation International Limited**
Union Bank of Switzerland (Securities) Limited	**S. G. Warburg & Co. Ltd.**

May 25, 1984

Figure 3.5
Bundling creates a
complex security.

3,000,000 Shares

The Chubb Corporation

$4.25 Convertible Exchangeable Preferred Stock

(Stated Value $50 Per Share)

The $4.25 Convertible Exchangeable Preferred Stock (the "Preferred Stock"), $1.00 par value, of The Chubb Corporation (the "Corporation") offered hereby is convertible at the option of the holder at any time, unless previously redeemed, into Common Stock, $1.00 par value, of the Corporation (the "Common Stock") at the rate of .722 shares of Common Stock for each share of Preferred Stock (equivalent to a conversion price of $69.25 per share), subject to adjustment under certain conditions. On March 25, 1985, the last reported sale price of the Common Stock on the New York Stock Exchange was $57¼ per share.

The Preferred Stock also is exchangeable in whole at the sole option of the Corporation on any dividend payment date beginning April 15, 1988 for the Corporation's 8¹/₂% Convertible Subordinated Debentures due April 15, 2010 (the "Debentures") at the rate of $50 principal amount of Debentures for each share of Preferred Stock. See "Description of Debentures".

The Preferred Stock is redeemable for cash at any time, in whole or in part, at the option of the Corporation at redemption prices declining to $50 on April 15, 1995, plus accrued and unpaid dividends to the redemption date. However, the Preferred Stock is not redeemable prior to April 15, 1988 unless the closing price of the Common Stock on the New York Stock Exchange shall have equaled or exceeded 140% of the then effective conversion price per share for at least 20 consecutive trading days ending within 5 days prior to the notice of redemption. Dividends on the Preferred Stock will be cumulative and are payable quarterly on January 15, April 15, July 15 and October 15. The initial dividend will be payable on July 15, 1985 and will accrue from the date of issuance. See "Description of Preferred Stock".

Application will be made to list the Preferred Stock on the New York Stock Exchange.

THESE SECURITIES HAVE NOT BEEN APPROVED OR DISAPPROVED BY THE
SECURITIES AND EXCHANGE COMMISSION NOR HAS THE COMMISSION
PASSED UPON THE ACCURACY OR ADEQUACY OF THIS PROSPECTUS.
ANY REPRESENTATION TO THE CONTRARY IS A CRIMINAL OFFENSE.

	Initial Public Offering Price	Underwriting Discount	Proceeds to Corporation(1)
Per Share	$50.00	$1.375	$48.625
Total	$150,000,000	$4,125,000	$145,875,000

(1) Before deducting expenses payable by the Corporation estimated at $500,000.

The shares of Preferred Stock are offered severally by the Underwriters, as specified herein, subject to receipt and acceptance by them and subject to their right to reject any order in whole or in part. It is expected that certificates for the shares of Preferred Stock will be ready for delivery at the offices of Goldman, Sachs & Co., New York, New York on or about April 2, 1985.

Goldman, Sachs & Co.

The date of this Prospectus is March 26, 1985.

Figure 3.6
Unbundling of
mortgages into
principal- and
interest-only
securities.

$200,000,000*

Federal National Mortgage Association

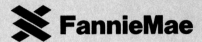 **FannieMae**

Stripped Mortgage-Backed Securities

**Principal and Interest payable on the 25th day of
each month, commencing August 25, 1987**

SMBS Trust 20-CL—Fixed-Rate Residential Mortgage Loans

SMBS Class 1: 100% of Principal Payments on Underlying
9¹/₂% Fannie Mae Guaranteed Mortgage Pass-Through Certificates

SMBS Class 2: 100% of Interest Payments on Underlying
9¹/₂% Fannie Mae Guaranteed Mortgage Pass-Through Certificates

---

The obligations of Fannie Mae under its guaranty of the SMBS Certificates are
obligations of Fannie Mae and are not backed by the full faith and credit of the United
States. The SMBS Certificates are exempt from the registration requirements of the
Securities Act of 1933 and are "Exempted Securities" within the meaning of the
Securities Exchange Act of 1934.

Class 1 $200,000,000 Principal Amount*
Class 2 $200,000,000 Notional Principal Amount*

Goldman, Sachs & Co.

July 9, 1987   *Approximate

Summary

1.   Real assets represent wealth. Financial assets represent claims to parts or all of that wealth. Financial assets determine how the ownership of real assets is distributed among investors.

2.   Financial intermediaries pool investor funds and invest them efficiently. Their services are in demand because small investors cannot efficiently gather information, diversify, and monitor portfolios. The financial intermediary sells its own securities to the small investors. The intermediary invests the funds thus raised, uses the proceeds to pay small investors, and profits from the difference (the spread).

3.   Banks pool investor funds in order to invest in all types of loans. Investments in other types of assets are undertaken by investment companies.

4.   Investment banking brings efficiency to corporate fund-raising. Investment bankers develop expertise in pricing new issues and in marketing them to investors.

5.   Investor demand is behind the creation of new investment vehicles that will appeal to a variety of purchasers. In many cases, these vehicles are derivative securities. Such financial assets pay off parts of the income from the underlying assets as specified on the derivative contract. Many financial innovations evolve as a response to taxation and regulation.

6.   The primary role of banks is to provide liquidity through demand deposits. The bank profits by investing a large proportion of these deposits in risky loans. A run on the bank may necessitate liquidation of loans, causing new losses to the bank, making it less able to meet depositors' demand for cash. Depositors will reclaim deposits whenever they suspect the bank may have negative net worth. Deposit insurance guards against the prospect of bank runs.

7.   The S&L debacle has its roots in a failure of regulators. They did not realize (or were tempted to ignore) that insured deposits give incentive to maximize the interest spread by increasing the riskiness of the loan portfolio.

8.   Risk pooling is effected by investing in independent risky assets, to reduce the probability of large losses. The reduction of the probability of large losses is called the insurance principle. Risk sharing is the distribution of a given risk to many investors. It is the way the insurance industry works.

9.   Risk can be reduced in three ways: shifting from risky to risk-free (money market) assets, insuring specific risks, and efficiently diversifying the funds placed under risk. The last is the role of investment companies.

10.   There are four types of financial markets. Direct search markets are the least efficient and sophisticated, where each transactor must find a counterpart. In brokered markets, brokers specialize in advising and finding counterparts for fee-paying transactors. Dealers provide a step up in convenience. They keep an inventory of the asset and stand ready to buy or sell on demand, profiting from the bid-ask spread. Auction markets allow a transactor to benefit from direct competition. All interested parties bid for the goods or services.

11.   Recent trends in financial markets include globalization, securitization, credit enhancement, and bundling/unbundling of assets.

Key Terms

auction market, 69	globalization, 70	primitive securities, 62
bundling, 73	insurance principle, 66	real assets, 54
credit enhancement, 73	investment bankers, 59	risk pooling, 66
dealer markets, 69	investment	risk premium, 66
derivative securities, 62	companies, 57	risk sharing, 67
financial assets, 54	pass-through	secondary market, 69
financial	securities, 61	securitization, 73
intermediaries, 57	primary market, 69	unbundling, 73

Selected Readings

An excellent discussion of financial innovation may be found in:
Miller, Merton H. "Financial Innovation: The Last Twenty Years and the Next."
Journal of Financial and Quantitative Analysis 21 (December 1986), pp. 459–71.

Detailed discussions of a variety of financial markets and market structure are provided in:
Garbade, Kenneth D. *Securities Markets.* New York: McGraw-Hill, 1982; and
Wood, John H., and Norm L. Wood. *Financial Markets.* San Diego: Harcourt Brace Jovanovitch, 1985.

A thorough discussion of deposit insurance and its problems is in:
Kane, Edward J. *How Incentive-Incompatible Deposit-Insurance Funds Fail.* Working Paper No. 2836 of the National Bureau of Economic Research, February 1989.

Problem Sets

1. Suppose you discover a treasure chest of $10 billion in cash.
   a. Is this a real or financial asset?
   b. Is society any richer for the discovery?
   c. Are you wealthier?
   d. Can you reconcile your answers to (b) and (c)? Is anyone worse off as a result of the discovery?
2. Examine the balance sheet of the financial sector. What is the ratio of tangible assets to total assets? What is that ratio for nonfinancial firms? Why should this difference be expected?
3. In the 1960s, the U.S. government instituted a 30% withholding tax on interest payments on bonds sold in the United States to overseas investors. (It has since been repealed.) What connection does this have to the contemporaneous growth of the huge Eurobond market, where U.S. firms issue dollar-denominated bonds overseas?
4. Consider Figure 3.7, on page 80, which describes an issue of American gold certificates.
   a. Is this issue a primary or secondary market transaction?
   b. Are the certificates primitive or derivative assets?
   c. What market niche is filled by this offering?
5. Why would you expect securitization to take place only in highly developed capital markets?
6. Suppose that you are an executive of General Motors, and that a large share of your potential income is derived from year-end bonuses that depend on GM's annual profits
   a. Would purchase of GM stock be an effective hedging strategy for the executive who is worried about the uncertainty surrounding his bonus?
   b. Would purchase of Toyota stock be an effective hedge strategy?

Figure 3.7
A gold-backed
security.

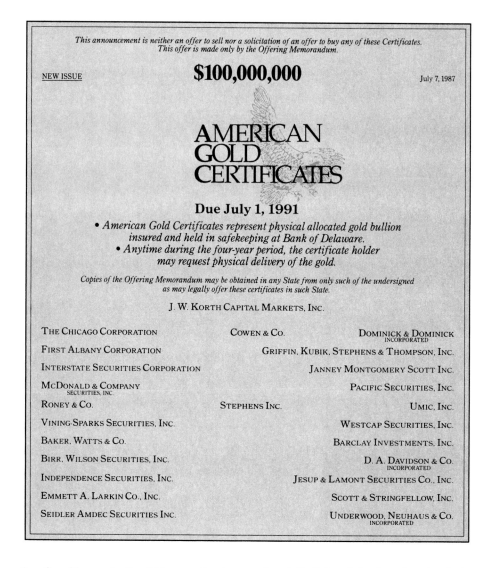

7. Consider again the GM executive in question 6. In light of the fact that the design of the annual bonus exposes the executive to risk that she would like to shed, why doesn't GM instead pay her a fixed salary that doesn't entail this uncertainty?

8. What is the relationship between securitization and the role of financial intermediaries in the economy? What happens to financial intermediaries as securitization progresses?

9. Although we stated that real assets comprise the true productive capacity of an economy, it is hard to conceive of a modern economy without well-developed financial markets and security types. How would the productive capacity of the U.S. economy be affected if there were no markets in which one could trade financial assets?

10. In Section 3.5 the possibility of the securitization of third-world debt was raised. How might such a third-world pass-through security be designed?

11. Why does it make sense that the first futures markets introduced in nineteenth century America were for trades in agricultural products? For example, why did we not see instead futures markets for goods such as paper or pencils?

Chapter

Financial Markets and Instruments

This chapter provides an overview of the major financial markets and instruments. We first describe money market instruments and how to measure their yield. We then move on to fixed-income and equity securities. We explain the structure of various stock market indexes in this chapter because market benchmark portfolios play an important role in portfolio construction and evaluation. Finally, we survey the derivative security markets for options and futures contracts. A summary of the markets, instruments, and indexes covered in this chapter appears in Table 4.1. After studying this chapter you should be able to:

- Distinguish among the major assets that trade in money markets and in capital markets.
- Describe the construction of stock market indexes.
- Calculate the profit or losses on investments in option and futures contracts.

 4.1   The Money Market

Money market
Includes short-term, highly liquid, and relatively low-risk debt instruments.

Capital markets
Includes longer-term, relatively riskier securities.

Financial markets are traditionally segmented into **money markets** and **capital markets.** This classification is consistent with the decomposition of a portfolio to safe and risky assets. Money market instruments include short-term, marketable, liquid, low-risk debt securities. Money market instruments are sometimes called *cash equivalents,* or just *cash* for short. Capital markets, in contrast, include longer-term and riskier securities. Securities in the capital market are much more diverse than those found within the money market. For this reason, we will subdivide the capital market into four segments: longer-term fixed-

81

Table **4.1**   *Financial Markets and Indexes*

The Money Market
  Treasury bills
  Certificates of deposit
  Commercial paper
  Bankers' acceptances
  Eurodollars
  Repos and reverses
  Federal funds
  Brokers' calls

Indexes
  Dow Jones averages
  Standard and Poor's indexes
  Bond market indicators
  International indexes

The Fixed-Income Capital Market
  Treasury bonds and notes
  Federal agency debt
  Municipal bonds
  Corporate bonds
  Mortgages and mortgage-backed securities

Equity Markets
  Common stocks
  Preferred stocks

Derivative Markets
  Options
  Futures and Forwards

Table **4.2**   *Components of the Money Market (November 1990)*

	$ Billion
Overnight repurchase agreements*	77.6
Term repurchase agreements	91.4
Small-denomination time deposits†	1156.0
Large-denomination time deposits‡	506.6
Term Eurodollars	72.6
Short-term Treasury securities	347.9
Bankers' acceptances	34.0
Commercial paper	357.7
Money market deposit accounts	507.0

Data from *Economic Report of the President,* U.S. Government Printing Office, 1990.

*Includes overnight Eurodollars.

†Less than $100,000 denomination.

‡More than $100,000 denomination.

income markets, equity markets, and the derivative markets for options and futures.

The money market is a subsector of the bond market. It consists of very short-term debt securities that are highly marketable. Many of these securities trade in large denominations, and so are out of the reach of individual investors. Money market mutual funds, however, are easily accessible to small investors. These mutual funds pool the resources of many investors and purchase a wide variety of money market securities on their behalf.

Figure 4.1 is a reprint of a money rates listing from *The Wall Street Journal.* It includes the various instruments of the money market that we describe in detail below. Table 4.2 lists outstanding volume in 1990 of the major instruments of the money market.

Figure 4.1
Rates on money market securities.
Reprinted by permission of *THE WALL STREET JOURNAL*, © 1991 Dow Jones & Company, Inc. All Rights Reserved Worldwide.

MONEY RATES

Tuesday, May 7, 1991

The key U.S. and foreign annual interest rates below are a guide to general levels but don't always represent actual transactions.

PRIME RATE: 8½%. The base rate on corporate loans at large U.S. money center commercial banks.

FEDERAL FUNDS: 5¾% high, 5 11/16% low, 5⅝% near closing bid, 5 11/16% offered. Reserves traded among commercial banks for overnight use in amounts of $1 million or more. Source: Babcock Fulton Prebon (U.S.A.) Inc.

DISCOUNT RATE: 5½%. The charge on loans to depository institutions by the New York Federal Reserve Bank.

CALL MONEY: 7½% to 8½%. The charge on loans to brokers on stock exchange collateral.

COMMERCIAL PAPER placed directly by General Motors Acceptance Corp.: 5.80% 15 to 50 days; 5.50% 51 to 59 days; 5.825% 60 to 119 days; 5.85% 120 to 149 days; 5.875% 150 to 179 days; 5.85% 180 to 244 days; 5.90% 245 to 270 days.

COMMERCIAL PAPER: High-grade unsecured notes sold through dealers by major corporations in multiples of $1,000: 5.92% 30 days; 5.92% 60 days; 5.92% 90 days.

CERTIFICATES OF DEPOSIT: 5.65% one month; 5.68% two months; 5.68% three months; 5.74% six months; 6.10% one year. Average of top rates paid by major New York banks on primary new issues of negotiable C.D.s, usually in amounts of $1 million and more. The minimum unit is $100,000. Typical rates in the secondary market: 5.91% one month; 5.95% three months; 6% six months.

BANKERS ACCEPTANCES: 5.75% 30 days; 5.74% 60 days; 5.74% 90 days; 5.74% 120 days; 5.74% 150 days; 5.74% 180 days. Negotiable, bank-backed business credit instruments typically financing an import order.

LONDON LATE EURODOLLARS: 6% — 5⅞% one month; 6% — 5⅞% two months; 6 1/16% — 5 15/16% three months; 6⅛% — 6% four months; 6 3/16% — 6 1/16% five months; 6 3/16% — 6 1/16% six months.

LONDON INTERBANK OFFERED RATES (LIBOR): 5 15/16% one month; 6 1/16% three months; 6 3/16% six months; 6⅝% one year. The average of interbank offered rates for dollar deposits in the London market based on quotations at five major banks. Effective rate for contracts entered into two days from date appearing at top of this column.

FOREIGN PRIME RATES: Canada 9.75%–10.25%; Germany 10.50%; Japan 7.88%; Switzerland 10.63%; Britain 12%. These rate indications aren't directly comparable; lending practices vary widely by location.

TREASURY BILLS: Results of the Monday, May 6, 1991, auction of short-term U.S. government bills, sold at a discount from face value in units of $10,000 to $1 million: 5.50% 13 weeks; 5.61% 26 weeks.

FEDERAL HOME LOAN MORTGAGE CORP. (Freddie Mac): Posted yields on 30-year mortgage commitments for delivery within 30 days. 9.38%, standard conventional fixed-rate mortgages; 6.625%, 2% rate capped one-year adjustable rate mortgages. Source: Telerate Systems Inc.

FEDERAL NATIONAL MORTGAGE ASSOCIATION (Fannie Mae): Posted yields on 30 year mortgage commitments for delivery within 30 days (priced at par). 9.33%, standard conventional fixed rate-mortgages; 7.15%, 6/2 rate capped one-year adjustable rate mortgages. Source: Telerate Systems Inc.

MERRILL LYNCH READY ASSETS TRUST: 5.70%. Annualized average rate of return after expenses for the past 30 days; not a forecast of future returns.

Treasury Bills

Treasury bills   Short-term government securities issued at a discount from the face value and returning the face amount at maturity.

U.S. **Treasury bills** (T-bills, or just bills, for short) are the most marketable of all money market instruments. T-bills represent the simplest form of borrowing. The government raises money by selling bills to the public. Investors buy the bills at a discount from the stated maturity value. At the bill's maturity, the holder receives from the government a payment equal to the face value of the bill. The difference between the purchase price and the ultimate maturity value represents the investor's earnings.

T-bills with initial maturities of 91 and 182 days are issued weekly. Offerings of 52-week bills are made monthly. Sales are conducted by an auction where investors can submit competitive or noncompetitive bids.

A competitive bid is an order for a given quantity of bills at a specific offered price. The order is filled only if the bid is high enough relative to other bids to be accepted. If the bid is high enough to be accepted, the bidder gets the order at the bid price. Thus, the bidder risks paying one of the highest prices for the same bill (bidding at the top), against the hope of bidding "at the tail," that is, making the cutoff at the lowest price.

A noncompetitive bid is an unconditional offer to purchase bills at the average price of the successful competitive bids. The Treasury rank orders bids by offering price and accepts bids in order of descending price until the entire issue is absorbed by the competitive plus noncompetitive bids. Competitive bidders face two dangers: They may bid too high and overpay for the bills or bid too low and be shut out of the auction. Noncompetitive bidders by contrast pay the average price for the issue, and all noncompetitive bids are accepted up to a maximum of $1 million per bid. In recent years, noncompetitive bids have absorbed between 10 and 25 percent of the total auction.

Individuals can purchase T-bills directly at the auction or on the secondary market from a government securities dealer. T-bills are highly liquid; that is, they are easily converted to cash and sold at low transaction cost and with little price risk. Unlike most other money market instruments, which sell in minimum denominations of $100,000, T-bills sell in minimum denominations of only $10,000. The income earned on T-bills is exempt from all state and local taxes, another characteristic distinguishing them from other money market instruments.

Bank Discount Yields

Distinguishing between HPRs (holding-period returns) and annualized rates is critical when evaluating investment prospects. HPRs are rates effectively earned (or expected to be earned) during a particular time period. It often is convenient to consider a holding period equal to the period between cash disbursements from the asset (e.g., six months for a semiannual coupon bond or one month for a mortgage that is paid monthly). Alternatively, the holding period may be determined by contractual compounding frequency (e.g., some banks compound interest daily). We will denote the number of holding periods in a year by m, which is 2 for the bond and 12 for the mortgage.

If we wish to compare rates of return on different instruments, say a semiannual coupon bond offering an HPR of 6.1 percent per half year with a monthly mortgage offering an HPR of 1 percent per month, we must examine their rates of return over a common period. By convention, we compare returns on instruments on an annual basis, so HPRs are most often annualized.

Annual percentage rate Annualized interest rate that is computed by multiplying the holding period return by the number of compounding periods per year.

One can annualize an HPR in two ways. Using the simple interest method, the **annual percentage rate** (APR) multiplies the HPR by m, the number of compounding periods per year. Thus, the bond in our example yields an APR of 6.1 × 2 = 12.2 percent, and the mortgage has an APR of 1 × 12 = 12 percent.

The APR does not account for compounding *within* the year, however, and therefore understates the true earning power of the investment. In our example, the APR methodology for annualization more heavily penalizes the mortgage that pays monthly, because the early interest payments may be reinvested longer within the year.

In contrast to the APR, the **effective annual rate** compounds the HPR for *m* periods, arriving at the total annual rate that would be earned if each receipt within the year were reinvested until the end of the year. Whenever we have more than one compounding period within the year, *m* > 1, the effective annual rate will exceed the APR. Thus, the effective annual rate on the bond is 12.57 percent ($1.061^2 - 1$) and on the mortgage, 12.68 percent ($1.01^{12} - 1$), better by 11 basis points. Most financial calculators can directly convert APRs to annual effective rates and vice versa.

Unfortunately, the financial community reports yields using conventions that evolved before the advent of the financial calculator in order to minimize algebraic calculations. We therefore must learn to interpret these "bank discount yields" and "bond equivalent yields."

T-bill yields are not quoted in the financial pages as effective annual rates of return. Instead, the **bank discount method** is used. To illustrate this method, consider a $10,000 par value T-bill sold at $9,600 with a maturity of a half-year, or 182 days. Using the bank discount method, the bill's discount from par value, which here equals $400, is "annualized" based on a 360-day year. The $400 discount is annualized as follows: $400 × (360/182) = $791.21. This figure is divided by the $10,000 par value to obtain a bank discount yield of 7.912 percent per year. Rather than report T-bill prices, the financial pages report these discount yields.

The bank discount yield understates the effective annual rate of return. To see this, note that the half-year holding period return on the bill is 4.17 percent: the $9,600 investment provides $400 in earnings, and 400/9,600 = .0417. The effective annual rate of return is therefore $1.0417^2 - 1 = .0851$, or 8.51 percent.

We can highlight the source of the discrepancy between the bank discount yield and effective annual yield by examining the bank discount formula.

$$r_{BD} = \frac{10,000 - P}{10,000} \times \frac{360}{n} \qquad \textbf{(4.1)}$$

where *P* is the bond price, *n* is the maturity of the bill in days, and r_{BD} is the bank discount yield. Actually, because of the convention of skip-day settlement, two business days are subtracted from *n* because the T-bill sale is consummated, that is, cash has to be disbursed, two business days after the date on which the price is quoted.

Three drawbacks to this technique all combine to reduce the bank discount yield compared to the effective annual yield. First, the HPR is underestimated because the denominator in the first term in Equation 4.1 is the par value, $10,000, rather than the purchase price of the bill, *P* = $9,600. Second, the bank discount yield is annualized by using a 360-day rather than a 365-day year. Finally, as an APR (simple interest) it is even lower relative to the annual effective rate.

Figure 4.2 shows Treasury bill listings from *The Wall Street Journal* for May 8, 1991. The discount yield on the bill maturing June 6 is 5.35 percent based on the bid price of the bond and 5.31 percent based on the ask price. (The bid price is the price at which a customer can sell the bill to a dealer in the security, while the ask price is the price at which the customer can buy a security from a dealer. The difference in bid and ask prices is a source of profit to the dealer.)

Effective annual rate   Annualized interest rate on a security computed using compound interest techniques.

Bank discount method   An annualized interest rate assuming simple interest, a 360-day year, and using the face value of the security rather than the purchase price to compute return per dollar invested.

Figure 4.2
Treasury bill listing.

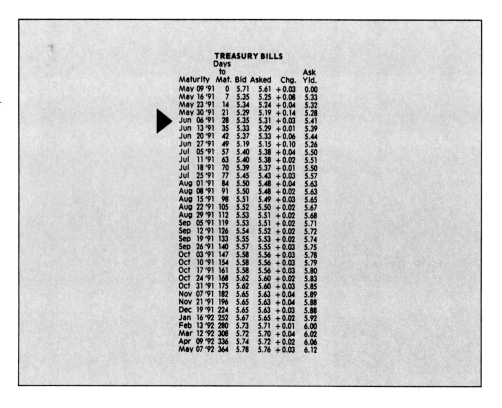

To determine the bill's true market price, we must solve Equation 4.1 for P. Rearranging 4.1, we obtain,

$$P = 10,000 \times [1 - r_{BD} \times (n/360)] \tag{4.2}$$

Equation 4.2 in effect first "deannualizes" the bank discount yield to obtain the actual proportional discount from par, then finds the fraction of par for which the bond sells (which is the expression in brackets), and finally multiplies the result by par value, or $10,000. In the case at hand, $n = 28$ days for the July 17 maturity bond (the table subtracts the 2 skip settlement days from the 30 days of maturity). The discount yield based on the ask price is 5.31 percent, or .0531, so the ask price of the bill is found to be

$$\$10,000 \times [1 - .0531 \times (28/360)] = \$9,958.70$$

Concept Check

Question 1. Find the bid price of this bill based on the bank discount yield at bid.

**Bond equivalent
yield** *Bond yield
calculated on an
annual percentage
rate method.*

The "yield" column in Figure 4.2 is the **bond equivalent yield** of the T-bill. This is the bill's APR, assuming it is purchased for the asking price. The bond equivalent yield is computed as

$$r_{BEY} = \frac{10,000 - P}{P} \times \frac{365}{n} \tag{4.3}$$

In Equation 4.3, the HPR of the bill is computed in the first term on the right-hand side as the price increase of the bill if held until maturity per dollar paid for the bill (the capital gains rate). The second term annualizes that yield. Note that the bond equivalent yield is a correct APR because it uses the price (*P*) of the bill in the denominator of the first term and uses a 365-day year in the second term to annualize.

The bond equivalent yield (*BEY*) in Equation 4.3 still is an APR, so a problem remains in comparing yields on bills with different maturities. The reality is, however, that yields on most securities with less than a year to maturity are published as APRs.

Thus, for our demonstration T-bill,

$$r_{BEY} = \frac{10,000 - 9,958.70}{9,958.70} \times \frac{365}{28} = .05406$$

or 5.41 percent as reported in *The Wall Street Journal*.

A convenient formula relating the bond equivalent yield to the bank discount yield is

$$r_{BEY} = \frac{365 \times r_{BD}}{360 - (n \times r_{BD})}$$

Here, $r_{BD} = .0531$, so that

$$r_{BEY} = \frac{365 \times .0531}{360 - (28 \times .0531)} = .05406$$

Finally, the effective annual yield on the bill based on the ask price, $9,958.70, is 5.54 percent. Its 28-day HPR equals $(10,000 - 9,958.70)/9,958.70$, or .4147 percent. Annualizing this return, we obtain $(1.004147)^{365/28} = 1.0554$, implying an effective annual rate of 5.54 percent.

This example illustrates the general rule that the bank discount yield is less than the bond equivalent yield, which in turn is less than the effective annual yield.

Certificates of Deposit

Certificate of deposit
A bank time deposit.

A **certificate of deposit** (CD) is a time deposit with a bank. Time deposits may not be withdrawn on demand. The bank pays interest and principal to the depositor only at the end of the fixed term of the CD. CDs issued in denominations larger than $100,000 are usually negotiable, however; that is, they can be sold to another investor if the owner needs to cash in the certificate before its maturity date. Short-term CDs are highly marketable, although the market significantly thins out for maturities of six months or more. CDs are treated as bank deposits by the Federal Deposit Insurance Corporation, so they are insured for up to $100,000 in the event of a bank insolvency.

Commercial Paper

The average corporation is a net borrower of both long-term funds (for capital budgets) and short-term funds (for working capital). Large, well-known companies often issue their own short-term unsecured debt notes directly to the pub-

Commercial paper
Short-term unsecured debt issued by large corporations.

lic, rather than borrowing from banks. These notes are called **commercial paper** (CP). Sometimes, CP is backed (secured) by a bank line of credit, which gives the borrower access to cash that can be used (if needed) to pay off the paper at maturity.

CP maturities range up to 270 days; longer maturities require registration with the Securities and Exchange Commission and so are almost never issued. CP most commonly is issued with maturities of less than one or two months in denominations of multiples of $100,000. Therefore, small investors can invest in commercial paper only indirectly, through money market mutual funds.

CP is considered to be a fairly safe asset, given that a firm's condition presumably can be monitored and predicted over a term as short as one month. It is worth noting, though, that many firms issue commercial paper intending to roll it over at maturity, that is, issue new paper to obtain the funds necessary to retire the old paper. If lenders become lackadaisical about monitoring a firm's prospects and grant rollovers willy-nilly, they can suffer big losses. When Penn Central defaulted in 1970, it had $82 million of commercial paper outstanding— the only major default on commercial paper in the past 40 years.

CP trades in secondary markets and so is quite liquid. Except for junk CP, most issues are rated by at least one agency such as Standard & Poor's. The yield on CP will depend on the time to maturity and the credit rating.

Bankers' Acceptances

Banker's acceptance
An order to a bank by a customer to pay a sum of money at a future date.

A **bankers' acceptance** starts as an order to a bank by a bank's customer to pay a sum of money at a future date, typically within six months. At this stage, it is like a postdated check. When the bank endorses the order for payment as "accepted," it assumes responsibility for ultimate payment to the holder of the acceptance. At this point, the acceptance may be traded in secondary markets like any other claim on the bank. Bankers' acceptances are considered very safe assets, as they allow traders to substitute the bank's credit standing for their own. They are used widely in foreign trade where the creditworthiness of one trader is unknown to the trading partner. Acceptances sell at a discount from the face value of the payment order, just as T-bills sell at a discount from par value.

Eurodollars

Eurodollars *Dollar-denominated deposits at foreign banks or foreign branches of American banks.*

Eurodollars are dollar-dominated deposits at foreign banks or foreign branches of American banks. Despite the tag "Euro," these accounts need not be in European banks, although that is where the practice of accepting dollar-denominated deposits outside the United States began. Any bank located outside the United States is exempted from regulation by the Federal Reserve Board.

Most Eurodollar deposits are for large sums, and most are time deposits of less than six months' maturity. A variation on the Eurodollar time deposit is the Eurodollar certificate of deposit. A Eurodollar CD resembles a domestic bank CD except it is the liability of a non-U.S. branch of a bank, typically a London branch. The advantage of Eurodollar CDs over Eurodollar time deposits is that the holder can sell the asset to realize its cash value before maturity. Eurodollar CDs are considered less liquid and riskier than domestic CDs, however, and so offer higher yields. Firms also issue Eurodollar bonds, dollar-denominated bonds in Europe, although bonds are not a money market investment by virtue of their long maturities.

Repos and Reverses

Repurchase agreements (repos) *Short-term sales of government securities with an agreement to repurchase the securities at a higher price.*

Dealers in government securities use **repurchase agreements,** also called repos or RPs, as a form of short-term, usually overnight, borrowing. The dealer sells securities to an investor on an overnight basis, with an agreement to buy back those securities the next day at a slightly higher price. The increase in the price is the overnight interest. The dealer thus takes out a one-day loan from the investor. The securities serve as collateral for the loan.

A *term repo* is essentially an identical transaction, except the term of the implicit loan can be 30 days or more. Repos are considered very safe in terms of credit risk because the loans are backed by the government securities. A *reverse repo* is the mirror image of a repo. Here, the dealer finds an investor holding government securities and buys them with an agreement to resell them at a specified higher price on a future date.

The repo market was upset by several failures of government security dealers in 1985. In these cases, the dealers had entered into the typical repo arrangements with investors, pledging government securities as collateral. The investors did not take physical possession of the securities as they could have under the purchase and resale arrangement. Some of the dealers, unfortunately, fraudulently pledged the same securities as collateral in different repos; when the dealers went under, the investors found they could not collect the securities they had "purchased" in the first leg of the repo transaction. In the wake of the scandal, repo rates for nonprimary dealers increased, while rates for some well-capitalized firms fell as investors became more sensitive to credit risk. Investors can best protect themselves by taking delivery of the securities, either directly or through an agent such as a bank custodian.

Brokers' Calls

Individuals who buy stocks on margin borrow part of the funds to pay for the stocks from their broker. The broker in turn may borrow the funds from a bank, agreeing to repay the bank immediately (on call) if the bank requests it. The rate paid on such loans is usually about one percentage point higher than the rate on short-term T-bills.

Federal Funds

Federal funds *Funds in the accounts of commercial banks with the Federal Reserve Bank.*

Just as most of us maintain deposits at banks, banks maintain deposits of their own at the Federal Reserve Bank. Each member bank of the Federal Reserve System is required to maintain a minimum balance in a reserve account with the Fed. The required balance depends on the total deposits of the bank's customers. Funds in the bank's reserve account are called **Federal funds** or *Fed funds*. At any time, some banks have more funds than required at the Fed. Other banks, primarily big New York and other financial center banks, tend to have a shortage of Federal funds. In the Federal funds market, banks with excess funds lend to those with a shortage. These loans, which are usually overnight transactions, are arranged at a rate of interest called the Federal funds rate.

While the Fed funds rate is not directly relevant to investors, it is used as one of the barometers of the money market and so is widely watched by them.

The LIBOR Market

London Interbank Offer Rate (LIBOR)
Rate that the most creditworthy banks charge one another for loans in the London market.

The **London Interbank Offer Rate (LIBOR)** is the rate at which large banks in London are willing to lend money among themselves. This rate has become the premier short-term interest rate quoted in the European money market and serves as a reference rate for a wide range of transactions. A corporation might borrow at a rate equal to LIBOR plus 2 percentage points, for example. Like the Fed funds rate, LIBOR is a statistic widely followed by investors.

Yields on Money Market Instruments

Although most money market securities are of low risk, they are not risk free. As we noted earlier, the commercial paper market was rocked by the Penn Central bankruptcy, which precipitated a default on $82 million of commercial paper. Money market investors became more sensitive to creditworthiness after this episode, and the yield spread between low- and high-quality paper widened.

The securities of the money market do promise yields greater than those on default-free T-bills, at least in part because of greater relative riskiness. Investors who require more liquidity also will accept lower yields on securities such as T-bills that can be more quickly and cheaply sold for cash. Figure 4.3 shows that bank CDs, for example, consistently have paid a risk premium over T-bills. Moreover, that risk premium increases with economic crises such as the energy

Figure 4.3
Spread between 3-month CDs and T-bills.
(From Timothy Q. Cook, "Treasury Bills," in Timothy Q. Cook and Timothy D. Rowe, ed., *Instruments of the Money Market*, Federal Reserve Bank of Richmond, Richmond, Va., 1986).

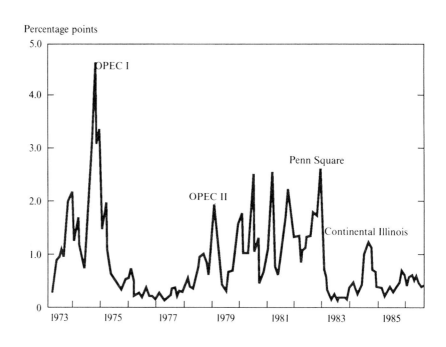

price shocks associated with the Organization of Petroleum Exporting Countries (OPEC) disturbances or the failures of Continental Illinois and Penn Square banks.

4.2   *The Fixed-Income Capital Market*

The fixed-income capital market is composed of longer-term borrowing instruments than those that trade in the money market. This market includes Treasury notes and bonds, corporate bonds, municipal bonds, mortgage securities, and federal agency debt.

The title "fixed-income" is given to these securities because most of them promise periodic (usually semiannual) interest payments. Payments are administered by the issuer, or a banking agent on the issuer's behalf. These payments are fixed unless the issuer is declared bankrupt.

Treasury Bonds and Notes

Treasury bond or note Debt obligations of the federal government that make semiannual payments and are sold at or near par value in denominations of $1,000 or more.

The U.S. government borrows funds in large part by selling **Treasury notes** and **bonds.** T-note maturities range up to 10 years, while bonds are issued with maturities ranging from 10 to 30 years. Both are issued in denominations of $1,000 or more. Both make semiannual coupon payments set at an initial level that enables the government to sell the securities at or near par value. Aside from their differing maturities at issuance, the only major distinction between T-notes and T-bonds is that T-bonds may be callable during a given period, usually the last five years of the bond's life. The call provision gives the Treasury the right to repurchase the bond at par value. While callable T-bonds still are outstanding, the Treasury no longer issues callable bonds.

Figure 4.4 is an excerpt from a listing of Treasury issues in *The Wall Street Journal*. The highlighted bond matures in August 2000. The coupon income or interest paid by the bond is 8¾ percent of par value, meaning that for a $1,000 face value bond, $87.50 in annual interest payments will be made in two semi-annual installments of $43.75 each. The numbers to the right of the colon in the bid and ask prices represent units of $\frac{1}{32}$ of a point.

The bid price of the highlighted bond is 104⁶/₃₂, or 104.1875. The ask price is 104⁸/₃₂, or 104.25. Although bonds are sold in denominations of $1,000 par value, the prices are quoted as a percent of par value. Thus, the ask price of 104.25 should be interpreted as 104.25 percent of par or $1,042.50 for the $1,000 par value bond. Similarly, the bond could be sold to a dealer for $1,041.875. The −2 bid change means the closing bid price on this day fell ²/₃₂ (as a percent of par value) from the previous day's closing bid price. Finally, the yield to maturity on the bond as based on the ask price is 8.09 percent. (Yield to maturity is discussed extensively in Chapter 15.) It is reported in the financial pages as an APR, calculated by doubling the semiannual yield to maturity, and hence is also the bond equivalent yield of the bond (discussed earlier).

Figure 4.4 shows that the yields on most bonds are fairly similar. Some bonds, however, such as the 3½ Nov 1998 bonds, offer seemingly low yields. These are special bonds known as *flower bonds* that may be used to settle federal estate taxes at par value under certain conditions. Because individuals using these

Figure 4.4
Listing of Treasury issues.
Reprinted by permission of *THE WALL STREET JOURNAL*, © 1991 Dow Jones & Company, Inc. All Rights Reserved Worldwide.

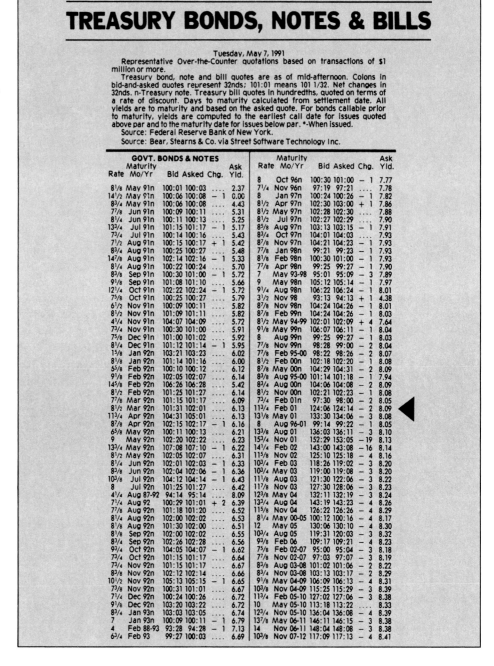

TREASURY BONDS, NOTES & BILLS

Tuesday, May 7, 1991

Representative Over-the-Counter quotations based on transactions of $1 million or more.

Treasury bond, note and bill quotes are as of mid-afternoon. Colons in bid-and-asked quotes represent 32nds; 101:01 means 101 1/32. Net changes in 32nds. n-Treasury note. Treasury bill quotes in hundredths, quoted on terms of a rate of discount. Days to maturity calculated from settlement date. All yields are to maturity and based on the asked quote. For bonds callable prior to maturity, yields are computed to the earliest call date for issues quoted above par and to the maturity date for issues below par. *-When issued.

Source: Federal Reserve Bank of New York.

Source: Bear, Stearns & Co. via Street Software Technology Inc.

bonds for estate-tax purposes may in effect sell them to the U.S. government for their full par value, these bonds sell at close to par value despite their low coupon payments. The Treasury no longer issues flower bonds.

You can pick out the callable bonds in Figure 4.4 because a range of years appears in the maturity date column. These are the years during which the bond is callable. Yields on premium bonds (bonds selling about par value) are calculated as the yield to the first call date, while yields on discount bonds are calculated as the yield to maturity date. Yields on premium bonds are computed to the first call date (rather than maturity) because, if interest rates do not rise (so that the bond continues to sell at a premium), it would be profitable for the issuer to call the bond early. Thus, the investor can expect to hold the bond only to the (earlier) first call date, rather than to maturity.

Concept Check

Question 2. Compute the yield to first call and the yield to maturity on one of the callable bonds in Figure 4.4. Do the results make sense to you?

Federal Agency Debt

Some government agencies issue their own securities to finance their activities. These agencies usually are formed for public policy reasons to channel credit to a particular sector of the economy that Congress believes is not receiving adequate credit through normal private sources. Figure 4.5 reproduces listings of some of these securities from *The Wall Street Journal*. The majority of the debt is issued in support of home mortgages and farm credit.

The major mortgage-related agencies are the Federal Home Loan Bank (FHLB), the Federal National Mortgage Association (FNMA, or Fannie Mae), the Government National Mortgage Assocation (GNMA, or Ginnie Mae), and the Federal Home Loan Mortgage Corporation (FHLMC, or Freddie Mac).

The FHLB borrows money by issuing securities and relends this money to savings and loan institutions to be lent to individuals borrowing for home mortgages.

Freddie Mac, Fannie Mae, and Ginnie Mae were organized to provide liquidity to the mortgage market. Until establishment of the pass-through securities sponsored by these government agencies, the lack of a secondary market in mortgages hampered the flow of investment funds into mortgages and made mortgage markets dependent on local, rather than national, credit availability. Pass-through financing initiated by these agencies represents one of the most important financial innovations of the 1980s.

The farm credit agencies are 12 district Banks for Cooperatives that make seasonal loans to farm cooperatives, 12 Federal Land Banks that make mortgage loans on farm properties, and 12 Federal Intermediate Credit Banks that provide short-term financing for production and marketing of crops and livestock.

Although the debt of federal agencies is not explicitly insured by the federal government, it is assumed the government would assist an agency nearing default. Thus, these securities are considered extremely safe assets, and their yield spread over Treasury securities is quite small.

Concept Check

Question 3. Compute yield to maturity on one of the agency bonds, and compare it to that of the T-bond with the nearest maturity date.

Figure 4.5 Listings of government securities.
Reprinted by permission of *THE WALL STREET JOURNAL*, © 1991 Dow Dow Jones & Company, Inc. All Rights Reserved Worldwide.

Municipal Bonds

Municipal bonds *Tax-exempt bonds issued by state and local governments.*

Municipal bonds ("munis") are issued by state and local governments. They are similar to Treasury and corporate bonds except their interest income is exempt from federal income taxation. The interest income also is exempt from state and local taxation in the issuing state. Capital gains taxes, however, must be paid on munis if the bonds mature or are sold for more than the investor's purchase price.

There are basically two types of municipal bonds. These are *general obligation bonds,* which are backed by the "full faith and credit" (i.e., the taxing power) of the issuer, and revenue bonds, which are issued to finance particular projects and are backed either by the revenues from that project or by the municipal agency operating the project. Typical issuers of revenue bonds are airports, hospitals, and turnpike or port authorities. Revenue bonds are riskier in terms of default than general obligation bonds.

A particular type of revenue bond is the industrial development bond, which is issued to finance commercial enterprises such as the construction of a factory that can be operated by a private firm. In effect, this device gives the firm access to the municipality's ability to borrow at tax-exempt rates. Figure 4.6 shows the volume of new offerings of municipal bonds in recent years. Note the increasing importance of revenue bonds.

Like Treasury bonds, municipal bonds vary widely in maturity. A good deal of the debt issued is in the form of short-term tax anticipation notes that raise funds to pay for expenses before actual collection of taxes. Other municipal debt may be long term and used to fund large capital investments. Maturities range up to 30 years.

The key feature of municipal bonds is their tax-exempt status. Because investors need not pay federal (and possibly state) taxes on the interest proceeds,

Figure 4.6
State and local government security issues.
(From *Historical Chart Book* of the Federal Reserve Board.)

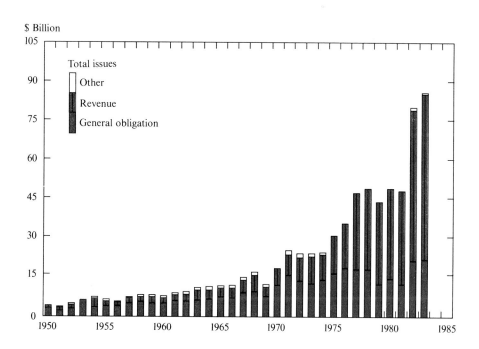

they are willing to accept lower yields on these securities. This represents a huge savings to state and local governments. Correspondingly, it is a huge drain of potential tax revenue from the federal government, which has shown some dismay over the explosive increase in the use of industrial development bonds. These so-called private purpose bonds increased from 22 percent of new municipal offerings in 1975 to 62 percent in 1983.

Because of concern that these bonds were being used to take advantage of the tax-exempt feature of municipal bonds rather than as a source of funds for publicly desirable investments, the Tax Reform Act of 1986 restricted their use. A state is now allowed to issue mortgage revenue and private purpose tax-exempt bonds only up to a limit of $50 per capita or $150 million, whichever is larger.

An investor choosing between taxable and tax-exempt bonds needs to compare after-tax returns on each bond. An exact comparison requires computation of after-tax rates of return with explicit recognition of taxes on income and realized capital gains. In practice, there is a simpler rule of thumb. If we let t denote the investor's marginal tax rate and r denote the total before-tax rate of return available on taxable bonds, then $r(1-t)$ is the after-tax rate available on those securities. If this value exceeds the rate on municipal bonds, r_m, the investor does better holding the taxable bonds. Otherwise, the tax-exempt municipals provide higher after-tax returns.

One way of comparing bonds is to determine the interest rate on taxable bonds that would be necessary to provide an after-tax return equal to that of municipals. To derive this value, we set after-tax yields equal and solve for the *equivalent taxable yield* of the tax-exempt bond. This is the rate a taxable bond would need to offer in order to match the after-tax yield on the tax-free municipal:

$$r(1 - t) = r_m \qquad\qquad (4.4)$$

or

$$r = r_m/(1 - t) \qquad\qquad (4.5)$$

Thus, the equivalent taxable yield is simply the tax-free rate divided by $1-t$. Table 4.3 presents equivalent taxable yields for several municipal yields and tax rates.

This table frequently appears in the marketing literature for tax-exempt mutual bond funds because it demonstrates to high tax-bracket investors that municipal bonds offer highly attractive equivalent taxable yields. Each entry is

Table 4.3   *Equivalent Taxable Yields Corresponding to Various Tax-Exempt Yields*

Marginal Tax Rate	Tax-Exempt Yield				
	4%	6%	8%	10%	12%
20%	5.0	7.5	10.0	12.5	15.0
30%	5.7	8.6	11.4	14.3	17.1
40%	6.7	10.0	13.3	16.7	20.0
50%	8.0	12.0	16.0	20.0	24.0

Figure 4.7
Ratio of yields on
tax-exempt bonds to
taxable bonds.
(Data from Moody's Investor
Service, 1991.)

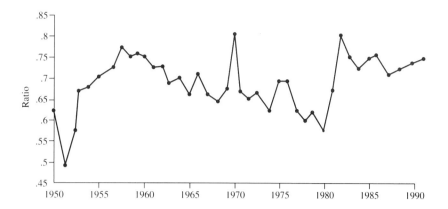

calculated from Equation 4.5. If the equivalent taxable yield exceeds the actual yields offered on taxable bonds, the investor is better off after taxes holding municipal bonds. The equivalent taxable interest rate increases with the investor's tax bracket; the higher the bracket, the more valuable the tax-exempt feature of municipals. Thus, high-bracket individuals tend to hold municipals.

We also can use Equations 4.4 or 4.5 to find the tax bracket at which investors are indifferent between taxable and tax-exempt bonds. The cutoff tax bracket is given by solving Equation 4.4 for the tax bracket at which after-tax yields are equal. Doing so, we find

$$t = 1 - r_m/r \tag{4.6}$$

Thus, the yield ratio r_m/r is a key determinant of the attractiveness of municipal bonds. The higher the yield ratio, the lower the cutoff tax bracket, and the more individuals will prefer to hold municipal debt.

Figure 4.7 graphs the yield ratio since 1950. The ratio seems to have risen over time. This implies municipals have become desirable to investors in progressively lower tax brackets.

Concept Check

Question 4. What economic policy changes in the 1980s might have contributed to the increase in the yield ratio?

Corporate Bonds

Corporate bonds
Long-term debt issued by private corporations typically paying semiannual coupons and returning the face value of the bond at maturity.

Corporate bonds are the means by which private firms borrow money directly from the public. These bonds are structured much like Treasury issues in that they typically pay semiannual coupons over their lives and return the face value to the bondholder at maturity. Where they differ most importantly from Treasury bonds is in risk.

Default risk is a real consideration in the purchase of corporate bonds. We treat this issue in considerable detail in Chapter 12. For now, we distinguish only among secured bonds, which have specific collateral backing them in the event of firm bankruptcy; unsecured bonds, called debentures, which have no collateral; and subordinated debentures, which have a lower priority claim to the firm's assets in the event of bankruptcy.

Corporate bonds usually come with options attached. Callable bonds give the firm the option to repurchase the bond from the holder at a stipulated call price. Convertible bonds give the bondholder the option to convert each bond into a stipulated number of shares of stock. These options are treated in more detail in Part Three.

Figure 4.8 is a partial listing of corporate bond prices from *The Wall Street Journal*. The listings are similar to those for Treasury bonds. The highlighted Du Pont bond has a coupon rate of 8½ percent and a maturity date of 2006. Its

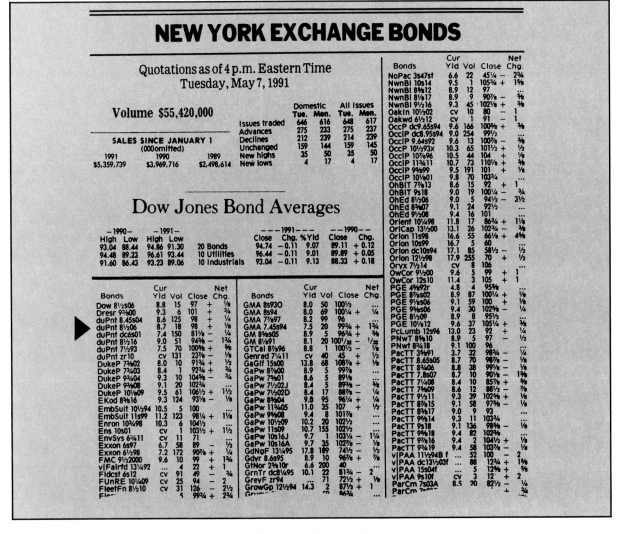

Listing of corporate bond prices.

current yield, defined as annual coupon income divided by price, is 8.7 percent. (Note that current yield is a different measure from yield to maturity. The differences are explored in Part Three.)

Only 1,800 Du Pont bonds traded on this day. The closing price of the bond was 98 percent of par, or $980, which was up ⅛ of a point from the previous day's close. In contrast to Treasury bonds, price quotes on corporate bonds use explicit fractions.

Mortgages and Mortgage-Backed Securities

Twenty years ago, your investments text probably would not have included a section on mortgage loans, for investors could not invest in these loans. Now, because of the explosion in mortgage-backed securities, almost anyone can invest in a portfolio of mortgage loans, and these securities have become a major component of the fixed-income market.

Until the 1970s, almost all home mortgages were written for a long term (15– to 30–year maturity), with a fixed interest rate over the life of the loan, and with equal, fixed monthly payments. These so-called conventional mortgages are still the most popular, but a diverse set of alternative mortgage designs have appeared.

Fixed-rate mortgages have created considerable difficulties for banks in years of increasing interest rates. Because banks commonly issue short-term liabilities (the deposits of their customers) and hold long-term assets such as fixed-rate mortgages, they suffer losses when interest rates increase. The rates they pay on deposits increase, while their mortgage income remains fixed.

A relatively recent introduction is the adjustable-rate mortgage. These mortgages require the borrower to pay an interest rate that varies with some measure of the current market interest rate. The interest rate, for example, might be set at two points above the current rate on one-year Treasury bills and might be adjusted once a year. Often a contract limits the maximum interest rate change within a year and over the life of the contract. The adjustable-rate contract shifts the risk of fluctuations in interest rates from the bank to the borrower.

Because of the shifting of interest rate risk to their customers, banks are willing to offer lower rates on adjustable-rate mortgages than on conventional fixed-rate mortgages. This encouraged borrowers during a period of high interest rates in the early 1980s. But as interest rates fell, conventional mortgages appear to have regained popularity. While adjustable-rate mortgages accounted for about half of all mortgage lending at year-end 1983, that figure fell to below 25 percent through the first half of 1991.

A *mortgage-backed security* is either an ownership claim in a pool of mortgages or an obligation that is secured by such a pool. These claims represent securitization of mortgage loans. Mortgage lenders originate loans and then sell packages of these loans in the secondary market. Specifically, they sell their claim to the cash inflows from the mortgages as those loans are paid off. The mortgage originator continues to service the loan, collecting principal and interest payments, and passes these payments along to the purchaser of the mortgage. For this reason, these mortgage-backed securities are called *passthroughs*.

Mortgage-backed pass-through securities were introduced by the Government National Mortgage Association (GNMA, or Ginnie Mae) in 1970. GNMA pass-throughs carry a guarantee from the U.S. government that ensures timely payment of principal and interest, even if the borrower defaults on the mortgage. This guarantee increases the marketability of the pass-through. Thus, investors can buy and sell GNMA securities like any other bond.

Other mortgage pass-throughs have since become popular. These are sponsored by FNMA (Fannie Mae) and FHLMC (Freddie Mac). The success of mortgage-backed pass-throughs has encouraged introduction of pass-through securities backed by other assets. For example, the Student Loan Marketing Association (SLMA, or Sallie Mae) sponsors pass-throughs backed by loans originated under the Guaranteed Student Loan Program and by other loans granted under various federal programs for higher education.

Although pass-through securities often carry guarantees as to payment of interest and principal, they do not promise a guaranteed rate of return. Holders of mortgage pass-throughs can be severely disappointed in their returns in years when interest rates drop significantly. This is because homeowners usually have an option to prepay the remaining principal outstanding on their mortgages ahead of schedule.

This right is essentially an option held by the borrower to "call back" the loan for the remaining principal balance, analogous to the option held by government or corporate issuers of callable bonds. The prepayment option gives the borrower the right to buy back the loan at the outstanding principal amount rather than at the present discounted value of the *scheduled* remaining payments.

When interest rates fall, so that the present value of the scheduled mortgage payments increases, the borrower may take out a new loan at today's lower interest rate and use the proceeds to prepay the outstanding mortgage. This refinancing pulls the rug out from under pass-through investors. They are liable to "receive a call" just when they might have anticipated capital gains from interest rate declines.

In most cases, a bank that originates a mortgage receives a large part of its profit in the form of points. Each point is a surcharge to the borrower of 1 percent of the mortgage.

While banks are required to make a statement to the borrower that shows the effective annual rate (inclusive of the points), the computation of the effective rate is complex and often poorly understood.

Compare a $100,000, 30-year mortgage, at an APR of 12 percent with no points, to a similar mortgage at an APR of "only" 11.75 percent, but with two points. The first carries an effective annual rate of 12.68 percent ($1.01^{12} - 1$). To compute the rate for the second mortgage, we need to take the maturity into account, noting that we receive only $98,000 (since $1,000 is deducted for each point), while the payments are computed on a full $100,000, 11.75 percent mortgage, and amount to $1,009.41 per month.

These payments, when applied to a loan of only $98,000, imply a (monthly) HPR of 1.0015 percent, or an effective annual rate of 12.70 percent, slightly more than the first mortgage. As a rule, 1 point is worth 13 basis points on the APR of a 30-year mortgage and more on a shorter one. However, the right to prepay the mortgage makes the maturity of the loan uncertain, so shopping for the best mortgage becomes more complicated still.

4.3   *Equity Securities*

Common Stock as Ownership Shares

Common stock
Equities are ownership shares in a publicly held corporation. Shareholders have voting rights and may receive dividends.

Common stocks, also known as equity securities or equities, represent ownership shares in a corporation. Each share of common stock entitles its owner to one vote on any matters of corporate governance put to a vote at the corporation's annual meeting and to a share in the financial benefits of ownership[1] (e.g., the right to any dividends that the corporation may wish to distribute).

A corporation is controlled by a board of directors elected by the shareholders.[2] The board, which meets only a few times each year, selects managers who run the corporation on a day-to-day basis. Managers have the authority to make most business decisions without the board's approval. The board's mandate is to oversee the management to ensure that it acts in the best interests of shareholders.

The members of the board are elected at the annual meeting. Shareholders who do not attend the annual meeting can vote by proxy, empowering another party to vote in their name. Management usually solicits the proxies of shareholders and normally gets a vast majority of these proxy votes. Occasionally, however, a group of shareholders intent on unseating the current management or altering its policies will wage a proxy fight to gain the voting rights of shareholders not attending the annual meeting. Thus, while management usually has considerable discretion to run the firm as it sees fit, without daily oversight from the equity holders who actually own the firm, both oversight from the board and the possibility of a proxy fight serve as checks on management's jurisdiction.

In practice, where ownership is greatly diffused in widely held corporations, management controls are less stringent than in theory. In proxy fights, management defends its board member allies at corporate expense, while the outsiders must finance the fight from their own pockets. A typical proxy fight costs millions, and about three fourths of the attempts have historically failed—statistics that send chills down the spines of would-be proxy fighters.

Management theory recognizes that inherent conflicts between management and shareholders can result in significant losses to shareholders. These losses are called agency costs. Experts have come to believe that this is a major issue and that structuring governance procedures and management-contract incentives so as to minimize agency costs deserves great efforts.

In view of potentially large agency costs, the most effective check on management's discretion may be the possibility of a corporate takeover; that is, that an outside investor who believes the firm is mismanaged will attempt to acquire the firm. Usually, this is accomplished with a *tender offer,* which is an offer made to stockholders to purchase their shares at a stipulated price, usually substantially above the current market price. If the tender is successful, the acquir-

---

[1]Sometimes a corporation issues two classes of common stock, one bearing the right to vote, the other not. Because of its restricted rights, the nonvoting stocks sell for a lower price reflecting the value of control.

[2]The voting system specified in the corporate articles determines the chances of affecting the elections to specific directorship seats. In a majority voting system, each shareholder can cast one vote per share for each seat. A cumulative voting system allows shareholders to concentrate all their votes on one seat, enabling minority shareholders to gain representation.

ing investor can purchase enough shares to obtain control of the firm and can replace its management.

According to agency theory, it is beneficial to leave the (regulatory) door open for takeover activity. The threat of a takeover may be the most effective means to ensure that management acts in the best interests of shareholders.

The common stock of most large corporations can be bought or sold freely on one or more of the stock exchanges. A corporation whose stock is not publicly traded is said to be closely held. In most closely held corporations, the owners of the firm also take an active role in its management. Takeovers generally are not an issue.

Thus, while there is substantial separation of the ownership and the control of large corporations, there are at least some implicit controls on management that encourage it to act in the interest of the shareholders.

Characteristics of Common Stock

The two most important characteristics of common stock as an investment are its residual claim and limited liability features.

Residual claim means stockholders are the last in line of all those who have a claim on the assets and income of the corporation. In a liquidation of the firm's assets, the shareholders have claim to what is left after paying all other claimants, such as the tax authorities, employees, suppliers, bondholders, and other creditors. In a going concern, shareholders have claim to the part of operating income left after interest and income taxes have been paid. Management can either pay this residual as cash dividends to shareholders or reinvest it in the business to increase the value of the shares.

Limited liability means that the most shareholders can lose in event of failure of the corporation is their original investment. Shareholders are not like owners of unincorporated businesses, whose creditors can lay claim to the personal assets of the owner—house, car, furniture. In the event of the firm's bankruptcy, corporate stockholders at worst have worthless stock. They are not personally liable for the firm's obligations: their liability is limited.

Concept Check

Question 5. *a.* If you buy 100 shares of IBM common stock, what does that entitle you to? *b.* What is the most money you can make over the next year? *c.* If you pay $50 per share, what is the most money you could lose over the year?

Stock Market Listings

Figure 4.9 is a partial listing from *The Wall Street Journal* of stocks traded on the New York Stock Exchange. The NYSE is one of several markets in which investors may buy or sell shares of stock. We will examine issues of trading in these markets in the next chapter.

To interpret the information provided for each traded stock, consider the listing for Baltimore Gas and Electric, BaltimrGE. The first two columns provide the highest and lowest price at which the stock has traded in the last 52 weeks, $30⅞ and $24⅜, respectively. The 2.10 figure means that dividend payout to its shareholders over the last quarter was $2.10 per share at an annual rate.

NEW YORK STOCK EXCHANGE COMPOSITE TRANSACTIONS

Quotations as of 4:30 p.m. Eastern Time
Tuesday, May 7, 1991

Figure 4.9 Listing of stocks traded on the New York stock Exchange.
Reprinted by permission of THE WALL STREET JOURNAL, © 1991 Dow Jones & Company, Inc. All Rights Reserved Worldwide.

This value corresponds to a dividend yield of 7.2 percent, since BaltimrGE stock is selling at $29⅛ (the last recorded, or "close," price in the next-to-last column), so that the dividend yield is 2.10/29.125 = 0.0721, or 7.21 percent.

The stock listings show that dividend yields vary widely among firms. High dividend-yield stocks are not necessarily better investments than low-yield stocks. Total return to an investor comes from both dividends and capital gains, or appreciation in the value of the stock. Low dividend-yield firms presumably offer greater prospects for capital gains, or else investors would not be willing to hold the low-yield firms in their portfolios.

The P/E ratio, or price earnings ratio, is the ratio of the current stock price to last year's earnings. The P/E ratio tells us how much stock purchasers must pay per dollar of earnings the firm generates for each share. The P/E ratio also varies widely across firms. Where the dividend yield and P/E ratio are not reported in Figure 4.9, the firms have zero dividends, or zero or negative earnings. We shall have much to say about P/E ratios in Part Four.

The sales column shows that 844 hundred shares of BaltimrGE were traded on May 7, 1991. Shares commonly are traded in round lots of 100 shares each. Investors who wish to trade in smaller "odd lots" generally must pay higher commissions to their stockbrokers. The highest price and lowest price per share at which the stock traded on May 7 were $29\frac{3}{8}$ and $29\frac{1}{8}$, respectively. The last, or closing, price of $29\frac{1}{8}$ was down $\frac{1}{8}$ from the closing price of the previous day.

Preferred Stock

Preferred stock Non-voting shares in a corporation, usually paying a fixed stream of dividends.

Preferred stock has features similar to both equity and debt. Like a bond, it promises to pay to its holder a fixed stream of dividends each year. In this sense, preferred stock is similar to an infinite-maturity bond, that is, a perpetuity. It also resembles a bond in that it does not give the holder voting power regarding the firm's management.

Preferred stock is an equity investment, however, in the sense that failure to pay the dividend due does not set off corporate bankruptcy. Instead, preferred dividends are usually *cumulative;* that is, unpaid dividends cumulate and must be paid in full before any dividends may be paid to holders of common stock.

Preferred stock also differs from bonds in terms of its tax treatment for the firm. Because preferred stock payments are treated as dividends rather than as interest on debt, they are not tax-deductible expenses for the firm. This disadvantage is largely offset by the fact that corporations may exclude 70 percent of dividends received from domestic corporations in the computation of their taxable income. Preferred stocks, therefore, make desirable fixed-income investments for some corporations.

Even though it ranks after bonds in the event of corporate bankruptcy, preferred stock often sells at lower yields than corporate bonds. Presumably this reflects the value of the dividend exclusion, for risk considerations alone indicate that preferred stock ought to offer higher yields than bonds. Individual investors, who cannot use the 70 percent exclusion, generally will find preferred stock yields unattractive relative to those on other available assets.

Preferred stock is issued in variations similar to those of corporate bonds. It can be callable by the issuing firm, in which case it is said to be *redeemable.* It also can be convertible into common stock at some specified conversion ratio. A recent innovation in the market is adjustable-rate preferred stock, which, like adjustable-rate mortgages, ties the dividend rate to current market interest rates.

4.4 *Stock and Bond Market Indexes*

Stock Market Indexes

The daily performance of the Dow Jones Industrial Average is a staple portion of the evening news report. While the Dow is the best-known measure of the performance of the stock market, it is only one of several indicators. Other more broadly based indexes are computed and published daily. In addition, several indexes of bond market performance are widely available.

The ever-increasing role of international trade and investments has made indexes of foreign financial markets part of the general news. Thus, foreign stock exchange indexes such as the Nikkei Average of Tokyo and the Financial Times index of London are fast becoming household names.

Dow Jones Averages

Price-weighted average
An average computed by adding the prices of the stocks and dividing by a "divisor."

The Dow Jones Industrial Average of 30 large "blue-chip" corporations has been computed since 1896. Its long history probably accounts for its preeminence in the public mind. (The average covered only 20 stocks until 1928.) The Dow is a **price-weighted average,** which means it is computed by adding the prices of the 30 companies and dividing by a "divisor."

This makes the index performance a measure of the performance of a particular portfolio strategy that buys one share of each firm in the index. Therefore, the weight of each firm in the index is proportional to the share price rather than the total outstanding market value of the shares.

For example, if firm XYZ sells for $100 and has 1 million shares outstanding, while firm ABC sells for $25 but has 20 million shares outstanding, the "Dow portfolio" would have four times as much invested in XYZ as in ABC ($100 compared to $25), despite the fact that ABC is a more prominent firm in the economy ($500 million market value of equity versus only $100 million for XYZ).

Table 4.4 illustrates this point. Suppose ABC increases by 20 percent, from $25 to $30, while XYZ increases by only 10 percent, from $100 to $110. The return on a price-weighted average of the two stocks would come to only 12 percent, while the combined market value of the two stocks actually increases by more than 18 percent. Because of its lower price, the superior performance of ABC relative to XYZ has a smaller effect on the price-weighted average than it does on the actual combined value of the stocks.

History has seen many changes in the Dow list. The divisor was 20 when 20 stocks were included in the index, so originally the index was no more than the average price of the 20 stocks. However, the divisor is adjusted so as to leave the Dow average unchanged whenever one corporation replaces another in the group of 30 industrial firms. As stocks are split, the Dow divisor is also adjusted to leave the average unaffected by the change. In this way, the divisor changes considerably over time. You can see the divisor equal to 0.559(!) on a particularly interesting day (in Figure 4.10) when Caterpillar, J. P. Morgan, and Disney

Table 4.4 *Price-Weighted Returns*

Stock	Initial Price	Final Price	Shares (Million)	Initial Value of Outstanding Stock ($ Million)	Final Value of Outstanding Stock ($ Million)
ABC	25	30	20	500	600
XYZ	100	110	1	100	110
Average	62.5	70		Total market value 600	710

Increase in average price = 12% = 70/62.5 − 1
Increase in market value = 18.3% = 710/600 − 1

Table 4.5 *Price-Weighted Returns after a Stock Split*

Stock	Initial Price	Final Price	Shares (Million)	Initial value of Outstanding Stock ($ Million)	Final Value of Outstanding Stock ($ Million)
ABC	25	30	20	500	600
XYZ	50	55	2	100	110
Index value	$\frac{75}{1.20} = 62.5$	$\frac{85}{1.2} = 70.83$			
Market value				600	710

replaced Navistar International, Primemerica, and USX in the list of 30 industrials.

For example, if XYZ were to split two for one and its share price to fall to $50, we would not want the average to fall, as that would incorrectly indicate a fall in the general level of market prices. Following a split, the divisor must be reduced to a value that leaves the average unaffected by the split. Table 4.5 illustrates this point. The initial share price of XYZ, which was $100 in Table 4.4, falls to $50 if the stock splits at the beginning of the period. Notice that the number of shares outstanding doubles, leaving the market value of the total shares unaffected. The divisor, *d,* which originally was 2.0 when the two-stock average was initiated, must be reset to a value that leaves the average unchanged. Because the sum of the postsplit stock prices is 75, and the presplit average price was 62.5, we calculate the new value of *d* by solving $75/d = 62.5$. The value of *d,* therefore, falls from its original value of 2.0 to $75/62.5 = 1.20$, and the initial value of the average is unaffected by the split: $75/1.20 = 62.5$.

At period-end, ABC will sell for $30, while XYZ will sell for $55, representing the same 10 percent return it was assumed to earn in Table 4.4. The new value of the price-weighted average is $(30 + 55)/1.20 = 70.83$, and the "rate of return" on the average is $70.83/62.5 - 1 = .133$, or 13.3 percent.

This return is greater than that calculated in Table 4.4. The relative weight of XYZ, which is the poorer-performing stock, is lower after the split because its price is lower; so the performance of the average improves. This example illustrates again that the implicit weighting scheme of a price-weighted average is somewhat arbitrary, being determined by the prices rather than by the outstanding market values of the shares in the average.

Concept Check

Question 6. Suppose XYZ increases in price to $110, while ABC falls to $20. Find the percentage change in the price-weighted average of these two stocks. Compare that to the percentage return of a portfolio that holds one share in each company.

Dow Jones & Company also computes a Transportation Average of 20 airline, trucking, and railroad stocks; a Public Utility Average of 15 electric and natural gas utilities; and a Composite Average combining the 65 firms of the three separate averages. Each is a price-weighted average, and so overweights the performance of high-priced stocks.

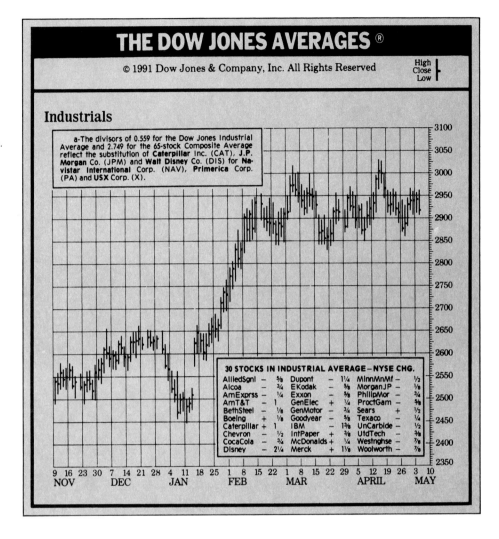

Figure 4.10 reproduces some of the data reported on the Dow Jones Averages from *The Wall Street Journal* (which is owned by Dow Jones & Company). The bars show the range of values assumed by the average on each day. The cross-hatch indicates the closing value of the average.

Standard & Poor's Indexes

Market value-weighted index   Computed by calculating a weighted average of the returns of each security in the index, with weights proportional to outstanding market value.

The Standard & Poor's Composite 500 stock index improves on the Dow Jones in two ways. First, it is a more broadly based index of 500 firms. Secondly, it is a **market value-weighted index.** In the case of the firms XYZ and ABC discussed above, the S&P 500 would give ABC five times the weight given to XYZ because the market value of its outstanding equity is five times larger.

The S&P 500 is computed by calculating the total market value of the 500 firms in the index and the total market value of those firms on the previous day of trading. The percentage increase in the total market value from one day to the next represents the increase in the index. The rate of return of the index

Figure 4.10 (concluded)

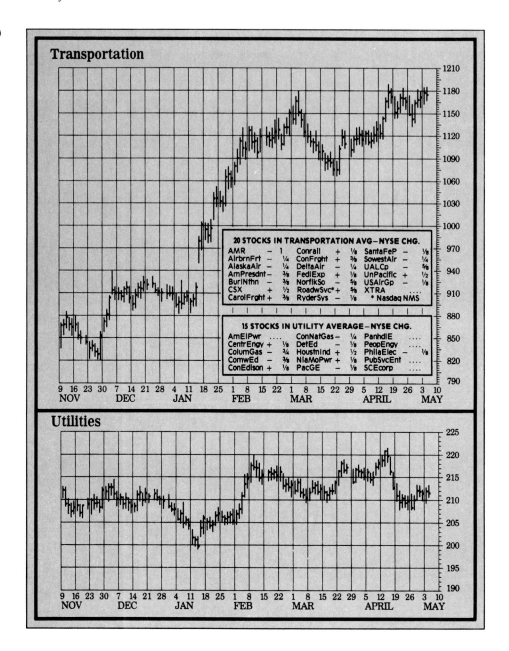

equals the rate of return that would be earned by an investor holding a portfolio of all 500 firms in the index in proportion to their market value, except that the index does not reflect cash dividends paid by those firms.

To illustrate, look again at Table 4.4. If the initial level of a market value-weighted index of stocks ABC and XYZ were set equal to an arbitrarily chosen starting value such as 100, the index value at year-end would be 100(710/600) = 118.3. The increase in the index reflects the 18.3 percent return earned on a portfolio consisting of those two stocks held in proportion to outstanding market values.

Note also from Tables 4.4 and 4.5 that market value-weighted indexes are unaffected by stock splits. The total market value of the outstanding XYZ stock increases from $100 million to $110 million regardless of the stock split, thereby rendering the split irrelevant to the performance of the index.

A nice feature of both market value-weighted and price-weighted indexes is that they reflect the returns to buy-and-hold portfolio strategies. If one were to buy each share in the index in proportion to its outstanding market value, the value-weighted index would perfectly track capital gains on the underlying portfolio. Similarly, a price-weighted index tracks the returns on a portfolio comprised of equal shares of each firm.

Investors today can purchase shares in mutual funds that hold shares in proportion to their representation in the S&P 500. These *index funds* yield a return equal to that of the S&P 500 index and so provide a low-cost passive investment strategy for equity investors.

Standard & Poor's also publishes a 400-stock Industrial Index, a 20-stock Transportation Index, a 40-stock Utility Index, and a 40-stock Financial Index.

Concept Check

Question 7. Reconsider companies XYZ and ABC from Question 6. Calculate the percentage change in the market value-weighted index. Compare that to the rate of return of a portfolio that holds $500 of ABC stock for every $100 of XYZ stock (i.e., an index portfolio).

Other Market Value Indexes

The New York Stock Exchange publishes a market value-weighted composite index of all NYSE-listed stocks, in addition to subindexes for industrial, utility, transportation, and financial stocks. The American Stock Exchange, or AMEX, also computes a market value-weighted index of its stocks. These indexes are even more broadly based than the S&P 500. The National Association of Securities Dealers publishes an index of nearly 3,000 OTC firms using the National Association of Securities Dealers Automatic Quotations (NASDAQ) service.

The ultimate equity index so far computed is the Wilshire 5000 index of the market value of all NYSE and AMEX stocks plus actively traded OTC stocks. Figure 4.11 reproduces a *Wall Street Journal* listing of stock index performance. Vanguard offers a mutual fund to small investors (the Extended Market Portfolio) that in conjunction with its Index 500 Portfolio enables investors to match the performance of the Wilshire 5000 index.

Equally Weighted Indexes

Market performance is sometimes measured by an equally weighted average of the returns of each stock in an index. Such an averaging technique, by placing equal weight on each return, calls for a portfolio strategy that places equal dollar values in each stock. This is in contrast to both price weighting, which requires equal numbers of shares of each stock, and market value weighting, which requires investments in proportion to outstanding value.

Equally weighted index An index computed from a simple average of returns.

Unlike price- or market value-weighted indexes, **equally weighted indexes** do not correspond to buy-and-hold portfolio strategies. Suppose you start with equal dollar investments in the two stocks of Table 4.4, ABC and XYZ. Because

Figure 4.11
Listing of stock index performance.
Reprinted by permission of *THE WALL STREET JOURNAL*, © 1991 Dow Jones & Company, Inc. All Rights Reserved Worldwide.

STOCK MARKET DATA BANK   5/7/91

MAJOR INDEXES

HIGH	LOW	(12 MOS)	CLOSE	NET CHG	% CHG	12 MO CHG	% CHG	FROM 12/31	% CHG
DOW JONES AVERAGES									
3004.46	2365.10	30 Industrials	x2917.49	− 24.15	− 0.82	+ 183.93	+ 6.73	+ 283.83	+ 10.78
1212.77	821.93	20 Transportation	1175.07	− 2.47	− 0.21	+ 10.06	+ 0.86	+ 264.84	+ 29.10
220.89	190.96	15 Utilities	211.52	− 0.44	− 0.21	− 0.57	− 0.27	+ 1.82	+ 0.87
1070.03	839.00	65 Composite	x1049.29	− 5.87	− 0.56	+ 38.38	+ 3.80	+ 128.68	+ 13.98
364.73	272.91	Equity Mkt. Index	352.40	− 2.35	− 0.66	+ 34.18	+ 10.74	+ 46.81	+ 15.32
NEW YORK STOCK EXCHANGE									
213.21	162.20	Composite	206.65	− 1.34	− 0.64	+ 19.54	+ 10.44	+ 26.16	+ 14.49
267.25	200.80	Industrials	259.11	− 1.78	− 0.68	+ 29.79	+ 12.99	+ 35.51	+ 15.88
95.87	80.96	Utilities	91.65	− 0.58	− 0.63	− 0.11	− 0.12	+ 0.35	+ 0.38
182.55	127.25	Transportation	170.89	− 0.79	− 0.46	− 1.35	− 0.78	+ 29.40	+ 20.78
158.19	103.26	Finance	151.56	− 0.75	− 0.49	+ 11.99	+ 8.59	+ 29.49	+ 24.16
STANDARD & POOR'S INDEXES									
390.45	295.46	500 Index	377.32	− 2.76	− 0.73	+ 35.31	+ 10.32	+ 47.10	+ 14.26
463.12	346.86	Industrials	448.31	− 3.10	− 0.69	+ 50.29	+ 12.64	+ 60.89	+ 15.72
291.30	208.77	Transportation	284.20	− 0.76	− 0.27	+ 8.43	+ 3.06	+ 49.53	+ 21.11
147.30	124.60	Utilities	140.34	− 1.04	− 0.74	− 1.21	− 0.85	− 3.25	− 2.26
31.69	18.80	Financials	29.90	− 0.24	− 0.80	+ 2.02	+ 7.25	+ 6.47	+ 27.61
NASDAQ									
511.31	325.44	Composite	491.51	+ 0.03	+ 0.01	+ 59.67	+ 13.82	+ 117.67	+ 31.48
575.67	344.11	Industrials	546.30	− 0.09	− 0.02	+ 91.67	+ 20.16	+ 140.25	+ 34.54
585.08	379.36	Insurance	558.06	+ 1.02	+ 0.18	+ 73.71	+ 15.22	+ 106.22	+ 23.51
357.28	235.25	Banks	327.02	− 2.99	− 0.91	− 20.24	− 5.83	+ 72.11	+ 28.29
225.92	142.41	Nat. Mkt. Comp.	216.76	− 0.03	− 0.01	+ 27.66	+ 14.63	+ 51.59	+ 31.23
229.93	135.93	Nat. Mkt. Indus.	217.53	− 0.09	− 0.04	+ 38.13	+ 21.25	+ 55.19	+ 34.00
OTHERS									
373.40	287.79	Amex	362.91	+ 0.07	+ 0.02	+ 15.33	+ 4.41	+ 54.80	+ 17.79
250.56	179.55	Value-Line (geom.)	239.79	− 0.55	− 0.23	+ 2.36	+ 0.99	+ 43.80	+ 22.36
178.70	118.82	Russell 2000	173.96	+ 0.18	+ 0.10	+ 13.07	+ 8.12	+ 41.77	+ 31.60
3731.48	2772.31	Wilshire 5000	3611.16	− 21.54	− 0.59	+ 343.00	+ 10.50	+ 509.81	+ 16.44

ABC increases in value by 20 percent over the year, while XYZ increases by only 10 percent, your portfolio no longer is equally weighted but is now more heavily invested in ABC. To reset the portfolio to equal weights, you would need to rebalance: either sell some ABC stock and/or purchase more XYZ stock. Such rebalancing would be necessary to align the return on your portfolio with that on the equally weighted index.

Foreign and International Stock Market Indexes

Development in financial markets worldwide includes the construction of indexes for these markets. The popular indexes are broader than the Dow Jones average and are value weighted.

The most important are the Nikkei and FTSE (pronounced "footsie"). The Nikkei averages are based on 225 of the largest Tokyo Stock Exchange (TSE) stocks. Both value- and price-weighted Nikkei averages are computed. FTSE is

Figure 4.12
Listing of foreign
stock market indexes.
Reprinted by permission of
*THE WALL STREET
JOURNAL*, © 1991 Dow
Jones & Company, Inc. All
Rights Reserved Worldwide.

Stock Market Indexes

EXCHANGE	5/7/91 CLOSE	NET CHG	PCT CHG
Tokyo Nikkei Average	26342.14	− 135.72	− 0.51
Tokyo Topix Index	1996.71	− 4.78	− 0.24
London FT 30-share	1989.7	+ 15.8	+ 0.80
London 100-share	2540.5	+ 17.8	+ 0.71
London Gold Mines	141.2	− 2.3	− 1.60
Frankfurt DAX	1627.46	+ 3.47	+ 0.21
Zurich Credit Suisse	545.8	+ 0.2	+ 0.04
Paris CAC 40	1830.19	+ 1.41	+ 0.06
Milan Stock Index	1132	− 9.0	− 0.79
Amsterdam ANP-CBS General	202.4	− 0.2	− 0.10
Stockholm Affarsvarlden	1041.9	− 1.0	− 0.10
Brussels Bel-20 Index	1176.00	− 1.27	− 0.11
Australia All Ordinaries	1537.8	+ 15.4	+ 1.01
Hong Kong Hang Seng	3741.51	+ 37.08	+ 1.00
Singapore Straits Times	1525.03	+ 6.23	+ 0.41
Johannesburg J'burg Gold	1041	unch	
Madrid General Index	280.04	+ 1.36	+ 0.49
Toronto 300 Composite	3478.82	− 8.85	− 0.25
Euro, Aust, Far East MSCI-p	860.6	+ 6.1	+ 0.71

p-Preliminary
na-Not available

published by the Financial Times of London and makes up the value-weighted index of 100 of the largest London Stock Exchange corporations.

Figure 4.12 shows the list of foreign stock exchange indexes published daily by *The Wall Street Journal*. Other indexes such as J.P. Morgan's provide a richer picture for professional investors.

Bond Market Indicators

Just as stock market indexes provide guidance concerning the performance of the overall stock market, several bond market indicators measure the performance of various categories of bonds. The two most well-known groups of indexes are the Shearson Lehman Hutton indexes and Salomon Brothers indexes. Table 4.6 summarizes the major indexes compiled by Shearson Lehman Hutton.

The indexes are all computed monthly, and all measure total returns as the sum of capital gains plus interest income derived from the bonds during the month. Any intramonth cash distributions received from the bonds are assumed to be invested during the month at the T-bill rate.

The major problem with these indexes is that true rates of return on many bonds are difficult to compute because bonds trade infrequently, which makes it hard to get reliable up-to-date prices. In practice, prices often must be estimated from bond valuation models. These so-called matrix prices may differ substantially from true market values.

4.5   *Derivative Markets*

*Derivative security   A
security with a payoff
that depends on the
prices of other
securities.*

A significant development in financial markets in recent years has been the growth of futures and options markets. Futures and options provide payoffs that depend on the values of other assets such as commodity prices, bond and stock prices, or market index values. For this reason, these instruments sometimes are called **derivative assets** or **contingent claims.** Their values derive from or are contingent on the values of other assets. We discuss derivative assets in detail in Part Five.

Table 4.6   *Shearson Lehman Hutton Bond Market Indexes*

	Averages				**Total Market Value ($ Million)**	**Total Index (%)**	
	Duration*	**Coupon**	**Maturity**	**Price**	**Yield**		**Gov./Corp.**	**Aggregate**
Government/Corporate Bond Index	5.12	8.96	9.48	101.91	8.13	1642854	100.00	71.33
Government bond index	4.63	9.03	8.13	104.30	7.72	1230452	74.90	53.42
Corporate bond index	6.58	8.78	13.49	95.38	9.35	412402	25.10	17.91
Mortgage-backed securities index	5.79	9.41	10.40	99.65	9.21	607938	100.00	26.40
Yankee bond index	6.67	9.80	13.40	102.46	9.11	52377	100.00	2.27
Aggregate bond index	5.33	9.10	9.81	101.31	8.44	2303169	0.00	100.00
Government/Corporate Bond Index	5.12	8.96	9.48	101.91	8.13	1642854	100.00	71.33
Intermediate	3.30	8.94	4.13	103.12	7.75	1157988	70.49	50.28
Long term	9.48	9.01	22.25	99.11	9.05	484866	29.51	21.05
Government Bond Index	4.63	9.03	8.13	104.30	7.72	1230452	74.90	53.42
Intermediate	3.10	8.97	3.83	104.03	7.49	952805	58.00	41.37
Long term	9.88	9.22	22.90	105.25	8.55	277647	16.90	12.05
Treasury	4.78	9.26	8.67	107.17	7.70	1053525	64.13	45.74
Intermediate	3.08	8.94	3.79	104.23	7.42	784468	47.75	34.06
Long term	9.74	10.30	22.87	116.76	8.53	269058	16.38	11.68
Agency	3.76	7.86	4.95	89.96	7.85	176927	10.77	7.68
Intermediate	3.23	9.11	4.00	103.07	7.79	168337	10.25	7.31
Long term	14.30	1.76	23.57	25.75	8.96	8589	0.52	0.37
Corporate Bond Index	6.58	8.78	13.49	95.38	9.35	412402	25.10	17.91
Intermediate	4.20	8.80	5.51	99.13	8.97	205183	12.49	8.91
Long term	8.94	8.76	21.39	91.93	9.72	207220	12.61	9.00
Industrial	6.70	9.12	13.66	96.98	9.46	118010	7.18	5.12
Intermediate	4.48	9.17	5.98	100.19	9.09	58597	3.57	2.54
Long term	8.89	9.08	21.23	94.02	9.81	59412	3.62	2.58
Utility	7.97	8.78	18.50	94.53	9.60	153195	9.32	6.65
Intermediate	4.78	8.09	6.35	95.27	9.17	38539	2.35	1.67
Long term	9.04	9.01	22.58	94.29	9.74	114656	6.98	4.98
Finance	4.98	8.50	7.92	94.98	8.98	141198	8.59	6.13
Intermediate	3.85	8.87	4.96	100.00	8.82	108047	6.58	4.69
Long term	8.68	7.50	17.57	81.61	9.48	33151	2.02	1.44

Modified from *The Bond Market Report*, Shearson Lehman Hutton Inc., February 1988.

*Duration is defined and discussed in Chapter 13.

Options

Call option   *The right to buy an asset at a specified price on or before a specified expiration date.*

A **call option** gives its holder the right to purchase an asset for a specified price, called the *exercise or strike price,* on or before some specified expiration date. A July call option on IBM stock with exercise price $120, for example, entitles its owner to purchase IBM stock for a price of $120 at any time up to and including the option's expiration date in July. Each option contract is for the purchase of 100 shares, with quotations made on a per share basis. The holder of the call need not exercise the option; it will be profitable to exercise only if the market value of the asset that may be purchased exceeds the exercise price.

When the market price exceeds the exercise price, the option holder may "call away" the asset for the exercise price and reap a profit equal to the difference between the stock price and the exercise price. Otherwise, the option will be left unexercised. If not exercised before the expiration date, the option expires and no longer has value. Calls, therefore, provide greater profits when stock prices increase and so represent bullish investment vehicles.

Put option   The right to sell an asset at a specified exercise price on or before a specified expiration date.

A **put option** gives its holder the right to sell an asset for a specified exercise price on or before a specified expiration date. A July put on IBM with exercise price $120 thus entitles its owner to sell IBM stock to the put writer at a price of $120 at any time before expiration in July even if the market price of IBM is lower than $120. While profits on call options increase when the asset increases in value, profits on put options increase when the asset value falls. The put is exercised only if its holder can deliver an asset worth less than the exercise price in return for the exercise price.

Figure 4.13 gives listed stock option quotations from *The Wall Street Journal*. The first option listed on the Chicago Board Options Exchange is for shares of Alcoa. The numbers below Alcoa indicate the last recorded price for Alcoa stock was $70⅞ per share. Options are traded on Alcoa with exercise prices of $65, $70, and $75. These values, the exercise price or strike price, are given in the first column of numbers. The exercise prices bracket the recorded price for Alcoa.

The next three columns of numbers provide the prices of call options on Alcoa shares with expiration dates of May, June, and July. The prices of Alcoa call options decrease as one moves down each column, corresponding to progressively higher exercise prices. This makes sense, as the right to purchase a share of Alcoa at a higher exercise price is worth less.

For example, with an exercise price of $65, the July call sells for $7¾ per share, while the option to purchase the stock for an exercise price of $75 is worth only $1¾. The footnote *r* indicates the option was not traded on that day, while *s* indicates the option with that exercise price and expiration date has not been introduced by the exchange.

The last three columns report prices of put options with various strike prices and times to maturity. Put prices increase with the exercise price. The right to sell a share of Alcoa at a price of $65 is less valuable than the right to sell it at $75.

Concept Check

Question 8.   What would be the profit or loss per share of stock to an investor who bought the July maturity Alcoa call option with exercise price $70 on May 9, 1991, if the stock price at the expiration of the option is $78? What about a purchaser of the put option with the same exercise price and maturity?

Futures Contracts

Futures contract   Obliges traders to purchase or sell an asset at an agreed-upon price on a specified future date.

A **futures contract** calls for delivery of an asset or its cash value at a specified delivery or maturity date, for an agreed-upon price called the *futures price* to be paid at contract maturity. The long position is held by the trader who commits to purchasing the commodity on the delivery date. The trader who takes the short position commits to delivering the commodity at contract maturity.

Figure 4.14 illustrates the listing of several financial futures contracts as they appear in *The Wall Street Journal*. The top line in boldface type gives the contract name, the exchange on which the futures contract is traded (in parentheses), and the contract size. Thus, the first contract listed is for the S&P 500 index, traded on the Chicago Mercantile Exchange (CME). Each contract calls for delivery of 500 times the value of the S&P 500 stock price index.

The next several rows detail price data for S&P 500 contracts expiring on various dates. The June 1991 maturity contract opened during the day at a fu-

Figure 4.13
Listing of stock
option quotations.
Reprinted by permission of
*THE WALL STREET
JOURNAL,* © 1991 Dow
Jones & Company, Inc. All
Rights Reserved Worldwide.

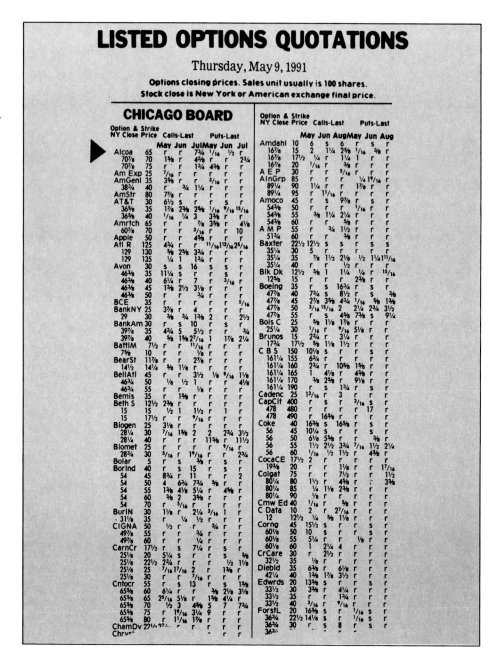

tures price of $380.45 per unit of the index. (The last line of the entry shows that the S&P 500 index was at $383.25 at close of trading on the day of the listing.) The highest futures price during the day was $385.20, the lowest was $379.65, and the settlement price (a representative trading price during the last few minutes of trading) was $384.60. The settlement price increased by $4.55 from the previous trading day. The highest and lowest futures prices over the contract's life to date have been $393.50 and $300.90, respectively. Finally, open interest, or the number of outstanding contracts, was 138,103. Corresponding information is given for each maturity date.

Figure 4.14
Listing of stock index
futures contracts.
Reprinted by permission of
*THE WALL STREET
JOURNAL,* © 1991 Dow
Jones & Company, Inc. All
Rights Reserved Worldwide.

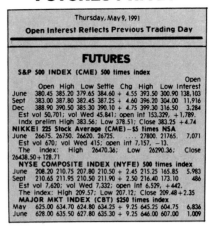

The trader holding the long position profits from price increases. Suppose that at expiration, the S&P 500 index is at 390. The long position trader who entered the contract at the futures price of $384.60 on May 9 would pay the previously agreed-upon $384.60 for each unit of the index, which at contract maturity would be worth $390.

Because each contract calls for delivery of 500 times the index, the profit to the long position, ignoring brokerage fees, would equal 500 × ($390 − 384.60) = $2,700. Conversely, the short position must deliver 500 times the value of the index for the previously agreed-upon futures price. The short position's loss equals the long position's profit.

The distinction between right to purchase the asset as opposed to the obligation to purchase is the difference between a call option and a long position in a futures contract. A futures contract *obliges* the long position to purchase the asset at the futures price; the call option merely *conveys the right* to purchase the asset at the exercise price. The purchase will be made only if it yields a profit.

Clearly, a holder of a call has a better position than the holder of a long position on a futures contract with futures price equal to the option's exercise price. This advantage, of course, comes only at a price. Call options must be purchased; futures investments are contracts only. The purchase price of an option is called the *premium*. It represents the compensation the holder of the call must pay for the ability to exercise the option only when it is profitable to do so. Similarly, the difference between a put option and a short futures position is the right as opposed to the obligation to sell an asset at an agreed-upon price.

Summary

1. Money market securities are very short-term debt obligations. They are usually highly marketable and have relatively low credit risk. Their low maturities and low credit risk ensure minimal capital gains or losses. These securities trade in large denominations, but they may be purchased indirectly through money market funds.

2. Much of U.S. government borrowing is in the form of Treasury bonds and notes. These are coupon-paying bonds usually issued at or near par value. Treasury bonds are similar in design to coupon-paying corporate bonds.

3. Municipal bonds are distinguished largely by their tax-exempt status. Interest payments (but not capital gains) on these securities are exempt from income taxes.

4. Mortgage pass-through securities are pools of mortgages sold in one package. Owners of pass-throughs receive all principal and interest payments made by the borrower. The firm that originally issued the mortgage merely services the mortgage, simply "passing through" the payments to the purchasers of the mortgage. The pass-through agency usually guarantees the payment of interest and principal on mortgages pooled into these pass-through securities.

5. Common stock is an ownership share in a corporation. Each share entitles its owner to one vote on matters of corporate governance and to a prorated share of the dividends paid to shareholders. Stock, or equity, owners are the residual claimants on the income earned by the firm.

6. Preferred stock usually pays a fixed stream of dividends for the life of the firm; it is a perpetuity. A firm's failure to pay the dividend due on preferred stock, however, does not set off corporate bankruptcy. Instead, unpaid dividends simply cumulate. New varieties of preferred stock include convertible and adjustable-rate issues.

7. Many stock market indexes measure the performance of the overall market. The Dow Jones Averages, the oldest and best-known indicators, are price-weighted indexes. Today, many broad-based, market value-weighted indexes are computed daily. These include the Standard & Poor's 500 stock index, the NYSE and AMEX indexes, the NASDAQ index, and the Wilshire 5000 index.

8. A call option is a right to purchase an asset at a stipulated exercise price on or before a maturity date. A put option is the right to sell an asset at some exercise price. Calls increase in value while puts decrease in value as the value of the underlying asset increases.

9. A futures contract is an obligation to buy or sell an asset at a stipulated futures price on a maturity date. The long position, which commits to purchasing, gains if the asset value increases, while the short position, which commits to delivering the asset, loses.

Key Terms

annual percentage
   rate, 84
bank discount
   method, 85
bankers'
   acceptance, 88
bond equivalent
   yield, 86
call option, 112
capital markets, 81
certificate of
   deposit, 87
commercial paper, 88
common stocks, 101

corporate bonds, 97
derivative asset/
   contingent
   claim, 111
effective annual
   rate, 85
equally weighted
   indexes, 109
Eurodollars, 88
Federal funds, 89
futures contract, 113
London Interbank Offer
   Rate (LIBOR), 90

market value-weighted
   index, 107
money markets, 81
municipal bonds, 95
preferred stock, 104
price-weighted
   average, 105
put option, 113
repurchase
   agreements, 89
Treasury bill, 83
Treasury bond, 91
Treasury notes, 91

Selected Readings

The standard reference to the securities, terminology, and organization of the money market is:
Stigum, Marcia. *The Money Market*. Homewood, Ill. Dow Jones-Irwin, 1983.

A more detailed treatment of money market securities is contained in the following collection of articles:
Cook, Timothy Q., and Timothy D. Rowe. *Instruments of the Money Market*. Richmond, Va.: Federal Reserve Bank of Richmond, 1986.

Collections of essays on a wide variety of fixed-income securities are:
Fabozzi, Frank J., and D. Fabozzi. *Bond Market Analysis and Strategies*. Englewood Cliffs, N. J.: Prentice Hall, 1989, and Fabozzi, Frank J. and Irving M. Pollack, eds. *The Handbook of Fixed Income Securities*. Homewood, Ill. Dow Jones-Irwin, 1987.

A good treatment of the institutional organization of option markets is contained in:
Reference Manual. Chicago Board Options Exchange, 1982.

Problem Sets

1. The following multiple-choice problems are based on questions that appeared in past CFA exams.
   a. Preferred stock
      (1) is actually a form of equity.
      (2) pays dividends not fully taxable to U.S. corporations.
      (3) is normally considered a fixed-income security.
      (4) all of the above.
   b. Straight preferred stock yields usually are lower than yields on straight bonds of the same quality because of
      (1) marketability.
      (2) risk.
      (3) taxation.
      (4) call protection.

2. The investment manager of a corporate pension fund has purchased a U.S. Treasury bill with 180 days to maturity at a price of $9,600 per $10,000 face value. The manager has computed the bank discount yield at 8 percent.
   a. Calculate the bond equivalent yield for the Treasury bill. Show calculations. (Ignore skip-day settlement.)
   b. Briefly state two reasons why a Treasury bill's bond equivalent yield is always different from the discount yield.

3. . A bill has a bank discount yield of 6.81 percent based on the bid price and 6.90 percent based on the ask price. The maturity of the bill (already accounting for skip-day settlement) is 60 days. Find the bid and ask prices of the bill.

4. Reconsider the T-bill in problem 3. Calculate its bond equivalent yield and effective annual yield based on the ask price. Confirm that these yields exceed the discount yield.

5. a. Which security offers a higher effective annual yield?
      (1) A three-month bill selling at $9,764.
      (2) A six-month bill selling at $9,539.
   b. Calculate the bank discount yield on each bill.

6. Find the after-tax return to a corporation that buys a share of preferred stock at $40, sells it at year-end at $40, and receives a $4 year-end dividend. The firm is in the 30 percent tax bracket.

7. Consider the three stocks in the following table. P_t represents price at time t, and

Q_t represents shares outstanding at time t. Stock C splits two for one in the last period.

	P_0	Q_0	P_1	Q_1	P_2	Q_2
A	90	100	95	100	95	100
B	50	200	45	200	45	200
C	100	200	110	200	55	400

    a. Calculate the rate of return on a price-weighted index of the three stocks for the first period ($t = 0$ to $t = 1$).

    b. What must happen to the divisor for the price-weighted index in year 2?

    c. Calculate the price-weighted index for the second period ($t = 1$ to $t = 2$).

8. Using the data in problem 7, calculate the first period rates of return on the following indexes of the three stocks:

    a. a market value-weighted index.

    b. an equally weighted index.

    c. a geometric index.

9. An investor is in a 28 percent tax bracket. If corporate bonds offer 9 percent yields, what must municipals offer for the investor to prefer them to corporate bonds?

10. Which security should sell at a greater price?

    a. A 10-year Treasury bond with a 9 percent coupon rate or a 10-year T-bond with a 10 percent coupon.

    b. A three-month maturity call option with an exercise price of $40 or a three-month call on the same stock with an exercise price of $35.

    c. A put option on a stock selling at $50 or a put option on another stock selling at $60. (All other relevant features of the stocks and options are assumed to be identical.)

    d. A three-month T-bill with a discount yield of 6.1 percent or a three-month bill with a discount yield of 6.2 percent.

11. Why do call options with exercise prices higher than the price of the underlying stock sell for positive prices?

12. Both a call and a put currently are traded on stock XYZ; both have strike prices of $50 and maturities of six months. What will be the profit to an investor who buys the call for $4 in the following scenarios for stock prices in six months? (*a*) $40. (*b*) $45. (*c*) $50. (*d*) $55. (*e*) $60.

What will be the profit in each scenario to an investor who buys the put for $6?

13. Explain the difference between a put option and a short position in a futures contract.

14. Examine the first 25 stocks listed in Figure 4.9. For how many of these stocks is the 52-week high price at least 50 percent greater than the 52-week low price? What do you conclude about the volatility of prices on individual stocks?

Chapter

5

How Securities Are Traded

The first time a security trades is when it is issued. Therefore, we begin our examination of trading with investment bankers, the midwives of securities. Next, we describe the markets in which securities are traded. Finally, we turn to the mechanics of trading in these markets.

We then describe the essentials of specific transactions such as buying on margin and short sales, and we discuss relevant regulations that govern security trading.

The selection of a broker and cost implications of the decision are also reviewed. Finally, we discuss alternatives to trading securities directly, that is, investing with investment companies. After studying this chapter, you should be able to:

- Describe the role of investment bankers in primary issues.
- Identify the various security markets.
- Describe the role of brokers.
- Describe how to invest with investment companies.

5.1 How Firms Issue Securities

Primary market   New issues of securities are offered to the public here.

When firms need to raise capital they may choose to sell securities (*float new issues*). These new issues of stocks, bonds, or other securities typically are marketed to the public by investment bankers in what is called the **primary market.** Purchase and sale of already-issued securities among investors occur in the **secondary market.**

Secondary market
Already-existing secur-
ities are bought and
sold in this market.

Initial public offerings
(IPOs) *Stocks issued*
to the public for the
first time by a formerly
privately owned
company.

There are two types of primary market issues of common stock. **Initial public offerings,** or **IPOs,** are stocks issued by a formerly privately owned company that is going public, that is, selling stock to the public for the first time. *Seasoned* new issues are offered by companies that already have floated equity. A sale by IBM of new shares of stock would constitute a seasoned new issue, for example.

In the case of bonds, we also distinguish between two types of primary market issues, a *public offering* and a *private placement*. The former refers to an issue of bonds sold to the general investing public that can then be traded on the secondary market. The latter refers to an issue that usually is sold to one or a few institutional investors and is generally held to maturity.

Investment Banking

Underwriters *Under-*
writers (investment
bankers) purchase
securities from the
issuing company and
resell them.

Public offerings of both stocks and bonds typically are marketed by investment bankers who in this role are called **underwriters.** More than one investment banker usually markets the securities. A lead firm forms an underwriting syndicate of other investment bankers to share the responsibility for the stock issue.

Prospectus *A descrip-*
tion of the firm and
the security it is
issuing.

Investment bankers advise the firm regarding the terms on which it should attempt to sell the securities. A preliminary registration statement must be filed with the Securities and Exchange Commission (SEC) describing the issue and the prospects of the company. This preliminary prospectus is known as a red herring because it includes a statement printed in red stating the company is not attempting to sell the security before the registration is approved. When the statement is in final form and approved by the SEC, it is called the **prospectus.** At this point, the price at which the securities will be offered to the public is announced.

In a typical underwriting arrangement, the investment bankers purchase the securities from the issuing company and then resell them to the public. The issuing firm sells the securities to the underwriting syndicate for the public offering price less a spread that serves as compensation to the underwriters. This procedure is called a *firm commitment;* the underwriters receive the issue and assume the full risk that the shares cannot be sold to the public at the stipulated offering price.

An alternative to this arrangement is the *best-efforts* agreement. In this case, the investment banker does not actually purchase the securities but agrees to help the firm sell the issue to the public. The banker simply acts as an intermediary between the public and the firm and does not bear the risk of not being able to resell purchased securities at the offering price. The best-efforts procedure is more common for initial public offerings of common stock, where the appropriate share price is less certain.

Corporations engage investment bankers either by negotiation or competitive bidding. Negotiation is more common. In addition to the compensation resulting from the spread between the purchase price and the public offering price, an investment banker may receive shares of common stock or other securities of the firm.

In the case of competitive bidding, a firm may announce its intent to issue securities and invite investment bankers to submit bids for the underwriting.

Such a bidding process may reduce the cost of the issue; it might also bring fewer services from the investment banker. Many public utilities are required to solicit competitive bids from underwriters.

Shelf Registration

An important innovation in the issuing of securities was introduced in 1982 when the SEC approved Rule 415, which allows firms to register securities and gradually sell them to the public for two years following the initial registration. Because the securities are already registered, they can be sold on short notice, with little additional paperwork. Moreover, they can be sold in small amounts without incurring substantial flotation costs. The securities are "on the shelf," ready to be issued, which has given rise to the term *shelf registration*.

Concept Check

Question 1. Why is shelf registration limited in time?

Underpricing

Underwriters face a peculiar conflict of interest. If they are acting in the best interests of the issuing firm, they should attempt to market securities to the public at the highest possible price, thereby maximizing the revenue the issuer realizes from the offering. At the same time, if investment bankers set the offering price higher than the public will pay, they will be unable to market the securities to customers. Underwriters left with unmarketable securities are forced to sell them at a loss on the secondary market.

The underwriter must trade off its own interests against those of its clients. The lower the public offering price, the less capital the firm raises, but the greater the chance the securities can be sold. Also, the lower the price, the less effort needed to find investors to purchase the securities. At a low enough price, investors will beat down the doors to purchase the securities.

Some evidence suggests IPOs of common stock often are underpriced compared to the price at which they could be marketed. In a study of the pricing of 112 IPOs, Ibbotson (1975) found that an investor who purchased shares of each issue at the initial offering price and then resold the stock one month later would have earned an average abnormal return of 11.4 percent.[1] This would indicate the stock was offered to the public at a price substantially below the price investors were willing to pay. Such underpricing would imply that IPOs commonly are oversubscribed; that is, there is more demand from the public for the share at the offering price than there are shares being offered.

---

[1] Abnormal return measures the return on the investment net of the portion that can be attributed to general market movements. See the discussion on this concept in Chapter 10.

5.2   *Where Securities Are Traded*

Once securities are issued to the public, investors may trade them among themselves. Purchase and sale of already-issued securities occur in the secondary markets, which are (1) national and local securities exchanges, (2) the over-the-counter market, and (3) direct trading between two parties.

The Secondary Markets

Stock exchanges
Secondary markets where already-issued securities are bought and sold by members.

There are nine major **stock exchanges** in the United States. Two of these, the New York Stock Exchange (NYSE, or the Big Board) and the American Stock Exchange (AMEX), are national in scope and are located in New York City. The others are to a considerable extent regional exchanges, which tend to list firms located in a particular geographic area. There also are several exchanges for the trading of options and futures contracts, which we will discuss later in the options and futures chapters.

An exchange provides a facility for its members to trade securities, and only members of the exchange may trade there. Therefore, memberships or *seats* on the exchange are valuable assets. The exchange member charges investors for executing trades on their behalf; that is, brokerage firms own seats on exchanges, and advertise their willingness to execute trades for customers for a fee.

As private associations, the exchanges limit the number of seats; there are 1,366 on the NYSE and 661 on the AMEX. The commissions that members can earn through this activity determine the market value of a seat. A seat on the NYSE has sold over the years for $4,000 in 1878, $35,000 in 1977, and as high as $1,150,000 in 1987 before falling considerably after that (see Table 5.1).

The NYSE is by far the largest single exchange. The shares of approximately 1,500 firms trade there, and more than 2,000 stock issues (common plus preferred stock) are listed. Daily trading volume on the NYSE regularly exceeds 100 million shares. Table 5.2 shows the market value of securities listed on the nine stock exchanges as of July 1986, as well as trading volume on each exchange during the previous year. The NYSE accounts for about 80 percent of the market value of shares traded on the exchanges.

The American Stock Exchange also is national in scope, but it focuses on listing smaller and younger firms than the NYSE. The national exchanges are willing to list a stock (allow trading in that stock on the exchange) only if it

Table 5.1   *Seat Prices on the NYSE*

Year	High	Low	Year	High	Low
1875	$ 6,800	$ 4,300	1985	$ 480,000	$310,000
1905	85,000	72,000	1986	600,000	455,000
1935	140,000	65,000	1987	1,150,000	605,000
1965	250,000	190,000	1988	820,000	580,000
1975	138,000	55,000	1989	675,000	420,000
1980	275,000	175,000	1990	430,000	250,000

From the New York Stock Exchange *Fact Book*, 1991.

Table 5.2 *Stock Exchanges*

	Market Value of Listed Securities ($ Million)	% of Total	Trading Volume During the Year (Thousands of Shares)	% of Total
New York	124,179	87.10	4,373,747	82.94
Midwest	7,684	5.39	285,541	5.41
Pacific	3,748	2.63	177,661	3.37
American	2,899	2.03	279,960	5.31
Boston	1,867	1.31	72,074	1.37
Philadelphia	1,503	1.05	59,821	1.13
Cincinnati	682	0.48	22,402	0.42
Spokane	2	0.00	2,283	0.04
Intermountain	0	0.00	0	0.00
Total	**142,564**	**100.00**	**5,273,489**	**100.00**

From the Securities and Exchange Commission *Monthly Statistical Review* 47 (February 1988).

Table 5.3 *Initial Listing Requirements for the NYSE*

Pretax income in last year	$ 2,500,000
Average annual pretax income in previous 2 years	$ 2,000,000
Net tangible assets	$18,000,000
Market value of publicly held stock	$18,000,000
Shares publicly held	1,100,000
Number of holders of 100 shares or more	2,000

Data from the New York Stock Exchange *Fact Book*, 1991.

meets certain criteria of size and stability. Regional exchanges provide a market for the trading of shares of local firms that do not meet the listing requirements of the national exchanges.

Table 5.3 gives the initial listing requirements for the NYSE. These requirements ensure that firms are of significant trading interest before the NYSE will allocate facilities for it to be traded on the floor of the exchange. If a listed company suffers a decline and fails to meet the criteria in Table 5.3, it may be delisted.

Regional exchanges also sponsor trading of some firms that are traded on national exchanges. This dual listing enables local brokerage firms to trade in shares of large firms without purchasing a membership on the NYSE.

While most common stocks are traded on the exchanges, the reverse is true for bonds and other fixed-income securities. Corporate bonds are traded both on the exchanges and over the counter, but all federal and municipal government bonds are traded over the counter.

The Over-the-Counter Market

Over-the-counter (OTC) market An informal network of brokers and dealers

Nearly 7,000 issues are traded on the **over-the-counter market,** but the OTC market is not a formal exchange. There are no membership requirements for trading or listing requirements for securities. Thousands of brokers register with the SEC as dealers in OTC securities, and any security may be traded. Security dealers quote prices at which they are willing to buy or sell securities. A broker executes a trade by contacting the dealer listing an attractive quote.

Before 1971, all OTC quotations of stock were recorded manually and published daily. The so-called pink sheets were the means by which dealers communicated their interest in trading at various prices. This was a cumbersome and inefficient technique, and published quotes were a day out of date. In 1971, the National Association of Securities Dealers Automatic Quotation system, or **NASDAQ,** was developed to offer via a computer-linked system immediate information on bid and ask prices for stocks offered by various dealers. The **bid price** is the price at which a dealer is willing to purchase a security; the **ask price** is the one at which the dealer will sell a security. Hence, the ask price is always higher than the bid price, and the difference, *the bid-ask spread,* makes up the dealer's profit. The system allows a broker who receives a buy or sell order from an investor to examine all current quotes, call the dealer with the best quote, and execute a trade. About 3,500 stocks are quoted on the NASDAQ system.

To be listed on NASDAQ, a firm must satisfy one of two sets of criteria:

1. *a.* 350,000 publicly held shares.
    b. Market value of publicly held shares of $2 million.
    c. Minimum bid price of $3.
    d. Annual net income of $300,000 in either the last fiscal year, or two of the last three years.

or

2. *a.* 800,000 publicly held shares.
    b. Market value of publicly held shares of $8 million.
    c. Net worth of $8 million.
    d. Incorporation of at least 4 years.

NASDAQ has three levels of subscribers. The highest, level 3 subscribers, are for firms dealing, or "making markets," in OTC securities. These market makers maintain inventories of a security and constantly stand ready to buy or sell these shares from or to the public at the quoted bid and ask prices. They earn profits from the spread between the bid and ask price.

Level 3 subscribers may enter the bid and ask prices at which they are willing to buy or sell stocks into the computer network and may update these quotes as desired.

Level 2 subscribers receive all bid and ask quotes, but they cannot enter their own quotes. These subscribers tend to be stockbrokers who execute trades for clients but do not actively deal in the stocks on their own account. Brokers attempting to buy or sell shares call the market maker (a level 3 subscriber) with the best quote in order to execute a trade.

Level 1 subscribers receive only the median, or "representative," bid and ask prices on each stock. Level 1 subscribers are investors who are not actively buying and selling securities but want information on current prices.

For bonds, the over-the-counter market is a loosely organized network of dealers linked by a computer quotation system. In practice, the corporate bond market often is quite "thin," in that there may be few investors interested in trading a given bond at any particular time. As a result, the bond market is subject to a type of liquidity risk, for it can be difficult to sell one's holdings quickly if the need arises.

The Third and Fourth Markets

Third market *Trading of exchange-listed securities on the OTC market.*

The **third market** refers to trading of exchange-listed securities on the over-the-counter market. In the past, members of an exchange were required to execute all their trades of exchange-listed securities on the exchange and to charge commissions according to a fixed schedule. This procedure was disadvantageous to large traders when it prevented them from realizing economies of scale on large trades. Because of this restriction, brokerage firms that were not members of the NYSE, and so not bound by its rules, established trading in the OTC market of large NYSE-listed stocks. These trades could be accomplished at lower commissions than would have been charged on the NYSE, and the third market grew dramatically until 1972, when the NYSE allowed negotiated commissions on orders exceeding $300,000. On May 1, 1975, frequently referred to as "May Day," commissions on all NYSE orders became negotiable, and they have been since. See the accompanying box for evidence of the growth of the third market.

Fourth market *Direct trading in exchange-listed securities between one investor and another without the benefit of a broker.*

The **fourth market** refers to direct trading between investors in exchange-listed securities without the benefit of a broker. Large institutions that wish to avoid brokerage fees may engage in direct trading.

The National Market System

The Securities Act Amendments of 1975 directed the Securities and Exchange Commission to implement a national competitive securities market. Such a market would entail centralized reporting of transactions and a centralized quotation system, with the aim of enhanced competition among market makers.

In 1975, Consolidated Tape began reporting trades on the NYSE, AMEX, and major regional exchanges, as well as trades of NASDAQ-listed stocks. In 1977, the Consolidated Quotations Service began providing on-line bid and ask quotes for NYSE securities also traded on various other exchanges. This enhances competition by allowing traders to find the best exchange for a desired trade. In 1978, the Intermarket Trading System was implemented to link seven exchanges by computer (NYSE, AMEX, Boston, Cincinnati, Midwest, Pacific, and Philadelphia). Brokers and market makers can display quotes on all markets and execute cross-market trades.

A central *limit order* book giving orders that are conditional on prices and dates, and thus not immediately executable, would be the ultimate centralization of the marketplace. In such a system, orders from all exchanges would be listed centrally. All traders could compete for all orders.

5.3 *Trading On Exchanges*

Most of the information we discuss here applies to all securities traded on exchanges. Some of it, however, applies just to stocks, and in such cases we use the specific words, *stocks* or *shares*.

The Participants

We start our discussion of the mechanics of exchange trading with a brief description of the potential parties to a trade. When an investor instructs a broker to buy or sell securities, a number of players must act to consummate the deal.

'Third-Market' Trading Crowds Stock Exchanges

NEW YORK—The "third market" is coming on strong in competition with stock exchanges for trading business.

And one big third-market player is speeding the growth by *paying* brokers to funnel their customers' orders through his system.

The third market is off-exchange trading in stocks that are listed on exchanges. The growth in trade and share volume in the third market is a serious concern for executives at the New York Stock Exchange, which still dominates the activity in its own listings but lately has lost business to others, including regional exchanges.

In 1989, the third market became the third-largest trading arena for New York Stock Exchange listed stocks, behind the Big Board itself and the Midwest Stock Exchange in Chicago. The third market increased its volume by 47 percent last year to 1.59 billion shares, or 3.2 percent of total volume in Big Board stocks.

The regional exchanges, too, are feeling the heat from the third market. "I can hardly be indifferent because it is turning our market share," says Charles Doherty, president of the Midwest exchange. "I am tremendously concerned."

Exchanges See Unfair Match
What's especially frustrating, regional exchange executives say, is that the third market plays by different rules. "We are being forced to play full-contact football in tennis whites," says Caroline B. Austin, president of the Midwest specialist firm Dempsey & Co. " We must abide by the rules of the exchange, while competing in a relatively deregulated environment."

Nothing can be more deregulated than paying brokers for their business. That's what Bernard L. Madoff Investment Securities, a New York firm, is doing. Mr. Madoff gives brokers a rebate of one cent a share on orders of 3,000 shares or less.

Mr. Madoff started this practice more than two years ago, but only since Wall Street's recession increased the emphasis on cost-cutting has the rebate overcome brokers' longstanding alliances with exchanges. Now that retail order desks are getting paid for trades, "suddenly they are heroes," says Mr. Doherty, the Midwest exchange's president.

A 500-share order would cost a broker about 80 cents to trade on the Midwest exchange. That order can earn the broker $5 when traded with Mr. Madoff.

Trading business "is a valuable commodity that we want to pay for," says Mr. Madoff, defending his rebates. He contends the rebates to brokers are returned to customers in the form of cheaper commissions. He adds that other brokerage firms "pay" for business through "free" research and other services.

Mr. Madoff can make money even with rebates by rapidly turning over those transactions at slightly better prices elsewhere, often on the very exchanges he competes with. He also boasts he can hedge his order book faster than any specialist.

Exchanges "have a competitive disadvantage, which is their own choice," says Mr. Madoff.

"We have more efficient, faster execution than any exchange, and absolutely at a competitive price," says Mr. Madoff, "The penny-per-share rebate is an added inducement to trade with us."

The investor places an order with a broker. The brokerage firm for which the broker works, and which owns a seat on the exchange, contacts its *commission broker,* who is on the floor of the exchange, to execute the order. When the firm's commission brokers are overloaded and have too many orders to handle, they will use the services of *floor brokers* who are independent members of the exchange (and own seats) to execute orders.

Registered traders are frequent traders who use their membership to execute trades for their own accounts. By trading directly, they avoid the commissions that would be incurred if they had to trade through a broker.

The specialist is central to the trading process. Specialists maintain a market in one or more listed securities. We examine their role in detail below.

Big Boom in Small Orders

Mr. Madoff's average order is for 500 stocks, and he handles about 15,000 such orders a day. Most of the third market's gains are coming in the form of small orders, one of the most sought-after staples of any exchange.

In the past five years, the third market's share of transactions under 1,100 shares has grown 328 percent to nearly 6 percent of all trades of that order size last year. Exchanges estimate Mr. Madoff's firm is handling about 70 percent of the business.

"Our volume, in any way you would measure it, has grown," says Mr. Madoff, who has been handling off-exchange trades for 15 years.

"Bernie has been a very effective competitor," says Richard Grasso, president of the New York Stock Exchange.

Mr. Madoff won't talk about his customers. But people close to the situation say they include many brokers that specialize in small investor orders: Alex. Brown & Sons Inc.; A.G. Edwards & Sons Inc. and Charles Schwab & Co., among others. Janney Montgomery Scott Inc. recently signed up with Mr. Madoff to give his fast electronic trading system a try.

Mr. Madoff says the exchanges feel threatened by automated trading systems, which are proving to be faster and cheaper than the specialists who handle trading on the exchange floor.

The exchanges, however, concentrate their criticism on Mr. Madoff's rebates and the fact that trades he handles don't occur through an exchange system.

Exchanges say they doubt Mr. Madoff's claim that his broker clients are passing along the rebates to public customers. "The fact that Madoff is paying for order flow raises the issue of whether the customer is getting the benefit of that payment," said Nicholas Giordano, president of the Philadelphia Stock Exchange. "If he is not, then what is it exactly?"

Exchanges also challenge the notion that an off-exchange market provides better pricing for customers. Mr. Grasso, the Big Board president, estimates the exchange will save investors some $400 million this year by getting a better price for them through the auction market that attempts to match public buyer with public seller without the dealer as an intermediary.

"To the extent the investor is trading in (dealer) markets, he is losing the opportunity for price improvement," said Mr. Grasso.

Mr. Madoff contests that statement. He says that in the biggest stocks, the mainstay of his business, competition keeps the prices at the most efficient levels.

While this debate goes on, Mr. Madoff and his automated trading system seem to be winning the business. Even Mr. Doherty of the Midwest exchange acknowledges that money talks louder than tradition. "We've tried quality of execution, we've tried promising a lot of things on quality," he says. "We talked to customers and they said, 'what you have to do to compete is pay us' " for trades.

Figure 5.1 provides a graphic view of the location of various activities on the NYSE.

Types of Orders

Investors may issue several types of orders to their brokers. *Market orders* are simply buy or sell orders that are to be executed immediately at current market prices.

Investors also may choose to place a *limit offer,* where they specify prices at which they are willing to buy or sell a security. If the stock falls below the limit on a limit buy order, then the trade is to be executed. If stock XYZ is selling at

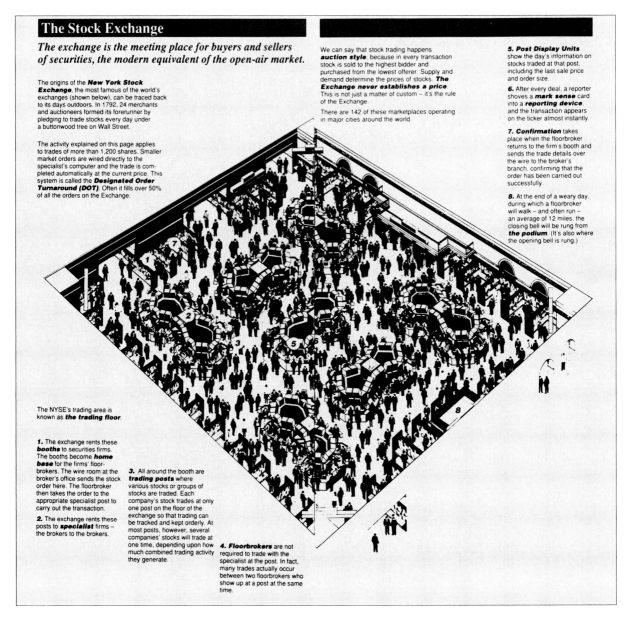

Figure 5.1 Trading on a stock exchange.

$45, for example, a limit buy order may instruct the broker to buy the stock if and when the share price falls *below* $43. Correspondingly, a limit sell order instructs the broker to sell as soon as the stock price goes *above* the specified limit.

Orders also can be limited by a time period. Day orders, for example, expire at the close of the trading day. If it is not executed on that day, the order is canceled. Open or good-till-canceled orders, in contrast, remain in force for up to six months, unless canceled by the customer.

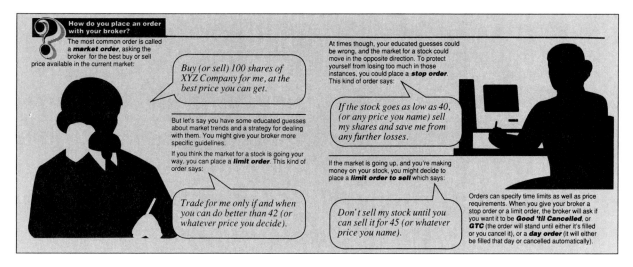

Figure 5.2   Types of orders.

Stop-loss orders are similar to limit orders in that the trade is not to be executed unless the stock hits a price limit. Here, however, the stock is to be *sold* if its price falls *below* a stipulated level. As the name suggests, the order lets the stock be sold to stop further losses from accumulating. Similarly, stop-buy orders specify that a stock should be bought when its price rises above a limit. These trades often accompany *short sales* (sale of securities you don't own but have borrowed from your broker) and are used to limit potential losses from the short position. Short sales are discussed in greater detail later in this chapter. Figure 5.2 highlights the order flow on some types of trades.

Specialists and the Execution of Trades

The specialist is the central figure in the execution of trades. The specialist is the broker's broker. When no other broker can be found to take the other side of a trade, specialists will do so even if it means they must buy for or sell from their own accounts. The NYSE commissions these companies to perform this service and monitors their performance.

Specialist *A trader who makes a market in the shares of one or more firms and who maintains a "fair and orderly market" by dealing personally in the market.*

A **specialist** "makes a market" in the shares of one or more firms. Part of this task is simply mechanical. The specialist maintains a "book" listing of all outstanding unexecuted limit orders entered by brokers on behalf of clients. Actually, the book is now a computer console. When limit orders can be executed at market prices, the specialist does the trade.

The specialist is required to use the highest outstanding offered purchase price and lowest outstanding offered selling price when matching trades. Therefore, the specialist system results in an auction market, meaning all buy and all sell orders come to one location, and the best bids "win" the trades. In this role, the specialist acts merely as a facilitator.

The more interesting function of the specialist is to maintain a "fair and orderly market" by dealing personally in the stock. In return for the exclusive right to make the market in a specific stock on the exchange, the specialist is required by the exchange to maintain an orderly market by buying and selling shares from inventory. Specialists maintain bid and ask prices at which they are obligated to meet at least a limited amount of market orders. If market buy orders come in, specialists must sell shares from their own accounts at the maintained ask price; if sell orders come in, they must stand willing to buy at the listed bid price.

Ordinarily, in an active market, specialists can match buy and sell orders without using their own accounts. That is, the specialist's own inventory need not be the primary means of order execution. Sometimes, the specialist's bid and ask prices are better than those offered by any other market participant. Therefore, at any point, the effective ask price in the market is the lower of either the specialist's offered ask price or the lowest of the unfilled limit-sell orders. Similarly, the effective bid price is the highest of the unfilled limit-buy orders or the specialist's bid. These procedures ensure that the specialist provides liquidity to the market.

By standing ready to trade at quoted bid and ask prices, the specialist is exposed to exploitation by other traders. Larger traders with ready access to late-breaking news will trade with specialists only if the specialist's quotes are temporarily out of line with assessments based on the trader's (possibly superior) information. Specialists who cannot match the information resources of large traders will be at a disadvantage when their quoted prices may offer profit opportunities to more advantaged traders.

You might wonder why specialists do not protect their interests by setting a low bid price and a high ask price. Specialists using that strategy would not suffer losses if they maintained a too-low ask or a too-high bid price in a period of dramatic movements in the stock price. In contrast, specialists who offer a narrow spread between the bid and ask price have little leeway for error and must constantly monitor market conditions to avoid offering other investors advantageous terms.

Large bid-ask spreads are not viable options for the specialist for two reasons. First, one source of the specialist's income is frequent trading at the bid and ask prices, with the spread as a trading profit. A too-large spread would discourage investors from trading, and the specialist's business would dry up. Another reason specialists cannot use large bid-ask spreads to protect their interests is that they are obligated to provide *price continuity* to the market.

To illustrate the principle of price continuity, suppose the highest limit buy order for a stock is $30 while the lowest limit sell order is $32. When a market buy order comes in, it is matched to the best limit sell at $32. A market sell order would be matched to the best limit buy at $30. As market buys and sells come to the floor randomly, the stock price would fluctuate between $30 and $32. The exchange authorities would consider this excessive volatility, and the specialist would be expected to step in with bid and/or ask prices between these values to reduce the bid-ask spread to an acceptable level, such as a quarter or a half point.

Specialists earn income both from commissions for acting as brokers for orders and from the spreads at which they buy and sell securities. Some believe specialists' access to their "book" of limit orders gives them unique knowledge about the probable direction of price movement over short periods of time; although, these days, interested floor traders also have access to the consoles of outstanding limit orders.

For example, suppose the specialist sees that a stock now selling for $45 has limit buy orders for over 100,000 shares at prices ranging from $44.50 to $44.75. This latent buying demand provides a cushion of support, in that it is unlikely that enough sell pressure could come in during the next few hours to cause the price to drop below $44.50. If there are very few limit sell orders above $45, in contrast, some transient buying demand could raise the price substantially.

The specialist in such circumstances realizes that a position in the stock offers little downside risk and substantial upside potential. Such access to the trading intentions of other market participants seems to allow a specialist and agile floor traders to earn profits on personal transactions and for selected clients. One can easily overestimate such advantages because ever more of the large orders are negotiated "upstairs," that is, as fourth-market deals.

The market crash of October 19, 1987, when the market lost almost a quarter of its value in one day, subjected the specialist system to extraordinary demands. Specialists as a group bought $486 million of stock on this one day, in the face of overwhelming sell pressures.[2] As prices continued to fall, these market makers suffered enormous losses, eliminating much of their net worth. Banks hesitated to lend additional funds to specialist firms, which threatened to shut specialists out of the market. Only assurances by the Federal Reserve to make ample credit available to the financial system reestablished banks' willingness to lend. The stock market came close to grinding to a halt.

Moreover, analysis in the wake of the market collapse revealed many specialists apparently decided not to sacrifice their own capital in what seemed like a hopeless effort to shore up prices. While specialists as a whole were net purchasers of stock, fully 30 percent of the specialists in a sample of large stocks were net sellers October 19. These firms were criticized for failing to live up to their mandate to support an orderly market.

In the wake of the crash and the Brady Commission's report, the exchanges have instituted "circuit breakers." When the broad market indexes fall or rise by large amounts, trading is halted temporarily and later reopened much the same way as the regular morning opening. This allows bargain hunters to react and support reasonable prices.

Block Sales

Block transactions
Large transactions in which at least 10,000 shares of stock are bought or sold.

Institutional investors frequently trade blocks of tens of thousands shares of stock. Table 5.4 shows that **block transactions** of over 10,000 shares now account for about half of all trading. The larger block transactions are often too large for specialists to handle, as they do not wish to hold such large blocks of stock in their inventory.

"Block houses" have evolved to aid in the placement of block trades. Block houses are brokerage firms that specialize in matching block buyers and sellers. Once a buyer and a seller have been matched, the block is sent to the exchange floor where specialists execute the trade. If a buyer cannot be found, the block house might purchase all or part of a block sale for its own account. The block house then can resell the shares to the public.

---

[2]This discussion is based on the Brady Commission report. See the Selected Readings.

Table 5.4   *Block Transactions on the New York Stock Exchange*

Year	Shares (Thousands)	Percentage of Reported Volume	Average Number of Block Transactions per Day
1965	48,262	3.1	9
1970	450,908	15.4	68
1975	778,540	16.6	136
1980	3,311,132	29.2	528
1985	14,222,272	51.7	2,139
1986	17,811,335	49.9	2,631
1987	24,497,241	51.2	3,639
1988	22,270,680	54.5	3,037
1989	21,316,132	51.1	3,464
1990	19,681,849	49.6	3,333

Data from the New York Stock Exchange *Fact Book*, 1991.

Settlement

An order executed on the exchange must be settled within five working days. The purchaser must deliver the cash, and the seller must deliver the stock to the broker, who in turn delivers it to the buyer's broker. Frequently, a firm's clients keep their securities in *street name,* which means the broker holds the shares registered in the firm's own name on behalf of the client. This convention can speed security transfer.

Settlement is simplified further by existence of a clearinghouse. The trades of all exchange members are recorded each day, with members' transactions netted out, so that each member need transfer or receive only the net number of shares sold or bought that day. An exchange member settles with the clearinghouse instead of individually with every firm with which it made trades.

5.4   *Trading on the OTC Market*

On the exchanges, all trading occurs through a specialist. On the OTC market, however, trades are negotiated directly through dealers who maintain an inventory of selected securities. Dealers sell from their inventories at ask prices and buy for them at bid prices.

An investor who wishes to purchase or sell shares OTC engages a broker who tries to locate the dealer offering the best deal on the security. This contrasts with exchange trading, where all buy or sell orders are negotiated through the specialist, who arranges for the best bids to get the trade. In the OTC market, brokers must search the offers of dealers directly to find the best trading opportunity.

If exchange trading is effectively an auction market, OTC trading is a dealer market. The NASDAQ system facilitates access. Subscribers to the NASDAQ level 2 or 3 service can obtain a full set of dealer bid and ask quotes. Dealers who make a market in securities will subscribe to the level 3 service, which allows them to list their offers as well as view those of other dealers. Brokers need only level 2 subscriptions to gain access to all offers.

Because this system does not use a specialist, OTC trades do not require a centralized trading floor as do exchange-listed stocks. Dealers can be located anywhere that they can communicate effectively with other buyers and sellers.

5.5   *Buying on Margin*

When purchasing securities, investors have easy access to a source of debt financing called *broker's call loans*. The act of taking advantage of broker's call loans is called *buying on margin*.

Margin   Describes securities purchased with money borrowed in part from a broker.

Purchasing stocks on **margin** means the investor borrows part of the purchase price of the stock from a broker. The brokers in turn borrow money from banks at the call money rate to finance these purchases; they then charge their clients that rate (defined in Chapter 4), plus a service charge for the loan. All securities purchased on margin must be maintained with the brokerage firm in street name, for the securities are collateral for the loan.

The Board of Governors of the Federal Reserve System limits the extent to which stock purchases can be financed using margin loans. The current maximum margin is 50 percent, meaning that at most 50 percent of the purchase price may be borrowed.

The percentage margin is defined as the ratio of the net worth, or "equity value," of the account to the market value of the securities. To demonstrate, suppose an investor initially pays $6,000 toward the purchase of $10,000 worth of stock (100 shares at $100 per share), borrowing the remaining $4,000 from a broker. The balance sheet looks like this:

Assets		Liabilities and Owner's Equity	
Value of stock	$10,000	Loan from broker	$4,000
		Equity	$6,000

The initial percentage margin is $6,000/$10,000 = 60 percent. If the stock's price declines to $70 per share, the account balance becomes:

Assets		Liabilities and Owner's Equity	
Value of stock	$7,000	Loan from broker	$4,000
		Equity	$3,000

The assets in the account fall by the full decrease in the stock value, and so does the equity. The percentage margin is now $3,000/$7,000 = 43 percent.

If the stock value were to fall below $4,000, owner's equity would become negative, meaning the value of the stock is no longer sufficient collateral to cover the loan from the broker. To guard against this possibility, the broker sets a *maintenance margin.* If the percentage margin falls below the maintenance level, the broker will issue a *margin call,* which requires the investor to add new cash or securities to the margin account. If the investor does not act, the broker may sell the securities from the account to pay off enough of the loan to restore the percentage margin to an acceptable level.

Suppose the maintenance margin is 30 percent. How far could the stock price fall before the investor would get a margin call? To answer this question requires some algebra.

Let P be the price of the stock. The value of the investor's 100 shares is then $100P$, and the equity in the account is $100P - \$4,000$. The percentage margin is $(100P - \$4,000)/100P$. The price at which the percentage margin equals the maintenance margin of 0.3 is found by solving the equation:

$$\frac{100P - 4,000}{100P} = .3$$
$$100P - 4,000 = 30P$$
$$P = \$57.14$$

If the price of the stock were to fall below $57.14 per share, the investor would get a margin call.

Concept Check

Question 2. If the maintenance margin in the example we have discussed were 40 percent, how far could the stock price fall before the investor would get a margin call?

Financing part of the investment with margin (debt) lets investors achieve greater upside potential, but it also exposes them to greater downside risk.

Suppose an investor is bullish on IBM stock, which is selling for $100 per share. An investor with $10,000 to invest expects IBM to go up in price by 30 percent during the next year. Ignoring any dividends, the expected rate of return would be 30 percent if the investor invested $10,000 to buy 100 shares.

But now assume the investor borrows another $10,000 from the broker and invests it in IBM, too. The total investment in IBM would be $20,000 (for 200 shares). Assuming an interest rate on the margin loan of 9 percent per year, what will the investor's rate of return be now (again ignoring dividends) if IBM stock goes up 30 percent by year's end?

The 200 shares will be worth $26,000. Paying off $10,900 of principal and interest on the margin loan leaves $15,100 ($26,000 − $10,900). The HPR in this case will be

$$\frac{\$15,100 - \$10,000}{\$10,000} = 51 \text{ percent.}$$

The investor has parlayed a 30 percent rise in the stock's price into a 51 percent rate of return on the $10,000 investment.

Doing so, however, magnifies the downside risk. Suppose that, instead of going up by 30 percent, the price of IBM stock goes down by 30 percent to $70 per share. In that case, the 200 shares will be worth $14,000, and the investor

Table 5.5 *Illustration of Buying Stock on Margin*

Change in Stock Price	End of Year Value of Shares	Repayment of Principal and Interest*	Investor's Rate of Return
30% increase	$26,000	$10,900	51%
No change	20,000	10,900	−9%
30% decrease	14,000	10,900	−69%

*Assuming the investor buys $20,000 worth of stock by borrowing $10,000 at an interest rate of 9% per year.

is left with $3,100 after paying off the $10,900 of principal and interest on the loan. The result is a disastrous HPR of

$$\frac{3,100 - 10,000}{10,000} = -69 \text{ percent.}$$

Table 5.5 summarizes the possible results of these hypothetical transactions. If there is no changes in IBM's stock price, the investor loses 9 percent, the cost of the loan.

Concept Check

Question 3. Suppose that in the previous example, the investor borrows only $5,000 at the same interest rate of 9 percent per year. What will the rate of return be if the price of IBM goes up by 30 percent? If it goes down by 30 percent? If it remains unchanged?

5.6 Short Sales

Short sale The sale of shares not owned by the investor but borrowed through a broker and later purchased to replace the loan.

Normally an investor would first buy a stock and later sell it. With a short sale, the order is reversed. First, you sell and then you buy the shares. In both cases, you begin and end with no shares.

A **short sale** allows investors to profit from a decline in a security's price. Instead of buying, an investor borrows a share of stock from a broker and sells it. Later, the short-seller must purchase a share of the same stock in the market in order to replace the share that was borrowed. This is called *covering the short position.*

The short-seller anticipates the stock price will fall, and the share can be purchased at a lower price than it initially sold for; therefore, the short-seller reaps a profit. Short-sellers must not only return the shares but also give the lender of the security any dividends paid during the short sale.

Brokers fill short sales by borrowing shares from street-name accounts. Investors who keep their securities in street-name accounts benefit from the free safekeeping and insurance, and brokers benefit from the privilege of borrowing the shares for short sales, on which they earn a fee.

Exchange rules permit short sales only after an *uptick,* that is, only when the last recorded change in the stock price is positive. This rule apparently is meant to prevent waves of speculation against the stock. In essence, the votes of "no confidence" in the stock that short sales represent may be entered only after a price increase.

Finally, exchange rules require that proceeds from a short sale must be kept on account with the broker. The short-seller cannot invest these funds to generate income. Short-sellers also are required to post margin (cash or collateral) with the broker to cover losses should the stock price rise during the short sale.

To illustrate the mechanics of short-selling, suppose you are bearish (pessimistic) on Xerox stock, and that its market price is $100 per share. You tell your broker to sell short 1,000 shares. The broker borrows 1,000 shares either from another customer's accounts or from another broker.

The $100,000 cash proceeds from the short sale are credited to your account. Suppose the broker has a 50 percent margin requirement on short sales. This means you must have other cash or securities in your account worth at least $50,000 that can serve as margin on the short sale. Let's say that you have $50,000 in Treasury bills. Your account with the broker after the short sale will then be:

Assets		Liabilities and Owner's Equity	
Cash	$100,000	Short position in Xerox stock (1,000 shares owed)	$100,000
T-bills	$ 50,000	Equity	$ 50,000

Now, if you are right and Xerox falls to $70 per share, you will be able to cover your short sale for a profit of $30,000. If the price of Xerox goes up unexpectedly while you are short, you may get a margin call from your broker.

Suppose the broker has a maintenance margin of 30 percent on short sales. This means the equity in your account must be at least 30 percent of the value of your short position at all times. How far can the price of Xerox stock go up before you get a margin call?

Let P be the price of Xerox stock. Then the value of your short position is $1,000P$, and the equity in your account is $\$150,000 - 1,000P$. Your short position margin ratio is $(150,000 - 1,000P)/1,000P$. The critical value of P is thus:

$$\frac{150,000 - 1,000P}{1,000P} = .3$$
$$150,000 - 1,000P = 300P$$
$$P = \$115.38 \text{ per share}$$

If Xerox stock should *rise* above $115.38 per share, you will get a margin call, and you will either have to put up additional cash or cover your short position.

Concept Check

Question 4.   a. Construct the balance sheet if Xerox goes up to $110. *b.* If the short position maintenance margin in the Xerox example were 40 percent, how far could the stock price rise before the investor would get a margin call?

5.7 *Regulation of Securities Markets*

Trading in securities markets in the United States is regulated by a myriad of laws. The major governing legislation includes the Securities Act of 1933 and the Securities Exchange Act of 1934. The 1933 Act requires full disclosure of relevant information relating to the issue of new securities. This is the act that requires registration of new securities and issuance of a prospectus that details the financial prospects of the firm. SEC approval of a prospectus or financial report is not an endorsement of the security as a good investment. The SEC cares only that the relevant facts are disclosed; investors make their own evaluations of the security's value.

The 1934 Act established the Securities and Exchange Commission to administer the provisions of the 1933 Act. It also extended the disclosure principle of the 1933 Act by requiring periodic disclosure of relevant financial information by firms with already-issued securities on secondary exchanges.

The 1934 Act also empowers the SEC to register and regulate securities exchanges, OTC trading, brokers, and dealers. While the SEC is the administrative agency responsible for broad oversight of the securities markets, it shares responsibility with other regulatory agencies. The Commodity Futures Trading Commission (CFTC) regulates trading in futures markets, while the Federal Reserve has broad responsibility for the health of the U.S. financial system. In this role, the Fed sets margin requirements on stocks and stock options and regulates bank lending to securities markets participants.

The Securities Investor Protection Act of 1970 established the Securities Investor Protection Corporation (SIPC) to protect investors from losses if their brokerage firms fail. Just as the Federal Deposit Insurance Corporation provides depositors with federal protection against bank failure, the SIPC ensures that investors will receive securities held for their account in street name by a failed brokerage firm up to a limit of $500,000 per customer. The SIPC is financed by levying an "insurance premium" on its participating, or member, brokerage firms. It also may borrow money from the SEC if its own funds are insufficient to meet its obligations.

In addition to federal regulations, security trading is subject to state laws, known generally as *blue sky laws* because they are intended to give investors a clearer view of the investment prospects. State laws to outlaw fraud in security sales existed before the Securities Act of 1933. Varying state laws were somewhat unified when many states adopted portions of the Uniform Securities Act, which was enacted in 1956.

Inside information
Nonpublic knowledge about a corporation possessed by corporate officers, major owners, or other individuals with privileged access to information about the firm.

One of the important restrictions involves insider trading. It is illegal for anyone to transact in securities to profit from **inside information,** that is, private information held by officers, directors, or major stockholders that has not yet been divulged to the public. But the definition of insiders can be ambiguous. While it is obvious that the chief financial officer of a firm is an insider, it is less clear whether the firm's biggest supplier can be considered an insider. Yet a supplier may deduce the firm's near-term prospects from significant changes in orders. This gives the supplier a unique form of private information, yet the supplier is not technically an insider.

These ambiguities plague security analysts, whose job is to uncover as much information as possible concerning the firm's expected prospects. The distinc-

Cloudy Cases: Insider-Trading Law Leads to an Array of Interpretations

You go to a party and meet a lawyer who advises Rupert Omnivore, a notorious corporate raider. The lawyer gives you a tip: Mr. Omnivore will soon "make a run at" Deadwood Industries Inc. You promptly buy stock in Deadwood. A week later, its share price surges as Mr. Omnivore goes public with his intentions.

Are you guilty of insider trading?

That sort of hypothetical question has legal experts, investment bankers, and stock-market investors tied up in knots these days. Nicholas Brady, chairman of Dillon, Read & Co., said in Senate testimony last month that he is confused about what is permissible and what isn't. "There needs to be clarification of exactly what conduct is to be prohibited by the concept of insider trading," said Mr. Brady.

Some practices clearly are illegal, as shown by the recent guilty pleas in Wall Street's widening insider-trading scandal. Just last week, investment banker Martin Siegel pleaded guilty to leaking information about pending takeovers to arbitrageur Ivan Boesky. Mr. Siegel's payoff: briefcases filled with cash, which he would pick up in secret meetings with Mr. Boesky's couriers.

But there are plenty of gray areas in insider-trading law. In fact, the Securities and Exchange Commission says it has resisted efforts to spell out precise guidelines, partly because it worries that shrewd market players may find ways to evade the spirit of the law, while just barely complying with the letter. "The current approach gives the SEC a lot more scope," says Irwin Schneiderman, a securities lawyer at the New York firm of Cahill, Gordon & Reindel. Mr. Schneiderman represents the investment banking firm of Drexel Burnham Lambert Inc., which has been a focus of the government's current insider-trading investigations.

Here are some examples of what legal experts say are ambiguous areas that ordinary investors may have to worry about—along with some sense of how the law currently stands.

The Raider's Tip

To some top lawyers, the example at the start of this story looks like a big loophole in current law. Unlike Mr. Siegel's situation, where he breached clients' confidences when he leaked information, raiders may be perfectly willing to have intermediaries tip off other investors about their next move. That's because such leaks can help move shares into "sympathetic hands," aiding raiders in later stages of a battle for corporate control.

"There is a real debate" about whether such practices are illegal, says Dillon Read's Mr. Brady. Lawyers generally say they aren't too comfortable with raiders leaking their intentions, and they certainly aren't about to assure a raider that it's safe to do so. But so far, there hasn't been a test case, says Philip Parker, chief counsel in the SEC's enforcement division.

A critical issue is whether a tender offer is involved, says John Coffee, a securities-law professor at Stanford University. If so, Rule 14e-3 under the Securities Exchange Act strictly limits trading by interested parties. But if a raider hasn't yet decided how to wage a fight, Rule 14e-3 might not apply, lawyers say.

Still, buying on the basis of a tip may have another set of worries for investors, says Geoffrey Hazard, a professor at Yale Law School. If they are acting in concert with the raider, the entire group may be required to disclose its holdings, once these exceed 5 percent of a company's stock.

"Insider trading isn't the only law pertaining to these situations," says Prof. Hazard. "That's a point worth remembering when people hem and haw about the ambiguities of insider-trading law."

The Chain

You're an officer of Ennui Enterprises, and you're about to report disappointing quarterly earnings. You know not to sell before the news, but you tell your college roommate. He tells his daughter, who's

tion between legal private information and illegal inside information can be fuzzy (see accompanying box).

The SEC requires officers, directors, and major stockholders to report all transactions in their firm's stock. A compendium of insider trades is published monthly in the SEC's *Official Summary of Securities Transactions and Holdings*.

married to a stockbroker. The broker tells his clients. They dump their stock in Ennui—hours before the earnings are reported and the stock falls.

Have the clients done anything wrong? Have you?

Lawyers say the critical question for recipients of such tips is whether they knew, or had reason to know, that any of the sources were breaching a fiduciary duty in leaking information. If so, tip recipients shouldn't trade on the information.

In practical terms, the longer the chain, the less likely regulators are to pursue the case. Bevis Longstreth, a former SEC commissioner, recalls one inquiry that led from former Deputy Defense Secretary Paul Thayer to a series of brokers to a group of world-class backgammon players. "It was pretty remote," he recalls, "and ultimately we didn't go after the backgammon players." (Officials did, successfully, bring a case against Mr. Thayer.)

Law-enforcement officials do pursue some chains, and the original leaker can face heavy sanctions. Just this week, criminal charges were filed against Israel Grossman, New York lawyer who allegedly leaked nonpublic information to six friends and relatives about Colt Industries Inc.'s 1986 recapitalization. The recipients of the leak weren't criminally charged but were charged in a civil case.

Early Word of News Stories

It could involve television, the business press, or a medical journal. But you know in advance about a news report that should boost a company's stock. Is it legal to trade on this information?

The law is still in flux here, says Stanford's Prof. Coffee. A former *Wall Street Journal* reporter, R. Foster Winans, was convicted of securities fraud for leaking information about future *Journal* articles. His case is due to be reviewed by the Supreme Court.

On the other hand, the SEC chose not to bring a case against an Arizona researcher who traded in G. D. Searle options before appearing on CBS-TV

to discuss Searle's Aspartame sweetener. The researcher said of his trading at the time: "I don't feel it's unethical. I feel it's the American way."

An important test here is how such traders learned of the future news reports, says Prof. Coffee. If they misappropriated information from their employer, in violation of company policy, they would seem to be guilty of insider trading under the current Winans ruling. But it's questionable whether any insider-trading offense would occur if the investor didn't have a fiduciary duty to the news organization.

The Overheard Tip

Tired of your duties at Ennui Enterprises, you take off for the golf course instead. You can't help overhearing another group talking about their corporate acquisition plans. You buy the stock they mention. Sure enough, their bid comes a week later, bringing you big profits.

Have the other executives done anything wrong? Have you?

If the leak really was inadvertent, despite sensible precautions to avoid it, the overheard executives face little legal risk, experts say. They add that accidental tip recipients are probably in the clear, too, as long as they haven't taken unusual steps to glean the information.

But enforcement officials may ask a lot of questions before they're convinced that a leak was an accident. And Mr. Lonstreth, currently a partner in the New York law firm of Debevoise & Plimpton, says investors should think a little about their conscience, as well as the law.

"For all the talk about gray areas, my clients can sense what's all right and what isn't," he says. "They don't call me and say: 'Where's the line, so I can stay just barely on the safe side of it.'"

The idea is to inform the public of any implicit votes of confidence or no confidence made by insiders.

Insiders *do* exploit their knowledge. Two forms of evidence support this conclusion. First, there have been well-publicized convictions of principals in insider trading schemes. An example is the Boesky case.

Second, there is considerable evidence of "leakage" of useful information to some traders before any public announcement of that information. For example, share prices of firms announcing dividend increases (which the market interprets as good news concerning the firm's prospects) commonly increase in value a few days *before* the public announcement of the increase. Clearly, some investors are acting on the good news before it is released to the public. Similarly, share prices tend to increase a few days before the public announcement of above-trend earnings growth. Share prices still rise substantially on the day of the public release of good news, however, indicating that insiders, or their associates, have not fully bid up the price of the stock to the level commensurate with the news.

Yet another sort of evidence on insider trading has to do with returns earned on trades by insiders. Researchers have examined the SEC's summary of insider trading to measure the performance of insiders. In one of the best known of these studies, Jaffee (1974) examined the abnormal return of stocks over the months following purchases or sales by insiders. For months in which insider purchasers of a stock exceeded insider sellers of the stock by three or more, the stock had an abnormal return in the following eight months of about 5 percent. Moreover, when insider sellers exceeded insider buyers, the stock tended to perform poorly.

Restriction of the use of inside information is not universal. Japan has no such prohibition. An argument in favor of free use of inside information is that investors are not misled to believe that the financial market is a level playing field for all; they can act appropriately to protect themselves when they expect insiders to have an advantage. At the same time, free use of inside information speeds up its dissemination.

Most Americans believe, however, that it is valuable as well as virtuous to take the moral high ground and outlaw such advantage, even if less-than-perfect enforcement may leave the door open for some profitable violation of the law.

Much of the securities industry relies on self-regulation. The SEC has delegated considerable responsibility for day-to-day oversight of trading to secondary exchanges. Similarly, the National Association of Securities Dealers oversees trading of OTC securities. The Institute of Chartered Financial Analysts' (ICFA) code of ethics and professional conduct sets out principles that govern the behavior of CFAs.

The market crash of October 19, 1987, prompted several suggestions for regulatory change. For example, the Brady Commission studying the event has suggested:

1. A single regulatory agency to coordinate issues that affect several financial markets.
2. Unified clearing systems across markets.
3. Consistent margin requirements across markets.
4. Circuit breakers to halt trading under certain market conditions.
5. Coordination of information gathering and dissemination across markets.

Of these recommendations, the institution of circuit breakers is the only measure adopted by the exchanges, and that is only on a voluntary basis.

5.8   *Selecting a Broker*

Individuals may choose from two kinds of brokers: full-service or discount brokers. Full-service brokers who provide a variety of services often are referred to as account executives or financial consultants. Table 5.6 lists brokerage firms ranked by capital and customers.

Besides carrying out the basic services of executing orders, holding securities for safekeeping, extending margin loans, and facilitating short sales, brokers routinely provide information and advice relating to investment alternatives.

Full-service brokers usually depend on a research staff that prepares analyses and forecasts of general economic as well as industry and company conditions and often makes specific buy or sell recommendations. Some customers take the ultimate leap of faith and allow a full-service broker to make buy and sell decisions for them by establishing a *discretionary account*. In this account, the broker can buy and sell prespecified securities whenever deemed fit. The broker cannot withdraw any funds, though. This action requires an unusual degree of trust on the part of the customer, for an unscrupulous broker can "churn" an account, that is, trade securities excessively with the sole purpose of generating commissions.

Table 5.6   *Top U.S. Brokerage Firms*

Ranked by Total Capital (Figures in millions of dollars)			
Firm	**12/80**	**Firm**	**1/1/88**
Merrill Lynch, Pierce, Fenner & Smith Inc.	$969	Shearson Lehman Brothers*	$4,584
Shearson Loeb Rhoades Inc.	470	Salomon Brothers Inc.	3,133
EF Hutton	448	Merrill Lynch, Pierce, Fenner & Smith Inc.	2,903
Salomon Holding Co.	330	Goldman, Sach & Co.	2,400
Dean Witter	274	Drexel Burnham Lambert Group	2,300
Bache Halsey Stewart Shields Inc.	252	First Boston Corporation	1,486
PaineWebber	243	PaineWebber Group Inc.	1,437
Goldman, Sachs & Co.	219	Dean Witter Reynolds, Inc.	1,344
Stephens Inc.	167	Bear Stearns & Co. Inc.	1,320

Ranked by Customer Accounts in 1988		
Firm	**Brokers**	**Customer Accounts**
Merrill Lynch, Pierce, Fenner & Smith Inc.	13,300	5,800,000
Shearson Lehman Hutton Inc.	11,750	4,600,000
Dean Witter Reynolds, Inc.	7,758	2,200,000
Prudential-Bache Securities, Inc.	6,082	1,900,000
PaineWebber Incorporated	4,350	1,870,000
A. G. Edwards & Sons Inc.	3,250	541,000
Thomson McKinnon Securities Inc.	2,400	500,897
Smith Barney, Harris Upham & Co., Inc.	2,311	500,000
Kidder Peabody & Co, Inc.	2,178	520,015
Bear Stearns & Co. Inc.	2,166	145,000

*Had not yet merged with EF Hutton.

Source: Securities Industry Association.

Discount brokers, on the other hand, provide "no-frills" services. They buy and sell securities, hold them for safekeeping, offer margin loans, and facilitate short sales, and that is all. The only information they provide about the securities they handle is price quotations.

Discount brokerage services have become increasingly available in recent years. Many banks, thrift institutions, and mutual fund management companies now offer such services to the investing public as part of a general trend toward the creation of one-stop "financial supermarkets."

One important service most full-service and discount brokers offer their customers is an automatic cash management feature. Cash generated from the sale of securities or the receipt of dividends and interest is automatically invested in a money market fund. This ensures that cash will not be idle and will always earn interest.

5.9   *Cost of Trading*

The cost of buying or selling a security is not as obvious as you may expect. In general, it is made up of three components: commission to your broker, the dealer's bid-ask spread, and the potential impact of your own order on the current quoted price (the "price concession"). The broker's commission is explicit. The dealer's **bid-ask spread,** on the other hand, is implicit in the stated transaction price. Sometimes the broker is a dealer in the security being traded and will charge no commission but instead collect the entire fee through the bid-ask spread.

Bid-ask spread *The difference between a dealer's bid and asked price.*

The price concession is almost always impossible to identify. It is an implicit cost of trading that an investor may be forced to make pay for trading in any quantity that exceeds the quantity the dealer is willing to trade at the posted bid or ask price. Dealers' quotes are binding on 100-lot shares. Larger trades allow the dealer to adjust the price to the "selling pressure."

Commissions on common stocks trades may range from 30 percent of the value of a small retail transaction by a full-service broker to less than 0.25 percent in institutional transactions. Before 1975, the commission schedule was fixed, but today there is substantial flexibility. On some trades, full-service brokers may offer even lower commissions than discount brokers. As Table 5.7 shows, it pays investors to shop around. (See also the accompanying box on big investors' commissions.)

Total trading costs can be substantial if we add up commissions, dealer bid-ask spread, and the price concession. According to one study (Loeb, 1983), the round-trip costs of trading large blocks of small capitalization stocks can be as high as 30 percent.

5.10   *Mutual Funds and Other Investment Companies*

As an alternative to investing in securities through a broker (or in addition to it), many individuals invest in mutual funds sponsored by investment companies. This section explains how these institutions work.

Table 5.7 *How Discount Brokerage Commissions Compare*

Commission charges quoted by several discounters for buying or selling various amounts of a $26 stock and charges at two full-service firms. (Prices to nearest dollar.)

Brokerage Firm	Number of Shares Traded				
	100	200	400	1,000	2,500
Fidelity Investments					
Brokerage account	$51	$ 86	$106	$151	$216
FidelityPlus	48	82	100	143	206
Spartan Brokerage	44	44	52	94	192
Andrew Peck	50	56	72	90	140
Quick & Reilly	49	61	85	121	175
Charles Schwab*	49	82	100	143	206
Waterhouse Securities	35	35	60	128	240
Jack White & Co.	48	71	89	132	210
York Securities	35	35	53	75	125
Merrill Lynch	80	132	228	418	728
Shearson Lehman	75	139	241	497	878

Note: Many firms offer additional discounts or rebates for active traders, with the amount linked to trading activity.

From *The Wall Street Journal*, March 6, 1991. Reprinted by permission of THE WALL STREET JOURNAL, © 1991 Dow Jones & Company, Inc. All Rights Reserved Worldwide.

Mutual Funds

Mutual funds are firms that manage pools of other people's money. Individuals buy shares of mutual funds, and the funds invest the money in certain specified types of assets, for example, common stocks, tax-exempt bonds, or mortgages. The shares issued to the investors entitle them to a pro rata portion of the income generated by these assets.

Mutual funds perform several important functions for their shareholders:

1. Recordkeeping and administration. A mutual fund issues periodic status reports and may reinvest dividends and interest.
2. Diversification and divisibility. By pooling their money, investment companies enable shareholders to hold fractional shares of many different securities. Funds can act as large investors even if any individual shareholder cannot.
3. Professional management. Many, but not all, mutual funds have full-time staffs of security analysts and portfolio managers who attempt to achieve superior investment results for their shareholders.
4. Lower transaction costs. Because they trade large blocks of securities, investment companies can achieve substantial savings on brokerage fees and commissions.

There are two types of mutual funds: *closed-end* and *open-end funds*. Open-end funds stand ready to redeem or issue shares at their net asset value (NAV), which is the market value of all cash and securities held by the fund divided by the number of shares outstanding. The number of shares outstanding of an open-end fund changes daily as investors buy new or redeem old shares. Closed-

Big Investors' Commission Rates May Have Hit a Low

NEW YORK—Commission rates paid by large investors on stock trades, which have been falling for more than a decade, may have finally hit a low point.

While skeptics dismiss it as no more than wishful thinking by brokers, indications that institutional commission rates have firmed—and may even increase—have surfaced in a new study by Greenwich Associates, Greenwich, Conn., consultants who do exhaustive research on the investment industry.

Greenwich's latest survey of 600 institutional investors found that the 115 largest, each of which pays $5 million or more in annual commissions, expect their per share costs to rise this year. Though the expected climb is tiny—to an average of 6.6 cents a share from 6.5 cents in 1989—it marks the first time since 1980 that Greenwich turned up evidence that large institutional commissions are on the rise. Greenwich has been conducting the study for 17 years.

"One-tenth of a cent does not a trend make, but it is the first time that it hasn't gone south" in a decade, Greenwich consultant James A. Bennett Jr. said of the institutional rate. But the aggregate forecast from all 600 institutional investors surveyed showed that commissions are expected to slip to 8.7 cents a share from 8.9 cents this year.

Even if commission rates for big investors have hit bottom at about 6.6 cents a share, they are still too low for brokers to make a profit trading stocks for customers, said Kevin L. Risen, brokerage analyst at Banc One Asset Management Corp. "Eight to 10 cents a share is what I consider to be a level they can make a profit at," he said.

And stock trading executives see little inclination by any of their customers to allow rates to move up quickly.

Robert M. Dewey Jr., managing director, equity trading and sales, at Donaldson, Lufkin & Jenrette Securities Corp., said that while institutions are talking about paying a bit more, few are taking action. "You could put on one hand all the people that have stepped up to the plate and said, 'I want to take my seven-cent commission up to eight cents,'" he said.

With Wall Street's trading capacity still far larger than necessary to handle the available business, many brokerage executives remain doubtful that the slide in institutional commission rates is over.

"From what we have seen in the first quarter, there is no indication that commissions are going up," said Stanley S. Abel, chairman of Abel/Noser Corp., which specializes in measuring stock trading costs. Brokers, he said, are "trying to talk rates up," but customers still hold the upper hand.

Ever since brokerage firms were forced to end their system of fixed stock-commission rates in 1975, per-share trading costs paid by big investors have declined steadily, squeezing Wall Street's stock trading profits. And according to a big securities firm, which declined to be identified, commission rates kept tumbling in the first quarter of this year. An executive at this firm said that from 1988 to 1989, average commissions paid to the firm fell 4.79 percent to 6.56 cents a share. For the first quarter of this year, commissions fell another 2 percent to 6.42 cents a share, the lowest in this firm's history.

Some big investment firms are paying even less. Independence Investment Associates, a money-

end funds do not redeem or issue shares at net asset value. Shares of closed-end funds are traded through brokers just like other common stocks, and their price can differ from NAV.[3]

Figure 5.3 shows a listing of closed-end funds' NAVs and prices from *The Wall Street Journal*. The list of these "Publicly Traded Funds" appears weekly

---

[3]The divergence of the market price of a closed-end fund's shares from NAV has yet to be fully explained by finance theorists.

management arm of John Hancock Mutual Life Insurance Co., is typical of the big investors that have significantly lowered their trading costs. Independence's per-share commissions have fallen an average of 10 percent annually in the past 15 years to 5.3 cents in 1989 from 25.6 cents in 1974.

Still, some institutional investors said they are worried that the drop in rates has gotten to the point that they are paying hidden costs through the pricing and timing of their stock trades.

"We're starting to get a little concerned that we've pushed these [commission] costs so low that maybe it is affecting prices," said William F. Quinn, president of AMR Investment Services Inc., which manages $6 billion for employees of AMR Corp.'s American Airlines and other clients. "We're hearing from a broad base of [money] managers that liquidity isn't what it used to be," he said.

As a result, Mr. Quinn said, he has authorized his outside money managers to pay higher commissions if necessary, which has resulted in AMR's per-share rate rising by perhaps half a penny above its previous five-cents-a-share cost. "We've said to managers that if they need to pay a little more [commission] to get a trade done at the best price, they should do it," he said.

Joseph W. Perrone, chief investment officer of the $24 billion Texas Teacher Retirement System, also believes big investors may have pushed Wall Street as hard as they can. For the Texas teachers fund, with $9.5 billion in stocks, saving a penny on the fund's average commission cost of six to seven cents a share could easily get lost "in the noise level," Mr Perrone said. "While I'm sitting there negotiating for one cent a share, I could lose $100,000 in the market."

"You've got to let those guys make some money or they can't stay in business," he said. "We can just tell the brokers not to write *any* commissions and they will just mark up the stock."

Mr. Dewey of Donaldson Lufkin said that despite customers' haggling over ordinary business, large blocks that require his firm to put up money to facilitate the trade are commanding higher commissions. "When it comes to using our capital to do a trade—almost everybody is willing to pay for that," he said.

But some investors still believe the cost of trading is too high in many cases. "I don't think it's low enough for large traders," said Greta Marshall, former chief investment officer of the $56 billion California Public Employees Retirement System and now a money manager heading her own firm.

While she was at the California pension fund, Ms. Marshall helped halve its average commission rate to five cents a share, cutting off brokers who refused to adjust their fees. But she noted that a nickel-a-share commission still amounts to $500 on a 10,000-share trade. "It just doesn't cost that much for a [trade] ticket," she said.

Brokers, Ms. Marshall said, should boost charges to very active traders, such as hedge funds, and cut them for those who are usually in less of a hurry to get trades done, such as pension funds.

"The Street says, 'We're not making any money,'" Ms. Marshall said. "I say, 'Maybe that's because you're inefficient and you're not making people pay for things that they use.'"

James A. White, "Big Investors' Commission Rates May Have Hit Low," *The Wall Street Journal*, April 24, 1990. Reprinted by permission of *THE WALL STREET JOURNAL,* © 1990 Dow Jones & Company, Inc. All Rights Reserved Worldwide.

on Mondays. In most cases, the stock price is different from the NAV, and many funds are trading below NAV.

Many investors consider closed-end fund shares selling at a discount to their NAV to be a bargain. Even if the market price never rises to the level of NAV, the dividend yield on an investment in the fund at this price could (if always paid out by the fund management) exceed the dividend yield on the same securities held outside the fund.

To see this, imagine a fund with an NAV of $10 per share holding a portfolio that pays an annual dividend of $1 per share; that is, the dividend yield to inves-

PUBLICLY TRADED FUNDS

Friday, May 17, 1991
Following is a weekly listing of unaudited net asset values
of publicly traded investment fund shares, reported by the
companies as of Friday's close. Also shown is the closing
listed market price or a dealer-to-dealer asked price of
each fund's shares, with the percentage of difference.

Fund Name	Stock Exch.	N.A. Value	Stock Price	% Diff.
Diversified Common Stock Funds				
Adams Express	NYSE	19.03	17	− 10.67
Baker Fentress	NYSE	21.04	16 7/8	− 19.80
Blue Chip Value	NYSE	7.65	7 1/8	− 6.86
Clemente Global Gro	NYSE	b10.99	9 1/8	− 16.97
Gemini II Capital	NYSE	15.27	12 3/4	− 16.50
Gemini II Income	NYSE	9.43	12 3/4	+ 35.21
General Amer Invest	NYSE	25.70	22	− 14.40
Growth Stock Outlook	NYSE	10.43	9 7/8	− 5.32
Liberty All-Star Eqty	NYSE	10.06	9 3/8	− 6.81
Niagara Share Corp.	NYSE	15.92	13 1/2	− 15.20
Nicholas-Applegate	NYSE	11.95	11 7/8	− 0.63
Quest For Value Cap	NYSE	19.23	14	− 27.20
Quest For Value Inco	NYSE	11.59	13 1/2	+ 16.48
Royce Value Trust	NYSE	10.54	9 7/8	− 6.31
Salomon Fd	NYSE	14.95	12 5/8	− 15.55
Source Capital	NYSE	40.43	42 3/4	+ 5.74
Tri-Continental Corp.	NYSE	27.35	24 5/8	− 9.96
Worldwide Value	NYSE	16.64	14	− 15.87
Zweig Fund	NYSE	11.17	12 1/4	+ 9.67
Closed End Bond Funds				
CIM High Yield Secs	AMEX	6.64	6 3/8	− 3.99
Franklin Multi Inc Tr	NYSE	b8.77	8 3/8	− 4.50
Franklin Prin Mat Tr	NYSE	b7.82	7 5/8	− 2.49
Franklin Universal Tr	NYSE	b6.93	6 1/2	− 6.20
Municipal High Inco	NYSE	a9.32	9 1/4	− 0.75
Zenix Income Fund	NYSE	a5.61	5 3/4	+ 2.50
Flexible Portfolio Funds				
America's All Seasn	OTC	5.75	4 1/2	− 21.74
European Warrant Fd	NYSE	9.71	7 1/2	− 22.76
Zweig Total Return Fd	NYSE	9.24	9 3/4	+ 5.52
Specialized Equity and Convertible Funds				
Alliance Global Env Fd	NYSE	13.62	12	− 11.89
American Capital Conv	NYSE	20.13	17 1/2	− 13.07
ASA Ltd	NYSE	bcv42.87	45 3/8	+ 5.84
Asia Pacific	NYSE	14.76	13 1/4	− 10.23
Austria Fund	NYSE	11.62	9 5/8	− 17.17
Bancroft Convertible	AMEX	20.42	17 7/8	− 12.46
Bergstrom Capital	AMEX	80.35	81 1/2	+ 1.43
BGR Precious Metals	TOR	be8.74	7 1/4	− 17.05
Brazil	NYSE	11.59	13	+ 12.17
CNV Holdings Capital	NYSE	10.00	6	− 40.00
CNV Holdings Income	NYSE	9.50	11	+ 15.79
Castle Convertible	AMEX	22.15	18 3/4	− 15.35
Central Fund Canada	AMEX	b4.42	4 3/16	− 5.26
Central Securities	AMEX	11.39	9 1/4	− 18.79
Chile Fund	NYSE	25.36	22 1/8	− 12.76
Couns Tandem Secs	NYSE	13.92	11 7/8	− 14.69
Cypress Fund	AMEX	5.82	4 7/8	− 16.24
Duff&Phelps Sel Utils	NYSE	8.50	8 7/8	+ 4.41
Ellsw Conv Gr&Inc	AMEX	8.18	7 1/8	− 12.90
Emerging Ger Fd	NYSE	8.82	8 1/8	− 7.88
Engex	AMEX	8.97	7 5/8	− 14.99
Europe Fund	NYSE	13.11	11	− 16.09
1stAustralia	AMEX	10.16	9 1/8	− 10.19
First Financial Fund	NYSE	6.87	7	+ 1.89
First Iberian	AMEX	9.50	8 3/4	− 7.89
First Philippine Fund	NYSE	10.55	7 7/8	− 25.36
France Growth Fund	NYSE	10.23	8 3/8	− 18.13
Future Germany Fund	NYSE	13.59	12 1/4	− 9.86
Gabelli Equity Trust	NYSE	11.38	11 1/4	− 1.14
Germany Fund	NYSE	10.62	11 1/8	+ 4.76
Growth Fund Spain	NYSE	11.54	10 1/8	− 12.26
GT Greater Europe Fd	NYSE	11.69	9 3/4	− 16.60
H&Q Healthcare Inv	NYSE	15.54	14 3/4	− 5.08
Hampton Utils Tr Cap	AMEX	b12.65	10 7/8	− 14.03

tors that hold this portfolio directly is 10 percent. Now suppose the market price of a share of this closed-end fund is $9. If management pays out the portfolio dividends as they come in, then the dividend yield to those that hold the same portfolio through the closed-end fund will reach 1/9, or 11.1 percent.

The market price of open-end funds, on the other hand, cannot fall below NAV because these funds redeem shares at NAV. The offer price will exceed

Load *A sales commission charged on a mutual fund.*

No-load fund *A mutual fund with no sales charge involved.*

NAV, however, if the fund carries a **load.** A load is in effect a sales commission, usually from 3 percent to 8.5 percent of NAV, which is paid to the seller. Load funds are sold by security brokers, many insurance brokers, and others.

Shares of a **no-load fund** are bought directly from the fund at NAV and involve no sales charge. The investment performance of the average no-load fund, taking into account all other fees and expenses, does not differ systematically from a load fund's performance, so it would seem that, on average, investors who buy into load funds are simply paying the retail price for an item that is readily available wholesale.

Judging the performance of mutual funds is far from trivial, however. In the context of the risk-return trade-off, we are required to take the risk of the fund portfolio into account. We discuss this issue in detail in Chapter 11.

Figure 5.4 shows part of the listings for mutual funds published every weekday in *The Wall Street Journal.* Load funds are the ones whose offer price exceeds their NAV.

At the end of 1991, there were about 3,000 open-end mutual funds with assets exceeding $700 billion. Of these, over 400 were money market funds (including tax-free money market funds). Table 5.8 breaks down the number of mutual funds and their assets by size of fund and type of fund as of the end of 1986. A brief description of various objectives of mutual funds and the reasons investors put money in mutual funds is given in Table 5.9.

Management Companies and Mutual Fund Investment Policies

Management companies are firms that manage a family of mutual funds. They typically organize the various funds and then collect a management fee for operating them. Some of the most well-known management companies are Fidelity, Dreyfus, and Vanguard. Each offers an array of open-end mutual funds with different investment policies. Table 5.10 lists the 12 largest mutual fund families with some of their features.

Figure 5.5 lists the funds offered by the Fidelity Group. The name of a fund often describes its investment policy. Fidelity Massachusetts Tax-Free Bond Fund (Mass TF), for example, invests exclusively in bonds that are tax-exempt in the Commonwealth of Massachusetts. Some funds have promotional names such as the High Income Fund, which invests in "junk" bonds (risky bonds of highly levered corporations). Other names of common stock funds give little or no clue as to their investment policies. An example is Fidelity's Puritan Fund.

Wiesenberger's (an investment service company) manual *Investment Companies* classifies common stock funds as having the following objectives:

1. Maximum capital gain.
2. Growth.
3. Growth and income.
4. Income.
5. Income and security.

"arranged in descending order of emphasis on capital appreciation and, consequently, in ascending order of the importance placed on current income and relative price stability." (More sources of information on the finance industry are listed in Appendix A.)

Figure 5.4
Listing for mutual funds.

From *The Wall Street Journal*, May 10, 1991. Reprinted by permission of *THE WALL STREET JOURNAL*, © Dow Jones & Company, Inc. All Rights Reserved Worldwide.

MUTUAL FUND QUOTATIONS

Thursday, May 9, 1991
Price ranges for investment companies, as quoted by the National Association of Securities Dealers. NAV stands for net asset value per share; the offering includes net asset value plus maximum sales charge, if any.

	NAV	Offer NAV Price	NAV Chg.
AAL Mutual:			
CaGr p	12.67	13.30	+.14
Inco p	9.75	10.24	...
MuBd p	10.15	10.66	+.01
AARP Invst:			
CaGr	28.99	NL	+.35
GiniM	15.34	NL	...
GthInc	26.03	NL	+.19
HQ Bd	15.21	NL	...
TxFBd	17.01	NL	+.03
TxFSh	15.27	NL	+.01
ABT Funds:			
Emrg p	9.73	10.22	+.09
FL TF	10.42	10.94	+.01
Gthin p	9.72	10.20	+.09
Utilin p	12.12	12.72	+.03
AdsnCa p	19.65	20.26	+.17
AEGON USA:			
CapApp	4.10	4.30	+.04
HiYld	9.71	10.19	...
Gwth	5.99	6.29	+.08
AFA NAv	10.89	11.43	+.13
AFA Tele	15.59	16.37	+.28
AHA Bal	11.27	NL	+.11
AHA LtM	10.16	NL	...
AIM Funds:			
Chart p	7.82	8.28	+.08
Const p	10.07	10.66	+.14
CvYld p	11.38	11.95	+.12
HiYld p	5.16	5.42	−.03
LimM p	9.95	10.13	...
Sumit	9.14	...	+.12
Weing p	14.81	15.67	+.19
A M A Family:			
ClaGt p	7.95	8.35	+.08
GlbGt p	21.83	22.92	+.16
Glbin p	18.73	19.66	...
USGv p	8.67	9.10	...
AMEV Funds:			
AstAl p	12.48	13.07	+.09
Capitl p	15.38	16.15	+.23
CaAp p	16.81	17.60	+.25
Fidcr p	24.66	25.82	+.39
GvTR p	8.94	9.36	−.01
Grwth p	22.17	23.28	+.43
HiYld p	7.07	7.40	...
TF MN	9.83	10.29	+.01
TF Nat	10.04	10.51	+.01
US Gvt	9.73	10.19	...
AMF Funds:			
Cp Bd	9.30	NL	...
IntlLiq	10.54	NL	...
MtgSc	10.92	NL	−.02
ASO Eq	12.77	13.16	+.11
AcornF	41.26	41.26	+.22
Afuture	12.13	NL	+.33
Advance America:			
EqInc	9.89	10.38	+.09
TF In p	9.87	10.36	...
US Gv p	9.29	9.75	...
Advest Advant:			
Govt p	8.54	8.54	...
Gwth p	14.86	14.86	+.16
HY Bd p	7.47	7.47	+.02
Inco p	10.96	10.96	+.07
Spcl p	13.80	13.80	+.11
AlgrSCp †	19.18	19.18	+.19
AlgerG †	16.51	16.51	+.25
Alliance Cap:			
Alian p	6.40	6.77	+.10
Balan p	12.52	13.25	+.12
Canad p	5.95	6.30	+.03
Conv p	7.62	8.06	+.07
Count p	10.49	10.77	+.19

	NAV	Offer NAV Price	NAV Chg.
MedRs	16.67	17.50	+.07
PBHG	11.66	12.24	+.16
Ray El	6.75	7.09	+.06
Trend	13.93	14.62	+.17
CarilCa	12.02	12.65	+.06
Carneg Cappielo:			
EmGr p	10.19	10.67	+.09
Grow p	18.76	19.64	+.18
TRetn p	11.62	12.17	+.09
Carnegie Funds:			
Govt p	9.23	9.66	...
TEOhG	9.24	9.68	...
TENHi	9.64	10.09	+.01
Cardnl	11.54	12.62	+.10
CrdnlGv	8.89	9.31	...
Cnt Shs	19.82	NL	+.18
ChartBC	11.18	11.18	+.16
Chestnt	110.77	NL	+1.55
CIGNA Funds:			
Agrsv p	15.82	16.65	+.11
GvSc p	9.98	10.51	+.01
Grth p	15.02	15.81	+.22
HiYld p	8.16	8.59	+.01
Inco p	7.56	7.96	...
MunB p	7.84	8.25	...
Util p	12.90	13.58	+.06
Value p	16.44	17.31	+.15
Citibank IRA-CIT:			
Balan f	2.51	NL	+.01
Equit f	2.80	NL	...
Incom f	2.17	NL	...
ShtTr f	1.80	NL	...
Clipper	45.44	45.44	+.41
Colonial Funds:			
AGold p	15.41	16.35	...
CalTE	7.03	7.38	+.01
CpCsh p	44.79	45.70	−.03
Dvsdln	6.68	7.01	+.02
Fund p	20.33	21.57	+.15
GvSec p	10.63	11.16	...
Gwth p	12.97	13.76	+.12
HiYld p	5.37	5.64	−.01
Incom p	6.19	6.50	−.01
IntEq p	16.28	17.27	+.04
MATx	7.22	7.58	+.01
MI TE	6.62	6.95	+.01
MN TE	6.96	7.31	...
NY TE	6.68	7.01	...
OhTE	6.95	7.30	+.01
Smlin p	12.08	12.82	+.07
TXIns p	7.79	8.18	+.01
TxEx p	13.04	13.69	+.02
US Gv p	7.01	7.36	...
US Id p	18.80	19.95	+.24
Colonial VIP:			
DvRet †	11.21	11.21	+.02
FdSec †	9.89	9.89	...
Gwth †	11.61	11.61	+.06
Hiinc †	8.53	8.53	−.01
HYMu †	9.65	9.65	+.01
InfHd †	10.19	10.19	+.02
Columbia Funds:			
Fixed	12.86	NL	...
Govt	8.49	NL	...
Grth	25.90	NL	+.33
Muni	11.84	NL	...
Specl	46.62	NL	+.54
Common Sense:			
Govt	11.09	11.89	...
Grwth	14.59	15.95	+.21
GrInc	14.00	15.30	+.18
MunB	12.58	13.21	+.01
CwithBl	2.08	2.25	+.01
Comm— —ital:			

Table 5.8   *Classification of Mutual Funds by Size and Type*
(As of December 31, 1986)

	Number of Funds	Combined Assets (Thousands)	Total (%)
Size of Fund			
Over $1 billion	167	$442,851,500	63.3
$500 million–$1 billion	159	111,655,000	16.0
$300 million–500 million	123	47,411,400	6.7
$100 million–$300 million	369	68,954,600	9.8
$50 million–$100 million	235	17,195,300	2.5
$10 million–$50 million	380	10,330,700	1.5
$1 million–$10 million	206	1,046,500	0.2
Under $1 million	30	16,000	0.0
	1,669	$699,461,000	100.0
Type of Fund			
Common Stock:			
Maximum capital gain	99	$ 31,842,200	4.6
Growth	268	44,826,600	6.4
Growth and income	134	50,970,000	7.3
Specialized:			
Canadian and international	44	9,182,800	1.3
Gold and precious metals	18	1,177,900	0.2
Industry	49	3,803,400	0.5
Government securities	113	118,589,100	16.9
Tax-exempt bond funds	270	80,628,000	11.5
Technology	5	283,100	0.0
Other	13	2,852,900	0.4
Balanced	26	5,290,000	0.8
Income	199	61,053,300	8.7
Bond and preferred stock	45	14,413,700	2.1
Money market	280	217,569,600	31.1
Tax-free money markets	106	56,978,400	8.2
	1,669	$699,461,000	100.0

From *Investment Companies 1987*, Wiesenberger Investment Companies Services.

Some funds are designed to be candidates for an individual's whole investment portfolio. Wiesenberger's manual classifies such funds, which hold both equities and fixed-income securities, as *income* or *balanced funds*. Income funds "provide as liberal a current income from investments as possible," while balanced funds "minimize investment risks so far as this is possible without unduly sacrificing possibilities for long-term growth and current income."

Index fund   A mutual fund holding shares in proportion to their representation in a market index such as the S&P 500.

Finally, an **index fund** tries to match the performance of a broad market index. For example, Vanguard Index Trust and Fidelity Spartan Market Index Fund are no-load mutual funds that replicate the composition of the Standard & Poor's 500 stock index. Investment in an index fund is a relatively low-cost way for small investors to pursue a passive common stock investment strategy.

An individual investor choosing a mutual fund should consider not only the fund's stated investment policy but also its management fees and other expenses. Comparative data on virtually all important aspects of mutual funds are

Table 5.9   *Funds for Different Objectives*

Funds for Different Objectives

Not long ago, mutual funds were simply broad-based investments. Today, they can be highly specialized, and they serve very specific investment objectives.

What are the goals of the different funds?

There are mutual funds to meet almost any investment objective.

goal	kind of fund	potential price rise	potential current income	safety
maximum price rise	**aggressive growth funds** invest in common stock of fledgling companies and industries, out-of-favor companies and industries	very high	very low	low to very low
high capital gains	**growth funds** invest in common stock of settled companies and industries	high to very high	very low	low
price rise and current income	**growth and income funds** invest in companies with solid track records of consistent dividend payments	moderate	moderate	low to moderate
high current income	**fixed income and equity income funds** both invest in high-yielding stocks and bonds	very low	high to very high	low to moderate
high current income	**option income funds** invest in dividend paying common stock on which call options are traded	moderate	high to very high	low to moderate
current income and maximum safety	**general money market funds** invest in short-term debt securities **US Gov't money market funds** invest in treasury and agency issues	none	moderate to high	very high
current income, long-term growth and safety	**balanced funds** invest in a mixture of bonds, preferred stock and common stock	low	moderate to high	high
tax-free income and safety	**tax-free money market funds** invest in short-term municipal notes and bonds	none	moderate to high	very high
tax-free income	**municipal bond funds** invest in bonds exempt from state, local and federal taxes	low to moderate	moderate to high	moderate

Why investors choose mutual funds over other financial investments

	more diversification	professional management	higher returns	expert management	easier to invest in
	60%	45%	44%	37%	23%

Figure 5.5
Listing of funds offered by the Fidelity Group.
From *The Wall Street Journal,* May 10, 1991. Reprinted by permission of *THE WALL STREET JOURNAL,* © 1991 Dow Jones & Company, Inc. All Rights Reserved Worldwide.

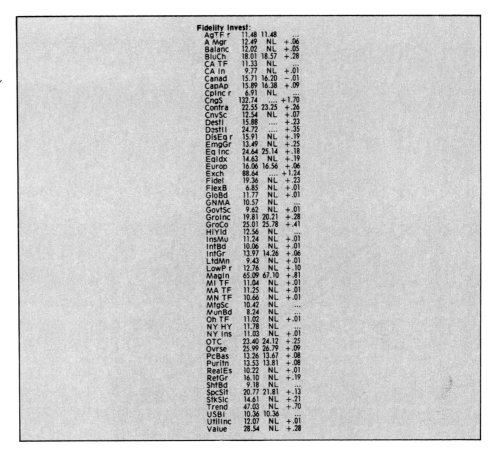

Fidelity Invest:			
AgTF r	11.48	11.48	...
A Mgr	12.49	NL	+.06
Balanc	12.02	NL	+.05
BluCh	18.01	18.57	+.28
CA TF	11.33	NL	...
CA In	9.77	NL	+.01
Canad	15.71	16.20	−.01
CapAp	15.89	16.38	+.09
CpInc r	6.91	NL	...
CngS	132.74	....	+1.70
Contra	22.55	23.25	+.26
CnvSc	12.54	NL	+.07
DestI	15.88	....	+.23
DestII	24.72	....	+.35
DisEq r	15.91	NL	+.19
EmgGr	13.49	NL	+.25
Eq Inc	24.64	25.14	+.18
EqIdx	14.63	NL	+.19
Europ	16.06	16.56	+.06
Exch	88.64	....	+1.24
Fidel	19.36	NL	+.23
FlexB	6.85	NL	+.01
GloBd	11.77	NL	+.01
GNMA	10.57	NL	...
GovtSc	9.62	NL	+.01
GroInc	19.81	20.21	+.28
GroCo	25.01	25.78	+.41
HiYld	12.56	NL	...
InsMu	11.24	NL	+.01
IntBd	10.06	NL	+.01
IntGr	13.97	14.26	+.06
LtdMn	9.43	NL	+.01
LowP r	12.76	NL	+.10
MagIn	65.09	67.10	+.81
MI TF	11.04	NL	+.01
MA TF	11.25	NL	+.01
MN TF	10.66	NL	+.01
MtgSc	10.42	NL	...
MunBd	8.24	NL	...
Oh TF	11.02	NL	+.01
NY HY	11.78	NL	...
NY Ins	11.03	NL	+.01
OTC	23.40	24.12	+.25
Ovrse	25.99	26.79	+.09
PcBas	13.26	13.67	+.08
Puritn	13.53	13.81	+.08
RealEs	10.22	NL	+.01
RetGr	16.10	NL	+.19
ShtBd	9.18	NL	...
SpcSit	20.77	21.81	+.13
StkSlc	14.61	NL	+.21
Trend	47.03	NL	+.70
USBI	10.36	10.36	...
UtilInc	12.07	NL	+.01
Value	28.54	NL	+.28

available in the annual volumes prepared by Wiesenberger Investment Companies Services, which can be found in most academic libraries.

Unit Investment Trusts

Unit investment trusts are pools of money invested in a portfolio that, in contrast to mutual funds, is fixed for the life of the fund. To form a unit trust, a sponsor, typically a brokerage firm, buys a set of securities and sells shares called *redeemable trust certificates* to investors at a premium (which is the trustee's fee) above NAV. All income and repayments of principal are paid out by the fund's trustee (a bank or trust company) to the shareholders. Most unit trusts hold fixed-income securities and expire at their maturity. There is no active management of a unit trust because the portfolio composition is fixed.

Commingled Funds

Commingled funds are investment pools managed by banks and insurance companies for trust or retirement accounts that are too small to warrant managing on a separate basis.

A commingled fund is similar in form to an open-end mutual fund. Instead of shares, though, the fund offers units that are bought and sold at net asset value.

Table 5.10   *The Major Mutual Fund Families*

Family	Total Net Assets ($ Billions)*	Number of Funds*	Range of Upfront or Deferred Sales Charges (%)	Basic Switching Limits or Charges‡	Comments
American Funds Group	$16.5	19	4.75 to 8.5	None	Vaunted 60-person research staff deserves much of the credit for strong overall family performance.
Dean Witter	20.0	14	4 to 5.5	None	Highly sales-driven group: last year 7,500 brokers hawked $1.2 billion in bond funds in 22 days.
Dreyfus Group	14.0	36	0 to 4.5	None	Chairman Howard Stein's launch of six risky (but top-gaining) strategic funds revitalized group.
Fidelity Investments	35.7	89	0 to 3.0†	4 switches a year	Incentive plan can boost fund managers' pay as much as 50% for market-whipping performance.
Franklin Group	30.0	42	4.0	$5 per switch	Early marketers of triple-tax-free muni funds; beware of 2.5% to 4% load on reinvested dividends.
Kemper	17.4	19	4.5 to 8.5	2 switches a month	High expense ratios (2% on average) cripple returns on popular, broker-sold Investment Portfolio series.

Modified from *Money*, May 1988.
*Excludes money market, institutional, and closed-end funds. Totals as of 12/31/87.
†Contractual-plan funds carry higher fees.
‡Excludes sector and international funds; rules for some funds may differ.
¶Switch out and return equals one round trip.

A bank or insurance company may offer an array of different commingled funds for trust or retirement accounts to choose from. Examples are a money market fund, a bond fund, and a common stock fund.

Real Estate Investment Trusts (REITs)

A REIT is similar to a closed-end mutual fund. REITs invest in real estate or loans secured by real estate. Besides issuing shares, they raise capital by borrowing from banks and issuing bonds and mortgages. Most of them are highly leveraged, with a typical debt ratio of 70 percent.

There are two principal kinds of REITs. *Equity trusts* invest in real estate directly, while *mortgage trusts* invest primarily in mortgage and construction

Table 5.10 *(concluded)*

Family	Total Net Assets ($ Billions)*	Number of Funds*	Range of Upfront or Deferred Sales Charges (%)	Basic Switching Limits or Charges‡	Comments
Merrill Lynch	23.0	27	0 to 6.5	2 switches a month	Standout growth-and-income managers generally follow relatively low-risk, value-oriented approach.
Putnam	29.7	30	4.75 to 8.5	$5 per switch	Excellent research, superior stock and muni bond fund performance, but, oh, those 8.5% loads.
Scudder	11.1	30	None	3 round trips per year¶	First big group to offer international funds (1953); Japan Fund, up 233%, among top 3-year gainers.
T. Rowe Price	8.3	20	None	2 switches per 120 days	First-rate service but middling overall performance; exceptions; international stock and bond funds.
Twentieth Century Investors	4.5	10	0 to 0.5	1 switch a month	Fee on small stock funds compensates existing shareholders with 0.5 % of new investments or withdrawals.
Vanguard Group	18.4	38	None	2 switches a year	Lowest expense ratios in the business (average: 0.4%) help bond and money market fund returns.

loans. REITs generally are established by banks, insurance companies, or mortgage companies, which then serve as investment managers to earn a fee.

REITs are exempt from taxes as long as at least 95 percent of their taxable income is distributed to shareholders. For shareholders, however, the dividends are taxable as personal income.

Summary

Firms issue securities to raise the capital necessary to finance their investments. Investment bankers market these securities to the public on the primary market. Investment bankers generally act as underwriters who purchase the securities from the firm and resell them to the public at a markup. Before the securities may be sold to the public, the firm must publish an SEC-approved prospectus that provides information on the firm's prospects.

2. Already-issued securities are traded on the secondary market, that is, on organized stock exchanges. Securities also trade on the over-the-counter market and, for large traders, through direct negotiation. Only members of exchanges may trade on the exchange. Brokerage firms holding seats on the exchange sell their services to individuals, charging commissions for executing trades on their behalf. The NYSE and, to a lesser extent, the AMEX have fairly strict listing requirements. Regional exchanges provide listing opportunities for local firms that do not meet the requirements of the national exchanges.

3. Trading of common stocks on exchanges occurs through specialists. The specialist acts to maintain an orderly market in the shares of one or more firms. The specialist maintains "books" of limit buy and sell orders and matches trades at mutually acceptable prices. Specialists also will accept market orders by selling from or buying for their own inventory of stocks when there is an imbalance of buy and sell orders.

4. The over-the-counter market is not a formal exchange but an informal network of brokers and dealers who negotiate sales of securities. The NASDAQ system provides on-line computer quotes offered by dealers in the stock. When an individual wishes to purchase or sell a share, the broker can search the listing of offered bid and ask prices, call the dealer with the best quote, and execute the trade.

5. Block transactions are a more recent, but fast-growing segment of the securities market that currently accounts for about half of trading volume. These trades often are too large to be handled readily by specialists and so have given rise to block houses that specialize in identifying potential trading partners for their clients.

6. Buying on margin means borrowing money from a broker in order to buy more securities than can be purchased with one's own money alone. By buying securities on a margin, an investor magnifies both the upside potential and the downside risk. If the equity in a margin account falls below the required maintenance level, the investor will get a margin call from the broker.

7. Short-selling is the practice of selling securities that the seller does not own. The short-seller borrows the securities sold through a broker and may be required to cover the short position at any time on demand. The cash proceeds of a short sale are always kept in escrow by the broker, and the broker usually requires that the short-seller deposit additional cash or securities to serve as margin (collateral) for the short sale.

8. Securities trading is regulated by the Securities and Exchange Commission as well as by self-regulation of the exchanges. Many of the important regulations have to do with full disclosure of relevant information concerning the securities in question. Insider trading rules also prohibit traders from attempting to profit from inside information.

9. In addition to providing the basic services of executing buy and sell orders, holding securities for safekeeping, making margin loans, and facilitating short sales, full-service brokers offer investors information, advice, and even investment decisions. Discount brokers offer only the basic brokerage services but usually charge less.

10. Total trading costs consist of commissions, the dealer's bid-ask spread, and price concessions. These costs can represent as much as 30 percent of the value of the securities traded.

11. As an alternative to investing in securities through a broker, many individuals invest in mutual funds and other investment companies. Mutual funds free the individual from many of the administrative burdens of owning individual securities and offer the prospect of superior investment results. Mutual funds are classified according to whether they are open- or closed-end, load or no-load, and by the type of securities they invest in. REITs are specialized investment companies that invest in real estate and loans secured by real estate.

Key Terms

ask price, 124	inside information, 137	primary market, 119
bid-ask spread, 142	load, 147	prospectus, 120
bid price, 124	margin, 133	secondary market, 119
block transactions, 131	NASDAQ, 124	short sales, 135
fourth market, 125	no-load fund, 147	specialist, 129
index fund, 149	Over-the-counter (OTC)	stock exchanges, 122
initial public offerings	market, 123	third market, 125
(IPOs), 120		underwriter, 120

Selected Readings

A good treatment of investment banking is:
> Smith, Clifford W. "Investment Banking and the Capital Acquisition Process." *Journal of Financial Economics* 15 (January–February 1986).

An overview of securities markets is provided in:
> Garbade, Kenneth D. *Securities Markets*. McGraw-Hill, New York, 1982.

The specialist system is examined in:
> Stoll, Hans R. "The Stock Exchange Specialist System: An Economic Analysis." *Monograph Series in Finance and Economics*. Graduate School of Business Administration, New York University, 1985.

An examination of market functioning during the October 1987 crash is in the so-called Brady Commission report, formally, the Report of the Presidential Task Force on Market Mechanisms.

The New York Stock Exchange Fact Book contains extensive data on exchange trading.

The behavior of IPOs is examined in:
> Ibbotson, Roger G. "Price Performance of Common Stock New Issues." *Journal of Financial Economics* 2 (September 1975), pp. 235–72; Rock, Kevin. "Why New Issues Are Underpriced." *Journal of Financial Economics* 15, pp. 187–212; and Ritter, Jay R. "The 'Hot Issue Market' of 1980." *Journal of Business* 57, pp. 215–40.

Problem Sets

1. FBN, Inc., has just sold 100,000 shares in an initial public offering. The underwriter's explicit fees were $70,000. The offering price for the shares was $50, but immediately upon issue, the share price jumped to $53.

  a. What is your best guess as to the total cost to FBN of the equity issue?

  b. Is the entire cost of the underwriting a source of profit to the underwriters?

2. Suppose you short-sell 100 shares of IBM, now selling at $120 per share.
   a. What is your maximum possible loss?
   b. What happens to the maximum loss if you simultaneously place a stop-buy order at $128?

3. An expiring put will be exercised and the stock sold if the stock price is below the exercise price. A stop loss order causes a stock sale when the stock price falls below some limit. Compare and contrast the two strategies of purchasing put options versus issuing a stop loss order.

4. Compare call options and limit buy orders.

5. Do you think it is possible to replace market-making specialists by a fully automated computerized trade matching system?

6. Consider the following limit order book of a specialist. The last trade in the stock occurred at a price of $50.

Limit Buy Orders		Limit Sell Orders	
Price	Shares	Price	Shares
49.75	500	50.25	100
49.50	800	51.50	100
49.25	500	54.75	300
49.00	200	58.25	100
48.50	600		

   a. If a market buy order for 100 shares comes in, at what price will it be filled?
   b. At what price would the next market buy order be filled?
   c. If you were the specialist, would you want to increase or decrease your inventory of this stock?

7. Consider the following data:

Year	Market Value of Shares Traded on NYSE ($ Millions)	Price on an NYSE Seat	
		High	Low
1965	73,200	$250,000	$190,000
1970	102,494	320,000	130,000
1975	131,705	138,000	55,000
1980	382,447	275,000	175,000
1985	980,772	480,000	310,000
1989	1,556,008	675,000	420,000

From New York Stock Exchange *Fact Book*, 1990.

   a. What do you conclude about the relationship between trading volume and the price of a seat?
   b. What happened in 1975 to upset this relationship?

8. You are bullish on AT&T stock. The current market price is $50 per share, and you have $5,000 of your own to invest. You borrow an additional $5,000 from your broker at an interest rate of 8 percent per year and invest $10,000 in the stock.

     a. What will be your rate of return if the price of AT&T stock goes up by 10 percent during the next year? (Ignore the expected dividend.)

     b. How far does the price of AT&T stock have to fall for you to get a margin call if the maintenance margin is 30 percent?

9. You are bearish on AT&T and decide to sell short 100 shares at the current market price of $50 per share.

     a. How much in cash or securities must you put into your brokerage account if the broker's initial margin requirement is 50 percent of the value of the short position?

     b. How high can the price of the stock go before you get a margin call if the maintenance margin is 30 percent of the value of the short position?

10. Call one full-service broker and one discount broker and find out the transaction costs of implementing the following strategies:

     a. Buying 100 shares of IBM now and selling them six months from now.

     b. Investing an equivalent amount in six-month at-the-money call options on IBM stock now and selling them six months from now.

Chapter

Risk and Return: The Basics

T his chapter introduces some key concepts and issues central to informed investment decision making. The material here is basic to the development of the theory in subsequent parts of the book. We start with what determines interest rates and risk premiums on risky securities. Then we review the historical record of rates of return on investments in the major asset classes—stocks, Treasury bonds, and Treasury bills—and of the rate of inflation. We also distinguish between real and nominal risk. We conclude by introducing the law of one price, which states that securities or combinations of securities will be priced so that no investor can make risk-free arbitrage profits by trading them. After studying this chapter you should be able to:

- Analyze the determinants of equilibrium real and nominal rates of interest.
- Cite the order of magnitude of historical means, standard deviations, and risk premiums of returns in major asset classes.
- Distinguish between real and nominal risk.
- Identify the law of one price and arbitrage.

6.1 *Determinants of the Level of Interest Rates*

Perhaps the single most important factor in investment decision making is the level of interest rates. Decisions depend to a great extent on forecasts of interest rates.

For example, suppose you have $10,000 in a savings account. The bank pays you a variable interest rate tied to some short-term reference rate such as the 30-day Treasury bill rate. You have the option of moving some or all of your money into a longer-term certificate of deposit that offers a fixed rate over the term of the deposit.

Your decision depends critically on your outlook for interest rates. If you think rates will fall, you will want to lock in the current higher rates by investing in a relatively long-term CD. If you expect rates to rise, you will want to postpone committing any funds to long-term CDs.

Forecasting interest rates is one of the most notoriously difficult parts of applied macroeconomics. Nonetheless, we do have a good understanding of the fundamental factors that determine the level of interest rates:

1. The supply of funds from savers, primarily households.
2. The demand for funds from businesses to be used to finance physical investments in plant, equipment, and inventories (real assets or capital formation).
3. The government's net supply and/or demand for funds as modified by actions of the Federal Reserve Bank.

Before we elaborate on these forces and resultant interest rates, we need to distinguish real from nominal interest rates.

Real and Nominal Rates of Interest

Suppose exactly one year ago you deposited $1,000 in a one-year time deposit guaranteeing a rate of interest of 10 percent. You are about to collect $1,100 in cash.

Is your $100 return for real? That depends on what money can buy these days, relative to what you *could* buy a year ago. The consumer price index (CPI) measures purchasing power by averaging the prices of goods and services in the consumption basket of an average urban family of four. While this basket may not represent your particular consumption plan, suppose for now that it does.

Suppose the rate of inflation (percent change in the CPI, denoted by i) for the last year amounted to $i = 6$ percent. This tells you the purchasing power of money is reduced by 6 percent a year. The value of each dollar depreciates by six percent a year in terms of the goods it can buy. Therefore, part of your interest earnings are offset by the reduction in the purchasing power of the dollars you will receive at the end of the year. With a 10 percent interest rate, after you net out the 6 percent reduction in the purchasing power of money, you are left with a net increase in purchasing power of about 4 percent. Thus, we need to distinguish between a **nominal interest rate**—the growth rate of your money— and a **real interest rate**—the growth rate of your purchasing power. If we call R the nominal rate, r the real rate, and i the inflation rate, then we conclude

$$r \approx R - i.$$

In words, the real rate of interest is the nominal rate reduced by the loss of purchasing power resulting from inflation.

In fact, the exact relationship between the real and nominal interest rate is given by:

$$1 + r = \frac{1 + R}{1 + i}$$

This is because the growth factor of your purchasing power, $1 + r$, equals the growth factor of your money, $1 + R$, divided by the new price level, that is

Nominal interest rate The interest rates in terms of nominal (not adjusted for purchasing power) dollars.

Real interest rate The excess of the interest rate over the inflation rate. The growth rate of purchasing power derived from an investment.

$1 + i$ times its value in the previous period. The exact relationship can be rearranged to

$$r = \frac{R - i}{1 + i}$$

that shows that the approximation rule overstates the real rate by the factor $1 + i$.

For example, if the interest rate on a one-year CD is 8 percent, and you expect inflation to be 5 percent over the coming year, then using the approximation formula, you expect the real rate to be $r = 8$ percent $- 5$ percent $= 3$ percent. Using the exact formula, the real rate is $r = \dfrac{.08 - .05}{1 + .05} = .0286$, or 2.86 percent. Therefore, the approximation rule overstates the expected real rate by only 0.14 percentage points. The approximation rule is more exact for small inflation rates and is perfectly exact for continuously compounded rates. We discuss further details in the appendix to this chapter.

Before the decision to invest, you would realize that conventional certificates of deposit offer a guaranteed *nominal* rate of interest. Thus, you can only infer what the expected real rate is by subtracting your expectation of what the rate of inflation will be.

It is always possible to calculate the real rate after the fact. The inflation rate is published by the Bureau of Labor Statistics (BLS). The future real rate, however, is unknown, and one has to rely on expectations. In other words, because future inflation is risky, the real rate of return is risky even if the nominal rate is risk free.

From January 1988 until recently, the Franklin Savings and Loan Association of Ottawa, Kansas, issued certificates of deposit that offered a guaranteed real rate of interest for maturities ranging from 1 to 10 years. Called "Inflation-Plus CDs," they were insured by the Federal Savings and Loan Insurance Corporation. The actual nominal rate of interest credited to your account was the promised real rate plus the rate of inflation as measured by the proportional increase in the CPI. Unfortunately, no other institution followed Franklin's lead, and that bank has gone under, so we still need to forecast real rates by inferring the expected rate of inflation that is impounded in nominal rates.

The Equilibrium Real Rate of Interest

Three basic factors—supply, demand, and government actions—determine the *real* interest rates. The nominal interest rate, which is the rate we actually observe, is the real rate plus the expected rate of inflation. So a fourth factor affecting the interest rate is the expected rate of inflation.

Although there are many different interest rates economywide (as many as there are types of securities), economists frequently talk as if there were a single representative rate. We can use this abstraction to gain some insights into determining the real rate of interest if we consider the supply and demand curves for funds.

Figure 6.1 shows a downward-sloping demand curve and an upward-sloping supply curve. On the horizontal axis, we measure the quantity of funds, and on the vertical axis, we measure the real rate of interest.

Figure 6.1
Determination of the equilibrium real rate of interest.

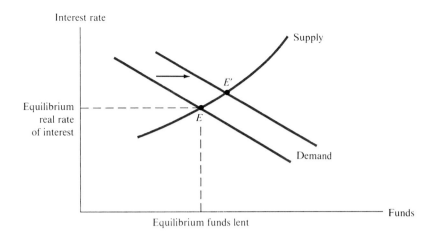

The supply curve slopes up from left to right because the higher the real interest rate, the greater the supply of household savings. The assumption is that at higher real interest rates households will choose to postpone some current consumption and set aside or invest more of their disposable income for future use.[1]

The demand curve slopes down from left to right because the lower the real interest rate, the more businesses will want to invest in physical capital. Assuming that businesses rank projects by the expected real return on invested capital, firms will undertake more projects the lower the real interest rate on the funds needed to finance those projects.

Equilibrium is at the point of intersection of the supply and demand curves, point *E* in Figure 6.1.

The government and the central bank (Federal Reserve) can shift these supply and demand curves either to the right or to the left through fiscal and monetary policies. For example, consider an increase in the government's budget deficit. This increases the government's borrowing demand and shifts the demand curve to the right, which causes the equilibrium real interest rate to rise to point *E'*. That is, a forecast that indicates higher than previously expected government borrowing increases expected future interest rates. The Fed can offset such a rise through an expansionary monetary policy, which will shift the supply curve to the right.

The Treasury and the Fed cannot shift the equilibrium rate of interest that easily, however. Short-term shifts in the interest rates achieved by increasing the money supply may result in changes in expected inflation that increase longer-term interest rates.

Thus, while the fundamental determinants of the real interest rate are the propensity of households to save and the expected productivity (or we could say profitability) of investment in physical capital, the real rate can be affected as well by government fiscal and monetary policies.

---

[1]There is considerable disagreement among experts on the issue of whether household saving does go up in response to an increase in the real interest rate.

The Equilibrium Nominal Rate of Interest

We've seen that the real rate of return on an asset is approximately equal to the nominal rate minus the inflation rate. Because investors should be concerned with their real returns—the increase in their purchasing power—we would expect that as the inflation rate increases, investors will demand higher nominal rates of return on their investments. This higher rate is necessary to maintain the expected real return offered by an investment.

Irving Fisher (1930) argued that the nominal rate ought to increase one for one with increases in the expected inflation rate. If we use the notation $E(i)$ to denote the current expectation of the inflation rate that will prevail over the coming period then we can state the so-called Fisher equation formally as:

$$R = r + E(i).$$

This relationship has been debated and empirically investigated. The equation implies that if real rates are reasonably stable, then increases in nominal rates ought to predict higher inflation rates. The results are mixed; while the data do not strongly support this relationship, nominal interest rates seem to predict inflation as well as alternative methods, in part because we are unable to forecast inflation well with any method.

One reason it is difficult to determine the empirical validity of the Fisher hypothesis that changes in nominal rates predict changes in future inflation rates is that the real rate also changes unpredictably over time. Nominal interest rates can be viewed as the sum of the required real rate on nominally risk-free assets, plus a "noisy" forecast of inflation.

In Part Three, we discuss the relationship between short- and long-term interest rates. Longer rates incorporate forecasts for long-term inflation. For this reason alone, interest rates on bonds of different maturity may diverge. In addition, we will see that prices of longer-term bonds are more volatile than those of short-term bonds. This implies that expected returns on longer-term bonds may include a risk premium, so that the expected real rate offered by bonds of varying maturity also may vary.

Concept Check

> *Question 1.*   *a.*   Suppose the real interest rate is 3 percent per year and the expected inflation rate is 8 percent. What is the nominal interest rate? *b.*   Suppose the expected inflation rate rises to 10 percent, but the real rate is unchanged. What happens to the nominal interest rate?

Taxes and the Real Rate of Interest

Tax liabilities are based on *nominal* income and the tax rate determined by the investor's tax bracket. Congress recognized the resultant "bracket creep" (when nominal income grows due to inflation and pushes taxpayers into higher brackets) and mandated index-linked tax brackets in the Tax Reform Act of 1986.

Index-linked tax brackets do not provide relief from the effect of inflation on the taxes of savings, however. Given a tax rate (t) and a nominal interest rate

(R), the after-tax interest rate is $R(1 - t)$. The real, after-tax rate is approximately the after-tax nominal rate minus the inflation rate:

$$R(1 - t) - i = (r + i)(1 - t) - i = r(1 - t) - it$$

Thus, the after-tax real rate of return falls as the inflation rate rises. Investors suffer an inflation penalty equal to the tax rate times the inflation rate. If, for example, you are in a 30 percent tax bracket and your investments yield 12 percent, while inflation runs at the rate of 8 percent, then your before-tax real rate is 4 percent, and you *should,* in an inflation-protected tax system, net after taxes $4(1 - .3) = 2.8$ percent. But the tax code does not recognize that the first 8 percent of your return is no more than compensation for inflation—not real income—and hence your tax includes an additional 8 percent $\times$ .3 = 2.4 percent, so that your after-tax real interest rate, at 0.4 percent, is almost wiped out.

6.2   *Risk and Risk Premiums*

Risk means uncertainty about future rates of return. We can quantify that uncertainty using probability distributions.

For example, suppose you are considering investing some of your money, now all invested in a bank account, in a stock market index fund. The price of a share in the fund is currently $100, and your *time horizon* is one year. You expect the cash dividend during the year to be $4, so your expected *dividend yield* is 4 percent.

Your total holding-period return (HPR) will depend on the price you expect to prevail one year from now. Suppose your best guess is that it will be $110 per share. Then your *capital gain* will be $10 and your HPR 14 percent. The definition of the holding period return in this context is capital gain income plus dividend income per dollar invested in the stock at the start of the period:

$$\text{HPR} = \frac{\text{Ending price of a share} - \text{Beginning price} + \text{Cash dividend}}{\text{Beginning price}}$$

In our case we have:

$$\text{HPR} = \frac{\$110 - \$100 + \$4}{\$100} = .14, \text{ or 14 percent.}$$

This definition of the HPR assumes the dividend is paid at the end of the holding period. To the extent that dividends are received earlier, the HPR ignores reinvestment income between the receipt of the payment and the end of the holding period. Recall also that the percent return from dividends is called the dividend yield, and so the dividend yield plus the capital gains yield equals HPR.

There is considerable uncertainty about the price of a share a year from now, however, so you cannot be sure about your eventual HPR. We can try to quantify our beliefs about the state of the economy and the stock market, however, in terms of three possible scenarios with probabilities as presented in Table 6.1.

How can we evaluate this probability distribution? Throughout this book we will characterize probability distributions of rates of return in terms of their expected or mean return, $E(r)$, and their standard deviation, σ. The expected

Table 6.1.   *Probability Distribution of HPR on the Stock Market*

State of the Economy	Probability	Ending Price	HPR
Boom	.25	$140	44%
Normal growth	.50	110	14
Recession	.25	80	−16

rate of return is a probability-weighted average of the rates of return in all scenarios. Calling $p(s)$ the probability of each scenario and $r(s)$ the HPR in each scenario, where scenarios are labeled or "indexed" by the variable s, we may write the expected return as:

$$E(r) = \sum_s p(s)r(s) \qquad (6.1)$$

Applying this formula to the data in Table 6.1, we find that the expected rate of return on the index fund is:

$$E(r) = .25 \times 44\% + .5 \times 14\% + .25 \times (-16\%) = 14\%.$$

The standard deviation of the rate of return (σ) is a measure of risk. It is defined as the square root of the variance, which in turn is defined as the expected value of the squared deviations from the expected return. The higher the volatility in outcomes, the higher will be the average value of these squared deviations. Therefore, variance and standard deviation measure the uncertainty of outcomes. Symbolically,

$$\sigma^2 = \sum_s p(s) [r(s) - E(r)]^2 \qquad (6.2)$$

Therefore, in our example,

$$\sigma^2 = .25(44 - 14)^2 + .5(14 - 14)^2 + .25(-16 - 14)^2 = 450$$

and

$$\sigma = 21.21\%.$$

Clearly, what would trouble potential investors in the index fund is the downside risk of a −16 percent rate of return, not the upside potential of a 44 percent rate of return. The standard deviation of the rate of return does not distinguish between these two; it treats both as deviations from the mean. As long as the probability distribution is more or less symmetric about the mean, however, σ is an adequate measure of risk. In the special case where we can assume that the probability distribution is normal—represented by the well-known bell-shaped curve—$E(r)$ and σ are perfectly adequate to characterize the distribution.

Getting back to the example, how much, if anything, should you invest in the index fund? First, you must ask how much of an expected reward is offered for the risk involved in investing money in stocks.

Risk-free rate   The interest rate that can be earned with certainty.

We measure the reward as the difference between the expected HPR on the index stock fund and the **risk-free rate,** that is, the rate you can earn by leaving money in risk-free assets such as T-bills, money market funds, or the bank. We

Risk premium   An expected return in excess of that on risk-free securities.

Risk aversion   A risk-averse investor will consider risky portfolios only if they offer a risk premium.

call this difference the **risk premium** on common stocks. If the risk-free rate in the example is 6 percent per year, and the expected index fund return is 14 percent, then the risk premium on stocks is 8 percent per year.

The degree to which investors are willing to commit funds to stocks depends on **risk aversion.** CFAs and finance theorists generally assume investors are risk averse in the sense that, if the risk premium were zero, people would not be willing to invest any money in stocks. In theory then, there must always be a positive risk premium on stocks in order to induce risk-averse investors to hold the existing supply of stocks instead of placing all their money in risk-free assets.

Although this simple scenario analysis illustrates the concepts behind the quantification of risk and return, you may still wonder how to get a more realistic estimate of $E(r)$ and σ for common stocks and other types of securities. Here history has insights to offer.

6.3   *The Historical Record*

Bills, Bonds, and Stocks, 1926–1990

The record of past rates of return is one possible source of information about risk premiums and standard deviations. We can estimate the historical risk premium by taking an average of the past differences between the HPRs on an asset class and the risk-free rate. Table 6.2 presents the annual HPRs on three asset classes for the period 1926–1990.

The fourth column shows the one-year HPR on a policy of "rolling over" 30-day Treasury bills as they mature. Because T-bill rates can change from month to month, the total rate of return on T-bills is riskless only for 30-day holding periods. The third column presents the annual HPR an investor would have earned by investing in U.S. Treasury bonds with 20-year maturities. The second column is the HPR on the Standard & Poor's Composite Index of common stocks, the value-weighted stock portfolio of 500 of the largest corporations in the United States. Finally, the last column gives the annual inflation rate as measured by the rate of change in the CPI.

At the bottom of each column are four descriptive statistics. The first is the arithmetic mean or average HPR. For bills, it is 3.73 percent; for bonds, 4.90 percent; and for common stock, 12.13 percent. These numbers imply an average risk premium of 1.17 percent per year on bonds and 8.40 percent on stocks (the average risk premium is the average HPR less the average risk-free rate of 3.73 percent).

The second statistic reported at the bottom of Table 6.2 is the standard deviation. The higher the standard deviation, the higher the variability of the HPR.

This standard deviation is based on historical data rather than forecasts of *future* scenarios as in Equation 6.2. The formula for historical variance, however, is similar to Equation 6.2:

$$\sigma^2 = \frac{n}{n-1} \sum_{t=1}^{n} \frac{(r_t - \bar{r})^2}{n}$$

Table 6.2. *Rates of Return, 1926 to 1990*

Date	Stocks	Long-Term Government Bonds	Treasury Bills	Inflation (CPI)
1926	0.1162	0.0777	0.0327	−0.0149
1927	0.3749	0.0893	0.0312	−0.0208
1928	0.4361	0.001	0.0324	−0.0097
1929	−0.0842	0.0342	0.0475	0.0019
1930	−0.249	0.0466	0.0241	−0.0603
1931	−0.4334	−0.0531	0.0107	−0.0952
1932	−0.0819	0.1684	0.0096	−0.103
1933	0.5399	−0.0008	0.003	0.0051
1934	−0.0144	0.1002	0.0016	0.0203
1935	0.4767	0.0498	0.0017	0.0299
1936	0.3392	0.0751	0.0018	0.0121
1937	−0.3503	0.0023	0.0031	0.031
1938	0.3112	0.0553	−0.0002	−0.0278
1939	−0.0041	0.0594	0.0002	−0.0048
1940	−0.0978	0.0609	0	0.0096
1941	−0.1159	0.0093	0.0006	0.0972
1942	0.2034	0.0322	0.0027	0.0929
1943	0.259	0.0208	0.0035	0.0316
1944	0.1975	0.0281	0.0033	0.0211
1945	0.3644	0.1073	0.0033	0.0225
1946	−0.0807	−0.001	0.0035	0.1817
1947	0.0571	−0.0263	0.005	0.0901
1948	0.055	0.034	0.0081	0.0271
1949	0.1879	0.0645	0.011	−0.018
1950	0.3171	0.0006	0.012	0.0579
1951	0.2402	−0.0394	0.0149	0.0587
1952	0.1837	0.0116	0.0166	0.0088
1953	−0.0099	0.0363	0.0182	0.0063
1954	0.5262	0.0719	0.0086	−0.005
1955	0.3156	−0.013	0.0157	0.0037
1956	0.0656	−0.0559	0.0246	0.0286
1957	−0.1078	0.0745	0.0314	0.0302
1958	0.4336	−0.061	0.0154	0.0176
1959	0.1196	−0.0226	0.0295	0.015
1960	−0.0047	0.1378	0.0266	0.0148
1961	0.2689	0.0097	0.0213	0.0067

Here, each year's outcome (r_t) is taken as a possible scenario. (We multiply by $n/(n-1)$ to eliminate statistical bias in the estimate of variance.) Deviations are simply taken from the historical average, $\bar{r}$, instead of the expected value $E(r)$. Each historical outcome is taken as equally likely and given a "probability" of $1/n$.

Figure 6.2 gives a graphic representation of the relative variabilities of the annual HPR for the three different asset classes. We have plotted the three time series on the same set of axes, each in a different color. The graph shows very clearly that the annual HPR on stocks is the most variable series. The standard deviation of stock returns has been 20.6 percent compared to 8.5 percent for bonds and 3.4 percent for bills. Here is evidence of the risk-return trade-off that

Table 6.2 *(concluded)*

Date	Stocks	Long-Term Government Bonds	Treasury Bills	Inflation (CPI)
1962	−0.0873	0.0689	0.0273	0.0122
1963	0.228	0.0121	0.0312	0.0165
1964	0.1648	0.0351	0.0354	0.0119
1965	0.1245	0.0071	0.0393	0.0192
1966	−0.1006	0.0365	0.0476	0.0335
1967	0.2398	−0.0919	0.0421	0.0304
1968	0.1106	−0.0026	0.0521	0.0472
1969	−0.085	−0.0508	0.0658	0.0611
1970	0.0401	0.121	0.0653	0.0549
1971	0.1431	0.1323	0.0439	0.0336
1972	0.1898	0.0568	0.0384	0.0341
1973	−0.1466	−0.0111	0.0693	0.088
1974	−0.2647	0.0435	0.08	0.122
1975	0.372	0.0919	0.058	0.0701
1976	0.2384	0.1675	0.0508	0.0481
1977	−0.0718	−0.0067	0.0512	0.0677
1978	0.0656	−0.0116	0.0718	0.0903
1979	0.1844	−0.0122	0.1038	0.1331
1980	0.3242	−0.0395	0.1124	0.124
1981	−0.0491	0.0185	0.1471	0.0894
1982	0.2141	0.4035	0.1054	0.0387
1983	0.2251	0.0068	0.088	0.038
1984	0.0627	0.1543	0.0985	0.0395
1985	0.3216	0.3097	0.0772	0.0377
1986	0.1847	0.2444	0.0616	0.0113
1987	0.0523	−0.0269	0.0547	0.0441
1988	0.1681	0.0967	0.0635	0.0442
1989	0.3149	0.1811	0.0837	0.0465
1990	−0.0317	0.0618	0.0781	0.0611
Average	0.1213	0.0490	0.0373	0.0325
Standard deviation	0.2064	0.0846	0.0336	0.0471
Minimum	−0.4334	−0.0919	−0.0002	−0.1030
Maximum	0.5399	0.4035	0.1471	0.1817

Data from the Center for Research of Security Prices, University of Chicago, Chicago.

characterizes security markets: The markets with the highest average returns also are the most volatile.

The other summary measures at the end of Table 6.2 show the highest and lowest annual HPR (the range) for each asset over the 65-year period. The extent of this range is another measure of the relative riskiness of each asset class. It, too, confirms the ranking of stocks as the riskiest and bills as the least risky of the three asset classes.

An all-stock portfolio with a standard deviation of 20.6 percent would represent a very volatile investment. For example, if stock returns are normally distributed with a standard deviation of 20.6 percent and an expected rate of return of 12.1 percent (the historical average), in roughly one year out of three, returns

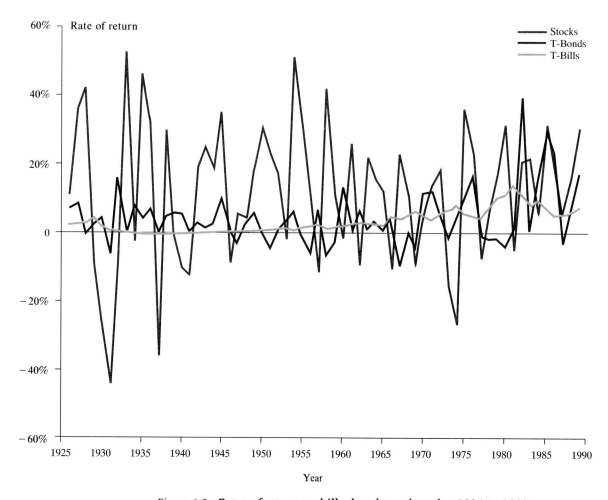

Figure 6.2 **Rates of return on bills, bonds, and stocks, 1926 to 1990.**

will be less than −8.5 percent (12.1 − 20.6) or greater than 32.7 percent (12.1 + 20.6).

Figure 6.3 is a graph of the normal curve with mean 12.1 percent and standard deviation 20.6 percent. The graph shows the theoretical probability of rates of return within various ranges given these parameters.

Figure 6.4 presents another view of the historical data, the actual frequency distribution of returns on various asset classes over the period 1926–1989. Again, the greater range of stock returns relative to bill or bond returns is obvious. Figure 6.4 suggests a risk-return trade-off in the security market. Common stocks, which are represented by the S&P 500 Index, have shown greater volatility of returns than bonds, but have offered higher average returns to investors. Similarly, examining the returns of small stocks, we see even more volatility than for the S&P 500, and correspondingly higher average returns.

We should stress that variability of HPR in the past can be an unreliable guide to risk, at least in the case of the risk-free asset. For an investor with a holding period of one year, for example, a one-year T-bill is a riskless investment, at least in terms of its nominal return, which is known with certainty. However, the standard deviation of the one-year T-bill rate estimated from historical data

Figure 6.3
**The normal
distribution.**

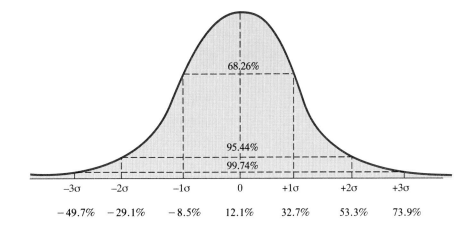

Figure 6.4
**Frequency
distributions of the
annual HPR on five
asset classes.**
(Modified from *Stocks,
Bonds, Bills and
Inflation*[SBBI]: *1990
Yearbook*, (Chicago:
Ibbotson Associates).

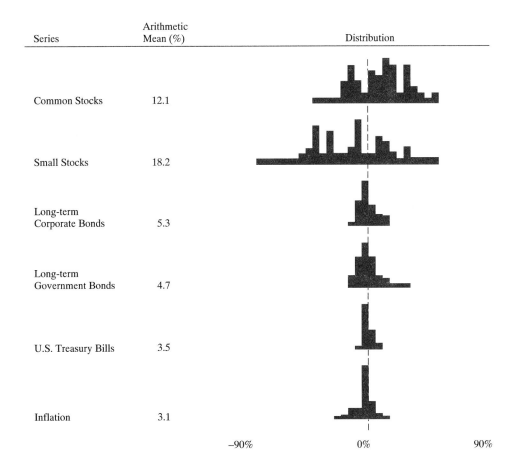

is not zero: This reflects variation in expected returns rather than fluctuations of actual returns around prior expectations.

Does the risk of the HPR on a financial asset reflect the risk of the cash flows from the real assets on which the financial assets are a claim? This is one of the most interesting and elusive questions in empirical finance. Ideally, the answer would be in the affirmative, reflecting prudent and competitive investment practices. So far, the evidence is inconclusive.

The risk of cash flows of real assets reflects both *business risk* (profit fluctuations due to business conditions) and *financial risk* (increased profit fluctuations due to leverage). This reminds us that an all-stock portfolio represents claims to corporate levered equity. Most corporations carry some debt, the service of which is a fixed cost. Greater fixed cost makes profits riskier; thus, leverage increases equity risk.

Concept Check

▪ ▪ ▪ ▪ ▪ ▪ ▪

Question 2.   Compute the average excess return on stocks (over the T-bill rate) and its standard deviation for the years 1926–1934.

Bills and Inflation, 1950–1990

A very important empirical relationship is the connection between inflation and the rate of return on T-bills. This is apparent in Figure 6.5, which plots both time series on the same set of axes. Both series tend to move together, which is consistent with our previous statement that expected inflation is a significant force determining the nominal rate of interest.

In the case of a holding period of 30 days, the difference between actual and expected inflation is not large. The 30-day bill rate will adjust rapidly to changes in expected inflation induced by observed changes in actual inflation. It is not surprising that we see nominal rates on bills move roughly in tandem with inflation over time.

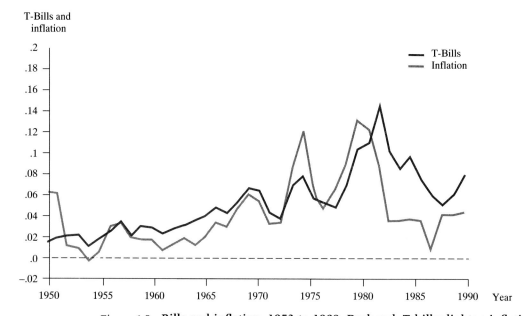

Figure 6.5   **Bills and inflation, 1953 to 1989. Dark red, T-bills: lighter, inflation.**

Investing: What to Buy When?

In making broad-scale investment decisions, investors may want to know how various types of investments have performed during booms, recessions, high inflation, and low inflation. The table shows how 10 asset categories performed during representative years since World War II. But history rarely repeats itself, so historical performance is only a rough guide to the future.

Investment	Average Annual Return on Investment*			
	Recession	Boom	High Inflation	Low Inflation
Bonds (long-term government)	17%	4%	−1%	8%
Commodity index	1	−6	15	−5
Diamonds (1-carat investment grade)	−4	8	79	15
Gold† (bullion)	−8	−9	105	19
Private home	4	6	6	5
Real estate‡ (commercial)	9	13	18	6
Silver (bullion)	3	−6	94	4
Stocks (blue chip)	14	7	−3	21
Stocks (small growth-company)	17	14	7	12
Treasury bills (3-month)	6	5	7	3

Modified from *The Wall Street Journal*, November 13, 1987. Reprinted by permission of *THE WALL STREET JOURNAL*, © 1987 Dow Jones & Company, Inc. All Rights Reserved Worldwide.

*In most cases, figures are computed as follows: Recession—average of performance during calendar years 1946, 1975, and 1982; boom—average of 1951, 1965, and 1984; high inflation—average of 1947, 1974, and 1980; low inflation—average of 1955, 1961, and 1986.

†Gold figures are based only on data since 1971 and may be less reliable than others.

‡Commercial real estate figures are based only on data since 1978 and may be less reliable than others.

Sources: Commerce Dept.; Commodity Research Bureau; DeBeers Inc.; Diamond Registry; Dow Jones & Co.; Dun & Bradstreet; Handy & Harman; Ibbotson Associates; Charles Kroll (Diversified Investor's Forecast); Merril Lynch; National Council of Real Estate Investment Fiduciaries; Frank B. Russell Co.; Shearson Lehman Bros.; T. Rowe Price New Horizons Fund.

6.4   *Real versus Nominal Risk*

The distinction between the real and the nominal rate of return is crucial in making investment choices when investors are interested in the future purchasing power of their wealth. Thus, a U.S. Treasury bond that offers a "risk-free" *nominal* rate of return is not truly a risk-free investment—it does not guarantee the future purchasing power of its cash flow.

An example might be a bond that pays $1,000 on a date 20 years from now but nothing in the interim. While some people see such a zero-coupon bond as a convenient way for individuals to lock in attractive, risk-free, long-term interest rates (particularly in IRA or Keogh[2] accounts), the evidence in Table 6.3 is rather discouraging about the value of $1,000 in 20 years in terms of today's purchasing power.

[2]A tax shelter for self-employed individuals.

Table 6.3   *Purchasing Power of $1,000 20 Years from Now and 20-Year Real Annualized HPR*

Assumed Annual Rate of Inflation	Number of Dollars Required 20 Years from Now to Buy What $1 Buys Today	Purchasing Power of $1,000 to Be Received in 20 Years	Annualized Real HPR
4%	$2.19	$456.39	7.69%
6	3.21	311.80	5.66
8	4.66	214.55	3.70
10	6.73	148.64	1.82
12	9.65	103.67	

Purchase price of bond is $103.67

Nominal 20-year annualized HPR is 12% per year.

Purchasing power = $1,000/(1 + inflation rate)^{20}.

Real HPR, R, is computed from the following relationship:
$$R = (1 + r)/(1 + i) - 1$$
$$= 1.12/(1 + i) - 1$$

Suppose the price of the bond is $103.67, giving a nominal rate of return of 12 percent per year (since $103.67 \times 1.12^{20} = 1,000$). We can compute the real annualized HPR for each inflation rate.

A revealing comparison is at a 12 percent rate of inflation. At that rate, Table 6.3 shows that the purchasing power of the $1,000 to be received in 20 years would be $103.67, what was paid initially for the bond. The real HPR in these circumstances is zero. When the rate of inflation equals the nominal rate of interest, the price of goods increases just as fast as the money accumulated from the investment, and there is no growth in purchasing power.

At an inflation rate of only 4 percent per year, however, the purchasing power of $1,000 will be $456.39 in terms of today's prices; that is, the investment of $103.67 grows to a real value of $456.39, for a real 20-year annualized HPR of 7.69 percent per year.

Again looking at Table 6.3, you can see that an investor expecting an inflation rate of 8 percent per year anticipates a real annualized HPR of 3.70 percent. If the actual rate of inflation turns out to be 10 percent per year, the resulting real HPR is only 1.82 percent per year. These differences show the important distinction between expected and actual inflation rates.

Even professional economic forecasters acknowledge that their inflation forecasts are hardly certain even for the next year, not to mention the next 20. When you look at an asset from the perspective of its future purchasing power, you can see that an asset that is riskless in nominal terms can be very risky in real terms.

Concept Check

Question 3.   Suppose the rate of inflation turns out to be 13 percent per year. What will be the real annualized 20-year HPR on the nominally risk-free bond?

6.5   *Risk in a Portfolio Context*

Hedging Investing in an asset to reduce the overall risk of a portfolio.

The riskiness of a security cannot be judged in isolation from an investor's entire portfolio of assets. Sometimes, adding a seemingly risky asset to a portfolio actually reduces the risk of the portfolio as a whole. Investing in an asset in order to reduce the overall risk of a portfolio is called **hedging.**

The most direct example of hedging is an insurance contract, which is a legal arrangement transferring a specific risk from the insured to the insurer for a specified cost (the insurance premium). Suppose you own a $100,000 house and have total net worth of $300,000. There is a small possibility that your house will burn to the ground within the coming year. If it does, your net wealth will be reduced by $100,000. If it does not, your wealth remains unchanged (independent of any income from this and other investments, which we shall ignore to simplify the example).

Say your probability assessment of the event "the house will burn to the ground during the coming year" is 0.002. Your expected loss (0.002 × $100,000 = $200) is small in terms of your overall wealth. On the other hand, a fire would reduce your wealth by a full one third.

An insurance contract to cover this risk might cost $220, a price that exceeds the expected loss and thereby provides expected profit to the insurer. If we evaluate the payoff to the insurance contract in isolation, insurance looks like a risky security.

Not only is the expected profit of the policy negative (−$20), and the expected rate of return negative (−20/220 = −9.09 percent), but the risk also seems to be substantial. The standard deviation of the policy's payoff is identical to that of the uninsured house. You receive either $100,000 (with probability 0.002) or nothing (with probability 0.998), a payoff structure that might remind you of a lottery.

Does this mean only risk lovers should purchase insurance? Clearly not. Instead, the example illustrates the fallacy of evaluating the risk of an asset (the insurance contract) separately from the other assets owned by the investor.

Consider the insured house as a *portfolio* that includes the insurance contract and the house.

Portfolio Component	Value if No Fire	Value if Fire
House	$100,000	0
Insurance contract	0	$100,000

The portfolio payoff in the two outcomes is identical and equal to $100,000 because the house is insured for its precise value, and the insurance kicks in only when the value of the house goes to zero (in the event of a fire). Thus, the portfolio's overall risk has been reduced to zero.

Hedging can be expected to have some costs, the insurance premium in this example. Adding the cost of the insurance premium to the house, you have an investment of $100,220.

The lesson of this example is that while people are concerned about the volatility of the value of their overall portfolios, they do *not* necessarily dislike volatility in individual components of their portfolios. This has important implications for the measurement of asset risk, the topic of Chapter 9. Most risk-averse people would invest in the "risky" insurance policy we describe, even with its negative expected HPR.

6.6   *The Law of One Price and Arbitrage*

Arbitrage   A zero-risk, zero-net investment strategy that still generates profits.

One of the most fundamental concepts in investments is arbitrage, as you will see again and again throughout this book. **Arbitrage** is the act of buying an asset at one price and simultaneously selling it or its equivalent at a higher price.

If you can buy Kodak stock over the counter for $128.00 per share and sell it on the New York Stock Exchange for $128.50, you can make a risk-free arbitrage profit of 50 cents per share. Furthermore, by synchronizing the purchase and sale you might not have to tie up any of your own funds in the transaction. You can use the proceeds from the sale at $128.50 to finance the purchase at $128 and clear the 50 cents without investing any of your own money.

Pure arbitrage opportunities of this sort are understandably rare, because it takes the participation of only a few (maybe only one) arbitrageurs to eliminate the price differential. The increased demand for Kodak by arbitrageurs buying on the OTC market would tend to drive the price above $128, and the increased supply of Kodak on the NYSE would drive the price down, until the stock would reach a single price in both markets.

This is of course a simplified example of arbitrage and the activity of arbitrageurs. In practice, there are transaction costs to deal with, and often the arbitrage opportunity involves not one security but combinations of securities. We will see in later chapters that Kodak stock can be created synthetically, using Kodak options plus T-bills, and arbitrage considerations, therefore, dictate a pricing relationship that must hold among these securities.

Practitioners and academicians may often disagree about the right way to characterize equilibrium yield and price relationships, but almost everyone would agree that the *law of one price* holds almost all of the time in the securities markets. Stated simply, the law of one price is that equivalent securities or bundles of securities are priced so that risk-free arbitrage is not possible.

Summary

1.   The economy's equilibrium level of real interest rates depends on the willingness of households to save, as reflected in the supply curve of funds, and on the expected profitability of business investment in plant, equipment, and inventories, as reflected in the demand curve for funds. It depends also on government fiscal and monetary policy.

2.   The nominal rate of interest is the equilibrium real rate plus the expected rate of inflation. In general, we can directly observe only nominal interest rates; from them, we must infer expected real rates, using inflation forecasts. The existence of securities that offer a guaranteed real rate allows us to observe ex-

pected inflation, by subtracting that real rate from the nominal rate on nominally risk-free bonds.

3. The equilibrium expected rate of return on any security is the sum of the equilibrium real rate of interest, the expected rate of inflation, and a security-specific risk premium.

4. Investors face a trade-off between risk and expected return. Historical data confirm our intuition that assets with low degrees of risk provide lower returns on average than do those of higher risk.

5. Assets with guaranteed nominal interest rates are risky in real terms because the future inflation rate is uncertain.

6. The riskiness of a security should always be viewed in the context of an investor's total portfolio of assets. Some securities, such as insurance contracts, that would seem quite risky in isolation actually help reduce the risk of an investor's overall portfolio.

7. The "law of one price" says two securities or groups of securities with the same payoff structure must sell for the same price. If two identical securities (or packages of securities) are selling in two markets at different prices, it should be profitable to buy the security in the low-priced market and sell it in the high-proceed market simultaneously. In the process, arbitrageurs, who engage in this activity for a profit, drive up the price in the low-price market and drive down the price in the high-priced market, eliminating the price differential.

Key Terms

arbitrage, 174   real interest rate, 159   risk-free rate, 164
hedging, 173   risk aversion, 165   risk premium, 165
nominal interest
  rate, 159

Selected Readings

The classic work on the determination of the level of interest rates is:
  Fisher, Irving. *The Theory of Interest: As Determined by Impatience to Spend Income and Opportunity to Invest It.* New York: Augustus M. Kelley, Publishers, 1965, originally published in 1930.

The standard reference for historical returns on a variety of instruments, updated annually is:
  Stocks, Bonds, Bills and Inflation: 1991 Yearbook. Chicago: Ibbotson Associates, Inc., 1991.

For an in-depth treatment of the distinction between real and nominal risk read:
  Bodie, Zvi. "Investment Strategy in an Inflationary Environment." In *The Changing Roles of Debt and Equity in Financing U.S. Capital Formation*, Benjamin M. Friedman, ed. Chicago: University of Chicago Press, 1982.

Problem Sets

1. You have $5,000 to invest for the next year and are considering three alternatives:
  a. A money market fund with an average maturity of 30 days offering a current yield of 6 percent per year.
  b. A one-year savings deposit at a bank offering an interest rate of 7.5 percent.

 c. A 20-year U.S. Treasury bond offering a yield to maturity of 9 percent per year.

What role does your forecast of future interest rates play in your decisions?

2. Use Figure 6.1 in the text to analyze the effect of the following on the level of real interest rates:

   a. Businesses become more optimistic about future demand for their products and decide to increase their capital spending.

   b. Households are induced to save more because of increased uncertainty about their future social security benefits.

   c. The Federal Reserve Board undertakes open market sales of U.S. Treasury securities in order to reduce the supply of money.

3. You are considering the choice between investing $50,000 in a conventional one-year bank CD offering an interest rate of 8 percent and a one-year Inflation-Plus CD offering 3 percent per year plus the rate of inflation.

   a. Which is the safer investment?

   b. Which offers the higher expected return?

   c. If you expect the rate of inflation to be 4 percent over the next year, which is the better investment? Why?

   d. If we observe a risk-free nominal interest rate of 8 percent per year and a risk-free real rate of 3 percent, can we infer that the market's expected rate of inflation is 5 percent per year?

4. Look at Table 6.1 in the text. Suppose you now revise your expectations regarding the stock market as follows:

State of the Economy	Probability	Ending Price	HPR
Boom	.3	$140	44%
Normal growth	.4	110	14
Recession	.3	80	−16

Use Equations 6.1 and 6.2 to compute the mean and standard deviation of the HPR on stocks. Compare your revised parameters with the ones in the text.

5. Derive the probability distribution of the one-year HPR on a 30-year U.S. Treasury bond with a 9 percent coupon if it is currently selling at par and the probability distribution of its yield to maturity a year from now is as follows:

State of the Economy	Probability	YTM
Boom	.25	12.0%
Normal growth	.50	9.0
Recession	.25	7.5

For simplicity, assume the entire 9 percent coupon is paid at the end of the year rather than every six months.

6. Using the historical risk premiums as your guide, what is your estimate of the expected annual HPR on the S&P 500 stock portfolio if the current risk-free interest rate is 8 percent?

7. Compute the means and standard deviations of the annual HPR listed in Table 6.2 of the text using only the last 30 years, 1961–1990. How do these statistics

compare with those computed from the data for the period 1926–1941? Which do you think are the most relevant statistics to use for projecting into the future?

8. During a period of severe inflation, a bond offered a nominal HPR of 80 percent per year. The inflation rate was 70 percent per year.
   a. What was the real HPR on the bond over the year?
   b. Compare this real HPR to the approximation $R = r - i$.

9. You own a house worth $250,000 and intend to insure it fully against fire for the next year. Suppose the probability of its burning to the ground during the year is 0.001 and that an insurance policy covering the full value costs $500.
   Consider the insurance policy as a security.
   a. What is its expected holding-period return?
   b. What is the standard deviation of its HPR?
   c. Is the policy a risky asset? Why?

10. Suppose that the inflation rate falls to 3 percent in the near future. Using the historical data provided in this chapter, what would be your predictions for:
    a. The T-bill rate?
    b. The expected rate of return on the stock market?
    c. The risk premium on the stock market?

11. The unification of Germany has led to forecasts of huge amounts of capital investment in what was formerly East Germany. How might this development affect real interest rates?

12. Would anyone ever rationally invest in a stock if the expected total rate of return on the stock were less than the rate available on riskless T-bills? Relate your answer to the insurance example presented in the chapter.

Problems 13–14 represent a greater challenge. You may need to review the definitions of call and put options in Chapter 4.

13. You are faced with the probability distribution of the HPR on the stock market index fund given in Table 6.1 of the text. Suppose the price of a put option on a share of the index fund with exercise price $110 and maturity of one year is $12.
    a. What is the probability distribution of the HPR on the put option?
    b. What is the probability distribution of the HPR on a portfolio consisting of one share of the index fund and a put option?
    c. In what sense does buying the put option constitute a purchase of insurance in this case?
    d. Why can't the market price of the put option be less than $10 as long as the market price of the underlying stock is $100?

14. Take as given the conditions described in the previous question, and suppose the risk-free interest rate is 6 percent per year. You are contemplating investing $107.55 in a one-year CD and simultaneously buying a call option on the stock market index fund with an exercise price of $110 and a maturity of one year.
    a. What is the probability distribution of your dollar return at the end of the year?
    b. What must be the market price of the call option and why?

Appendix   *Continuous Compounding*

Suppose your money earns interest at an annual percentage rate (APR) of 6 percent per year compounded semiannually. What is your *effective* annual rate of return, accounting for compound interest?

We find the answer by first computing the per (compounding) period rate, 3 percent per half year, and then computing the future value (FV) at the end of the year per dollar invested at the beginning of the year. In this example, we get

$$FV = (1.03)^2 = 1.0609.$$

The effective annual rate (r_{EFF}) is just this number minus 1.0.

$$r_{EFF} = 1.0609 - 1 = .0609 = 6.09 \text{ percent per year.}$$

The general formula for the effective annual rate is:

$$r_{EFF} = \left(1 + \frac{APR}{n}\right)^n - 1$$

where APR is the annual percentage rate, and n the number of compounding periods per year. Table 6A.1 presents the effective annual rates corresponding to an annual percentage rate of 6 percent per year for different compounding frequencies.

As the compounding frequency increases, $(1 + APR/n)^n$ gets closer and closer to e^{APR} where e is the number 2.71828 (rounded off to the fifth decimal place). In our example, $e^{.06} = 1.0618365$. Therefore, if interest is continuously compounded, $r_{EFF} = .0618365$, or 6.18365 percent per year.

Using continuously compounded rates simplifies the algebraic relationship between real and nominal rates of return. To see how, let us compute the real rate of return first using annual compounding and then using continuous compounding. Assume the nominal interest rate is 6 percent per year compounded annually and the rate of inflation is 4 percent per year compounded annually. Using the relationship

$$\text{Real rate} = \frac{1 + \text{Nominal rate}}{1 + \text{Inflation rate}} - 1$$

$$r = \frac{(1 + R)}{(1 + i)} - 1 = \frac{R - i}{1 + i}$$

we find that the effective annual real rate is:

$$r = 1.06/1.04 - 1 = .01923 = 1.923 \text{ percent per year.}$$

With continuous compounding, the relationship becomes:

$$e^r = e^R/e^i = e^{R-i}.$$

Table 6A.1 *Effective Annual Rates for an APR of 6 percent*

Compounding Frequency	n	r_{EFF} (%)
Annually	1	6.00
Semiannually	2	6.09
Quarterly	4	6.13636
Monthly	12	6.16778
Weekly	52	6.17998
Daily	365	6.18313

Taking the natural logarithm we get:

$$r = R - i$$
Real rate = Nominal rate − Inflation rate

all expressed as annual, continuously compounded percentage rates.

Thus, if we assume a nominal interest rate of 6 percent per year compounded continuously and an inflation rate of 4 percent per year compounded continuously, the real rate is 2 percent per year compounded continuously.

To pay a fair interest rate to a depositor, the compounding frequency must be at least equal to the frequency of deposits and withdrawals. Only when you compound at least as frequently as transactions in an account, can you assure that each dollar will earn the full interest due for the exact duration it has been in the account. These days, on-line computing for deposits is feasible, so one expects the frequency of compounding to grow until the use of continuous compounding becomes the norm.

Part Two
Portfolio Theory

■ ■

Chapter

7

Capital Allocation to Risky Assets

The investment process consists, broadly speaking, of two tasks. One is security and market analysis, by which we assess the risk and expected return of the entire set of available investment vehicles. The second is construction of the optimal portfolio of assets, where we identify the set of efficient portfolios, those with the best risk-return characteristics.

We start our analysis of investments with the latter task and discuss the specifics of security, industry, and market analysis in later chapters.

This chapter introduces three broad themes of investment strategy, all related to risk:

1. Investors are risk averse and demand a risk premium for making risky investments.
2. Portfolio risk can be quantified by standard deviation and investors categorized by degree of risk aversion. The degree of risk aversion determines the risk premium an investor will demand given the standard deviation of the overall portfolio.
3. The risk of an individual asset must be assessed in the context of the portfolio of which it is a part. A proper measure of the risk of an individual asset is its impact on the volatility of the entire investment portfolio. Thus, seemingly risky securities may be portfolio stabilizers and actually low-risk assets.

There are two ways to control investment risk: (1) shift funds out of risky securities into safe (money market) assets, and (2) construct the risky portfolio efficiently, purging it of unnecessary risk. This chapter concentrates on the first technique. We call this an *asset allocation decision* because it requires choosing among broad asset classes; here, the choice is between risky versus money market securities.

In a "top-down" approach, we begin with asset allocation: how to mix the broad asset classes of an investor's portfolio. Only then do we consider how to select the securities within each asset class. This treatment offers a bird's-eye view of portfolio construction that helps us focus on fundamentals without getting lost in the intricacies of security selection. Our assumption is that asset allocation theory provides a greater perspective as background for the analytically more difficult security selection decision. After studying this chapter, you should be able to:

- Use the mean-variance framework to rank portfolios.
- Calculate the effect of a shift between risky and risk-free assets on the expected return and standard deviation of the complete portfolio.
- Choose among portfolios for investors with different degrees of risk aversion.

7.1 Risk and Risk Aversion

Risk with Simple Prospects

The presence of risk means more than one outcome is possible. A *simple prospect* is an investment opportunity in which a certain initial wealth is placed at risk, and there are only two possible outcomes. For the sake of simplicity, it is useful to begin our analysis and elucidate some basic concepts using simple prospects.

Take as an example initial wealth, W, of \$100,000, and assume two possible results. With a probability of $p = .6$, the favorable outcome will occur, leading to final wealth of $W_1 = \$150,000$. Otherwise, with probability $1-p = .4$, a less favorable outcome, $W_2 = \$80,000$, will occur. We can represent the simple prospect using an event tree:

$$W = \$100,000 \begin{cases} p = .6 & W_1 = \$150,000 \\ 1 - p = .4 & W_2 = \$80,000 \end{cases}$$

Suppose an investor, Susan, is offered an investment portfolio with a payoff in one year that is described by such a simple prospect. How can she evaluate this portfolio?

First, she could try to summarize it using descriptive statistics. For instance, her mean or expected end-of-year wealth, denoted $E(W)$, is

$$E(W) = pW_1 + (1-p)W_2$$
$$= [.6 \times 150,000] + [.4 \times 80,000] = \$122,000.$$

The expected profit on the \$100,000 investment portfolio is \$22,000: 122,000 − 100,000. The variance, σ^2, of the portfolio's payoff is calculated as the expected value of the squared deviations of each possible outcome from the mean:

$$\sigma^2 = p[W_1 - E(W)]^2 + (1 - p)[W_2 - E(W)]^2$$
$$= .6(150,000 - 122,000)^2 + .4(80,000 - 122,000)^2$$
$$= 1,176,000,247.$$

The standard deviation, σ, which is the square root of the variance, is $34,292.86.

Clearly, this is risky business. The standard deviation of the payoff is large, much larger than the expected profit of $22,000. Whether the expected profit is large enough to justify such risk depends on the alternative portfolios.

Suppose Treasury bills are one alternative to Susan's risky portfolio and that at the time of the decision, a one-year T-bill offers a rate of return of 5 percent; $100,000 can be invested to yield a sure profit of $5,000. We can now draw Susan's decision tree as

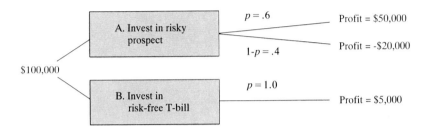

Earlier, we showed the expected profit on the portfolio to be $22,000. Therefore, the expected marginal, or incremental, profit of the risky portfolio over investing in safe T-bills is:

$$\$22,000 - \$5,000 = \$17,000,$$

meaning that one can earn a *risk premium* (expected return in excess of the risk-free return) of $17,000 as compensation for the risk of the investment.

The question of whether a given risk premium provides adequate compensation for the investment's risk is age-old. One of the central concerns of finance theory (and much of this text) is the measurement of risk and the determination of the risk premiums that investors can expect of risky assets in well-functioning capital markets.

Concept Check

Question 1. *a.* What is the risk premium of Susan's risky portfolio in terms of rate of return rather than dollars? *b.* What is the standard deviation of the rate of return?

Risk, Speculation, and Gambling

Speculators assume risk voluntarily and are often confused with gamblers, who also seek risk. The business of investors is speculation, so it is well to start by distinguishing them from gamblers.

One dictionary's definition of speculation is "the assumption of considerable business risk in obtaining commensurate gain." While this definition is fine linguistically, it is vague if we cannot specify what is meant by "considerable risk" and "commensurate gain."

By "considerable risk" we mean the risk is sufficient to affect the decision. An investor might reject an investment that offers a significant rate of return that is insufficient to make up for the risk involved. By "commensurate gain" we mean an expected return that is sufficiently greater than the risk-free alternative. This risk premium is the *incremental* expected return from taking on the risk.

To gamble is defined as "to bet or wager on an uncertain outcome." Compared to speculation, the central difference is the lack of "commensurate gain," the risk premium. Gambling is the assumption of risk for no purpose beyond the enjoyment of the risk itself, while speculation is undertaken despite the risk, because the speculator sees a favorable risk-return trade-off. Hence, risk aversion and speculation are not inconsistent. A gamble can be turned into a speculative investment if it is sweetened with an adequate risk premium to compensate risk-averse investors.

The financing of business activity involves the sale of risky financial assets. Thus, speculation is an integral part of the generation of real assets, and speculators are rewarded with a share of the wealth generated with their funds.

To offer gambling opportunities, risk must be created, as in the case of casino gambling, or at least administered, when the gamblers bet on events such as competitive sports. These costs must be born by the gamblers; hence, gambling must carry a negative risk premium. Moreover, compulsive gambling, which leads a gambler to participate (over time) in a large number of gambles, almost assures a negative average rate of return.

In some cases, a gamble may seem more like speculation to the participants. Suppose two investors disagree about the future exchange rate of the U.S. dollar against the Japanese yen. They decide to bet on their beliefs. Paul will pay Mary $100 if the value of $1 exceeds ¥150, or Mary will pay the same to Paul if $1 is worth ¥150 or less one year from now. There are two possible outcomes. If Paul and Mary agree on the probabilities, and if neither party anticipates a loss, then it must be that both assign $p = .5$ to each outcome. In that case, both *expect* a profit of zero, and each has entered a gambling prospect.

What is more likely, however, is that the bet results from a difference in the probabilities Paul and Mary assign to the event "one year from now, $1 will exceed ¥150." Mary assigns it $p > .5$, while Paul's assessment is $p \leq .5$. They perceive, subjectively, two different prospects. Economists call this a case of "heterogeneous expectations." In such cases, investors on each side of a financial position see themselves as speculating rather than gambling.

Both Paul and Mary should be wondering why the other is willing to invest on the side of a risky financial position that seemingly offers a negative expected return. (This is a variation of the Groucho Marx statement: "I would not be member of any club that would let me join.")

One way to resolve heterogeneous expectations is for Paul and Mary to "merge their information sets," that is, for each party to verify that he or she possesses and properly processes all relevant information. Of course, the acquisition of information and the extensive communication required to eliminate all heterogeneity in expectations are costly. Hence, up to a point, heterogeneous expectations cannot be taken as irrational. If, however, Paul and Mary enter such contracts frequently, they will recognize the information problem in one of two ways: if they each win half of the bets, they will realize they have been creating gambles. Otherwise, the consistent loser must admit to betting on inferior forecasts.

Concept Check

Question 2. A dollar-denominated T-bill in the United States and a pound-denominated bill in the United Kingdom offer equal yields. Both are short-term assets, free of default risk, and neither offers investors a risk premium. However, a U.S. investor who holds U.K. bills is subject to exchange rate risk, because the pounds earned on the U.K. bills eventually will be exchanged for dollars at the future exchange rate. Is the U.S. investor speculating or gambling?

A risky asset offering a zero risk premium, so that its expected return equals that of the risk-free asset, is called a *fair game*. For example, a gamble of "double or nothing," with probability of 0.5 has an expected rate of return of zero. Since no cash is put upfront for any considerable time, the opportunity cost in terms of the time value of money is also zero. Thus, this gamble is a fair game. If the probability of winning were increased, the game would become better than fair.

Risk-averse investors will reject investments that are fair games or worse. They are willing to consider only risk-free or speculative prospects (that by definition offer a positive risk premium).

Loosely speaking, a risk-averse investor "penalizes" the expected rate of return of a risky portfolio by a certain percentage to account for the risk involved. The greater the risk the investor associates with the asset, the larger the penalty. Observation of capital asset pricing in financial markets confirms this hypothesis for the average investor. The average investor engages in insurance (accepting a negative expected return in exchange for the risk-reducing profile of returns), and, more generally, observed risk premiums on financial assets are positively associated with risk.

Utility The measure of the welfare or satisfaction of an investor.

To formalize this notion of a risk penalty system, we will assume that each investor can assign a welfare or **utility** score to competing investment portfolios according to the expected return and risk of those portfolios. The utility score is a means of ranking portfolios. Higher utility values are assigned to portfolios with more attractive risk-return profiles. Portfolios receive higher utility scores for higher expected returns and lower scores for higher volatility.

Many scoring systems are legitimate. One reasonable function that is commonly employed by CFAs and financial theorists assigns a portfolio with expected return $E(r)$ and variance of returns σ^2 the following utility score:

$$U = E(r) - (1/2)A\sigma^2 \tag{7.1}$$

where U is the utility value, and A is an index of the investor's aversion to taking on risk. The factor of ½ is a scaling convention that has no economic significance.

Equation 7.1 is consistent with the notion that for risk-averse investors, utility is enhanced by high expected returns and diminished by high risk as measured by the variance.

The extent to which variance lowers utility depends on the magnitude of A, the investor's degree of risk aversion. More risk-averse investors (who have the larger As) penalize risky investments more severely. Investors choosing among competing investment portfolios will select the one providing the highest utility value.

To demonstrate, consider the choice between a portfolio with expected return $E(r) = .22$ (22 percent) and standard deviation $\sigma = .34$ (34 percent), and an investment in T-bills providing a risk-free return of $r_f = .05$ (5 percent). The risk premium on the risky portfolio is large, $E(r) - r_f = 22 - 5 = 17$ percent, but so is the portfolio risk. An investor need not be very risk averse to choose the safe all-bills strategy. Even for $A = 3$, a moderate risk-aversion parameter, Equation 7.1 shows the risky portfolio's utility value as 4.66 percent ($.22 - .5 \times 3 \times .34^2 = .0466$), which is lower than the risk-free rate.

The downward adjustment of the expected return as a penalty for risk is $.5 \times 3 \times .34^2 = .1734$ (17.34 percent). A less risk-averse (more risk-tolerant) investor, with, say $A = 2$, would adjust the expected rate of return downward by only 11.56 percent. In that case, the utility level of the portfolio would be 10.44 percent, more than the risk-free rate. Therefore, more risk-tolerant investors will choose the risky portfolio over T-bills.

In fact, the critical level of risk aversion, above which investors will choose T-bills over the portfolio in the example, can be calculated from Equation 7.1 as: the risk premium, $E(r) - r_f$, divided by half the variance. In our example, $.17/(.5 \times .34^2) = 2.9$.

To illustrate the plausibility of various values for the coefficient of risk aversion (A), consider the compensation an individual will require when asked to put up \$1,000 in a gamble of "double or nothing," with a probability of 0.5. The probability distribution in terms of rates of return is: plus or minus 1.0 (100 percent) with $p = .5$, implying a variance of $\sigma^2 = 1.0$.

To make the utility of the gamble as high as that of not participating, for which $U = 0$, we need to satisfy: $0 = E(r) - (\frac{1}{2})A$. Hence, an individual with $A = 3$ will require a rate of return of 150 percent, that is, the gamble would have to be "2.5 times or 0.5" instead of "double or nothing." (Try this for different levels of A. What is your degree of risk aversion?)

Concept Check

▪ ▪ ▪ ▪ ▪ ▪ ▪ ▪

Question 3.   A portfolio has an expected rate of return of 0.20 and standard deviation of 0.20. Bills offer a sure rate of return of 0.07. Which investment alternative will be chosen by an investor with $A = 4$? Find the critical level of risk aversion above which investors will prefer T-bills to the portfolio in question.

As Equation 7.1 implies, the utility of a risk-free (zero-variance) portfolio is simply the rate of return on the portfolio. An investment with zero variance is not penalized for risk. This gives us a convenient benchmark for evaluating portfolios.

Certainty equivalent rate   The certain return providing the same utility as a risky portfolio.

Because we can compare utility values to the rate offered on risk-free investments in choosing between a risky portfolio and a safe one, we may interpret a portfolio's utility value as its "certainty equivalent" rate of return to an investor. That is, the **certainty equivalent rate** of a portfolio is the rate that risk-free investments would need to offer to be considered as attractive as the risky portfolio.

Now we can say that a portfolio is desirable only if its certainty equivalent return exceeds that of the risk-free alternative. Sufficiently risk-averse investors will assign any risky portfolio, even one with a great risk premium, a certainty equivalent rate of return that is below the risk-free rate. Such investors will reject the portfolio.

At the same time, less risk-averse (more risk-tolerant) investors will assign the same portfolio a certainty equivalent rate that exceeds the risk-free rate and thus will prefer the portfolio to the risk-free alternative. If the risk premium is zero or negative to begin with, any downward adjustment to utility only makes the portfolio look worse. Its certainty equivalent rate will be below that of the risk-free alternative for all risk-averse investors.

Risk neutral A risk-neutral investor finds the level of risk irrelevant and considers only the expected return of risk prospects.

Risk loving A risk lover is willing to accept lower expected returns on prospects with higher amounts of risks.

In contrast to risk-averse investors, **risk-neutral** investors judge risky prospects solely by their expected rates of return. Their portfolio choice is expressed by a value $A = 0$ for the coefficient of risk aversion. The level of risk is irrelevant to the risk-neutral investor, meaning investments are not penalized for risk. For risk-neutral investors, a portfolio's certainty equivalent rate is simply its expected rate of return.

A **risk-loving** investor is willing to engage in fair games and gambles; this investor adjusts the expected return upward to take into account the "fun" of confronting the prospect's risk. Risk lovers will always take a fair game because their upward adjustment of utility for risk gives the fair game a certainty equivalent that exceeds the alternative of the risk-free investment.

We can depict the individual's trade-off between risk and return by plotting the characteristics of potential investment portfolios on a graph with axes measuring portfolio expected returns and standard deviation. Figure 7.1 plots the characteristics of one portfolio.

Portfolio P, with expected return $E(r_P)$ and standard deviation σ_P, is preferred by risk-averse investors to any portfolio in quadrant IV because it has an equal or *greater* expected return and an equal or *smaller* standard deviation than any portfolio in that quadrant. Conversely, any portfolio in quadrant I is preferable to portfolio P because its expected return is equal to or greater than P's and its standard deviation is equal to or smaller than P's.

Figure 7.1
The trade-off between risk and return of a potential investment portfolio.

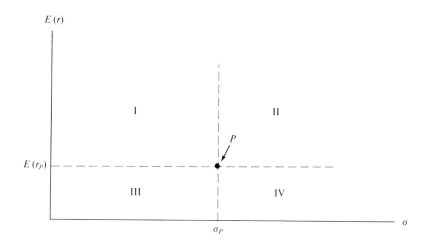

*Mean variance
criterion   The selec-
tion of portfolios based
on the means and var-
iances of their returns.
The choice of the
higher expected return
portfolio for a given
level of variance or the
lower variance port-
folio for a given ex-
pected return.*

This is the mean-standard deviation, or equivalently, **mean-variance (M-V)
criterion.** It can be stated as: investment A dominates investment B if

$$E(r_A) \geq E(r_B)$$

and

$$\sigma_A \leq \sigma_B$$

and at least one inequality is strict.

In the expected return-standard deviation graph, the preferred direction is
northwest because in this direction we simultaneously increase the expected return and decrease the standard deviation of the rate of return. This means any
portfolio that lies northwest of *P* is superior to *P*.

The desirability of portfolios in quadrants II and III, compared with *P*, depends on the investor's risk aversion. Starting at *P,* an increase in standard
deviation lowers utility; it must be offset by an adequate increase in expected
return. Thus, point *Q* in Figure 7.2 represents a portfolio that is as desirable to
this investor as portfolio *P*.

For any degree of risk aversion, investors may be attracted as much to portfolios with high risk and high expected returns as to other portfolios with lower
risk but lower expected returns. These equally preferred portfolios will lie on a
curve in the mean-standard deviation graph that connects all portfolio points
with the same utility value (see Figure 7.2). This is called the **indifference curve.**

*Indifference curve   A
curve connecting all
portfolios with the
same utility value.*

To determine some of the points that appear on the indifference curve, examine Table 7.1, which gives the utility values of several possible portfolios for
an investor with $A = 4$. Each portfolio offers identical utility because the high-
return portfolios also have high risk. Although in practice the exact indifference curves of various investors cannot be known, this sort of approach can
take us a long way in determining appropriate principles for portfolio selection
strategy.

Figure 7.2
**The indifference
curve.**

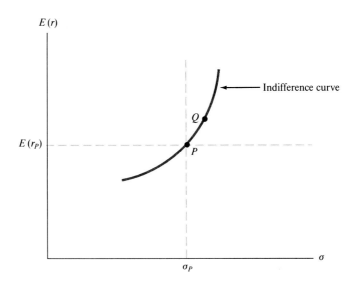

Table 7.1 *Utility Values of Possible Portfolios*

Expected Return, E(r)	Standard Deviation, σ	Utility = E(r) − 1/2Aσ²
.10	.200	.10 − .5 × 4 × .04 = .02
.15	.255	.15 − .5 × 4 × .065 = .02
.20	.300	.20 − .5 × 4 × .09 = .02
.25	.339	.25 − .5 × 4 × .115 = .02

Concept Check

> **Question 4.** How will the indifference curve of a less risk-averse investor compare to the indifference curve drawn in Figure 7.2? Draw both indifference curves passing through point *P*.

7.2 *Asset Allocation with One Risky Asset and One Risk-Free Asset*

Now we can talk about combining assets. We start by considering investors holding a risky portfolio, called *P*, along with some money market securities such as T-bills, which we will refer to as the risk-free asset *F*.

The Risky Asset

When we shift wealth from the risky portfolio (*P*) to the risk-free asset, we do not change the relative proportions of the various risky assets within the risky portfolio. Rather, we reduce the relative weight of the risky portfolio as a whole in favor of risk-free assets.

A simple example demonstrates the procedure. Assume the total market value of an initial portfolio is $300,000. Of that, $90,000 is invested in the Ready Assets money market fund, a risk-free asset. The remaining $210,000 is in risky securities, say $113,400 in the Vanguard market index fund (called the Index Trust 500 Portfolio) and $96,600 in Shearson Lehman's High-Yield Bond Fund.

The Vanguard fund (*V*) is a passive equity fund that replicates the S&P 500 portfolio. The Shearson Lehman High-Yield Bond Fund (*SL*) invests about 80 percent in high-yield (junk) bonds and the remainder in other assets. We choose these two funds for the risky portfolio in the spirit of a low-cost, well-diversified portfolio. While in the next chapter we discuss portfolio optimization, here we simply assume the investor considers the given weighting of *V* and *SL* to be optimal.

The holdings in Vanguard and Shearson Lehman make up the risky portfolio, with 54 percent in *V* and 46 percent in *SL*:

$$w_V = 113,400/210,000 = .54 \text{ (Vanguard Index Trust Fund)}$$
$$w_{SL} = 96,600/210,000 = .46 \text{ (Shearson's High-Yield Bond Fund)}$$

Complete portfolio
The entire portfolio,
including risky and
risk-free assets.

The weight of the risky portfolio, *P,* in the **complete portfolio,** *including* risk-free investments, is denoted by *y,* and so the weight of the money market fund in *P* is 1 − *y:*

$$y = 210,000/300,000 = .7 \text{ (risky assets, portfolio } P)$$
$$1 - y = \ 90,000/300,000 = .3 \text{ (risk-free assets)}$$

The weights of the individual assets in the complete portfolio (*C*) are:

Vanguard	113,400/300,000 =	.378
Shearson	96,600/300,000 =	.322
Portfolio *P*	210,000/300,000 =	.700
Ready Assets *F*	90,000/300,000 =	.300
Portfolio *C*	300,000/300,000 =	1.000

Suppose the investor decides to decrease risk by reducing the exposure to the risky portfolio from *y* = .7 to *y* = .56. The risky portfolio would total only .56 × 300,000 = $168,000, requiring the sale of $42,000 of the original $210,000 risky holdings, with the proceeds used to purchase more shares in Ready Assets. Total holdings in the risk-free asset will increase to 300,000(1 − .56) = $132,000 (the original holdings plus the new contribution to the money market fund: 90,000 + 42,000 = $132,000).

The key point is that we leave the proportion of each asset in the risky portfolio unchanged. Because the weights of Vanguard and Shearson in the risky portfolio are 0.54 and 0.46, respectively, we sell .54 × 42,000 = $22,680 of Vanguard and .46 × 42,000 = $19,320 of Shearson. After the sale, the proportions of each share in the risky portfolio are unchanged:

$$w_V = \frac{113,400 - 22,680}{210,000 - 42,000} = .54 \text{ (Vanguard)}$$

$$w_{SL} = \frac{96,600 - 19,320}{210,000 - 42,000} = .46 \text{ (Shearson)}$$

This procedure shows that rather than thinking of our risky holdings as Vanguard and Shearson separately, we may view our holdings as if they are in a single fund holding Vanguard and Shearson in fixed proportions. In this sense, we treat the risky fund as a single risky asset, that asset being a particular bundle of securities. As we shift in and out of safe assets, we simply alter our holdings of that bundle of securities commensurately.

Given this simplification, we can now turn to the desirability of reducing risk by changing the risky/risk-free asset mix, that is, reducing risk by decreasing the proportion *y.* Because we do not alter the weights of each asset within the risky portfolio, the probability distribution of the rate of return on the risky portfolio remains unchanged by the asset reallocation. What will change is the probability distribution of the rate of return on the *complete portfolio* that is made up of the risky and risk-free assets.

Concept Check

Question 5. What will be the dollar value of your position in Vanguard, and its proportion in your complete portfolio, if you decide to hold 50 percent of your investment budget in Ready Asset?

The Risk-Free Asset

The power to tax and to control the money supply lets the government, and only the government, issue default-free bonds. The default-free guarantee by itself is not sufficient to make the bonds risk-free in real terms, as you saw in the discussion of real versus nominal risk in Chapter 6. The only risk-free asset in real terms would be a perfectly price-indexed bond. Even then, a default-free, perfectly indexed bond offers a guaranteed real rate to an investor only if the maturity of the bond is identical to the investor's desired holding period. Even indexed bonds are subject to interest rate risk, because real interest rates change unpredictably through time. When future real rates are uncertain, so is the future price of perfectly indexed bonds.

These qualifications notwithstanding, it is common to view Treasury bills as *the* risk-free asset. Because they are short-term investments, they are relatively insensitive to interest rate fluctuations. An investor can lock in a short-term nominal return by buying a bill and holding it to maturity. Any inflation uncertainty over the course of a few weeks, or even months, is negligible compared to the uncertainty of stock market returns.

In practice, most investors use a broader range of money market instruments as a risk-free asset. All the money market instruments are virtually immune to interest rate risk (unexpected fluctuations in the price of a bond due to changes in market interest rates) because of their short maturities, and all are safe in terms of default or credit risk.

Money market funds hold, for the most part, three types of securities: Treasury bills, bank certificates of deposit (CDs), and commercial paper (CP). The instruments differ slightly in their default risk. The yields to maturity on CDs and CP, for identical maturities, are always slightly higher than those of T-bills. A history of this yield spread for 90-day CDs is shown in Figure 7.3.

Money market funds have changed their relative holdings of these securities over time, but by and large, T-bills make up only about 15 percent of their portfolios. Nevertheless, the risk of such blue-chip, short-term investments as CDs and CP is minuscule compared with that of most other assets, such as long-term corporate bonds, common stocks, or real estate. Hence, we treat money market funds as representing the most easily accessible risk-free asset for most investors.

Portfolio Expected Return and Risk

In this section, we examine the risk-return combinations available to investors. This is the "technical" part of asset allocation; it deals only with the opportunities available to investors given the features of the asset markets in which they can invest. In the next section, we address the "personal" part of the problem, the specific individual's choice of the best risk-return combination from the set of feasible combinations, given his or her level of risk aversion.

Since we assume the composition of the optimal risky portfolio (P) has already been determined, the concern here is with the proportion of the investment budget (y) to be allocated to the risky portfolio. The remaining proportion $(1 - y)$ is to be invested in the risk-free asset (F).

We denote the risky rate of return by r_P, the expected rate of return on P by $E(r_p)$, and its standard deviation by σ_P. The rate of return on the risk-free asset

Yield spread

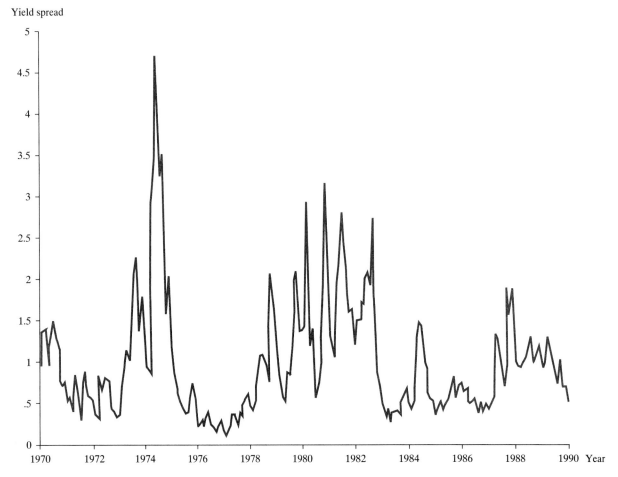

Figure 7.3 The pattern of the yield spread for 90-day certificates of deposit over 3-month Treasury bills.

is denoted as r_f. In the numerical example, we assume $E(r_P) = 15$ percent, $\sigma_P = 22$ percent, and $r_f = 7$ percent. Thus, the risk premium on the risky asset is $E(r_P) - r_f = 8$ percent.

With a proportion y in the risky portfolio and $1-y$ in the risk-free asset, the rate of return on the *complete* portfolio (C) is r_C where

$$r_C = yr_P + (1-y)r_f.$$

The expectation of this portfolio's rate of rate of return is

$$
\begin{aligned}
E(r_C) &= yE(r_P) + (1-y)r_f \\
&= r_f + y[E(r_P) - r_f] \\
&= .07 + y(.15 - .07).
\end{aligned}
\tag{7.2}
$$

This result is easily interpreted. The base rate of return for any portfolio is the risk-free rate. Beyond this, the portfolio is *expected* to earn a risk premium that depends on the risk premium of the risky portfolio, $E(r_P) - r_f$, and the inves-

Figure 7.4
Expected return-
standard deviation
combinations.

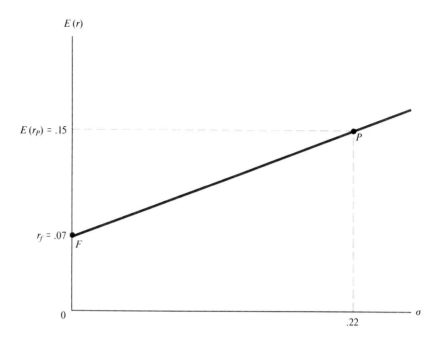

tor's exposure to the risky asset, y. Investors are assumed to be risk averse and, therefore, demand a positive risk premium.

When combining a risky asset (P) and a risk-free asset (F) into the complete portfolio (C), the standard deviation of portfolio C is simply the standard deviation of the risky asset (σ_P) times the weight (y) of the risky asset in the portfolio. Hence,

$$\sigma_C = y\sigma_P = .22y \qquad (7.3)$$

which makes sense because the standard deviation of the portfolio is proportional to both the standard deviation of the risky asset and the proportion invested in it. The bottom line is that the rate of return of the complete portfolio will have expected return $E(r_C) = r_f + y[E(r_P) - r_f] = .07 + .08y$ and standard deviation $\sigma_C = .22y$.

The next step is to plot the portfolio characteristics (for various values of y) in the expected return-standard deviation plane. This is done in Figure 7.4. The expected return-standard deviation combination for the risk-free asset (F) appears on the vertical axis where the standard deviation is zero. The risky asset is plotted with a standard deviation of $\sigma_P = .22$ and expected return of $E(r_P) = .15$.

If an investor chooses to invest solely in the risky asset, then $y = 1.0$, and the complete portfolio (C) is simply P. If the chosen position is $y = 0$, then $1 - y = 1.0$, and the complete portfolio is simply the risk-free asset F.

Midrange portfolios, where y is set between 0 and 1, will graph on the straight line connecting points F and P. The slope of that line is simply $[S = E(r_P) - r_f]/\sigma_P$ (or rise/run); in this case, $S = .08/.22$.

The conclusion is straightforward. Increasing the fraction of the complete portfolio invested in the risky asset increases the expected return by the risk premium of Equation 7.2, which is 0.08. It also increases portfolio standard deviation according to Equation 7.3 at the rate 0.22. The extra return per extra risk is $S = .08/.22 = .36$.

To derive the exact equation for the straight line between F and P, we rearrange Equation 7.3 to find that $y = \sigma_C/\sigma_P = \sigma_C/.22$, and substitute for y in Equation 7.2 to describe the expected return-standard deviation trade-off:

$$E[r_C(y)] = r_f + y[E(r_P) - r_f]$$

$$= r_f + \frac{[E(r_P) - r_f]}{\sigma_P}\sigma_C \qquad (7.4)$$

$$= .07 + .36\sigma_C.$$

Thus, the expected return of the portfolio as a function of its standard deviation is a straight line, with intercept r_f and slope

$$S = \frac{E(r_P) - r_f}{\sigma_P} = .36. \qquad (7.5)$$

The Capital Allocation Line

Figure 7.5 graphs the investment opportunity set, which is the set of feasible expected return and standard deviation pairs of all portfolios resulting from different values of y. The graph is a straight line originating at r_f and going through the risky asset P.

Capital allocation line (CAL)   A graph showing all feasible risk-return combinations using a risky and risk-free asset.

The straight line in Figure 7.5 is called the **capital allocation line** (CAL). It depicts all the risk-return combinations available to investors. The slope (S) of the CAL equals the increase in the expected return of the chosen portfolio per unit of additional standard deviation, or more directly, the measure of extra return per extra risk. For this reason, the slope is also called the **reward-to-variability ratio.**

Reward-to-variability ratio   Ratio of excess return to portfolio standard deviation.

A portfolio equally divided between the risky asset and the risk-free asset, that is, where $y = .5$, will have an expected rate of return of $E(r_C) = .07 + (.5 \times .08) = .11$, implying a risk premium of 4 percent, and a standard deviation of $\sigma_C = .5 \times .22 = .11$, or 11 percent. It will plot on the line FP midway between F and P. The reward-to-variability ratio is $S = .08/.22 = .36$.

Concept Check

Question 6.   Can the reward-to-variability ratio, $S = [E(r_C) - r_f]/\sigma_C$, of any combination of the risky and risk-free assets be different from the ratio for the risky asset taken alone, $[E(r_P) - r_f]/\sigma_P$, which in this case is 0.36?

What about points on the line to the right of portfolio P in the investment opportunity set? If investors can borrow at the (risk-free) rate of $r_f = 7$ percent, they can construct portfolios that plot on the CAL to the right of P.

Suppose the investment budget is $300,000, and our investor borrows an additional $120,000, investing the $420,000 in the risky asset. This is a levered position in the risky asset, which is financed in part by borrowing. In that case,

$$y = \frac{420,000}{300,000} = 1.4$$

Figure 7.5
The investment opportunity set with a risky asset and a risk-free asset.

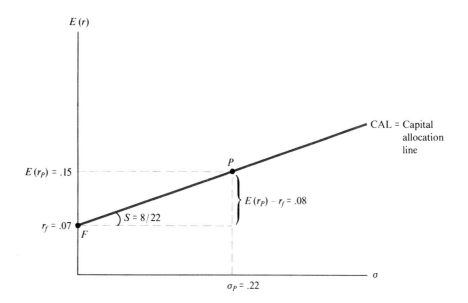

and $1 - y = 1 - 1.4 = -.4$, reflecting a short position in the risk-free asset, or a borrowing position. Rather than lending at a 7 percent interest rate, the investor borrows at 7 percent. The portfolio rate of return still exhibits the same reward-to-variability ratio because:

$$E(r_C) = .07 + (1.4 \times .08) = .182$$
$$\sigma_C = 1.4 \times .22 = .308$$
$$S = \frac{E(r_C) - r_f}{\sigma_C} = \frac{.112}{.308} = .36.$$

As you might expect, the levered portfolio has a higher standard deviation than an unlevered position in the risky asset.

Of course, nongovernment investors cannot borrow at the risk-free rate. The risk of a borrower's default leads lenders to demand higher interest rates on loans. Therefore, the nongovernment investor's borrowing cost will exceed the lending rate of $r_f = 7$ percent.

Suppose the borrowing rate is $r_B = 9$ percent. Then, for y greater than 1.0 (the borrowing range), the reward-to-variability ratio (the slope of the CAL), will be: $[E(r_P) - r_B]/\sigma_P = .06/.22 = .27$. Here, the borrowing rate (r_B) replaces the lending rate (r_f), reducing the "reward" (numerator) in the reward-to-variability ratio. The CAL will be "kinked" at point P as in Figure 7.6. To the left of P, where $y < 1$ the investor is lending at 7 percent, and the slope of the CAL is 0.36. To the right of P, where $y > 1$, the investor is borrowing (at a higher than the risk-free rate) to finance extra investments in the risky asset, and the slope is 0.27.

In practice, borrowing to invest in the risky portfolio is easy and straightforward if you have a margin account with a broker. All you have to do is tell your broker you want to buy "on margin." Margin purchases may not exceed 50 percent of the purchase value. Therefore, if your net worth in the account is $300,000, the broker is allowed to lend you up to $300,000 to purchase additional

Figure 7.6
The opportunity set with differential borrowing and lending rates.

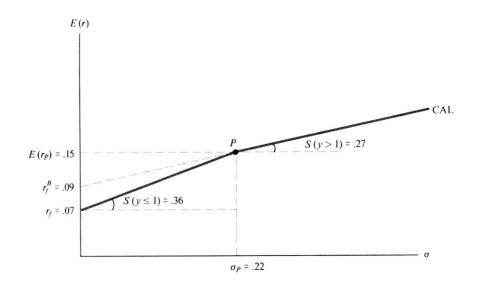

stock. You would then have $600,000 on the asset side of your account, and $300,000 on the liability side, resulting in $y = 2.0$.

Concept Check

> *Question 7.* Suppose there is a shift upward in the expected rate of return on the risky asset, from 15 percent to 17 percent. If all other parameters remain Gunchanged, what will be the slope of the CAL for $y \leq 1$ and $y > 1$?

Risk Tolerance and Asset Allocation

We have shown how to develop the CAL, the graph of all feasible risk-return combinations available from different asset allocation choices. The investor confronting the CAL now must choose one optimal combination from the set of feasible choices. This choice entails a trade-off between risk and return. Individual investors of different levels of risk aversion, given an identical opportunity set (as described by a risk-free rate and a reward-to-variability ratio), will choose different positions in the risky asset. Specifically, the more risk-averse investors will choose to hold *less* of the risky asset and more of the risk-free asset.

To develop the entire optimization process, we go back to the representation of utility:

$$U = E(r) - (1/2)A\sigma^2$$

where the objective now is to choose a complete portfolio with expected return and standard deviation that will maximize the level of utility. The decision variable is the proportion (y) to be invested in the risky portfolio (P), and we know the expected return and variance arising from a choice of y are:

$$E(r_C) = r_f + y[E(r_P) - r_f]$$

and

$$\sigma_C^2 = y^2\sigma_P^2.$$

The problem of maximizing utility (U) by choosing the best allocation to the risky asset is usually written as:

$$\text{Max } U = E(r_C) - (1/2)A\sigma_C^2 = r_f + y[E(r_P)-r_f] - y^2(1/2)A\sigma_P^2$$

Solving for y (this can be done analytically using calculus, or graphically) yields the optimal position for risk-averse investors in the risky asset, y^*:

$$y^* = \frac{E(r_P)-r_f}{A\sigma_P^2} \qquad (7.6)$$

This solution shows that the optimal position in the risky asset is, as one would expect, *inversely* proportional to the level of risk aversion as well as to the level of risk as measured by the *variance*. The optimal position is directly proportional to the risk premium offered by the risky asset.

Going back to our numerical example [$r_f = 7$ percent, $E(r_P) = 15$ percent and $\sigma_P = 22$ percent], we can find the optimal solution for an investor with a coefficient of risk aversion $A = 4$:

$$y^* = \frac{.15 - .07}{4 \times .22^2} = .41.$$

This investor will invest 41 percent of the investment budget in the risky asset and 59 percent in the risk-free asset. Note that r_f, $E(r_P)$, and σ_P must be expressed as decimal fractions or else it will be necessary to change the scale of A.

With 41 percent invested in the risky asset, the complete portfolio will have an expected return and standard deviation of:

$$E(r_C) = .07 + .41 \times (.15 - .07) = .1028$$
$$\sigma_C = .41 \times .22 = .0902.$$

The risk premium of the complete portfolio is $E(r_C)-r_f = 3.28$ percent, and entails a standard deviation of 9.02 percent. The reward-to-variability ratio is $3.28/9.02 = .36$ as assumed for this problem.

A less mathematical way of presenting this decision problem is to use indifference curve analysis. Recall that the indifference curve is a graph in the expected return-standard deviation plane of all points that result in a given level of utility. The curve then displays the investor's required trade-off between expected return and standard deviation.

As an example, suppose the complete portfolio under consideration is the risky asset itself, $y = 1$. The dark red curve in Figure 7.7 represents the indifference curve for an investor with a degree of risk aversion, $A = 4$, that passes through the risky asset with $E(r_P) = 15$ percent and $\sigma_P = 22$ percent. A second, light colored curve, by contrast, shows an indifference curve also going through P, but with a smaller degree of risk aversion, $A = 2$. The second indifference curve is flatter; it shows that the less risk-averse investor requires a smaller increase in expected return to compensate for a given increase in standard deviation.

The intercept of the indifference curve with the vertical axis is the *certainty equivalent* of the risky portfolio's expected rate of return because it gives a risk-free return with the same utility as the risky portfolio. In Figure 7.7, the less risk-averse investor (with $A = 2$) has a certainty equivalent for a risky portfolio such as P that is *higher* that that of the more risk-averse ($A = 4$) investor.

Figure 7.7
**Two indifference
curves through a
risky asset.**

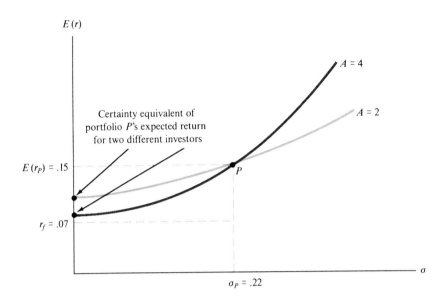

Figure 7.8
**A set of indifference
curves.**

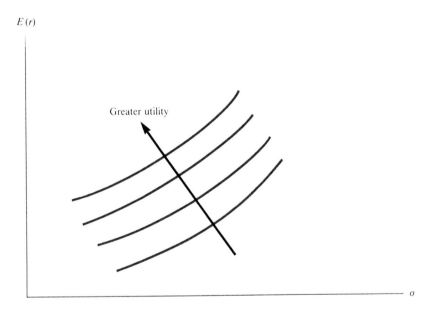

Indifference curves can be drawn for many benchmark portfolios, according to various levels of utility. Figure 7.8 shows such a set of graphs for $A = 4$.

To show how to use indifference curve analysis to determine the choice of the optimal portfolio for a specific CAL, we provide Figure 7.9, which superimposes the graphs of the indifference curves on the graph of the investment opportunity set (the CAL).

The investor is looking for the position with the highest feasible level of utility, represented by the highest possible indifference curve that touches the investment opportunity set. This is the indifference curve tangent to the CAL.

Figure 7.9
The graphical
solution to the
portfolio decision.

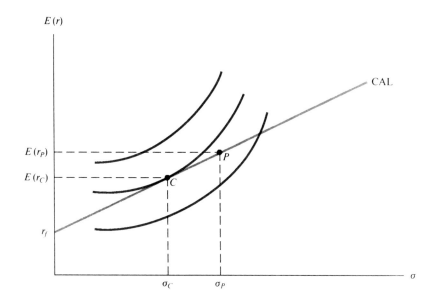

This optimal complete portfolio is represented by point C on the investment opportunity set. Using this graphical approach yields the same solution as the algebraic approach: $E(r_C) = .1028$ and $\sigma_C = .0902$, which means $y^* = .41$.

In summary, the asset allocation process can be broken down into two steps: (1) determine the capital allocation line, and (2) find the point of highest utility along that line.

Concept Check

Question 8. *a.* If an investor's coefficient of risk aversion is $A = 3$, how does the optimal asset mix change? What are the new $E(r_C)$ and σ_C? *b.* Suppose the borrowing rate $r_B = 9$ percent is greater than the lending rate, $r_f = 7$ percent. Show in a graph how the optimal portfolio choice of some investors will be affected by the higher borrowing rate. Which investors will *not* be affected by the borrowing rate?

7.3 *Passive Strategies: The Capital Market Line*

Passive strategy
Buying a well-diversified portfolio to represent a broad-based market index without attempting to search out mispriced securities.

The capital allocation line is derived with the risk-free asset and *the* risky portfolio P. Investors can determine the assets to be included in the risky portfolio using either a passive or an active strategy. A **passive strategy** describes an investment decision that avoids *any* security analysis. At first blush, a passive strategy would appear to be naive, yet the efficient market hypothesis (EMH discussed in Chapter 10) predicts that forces of supply and demand in large capital markets (to be discussed in Chapters 8–10) may make such a strategy a reasonable choice for many investors.

Data support development of various passive strategies. The University of Chicago's Center for Research in Security Prices (CRSP) has an extensive computer data base that includes rates of return on 30-day T-bills, long-term

Index Funds Emerge as Hot Turf of 1990

Marketing Efforts Target Individuals

NEW YORK—Just as money-market funds were the hot product in 1989, so stock-index funds are quickly becoming the scene of this year's biggest mutual fund marketing battle.

Following the stellar performance of Vanguard Group's index funds, both Dreyfus Corp. and Fidelity Investments have weighed in with index funds of their own. In recent weeks, both funds groups have come out with unmanaged portfolios of the stocks that make up the Standard & Poor's 500 stock index; these funds are designed to closely track the S&P 500's performance.

Small investors are just waking up to the virtues of index investments, which have already attracted about $250 billion from giant institutions. The oldest and largest of the index mutual funds, Van-

guard's Index Trust-500 Portfolio, notched up an annualized total return of 17 percent in the 1980s, putting it in the top quarter of all stock mutual funds. At the same time, the average stock fund returned just 15.5 percent a year.

As reported here earlier this year, the investment success of Vanguard's index funds was long ignored by Vanguard's competitors. Not any more. Both Dreyfus and Fidelity are now running full page advertisements as they seek to wrestle a share of the index-fund business away from Vanguard.

'Magical Product'

"As far as a mutual fund manager is concerned, an index fund is a magical product," says one analyst. "It already has a performance record—that of the

Keeping Up With The Averages

After years of being ignored by the fund Industry, index funds are starting to proliferate. Here are some of the no-load Index funds with the lowest annual expenses.

	ANNUAL EXPENSES	INVESTMENT MINIMUM[1]	TELEPHONE
RUSSELL 2000 Vanguard Small Company	0.35%	$3,000	(800) 662–7447
STANDARD & POOR'S 500: Peoples Index Fund (Dreyfus)	0	2,5000	(800) 782–6620
Spartan Market Index (Fidelity)	0.28	10,000	(800) 544–6666
Vanguard 500 Portfolio	0.20	3,000	(800) 662–7447
WILSHIRE 4,500[2] Vanguard Extended Market	0.23	3,000	(800) 662–7447

[1]Minimum for IRA accounts may be less   [2]Wilshire 5,000 minus the S&P 500 Stocks

T-bonds, long-term corporate bonds, and common stocks. The CRSP tapes provide a monthly rate of return series for the period 1926 through the present and, for common stocks, a daily rate of return series from 1962 through the present.

To avoid the costs of acquiring information on any individual stock or group of stocks, we may follow a "neutral" diversification approach. A natural strategy is to select a diversified portfolio of common stocks that mirrors the corporate sector of the U.S. economy. This results in a value-weighted portfolio, which, for example, invests a proportion in GM stock that is equal to the ratio of GM's market value to the market value of all listed stocks.

The CRSP data base offers a choice of the value-weighted or the equally weighted stock portfolio of either the Standard & Poor's Composite Index of 500 of the largest capitalization corporations (S&P 500) or the entire list of corporations that trade on the NYSE. Table 7.2 summarizes the historical record

index. I'm hard pressed to figure out why they didn't bring these funds out earlier."

Though it's still early, it seems that Dreyfus's and Fidelity's index funds are proving a tough sell even though they are holding down fees. So far, Dreyfus's Peoples Index Fund has assets of just $3.3 million (including $3 million of the company's own seed capital). And Fidelity's Spartan Market Index Fund has $16 million (including $4 million in seed capital).

If Dreyfus and Fidelity thought that this year's index funds would match the popularity of last year's money market funds, they have clearly been disappointed. Early in 1989, both Dreyfus and Fidelity brought out low-cost, money market funds, jumping into an area previously dominated by Vanguard. Dreyfus's Worldwide Dollar Fund has since pulled in $7.3 billion. Fidelity's Spartan Money Market Fund has snagged $8.3 billion.

'Education Problem'

"They are jumping onto the index fund bandwagon, and they're trying to get some attention by waiving the fees," says John Bogle, Vanguard's chairman. "Fees are the only thing that distinguishes one money market fund from another. When you get to an index fund, fees are just one of the things that affect return. Only a moron would buy a stock fund to avoid a 0.5 percent expense ratio for two weeks or two months. Apparently the marketplace is smarter than the fund sponsors."

Dreyfus Chairman Howard Stein concedes that the Peoples Index Fund may not be the immediate success that the Worldwide Dollar Fund was. "Yes, there is an education problem," he says. "Yes, it will take time." A spokesman for Dreyfus notes that while the fund group has been advertising the Peoples Index Fund for some time, prospectuses only became available on May 4.

For years, Vanguard has had a virtual stranglehold on the index-fund market. It offers index funds that track a bond-market index, two international stock indexes and two small-company stock indexes. But its biggest winner has been the 500 Portfolio, which now has assets of $2.2 billion and so far this year has been the fund group's best-selling stock fund.

As with its other funds, Vanguard's edge in the index-fund business comes from its extremely low annual-expense ratios. The 500 Portfolio charges just 0.2 percent of assets annually, well below the 1.5 percent typically charged by an actively managed stock fund.

To compete, both Dreyfus and Fidelity are holding down expenses on their index funds. Dreyfus is absorbing all expenses until the end of the year or until the fund hits $100 million in assets, whichever comes first. Fidelity has promised to keep its expenses at 0.28 percent of assets until May 1, 1991.

From Jonathan Clements, "Index Funds Emerge as Hot Turf of 1990," *The Wall Street Journal*, May 18, 1990. Reprinted by permission of *THE WALL STREET JOURNAL*, © 1990 Dow Jones & Company, Inc. All Rights Reserved Worldwide.

of the value-weighted S&P 500 portfolio and one-month T-bills. The last pair of columns shows the average risk premium over T-bills and the standard deviation of the common stock portfolio.

Capital market line
The capital allocation line using the market index portfolio as the risky asset.

We call the capital allocation line provided by one-month T-bills and a broad index of common stocks the **capital market line** (CML). That is, a passive strategy based on stocks and bills generates an investment opportunity set that is represented by the CML.

How reasonable is it for an investor to pursue a passive strategy? We cannot answer such a question definitively without comparing passive strategy results to the costs and benefits accruing to an active portfolio strategy. Some issues are worth considering, however.

First, the alternative active strategy entails costs. Whether you choose to invest your own time (which has a value) to acquire the information needed to

Table 7.2 *Average Rates of Return and Standard Deviations for Common Stocks and One-Month Bills, and the Risk Premium over Bills on Common Stock*

	Common Stocks		One-Month Bills		Risk Premium over Bills on Common Stocks	
	Mean	S.D.	Mean	S.D.	Mean	S.D.
1926–1941	7.3	29.6	1.3	1.5	6.0	29.6
1942–1957	17.3	16.4	1.1	.8	16.2	16.7
1958–1973	10.2	15.3	4.1	1.6	6.2	16.3
1974–1990	13.6	16.7	8.2	2.5	5.4	17.0
1926–1990	12.1	20.6	3.7	3.4	8.4	21.1

generate an optimal active portfolio of risky assets or whether you delegate the task to a professional who will charge a fee, constructing an active portfolio is more expensive than constructing a passive one. The passive portfolio requires only small commissions on purchases of U.S. T-bills (or zero commissions if you purchase bills directly from the government) and management fees to a mutual fund company that offers a market index fund to the public. An index fund has the lowest operating expenses of all mutual stock funds because it requires minimum effort.

A second argument supporting a passive strategy is the free-rider benefit. If you assume there are many active, knowledgeable investors who quickly bid up prices of undervalued assets and offer down overvalued assets (by selling), you have to conclude that most of the time most assets will be fairly priced. Therefore, a well-diversified portfolio of common stock will be a reasonably fair buy, and the passive strategy may not be inferior to that of the average active investor. (We will explain this assumption and provide a more comprehensive analysis of the relative success of passive strategies in Chapter 10.) The growing popularity of passive index funds is explored in the nearby box.

To summarize, a passive strategy involves investment in two passive portfolios: virtually risk-free short-term T-bills (or a money market fund), and a fund of common stocks that mimics a broad market index. The capital allocation line representing such a strategy is called the *capital market line*. Using the last pair of columns of Table 7.2, we see that using 1926 to 1990 data, the passive risky portfolio has offered an average risk premium of 8.4 percent and a standard deviation of 21.1 percent, resulting in a reward-to-variability ratio of 0.41.

We can use our analysis to deduce a typical investor's risk-aversion measure. The total market value of the S&P 500 stocks is about four times as large as the market value of all outstanding T-bills of less than six months to maturity. If we ignore all other assets (long-term bonds and real estate for example) and pretend all investors followed a passive strategy, then the average investor's position in the risky asset (the S&P 500) was

$$y = \frac{1}{1 + 4} = .8.$$

What degree of risk aversion must investors have had in order for this portfolio to be optimal? Assuming the average investor in 1990 uses the historical average risk premium (8.4%) and standard deviation (21.1%) to forecast future return and standard deviation, and using 0.8 as the weight in the risky portfolio, we can work out the average investor's risk tolerance as follows:

$$y^* = \frac{E(r_M) - r_f}{A\sigma_M^2} = .8 = \frac{.084}{A \times .211^2}$$

which implies a coefficient of risk aversion of

$$A = \frac{.084}{.8 \times .211^2} = 2.36.$$

This is, however, speculation. We have assumed without any basis that the average 1990 investor holds the naive view that historical average rates of return and standard deviations are the best estimates of expected rates of return and risk looking into the future. To the extent that the average investor takes advantage of contemporary information in addition to simple historical data, our estimate of $A = 2.36$ would be an unjustified inference. At the same time, studies that consider the full range of available assets place the representative investor's degree of risk aversion somewhere in this range.

Concept Check

Question 9. Suppose expectations about the S&P 500 index and the T-bill rate are the same today as they were in 1990, but you find there is a greater proportion invested in T-bills now than in 1990. What can you conclude about the change in risk tolerance since 1990?

Summary

1. Speculation is the undertaking of a risky investment for its risk premium. The risk premium has to be large enough to compensate a risk-averse investor for the risk of the investment.

2. A fair game is a zero-risk-premium risky prospect. It will not be undertaken by a risk-averse investor.

3. Investors' preferences about the expected return and volatility of a portfolio may be expressed by a utility function that is higher for higher expected returns and lower for higher portfolio variances. More risk-averse investors will apply greater penalties for risk. We can describe these preferences graphically using indifference curves.

4. The desirability of a risky portfolio to a risk-averse investor may be expressed by the certainty equivalent value of the portfolio. The certainty equivalent rate of return is a value that, if received with certainty, would yield the same utility as the risky portfolio.

5. Shifting funds from the risky portfolio to the risk-free asset is the simplest way to reduce risk. Another method involves diversification of the risky portfolio. We take up diversification in later chapters.

6. U.S. T-bills provide a perfectly risk-free asset in nominal terms only. Nevertheless, the standard deviation of real rates on short-term T-bills is small compared to that of assets such as long-term bonds and common stocks, so for the purpose of our analysis, we consider T-bills the risk-free asset. Besides

T-bills, money market funds hold short-term safe obligations such as CP and CDs. These entail some default risk but relatively little compared to most other risky assets. For convenience, we often refer to money market funds as risk-free assets.

7. A risky investment portfolio (referred to here as the risky asset) can be characterized by its reward-to-variability ratio. This ratio is the slope of the capital allocation line (CAL), the line that goes from the risk-free asset through the risky asset. All combinations of the risky and risk-free assets lie on this line. Investors would prefer a steeper sloping CAL, because that means higher expected returns for any level of risk. If the borrowing rate is greater than the lending rate, the CAL will be "kinked" at the point corresponding to investment of 100 percent of the complete portfolio in the risky asset.

8. An investor's degree of risk aversion is characterized by the slope of an indifference curve. Indifference curves show the required risk premium for taking on additional standard deviation. More risk-averse investors have steeper indifference curves because they require a greater risk premium for taking on more risk.

9. The optimal position in the risky portfolio is proportional to the risk premium and inversely proportional to the portfolio variance and to the degree of risk aversion. Graphically, this portfolio is at the tangency of an indifference curve to the CAL.

10. A passive investment strategy operates without security analysis, targeting instead the risk-free asset and a broad portfolio of risky assets such as the S&P 500 stock portfolio. If, in 1990, investors took the historical mean return and standard deviation of the S&P 500 as proxies for the expected return and standard deviation in the future, then the market values of outstanding T-bills and the S&P 500 stocks would imply a degree of risk aversion of about $A = 2.36$ for the average investor.

Key Terms

capital allocation line, 196	indifference curve, 190	risk loving, 189
capital market line, 203	mean-variance (M-V) criterion, 190	risk neutral, 189
certainty equivalent rate, 188	passive strategy, 201	utility, 187
complete portfolio, 192	reward-to-variability ratio, 196	

Selected Readings

A good work on risk aversion is:
Wells Fargo Investment Advisors. *Institutional Counsel Service Newsletter,* November 1981.

Practitioner-oriented approaches to asset allocation may be found in:
Maginn, John L., and Donald L. Tuttle. *Managing Investment Portfolios: A Dynamic Process.* New York: Warren, Gorham, and Lamont, 1990.
Sharpe, William. "Integrated Asset Allocation." *Financial Analysts Journal,* September–October 1987.

Estimation of the degree of risk aversion of investors is undertaken in:
Friend, I., and M. Blume. "The Demand for Risky Assets." *American Economic Review* 64 (1974), pp. 900–21; and in Grossman, S. J., and R. J. Shiller. "The De-

terminants of the Variability of Stock Market Prices." *American Economic Review* 71 (1981), pp. 222–27.

Problem Sets

1. Consider a risky portfolio. The end-of-year cash flow derived from the portfolio will be either $50,000 or $150,000 with equal probabilities of 0.5. The alternative riskless investment in T-bills pays 5 percent.

   a. If you require a risk premium of 10 percent, how much will you be willing to pay for the portfolio?

   b. Suppose the portfolio can be purchased for the amount you found in (*a*). What will the expected rate of return on the portfolio be?

   c. Now suppose you require a risk premium of 15 percent. What is the price you will be willing to pay now?

   d. Comparing your answers to (*a*) and (*c*), what do you conclude about the relationship between the required risk premium on a portfolio and the price at which the portfolio will sell?

2. Consider a portfolio that offers an expected rate of return of 10 percent and a standard deviation of 15 percent. T-bills offer a risk-free 8 percent. What is the maximum level of risk aversion at which the risky portfolio is still preferred over bills?

3. Draw the indifference curve in the expected return-standard deviation plane corresponding to a utility level of 0.05 for an investor with a risk-aversion coefficient of 3. (Hint: Choose several possible standard deviations, ranging from 0.05 to 0.25, and find the expected rates of return providing a utility level of 0.05. Then plot the expected return/standard deviation points so derived.)

4. Now draw the indifference curve corresponding to a utility level of 0.04 for an investor with risk-aversion coefficient $A = 4$. Comparing this curve with your answer to (3), what do you conclude?

5. Draw an indifference curve for a risk-neutral investor providing utility level 0.05.

6. What must be true about the sign of the risk-aversion coefficient (A) for a risk lover? Draw the indifference curve for a utility level of 0.05 for a risk lover.

7. Consider historical data showing that the annual rate of return on the S&P 500 portfolio over the past 65 years has averaged about 8.4 percent more than the Treasury bill return, with a standard deviation of about 21 percent per year. Assume these values are representative of investor expectations for future performance and that the current T-bill rate is 6 percent. Use these values in the following questions.

   a. Calculate the expected return and variance of portfolios invested in T-bills and the S&P 500 index with weights as follows:

w_{bills}	w_{market}
0	1.0
.2	.8
.4	.6
.6	.4
.8	.2
1.0	1.0

   b. Calculate the utility levels of each portfolio in (*a*) for an investor with $A = 3$.

   c. Repeat problem (*b*) for an investor with $A = 5$. Comparing the (*b*) and (*c*) solutions, what do you conclude?

For problems 8–14, assume that you manage a risky portfolio with an expected rate of return of 17 percent and a standard deviation of 27 percent. The T-bill rate is 7 percent.

8. *a.* Your client chooses to invest 70 percent of a portfolio in your fund and 30 percent in a T-bill money market fund. What is the expected return and standard deviation of your client's portfolio?

    b. Suppose your risky portfolio includes the following investments in the given proportions:

Stock A	27%
Stock B	33%
Stock C	40%

What are the investment proportions of your client's overall portfolio, including the position in T-bills?

    c. What is the reward-to-variability ratio (S) of your risky portfolio?

    d. Draw the CAL of your portfolio on an expected return-standard deviation diagram. What is the slope of the CAL? Show the position of your client on your fund's CAL.

9. Suppose the same client decides to invest in your portfolio a proportion (y) of the total investment budget so that the overall portfolio will have an expected rate of return of 15 percent.

    a. What is the proportion y?

    b. What are your client's investment proportions in your three stocks and the T-bill fund?

    c. What is the standard deviation of the rate of return on your client's portfolio?

10. Suppose your client prefers to invest in your fund a proportion (y) that maximizes the expected return on the overall portfolio subject to the constraint that the overall portfolio's standard deviation will not exceed 20 percent.

    a. What is the investment proportion, y?

    b. What is the expected rate of return on the overall portfolio?

11. Your client's degree of risk aversion is $A = 3.5$.

    a. What proportion, y, of the total investment should be invested in your fund?

    b. What is the expected value and standard deviation of the rate of return on your client's optimized portfolio?

12. You estimate that a passive portfolio (invested to mimic the S&P 500 stock index) yields an expected rate of return of 13 percent with a standard deviation of 25 percent. Draw the CML and your fund's CAL on an expected return-standard deviation diagram.

    a. What is the slope of the CML?

    b. Characterize in one short paragraph the advantage of your fund over the passive fund.

13. Your client wonders whether to switch the 70 percent that is invested in your fund to the passive portfolio.

    a. Explain to your client the disadvantage of the switch.

    b. Show your client the maximum fee you could charge (as a percent of the investment in your fund deducted at the end of the year) that would still leave the client at least as well off investing in your fund as in the passive one. (Hint: The fee will lower the slope of your client's CAL by reducing the expected return net of the fee.)

14. Consider the client in problem 11 with $A = 3.5$.

    a. If the client chose to invest in the passive portfolio, what proportion, y, would be selected?

    b. What fee (percent of the investment in your fund, deducted at the end of the year) can you charge to make the client indifferent between your fund and the passive strategy?

15. Look at the data in Table 7.2 on the average risk premium of the S&P 500 over bills and the standard deviation of that risk premium. Suppose the S&P 500 is your risky portfolio.

    a. If your risk aversion coefficient is 4, and you believe the entire 1926–1990 period is representative of future expected performance, what fraction of your portfolio should be allocated to bills and what to equity investment?

    b. What if you believe the 1974–1990 period is representative?

    c. What do you conclude on comparing your answers to (*a*) and (*b*)?

16. What do you think would happen to the expected return on stocks if investors perceived an increase in volatility of stocks?

Chapter

Efficient Diversification

In Chapter 7, we discussed *capital allocation,* the choice between the risk-free asset and a particular risky portfolio. This chapter describes how to make up the best risky portfolio. A central concept is diversification.

The notion of diversification is age old. The adage "don't put all your eggs in one basket" predates economic theory. It wasn't until 1952, however, that Harry Markowitz developed a formal model of portfolio selection embodying diversification principles, a feat for which he was awarded the Nobel Prize for economics in 1990. This chapter is developed mostly from his work.

Our discussion first explores how diversification can reduce the variability of portfolio returns and then casts this explanation in a factor model of security returns. Our basic approach is to conceptualize the investment decision in a top-down fashion. We already have discussed capital allocation with one risky and one risk-free asset. We next proceed to asset allocation among a small set of risky portfolios that may be representative of broad segments of the securities market, for example, a stock fund and a bond fund. Finally, we discuss security selection principles when choosing among the entire universe of risky assets.

First, we discuss asset allocation with two risky assets. Next, we add a risk-free asset to the menu, thereby using capital allocation with asset allocation to find both the composition of the optimal risky portfolio and the desired allocation to it and to the risk-free asset.

Moving beyond two risky assets, we generalize the analysis to security selection in a universe of many risky assets. We discuss the efficient set of risky portfolios and show how it leads us to the best attainable capital allocation line.

An appendix examines the common fallacy that long-term investment mitigates the risk of risky assets. We argue that what is perceived as a time diversification effect is an illusion, not real diversification. After studying this chapter you should be able to:

- Use factor models to analyze the risk characteristics of securities and portfolios.

- Construct efficient portfolios.
- Calculate the composition of the optimal risky portfolio.

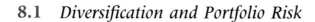

8.1 *Diversification and Portfolio Risk*

Suppose you have in your risky portfolio only one stock, say, Digital Equipment Corporation. What are the sources of risk affecting this "portfolio"?

We can identify two broad sources of uncertainty. The first is the risk that has to do with general economic conditions, such as the business cycle, the inflation rate, interest rates, exchange rates, and so forth. None of these macroeconomic factors can be predicted with certainty, and all affect the rate of return Digital stock eventually will provide. Then you must add to these macro factors firm-specific influences, such as Digital's success in research and development, management style and philosophy, and so on. Firm-specific factors are those that affect Digital without noticeably affecting other firms.

Now consider a naive diversification strategy, adding another security to the risky portfolio. If you invest half of your risky portfolio in Exxon, leaving the other half in Digital, what happens to portfolio risk? Because the firm-specific influences on the two stocks differ (statistically speaking, the influences are independent), this strategy should reduce portfolio risk. For example, when oil prices fall, hurting Exxon, computer prices might rise, helping Digital. The two effects are offsetting, which stabilizes portfolio return.

But why stop at only two stocks? Diversifying into many more securities continues to minimize exposure to firm-specific factors, so portfolio volatility should continue to fall. Ultimately, however, even with a large number of risky securities in a portfolio, there is no way to avoid all risk. To the extent that virtually all securities are affected by common (risky) macroeconomic factors, we cannot eliminate our exposure to general economic risk, no matter how many stocks we hold.

Figure 8.1 illustrates these concepts. When all risk is firm-specific, as in Figure 8.1A, diversification can reduce risk to low levels. With all risk sources independent, and with investment spread across many securities, exposure to any particular source of risk is negligible. This is just an application of the law

Figure 8.1
Portfolio risk as a function of the number of stocks in the portfolio.

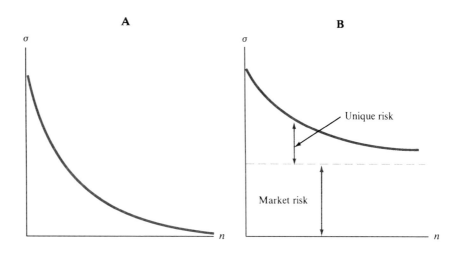

of averages. The reduction of risk to very low levels because of independent risk sources is sometimes called the *insurance principle*.

This analysis is borne out by empirical studies. Figure 8.2 shows the effect of portfolio diversification, using data on NYSE stocks. The figure shows the average standard deviations of equally weighted portfolios constructed by selecting stocks at random as a function of the number of stocks in the portfolio. On average, portfolio risk does fall with diversification, but the power of diversification to reduce risk is limited by common sources of risk.

When these common sources of risk affect all firms, even extensive diversification cannot eliminate risk. In Figure 8.1B, portfolio standard deviation falls as the number of securities increases, but it is not reduced to zero. The risk that remains even after diversification is called **market risk,** risk that is attributable to marketwide risk sources. Other names are **systematic risk** or **nondiversifiable risk.** The risk that *can* be eliminated by diversification is called **unique risk, firm-specific risk, nonsystematic risk,** or **diversifiable risk.**

Market risk, systematic risk, nondiversifiable risk   *Risk factors common to the whole economy.*

Diversifiable risk, unique risk, firm specific risk, nonsystematic risk   *Risk that can be eliminated by diversification.*

Risk Premiums, Inflation, and the Real Risk-Free Rate

Efficient investors never lose sight of the fact that the objective rate of return is the *real* rate on the *complete* portfolio. So here, again, the decomposition of the rate of return on a risky asset into the risk-free rate plus a risk premium is useful. Because the risk premium is a differential (between the total return and the risk-free rate), it is always an increment to the real rate and is, therefore, real.

Integration of expected inflation into the analysis can be neatly compartmentalized into two parts. First and most importantly, the nominal risk-free rate must be adjusted downward for expected inflation. Each investor must use a subjective forecast of inflation.

Figure 8.2
Portfolio diversification. The average standard deviation of returns of portfolios composed of only one stock was .554. The average portfolio risk fell rapidly as the number of stocks included in the portfolio increased. For 32 stocks, the portfolio standard deviation was down to .325.
From Lawrence Fisher, and James H. Lorie, "Some Studies of the Variability of Returns on Investments in Common Stocks," *Journal of Business,* 43, April 1970; published by the University of Chicago.

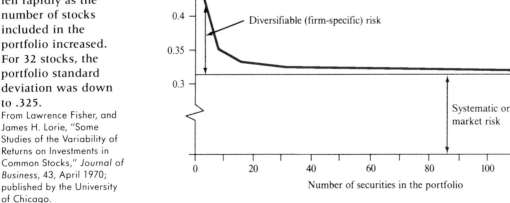

Second, inflation risk can be handled by introducing an inflation factor in risky-asset returns. When we develop the factor representation of security returns, this way of handling inflation risk will become clear.

A Single-Factor Asset Market

A world where security risk can be divided into macroeconomic factors that affect all securities and unique firm-specific factors can be represented by a factor model of capital markets. The first to use a factor model to explain the benefits of diversification was another Nobel Prize winner, William S. Sharpe (1963). We will introduce his major work (the capital asset pricing model) in the next chapter.

Let us use R_i to denote the *excess return* on a security, that is, the rate of return in excess of the risk-free rate: $R_i = r_i - r_f$. Then we can express the distinction between macroeconomic and firm-specific factors by decomposing this excess return in some holding period into three components:

$$R_i = E_i(R_i) + \beta_i M + e_i \qquad (8.1)$$

In Equation 8.1, $E(R_i)$ is the *expected* excess holding period return (HPR) at the start of the holding period. The next two terms reflect the impact of two sources of uncertainty. M quantifies the market or macroeconomic surprises (with zero meaning that there is "no surprise") during the holding period. β_i is the sensitivity of the security to the macroeconomic factor. Finally, e_i is the impact of unanticipated firm-specific events.

Beta *The sensitivity of a security's returns to the systematic or market factor.*

Both M and e_i have zero expected values because each represents the impact of unanticipated events, which by definition must average out to zero. The **beta** of the security (β_i) denotes the particular responsiveness of security i to macroeconomic events; this sensitivity will be different for different securities.

As an example of a factor model, suppose that the excess return on Digital stock is *expected* to be 9 percent in the coming holding period. However, on average, for every unanticipated increase of 1 percent in the vitality of the general economy, which we take as the macroeconomic factor M, Digital's stock return will be enhanced by 1.2 percent: Digital's β is 1.2. Finally, Digital is affected by firm-specific surprises as well. Therefore, we can write the realized excess return on Digital stock as follows:

$$R_D = 9\% + 1.2\, M + e_i$$

If the economy outperforms expectations by 2 percent, then we would revise upward our expectation of Digital's excess return by 1.2×2 percent, or 2.4 percent, resulting in a new expected excess return of 11.4 percent. Finally, the effects of Digital's firm-specific news during the holding period must be added to arrive at the actual holding period return on Digital stock.

Equation 8.1 describes a factor model for stock returns. This is a simplification of the situation; a more realistic decomposition of security returns would require more than one factor in Equation 8.1. We treat this issue in the next chapter, but for now, let us examine the single-factor case.

Specification of a Single-Index Model of Security Returns

A factor model description of security returns is of little use if we cannot specify a way to measure the factor that we say affects security returns. One reasonable

Index model A model of stock returns using a market index such as the S&P 500 to represent common or systematic risk factors.

approach is to use the rate of return on a broad index of securities, such as the S&P 500, as a proxy for the common macro factor. With this assumption, we can use the excess return on the market index, R_M, to measure the direction of macro shocks in any period.

The **index model** separates the realized rate of return on a security into macro (systematic) and micro (firm-specific) components much like Equation 8.1. The excess rate of return on each security is the sum of three components:

	Symbol
1. The stock's excess return if the market factor is neutral, that is, if the market's excess return is zero.	α_i
2. The component of return due to movements in the overall market (as represented by the index R_M); β_i is the security's responsiveness to the market.	$\beta_i R_M$
3. The component attributable to unexpected events that are relevant only to this security (firm-specific).	e_i

The HPR on the stock now can be stated as

$$R_i = \alpha_i + \beta_i R_M + e_i \qquad (8.2)$$

Equation 8.2 specifies the two sources of security risk: market or systematic risk ($\beta_i R_M$), attributable to the security's sensitivity as measured by beta (β) to the movements in the overall market, and firm-specific risk (e_i), which is the part of uncertainty independent of the factor. If we denote the variance of the return on the market as σ_M^2, then we can use Equation 8.2 to divide the variance of the rate of return on each security into two components:

	Symbol
1. The variance attributable to the uncertainty common to the entire market; this is the systematic risk.	$\beta_i^2 \sigma_M^2$
2. The variance attributable to firm-specific uncertainty.	$\sigma^2(e_i)$

Denoting the variance of the rate of return on security i as σ_i^2, and recalling that the firm-specific component and the market component are uncorrelated, we find that total volatility is the sum of systematic and firm-specific risk:

$$\sigma_i^2 = \beta_i^2 \sigma_M^2 + \sigma^2(e_i) \qquad (8.3)$$

This single index model is convenient. It relates security returns to a market index that investors follow. Moreover, as we shall soon see, its usefulness goes beyond mere convenience.

Statistical and Graphical Representation of the Single-Index Model

Equation 8.2, $R_i = \alpha_i + \beta_i R_M + e_i$, may be interpreted as a single-variable *regression equation* of R_i on the factor excess return R_M. The excess return on the security (R_i) is the dependent variable that is to be explained by the regres-

Figure 8.3
Scatter diagram for
DEC.

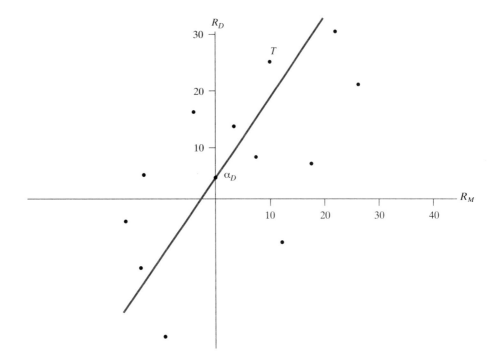

sion. On the right-hand side of the equation are the intercept α_i; the regression (or slope) coefficient beta, β_i, multiplying the independent (or explanatory) variable, R_M; and the security residual (unexplained) return, e_i. We can plot this regression as in Figure 8.3, which shows a scatter diagram for Digital Equipment Corporation (DEC) return against the market factor.

The horizontal axis of the scatter diagram measures the explanatory variable, here the market factor, R_M. The vertical axis measures the dependent variable, here DEC's excess return, R_D. The points on the scatter diagram represent a sample of pairs of returns (R_M, R_D) that might be observed for the chosen number of holding periods. Point T, for instance, describes a holding period when the excess return was 17 percent on the market and 27 percent on DEC.

Regression analysis lets us use the sample of historical returns to estimate a relationship between the dependent variable and the explanatory variable. The regression line in Figure 8.3 is drawn so as to minimize the sum of all the squared deviations around it. Hence, we say the regression line "best fits" the data in the scatter diagram. The line is sometimes called the *security characteristic line*.

The regression intercept (α_D) is measured from the origin to the intersection of the regression line with the vertical axis. Any point on the vertical axis represents zero market excess return, so the intercept gives us the *expected* excess return on DEC when market performance is neutral.

The slope of the regression line can be measured by dividing the rise of the line by its run. It is also expressed by the number multiplying the explanatory variable, which is called the regression coefficient, or the slope coefficient, or simply the beta. The regression beta is a natural measure of systematic risk since it measures the typical response of the security return to market fluctuations.

The regression line does not represent the *actual* returns; that is, the points on the scatter diagram almost never lie on the regression line, although the actual returns are used to calculate the regression coefficients. Rather, the line represents average tendencies; it shows the effect of the index return on our *expectation* of R_D. The algebraic representation of the regression line is

$$E(R_D|R_M) = \alpha_D + \beta_D R_M \qquad (8.4)$$

which reads: The expectation of R_D *given* a value of R_M equals the intercept plus the slope coefficient times the given value of R_M.

Because the regression line represents expectations, and because these expectations may not be realized in any or all of the actual returns (as the scatter diagram shows), the *actual* security returns also include a residual, the firm-specific surprise, e_i. This surprise (at point T, for example) is measured by the vertical distance between the point of the scatter diagram and the regression line.

Equation 8.3 shows that the greater the beta of the security, that is, the greater the slope of the regression, the more the security's systematic risk ($\beta_D^2 \sigma_M^2$), as well as its total variance (σ_D^2). The *average security* has a slope coefficient (beta) of 1.0: because the market is composed of all securities, the typical response to a market movement must be one for one. An "aggressive" investment will have a beta higher than 1.0; that is, the security has above-average market risk. In Figure 8.3, DEC's beta is 1.4. Similarly, securities with betas lower than 1.0 are called defensive.

A security may have a negative beta. Its regression line will then slope downward, meaning that for more favorable macro events (higher R_M), we would expect a *lower* return, and vice versa. The latter means that when the macro economy goes bad (negative R_M), while other securities with positive beta are expected to have negative excess returns, the negative-beta security will shine. The result is that a negative-beta security carries *negative* systematic risk, that is, provides a hedge against systematic risk.

The scale of the scatter of actual returns about the regression line is determined by the residual variance $\sigma^2(e_D)$, which measures the effects of the firm-specific events independent of market movements. The magnitude of firm-specific risk varies across securities. One way to measure the relative weight of systematic risk is to measure the ratio of systematic variance to total variance:

$$\rho^2 = \frac{\text{Systematic or explained variance}}{\text{Total variance}}$$
$$= \frac{\beta_D^2 \sigma_M^2}{\sigma_D^2} = \frac{\beta_D^2 \sigma_M^2}{\beta_D^2 \sigma_D^2 + \sigma^2(e_D)} \qquad (8.5)$$

ρ is the correlation coefficient between R_D and R_M. Its square measures the ratio of explained variance to total variance. But if beta is negative, so is the correlation coefficient, an indication the explanatory and dependent variables are expected to move in opposite directions.

At the extreme, when the correlation coefficient is either 1.0 or -1.0, the security return is fully explained by the market return, that is, there are no firm-specific effects. All the scatter diagram points will lie exactly on the line. This is called perfect correlation (either positive or negative); the return on the security is perfectly predictable from the factor return. A large correlation coeffi-

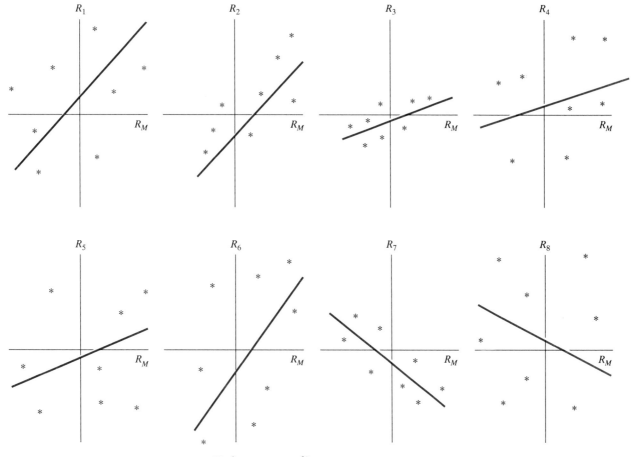

Figure 8.4 Various scatter diagrams.

cient (in absolute terms) means systematic variance dominates the total variance; that is, firm-specific variance is relatively unimportant. When the correlation coefficient is small (in absolute terms), the market factor plays a relatively unimportant part in explaining the variance of the asset, and firm-specific factors predominate.

Concept Check

Question 1. Explain the economic meaning of the differences in the eight scatter diagrams of Figure 8.4.

Diversification in a Single-Factor Security Market

Imagine a portfolio that is divided equally among securities whose returns are given by the single-index Equation 8.2. What is the systematic and nonsystematic (firm-specific) variance of this portfolio?

You hardly need arithmetic to see that the beta of the portfolio is the simple average of the individual security betas, which we denote β_P. Hence, the systematic variance equals $\beta_P^2 \sigma_M^2$. This is the level of market risk in Figure 8.1B. The factor variance (σ_M^2) and the degree of aggressiveness of the portfolio (β_P^2) determines the market risk of the portfolio. By choosing β_P^2, we decide the systematic variance.

The systematic part of each security return, $\beta_i R_M$, is fully determined by the market factor and therefore is perfectly correlated with the systematic part of any other security return. Hence, there are no diversification effects on systematic risk no matter how many securities are involved. As far as *market risk* goes, a single-security portfolio with a small beta will result in a low market-risk portfolio. The number of securities makes no difference.

It is quite different with unique risk. If you choose securities with small residual variances for a portfolio, it, too, will have low unique risk. But you can do even better by simply holding more securities, even if each has a large residual variance. Because the firm-specific effects are independent of each other, their risk effects are offsetting. This is the insurance principle applied to the firm-specific component of risk. The portfolio ends up with a negligible level of nonsystematic risk.

In sum, when we control the systematic risk of the portfolio by manipulating the average beta of the component securities, the number of securities is of no consequence. But in the case of *nonsystematic* risk, the number of securities involved is more important than the firm-specific variance of the securities. Sufficient diversification can virtually eliminate firm-specific risk. Understanding this distinction is essential to understanding the role of diversification in portfolio construction.

We have just seen that when forming highly diversified portfolios, firm-specific risk becomes *irrelevant*. Only systematic risk remains. We conclude that in mesuring security risk for diversified investors, we should focus our attention on the security's systematic risk. This means that for diversified investors the relevant risk measure for a security will be the security's beta, β, since firms with higher β have greater sensitivity to broad market disturbances. As Equation 8.3 makes clear, systematic risk will be determined by the product of market volatility, σ_M, and the firm's sensitivity to the market, β.

8.2   *Asset Allocation with Two Risky Assets*

A two-risky-asset allocation decision will rarely, if ever, involve two stocks. Investors are more likely to hold two risky mutual funds from different components of the capital market, such as a bond and a stock fund. Therefore, we consider a two-risky *funds* allocation problem, where the choice is between a well-diversified risky bond fund and a well-diversified stock fund. This distinction lets us analyze the allocation decision more clearly. Let us denote the bond fund by B and the stock fund by S.

The Three Rules of Two-Risky-Asset Portfolios

Suppose a proportion denoted by w_B is invested in the bond fund, and the remainder $1 - w_B$, denoted w_S, is invested in the stock fund. We approach the analysis following three rules (which apply the rules of statistics governing combinations of random variables):

Rule 1. The rate of return on the portfolio is a weighted average of the component securities returns, with the investment proportions as weights.

$$r_P = w_B r_B + w_S r_S \tag{8.6}$$

Rule 2. The *expected* rate of return on the portfolio is always a weighted average of the *expected* returns on the component securities, with the same portfolio proportions as weights. In symbols, the expectation of Equation 8.6 is:

$$E(r_P) = w_B E(r_B) + w_S E(r_S). \tag{8.7}$$

The first two rules are simple linear expressions. This is not so in the case of the portfolio variance, as the third rule shows.

Rule 3. The variance of the rate of return on the two-risky-asset portfolio is:

$$\sigma_P^2 = (w_B \sigma_B)^2 + (w_S \sigma_S)^2 + 2(w_B \sigma_B)(w_S \sigma_S)\rho_{BS} \tag{8.8}$$

where ρ_{BS} is the correlation coefficient between the returns on the stock and bond funds.

The variance of the portfolio is a *sum* of the contributions of the component security variances *plus* a term that involves the correlation coefficient between the component securities. This complication has a virtue: it holds a tremendous potential for gains from efficient diversification.

The Risk-Return Trade-Off with Two-Risky-Asset Portfolios

Suppose the standard deviation of bonds is 12 percent and of stocks is 25 percent, and there is zero correlation between the return on the bond fund and the return on the stock fund. A correlation coefficient of zero means a regression of bond returns on stock returns yields a beta of zero. In other words, stock returns do not help us predict bond returns, and bond returns do not help us predict stock returns.

Say we start out with a position of 100 percent in bonds, and we now consider a shift: invest 50 percent in bonds and 50 percent in stocks. We can compute the portfolio variance as in Equation 8.8:

Input data: $\sigma_B = .12$; $\sigma_S = .25$; $\rho_{BS} = 0$; $w_B = .5$; $w_S = .5$
Portfolio variance: $\sigma_P^2 = (.5 \times .12)^2 + (.5 \times .25)^2 + 2(.5 \times .12) \times (.5 \times 25) \times 0$
$$= .019225$$

The standard deviation of the portfolio (the square root of the variance, 0.019225) is 0.1387 (13.87 percent). Had we mistakenly analyzed the shift from investing 100 percent in bonds to investing 50 percent in stocks by averaging the two standard deviations, we would have incorrectly inferred an increase in the portfolio standard deviation by a full 6.50 percentage points to 18.5 percent, ([25 + 12]/2). Instead, the portfolio variance equation shows that the addition of stocks to the portfolio actually increases the portfolio standard deviation by only 1.87 percentage points. So the gain from diversification can be seen as a full 4.63 percent.

This gain is cost free in the sense that diversification allows us to experience the full contribution of the stock's higher expected return, while keeping the standard deviation below the average of the component standard deviations. As

Figure 8.5
Investment
opportunity set for
bond and stock
funds.

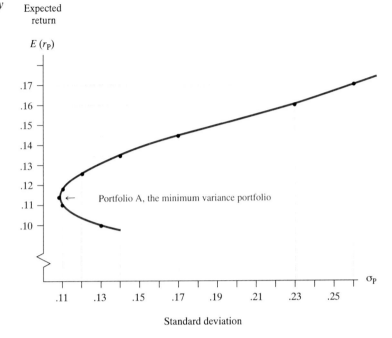

Equation 8.7 shows, the portfolio expected return is the weighted average of expected returns of the component securities. If the expected return on bonds is 10 percent and on stocks 17 percent, then shifting from 0 percent to 50 percent investment in stocks will increase our expected return from 10 percent to 13.5 percent.

What if we invest 75 percent in bonds and only 25 percent in stocks? We can construct a portfolio with an expected return higher than bonds (.75 × 10) + (.25 × 17) = 11.75 percent and, at the same time, a standard deviation that is less than bonds. Using Equation 8.8 again, we find that the portfolio variance is 0.012 and, accordingly, the portfolio standard deviation is 10.96 percent—less than the standard deviation of either bonds or stocks alone and less than the standard deviation of the 50–50 portfolio. Taking on a riskier asset (stocks) actually reduces portfolio risk! Such is the power of the unique bond and stock effects to diversify each other.

We can find investment proportions that will reduce risk further. The variance-minimizing proportions will be 81.27 percent in bonds and 18.73 percent in stocks.[1] Thus, the lowest-risk portfolio standard deviation will be 10.82 percent, and the portfolio's expected return will be 11.31 percent.

Is this portfolio preferable to the one with 25 percent in the stock fund? That depends on investor preferences, because the portfolio with the smaller variance also has a smaller expected return.

What the analyst can and must do, however, is to show investors the entire **investment opportunity set** as we do in Figure 8.5. This is the set of all attainable combinations of risk and return offered by portfolios formed using the available assets in differing proportions.

*Investment opportunity
set Set of available
portfolio risk-return
combinations.*

---

[1]With a zero correlation coefficient, the variance minimizing proportion in the bond fund is given by the expression: $\sigma^2_S/(\sigma^2_B + \sigma^2_S)$.

Table 8.1 *Investment Opportunity Set for Bond and Stock Funds*

Investment Proportions		Expected Return $E(r_P)$	Standard Deviation σ_P
w_B	w_S		
0.	1.0	.17	.25
.2	.8	.156	.2014
.4	.6	.142	.1575
.5	.5	.135	.1387
.6	.4	.128	.1232
.8	.2	.114	.10824
.8127*	.1873*	.1131	.108218
1.0	0.	.10	.12

$$E(r_B) = .10 \qquad E(r_S) = .17 \qquad \sigma_B = .12 \qquad \sigma_S = .25 \qquad \rho_{BS} = 0$$

*Minimum variance portfolio.

Points on the investment opportunity set of Figure 8.5 can be found by varying the investment proportions and computing the resulting expected returns and standard deviations from Equations 8.7 and 8.8. We feed the data input and the two equations into a personal computer and let it draw the graph. With the aid of the computer, we can easily find the portfolio composition for any point on the opportunity set. Table 8.1 shows the investment proportions and mean and standard deviation for a few portfolios.

As risk-averse investors desire northwestern-most combinations of expected returns and standard deviations, all portfolios below the point of the minimum standard deviation on the graph (portfolio A) will be rejected out of hand as inefficient. Any of those portfolios can be strictly dominated by another feasible portfolio lying directly above it (on the upward sloping portion of the curve) that has higher expected return and lower standard deviation. Choice among the other portfolios depends on the investor's level of risk aversion.

So far we have assumed a correlation of zero between stock and bond returns. We know that low correlations aid diversification and that a higher correlation coefficient between stocks and bonds results in a reduced effect of diversification. What are the implications of perfect positive correlation between bonds and stocks?

Assuming the correlation coefficient is 1.0 simplifies Equation 8.8 for portfolio variance. Looking at it again, you will see that substitution of $\rho_{BS} = 1$ in Equation 8.8 means we can "complete the square" of the quantities $w_B\sigma_B$ and $w_S\sigma_S$ to obtain

$$\sigma_P^2 = (w_B\sigma_B + w_S\sigma_S)^2$$

and, therefore,

$$\sigma_P = w_B\sigma_B + w_S\sigma_S. \tag{8.9}$$

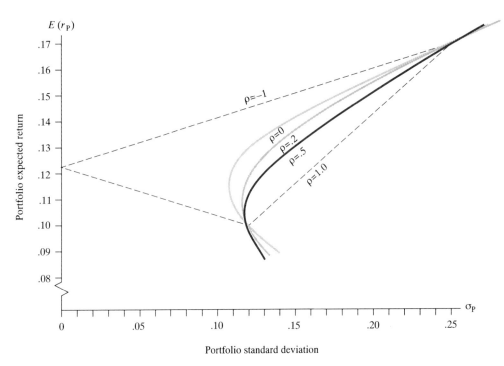

Figure 8.6 Investment opportunity sets for bonds and stocks with various
correlation coefficients.

Only in the special case of perfect positive correlation is the portfolio standard deviation a weighted average of the component security standard deviations, as is the case for expected returns. In this circumstance, there are no
gains to be had from diversification. Whatever the proportions of stocks and
bonds, both the portfolio mean and standard deviation are simply weighted averages. Figure 8.6 shows the opportunity set with perfect positive correlation—
a straight line through the component securities. No portfolio can be discarded
as inefficient in this case, and the choice among portfolios simply depends on
risk preference. Diversification in the case of perfect positive correlation is not
effective.

Our analysis has ranged from very attractive diversification benefits ($\rho_{BS} = 0$)
to no benefits at all ($\rho_{BS} = 1.0$). For ρ_{BS} within this range the benefits will be
somewhere in between. As Figure 8.6 illustrates, $\rho_{BS} = .5$ is a lot better for
diversification than perfect positive correlation and quite a bit worse than zero
correlation.

A realistic correlation coefficient between stocks and bonds based on historical experience actually is 0.20. The expected returns and standard deviations
that we have so far assumed also reflect historical experience, which is why we
include a graph for $\rho_{BS} = .2$ in Figure 8.6. Table 8.2 enumerates some of the
points on the various opportunity sets in Figure 8.6.

Negative correlation between a pair of assets is also possible. Where negative
correlation is present, there will be even greater diversification benefits. Again,
let us start with an extreme. With perfect negative correlation, we substitute

Table 8.2 *Investment Opportunity Sets for Bonds and Stocks with Various Correlation Coefficients*

w_B	$E(r_P)$	Portfolio Standard Deviation for Given Correlation				
		$\rho = -1.0$	$\rho = 0$	$\rho = .2$	$\rho = .5$	$\rho = 1.0$
0.	.17	.25	.25	.25	.25	.25
.2	.156	.176	.2014	.2061	.2130	.224
.4	.142	.102	.1575	.1664	.1789	.198
.6	.128	.028	.1232	.1344	.1496	.172
.8	.114	.046	.1082	.1168	.1285	.146
1.0	.10	.12	.12	.12	.12	.12
		Minimum Variance Portfolio				
w_B (min)*		.6757	.8127	.8706	1.0128	1.00
$E(r_P)$		.1227	.1131	.1091	.0981	.10
σ_P		.0	.108218	.1154	.1183	.12

$$*w_B \text{ (min)} = \frac{\sigma_S^2 - \sigma_B\sigma_S\rho_{BS}}{\sigma_B^2 + \sigma_S^2 - 2\sigma_B\sigma_S\rho_{BS}}$$

$\rho_{BS} = -1.0$ in Equation 8.8 and simplify it in the same way as with positive perfect correlation. Here, too, we can complete the square, this time, however, with different results:

$$\sigma_P^2 = (w_B\sigma_B - w_S\sigma_S)^2$$

and, therefore,

$$\sigma_P = ABS[w_B\sigma_B - w_S\sigma_S]. \tag{8.10}$$

The equation uses the absolute value because standard deviation is always positive.

With perfect negative correlation, the benefits from diversification stretch to the limit. Equation 8.10 points to the proportions that will reduce the portfolio standard deviation all the way to zero.[2] With our data, this will happen with $w_B = 67.57$ percent. While exposing us to zero risk, investing 32.43 percent in stocks (rather than placing all funds in bonds) will still increase the portfolio expected return to 12.27 percent. Of course, we can hardly expect results like this in reality.

Concept Check

Question 2. Suppose you are required to invest 40 percent in bonds.
a. What must be the correlation between stocks and bonds so that the portfolio standard deviation will be 15 percent?
b. What is the portfolio expected return?
c. Do you prefer this situation to being unrestricted with $\rho_{BS} = .2$?

---

[2]The proportion in bonds that will get the standard deviation to zero is: $w_B = \sigma_S/(\sigma_B + \sigma_S)$.

8.3   *The Optimal Risky Portfolio with a Risk-Free Asset*

In expanding the asset allocation problem to include a risk-free asset, let us assume a realistic correlation coefficient between stocks and bonds of 0.20. Suppose then that we are still confined to the risky bond and stock funds, but now can also invest in risk-free T-bills yielding 8 percent. Figure 8.7 shows the opportunity set generated from the bond and stock funds. This is the same opportunity set as graphed in Figure 8.6 with $\rho = .20$.

Two possible capital allocation lines (CALs) are drawn from the risk-free rate ($r_f = 8$ percent) to two feasible portfolios. The first possible CAL is drawn through the variance-minimizing portfolio (*A*), which invests 87.06 percent in bonds and 12.94 percent in stocks. Portfolio *A*'s expected return is 10.91 percent and its standard deviation is 11.54 percent. With a T-bill rate (r_f) of 8 percent, the reward-to-variability ratio of portfolio *A* (which is also the slope of the CAL that combines T-bills with portfolio *A*) is

$$S_A = \frac{E(r_A) - r_f}{\sigma_A}$$
$$= \frac{.1091 - .08}{.1154} = .25.$$

Now consider the CAL that uses portfolio *B* instead of *A*. Portfolio *B* invests 65 percent in bonds and 35 percent in stocks, providing an expected return of 12.45 percent with a standard deviation of 12.83 percent. Thus, the reward-to-variability ratio of any portfolio on the CAL of *B* is

$$S_B = \frac{.0445}{.1283} = .35.$$

This is significantly higher than the reward-to-variability ratio of the CAL of the variance-minimizing portfolio *A*.

Figure 8.7
The opportunity set using bonds and stocks and two capital allocation lines.

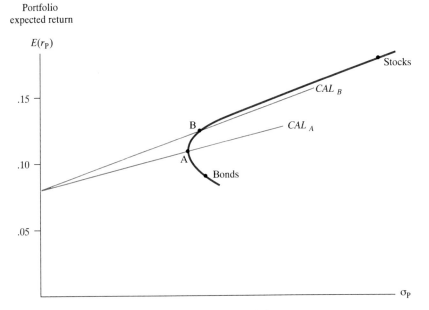

Portfolio standard deviation

If the CAL of B has a better reward-to-variability ratio, then, for any level of risk (standard deviation) that an investor is willing to bear, the expected return is higher with a portfolio on the CAL of B than of A. You can verify this from Figure 8.7, where the CAL of portfolio B lies above the CAL of portfolio A. In this sense, portfolio B dominates portfolio A.

In terms of profitability, the difference between the reward-to-variability ratios is

$$S_B - S_A = .10.$$

As a result, we get 10 extra basis points (0.1 percent) of expected return with CAL_B for each percentage point increase in standard deviation.

But why stop at portfolio B? We can continue to ratchet the CAL upward until it reaches the ultimate point of tangency with the investment opportunity set. This must yield the CAL with the highest feasible reward-to-variability ratio. Therefore, the tangency portfolio (O) in Figure 8.8 is the **optimal risky portfolio** to mix with T-bills, which may be defined as the risky portfolio resulting in the highest possible CAL. We can read the expected return and standard deviation of portfolio O (for "optimal") off the graph in Figure 8.8 as

$$E(r_O) = 14.36\%$$
$$\sigma_O = 17.07\%$$

which can be identified as the portfolio that invests 37.65 percent in bonds and 62.35 percent in stocks.[3] We can obtain a numerical solution to this problem using a computer program.

The CAL with our optimal portfolio has a slope of

$$S_O = \frac{.1436 - .08}{.1707} = .37$$

which is the reward-to-variability ratio of portfolio O. This slope exceeds the slope of any other feasible portfolio, as it must if it is to be the slope of the best feasible CAL.

In Chapter 7, we found the optimal *complete* portfolio given an optimal risky portfolio and the CAL generated by a combination of this portfolio and T-bills. Now that we have constructed the optimal risky portfolio (O), we can use the individual investor's degree of risk aversion (A) to calculate the optimal proportions of the complete portfolio.

An investor with $A = 4$ for risk aversion would take a position in portfolio O of

$$y = \frac{E(r_O) - r_f}{A\sigma_O^2} = \frac{.1436 - .08}{4 \times .1707^2} = .5457.$$

This means 54.57 percent of the investor's wealth will be invested in portfolio O and 45.43 percent in T-bills. Portfolio O is made up of 37.65 percent in the bond fund, so the percentage of wealth in bonds will be $yw_B = .5457 \times 37.65$

Optimal risky portfolio
The best combination of risky assets to be mixed with safe assets to form the complete portfolio.

---

[3]The proportion in bonds of portfolio O is:

$$w_B = \frac{[E(r_B) - r_f]\sigma_S^2 - [E(r_S) - r_f]\sigma_B \sigma_S \rho_{BS}}{[E(r_B) - r_f]\sigma_S^2 + [E(r_S) - r_f]\sigma_B^2 - [E(r_B) - r_f + E(r_S) - r_f]\sigma_B \sigma_S \rho_{BS}}$$

Figure 8.8
The optimal capital allocation line with bonds, stocks, and T-bills.

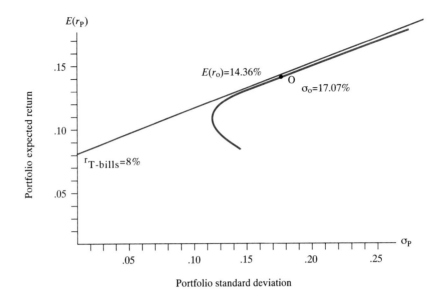

= 20.55 percent. Similarly, the investment in stocks will be yw_S = .5457 × 62.35 = 34.02 percent of wealth. The graphical representation of this solution is in Figures 8.9 and 8.10.

Concept Check

Question 3. A universe of securities includes a risky stock (X), a stock index fund (S), and T-bills. The data for the universe are:

	Expected Return	Standard Deviation
X	.25	.60
S	.20	.30
T-bills	.05	0.00

The correlation coefficient between X and S is −.2.
a. Draw the opportunity set of securities X and S.
b. Find the optimal risky portfolio (O) and its expected return and standard deviation.
c. Find the slope of the CAL supported by T-bills and portfolio O.
d. How much will an investor with A = 3.5 invest in X or S, and in T-bills?

8.4   *Efficient Diversification with Many Risky Assets*

We can extend this portfolio construction methodology to cover the case of many risky assets and a risk-free asset. First, we offer an overview. As in the two-risky-asset example, the problem has three separate steps. To begin, we

Figure 8.9
The complete portfolio with coefficient of risk aversion A = 4.

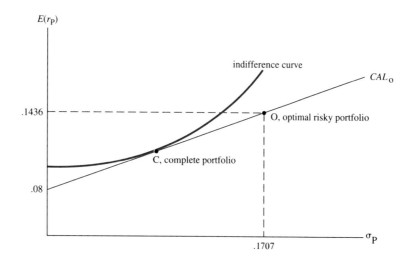

Figure 8.10
The composition of the complete portfolio.

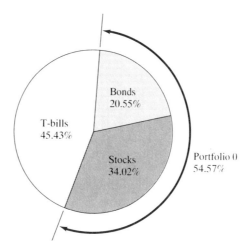

identify the best possible or *efficient* risk-return combinations available from the universe of risky assets. Next we determine the optimal portfolio of risky assets by finding the portfolio that supports the steepest CAL. Finally, we choose an appropriate complete portfolio by mixing the risk-free asset with the optimal risky portfolio.

The Efficient Frontier of Risky Assets

First, we determine the risk-return opportunity set. The aim is to construct the northwestern-most portfolios (in terms of expected return and standard deviation) from the universe of securities. The inputs are the expected return and standard deviation of each asset in the universe, along with the correlation coefficients between each pair of assets. These data come from security analysis, to be discussed in Part Four. The graph that connects all the northwestern-most

Figure 8.11

The efficient frontier of risky assets and individual assets.

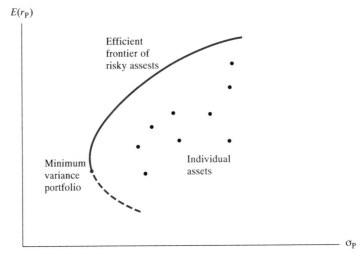

$E(r_P)$

Efficient
frontier of
risky assests

Minimum
variance
portfolio

Individual
assets

σ_P

Portfolio standard deviation

Efficient frontier
Graph representing a
set of portfolios that
maximize expected re-
turn at each level of
portfolio risk.

portfolios is called the **efficient frontier** of risky assets. It represents the set of portfolios that offer the highest possible expected rate of return for each level of portfolio standard deviation. These portfolios may be viewed as efficiently diversified. One such frontier is shown in Figure 8.11.

Expected return-standard deviation combinations corresponding to any *individual* asset ends up inside the efficient frontier, because single-asset portfolios are inefficient—as they are not efficiently diversified.

When we choose among portfolios on the efficient frontier, we can immediately discard portfolios below the variance-minimizing portfolio. These all may be dominated by portfolios on the upper half of the frontier with equal risk but higher expected returns. Therefore, the real choice is among portfolios on the efficient frontier above the minimum variance portfolio.

Various constraints may preclude a particular investor from choosing portfolios on the efficient frontier, however. If an institution is prohibited by law from taking short positions in any asset, for example, the portfolio manager must add constraints to the computer-optimization program that rule out negative (short) positions. In this case, the individual asset with the highest expected return in the universe will lie on the efficient frontier. The only way to obtain that rate of return, if short sales are ruled out, is to hold the highest-expected return asset alone as the entire risky portfolio.

Short sale restrictions are only one constraint. Some clients may want to assume a minimum level of expected *dividend yield*. In this case, data input must include a set of expected dividend yields. The optimization program is made to include a constraint to ensure the expected *portfolio* dividend yield will equal or exceed the desired level.

Another popular constraint is against investment in companies engaged in "undesirable social activity." The accompanying box reproduces a *Wall Street Journal* article about socially responsible funds that constrain portfolio choice according to several criteria.

Basically, portfolio managers can tailor the efficient frontier to meet any particular objective. Of course, satisfying constraints carries a price tag. An efficient frontier subject to a number of constraints will offer a lower reward-to-variability ratio than a less constrained one. Clients should be aware of this cost and may want to think twice about constraints that are not mandated by law.

Choosing the Optimal Risky Portfolio

The second step of the optimization plan involves the risk-free asset. Using the current risk-free rate, we search for the capital allocation line with the highest reward-to-variability ratio (the steepest slope), as shown in Figure 8.8.

The CAL that is supported by the optimal risky portfolio (*O*) will be tangent to the efficient frontier of risky assets discussed above. This CAL dominates all alternative feasible lines (the dashed lines that are drawn through the frontier). Portfolio *O*, therefore, is the optimal risky portfolio.

The Optimal Complete Portfolio and the Separation Property

Finally, in the third step, the investor chooses the appropriate mix between the optimal risky portfolio (*O*) and T-bills, exactly as in Figure 8.9.

A portfolio manager will offer the same risky portfolio (*O*) to all clients, no matter what their degree of risk aversion. Risk aversion comes into play only when clients select their desired point on the CAL. More risk-averse clients will invest more in the risk-free asset and less in the optimal risky portfolio *O* than less risk-averse clients, but both will use portfolio *O* as the optimal risky investment vehicle.

Separation property
The property that port-folio choice can be separated into two independent tasks: (1) determination of the optimal risky port-folio, which is a purely technical problem, and (2) the personal choice of the best mix of the risky portfolio and the risk-free asset.

This result is called a **separation property,** introduced by James Tobin (1958), the 1983 Nobel Laureate for economics; it implies that portfolio choice can be separated into two independent tasks. The first task, which includes steps one and two, determination of the optimal risky portfolio (*O*), is purely technical. Given the particular input data, the best risky portfolio is the same for all clients regardless of risk aversion. The second task, construction of the complete port-folio from bills and portfolio *O*, however, depends on personal preference. Here the client is the decision maker.

Of course, the optimal risky portfolio for different clients may vary because of portfolio constraints such as dividend yield requirements, tax considerations, or other client preferences. Our analysis, though, suggests that a few portfolios may be sufficient to serve the demands of a wide range of investors. We see here the theoretical basis of the mutual fund industry.

If the optimal portfolio is the same for all clients, professional management is more efficient and less costly. One management firm can serve a number of clients with relatively small incremental administrative costs.

The (computerized) optimization technique is the easiest part of portfolio construction. If different managers use different input data to develop different efficient frontiers, they will offer different "optimal" portfolios. Therefore, the real arena of the competition among portfolio managers is in the sophisticated security analysis that underlies their choices. The rule of GIGO (garbage in–garbage out) applies fully to portfolio selection. If the quality of the security analysis is poor, a passive portfolio such as a market index fund can yield better results than an active portfolio tilted toward seemingly favorable securities.

Doing Good and Doing All Right: Investors Applying Ethical Values

George Pillsbury, a wealthy Bostonian who spends a lot of time steering foundation money to liberal causes, decided last summer that his personal portfolio should more closely reflect his social views.

YOUR

MONEY

MATTERS

So he put $400,000 in the hands of Franklin Research & Development Corp., a Boston firm specializing in what it calls "socially responsible investing." A year later, Mr. Pillsbury's account had grown 44 percent, to $576,000, beating the return of the Standard & Poor's 500 stock index by about eight percentage points.

At a time when many states, cities, and universities are selling stock in companies that do business in South Africa, a growing number of individuals are putting their money where their ethical values are. Last year, says the Boston-based Social Investment Forum, individuals invested more than $8 billion with money managers using social and political criteria.

To some critics, avoiding a company to contest apartheid, industrial pollution, or a lack of women in positions of authority is like throwing money away. "If you make noneconomic choices, you will get noneconomic results—less profit," says Jack Albertine, vice chairman of Chicago-based Farley Industries Inc.

Being Charitable

Indeed, few investors can expect to match Mr. Pillsbury's good fortune over any extended time. And the performance of some money managers can be charitably described as only mediocre.

But individuals who exclude investments in companies that don't meet certain social or political criteria probably don't do any worse, on average, than the typical investor. While none of the nine "socially responsible" mutual funds tracked by Lipper Analytical Services Inc. outperformed the S&P 500 in the year through June 30, neither did the average mutual fund.

"By restricting your investments in any way, you cannot be better off," says Marshall Blume, a professor of finance at the University of Pennsylvania's Wharton School. In fact, he says, "you are probably worse off—but the amount may be so trivial that you can ignore it," particularly with a small personal portfolio.

Allan Emkin, vice president of Wilshire Associates, a Santa Monica, Calif., investment consulting firm, agrees. "When you limit the number of opportunities, you limit some of the potential for return," he says. By restricting investment choices for large institutional portfolios, he says, "you're going to forgo something."

PROFITS IN CONSCIENCE
"Socially Responsible" Mutual Funds

Fund	Assets (In millions)*	Total Return (In percent)†
New Alternatives	$ 1.0	35.4%
Calvert Social Investment Managed Growth Portfolio	52.4	32.9
Pioneer Three	520.8	30.4
Parnassus	1.9	28.9
Pioneer II	2,672.5	26.5
Pax World	40.8	25.2
Pioneer	1,526.4	24.3
Dreyfus Third Century	184.3	18.4
Pioneer Bond	26.1	15.3
Mutual Fund Average		27.7
Standard & Poor's 500-Stock Index		35.6

*On 3/31/86.

†12 months through 6/30/86.

Source: Lipper Analytical Services Inc.

The loss isn't necessarily great, however, because the universe of potential investments is huge even if one eliminates some companies. With small personal portfolios, which by their nature are limited in breadth, "it probably doesn't matter," Mr. Emkin says.

Richard Dixon, an associate with Wilshire, says the real problem isn't return, but market risk. Restricted portfolios tend to eliminate large multinational corporations, replacing them with smaller firms whose stock is more volatile, says Mr. Dixon. Investments with low market risk typically fall less rapidly than more volatile investments in a down market and rise less sharply in a bull market.

"The greater risk should actually improve return" over long periods of time because active stocks tend to gain more than they lose, he says. "But for the risk-averse investor, the greater volatility of smaller capitalization companies may be something to avoid."

A recent study by Wilshire compared hypothetical portfolios with and without South Africa-related securities from 1979 to 1984. The 21.1 percent return of the "South Africa-free" portfolio outperformed the unrestricted portfolio by almost seven points, says Mr. Dixon. But the stock of the generally smaller companies in the restricted portfolio reacted more severely to swings in the market, he adds.

When looking at actual mutual funds, however, the risk factor doesn't loom that large. Spero Kripotos, vice president of CDA Investment Technologies Inc., a Silver Spring, Md., firm that tracks mutual fund performance, says that mutual funds in general are investments with low to average risk. Comparisons by CDA show that funds using social and political investment criteria are no different.

Proponents of social investing, moreover, have little doubt of the wisdom of their approach. Robert J. Schwartz, a New York broker who encourages clients to set their own ethical standards, says he can shape portfolios to avoid investments in South Africa, nuclear utilities or weapons makers without sacrificing return. In 1985, he says, his "socially screened" equity and fixed-income accounts grew an average of 25.2 percent.

Julie Wendrich, a broker with E.F. Hutton Inc. in Cambridge, Mass., says concern about a company's social responsibility can actually improve return by helping investors avoid potential problems. "A company that will be spending millions to clean up its pollutions or on product liability suits . . . could get torn up," she says. By practicing what she preaches with her own money, Ms. Wendrich

says she turned $21,000 into $55,000 in the past nine months.

A Sacrifice?

Amy L. Domini, vice president of Franklin Research & Development, says she can't promise profits like Mr. Pillsbury's 44 percent first-year return. But she says Franklin, which handles $55 million in balanced portfolios for some 90 clients, had a 15.2 percent average annual return in the five years through 1985, about half a point better than the S&P 500. "Looking at our performance," she adds, "do you think our clients are sacrificing anything?"

At first glance, it might seem that social responsibility had been costly for investors in Dreyfus Third Century Fund. But Jeffrey Friedman, its portfolio manager, says the practice of excluding investments on ethical grounds isn't the reason the fund's total return in the 12 months through June 30 was only 18.4 percent, far short of the 27.7 percent mutual-fund average.

"Over the long run, the social criteria doesn't interfere," Mr. Friedman says. What hurt this past year, he says, was an old-fashioned mistake: being too cautious during a bull market. "I don't think the economy could support this kind of market."

Ultimately, investment performance is in the eye of the beholder. People who put their money in a do-good fund expect psychic returns in addition to profits.

Anne Kessler, a San Francisco banker who says she looks for ways to "put money to use for human value," invested $9,000 last year in the Parnassus Fund "because there wasn't a trade-off" between her social and financial goals. Parnassus, which combines social criteria with the contrarian approach of investing in out-of-favor businesses, has recently been edging out the industry average; it had a 28.9 percent return for the year ended June 30.

Says Ms. Kessler. "I want to invest in things I believe in long-term, as well as make money now."

Concept Check

Question 4. Two portfolio managers work for competing investment management houses. Each employs security analysts to prepare input data for the construction of the optimal portfolio. When all is completed, the efficient frontier obtained by manager A dominates that of manager B in that A's optimal risky portfolio lies northwest of B's. What would you say if A's manager advertised as "best choice" on the basis of these frontiers?

8.5   *Optimal Portfolios with Restrictions on Risk-Free Investments*

The availability of a risk-free asset greatly simplifies the portfolio decision. When all investors can borrow and lend at the risk-free rate, the result is a *unique* optimal risky portfolio that is appropriate for all investors. All investors use the same risky portfolio and differ only in the proportion they invest in it and in the risk-free asset. This portfolio maximizes the reward-to-variability ratio.

What if a risk-free asset is not available? Although T-bills are risk-free assets in nominal terms, inflation uncertainty makes them risky in real or price-adjusted terms. Without a risk-free asset, there is no tangency portfolio that is best for all investors. Investors must choose a portfolio from the efficient frontier of risky assets redrawn as in Figure 8.12.

Investors will superimpose their set of indifference curves on the efficient frontier as Figure 8.12 shows. The optimal portfolio (*P*) for the investor whose risk aversion is represented by the set of indifference curves in Figure 8.12 is tangent to the highest attainable indifference curve.

Investors who are more risk averse will have steeper indifference curves. Their tangency portfolios will have lower standard deviations and expected returns than portfolio *P*, such as portfolio *Q*.

The common feature of all these rational investors is that they choose portfolios on the efficient frontier; that is, they choose mean-variance efficient portfolios.

Figure 8.12
Individual portfolio selection without a risk-free asset.

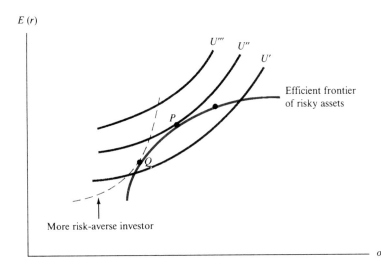

8.6 *Asset Allocation and Efficient Diversification*

The technique we have described does not differentiate asset allocation—choices among broad asset classes—from efficient diversification—choice of the specific securities held within each asset class. For a variety of organizational reasons, large institutions may decompose their investment decisions into two separate components, asset allocation and efficient diversification. Many practitioners are convinced that doing so is justified on grounds of efficiency.

In fact, some research (Binson, Hood, and Bibower, 1986) has used statistical techniques to divide professionally managed portfolio returns into components attributable to asset allocation decisions and security selection (within asset class) decisions. The results are interesting—asset allocation turns out the dominant factor.

Managers who believe in these results will put their best resources into asset allocation. That is, they will invest most heavily in analysis at the macro and industry level. Their asset-class portfolios may be passive funds. Active managers may use security analysis to improve on the index portfolio. We discuss this kind of operation in Part Six on active portfolio management.

Factor models facilitate the distinction between asset allocation and security selection. They also allow for the introduction of inflation as a distinct factor. This aspect will be discussed in Chapter 9.

Summary

1. The expected rate of return of a portfolio is the weighted average of the component asset expected returns with the investment proportions as weights.

2. The variance of a portfolio is a sum of the contributions of the component securities variance *plus* terms involving the correlation among assets.

3. Even if correlations are positive, the portfolio standard deviation will be less than the weighted average of the component standard deviations, as long as the assets are not *perfectly* positively correlated. Thus, portfolio diversification is of value as long as assets are less than perfectly correlated.

4. The contribution of an asset to portfolio variance arises from its correlation with the other assets in the portfolio, as well as on its own variance. An asset that is perfectly negatively correlated with a portfolio can be used to reduce the portfolio variance to zero. Thus, it can serve as a perfect hedge.

5. The efficient frontier of risky assets is the graphical representation of a set of portfolios that maximizes portfolio expected return for a given level of portfolio standard deviation. Rational investors will choose a portfolio on the efficient frontier.

6. A portfolio manager identifies the efficient frontier by first establishing estimates for the expected returns and standard deviations, and the correlations among them. The input data are then fed into an optimization program that produces the investment proportions, expected returns, and standard deviations of the portfolios on the efficient frontier.

7. In general, portfolio managers will identify different efficient portfolios because of differences in the methods and quality of security analysis. Managers

compete on the quality of their security analysis relative to their management fees.

8. If a risk-free asset is available and input data are identical, all investors will choose the same efficient frontier portfolio, the one that is tangent to the CAL. All investors with identical input data will hold the identical risky portfolio, differing only in how much each allocates to this optimal portfolio and to the risk-free asset. This result is characterized as the separation principle of portfolio selection.

9. When a risk-free asset is not available, investors choose a risky portfolio on the efficient frontier according to their degree of risk aversion.

Key Terms

beta, 213
diversifiable risk, 212
efficient frontier, 228
firm-specific risk, 212
index model, 214
investment opportunity
set, 220

market risk, 212
nondiversifiable
risk, 212
optimal risky
portfolio, 225

separation
property, 229
systematic risk, 212
unique risk, 212

Selected Readings

Three frequently cited papers on the impact of diversification on portfolio risk are:
Fisher, L., and J. H. Lorie. "Some Studies of the Variability of Returns on Investments in Common Stocks." *Journal of Business* 43 (April 1970), pp. 99–134.

Evans, John L., and Stephen H. Archer. "Diversification and the Reduction of Dispersion: An Empirical Analysis." *Journal of Finance*, December 1968.

Wagner, W. H., and S. C. Lau. "The Effect of Diversification on Risk." *Financial Analysts Journal*, November–December 1971.

The seminal works on portfolio selection, largely responsible for Harry Markowitz's Nobel prize are:
Markowitz, Harry M. "Portfolio Selection." *Journal of Finance*, March 1952, and *Portfolio Selection: Efficient Diversification of Investments*. New York: John Wiley & Sons, 1959.

Problem Sets

The following data apply to Questions 1–6:

A pension fund manager is considering three mutual funds. The first is a stock fund, the second is a long-term government and corporate bond fund, and the third is a T-bill money market fund that yields a sure rate of 9 percent. The probability distribution of the risky funds is:

	Expected Return	Standard Deviation
Stock fund (S)	.22	.32
Bond fund (B)	.13	.23

The correlation between the fund returns is 0.15.

1. Tabulate and draw the investment opportunity set of the two risky funds. Use investment proportions for the stock fund of 0 to 100 percent in increments of 20 percent. What expected return and standard deviation does your graph show for the minimum variance portfolio?

2. Draw a tangent from the risk-free rate to the opportunity set. What does your graph show for the expected return and standard deviation of the optimal risky portfolio?

3. What is the reward-to-variability ratio of the best feasible CAL?

4. Suppose now that your portfolio must yield an expected return of 15 percent and be efficient, that is, on the best feasible CAL.
   a. What is the standard deviation of your portfolio?
   b. What is the proportion invested in the T-bill fund and each of the two risky funds?

5. If you were to use only the two risky funds, and still require an expected return of 15 percent, what would be the investment proportions of your portfolio? Compare its standard deviation to that of the optimal portfolio in problem 4. What do you conclude?

6. Suppose you can invest in T-bills but cannot borrow. You wish to construct a portfolio with an expected return of 29 percent. What are the appropriate portfolio proportions and the resulting standard deviation? What reduction in standard deviation could you achieve if you were allowed to borrow at the risk-free rate?

7. Stocks offer an expected rate of return of 18 percent with a standard deviation of 22 percent, and gold offers an expected return of 10 percent with a standard deviation of 30 percent.
   a. In light of the apparent inferiority of gold to stocks with respect to both mean return and volatility, would anyone hold gold? If so, demonstrate graphically why one would do so.
   b. How would you answer *a* if the correlation coefficient between gold and stocks were 1.0? Draw a graph illustrating who would or would not hold gold. Could these expected returns, standard deviations, and correlation represent an equilibrium for the security market?

8. Suppose that many stocks are traded in the market, and it is possible to borrow at the risk-free rate, r_f. The characteristics of two of the stocks are as follows:

Stock	Expected Return	Standard Deviation
A	.08	.40
B	.13	.60
Correlation $= -1$		

Could the equilibrium r_f be greater than 0.10?

9. Assume expected returns and standard deviations for all securities, as well as the risk-free rate for lending and borrowing, are known. Will investors arrive at the same optimal risky portfolio? Explain.

10. What is the relationship of the portfolio standard deviation to the weighted average of the standard deviations of the component assets?

11. A project has a 0.7 chance of doubling your investment in a year and a 0.3 chance of halving your investment in a year. What is the standard deviation of the rate of return on this investment?

The following data apply to questions 12 through 14:

Hennessy & Associates manages a $30 million equity portfolio for the multi-manager Wilstead Pension Fund. Jason Jones, financial vice president of Wilstead, noted that Hennessy had rather consistently achieved the best record among the Wilstead's six equity managers. Performance of the Hennessy portfolio had been clearly superior to that of the S&P 500 in four of the past five years. In the one less favorable year, the shortfall was trivial.

Hennessy is a "bottom-up" manager. The firm largely avoids any attempt to "time the market." It also focuses on selection of individual stocks, rather than the weighting of favored industries.

There is no apparent conformity of style among the six equity managers. The five managers, other than Hennessy, manage portfolios aggregating $250 million made up of more than 150 individual issues.

Jones is convinced that Hennessy is able to apply superior skill to stock selection, but the favorable results are limited by the high degree of diversification in the portfolio. Over the years, the portfolio generally held 40–50 stocks, with about 2 percent to 3 percent of total funds committed to each issue. The reason Hennessy seemed to do well most years was because the firm was able to identify each year 10 or 12 issues which registered particularly large gains.

Based on this overview, Jones outlined the following plan to the Wilstead pension committee:

> Let's tell Hennessy to limit the portfolio to no more than 20 stocks. Hennessy will double the commitments to the stocks that it really favors, and eliminate the remainder. Except for this one new restriction, Hennessy should be free to manage the portfolio exactly as before.

All the members of the pension committee generally supported Jones's proposal, because all agreed that Hennessy had seemed to demonstrate superior skill in selecting stocks. Yet, the proposal was a considerable departure from previous practice, and several committee members raised questions. Respond to each of these questions:

12. Answer the following:
    a. Will the limitation of 20 stocks likely increase or decrease the risk of the portfolio? Explain.
    b. Is there any way Hennessy could reduce the number of issues from 40 to 20 without significantly affecting risk? Explain.
13. One committee member was particularly enthusiastic concerning Jones's proposal. He suggested that Hennessy's performance might benefit further from reduction in the number of issues to 10. If the reduction to 20 could be expected to be advantageous, explain why reduction to 10 might be less likely to be advantageous. (Assume that Wilstead will evaluate the Hennessy portfolio independently of the other portfolios in the fund.)
14. Another committee member suggested that, rather than evaluate each managed portfolio independently of other portfolios, it might be better to consider the effects of a change in the Hennessy portfolio on the total fund. Explain how this broader point of view could affect the committee decision to limit the holdings in the Hennessy portfolio to either 10 or 20 issues.

Appendix   *The Fallacy of Time Diversification*

In Chapter 1, we pointed out a common misunderstanding of the rationale behind the insurance industry. Many people believe risk pooling explains the industry, yet risk sharing is what attracts investors to become insurers. When insurers hold a small share of their portfolios in any given policy, then any risk, no matter how unique and "unpooled," will be tolerable. Of course, insurers have to worry about correlation among insured risks, lest the entire portfolio collapse from one shock and its ripple effect.

The root of the misconception lies in comparing portfolios of different sizes. Pooling risks means the portfolio grows in total size. Each additional life insurance policy that a company sells increases the dollar value of the entire portfolio, hence the dollar risk always goes up with risk pooling. Thus, while the properties of the larger pie may be better, it may still be too large to swallow. Risk sharing, on the other hand, means we take a given pie and split it into ever smaller parts, making each palatable for a small mouth. We take each life insurance policy and sell a small portion of it to many investors. In this way, the size of the pie that each investor holds can be made small enough.

A parallel version of this misconception is "time diversification." Consider the case of Mr. Frier. Planning to retire in five years makes him an investor with a five-year horizon. Confronted with the fact that the standard deviation of stock returns exceeds 20 percent per year, Mr. Frier has become aware of his acute risk aversion and is keeping most of his retirement portfolio in money market assets.

Recently, Mr. Frier has learned of the large potential gains from diversification. He wonders whether investing for as long as five years might not take the standard deviation sting out of stocks while keeping the expected return money.

Mr. Mavin, a highly recommended financial advisor, argues that the time factor is all important. He cites academic research showing that asset rates of return over successive holding periods are independent. Therefore, he argues that over a five-year period, returns in good years and bad years will cancel out, making the average rate of return on the portfolio over the investment period less risky than would appear from an analysis of single-year volatility. Because returns in each year are independent, Mr. Mavin tells Mr. Frier a five-year investment is equivalent to a portfolio of five equally weighted, independent assets.

Mr. Frier is convinced and intends to transfer his funds to a stock fund right away. Is his conviction warranted? Does Mr. Mavin's time diversification really reduce risk?

It is true that the standard deviation of the *average* annual rate of return over the five years really will be smaller than the one-year standard deviations, as Mr. Mavin claims. But what about the volatility of Mr. Frier's total retirement fund?

Mr. Mavin is wrong: time diversification does not reduce risk. While it is true that the per year *average* rate of return has a smaller standard deviation for a longer time horizon, it is also true that the uncertainty compounds over a greater number of years. Unfortunately, this latter effect dominates; that is, the total T-year return becomes more uncertain the longer the investment horizon (T years).

Investing for more than one holding period means the amount at risk is growing. This is analogous to an insurer taking on more insurance policies. The fact that these policies are independent does not offset the effect of placing more funds at risk. Focus on the standard deviation of the *average* rate of return should never obscure the more proper emphasis on the ultimate dollar value of a portfolio strategy.

Using the standard deviation of one-year returns to analyze Mr. Frier's problem is appropriate only if the dollar risk grows in direct proportion to the number of years at risk. If this assumption seems too moderate or too extreme, one can adjust it accordingly. Using the standard deviation of the average will almost never be the appropriate solution.

Chapter

9

Capital Asset Pricing and Arbitrage Pricing Theory

The capital asset pricing model, almost always referred to as the CAPM, is a centerpiece of modern financial economics. It was developed by William F. Sharpe, who was awarded the 1990 Nobel Prize for economics.

The CAPM gives us a precise prediction of the relationship we should observe between the risk of an asset and its expected return. This relationship serves two vital functions.

First, it provides a benchmark rate of return for evaluating possible investments. For example, a security analyst might want to know whether the expected return forecast for a stock is more or less than its "fair" return given risk. Second, the model helps us make an educated guess as to the expected return on assets that have not yet been traded in the marketplace. For example, how do we price an initial public offering of stock? How will a major new investment project affect the return investors require on a company's stock? Although the CAPM does not fully withstand empirical tests, it is widely used because of the insight it offers and because its accuracy suffices for many important applications.

As we saw in Chapter 6, the exploitation of security mispricing to earn risk-free economic profits is called arbitrage. It typically involves the simultaneous purchase and sale of equivalent securities (usually in different markets) in order to profit from discrepancies in their price relationship.

Perhaps the most basic principle of capital market theory is that equilibrium market prices are rational in that they rule out arbitrage opportunities. Pricing relationships that guarantee the absence of arbitrage possibilities are extremely powerful. If actual security prices allow for arbitrage, the result is strong pressure on security prices to restore equilibrium. Only a few investors need be aware of arbitrage opportunities to bring about a large volume of trades, and these trades will bring prices back into balance.

The first to introduce the concept of arbitrage into economics were Modigliani and Miller, both Nobel laureates (1985 and 1990). As an alternative model for pricing capital assets, arbitrage pricing theory (APT), developed by Stephen Ross, leads to the same relationship between expected return and risk as the CAPM, despite the different assumptions. We explore this relationship using well-diversified portfolios and discuss the similarities and differences between the APT and the CAPM. After studying this chapter you should be able to:

- Use the implications of capital market theory to compute security risk premiums.
- Construct and use the security market line.
- Take advantage of an arbitrage opportunity with a portfolio that includes mispriced securities.
- Use arbitrage pricing theory with more than one factor to identify mispriced securities.

9.1 *The Capital Asset Pricing Model*

Capital asset pricing model (CAPM) A model that relates the required rate of return for a security to its risk as measured by beta.

The **Capital Asset Pricing Model,** or **CAPM,** predicts the relationship between the risk and equilibrium expected returns on risky assets. We will approach the CAPM by posing "what if" questions in a simplified world. Thinking about an admittedly unrealistic world allows a relatively easy leap to the solution. With this accomplished, we can add complexity to the environment, one step at a time, and see how the theory must be amended. This process allows us to develop a reasonably realistic and comprehensible model.

We make a number of simplifying assumptions that lead to the basic version of the CAPM. One fundamental assumption is that individuals are as alike as possible, with the notable exceptions of initial wealth and risk aversion. Conformity of investor behavior vastly simplifies our analysis. The list of assumptions goes like this:

1. There are many investors, each with an endowment (wealth) that is small compared to the total endowment of all investors. Investors are price takers in that they act as though security prices are unaffected by their own trades. This is the usual perfect competition assumption of microeconomics.

2. All investors plan for one identical holding period. This behavior sometimes is said to be shortsighted, in that it ignores everything that might happen after the end of the single-period horizon. Myopic behavior is, in general, suboptimal.

3. Investments are confined to a universe of publicly traded financial assets, such as stocks and bonds, and to unlimited risk-free borrowing or lending arrangements. This assumption rules out investment in nontraded assets such as in education (human capital), private enterprises, and governmentally funded assets such as town halls and nuclear submarines.

4. Investors pay neither taxes on returns nor transaction costs (commissions and service charges) on trades in securities. In reality, investors are in different tax brackets, which frequently affects the type of assets they invest in. Income

from interest and dividends may present different tax implications than income from unrealized capital gains. Furthermore, trading costs money, and commissions and fees depend on the size of the trade and the good standing of the individual investor.

5. All investors are rational mean-variance optimizers, meaning they all attempt to construct efficient frontier portfolios.

6. All investors analyze securities in the same way and share the same economic view of the world. Hence, they all end with identical estimates of the probability distribution of future cash flows from investing in the available securities. This means that given a set of security prices and the risk-free interest rate, all investors use the same expected returns, standard deviations, and correlations to generate the efficient frontier and the unique optimal risky portfolio. This assumption is often called *homogeneous expectations*.

These assumptions represent the "if" part of the "what if" analysis. Obviously, they ignore many real-world complexities. With these assumptions, however, we can gain some powerful insights into the nature of equilibrium in security markets.

Next, we summarize the equilibrium that will prevail in this hypothetical world of securities and investors, that is, the "what" that follows from the assumptions in the "if" part. We explain these implications in the following sections.

Market portfolio The portfolio for which each security is held in proportion to its market value.

1. All investors will choose to hold the **market portfolio** (*M*), which includes all assets of the universe. For simplicity, we shall refer to all assets as stocks. The proportion of each stock in the market portfolio equals the market value of the stock (price per share times the number of shares outstanding) divided by the total market value of all stocks.

2. The market portfolio will be on the efficient frontier. Moreover, it will be the optimal risky portfolio, the tangency point of the CAL to the efficient frontier. As a result, the capital market line (CML), the line from the risk-free rate through the market portfolio, *M,* is also the best attainable capital allocation line (CAL). All investors hold *M* as their optimal risky portfolio, differing only in the amount invested in it as compared to investment in the risk-free asset.

3. The risk premium on the market portfolio will be proportional to the variance of the market portfolio and the market degree of risk aversion. Mathematically,

$$E(r_M) - r_f = A^* \sigma_M^2$$

where σ_M is the standard deviation of the market portfolio and A^* is the degree of risk aversion of the average investor.

4. The risk premium on individual assets will be proportional to the risk premium on the market portfolio (*M*) and to the *beta coefficient* of the security on the market portfolio. This implies the rate of return on the market portfolio is the single factor of the security market. The beta then measures the extent to which returns on the stock respond to the returns of the market portfolio. Formally, beta is the regression (slope) coefficient of the security return on the market portfolio return, representing the sensitivity of the stock return to fluctuations in the overall security market.

Why All Investors Hold the Market Portfolio

Given all our assumptions, it is easy to see why all investors hold identical risky portfolios. If all investors use identical mean-variance analysis (assumption 5), apply it to the same universe of securities (assumption 3), with an identical time horizon (assumption 2), use the same security analysis (assumption 6), and experience identical tax consequences (assumption 4), they all must arrive at the same determination of the optimal risky portfolio. That is, they all derive identical efficient frontiers and find the same tangency for the capital allocation line (CAL) from T-bills (risk-free rate, zero standard deviation) to that frontier, as in Figure 9.1.

With everyone choosing to hold the same risky portfolio, stocks will be represented in the aggregate risky portfolio in the same proportion as they are in each investor's (common) risky portfolio. If GM represents 1 percent in each common risky portfolio, GM will be 1 percent of the aggregate risky portfolio. This in fact is the market portfolio since the market is no more than the aggregate of all individual portfolios. Because each investor uses the market portfolio for the optimal risky portfolio, the CAL in this case is called the capital market line, or CML, as in Figure 9.1.

Suppose the optimal portfolio of our investors does not include the stock of some company, say, Delta Air Lines. When no investor is willing to hold Delta stock, the demand is zero, and the stock price will take a free fall. As Delta stock gets progressively cheaper, it begins to look more attractive, while all other stocks look (relatively) less attractive. Ultimately, Delta will reach a price where it is desirable to include it in the optimal stock portfolio, and investors will buy.

Figure 9.1
The efficient frontier
and the capital
market line.

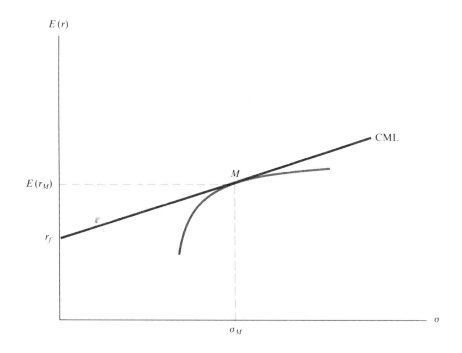

This price adjustment process guarantees that all stocks will be included in the optimal portfolio. The only issue is the price. At a given price level, investors will be willing to buy a stock, at another price not. The bottom line is this: if all investors hold an *identical* risky portfolio, this portfolio has to be the *market* portfolio.

The Passive Strategy Is Efficient

A passive strategy, using the CML as the optimal CAL, is a powerful alternative to an active strategy. The market portfolio proportions are a result of profit-oriented "buy" and "sell" orders that cease only when there is no more profit to be made. And in the simple world of the CAPM, all investors use precious resources in security analysis. An investor who takes a free ride by choosing the market portfolio benefits from the efficiency of the strategy. In fact, an active investor who chooses any other portfolio will end on a CAL that is less efficient than the CML where we may find passive investors.

*Mutual fund theorem
That all investors de-
sire the same portfolio
of risky assets and
therefore that all can
be satisfied by a single
mutual fund composed
of that portfolio.*

We sometimes call this result a **mutual fund theorem** because it implies that only one mutual fund of risky assets—the market portfolio—is sufficient to satisfy the investment demands of all investors. The mutual fund theorem is another incarnation of the separation property discussed in Chapter 8. Assuming all investors choose to hold a market index mutual fund, we can separate portfolio selection into two components—(1) the technical side, creation of an efficient mutual fund by professional management, and (2) the personal side that depends on an investor's risk aversion in the allocation of the complete portfolio between the mutual fund and risk-free asset. Here, all investors agree that the mutual fund they would like to hold is the market portfolio.

While different investment managers do create risky portfolios that differ from the market index, we attribute this in part to the use of different estimates as input. At the same time, a passive investor may view the market index as a reasonable first approximation to an efficient risky portfolio. The accompanying box shows that index mutual funds are increasingly popular investment strategies among individual investors.

The logical inconsistency of the CAPM is this: If a passive strategy is costless *and* efficient, why would anyone follow an active strategy? And if no one does any security analysis, how can a process exist that brings about the efficiency of the market portfolio?

We have acknowledged from the outset that the CAPM simplifies the real world in its search for a tractable solution. Its applicability to the real world depends on whether its predictions are accurate enough. The model's use is some indication that its predictions are reasonable. We discuss this issue in depth in Chapter 10 on market efficiency.

Concept Check

Question 1. If only a few investors perform security analysis and all others hold the market portfolio (*M*), would the CML still be the efficient CAL for investors who do not engage in security analysis? Explain.

The Risk Premium of the Market Portfolio

In Chapter 7, we discussed how individual investors decide how much to invest in the risky portfolio. Returning now to the decision of how much to invest in portfolio M and how much in the risk-free asset, what can we deduce about the equilibrium risk premium of portfolio M?

We asserted earlier that the equilibrium risk premium of the market portfolio, $E(r_M) - r_f$, will be proportional to the degree of risk aversion of the average investor and to the risk of the market portfolio, σ_M^2. Now we can explain this result.

Recall that an individual investor who has average risk aversion, A^*, will choose a proportion, y, allocated to the optimal portfolio (M) such that

$$y = \frac{E(r_M) - r_f}{A^*\sigma_M^2} \tag{9.1}$$

In the simplified CAPM economy, risk-free investments involve borrowing and lending among investors. Any borrowing position will be offset by the lending position of the creditor. This means net borrowing and lending summed across all investors, that is, lending by the average investor, must be zero. In consequence, the average investor's position in the *risky* portfolio must be $y = 1.0$. Using this argument in Equation 9.1 and rearranging results in

$$E(r_M) - r_f = A^*\sigma_M^2 \;, \tag{9.2}$$

that is, the risk premium on the market portfolio is proportional to its risk and to average risk aversion.

Concept Check

Question 2. Data from 1926 to 1990 for the S&P 500 index show an average excess return of 8.4 percent with standard deviation of 21 percent. To the extent that these averages approximate investor expectations for the period, what must have been the coefficient of risk aversion of the average investor? If the coefficient of risk aversion were 3.5, what risk premium would have been consistent with the market's historical standard deviation?

Expected Returns on Individual Securities

The CAPM is built on the insight that the appropriate risk premium on an asset will be determined by its contribution to the risk of investors' overall portfolios. Portfolio risk is what matters to investors, and portfolio risk is what governs the risk premiums they demand.

You learned in Chapter 8 that, in a single-factor security market, the contribution of a single security to the standard deviation of a large diversified portfolio depends only on the systematic risk of the security. In fact, the security's contribution to the standard deviation of the diversified portfolio is proportional to its beta relative to the factor and to the standard deviation of the factor. To illustrate the CAPM rationale in a relatively simple fashion, we now add assumption 7: our universe is a single-factor security market, and the return on

The Index Boom: It's No Longer Just the S&P 500 Stock Index

NEW YORK—There's an index explosion on Wall Street.

Time was when "index" investing meant one thing: buying and holding the stocks in Standard & Poor's 500 stock index to match the performance of the broad stock market.

No more. Today, indexing comes in more varieties than Baskin Robbins has flavors.

Pension funds and other big institutions are building portfolios that track a variety of market benchmarks: new indexes tied to small-company stocks; "value" stocks or "growth" stocks; international stocks; and other types of assets, such as mortgage-backed bonds.

Say you want an index fund of international stocks. There are index funds that match the benchmark Morgan Stanley Capital International Europe, Australia, Far East stock index. International index funds can be designed to invest in one region, such as the Pacific rim, and then modified for a particular investment strategy, such as including or excluding Japanese stocks.

One Pennsylvania bank offers an index fund that invests only in companies with operations in Pennsylvania. "You can come up with any benchmark you like" says Larry L. Martin, vice president of State Street Bank & Trust, Co.

Pioneered in the 1970s, indexing appeals to big investors for its simplicity. Investors make or lose money in line with moves in the broad stock market; and the investors can do so at lower cost than traditional stock pickers, who as a group generally lag behind the performance of the S&P 500, despite heavy spending on stock research and money-manager salaries. So straightforward is the strategy that

institutional investors have poured $275 billion into indexing.

The S&P 500 fund remains the grand-daddy of the indexing world, with 75 percent of the money invested in indexing still tied to the S&P index. Though many money managers predicted a falloff in S&P 500 indexing during last year's bear market, the drop didn't materialize. Big institutional investors still depend on the S&P 500 to track large-company stocks.

But as institutions diversify their holdings, many in the indexing industry think their best chance of attracting additional business is through the new flavors of indexing.

At Wells Fargo Nikko Investment Advisors, the largest index money manager overseeing $83 billion in assets, the biggest demand from new clients these days is for so-called style funds. These funds contain only stocks sharing certain attributes, such as low price/earnings ratios, often dubbed value stocks, or above-average earnings growth, called growth stocks.

Instead of using the S&P 500, which contains both value and growth stocks, as a benchmark, a value style fund can be constructed to follow specialized value-stock indexes, such as Frank Russell Co.'s Russell Price-Driven Index of 558 value stocks. A growth index fund might track Russell's Earnings Growth Index of 434 growth stocks.

"Over extended periods of time, it's the decisions about growth or value, and large or small stocks, that ultimately drive your investment returns," says Tom Stevens, chief investment officer of Wilshire Asset Management, which manages $700 million in style index funds.

---

the market portfolio can be treated as that factor. The average asset beta on the market portfolio is 1.0

In our security market, then, the contribution of a given stock, say DEC, to the standard deviation of the market portfolio is $\beta_D \sigma_M$.[1] The CAPM implies that DEC's risk premium (i.e., its expected rate of return in excess of the risk-free rate) is proportional to this contribution in the same way that the market portfolio's expected excess return is proportional to its risk.

---

[1]This is literally true with a sufficient number of securities that all nonsystematic risk is diversified away, and the weight of a single security in the market portfolio is negligible. In a market as diversified as the U.S. stock market, this would be true for all practical purposes.

Index Explosion

About 75% of the $275 billion in institutional index funds, still track the Standard & Poor's 500-stock Index. But other indexes are becoming popular, too.

TOTAL U.S. STOCK MARKET

Wilshire 5000
Russell 2000

SMALL STOCKS

Russell 2000
Wilshire Small-Company Growth
Wilshire Small-Company Value

VALUE STOCKS

Russell Price-Driven Index

GROWTH STOCKS

Russell Earnings Growth Index

MORTGAGE-BACKED SECURITIES

Eshman's

INTERNATIONAL STOCKS

Morgan Stanley Capital International
Non-U.S. Index

Other index managers say their strongest new business area is international. "We expect that to continue for the next 15 years," says Mr. Martin of Boston's State Street Bank & Trust, which oversees $60 billion, including $10 billion in stocks indexed outside the United States. Demand is coming from both U.S. and foreign institutions that want to put money to work around the world, international index managers say.

Individual investors can get into the act through mutual funds. Vanguard Group, for example, offers index funds tracking the S&P 500, the broader Wilshire 4500 index, the Russell 2000 small-company index, and a bond fund linked to Salomon Brothers Inc.'s Broad Investment Grade bond index, among others.

The proliferation of indexes is part of a larger trend toward computer-based investing techniques, often called "quantitative" investing. Unlike the "passive" approach of basic indexing, these quantitative techniques often combine active investment bets by portfolio managers with indexing, hoping to come up with the best of both worlds.

Money-management giants, such as the $35 billion General Electric Investment arm of General Electric Co., have embraced quantitative techniques in a big way. GE says that by mixing active and passive quantitative techniques, it has added as much one percentage point a year to the performance of its traditional index funds. Results like that have caused GE to have $5 billion invested in various quantitative techniques today, up from nothing as recently as 1984.

Patricia C. Dunn, president of Wells Fargo Nikko, says that institutional investors are blurring the dividing lines between traditional and quantitative investment management styles, and are looking for a marriage between the two. The differences between active and passive investing, she says, are becoming "increasingly obsolete."

From James A. White, "The Index Boom: It's No Longer Just the S&P 500-Stock Index," *The Wall Street Journal*, May 29, 1991. Reprinted by permission of *THE WALL STREET JOURNAL*, © 1991 Dow Jones & Company, Inc. All Rights Reserved Worldwide.

To be more specific, the investor's trade-off between risk and return using the optimal risky portfolio is given by the reward-to-variability ratio of the capital market line, $S = [E(r_M) - r_f]/\sigma_M$. Setting this value equal to what should be DEC's risk premium per unit *contribution* to the market's portfolio risk, we have

Expected return-beta relationship Implication of the CAPM that security risk premiums (expected excess returns) will be proportional to beta.

$$\frac{E(r_M) - r_f}{\sigma_M} = \frac{E(r_D) - r_f}{\beta_D \sigma_M}$$

from which we derive the CAPM's **expected return-beta relationship**

$$E(r_D) = r_f + \beta_D[E(r_M) - r_f] \tag{9.3}$$

In words, the rate of return on any asset exceeds the risk-free rate by a risk premium that is arrived at by multiplying the asset's systematic risk measure (its beta) and the risk premium of the (benchmark) market portfolio. This expected return-beta relationship is the most familiar expression of the CAPM to practitioners.

We see now why the assumptions that made individuals act similarly are so useful. If everyone holds an identical risky portfolio, then everyone will find that the beta of each asset on the market portfolio equals the asset's beta with their own risky portfolio. Hence, everyone will agree on the appropriate risk premium for each asset.

The fact that few real-life investors actually hold the market portfolio does not necessarily invalidate the CAPM. Recall from Chapter 8 that reasonably well-diversified portfolios shed (for practical purposes) firm-specific risk and are subject only to systematic or market risk. Even if one does not hold the precise market portfolio, a well-diversified portfolio will be so highly correlated with the market that a stock's beta relative to the market still will be a useful risk measure.

In fact, several researchers have shown that modified versions of the CAPM will hold despite differences among individuals that may cause them to hold different portfolios. A study by Brennan (see Selected Readings) examines the impact of differences in investors' personal tax rates on market equilibrium. Another by Mayers looks at the impact of nontraded assets such as human capital (earning power). Both find that while the market portfolio is no longer each investor's optimal risky portfolio, a modified version of the expected return-beta relationship still holds.

If the expected return-beta relationship holds for any individual asset, it must hold for any combination of assets. So that if some portfolio P has n stocks with weight w_k for stock k, we can obtain its expected return from the component securities using their CAPM representation. Writing out the CAPM Equation 9.3 for each stock and multiplying each equation by the weight of the stock in the portfolio, we obtain n equations that sum to the total portfolio:

$$
\begin{aligned}
w_1 E(r_1) &= w_1 r_f + w_1 \beta_1 [E(r_M) - r_f] \\
+ w_2 E(r_2) &= w_2 r_f + w_2 \beta_2 [E(r_M) - r_f] \\
\cdots &= \cdots \\
+ w_k E(r_k) &= w_k r_f + w_k \beta_k [E(r_M) - r_f] \\
\cdot &= \cdots \\
+ w_n E(r_n) &= w_n r_f + w_n \beta_n [E(r_M) - r_f] \\
\hline
E(r_P) &= r_f \quad + \beta_P [E(r_M) - r_f]
\end{aligned}
\tag{9.4}
$$

Summing each column shows that the CAPM holds for the overall portfolio, which has a beta that is the weighted average of the component securities. Incidentally, this result has to be true for the market portfolio itself:

$$
E(r_M) = r_f + \beta_M [E(r_M) - r_f]
$$

(Note that $\beta_M = 1$.)

Concept Check

Question 3. Suppose the risk premium on the market portfolio is estimated at 8 percent with a standard deviation of 22 percent. What is the risk premium on a portfolio invested 25 percent in GM with a beta of 1.15 and 75 percent in Ford with a beta of 1.25?

A word of caution: we are all accustomed to hearing that well-managed firms will provide high rates of return. We agree this is true if one measures the *firm's* return on investments in plant and equipment. The CAPM, however, predicts returns on investments in the *securities* of the firm.

Say that everyone knows a firm is well run. Its stock price should, therefore, be bid up, and returns to stockholders who buy at those high prices will not be extreme. Security *prices* reflect public information about a firm's prospects, but only the risk of the company (as measured by beta in the context of the CAPM) should affect *expected returns*. In a rational market, investors receive high expected returns only if they are willing to bear risk.

The Security Market Line

We can view the expected return-beta relationship as a reward-risk equation. The beta of a security is the appropriate measure of its risk because beta is proportional to the risk the security contributes to the optimal risky portfolio.

Risk-averse investors measure the risk of the optimal risky portfolio by its standard deviation. In this world, we would expect the reward, or the risk premium on individual assets, to depend on the risk an individual asset contributes to the overall portfolio. Because the beta of a stock measures the stock's contribution to the standard deviation of the market portfolio, we expect the required risk premium to be a function of beta. The CAPM confirms this intuition, stating further that the security's risk premium is directly proportional to both the beta and the risk premium of the market portfolio; that is, the risk premium equals $\beta[E(r_M) - r_f]$.

Security market line (SML) Graphical representation of the expected return-beta relationship of the CAPM.

The expected return-beta relationship can be graphed as the **security market line (SML)** in Figure 9.2. Its slope is the risk premium of the market portfolio. At the point where $\beta = 1.0$ (which is the beta of the market portfolio) on the horizontal axis, we can read off the vertical axis the expected return on the market portfolio.

It is useful to compare the security market line to the capital market line. The CML graphs the risk premiums of efficient portfolios (that is, complete portfolios made up of the risky market portfolio and the risk-free asset) as a function of portfolio standard deviation. This is appropriate because standard deviation is a valid measure of risk for portfolios that are candidates for an investor's complete (overall) portfolio.

The SML, in contrast, graphs *individual asset* risk premiums as a function of asset risk. The relevant measure of risk for individual assets (which are held as parts of a well-diversified portfolio) is not the asset's standard deviation; it is, instead, the contribution of the asset to the portfolio standard deviation as mea-

Figure 9.2
The security market line.

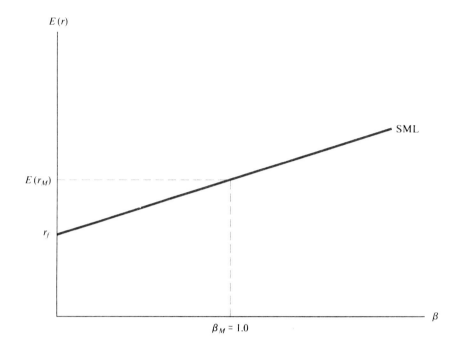

sured by the asset's beta. The SML is valid for both portfolios and individual assets.

The security market line provides a benchmark for evaluation of investment performance. Given the risk of an investment as measured by its beta, the SML provides the required rate of return that will compensate investors for the risk of that investment, as well as for the time value of money.

Because the security market line is the graphical representation of the expected return-beta relationship, "fairly priced" assets plot exactly on the SML. The expected returns of such assets are commensurate with their risk. Whenever the CAPM holds, all securities must lie on the SML in the market equilibrium. Underpriced stocks plot above the SML: given their betas, their expected returns are greater than is indicated by the CAPM. Overpriced stocks plot below the SML.

Alpha The abnormal rate of return on a security in excess of what would be predicted by an equilibrium model like the CAPM or APT.

The difference between the fair and actually expected rate of return on a stock is called the stock's **alpha,** denoted α. For example, if the return on the market is expected to be 14 percent, a stock has a beta of 1.2, and the T-bill rate is 6 percent, the SML would predict an expected return on the stock of $6 + 1.2(14 - 6) = 15.6$ percent. If one believes the stock will provide instead a return of 17 percent, its implied alpha would be 1.4 percent. (See Figure 9.3.)

Applications of the CAPM

One place the CAPM may be used is in the investment management industry. Suppose the SML is taken as a benchmark to assess the *fair* expected return on a risky asset. Then an analyst calculates the return he or she actually expects. (Notice that we depart here from the simple CAPM world in that some investors

Figure 9.3
The SML and a
positive-alpha stock.

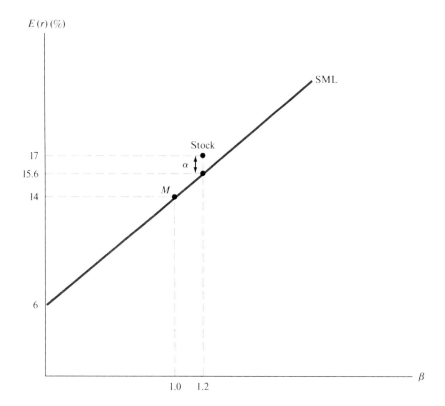

apply their own analysis to derive an "input list" that may differ from their competitors'.) If a stock is perceived to be a good buy, or underpriced, it will provide a positive alpha, that is, an expected return in excess of the fair return stipulated by the SML.

The CAPM also is useful in capital budgeting decisions. If a firm is considering a new project, the CAPM can provide the return the project needs to yield, given its beta, to be acceptable to investors. Managers can use the CAPM to obtain this cutoff internal rate of return (IRR) or "hurdle rate" for the project.

Suppose Silverado Springs Inc. is considering a new spring-water bottling plant. The business plan forecasts an internal rate of return of 14 percent on the investment. Research shows the beta of similar products is 1.3. Thus, if the risk-free rate is 9 percent, and the market excess return is estimated at 8 percent, the hurdle rate for the project should be 19.4 percent [9 + (1.3 × 8)]. Because the IRR is less than the risk-adjusted discount or hurdle rate, the project has a negative net present value and ought to be rejected.

Yet another use of the CAPM is in utility rate-making cases. Here the issue is the rate of return a regulated utility should be allowed to earn on its investment in plant and equipment. Suppose equity holders' investment in the firm is $100 million and the beta of the equity is 0.6. If the T-bill rate is 6 percent and the market risk premium is 8 percent, then a fair annual profit will be 6 + (.6 × 8) = 10.8 percent of $100 million, or $10.8 million. Since regulators accept the CAPM, they will allow the utility to set prices at a level expected to generate these profits.

Concept Check

Question 4. *a.* Stock XYZ has an expected return of 12 percent and risk of $\beta = 1.0$. Stock ABC is expected to return 13 percent with a beta of 1.5. The market expected return is 11 percent and $r_f = 5$ percent. According to the CAPM, which stock is a better buy? What is the alpha of each stock? Plot the SML and the two stocks and show the alphas on the graph.

b. The risk-free rate is 8 percent and the expected return on the market portfolio is 17 percent. A firm considers a project with an estimated beta of 1.3. What is the required rate of return on the project? If the IRR of the project is 19 percent, what is the project α?

9.2 The CAPM and Index Models

The CAPM has two limitations: it relies on the theoretical market portfolio, which includes *all* assets (such as real estate, foreign stocks, etc.), and it deals with *expected* as opposed to actual returns. To implement the CAPM, we cast it in the form of an *index model* and use realized, not expected, returns.

An index model uses actual portfolios, such as the S&P 500, rather than the theoretical market portfolio to represent the relevant factors in the economy. The important advantage of index models is that the composition and rate of return of the index is easily measured and unambiguous.

In contrast to an index model, the CAPM revolves around the "market portfolio." However, because many assets are not traded, investors would not have full access to the market portfolio even if they could exactly identify it. Thus, the pure theory behind the CAPM rests on a shaky real-world foundation. But, as in all science, a theory may be viewed as legitimate if its predictions approximate real-world outcomes with a sufficient degree of accuracy. In particular, the reliance on the "market portfolio" shouldn't faze us if we can verify that the predictions of the CAPM are sufficiently accurate when the index portfolio is substituted for the market.

We can start with one central prediction of the CAPM: the market portfolio is mean-variance efficient. An index model can be used to test this hypothesis by verifying that the chosen index is a mean-variance efficient portfolio.

Another aspect of the CAPM is that it predicts relationships among *expected* returns, while all we can observe are realized (historical) holding-period returns; actual returns in a particular holding period seldom, if ever, match our initial expectations. To test the mean-variance efficiency of an index portfolio, we would have to show that the reward-to-variability ratio of the index is not surpassed by any other portfolio. The reward-to-variability ratio, however, is set in terms of expectations, and we can measure it only in terms of realizations.

The Index Model, Realized Returns, and the Expected Return-Beta Relationship

To move from a model cast in expectations to a realized return framework, we start with a form of the single-index regression equation in realized excess returns, similar to that of Equation 8.2 in Chapter 8:

$$r_i - r_f = \alpha_i + \beta_i(r_M - r_f) + e_i \tag{9.5}$$

where r_i is the HPR on asset i, α_i and β_i are the intercept and slope of the regression line that relates asset i's realized excess return to the realized excess return of the index. We denote the index returns by r_M to emphasize that the index portfolio is proxying for the market. The e_i measures firm-specific effects during the holding period; it is the deviation of security i's realized HPR from the regression line, that is, the deviation from the forecast that accounts for the index's HPR. We set the relationship in terms of *excess* returns (over the risk-free rate, r_f), for consistency with the CAPM's logic of risk premiums.

Given that the CAPM is a statement about the expectation of asset returns, we look at the expected return of security i predicted by Equation 9.5. Recall that the expectation of e_i is zero (the firm-specific surprise is expected to average zero over time), so the relationship expressed in terms of expectations is:

$$E(r_i) - r_f = \alpha_i + \beta_i[E(r_M) - r_f]. \tag{9.6}$$

Comparing this relationship to the expected return-beta relationship (9.3) of the CAPM, reveals that the CAPM predicts $\alpha_i = 0$. Thus, we have converted the CAPM prediction about unobserved expectations of security returns relative to an unobserved market portfolio into a prediction about the intercept in a regression of observed variables: realized excess returns of a security relative to those of a specified index.

Operationalizing the CAPM in the form of an index model has a drawback, however. If intercepts of regressions of returns on an index differ substantially from zero, you will not be able to tell whether it is because you chose a bad index to proxy for the market or because the theory is not useful.

In actuality, few instances of positive significant alpha values have been identified; these will be discussed in the next chapter. Among them are: (1) small versus large stocks, (2) stocks of companies that have recently announced unexpected good earnings, and (3) stocks that have experienced recent sharp price declines. These alphas appear to be fading now that they are widely recognized, however, and finding new ones is not easy. Further, future alphas are practically impossible to predict from past values. The result is that index models are widely used to operationalize capital asset pricing theory.

Estimating and Predicting Betas

Even if a single-index model representation is not fully consistent with the CAPM, the concept of systematic versus diversifiable risk is still useful. Systematic risk is well approximated by the regression equation beta and nonsystematic risk by the residual variance of the regression.

Security characteristic line (SCL) A plot of a security's expected excess return over the risk-free rate as a function of the excess return on the market.

The regression line of a security is often called the **security characteristic line (SCL).** The slope of that regression is the security's beta. The residual variance, $\sigma^2(e)$, that describes the magnitude of deviations of the scatter diagram about the SCL serves two purposes. It measures the firm-specific (diversifiable) risk, and it also indicates the reliability of the estimate of beta. This information may be useful.

Often, we estimate betas in order to forecast the rate of return of an asset. The beta from the regression equation is an estimate based on past history; it will not reveal possible changes in future beta. As an empirical rule, it appears that betas exhibit a statistical property called "regression toward the mean." This means that high β ($\beta > 1$) securities in one period tend to exhibit a lower β in future periods, while low β (β < 1) securities exhibit a higher β in future periods. Researchers often adjust beta estimates from past data to account for regression toward the mean when they use them as predictors of future betas. For this reason, it is necessary to verify whether the estimates are already "adjusted betas."

9.3   Arbitrage Pricing Theory

In the 1970s, as researchers were working on test methodologies for variants of the CAPM, Stephen Ross (1976) stunned the world of finance with the arbitrage pricing theory (APT). Moving away from construction of mean-variance efficient portfolios, Ross instead calculated relations among expected rates of return that would rule out riskless profits by any investor in well-functioning capital markets. This generated a theory of risk and return similar to the CAPM.

Arbitrage Opportunities and Profits

Zero-investment portfolio A portfolio of zero net value, established by buying and shorting component securities, usually in the context of an arbitrage strategy.

To explain the APT, we begin by explaining the concept of arbitrage.

A riskless arbitrage opportunity arises when an investor can construct a **zero investment portfolio** that will yield a sure profit. Zero investment means investors need not use any of their own money. To construct a zero investment portfolio, one has to be able to sell short at least one asset and use the proceeds to purchase (go long) one or more assets. Even a small investor, using borrowed money in this fashion, can take a large position in such a portfolio.

An obvious case of an arbitrage opportunity arises in the violation of the law of one price (see Chapter 6). When an asset is trading at different prices in two markets (and the price differential exceeds transaction costs), a simultaneous trade in the two markets will produce a sure profit (the net price differential) without any net investment. One simply sells short the asset in the high-priced market and buys it in the low-priced market. The net proceeds are positive, and there is no risk because the long and short positions offset each other.

In modern markets with electronic communications and instantaneous execution, such opportunities have become rare but not extinct. The same technology that enables the market to absorb new information quickly also enables fast operators to make large profits by trading huge volumes at the instant an arbitrage opportunity opens. This is the essence of program trading and index arbitrage, to be discussed in Part Five.

From the simple case of a violation of the law of one price, let us proceed to a less obvious (yet just as profitable) arbitrage opportunity. Imagine that four stocks are traded in an economy with only four possible scenarios. The rates of return on the four stocks for each inflation-interest rate scenario appear in Table 9.1. The current prices of the stocks and rate of return statistics are shown in Table 9.2.

The rate of return data give no immediate clue to any arbitrage opportunity lurking in this set of investments. The expected returns, standard deviations, and correlations do not reveal any abnormality.

Consider, however, an equally weighted portfolio of the first three stocks (Apex, Bull, and Crush), and contrast its possible future rates of return with those of the fourth stock, Dreck. We do this in Table 9.3.

Table 9.1 *Rate of Return Projections*

	High Real Interest Rates		Low Real Interest Rates	
	High Inflation	**Low Inflation**	**High Inflation**	**Low Inflation**
Probability:	.25	.25	.25	.25
Stock				
Apex (A)	−20	20	40	60
Bull (B)	0	70	30	−20
Crush (C)	90	−20	−10	70
Dreck (D)	15	23	15	36

Table 9.2 *Rate of Return Statistics*

Stock	Current Price	Expected Return	Standard Deviation(%)	Correlation Matrix			
				A	**B**	**C**	**D**
A	$10	25	29.58	1.00	−.15	−.29	.68
B	$10	20	33.91	−.15	1.00	−.87	−.38
C	$10	32.5	48.15	−.29	−.87	1.00	.22
D	$10	22.25	8.58	.68	−.38	.22	1.00

Table 9.3 *Rate of Return Projections*

	High Real Interest Rates		Low Real Interest Rates	
	Rate of Inflation		Rate of Inflation	
	High	**Low**	**High**	**Low**
Equally weighted portfolio: A,B, and C	23.33	23.33	20.00	36.67
Dreck	15.00	23.00	15.00	36.00

Table 9.3 reveals that in all scenarios, the equally weighted portfolio will outperform Dreck. The rate of return statistics of the two alternatives are

	Mean	Standard Deviation	Correlation
Three-stock portfolio	25.83	6.40	
			.94
Dreck	22.25	8.58	

The two investments are not perfectly correlated and are not perfect substitutes. While there is no violation of the law of one price here, the equally weighted portfolio will fare better under *any* circumstances. Any investor, no matter how risk averse, can take advantage of this dominance by taking a short position in Dreck and using the proceeds to purchase the equally weighted portfolio. Let us see how it would work.

Suppose we sell short 300,000 shares of Dreck and use the $3 million proceeds to buy 100,000 shares each of Apex, Bull, and Crush. The dollar profits in each of the four scenarios will be

Stock	Dollar Investment	High Real Interest Rates Inflation Rate		Low Real Interest Rates Inflation Rate	
		High	Low	High	Low
Apex	$ 1,000,000	$ -200,000	$200,000	$ 400,000	$ 600,000
Bull	1,000,000	0	700,000	300,000	-200,000
Crush	1,000,000	900,000	-200,000	-100,000	700,000
Dreck	-3,000,000	-450,000	-690,000	-450,000	-1,080,000
Portfolio	$ 0	$ 250,000	$ 10,000	$ 150,000	$ 20,000

The first column verifies that the net investment in our portfolio is zero. Yet this portfolio yields a positive profit in all scenarios. It is a money machine. Investors will want to take an infinite position in such a portfolio, for larger positions entail no risk of losses, yet yield ever-growing profits. In principle, even a single investor would take such large positions the market would react to the buying and selling pressure: the price of Dreck will come down, and/or the prices of Apex, Bull, and Crush will go up. The pressure will persist until arbitrage opportunity is eliminated.

Concept Check

Question 5. Suppose Dreck's price starts falling without any change in its per share dollar payoffs. How far must the price fall before arbitrage between Dreck and the equally weighted portfolio is no longer possible? (Hint: account for the amount of the equally weighted portfolio that can be purchased with the proceeds of the short sale as Dreck's price falls.)

The critical property of an arbitrage portfolio is that any investor, regardless of risk aversion or wealth, will want to take an infinite position in it so that profits will be driven to an infinite level. Because those large positions will force some prices up and/or some down until the opportunity vanishes, we can derive restrictions on security prices that satisfy the condition that no arbitrage opportunities are left in the marketplace.

The idea that equilibrium market prices ought to be rational in the sense that they rule out arbitrage opportunities is perhaps the most fundamental concept in capital market theory. Violation of this principle would indicate the grossest form of market irrationality.

There is an important distinction between arbitrage and CAPM risk-versus-return dominance arguments in support of equilibrium price relationships. A dominance argument, as in the CAPM, holds that when an equilibrium price relationship is violated, many investors will make portfolio changes. Each individual investor will make a limited change, though, depending on wealth and degree of risk aversion. Aggregation of these limited portfolio changes over many investors is required to create a large volume of buying and selling, which restores equilibrium prices.

When arbitrage opportunities exist, by contrast, each investor wants to take as large a position as possible; in this case, it will not take many investors to bring about the price pressures necessary to restore equilibrium. Implications derived from the no-arbitrage argument, therefore, are stronger than implications derived from a risk-versus-return dominance argument, because they do not depend on a large, well-educated population of investors.

The CAPM argues that all investors hold mean-variance efficient portfolios. When a security (or a bundle of securities) is mispriced, investors will tilt their portfolios toward the underpriced and away from the overpriced securities. The resulting pressure on prices comes from many investors shifting their portfolios, each by a relatively small dollar amount. This assumption that a large number of investors are mean-variance optimizers is critical; in the case of the APT, even few arbitrageurs will mobilize large dollar amounts to take advantage of an arbitrage opportunity.

We have described pure arbitrage: the search for a costless sure profit. Practitioners often use the terms arbitrage and arbitrageurs more loosely. An arbitrageur may be a professional searching for mispriced securities in specific areas such as merger-target stocks, rather than one looking for strict (risk-free) arbitrage opportunities in the sense that no loss is possible. The search for mispriced securities is called risk arbitrage to distinguish it from pure arbitrage.

Well-Diversified Portfolios and the Arbitrage Pricing Theory

In futures and option markets, values are determined by the prices of the underlying securities. A call option on a stock, for example, has a value at maturity that will be fully determined by the price of the stock. Pure arbitrage is a practical possibility in these circumstances, and the condition of no arbitrage leads to exact pricing. In the case of stocks, whose values cannot be determined strictly by prices of other assets, however, we derive no-arbitrage conditions using diversification arguments.

Arbitrage pricing theory (APT)   A theory of risk-return relationships derived from no-arbitrage considerations in large capital markets.

Like the CAPM, **Arbitrage Pricing Theory,** or **APT,** predicts the relationship between the risk and expected rate of return of risky assets. The basic version of the arbitrage pricing theory assumes that only one systematic factor affects security returns. We start by reexamining the single-factor model introduced in Chapter 8. Uncertainty in asset returns has two sources: a common macroeconomic factor and a firm-specific cause. In the factor model, the common factor is meant to measure new information concerning the macro economy. New information has, by definition, zero expected value since new information is equally likely to be positive or negative. In contrast to the CAPM, there is no need to assume the factor can be proxied by the return on a market index portfolio.

If we call M the deviation of the common factor from its expected value, β_i, the sensitivity of firm i to that factor, and e_i the firm-specific residual, the factor model states that the actual return on firm i stock will equal its expected return plus a (zero expected value) random amount attributable to unanticipated economywide events, plus another (zero expected value) random amount attributable to firm-specific events.

We can formulate that rate of return as

$$r_i = E(r_i) + \beta_i M + e_i \tag{9.7}$$

where $E(r_i)$ is the expected return on stock i. The nonsystematic return (e_i) is uncorrelated with other assets and with the factor (M).

To make the factor model more concrete, consider an example. Suppose the macro factor is taken to be the unexpected percentage change in gross national product (GNP), and the consensus is that GNP will increase by 4 percent this year. Suppose also that a stock's beta is 1.2. If GNP increases by only 3 percent, then the value of M will be -1 percent, to represent the one percentage point deviation of actual from expected growth. Given the stock's beta, this disappointment will translate into a return on the stock that is 1.2 percent less than previously expected. This macro surprise, together with the firm-specific disturbance, e_i, determines the total departure of the stock's return from its originally expected value.

Now we look at the risk of a portfolio of stocks. As we know, if a portfolio is sufficiently diversified, its firm-specific risk will be reduced to negligible levels. Only factor (or systematic) risk remains. The required degree of diversification, how many stocks and the investment proportions in each, will depend on the level of nonsystematic risk of component securities. We shall call a **well-diversified portfolio** one that has a negligible level of diversifiable risk.

Well-diversified portfolio A portfolio diversified sufficiently to make nonsystematic risk negligible.

With a very large universe of securities we can construct many well-diversified portfolios with any desired beta. Large institutional investors can hold portfolios of hundreds and even thousands of securities, so the concept of well-diversified portfolios clearly is operational in contemporary financial markets.

Because a well-diversified portfolio, P, has for all practical purposes zero firm-specific risk, $e_P = 0$, its returns can be written as

$$r_P = E(r_P) + \beta_P M \tag{9.8}$$

Figure 9.4 plots two scatter diagrams and estimated security characteristic lines (SCLs). As the slopes of the SCLs show, both assets have a beta of one. Figure 9.4 Panel A plots well-diversified portfolio A. Here, all the returns plot on the SCL. The expected return is 10 percent: This is where the SCL crosses the vertical axis. At this point, the factor value is zero, implying no macro surprise. For positive values of the macro factor, the well-diversified portfolio re-

Figure 9.4
Returns as a function of the systematic factor. A, well-diversified portfolio, B, single stock.

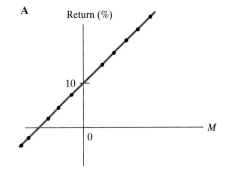

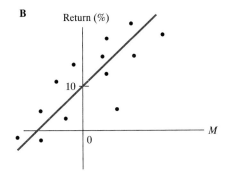

turn exceeds its expected value; otherwise the portfolio return falls short of its mean. Formally, the return on portfolio A is

$$r_A = E(r_A) + \beta_A M = .10 + 1.0 \times M.$$

Compare Figure 9.4 Panel A to Figure 9.4 Panel B, which is a similar graph for a single stock with $\beta = 1$. The undiversified stock is subject to nonsystematic risk, which is seen in a scatter of points about the line. The well-diversified portfolio's return, in contrast, is determined completely by the systematic factor.

Equation 9.8 and Figure 9.4 demonstrate why well-diversified portfolios are central to the APT. A well-diversified portfolio with a beta of *zero* has *no* risk at all. This is easy to achieve. The simplest way is to finance a long position in a well-diversified portfolio with a short position in another with equal beta. The short (hence negative) portfolio beta will offset the beta of the portfolio held long. The result is a zero beta, zero investment portfolio. No investment and no risk—the prescription for arbitrage.

We next need to determine what portfolio returns will prevent arbitrage, that is, will not let investors construct a zero beta, zero investment, well-diversified portfolio with a positive (sure) return.

Betas and Expected Returns

Now consider Figure 9.5 where the dashed line plots the return on another well-diversified portfolio, portfolio B, with an expected return of 8 percent and beta also equal to 1.0. Could portfolios A and B coexist? Clearly not: no matter what the systematic factor turns out to be, portfolio A outperforms portfolio B, leading to an arbitrage opportunity.

If you sell short $1 million of B and buy $1 million of A, a zero net investment strategy, your eventual proceeds would be $20,000, as follows:

from long position in A	$(.10 + 1.0 \times M) \times \$1$ million
from short position in B	$-(.08 + 1.0 \times M) \times \$1$ million
net proceeds	$.02 \times \$1$ million $= \$20,000$

Figure 9.5
Returns as a function of the systematic factor: an arbitrage opportunity.

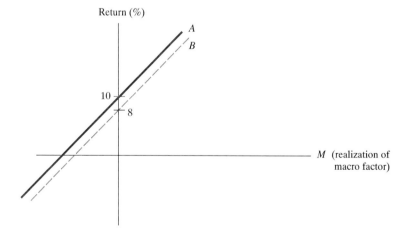

Figure 9.6
An arbitrage
opportunity.

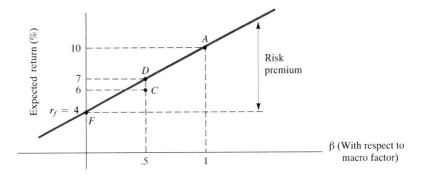

You make a risk-free profit because the factor risk cancels out across the long and short positions. Moreover, the strategy requires zero net investment. You should pursue it on an infinitely large scale until the return discrepancy between the two portfolios disappears. The conclusion is that portfolios with equal betas must have equal expected returns in market equilibrium, or arbitrage opportunities exist.

What about portfolios with different betas? We show now that their *risk premiums* must be proportional to beta. To see why, consider Figure 9.6. Suppose the risk-free rate is 4 percent and well-diversified portfolio *C*, with a beta of 0.5, has an expected return of 6 percent. Portfolio *C* plots below the line from the risk-free asset (*F*) to portfolio *A*. Consider, therefore, a new portfolio (*D*) that invests half in portfolio *A* and half in the risk-free asset *F*. Portfolio *D*'s beta will be $(.5 \times .0) + (.5 \times 1.0) = .5$, and its expected return will be $(.5 \times 4) + (.5 \times 10) = 7$ percent. Therefore, portfolio *D* has an equal beta but greater expected return than portfolio *C*. From our analysis in the previous paragraph, we know this constitutes an arbitrage opportunity.

We conclude that to preclude arbitrage opportunities, the expected return on any and all well-diversified portfolios must lie on the straight line from the risk-free asset (*F*) in Figure 9.6. The equation of this line will dictate the expected return on all well-diversified portfolios.

Notice in Figure 9.6 that risk premiums are proportional to portfolio betas. The risk premium is depicted by the vertical arrow in Figure 9.6, which measures the distance between the risk-free rate and the expected return on the portfolio. The risk premium is zero for a zero beta and rises in direct proportion to beta.

Concept Check

> ***Question 6.*** Suppose portfolio *E* is well diversified, with a beta of ⅔ and expected return of 9 percent. Would an arbitrage opportunity exist? Explain.

The Security Market Line of the APT

The market index portfolio is certainly one of the well-diversified portfolios. Therefore, it plots on the line in Figure 9.6. Moreover, because the return on the market index portfolio is perfectly correlated with the macro factor, nothing is lost by replacing the factor *M* with the return on the market index. Treating the index return as the macro factor, the beta of the market portfolio becomes 1.0, and we can use the index to determine the equation describing the line. As

Figure 9.7
The security market line.

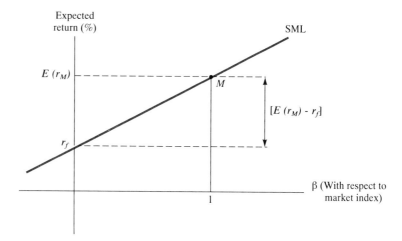

Figure 9.7 shows, the intercept is r_f and the slope is $E(r_M) - r_f$ [rise $= E(r_M) - r_f$; run $= 1$], implying that the equation of the line is

$$E(r_P) = r_f + \beta_P[E(r_M) - r_f] \tag{9.9}$$

and that Figures 9.6 and 9.7, as represented by Equation 9.9, are identical to the SML relation of the CAPM.

We have used the no-arbitrage condition to obtain an expected return-beta relationship identical to that of the CAPM, without one of the restrictive assumptions of the CAPM, namely, that all investors must be mean-variance optimizers. This suggests that despite its restrictive assumptions, the main conclusion of the CAPM, namely, the SML's expected return-beta relationship, is likely to be valid.

An advantage of the APT is that it does not require that the benchmark portfolio in the SML relationship be the true market portfolio. Any well-diversified portfolio lying on the SML of Figure 9.7 may serve as the benchmark portfolio. For example, one might define the benchmark portfolio as the well-diversified portfolio most highly correlated with whatever systematic factor is thought to affect stock returns.

The APT provides further support for use of the index model in the practical implementation of the SML relationship. Even if the index portfolio is not a precise proxy for the true market portfolio, we now know that if it is sufficiently well diversified, the SML relationship should still hold true according to the APT.

Individual Assets in the APT and the CAPM

We have said one of the conditions ruling out arbitrage opportunities in the case of well-diversified portfolios is that each portfolio's expected excess return must be proportional to its beta. For any two well-diversified portfolios P and Q, this can be written as

$$\frac{E(r_P) - r_f}{\beta_P} = \frac{E(r_Q) - r_f}{\beta_Q}.$$

Does this relationship tell us anything about the expected rates of return on the *individual assets* that make up these portfolios? If the relationship is to be satisfied by *all* well-diversified portfolios, it almost surely must be satisfied by all individual securities. If the relationship were violated by many individual securities, it would be virtually impossible for all well-diversified portfolios to satisfy the equation.

We say "almost" because, according to the APT, there is no guarantee that all individual assets will lie on the SML. If only a few securities violated the SML, their effect on well-diversified portfolios could conceivably be offsetting. In this sense, it is possible that the SML relationship is violated for single securities. If many securities violate the expected return-beta relationship, however, the relationship will no longer hold for well-diversified portfolios comprised of these securities, and arbitrage opportunities will be available.

The APT serves many of the same functions as the CAPM. It gives us a benchmark for fair rates of return that can be used for capital budgeting, security evaluation, or investment performance evaluation. Moreover, the APT highlights the crucial distinction between nondiversifiable risk (factor risk) that requires a reward in the form of a risk premium and diversifiable risk that does not.

Multifactor Generalization of the APT and CAPM

We've assumed all along that there is only one systematic factor affecting stock returns. This simplifying assumption may be too simplistic. It is easy to think of several factors that might affect stock returns: business cycles, interest rate fluctuations, inflation rates, oil prices, and so on. Presumably, exposure to any of these factors singly or together will affect a stock's perceived riskiness and appropriate expected rate of return. We can use a multifactor version of the APT to accommodate these multiple sources of risk.

Suppose we generalize the factor model expressed in Equation 9.7 to a two-factor model:

$$r_i = E(r_i) + \beta_{i1} M_1 + \beta_{i2} M_2 + e_i \qquad \textbf{(9.10)}$$

Factor 1 might be, for example, departures of GNP growth from expectations, while factor 2 might be unanticipated inflation. Each factor has a zero expected value because each measures the surprise in the systematic variable rather than the level of the variable. Similarly, the firm-specific component of unexpected return, e_i, also has zero expected value. Extending such a two-factor model to any number of factors is straightforward.

Establishing a multifactor APT proceeds along lines very similar to those we followed in the simple one-factor case. First, we introduce the concept of a **factor portfolio,** which is a well-diversified portfolio constructed to have a beta of 1.0 on one of the factors and a beta of 0 on any other factor. This is an easy restriction to satisfy because we have a large number of securities to choose from and a relatively small number of factors. Factor portfolios will serve as the benchmark portfolios for a multifactor generalization of the security market line relationship.

Suppose the two factor portfolios, here called portfolios 1 and 2, have expected returns $E(r_1) = 10$ percent and $E(r_2) = 12$ percent. Suppose further that

Factor portfolio A well-diversified portfolio constructed to have a beta of 1.0 on one factor and a beta of zero on any other factor.

the risk-free rate is 4 percent. The risk premium on the first factor portfolio becomes 6 percent, while that on the second factor portfolio is 8 percent.

Now consider an arbitrary well-diversified portfolio (A), with beta on the first factor, $\beta_{A1} = .5$, and on the second factor, $\beta_{A2} = .75$. The multifactor APT states the portfolio risk premium required as compensation to investors for each source of systematic risk must equal the sum of the risk premiums required as compensation to investors for each source of systematic risk. The risk premium attributable to risk factor 1 is the portfolio's exposure to factor 1, β_{A1}, times the risk premium earned on the first factor portfolio, $E(r_1) - r_f$. Therefore, the portion of portfolio A's risk premium that is compensation for its exposure to the first risk factor is $\beta_{A1}[E(r_1) - r_f] = .5(.10 - .04) = .03$, while the risk premium attributable to risk factor 2 is $\beta_{A2}[E(r_2) - r_f] = .75(.12 - .04) = .06$. The total risk premium on the portfolio, therefore, should be $3 + 6 = 9$ percent, and the total return on the portfolio should be 13 percent.

$$
\begin{array}{rl}
.04 & \text{risk-free rate} \\
+.03 & \text{risk premium for exposure to factor 1} \\
\underline{+.06} & \text{risk premium for exposure to factor 2} \\
.13 & \text{Total expected return.}
\end{array}
$$

To see why the expected return on the portfolio must be 13 percent, consider the following argument. Suppose the expected return on portfolio A is 12 percent rather than 13 percent. This return would give rise to an arbitrage opportunity. Form a portfolio from the factor portfolios with the same betas as portfolio A. This requires weights of 0.5 on the first factor portfolio, 0.75 on the second factor portfolio, and -0.25 on the risk-free asset. This portfolio has exactly the same factor betas as portfolio A: a beta of 0.5 on the first factor because of its 0.5 weight on the first factor portfolio and a beta of 0.75 on the second factor.

In contrast to portfolio A's 12 percent expected return, however, this portfolio's expected return is $(.5 \times 10) + (.75 \times 12) - (.25 \times 4) = 13$ percent. A long position in this portfolio and a short position in portfolio A would yield an arbitrage profit. The total proceeds per dollar long or short in each position would be

$$
\begin{array}{rl}
.13 + .5\,M_1 + .75\,M_2) & \text{long position in factor portfolios} \\
\underline{-(.12 + .5\,M_1 + .75\,M_2)} & \text{short position in portfolio } A \\
.01 &
\end{array}
$$

for a positive risk-free return on a zero net investment position. To generalize this argument, note that the factor exposure of any portfolio P is given by its betas, β_{P1} and β_{P2}. A competing portfolio, Q, can be formed from factor portfolios with weights: β_{P1} in the first factor portfolio, β_{P2} in the second factor portfolio, and $1 - \beta_{P2} - \beta_{P2}$ in T-bills. By construction, Q will have betas equal to those of portfolio P and expected return of

$$
\begin{aligned}
E(r_Q) &= \beta_{P1}E(r_1) + \beta_{P2}E(r_2) + (1 - \beta_{P1} - \beta_{P2})\,r_f \qquad \textbf{(9.11)} \\
&= r_f + \beta_{P1}[E(r_1) - r_f] + \beta_{P2}[E(r_2) - r_f].
\end{aligned}
$$

Hence, any well-diversified portfolio with betas β_{P1} and β_{P2} must have the return given in Equation 9.11 if arbitrage opportunities are to be ruled out. A comparison of Equations 9.9 and 9.11 shows that 9.11 is simply a generalization of the one-factor SML.

Finally, extension of the multifactor SML of Equation 9.11 to individual assets is precisely the same as for the one-factor APT. Equation 9.11 cannot be satisfied by every well-diversified portfolio unless it is satisfied by virtually every security taken individually. Equation 9.11, thus, represents the multifactor SML for an economy with multiple sources of risk.

The generalized APT must be qualified with respect to individual assets just as in the single-factor case. A multifactor CAPM would, at the cost of the additional assumption on investor mean-variance efficiency, apply to any and all individual assets. As we have seen, the result will be a security market equation (a multidimensional SML) that is identical to that of the multifactor APT.

Concept Check

Question 7. Using the factor portfolios just considered, find the fair rate of return on a security with $\beta_1 = .2$ and $\beta_2 = 1.4$.

Summary

1. The CAPM assumes investors are rational single-period planners who agree on a common input list from security analysis and seek mean-variance optimal portfolios.

2. The CAPM assumes ideal security markets in the sense that: (*a*) markets are large, and investors are price takers, (*b*) there are no taxes or transaction costs, (*c*) all risky assets are publicly traded, and (*d*) any amount can be borrowed and lent at a fixed, risk-free rate.

3. These assumptions mean that all investors will hold identical risky portfolios. The CAPM implies that, in equilibrium, the market portfolio is the unique mean-variance efficient tangency portfolio, which indicates that a passive strategy is efficient.

4. The market portfolio is a value-weighted portfolio. Each security is held in a proportion equal to its market value divided by the total market value of all securities.

5. If the market portfolio is efficient, and because the average investor overall neither borrows nor lends, the risk premium on the market portfolio is proportional to its variance, σ_M^2, and to the coefficient of risk aversion of the average investor (A^*).

6. The CAPM implies that the risk premium on any individual asset or portfolio is the product of the risk premium on the market portfolio and the asset's beta.

7. In a single-index security market, once an index is specified, any security beta can be estimated from a regression of the security's excess return on the index's excess return. This regression line is called the security characteristic line (SCL). The intercept of the SCL, called alpha, represents the average excess return on the security when the index excess return is zero. The CAPM implies that alphas should be zero.

8. Estimates of beta from past data often are adjusted when used to assess required future returns.

9. An arbitrage opportunity arises when the disparity between two or more security prices enables investors to construct a zero net investment portfolio that will yield a sure profit.

10. Rational investors will want to take infinitely large positions in arbitrage portfolios regardless of their degree of risk aversion.

11. The presence of arbitrage opportunities and the resulting volume of trades will create pressure on security prices that will persist until prices reach levels that preclude arbitrage. Only a few investors need to become aware of arbitrage opportunities to trigger this process because of the large volume of trades in which they will engage.

12. When securities are priced so that there are no arbitrage opportunities, the market satisfies the no-arbitrage condition. Price relationships that satisfy the no-arbitrage condition are important because we expect them to hold in real-world markets.

13. Portfolios are called *well diversified* if they include a large number of securities in such proportions that the residual risk of the portfolio is negligible.

14. In a single-factor security market, all well-diversified portfolios must satisfy the expected return-beta relationship of the SML in order to satisfy the no-arbitrage condition.

15. If all well-diversified portfolios satisfy the expected return-beta relationship, then all but a small number of securities also must satisfy this relationship.

16. The APT implies the same expected return-beta relationship as the CAPM yet does not require that all investors be mean-variance optimizers. The price of this generality is that the APT does not guarantee this relationship for all securities at all times.

17. A multifactor APT generalizes the single-factor model to accommodate several sources of systematic risk.

Key Terms

alpha, 248
arbitrage pricing theory
 (APT), 252
capital asset pricing
 model (CAPM), 239
expected return-beta
 relationship, 245

factor portfolio, 260
market portfolio, 240
mutual fund
 theorem, 242
security characteristic
 line, 251

security market line
 (SML), 247
well-diversified
 portfolio, 256
zero investment
 portfolio, 252

Selected Readings

A good introduction to the CAPM, now in its fifth edition, is:
 Malkiel, Burton G. *A Random Walk Down Wall Street.* New York: W. W. Norton & Company Inc., 1990.

The four articles that established the CAPM are:
 (1) Sharpe, William. "Capital Asset Prices: A Theory of Market Equilibrium." *Journal of Finance,* September 1964; (2) Lintner, John. "The Valuation of Risk Assets and the Selection of Risky Investments in Stock Portfolios and Capital Budgets." *Review of Economics and Statistics,* February 1965; (3) Mossin, Jan. "Equilibrium in a Capital Market." *Econometrica,* October 1966; (4) Treynor,

Jack. "Toward a Theory of Market Value of Risky Assets." Unpublished manuscript, 1961.

A review of the simple CAPM and its variants is contained in:
Jensen, Michael C. "The Foundation and Current State of Capital Market Theory." In *Studies in the Theory of Capital Markets*, ed. M. C. Jensen. New York: Praeger Publishers, 1972.

Three variants of the CAPM with less restrictive assumptions are discussed in:
Brennan, Michael J. "Taxes, Market Valuation, and Corporate Finance Policy." *National Tax Journal*, December 1973; Mayers, David. "Nonmarketable Assets and Capital Market Equilibrium under Uncertainty." In *Studies in the Theory of Capital Markets*, ed. M. C. Jensen. New York: Praeger, 1972; Black, Fisher. "Capital Market Equilibrium with Restricted Borrowing." *Journal of Business*, July 1972.

Excellent practitioner-oriented discussions of the CAPM appear in:
Mullins, David. "Does the Capital Asset Pricing Model Work." *Harvard Business Review*, January–February 1982; Rosenberg, Barr, and Andrew Rudd. "The Corporate Uses of Beta." In *The Revolution in Corporate Finance*, ed. J. M. Stern and D. H. Chew, Jr. New York: Basil Blackwell, 1986.

Stephen Ross developed the arbitrage pricing theory in two articles:
Ross, S. A. "Return, Risk and Arbitrage." In *Risk and Return in Finance*, ed. I. Friend and J. Bicksler. Cambridge, Mass.: Ballinger, 1976; Ross, S.A. "Arbitrage Theory of Capital Asset Pricing." *Journal of Economic Theory*, December 1976.

Articles exploring the factors that influence common stock returns are:
Bower, D. A., R. S. Bower, and D. E. Logue. "Arbitrage Pricing and Utility Stock Returns." *Journal of Finance*, September 1984; Chen, N. F., R. Roll, and S. Ross. "Economic Forces and the Stock Market: Testing the APT and Alternative Asset Pricing Theories." *Journal of Business*, July 1986; Sharpe, W. "Factors in New York Stock Exchange Security Returns, 1931–1979." *Journal of Portfolio Management*, Summer 1982.

Problem Sets

1. What is the beta of a portfolio with $E(r_P) = 20$ percent, if $r_f = 5$ percent and $E(r_M) = 15$ percent?

2. The market price of a security is \$40. Its expected rate of return is 13 percent. The risk-free rate is 7 percent, and the market risk premium is 8 percent. What will the market price of the security be if its beta doubles (and all other variables remain unchanged)? Assume the stock is expected to pay a constant dividend in perpetuity.

3. You are a consultant to a large manufacturing corporation considering a project with the following net after-tax cash flows (in millions of dollars)

Years from Now	After-Tax CF
0	−20
1–9	10
10	20

The project's beta is 1.7. Assuming $r_f = 9$ percent, and $E(r_M) = 19$ percent, what is the net present value of the project? What is the highest possible beta estimate for the project before its NPV becomes negative?

4. Are the following statements true or false? Explain.
    a. Stocks with a beta of zero offer an expected rate of return of zero.
    b. The CAPM implies that investors require a higher return to hold highly volatile securities.
    c. You can construct a portfolio with beta of 0.75 by investing 0.75 of the budget in T-bills and the remainder in the market portfolio.

5. Consider the following table, which gives a security analyst's expected return on two stocks for two particular market returns:

Market Return	Aggressive Stock	Defensive Stock
.05	.02	.035
.20	.32	.14

    a. What are the betas of the two stocks?
    b. What is the expected rate of return on each stock if the market return is equally likely to be 5 percent or 20 percent?
    c. If the T-bill rate is 8 percent, and the market return is equally likely to be 5 percent or 20 percent, draw the SML for this economy.
    d. Plot the two securities on the SML graph. What are the alphas of each?
    e. What hurdle rate should be used by the management of the aggressive firm for a project with the risk characteristics of the defensive firm's stock?

If the simple CAPM is valid, which of the situations in problems 6–12 below are possible? Explain. Consider each situation independently.

6.

Portfolio	Expected Return	Beta
A	.20	1.4
B	.25	1.2

7.

Portfolio	Expected Return	Standard Deviation
A	.30	.35
B	.40	.25

8.

Portfolio	Expected Return	Standard Deviation
Risk-free	.10	0
Market	.18	.24
A	.16	.12

9.

Portfolio	Expected Return	Standard Deviation
Risk-free	.10	0
Market	.18	.24
A	.20	.22

10.

Portfolio	Expected Return	Beta
Risk-free	.10	0
Market	.18	1.0
A	.16	1.5

11.

Portfolio	Expected Return	Beta
Risk-free	.10	0
Market	.18	1.0
A	.16	.9

12.

Portfolio	Expected Return	Standard Deviation
Risk-free	.10	0
Market	.18	.24
A	.16	.22

In problems 13–15 below, assume the risk-free rate is 8 percent and the expected rate of return on the market is 18 percent.

13. A share of stock is now selling for $100. It will pay a dividend of $9 per share at the end of the year. Its beta is 1.0. What do investors expect the stock to sell for at the end of the year?

14. I am buying a firm with an expected perpetual cash flow of $1,000 but am unsure of its risk. If I think the beta of the firm is zero, when the beta is really 1.0, how much *more* will I offer for the firm than it is truly worth?

15. A stock has an expected return of 6 percent. What is its beta?

16. Two investment advisors are comparing performance. One averaged a 19 percent return and the other a 16 percent return. However, the beta of the first advisor was 1.5 while that of the second was 1.0.

   a. Can you tell which advisor was a better predictor of individual stocks (aside from the issue of general movements in the market)?

   b. If the T-bill rate were 6 percent, and the market return during the period were 14 percent, which advisor would be the superior stock selector?

   c. What if the T-bill rate were 3 percent and the market return 15 percent?

17. In 1990, the yield on short-term government securities (perceived to be risk-free) was about 6 percent. Suppose the expected return required by the market for a portfolio with a beta of 1.0 is 15 percent. According to the capital asset pricing model:

   a. What is the expected return on the market portfolio?

   b. What would the expected return be on a zero beta stock?

   c. Suppose you consider buying a share of stock at a price of $40. The stock is expected to pay a dividend of $3 next year and to sell then for $41. The stock risk has been evaluated at $\beta = -.5$. Is the stock overpriced or underpriced?

18. Consider the following data for a one-factor economy. All portfolios are well diversified.

Portfolio	E(r)	Beta
A	10 percent	1.0
F	4	0

Suppose portfolio E is well diversified with a beta of $\frac{2}{3}$ and expected return of 9 percent. Would an arbitrage opportunity exist? If so, what would the arbitrage strategy be?

19. Following is a scenario for three stocks constructed by the security analysts of PF Inc.

		Scenario Rate of Return (%)		
Stock	Price($)	Recession	Average	Boom
A	10	−15	20	30
B	15	25	10	−10
C	50	12	15	12

   a. Construct an arbitrage portfolio using these stocks.
   b. How might these prices change when equilibrium is restored? Give an example where a change in stock C's price is sufficient to restore equilibrium, assuming the dollar payoffs to stock C remain the same.

20. Assume both portfolios A and B are well diversified, that $E(r_A) = .14$, and $E(r_B) = .148$. If the economy has only one factor, and $\beta_A = 1.0$ while $\beta_B = 1.1$, what must be the risk-free rate?

21. Assume a market index represents the common factor, and all stocks in the economy have a beta of 1.0. Firm specific returns all have a standard deviation of 0.30.

   Suppose an analyst studies 20 stocks and finds that one half have an alpha of 3 percent, and the other half an alpha of −3 percent. The analyst then buys $1 million of an equally weighted portfolio of the positive alpha stocks and sells short $1 million of an equally weighted portfolio of the negative alpha stocks.
   a. What is the expected profit (in dollars) and what is the standard deviation of the analyst's profit?
   b. How does your answer change if the analyst examines 50 stocks instead of 20? 100 stocks?

22. Assume security returns are generated by the single index model

$$R_i = \alpha_i + \beta_i R_M + e_i$$

where R_i is the excess return for security i, and R_M is the market's excess return. Suppose also that there are three securities A, B, and C characterized by these data:

Security	β	E(R)	$\sigma^2(e)$
A	.8	.10	.05
B	1.0	.12	.01
C	1.2	.14	.10

    a. If $\sigma_M^2 = .04$, calculate the variance of returns of securities A, B, and C.

    b. Now assume there are an infinite number of assets with return characteristics identical to those of A, B, and C, respectively. If one forms a well-diversified portfolio of type A securities, what will be the mean and variance of the portfolio's excess returns? What about portfolios composed only of type B or C stocks?

    c. Is there an arbitrage opportunity in this market? Analyze the opportunity using a graph.

23. If the APT is to be a useful theory, the numbers of systematic factors in the economy must be small. Why?

24. The APT itself does not provide information on the factors that one might expect to determine risk premiums. How should researchers decide which factors to investigate? Is industrial production a reasonable factor to test for a risk premium? Why or why not?

25. Suppose two factors are identified for the U.S. economy: the growth rate of industrial production, IP, and the inflation rate, IR. IP is expected to be 4 percent, and IR 6 percent. A stock with a beta of 1.0 on IP and 0.4 on IR currently is expected to provide a rate of return of 14 percent. If industrial production actually grows by 5 percent, while the inflation rate turns out to be 7 percent, what is your best guess for the rate of return on the stock?

26. Suppose there are two independent economic factors, M_1 and M_2. The risk-free rate is 7 percent, and all stocks have independent firm-specific components with a standard deviation of 50 percent. The following are well diversified portfolios:

Portfolio	Beta on M_1	Beta on M_2	Expected Return (%)
A	1.8	2.1	40
B	2.0	−0.5	10

What is the expected return-beta relationship in this economy?

Chapter

10

The Efficient Market Hypothesis

One of the early applications of computers in economics in the 1950s was to analyze economic time series. Business cycle theorists believed tracing the evolution of several economic variables over time would clarify and predict the progress of the economy through boom and bust periods. A natural candidate for analysis was the behavior of stock market prices over time. Assuming stock prices reflect the prospects of the firm, recurring patterns of peaks and troughs in economic performance ought to show up in those prices.

Maurice Kendall (1953) was one of the first to examine this proposition. He found to his great surprise that he could identify *no* predictable patterns in stock prices. Prices seemed to evolve randomly. They were as likely to go up as they were to go down on any particular day regardless of past performance. The data provided no way to predict price movements.

At first blush, Kendall's results disturbed some financial economists. They seemed to imply the stock market is dominated by erratic market psychology, or "animal spirits," that it follows no logical rules. In short, the results appeared to confirm the irrationality of the market. On further reflection, however, economists reversed their interpretation of Kendall's study.

It soon became apparent that random price movements indicated a well-functioning or efficient market, not an irrational one. In this chapter, we will explore the reasoning behind what may seem a surprising conclusion. We show how competition among analysts leads naturally to market efficiency, and we examine the implications of the efficient market hypothesis for investment policy. We also consider empirical evidence that supports and contradicts the notion of market efficiency. After studying this chapter you should be able to:

- Demonstrate why security price movements should be essentially unpredictable.
- Cite evidence that supports and contradicts the efficient market hypothesis.

■ Formulate investment strategies that make sense in informationally efficient markets.

10.1   *Random Walks and the Efficient Market Hypothesis*

Suppose Kendall had discovered that stock prices are predictable. Imagine the gold mine for investors! If they could use Kendall's equations to predict stock prices, investors would reap unending profits simply by purchasing stocks the computer model implied were about to increase in price and selling those stocks about to fall in price.

A moment's reflection should be enough to convince you that this situation could not persist for long. For example, suppose the model predicts with great confidence that XYZ stock price, currently at $100 per share, will rise dramatically in three days to $110. All investors with access to the model's prediction would place a great wave of immediate buy orders to cash in on the prospective increase in stock price. No one in the know holding XYZ, however, would be willing to sell, and the net effect would be an *immediate* jump in the stock price to $110. The forecast of a future price increase leads instead to an immediate price increase. Another way of putting this is that the stock price will immediately reflect the "good news" implicit in the model's forecast.

This simple example illustrates why Kendall's attempts to find recurring patterns in stock price movements was in vain. A forecast about favorable *future* performance leads instead to favorable *current* performance, as market participants all try to get in on the action before the price jump.

More generally, one could say that any publicly available information that might be used to predict stock performance, including information on the macro economy, the firm's industry, and its operations, plans, and management should already be impounded in stock prices. As soon as there is any information indicating a stock is underpriced and offers a profit opportunity, investors flock to buy the stock and immediately bid up its price to a fair level, where again only ordinary rates of return can be expected. These "ordinary rates" are simply rates of return commensurate with the risk of the stock.

But if prices are bid immediately to fair levels, given all available information, it must be that prices increase or decrease only in response to new information. New information, by definition, must be unpredictable; if it could be predicted, then that prediction would be part of today's information! Thus, stock prices that change in response to new (unpredictable) information also must move unpredictably.

Random walk
Describes the notion that stock price changes are random and unpredictable.

This is the essence of the argument that stock prices should follow a **random walk,** that is, that price changes should be random and unpredictable. Far from being a proof of market irrationality, randomly evolving stock prices are the necessary consequence of intelligent investors competing to discover relevant information on which to buy or sell stocks before the rest of the market becomes aware of that information.

Don't confuse randomness in price *changes* with irrationality in the *level* of prices. If prices are determined rationally, then only new information will cause them to change. Therefore, a random walk would be the natural evolution of prices that always reflect all current knowledge.

Efficient market hypothesis *The hypothesis that prices of securities fully reflect available information about securities.*

Indeed, if stock price movements were predictable, that would be damning evidence of stock market *in*efficiency, because the ability to predict prices would indicate that all available information was not already impounded in stock prices. Therefore, the notion that stocks already reflect all available information is referred to as the **efficient market hypothesis** (EMH).

Competition as the Source of Efficiency

Why should we expect stock prices to reflect all available information? After all, if you spend time and money gathering information, you would hope to turn up something that has been overlooked by the rest of the investment community. When information costs you money to uncover and analyze, you would expect your investment analysis calling for such expenditures to result in an increased expected return.

Investors will have an incentive to spend time and resources to analyze and uncover new information only if such activity is likely to generate higher investment returns. Therefore, in market equilibrium, efficient informational gathering activity should be fruitful.[1] While we would not go so far as to say you absolutely cannot come up with new information, it still makes sense to consider the competition.

Assume an investment management fund is managing a $5 billion portfolio. Suppose the fund manager can devise a research program that could increase the portfolio rate of return by one tenth of 1 percent per year, a seemingly modest amount. This program would increase the dollar return to the portfolio by $5 billion × .001, or $5 million. Therefore, the fund is presumably willing to spend up to $5 million per year on research to increase stock returns by a mere one tenth of 1 percent per year.

With such large rewards for such small increases in investment performance, is it any surprise that professional portfolio managers are willing to spend large sums on industry analysts, computer support, and research effort? With so many well-backed analysts willing to spend considerable resources on research, there cannot be many easy pickings in the market. Moreover, the incremental rates of return on research activity are likely to be so small that only managers of the largest portfolios will find them worth pursuing.

While it may not literally be true that *all* relevant information will be uncovered, it is virtually certain there are many investigators hot on the trail of any leads that may improve investment performance. Competition among these many well-backed, highly paid, aggressive analysts ensures that, as a general rule, stock prices ought to reflect available information regarding their proper levels.

Versions of the Efficient Market Hypothesis

It is common to distinguish among three versions of the EMH: the weak, semistrong, and strong forms of the hypothesis. These versions differ according to their notions of what is meant by the term *all available information.*

---

[1]A challenging and insightful discussion of this point may be found in Sanford J. Grossman and Joseph E. Stiglitz, "On the Impossibility of Informationally Efficient Markets," *American Economic Review* 70 (June 1980).

Weak-form EMH The assertion that stock prices already reflect all information contained in the history of past trading.

The **weak-form EMH** asserts that stock prices already reflect all information that can be derived by examining market trading data such as the history of past prices, trading volume, or short interest. This version of the hypothesis implies that trend analysis is fruitless. Past stock price data are publicly available and virtually costless to obtain. The weak-form hypothesis holds that if such data ever conveyed reliable signals about future performance, all investors would have learned long since to exploit the signals. Ultimately, the signals lose their value as they become widely known, because a buy signal for instance, would result in an immediate price increase.

Semistrong-form EMH The assertion that stock prices already reflect all publicly available information.

The **semistrong-form EMH** states that all publicly available information regarding the prospects of a firm must be reflected already in the stock price. Such information includes, in addition to past prices, fundamental data on the firm's product line, quality of management, balance sheet composition, patents held, earnings forecasts, accounting practices, and so forth. Again, if any investor has access to such information from publicly available sources, one would expect it to be reflected in stock prices.

Strong-form EMH The assertion that stock prices reflect all relevant information including inside information.

Finally, the **strong-form EMH** states that stock prices reflect all information relevant to the firm, even including information available only to company insiders. This version of the hypothesis is quite extreme. Few would argue with the proposition that corporate officers have access to pertinent information long enough before public release to enable them to profit from trading on that information. Indeed, much of the activity of the Securities and Exchange Commission is directed toward preventing insiders from profiting by exploiting their privileged situation. Rule 10b-5 of the Security Exchange Act of 1934 limits trading by corporate officers, directors, and substantial owners, requiring them to report trades to the SEC. Anyone trading on information supplied by insiders is considered in violation of the law.

Defining insider trading is not always easy, however. After all, stock analysts are in the business of uncovering information not already widely known to market participants. As we saw in Chapter 5, the distinction between private and inside information is sometimes murky.

Concept Check

Question 1. If the weak form of the efficient market hypothesis is valid, must the strong form also hold? Conversely, does strong-form efficiency imply weak-form efficiency?

10.2 *Implications of the EMH for Investment Policy*

Technical Analysis

Technical analysis Research on recurrent and predictable stock price patterns and on proxies for buy or sell pressure in the market.

Technical analysis is essentially the search for recurring and predictable patterns in stock prices. Although technicians recognize the value of information that has to do with future economic prospects of the firm, they believe such information is not necessary for a successful trading strategy. Whatever the fundamental reason for a change in stock price, if the stock price responds slowly enough, the analyst will be able to identify a trend that can be exploited during the adjustment period. Technical analysis assumes a sluggish response of stock prices to fundamental supply and demand factors. This assumption is diametrically opposed to the notion of an efficient market.

Technical analysts are sometimes called *chartists* because they study records or charts of past stock prices, hoping to find patterns they can exploit to make a profit. As an example of technical analysis, consider the *relative strength* approach. The chartist compares stock performance over a recent period to performance of the market or other stocks in the same industry. A simple version of relative strength takes the ratio of the stock price to a market indicator such as the S&P 500 index. If the ratio increases over time, the stock is said to exhibit relative strength, because its price performance is better than that of the broad market. Such strength presumably may continue for a long enough period to offer profit opportunities. We will explore this technique as well as several other tools of technical analysis further in Chapter 17.

The efficient market hypothesis predicts that technical analysis is without merit. The past history of prices and trading volume is publicly available at minimal cost. Therefore, any information that was ever available from analyzing past prices has already been reflected in stock prices. As investors compete to exploit their common knowledge of a stock's price history, they necessarily drive stock prices to levels where expected rates of return are commensurate with risk. At those levels, stocks are neither bad nor good buys. They are just fairly priced, meaning one should not expect abnormal returns.

Despite these theoretical considerations, some technically oriented trading strategies would have generated abnormal profits in the past. We will consider these strategies, and technical analysis more generally, in Chapter 17.

Fundamental Analysis

Fundamental analysis Research on determinants of stock value such as earnings and dividends prospects, expectations for future interest rates, and risk of the firm.

Fundamental analysis uses earnings and dividend prospects of the firm, expectations of future interest rates, and risk evaluation of the firm to determine proper stock prices. Ultimately, it represents an attempt to determine the present discounted value of all the payments a stockholder will receive from each share of stock. If that value exceeds the stock price, the fundamental analyst would recommend purchasing the stock.

Fundamental analysts usually start with a study of past earnings and an examination of company balance sheets. They supplement this analysis with further detailed economic analysis, ordinarily including an evaluation of the quality of the firm's management, the firm's standing within its industry, and the prospects for the industry as a whole. The hope is to attain some insight into the future performance of the firm that is not yet recognized by the rest of the market. Chapters 14 to 16 provide a detailed discussion of the types of analyses that underlie fundamental analysis.

Once again, the efficient market hypothesis predicts that *most* fundamental analysis adds little value. If analysts rely on publicly available earnings and industry information, one analyst's evaluation of the firm's prospects is not likely to be significantly more accurate than another's. There are many well-informed, well-financed firms conducting such market research, and in the face of such competition, it will be difficult to uncover data not also available to other analysts. Only analysts with a unique insight will be rewarded.

Fundamental analysis is much more difficult than merely identifying well-run firms with good prospects. Discovery of good firms does an investor no good in and of itself if the rest of the market also knows those firms are good. If the knowledge is already public, the investor will be forced to pay a high price for those firms and will not realize a superior rate of return.

The trick is not to identify firms that are good, but to find firms that are *better* than everyone else's estimate. Similarly, poorly run firms can be great bargains if they are not quite as bad as their stock prices suggest.

This is why fundamental analysis is difficult. It is not enough to do a good analysis of a firm; you can make money only if your analysis is better than that of your competitors, because the market price is expected already to reflect all commonly available information.

The quest for superior returns via fundamental analysis can serve a larger social purpose. Because stock prices may play an important role in firms' capital budgeting decisions, they can affect the allocation of capital across the economy. In this sense, it is important that stock prices be set efficiently so that they may serve as informative guides to investments in real assets. By helping ensure that stock prices reflect all economically relevant information, financial analysts may contribute to the efficiency of the real economy as well as to that of financial markets.

Active versus Passive Portfolio Management

Casual efforts to pick stocks are not likely to pay off. Competition among investors ensures that any easily implemented stock evaluation technique will be used widely enough so that any insights derived will be reflected in stock prices. Only serious, time-consuming, and expensive techniques are likely to generate the *differential* insight necessary to generate trading profits.

Moreover, these techniques are economically feasible only for managers of large portfolios. If you have only $100,000 to invest, even a 1 percent per year improvement in performance generates only $1,000 per year, hardly enough to justify herculean efforts. The billion-dollar manager, however, would reap extra income of $10 million annually from the same 1 percent increment.

If small investors are not in a favored position to conduct active portfolio management, what are their choices? The small investor probably is better off placing funds in a mutual fund. By pooling resources in this way, small investors can obtain the advantages of large size.

More difficult decisions remain, though. Can investors be sure that even large mutual funds have the ability or resources to uncover mispriced stocks? Further, will any mispricing be sufficiently large to repay the costs entailed in active portfolio management?

Proponents of the efficient market hypothesis believe active management is largely wasted effort and unlikely to justify the expenses incurred. Therefore, they advocate a **passive investment strategy** that makes no attempt to outsmart the market. A passive strategy aims only at establishing a well-diversified portfolio of securities without attempting to find under- or overvalued stocks. Passive management is usually characterized by a buy-and-hold strategy. Because the efficient market theory indicates stock prices are at fair levels, given all available information, it makes no sense to buy and sell securities frequently, as transactions generate large trading costs without increasing expected performance.

Passive investment strategy Buying a well-diversified portfolio without attempting to search out mispriced securities.

Index fund   A mutual fund holding shares in proportion to their representation in a market index such as the S&P 500.

One common strategy for passive management is to create an **index fund,** which is a fund designed to replicate the performance of a broad-based index of stocks. For example, in 1976, the Vanguard Group of mutual funds introduced a mutual fund called the Index 500 Portfolio that holds stocks in direct proportion to their weight in the Standard & Poor's 500 stock price index. The performance of the Index 500 fund replicates the performance of the S&P 500. Investors in this fund obtain broad diversification with relatively low management fees. The fees can be kept to a minimum because Vanguard does not need to pay analysts to assess stock prospects and does not incur transaction costs from high portfolio turnover. While the typical annual expense ratio for an actively managed fund is over 1 percent of assets, Vanguard charges only about 0.2 percent for the Index 500 Portfolio.

Indexing has grown in appeal considerably since 1976. *The Wall Street Journal* deemed stock index funds the hot product of 1990 in the mutual fund industry.[2] Vanguard's Index 500 Portfolio had approximately $2.2 billion in assets in early 1991, placing it among the 40 largest mutual funds. Both Fidelity and Dreyfus have now initiated S&P 500 index funds. Moreover, over $250 billion is now invested by institutional investors in indexed portfolios. Many institutional investors now hold indexed bond portfolios as well as indexed stock portfolios. These portfolios aim to replicate the features of well-known bond indexes such as the Shearson Lehman or Salomon Brothers indexes. In 1987, fully one third of all fixed-income investments of tax-exempt institutional investors went into index bond funds. Vanguard and Fidelity now offer index bond mutual funds for small investors.

Concept Check

Question 2.   What would happen to market efficiency if *all* investors attempted to follow a passive strategy?

The Role of Portfolio Management in an Efficient Market

If the market is efficient, why not throw darts at *The Wall Street Journal* instead of trying to choose a stock portfolio rationally? It's tempting to draw this sort of conclusion from the notion that security prices are fairly set, but it's a far too simple one. There is a role for rational portfolio management, even in perfectly efficient markets.

A basic principle in portfolio selection is diversification. Even if all stocks are priced fairly, each still poses firm-specific risk that can be eliminated through diversification. Therefore, rational security selection, even in an efficient market, calls for the selection of a well-diversified portfolio. Moreover, that portfolio should provide the systematic risk level the investor wants. Even in an efficient market, investors must choose the risk-return profiles they deem appropriate.

Rational investment policy also requires that investors take tax considerations into account in security choice. If you are in a high tax bracket, you generally will not want the same securities that low-bracket investors find favorable.

---

[2]See the Second Box in Chapter 7.

At an obvious level, high-bracket investors find it advantageous to buy tax-exempt municipal bonds despite their relatively low pretax yields, while those same bonds are unattractive to low-tax-bracket investors. At a more subtle level, high-bracket investors might want to tilt or specialize their portfolios toward securities that provide capital gains as opposed to dividend or interest income, because the option to defer the realization of capital gains income is more valuable, the higher the investor's current tax bracket. They also will be more attracted to investment opportunities where returns are sensitive to tax benefits, such as real estate ventures.

A third argument for rational portfolio management relates to the particular risk profile of the investor. For example, a General Motors executive whose annual bonus depends on GM's profits generally should not invest additional amounts in auto stocks. To the extent that his or her compensation already depends on GM's well-being, the executive is overinvested in GM now and should not exacerbate the lack of diversification.

Investors of varying ages also might warrant different portfolio policies with regard to risk bearing. For example, older investors who are essentially living off savings might avoid long-term bonds whose market values fluctuate dramatically with changes in interest rates. Because these investors rely on accumulated savings, they require conservation of principal. In contrast, younger investors might be more inclined toward long-term bonds. The steady flow of income over long periods that is locked in with long-term bonds can be more important than preservation of principal to those with long life expectancies.

In short, there is a role for portfolio management even in an efficient market. Investors' optimal positions will vary according to factors such as age, tax bracket, risk aversion, and employment. The role of the portfolio manager in an efficient market is to tailor the portfolio to these needs, rather than to attempt to beat the market.

10.3 Are Markets Efficient?

The Issues

Not surprisingly, the efficient market hypothesis is not universally hailed by professional portfolio managers. It implies that a great deal of the activity of portfolio managers—the search for undervalued securities—is at best wasted effort and possibly harmful to clients because it costs money and leads to imperfectly diversified portfolios. Consequently, the EMH has never been widely accepted on Wall Street, and debate continues today on the degree to which security analysis can improve investment performance. Before discussing empirical tests of the hypothesis, we want to note three factors that together imply the debate probably never will be settled: the magnitude issue, the selection bias issue, and the lucky event issue.

The Magnitude Issue

Consider an investment manager overseeing a $2 billion portfolio. If she can improve performance by only one tenth of 1 percent per year, that effort will be worth $.001 \times \$2$ billion = $2 million annually. This manager clearly would be worth her salary! Yet we, as observers, probably cannot statistically measure her contribution. A one tenth of 1 percent contribution would be swamped by the yearly volatility of the market. Remember, the annual standard deviation of the well-diversified S&P 500 index has been more than 20 percent per year. Against these fluctuations, a small increase in performance would be hard to detect. Nevertheless, $2 million remains an extremely valuable improvement in performance.

All might agree that stock prices are very close to fair values, and that only managers of large portfolios can earn enough trading profits to make the exploitation of minor mispricing worth the effort. According to this view, the actions of intelligent investment managers are the driving force behind the constant evolution of market prices to fair levels. Rather than ask the qualitative question "are markets efficient?" we ought instead to ask the more quantitative question "how efficient are markets?"

The Selection Bias Issue

Suppose you discover an investment scheme that could really make money. You have two choices: either publish your technique in *The Wall Street Journal* to win fleeting fame, or keep your technique secret and use it to earn millions of dollars. Most investors would choose the latter option, which presents us with a conundrum. Only investors who find that an investment scheme cannot generate abnormal returns will be willing to report their findings to the whole world. Hence, opponents of the efficient markets view of the world always can use evidence that various techniques do not provide investment rewards as proof that the techniques that do work simply are not being reported to the public. This is a problem in *selection bias;* the outcomes we are able to observe have been preselected in favor of failed attempts. Therefore, we cannot fairly evaluate the true ability of portfolio managers to generate winning stock market strategies.

The Lucky Event Issue

In virtually any month, it seems we read an article in *The Wall Street Journal* about some investor or investment company with a fantastic investment performance over the recent past. Surely the superior records of such investors disprove the efficient market hypothesis.

This conclusion is far from obvious, however. As an analogy to the "contest" among portfolio managers, consider a contest to flip the most heads out of 50 trials using a fair coin. The expected outcome for any person is 50 percent heads and 50 percent tails. If 10,000 people, however, compete in this contest, it would not be surprising if at least one or two contestants flipped more than 75 percent heads. In fact, elementary statistics tells us that the expected number of contestants flipping 75 percent or more heads would be two. It would be silly, though, to crown these people the head-flipping champions of the world. They are simply the contestants who happened to get lucky on the day of the event.

The analogy to efficient markets is clear. Under the hypothesis that any stock is fairly priced given all available information, any bet on a stock is simply a coin toss. There is equal likelihood of winning or losing the bet. Yet, if many investors using a variety of schemes make fair bets, statistically speaking, *some* of those investors will be lucky and win a great majority of the bets. For every big winner, there may be many big losers, but we never hear of these managers.

How to Guarantee a Successful Market Newsletter

Suppose you want to make your fortune publishing a market newsletter. You need first to convince potential subscribers that you have talent worth paying for. But what if you have no market prediction talent? The solution is simple: Start eight market newsletters.

In year one, let four of your newsletters predict an up market and four a down market. In year two, left half of the originally optimistic group of newsletters continue to predict an up market and the other half a down market. Do the same for the originally pessimistic group. Continue in this manner to obtain the following pattern of predictions (U = prediction of an up market, D = prediction of a down market).

Newsletter Predictions

Year	1	2	3	4	5	6	7	8
1	U	U	U	U	D	D	D	D
2	U	U	D	D	U	U	D	D
3	U	D	U	D	U	D	U	D

After three years, no matter what has happened to the market, one of the newsletters would have had a perfect prediction record. This is because after three years, there are $2^3 = 8$ outcomes for the market, and we've covered all eight possibilities with the eight letters. Now, we simply slough off the seven unsuccessful newsletters and market the eighth letter based on its perfect track record. If we want to establish a letter with a perfect track record over a four-year period, we need $2^4 = 16$ newsletters. A five-year period requires 32 newsletters, and so on.

After the fact, the one newsletter that was always right will attract attention for your uncanny foresight and investors will rush to pay large fees for its advice. Your fortune is made, and you never even researched the market!

WARNING: This scheme is illegal! The point, however, is that with hundreds of market newsletters, you can find one that has stumbled onto an apparently remarkable string of successful predictions without any real degree of skill. After the fact, *someone's* prediction history can seem to imply great forecasting skill. This person is the one we will read about in *The Wall Street Journal;* the others will be forgotten.

The winners, though, turn up in *The Wall Street Journal* as the latest stock market gurus; then they can make a fortune publishing market newsletters.

Our point is that after the fact there will have been at least one successful investment scheme. A doubter will call the results luck; the successful investor will call it skill. The proper test would be to see whether the successful investors can repeat their performance in another period, yet this approach is rarely taken. For an extreme version of the lucky event issue, see the accompanying box.

With these caveats in mind, we turn now to some of the empirical tests of the efficient market hypothesis.

Concept Check

Question 3. The Magellan Fund managed by Fidelity outperformed the S&P 500 in 11 of the 13 years ending in 1989, resulting in an average annual return for this period more than 10 percent better than that of the index. Is this performance sufficient to cause you to doubt the efficient markets theory? If not, would *any* performance record be sufficient to dissuade you?

Tests of Technical Analysis

Early tests of efficient markets were tests of the weak form. Could speculators find trends in past prices that would enable them to earn abnormal profits? This is essentially a test of the efficacy of technical analysis.

The work of Kendall (1953) and Roberts (1959), both of whom analyzed the possible existence of patterns in stock prices, suggests that such patterns are not to be found. Fama (1965) later analyzed "runs" of stock prices to see whether the stock market exhibits momentum that can be exploited. (A run is a sequence of consecutive price increases or decreases.) For example, if the last three changes in daily stock prices were positive, could we be more confident that the next move also would be up?

Fama classified daily stock price movements of each of the 30 Dow Jones industrial stocks as positive, zero, or negative in order to test persistence of runs. He found that neither positive nor negative runs persisted to an extent that could contradict the efficient market hypothesis. Although there was some evidence of runs over very short time intervals (less than one day), the tendency for runs to persist was so slight that any attempt to exploit them would generate trading costs in excess of the expected abnormal returns.

Filter rule   A rule for buying or selling stock according to recent price movements.

A more sophisticated version of trend analysis is a **filter rule.** A filter technique gives a rule for buying or selling a stock depending on past price movements. One rule, for example, might be: "Buy if the last two trades each resulted in a stock price increase." A more conventional one might be: "Buy a security if its price increases by 1 percent, and hold it until its price falls by more than 1 percent from the subsequent high." Alexander (1964) and Fama and Blume (1966) found that such filter rules generally could not generate trading profits.

Similar results were obtained by Levy (1971), who identified 32 standard chartist patterns and tested their predictive power. He concluded that none of the patterns produced better-than-average trading results for anyone who cannot buy and sell securities free of commissions. Moreover, the most bullish results tended to be generated by patterns that technical analysts typically describe as bearish!

The conclusion of the vast majority of weak-form tests is that stock market data validate the efficient market hypothesis. To be fair, however, one should note the criticism of efficient market skeptics, who argue that any filter rule or trend analysis that can be tested statistically is overly mechanical and cannot capture the finesse with which human investors can detect subtle but exploitable patterns in past prices.

One interesting technically based trading strategy that seems to have had value is employed by Value Line. It classifies stocks as good or bad buys based in part on earnings and price momentum. The strategy seems to have enjoyed considerable predictive success, although Value Line itself has not been able to translate this success into outstanding performance of its mutual funds. We consider the Value Line system in more detail in Chapter 17 on technical analysis.

Moreover, more sophisticated recent tests of the random walk hypothesis have found some interesting violations of the model. Lo and MacKinlay (1988), Fama and French (1987), Poterba and Summers (1987), and Jegadeesh (1990) all find evidence of serial correlation in movements in stock market indexes.

Serial correlation refers to the tendency for stock returns to be related to past returns. Positive serial correlation means positive returns tend to follow positive returns (a momentum type of property). Negative serial correlation means positive returns tend to be followed by negative returns (a reversal or "correction" property).

These studies find that there is short-term positive serial correlation in stock market prices but pronounced negative long-term serial correlation. The latter result has given rise to a "fads hypothesis," which asserts that stock prices might overreact to relevant news. Such overreaction leads to positive serial correlation (momentum) over short time horizons. Subsequent correction of the overreaction leads to poor performance following good performance and vice versa. The corrections mean a run of positive returns eventually will tend to be followed by negative returns, leading to negative serial correlation over longer horizons.

A related phenomenon relates to the finding of "excess volatility" in stock prices emphasized by Shiller (1981), and since intensively studied. Shiller compared the actual values over time of various stock market indexes to an estimate of the present value of all future dividends to be paid by the stocks in the indexes. This present value may be viewed as the intrinsic value of the stock index had investors been able to forecast dividends perfectly. Figure 10.1 shows the graph of *P**, the perfect-foresight intrinsic value of the S&P 500, to *P,* the actual value. (Both graphs are detrended, meaning all values are divided by the long-run growth factor to abstract from the general upward drift in prices.) The actual series fluctuates considerably around the intrinsic value, leading Shiller to conclude that actual prices exhibit excess volatility compared to the volatility of intrinsic value.

An alternative interpretation of these results holds that they do not necessarily imply stock market inefficiency but only that fair risk premiums vary systematically over time. As the risk premium and market discount rate varies over time, it can lead to the appearance of mean reversion and excess volatility in prices. In addition, it is not clear that these empirical results could be used to formulate trading strategies to yield abnormal profits after transaction costs.

More powerful trading strategies based essentially on technical-type analysis are suggested in studies by De Bondt and Thaler (1985), Jegadeesh (1990), and Lehman (1990). They find strong tendencies for very poorly performing stocks

Figure 10.1
Excess market volatility. Perfect foresight value of S&P 500 index, P*, versus actual value, *P*.
From Shiller (1981).

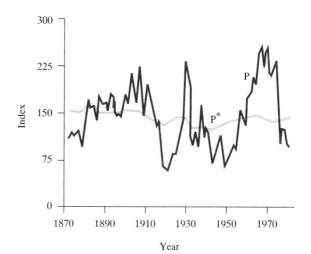

Reversal effect The tendency of poorly performing stocks and well-performing stocks in one period to experience reversals in the following period.

in one time period to experience sizable reversals over the subsequent period, while the best-performing stocks in a given period tend to follow with poor performance in the following period. This phenomenon, dubbed the **reversal effect,** is suggestive of overreaction of stock prices to relevant news. Here, however, the overreaction is stock-specific, rather than common to the entire market.

It is much harder to explain these results by appealing to time-varying risk premiums. Moreover, these tendencies seem pronounced enough to be exploited profitably and so present a strong challenge to market efficiency. Some funds are already being managed to exploit this apparent profit opportunity. The true test of market efficiency will be to see whether the reversal effect persists now that market participants are aware of it.

Portfolio Strategies: Tests of the Semistrong Hypothesis

Fundamental analysis calls on a much wider range of information to create portfolios than does technical analysis, and tests of the value of fundamental analysis, therefore, are correspondingly more difficult to evaluate. They have, however, revealed a number of so-called anomalies, that is, evidence that seems inconsistent with the efficient market hypothesis. We will review several such anomalies in the following pages.

One major problem with these tests is that most require risk adjustments to portfolio performance, and most tests use the CAPM to make the risk adjustments. We know that while beta seems to be a relevant descriptor of stock risk, the empirically measured quantitative trade-off between risk as measured by beta and expected return differs from the predictions of the CAPM. If we use the CAPM to adjust portfolio returns for risk, inappropriate adjustments might lead to the conclusion that various portfolio strategies can generate superior returns, when the risk adjustment procedure has failed.

Tests of risk-adjusted returns are *joint tests* of the efficient market hypothesis *and* the risk adjustment procedure. If it appears that a portfolio strategy can generate superior returns, we must then choose between rejecting the EMH or rejecting the risk adjustment technique. Usually, the risk adjustment technique is based on more questionable assumptions than the EMH; if we reject the procedure, we are left with no conclusion about market efficiency.

P/E effect Portfolios of low P/E stocks have exhibited higher average risk-adjusted returns than high P/E stocks.

An example of this problem is the discovery by Basu (1977, 1983) that portfolios of low price/earnings ratio stocks have higher average returns than high P/E portfolios. The **P/E effect** holds up even if returns are adjusted for portfolio beta. Is this a confirmation that the market systematically misprices stocks according to P/E ratio?

This would be a surprising and, to us, disturbing conclusion, because analysis of P/E ratios is such a simple procedure. While it may be possible to earn superior returns using hard work and much insight, it hardly seems likely that following such a basic technique is enough to generate abnormal returns.

One possible interpretation of these results is that the model of capital market equilibrium is at fault in that the returns are not properly adjusted for risk. This is the conclusion Basu reached in 1983.

Small-firm effect That stocks of small firms have earned abnormal returns, primarily in Januarys.

The Small-Firm Effect

One of the most frequently cited anomalies with respect to the efficient market hypothesis is the so-called size or **small-firm effect,** originally documented by

Banz (1981). Banz found that both total and risk-adjusted rates of return tend to fall with increases in the relative size of the firm, as measured by the market value of the firm's outstanding equity. Dividing all NYSE stocks into quintiles according to firm size, Banz found that the average annual return of firms in the smallest size quintile was 19.8 percent greater than the average return of firms in the largest size quintile.

This is a huge premium; imagine earning extra return of this amount on a billion-dollar portfolio. Yet it is remarkable that following a simple (even simplistic) rule such as "invest in low capitalization stocks" should enable an investor to earn excess returns. After all, any investor can measure firm size costlessly. One would not expect such minimal effort to yield such large rewards.

Later studies [Keim (1983), Reinganum (1983), and Blume and Stambaugh (1983)] showed that the small-firm effect occurs virtually entirely in the first two weeks of January. The size effect is in fact a small-firm-in-January effect.

Figure 10.2 illustrates the January effect. Keim ranked firms in order of increasing size as measured by market value of equity and then divided them into 10 portfolios grouped by the size of each firm. In each month of the year, he calculated the difference in the average excess return of firms in the smallest-firm portfolio and largest-firm portfolio. The average monthly differences over the years 1963–1979 appear in Figure 10.2. January clearly stands out as an exceptional month for small firms, with an average small firm premium of 0.714 percent (an annualized premium of 8.9 percent).

Some researchers believe the January effect is tied to tax loss selling at the end of the year. The hypothesis is that many people sell stocks that have declined in price during the previous months to realize their capital losses before the end of the tax year. Such investors do not put the proceeds from these sales back into the stock market until after the turn of the year. At that point, the rush of demand for stock prices places an upward pressure on prices that results in the January effect. Finally, the January effect is said to show up most dramatically for the smallest firms because the small-firm group includes, as an empirical matter, stocks with the greatest variability of prices during the year. The group, therefore, includes a relatively large number of firms that have declined sufficiently to induce tax-loss selling.

Some empirical evidence supports the belief that the January effect is connected to tax-loss selling. For example, Ritter (1988) shows that the ratio of

Figure 10.2

Average difference between daily excess returns (in percentages) of lowest-firm-size and highest-firm-size deciles by month between 1963 and 1979.

Data from Donald B. Keim (1983).

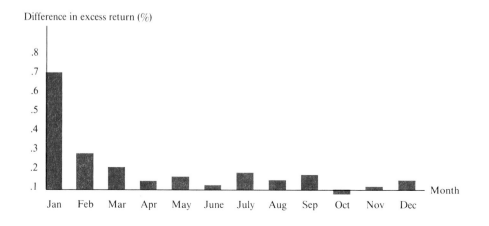

stock purchases to sales by individual investors is below normal in late December and above normal in early January. This is consistent with tax-loss rebalancing.

Reinganum (1983) found that within size class, firms that had declined more severely in price had larger January returns. This pattern is illustrated in Figure 10.3. Reinganum divided firms into quartiles based on the extent to which stock prices had declined during the year. Big price declines would be expected to generate big January returns if these firms tend to be unloaded in December and enjoy demand pressure in January. The figure shows that the lowest quartile (biggest tax loss) portfolios within the smallest size group show the greatest January effect.

Figure 10.3
Average daily returns of small firms in January for securities in the upper quartile and bottom quartile of the tax-loss selling distribution.
From Marc R. Reinganum, (1983).

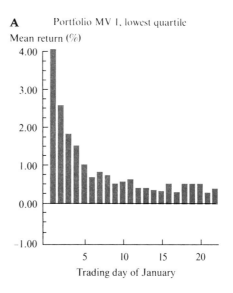

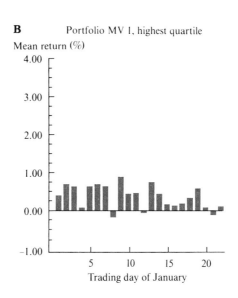

The fundamental question is why market participants do not exploit the January effect and thereby ultimately eliminate it by bidding stock prices to appropriate levels. One possible explanation lies in segmentation of the market into two groups: institutional investors who invest primarily in large firms, and individual investors who invest disproportionately in smaller firms. According to this view, managers of large institutional portfolios are the moving force behind efficient markets. It is professionals who seek out profit opportunities and bid prices to their appropriate levels. Institutional investors do not seem to buy at the small-size end of the market, perhaps because of limits on allowed portfolio positions, so the small-firm anomaly persists without the force of their participation.

Concept Check

> *Question 4.* Does this market segmentation theory get the efficient market hypothesis off the hook, or are there still market mechanisms that, in theory, ought to eliminate the small-firm anomaly?

The Neglected-Firm Effect

Arbel and Strebel (1983) give another interpretation of the small-firm effect. Because small firms tend to be neglected by large institutional traders, information about such firms is less available. This information deficiency makes smaller firms riskier investments that command higher returns. "Brand-name" firms, after all, are subject to considerable monitoring from institutional investors that assures high-quality information, and presumably investors do not purchase "generic" stocks without the prospect of greater returns.

Neglected-firm effect The tendency of investments in stock of less well-known firms to generate abnormal returns.

As evidence for the **neglected-firm effect,** Arbel (1985) measures the information deficiency of firms using the coefficient of variation of analysts' forecasts of earnings. (The coefficient of variation is the ratio of standard deviation to mean and measures the dispersion of forecasts. It is a "noise-to-signal" ratio.) The correlation coefficient between the coefficient of variation and total return was 0.676, quite high, and statistically significant. In a related test, Arbel divided firms into highly researched, moderately researched, and neglected groups based on the number of institutions holding the stock. Table 10.1 shows that the January effect was largest for the neglected firms.

The Day-of-the-Week Effect

The small-firm-in-January effect is one example of seasonality in stock market returns, a recurring pattern of turn-of-the-year abnormal returns. Another such pattern, and in several ways an even odder one, is the **weekend effect,** first documented by French (1980) and Gibbons and Hess (1981). These researchers studied the pattern of stock returns from close of trading on Friday afternoon to close on Monday to determine whether the three-day return spanning the weekend would be three times the typical return on a weekday. This was to be a test of whether the market operates on calendar time or trading time.

Weekend effect The tendency for the average stock return from Friday to Monday to be lower than average returns on any other weekday.

Surprisingly, the typical Friday to Monday return was not larger than that of other weekdays—in fact, it was negative! We show below the mean return of the S&P 500 portfolio for each day of the week from July 1962 through December

1978. The Monday return is based on closing price Friday to closing price Monday, the Tuesday return on Monday closing to Tuesday closing, and so on.

Day:	Monday	Tuesday	Wednesday	Thursday	Friday
Mean return:	−.134%	.002%	.096%	.028%	.084%

The negative Monday effect is extremely large. On an annualized basis, assuming 250 trading days a year, the return is −33.5 percent (−.134 × 250). Gibbons and Hess report, for the overall period, all 30 Dow Jones Industrial stocks had negative mean Monday returns. Thus, it is quite unlikely that the weekend effect can be attributed to statistical fluke.

The weekend effect poses a problem for efficient market theorists. In frictionless markets, we would expect this recurrent pattern to be "arbitraged away." If there is a predictable weekend effect, surely investors ought to shy away from purchases on Fridays, delaying them until Monday. Conversely, sales of stock originally scheduled for Monday optimally would be pushed up to the preceding Friday. This reshuffling of buying and selling would be enough to increase buy relative to sell pressure on Monday to the point where the weekend effect would be dissipated. Interestingly, research by Connolly (1989) suggests that the weekend effect has disappeared in recent years.

Inside Information

It would not be surprising if insiders were able to make superior profits trading in their firm's stock. The ability of insiders to trade profitability in their own stock has been documented in studies by Jaffee (1974), Seyhun (1986), Givoly and Palmon (1985), and others. Jaffee's was one of the earliest studies to show the tendency for stock prices to rise after insiders intensively bought shares and to fall after intensive insider sales.

Table 10.1 *January Effect by Degree of Neglect (1971–1980)*

S&P 500 Companies	Average January Return (%)	Average January Return minus Average Return during Rest of Year (%)	Average January Return after Adjusting for Systematic Risk(%)
Highly researched	2.48	1.63	−1.44
Moderately researched	4.95	4.19	1.69
Neglected	7.62	6.87	5.03
Non-S&P 500 Companies			
Neglected	11.32	10.72	7.71

From: Avner Arbel, "Generic Stocks: An Old Product in a New Package," *Journal of Portfolio Management*, Summer 1985, pp. 4–13.

To level the playing field, the Securities and Exchange Commission requires all insiders to register all their trading activity, and it publishes these trades in an *Official Summary of Insider Trading*. Once the *Official Summary* is published, the trades become public information. At that point, if markets are efficient, fully and immediately processing the information released, an investor should no longer be able to profit from following the pattern of those trades.

Surprisingly, early studies like Jaffee's seemed to indicate that following insider transactions, that is, buying after inside purchases were reported in the *Official Summary* and selling after insider sales, could offer substantial abnormal returns to an outside investor. This would be a clear violation of market efficiency, as the data in the *Official Summary* are publicly available. Work since then by Seyhun, who carefully tracked the public release dates of the *Official Summary,* found that following insider transactions would be to no avail. While there is some tendency for stock prices to increase even after the *Official Summary* reports insider buying, the abnormal returns are not of sufficient magnitude to overcome transaction costs.

The Value Line Enigma

The Value Line Investor Survey is an investment advisory service that ranks securities on a timeliness scale of one (best buy) to five (sell). Ranks are based on relative earnings and price performance across securities, price momentum, quarterly earnings momentum, and a measure of unexpected earnings in the most recent quarter. The Value Line technique is discussed in more detail in Chapter 17 on technical analysis.

Several studies have examined the predictive value of the Value Line recommendations. Black (1971) found that Portfolio 1 (the "buy" portfolio) had a risk-adjusted excess rate of return of 10 percent, while Portfolio 5 (the "sell" portfolio) had an abnormal return of −10 percent. These results imply a fantastic potential value to the Value Line forecasts. Copeland and Mayers (1982) performed a similar study using a more sophisticated risk-adjustment technique, which found that the difference in the risk-adjusted performance of Portfolios 1 and 5 was much smaller: Portfolio 1 earned an abnormal six-month rate of return of 1.52 percent, while Portfolio 5 earned an abnormal return of −2.97 percent. Even this smaller difference, however, seems to be a substantial deviation from the prediction of the efficient market hypothesis, although it is an open question as to whether the abnormal returns present profit opportunities after accounting for bid-ask spreads and transaction costs.

Given Value Line's apparent success in predicting stock performance, we would expect that changes in Value Line's timeliness rankings would result in abnormal returns for affected stocks. This seems to be the case. Stickel (1985) shows that Value Line rerankings generally are followed by abnormal stock returns in the expected direction. Interestingly enough, smaller firms tend to have more sensitivity to rerankings. This pattern is consistent with the neglected-firm effect in that the information contained in a reranking carries greater weight for firms that are less intensively monitored.

The Market Crash of October 1987

The market crash of October 1987 seems to be a glaring counterexample to the efficient market hypothesis. If prices reflect market fundamentals, then defenders of the EMH must look for news on the 19th of that month that was consistent with the 20 percent one-day decline in stock prices. Yet no events of such importance seem to have transpired on that date. The fantastic price swing is hard to reconcile with market fundamentals. The accompanying box offers an assessment of efficient market theory in light of the crash.

Concept Check

Question 5. Some say that continued worry concerning the U.S. trade deficit brought down the market on October 19. Is this explanation consistent with the EMH?

Mutual Fund Performance

We have documented some of the apparent chinks in the armor of efficient market proponents. Ultimately, however, from the perspective of portfolio management, the issue of market efficiency boils down to whether skilled investors can make consistent abnormal trading profits. The best test is simply to look at the performance of market professionals and see if that performance is superior to that of a passive index fund that buys and holds the market.

Casual evidence does not support claims that professionally managed portfolios can beat the market. In the decade ended in 1979, about 47 percent of equity fund managers outperformed the S&P 500. In the 1980s, only 37 percent beat the market (Bogle, 1991). Figure 10.4 shows year by year the percent of mutual fund managers whose performance was inferior to the S&P 500. Figure 10.5 shows the cumulative return of the S&P 500 over these two decades compared to the Lipper General Equity Fund average. The annualized return of the S&P 500 was 11.5 percent versus 9.4 percent for the funds. The 2.1 point margin is substantial. About 1.1 points of the S&P 500's margin can be attributed to fund operating costs, and about 0.7 points to transaction fees associated with trading (Bogle, 1991). Thus, it appears that even after accounting for the costs of operating and trading for the fund, there is little evidence of superior investment results.

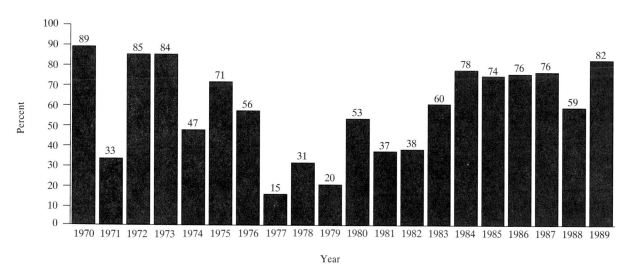

Figure 10.4 **Equity mutual funds outperformed by S&P 500 index.**
From John C. Bogle (1991).

The 'Efficient Market' Was a Good Idea—and Then Came the Crash

It Launched a Revolution, but the Theory Can't Explain Why Investors Panicked on Oct. 19

The Oct. 19 stock market collapse crushed more than $500 billion in investor wealth. It also struck a blow against one of the most powerful ideas in finance—the efficient market theory (EMT). "It was the nail in the coffin of the theory," says economist Bruce Greenwald, a staff member on the Brady commission, which studied the crash.

That theory bucked the popular view that stocks move on the latest fad or the speculative fever of the crowd. Well-informed investors could make a bundle, went the conventional wisdom. Not so, says the EMT. The stock market is an efficient information processing machine. Investors act rationally, and stock prices reflect whatever information people have about the fundamentals, such as present and future earnings. Stock prices change only on fresh news—and that doesn't include crowd psychology.

Herd Instinct

The theory had few believers back in the early 1960s. But the EMT ended up launching a market revolution. Finance professors and math whizzes built careers on Wall Street exploiting its insights. For instance, the theory says that you can't consistently outperform the market averages, since only unexpected news moves prices. Did the EMT catch on with big money? You bet. Many pension-fund sponsors turned their backs on money managers who claimed that they could beat the market and bought some $175 billion in index funds that track the market.

Then came Bloody Monday. Efficient market theory is useless in explaining the biggest stock market calamity in 58 years. What new information

jarred investors into slashing their estimate of the value of corporate America's assets by some 23 percent in the 6½ hours the New York Stock Exchange was open? Hardly enough news came out that day, or over the weekend, to account for the plunge.

Indeed, a survey by Yale University's Robert Shiller of nearly 1,000 big and small investors showed that the reason for selling was not a change in the fundamentals. Rather, it was the declines that took place in the market itself the Thursday and Friday before, as well as the sharp sell-off on the morning of Oct. 19. "Lots of nervous people came to believe the price drops themselves signaled a crash, and everyone tried to be the first out the door," says Shiller. Investors panicked because the market was falling like a stone. There was no rationality, only herd instinct.

The rout of the efficient markets theory holds important implications not only for investors but also for the idea that the market is the best possible way to channel capital to its most productive uses. According to this belief, investors allowed to choose in a competitive market will funnel money to those companies with the best prospects. It's no coincidence that the EMT was mainly developed at the University of Chicago, a laissez-faire bastion. Moreover, the so-called derivative securities—stock index futures and options—were conceived in the Windy City and traded on the Chicago exchanges largely because of the impetus from the university's free market theorists, who argued that the new instruments would make the stock market even more efficient.

Reason to Believe

But if crowd psychology, not rationality, rules stock prices, investors and policymakers might be getting

Of course, one might argue that there are good managers and bad managers, and the good managers can consistently outperform the index. The real test of this notion is to see whether managers with good performance in one year can repeat that performance in a following year. In other words, is the abnormal performance due to luck or skill? Jensen (1969) performed such a test using 10 years of data on 115 mutual funds, a total of 1,150 annual observations.

the wrong signals from the market. Money might flow to unproductive businesses, such as junk-bond-financed leveraged buyouts. Meanwhile, companies spending a lot on future products and cultivating markets could starve for cheap capital. Even Chicago's pioneering efficient-market theorist Eugene Fama admits the EMT is "a matter of belief" to him. If prices are not being set the way the theory assumes, then the free market system is not allocating resources efficiently, says Fama.

Signs that the EMT doesn't work began to show up in the stock market well before Bloody Monday. The crash is only the latest, most dramatic, instance of the theory's failure. A cottage industry has sprung up in academe documenting market "anomalies" inconsistent with the EMT. Take the "January effect." Small-capitalization stocks repeatedly show large returns during the first five trading days of the year. According to the EMT, the January effect shouldn't persist. Sophisticated investors, anticipating the easy gains, should have bid up prices well before the beginning of the year.

Other economists believe they have found further instances of investor irrationality. A study by economists Richard Thaler and Werner De Bondt shows that a stock portfolio made up of the 35 worst-performing NYSE issues consistently outperformed the market by an average of 19.6 percent over a period of three years. The reason, explains Thaler, is that investors overreacted to the bad news and drove the dogs way down—far below what they were truly worth. Stocks again and again overshoot the fundamentals, a finding that doesn't square with the EMT.

Never Say Die

The EMT is far from dead, however. Yale University's Stephen Ross challenges the view that there was little news to account for the crash. He says volatility rose as investors became nervous about the market weeks before Oct. 19. Under the circumstances, "only a small change in news can start an avalanche," says Ross.

The market should have been able to hold back the avalanche, says the EMT theorist, but the exchanges simply broke down. The Brady report pointed out that many NYSE specialists buckled under pressure on Oct. 19 and 20 and were selling, not buying. At the same time, the Big Board computers could not handle the volume. The institutions that make up the market failed, not the EMT.

Still, there is evidence that the stock market is not as competitive as the efficient-market theorists believe. The Brady report said that a handful of mutual and pension funds unleashed enormous selling pressure at the opening of the market on Bloody Monday, swamping the system. For the EMT to work, no one seller should be able to influence the market very much. More telling, four months after the crash, the Dow Jones industrial average is still some 800 points below its peak in August. What changes in U.S. business prospects can account for such a downgrading?

The arguments over the EMT are likely to continue. But the theory's apparent failure to explain the greatest stock market crash in history may suggest to policymakers and to the exchanges that the "market" is not all that it was cracked up to be.

Jensen first risk-adjusted all returns using the CAPM to obtain portfolio alphas, or returns in excess of required return given risk. Then he tested to see whether managers with positive alphas tended to repeat their performance in later years. If markets are efficient, and abnormal performance is due solely to the luck of the draw, the probability of following superior performance in one year with superior performance in the next year should be 50 percent: each

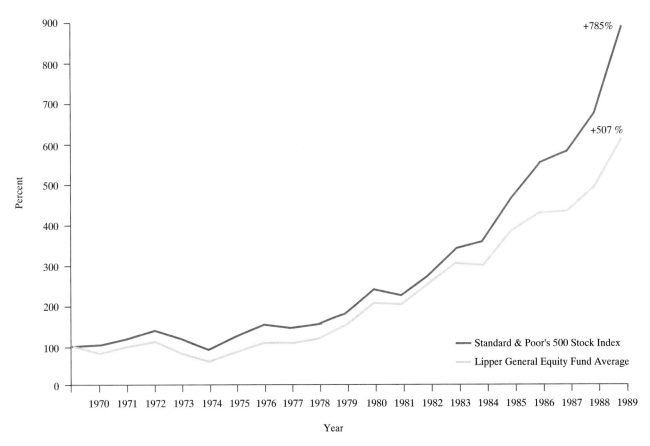

Figure 10.5 **Cumulative performance: 1970–1989.**
Cumulative total returns, December 31, 1969 = 100.
From John C. Bogle (1991).

year's abnormal return is essentially like the toss of a fair coin. This is precisely the pattern Jensen found. Table 10.2 is reproduced from Jensen's study.

In row 1, we see that 574 positive alphas were observed out of the 1,150 observations, virtually 50 percent on the nose. Of these 574 positive alphas, 50.4 percent were followed by positive alphas. So far, it appears that obtaining a positive alpha is pure luck, like a coin toss. Row 2 shows that 312 cases of two consecutive positive alphas were observed. Of these observations, 52.0 percent were followed by yet another positive alpha. Continuing, we see that 53.4 percent of three-in-a-row were followed by a fourth, and 55.8 percent of four-in-a-row were followed by a fifth.

The intriguing results seem to suggest that most positive alphas are obtained through luck. Yet as more and more stringent filters are applied, the remaining managers show greater tendency to follow good performance with more good performance. This might suggest there are a few, superior managers who can consistently beat the market. At this point, however, the pattern collapses. Only 46.4 percent of the five-in-a-row group repeats the superior performance, but

Table 10.2 *Mutual Fund Performance*

Number of Consecutive Positive Alphas so Far	Number of Observations	Percent of Cases in Which the Next Alpha Is Positive
1	574	50.4
2	312	52.0
3	161	53.4
4	79	55.8
5	41	46.4
6	17	35.3

From Michael Jensen (1969).

Table 10.3 *Quartile Comparison of Investment Results*

Base Period Quartile	Subsequent Period Quartile			
	Q1	Q2	Q3	Q4
Q1	26%	37%	11%	26%
Q2	10	25	25	40
Q3	25	30	40	10
Q4	30	14	35	20

From Patricia Dunn and Rolf D. Theisen, "How Consistently Do Active Managers Win?" *Journal of Portfolio Management* 9 (Summer 1983), pp. 47–53.

now, the sample size is too small to make statistically precise inferences about the population of managers.

The ultimate interpretation of these results is to some extent a matter of faith. At the minimum, it seems clear it is not wise to invest your money with an actively managed fund chosen at random. The average alpha of all funds was slightly negative even *before* subtracting all the costs of management.

In a more recent study, Dunn and Theisen (1983) examined the performance of several institutional portfolios for 1973–1982. Dividing the funds into four quarters based on total investment return for different subperiods, they posed the question: "Do funds that performed well in one period tend to perform well in subsequent periods?"

The answer seems to be no, suggesting that superior performance in any period usually is more a matter of luck than of underlying consistent ability. For example, Table 10.3 shows investment results for a base period 1973–1977 and subsequent period 1978–1982.

The first row shows the relative performance of the first-quartile managers from the 1973–1977 base period in the subsequent 1978–1982 period. Only 26 percent of those managers repeated their first-quartile performance; another 26 percent dropped to the *bottom* quartile in the latter period. Second-quartile performers in the base period also fared poorly in the subsequent period; only 10 percent ended up in the top quartile, and 25 percent continued in the second quartile. All told, we cannot reject the hypothesis that relative rank is independent from one period to the next.

So, Are Markets Efficient?

There is a telling joke about two economists walking down the street. They spot a $20 bill on the sidewalk. One starts to pick it up, but the other one says, "Don't bother; if the bill were real someone would have picked it up already."

The lesson here is clear. An overly doctrinaire belief in efficient markets can paralyze the investor and make it appear that no research effort can be justified. This extreme view is probably unwarranted. There are enough anomalies in the empirical evidence to justify the search for underpriced securities that clearly goes on.

Moreover, a small number of investment superstars—Peter Lynch (formerly of Fidelity's Magellan Fund), Warren Buffet (of Berkshire Hathaway), John Templeton (of Templeton Funds), and John Neff (of Vanguard's Windsor Fund) among them—have compiled career records that show a consistency of superior performance hard to reconcile with absolutely efficient markets. Nobel prize winner Paul Samuelson (1989) reviews this investment hall of fame but points out that the records of the vast majority of professional money managers offer convincing evidence that there are no easy strategies to guarantee success in the securities market.

The bulk of the evidence suggests that any supposedly superior investment strategy should be taken with many grains of salt. The market is competitive *enough* that only differentially superior information or insight will earn money; the easy pickings have been picked. In the end, it is likely that the margin of superiority that any professional manager can add is so slight that the statistician will not be able to detect it.

We conclude that markets are very efficient, but rewards to the especially diligent, intelligent, or creative may be waiting.

Summary

1. Statistical research has shown that stock prices seem to follow a random walk with no discernible predictable patterns that investors can exploit. Such findings are now taken to be evidence of market efficiency, that is, of evidence that market prices reflect all currently available information. Only new information will move stock prices, and this information is equally likely to be good news or bad news.

2. Market participants distinguish among three forms of the efficient market hypothesis. The weak form asserts that all information to be derived from past stock prices already is reflected in stock prices. The semistrong form claims that all publicly available information is already reflected. The strong form, usually taken only as a straw man, asserts that all information, including insider information, is reflected in prices.

3. Technical analysis focuses on stock price patterns and on proxies for buy or sell pressure in the market. Fundamental analysis focuses on the determinants of the underlying value of the firm, such as current profitability and growth prospects. As both types of analysis are based on public information, neither should generate excess profits if markets are operating efficiently.

4. Proponents of the efficient market hypothesis often advocate passive as opposed to active investment strategies. The policy of passive investors is to

buy and hold a broad-based market index. They expend resources neither on market research nor on frequent purchase and sale of stocks. Passive strategies may be tailored to meet individual investor requirements.

5. Empirical studies of technical analysis do not generally support the hypothesis that such analysis can generate trading profits. Only very short-term filters seem to offer any hope for profits, yet these are extremely expensive in terms of trading costs. These costs exceed potential profits even in the case of floor traders. However, the Value Line ranking system has had considerable success. Moreover, recent anomalies pertaining to excess price volatility and price reversals are yet to be reconciled with efficient markets.

6. Several anomalies regarding fundamental analysis have been uncovered. These include the P/E effect, the small-firm effect, and the neglected-firm effect.

7. By and large, the performance record of professionally managed funds lends little credence to claims that professionals can consistently beat the market.

Key Terms

efficient market
  hypothesis, 271
filter rule, 279
fundamental
  analysis, 273
index fund, 275
neglected-firm
  effect, 284

passive investment
  strategy, 274
P/E effect, 281
random walk, 270
reversal effect, 281
semistrong-form
  EMH, 272

small-firm effect, 281
strong-form EMH, 272
technical analysis, 272
weak-form EMH, 272
weekend effect, 284

Selected Readings

One of the best treatments of the efficient market hypothesis is:
Malkiel, Burton G. *A Random Walk Down Wall Street*. New York: W. W. Norton & Co., 1990, now in its fifth edition. This paperback book provides an entertaining and insightful treatment of the ideas presented in this chapter as well as fascinating historical examples of securities markets in action.

Nobel laureate Paul Samuelson discusses the status of the efficient market hypothesis and the records of investment superstars in his article:
"The Judgment of Economic Science on Rational Portfolio Management." *Journal of Portfolio Management* 16 (Fall 1989), pp. 4–12.

The lucky event issue and the performance of the Magellan Fund are discussed in:
Marcus, Alan "The Magellan Fund and Market Efficiency." *Journal of Portfolio Management* 17 (Fall 1990), pp. 85–88.

Problem Sets

1. If markets are efficient, what should be the correlation coefficient between stock returns for two nonoverlapping time periods?

2. Which of the following most appears to contradict the proposition that the stock market is *weakly* efficient? Explain.

a. Over 25 percent of mutual funds outperform the market on average.

        b. Insiders earn abnormal trading profits.

        c. Every January, the stock market earns above normal returns.

3. Suppose, after conducting an analysis of past stock prices, you come up with the following observations. Which would appear to *contradict* the *weak* form of the efficient market hypothesis? Explain.

        a. The average rate of return is significantly greater than zero.

        b. The correlation between the market return one week and the return the following week is zero.

        c. One could have made superior returns by buying stock after a 10 percent rise in price and selling after a 10 percent fall.

        d. One could have made higher than average capital gains by holding stock with low dividend yields.

4. Which of the following statements are true if the efficient market hypothesis holds?

        a. It implies perfect forecasting ability.

        b. It implies prices reflect all available information.

        c. It implies the market is irrational.

        d. It implies prices do not fluctuate.

5. Which of the following observations would provide evidence *against* the *strong form* of the efficient market theory? Explain.

        a. Mutual fund managers do not on average make superior returns.

        b. You cannot make superior profits by buying (or selling) stocks after the announcement of an abnormal rise in earnings.

        c. Managers who trade in their own stock make superior returns.

        d. In any year, approximately 50 percent of pension funds outperform the market.

6. A successful firm like IBM has consistently generated large profits for years. Is this a violation of the EMH?

7. Prices of stocks before stock *splits* show on average consistently positive abnormal returns. Is this a violation of the EMH?

8. "If the business cycle is predictable, and a stock has a positive beta, the stock's returns also must be predictable." Respond.

9. "The expected return on all securities must be equal if markets are efficient." Comment.

10. We know the market should respond positively to good news, and good news events such as the coming end of a recession can be predicted with at least some accuracy. Why, then, can we not predict that the market will go up as the economy recovers?

11. If prices are as likely to increase or decrease, why do investors earn positive returns from the market on average?

12. You know that firm XYZ is very poorly run. On a management scale of 1 (worst) to 10 (best), you would give it a score of 3. The market consensus evaluation is that the management score is only 2. Should you buy or sell the stock?

13. Some authors contend that professional managers are incapable of outperforming the market. Others come to an opposite conclusion. Compare and contrast the assumptions about the stock market that support (*a*) passive portfolio management and (*b*) active portfolio management.

14. You are a portfolio manager meeting a client. During the conversation that followed your formal review of her account, your client asked the following question:

    "My grandson, who is studying investments, tells me that one of the best ways to make money in the stock market is to buy the stocks of small-capitalization firms on a Monday morning late in December and to sell the stocks one month later. What is he talking about?"

a. Identify the apparent market anomalies that would justify the proposed strategy.

b. *Explain* why you believe such a strategy might or might not work in the future.

15. Which of the following phenomena would be either consistent with or a violation of the efficient market hypothesis? Explain briefly.

a. Nearly half of all professionally managed mutual funds are able to outperform the S&P 500 in a typical year.

b. Money managers that outperform the market (on a risk-adjusted basis) in one year are likely to outperform in the following year.

c. Stock prices tend to be predictably more volatile in January than in other months.

d. Stock prices of companies that announce increased earnings in January tend to outperform the market in February.

e. Stocks that perform well in one week perform poorly in the following week.

Chapter

11

Performance Evaluation

■ ■

In previous chapters, we derived predictions for expected return as a function of risk. In this chapter, we ask how we can evaluate the performance of a portfolio manager given the risk of his or her portfolio. Even measuring average portfolio returns is not as straightforward as it might seem. There also are difficulties in adjusting average returns for risk, which presents a host of other problems.

We begin with issues concerning the measurement of portfolio returns. From there, we move on to conventional approaches to risk adjustment. These use the risk measures developed in this part of the text to compare investment results. We show the problems with these approaches when you apply them in a real and complex world. Finally, we examine evaluation procedures used in the field. We show how overall investment results can be decomposed and attributed to the underlying asset allocation and security selection decisions of the portfolio manager. After studying this chapter you should be able to:

Compute time-weighted and dollar-weighted rates of return and determine when each of these measures is the more appropriate performance statistic.

Compute risk-adjusted rates of return.

Decompose excess returns into components attributable to asset allocation choices versus security selection choices.

11.1 *Measuring Investment Returns*

The rate of return on an investment is a simple concept in the case of a one-period investment. It is merely the holding period return: the total proceeds derived from the investment per dollar invested at the start of the period. Proceeds are defined broadly to include both cash distributions and capital gains.

For stocks, total returns are dividends plus capital gains. For bonds, total returns are coupon or interest paid plus capital gains.

To set the stage for discussing the more subtle issues below, let us start with a basic example. Consider a stock paying a dividend of $2 annually that currently sells for $50. You purchase the stock today and collect the $2 dividend, then sell the share for $53 at year's end. Your rate of return for the period is:

$$\frac{\text{Total proceeds}}{\text{Initial investment}} = \frac{\text{Income + Capital gain}}{50} = \frac{2 + (53 - 50)}{50} = .10$$

or 10 percent.

Another approach that is useful in the more difficult multiperiod case is to set up the investment as a discounted cash flow problem. Call r the rate of return that equates the present value of all cash flows from the investment with the initial outlay. In our example, the stock is purchased for $50 and generates cash flows at year-end of $2 (dividend) plus $53 (sale of stock). Therefore, we solve $50 = \dfrac{2 + 53}{1 + r}$ to find again that $r = .10$, or 10 percent.

Time-Weighted versus Dollar-Weighted Returns

When we consider investments over a period during which you added cash or withdrew it, measuring the rate of return becomes more difficult. To continue the example, suppose you were to purchase a second share of the same stock at the end of the first year and hold both shares until the end of year 2, at which point you sell each share for $54.

Total cash outlays are:

Time	Outlay
0	$50 to purchase first share
1	$53 to purchase second share a year later

Proceeds are:

Time	Proceeds
1	$2 dividend from initially purchased share
2	$4 dividend from the 2 shares held in the second year, plus $108 received from selling both shares at $54 each

Using the discounted cash flow approach, we can solve for the average return over the two years by equating the present values of the cash inflows and outflows:

$$50 + \frac{53}{1 + r} = \frac{2}{1 + r} + \frac{108 + 4}{(1 + r)^2}$$

resulting in $r = 7.117$ percent.

Dollar-weighted rate of return   The internal rate of return on an investment.

Time-weighted rate of return   An average of the period-by-period holding-period returns on an investment.

This value is called the internal rate of return or the **dollar-weighted rate of return** on the investment. It is "dollar weighted" because the second-year performance, when two shares of stock are held, has more influence on the average overall return than the first-year performance when only one share is held.

An alternative to the internal or dollar-weighted return is the **time-weighted rate of return,** which is simply an average of period-by-period returns. This method ignores the number of shares of stock held in each period. The stock return in the first year was 10 percent. (A $50 purchase provided $2 in dividends and $3 in capital gains.) In the second year, the stock had a starting value of $53 and sold at year-end for $54, for a total one-period rate of return of $3 ($2 dividend + $1 capital gain) divided by $53 (the stock price at the start of the second year), or 5.66 percent. The time-weighted return is the average of 10 percent and 5.66 percent, which is 7.83 percent. This average return considers only the period-by-period returns without regard to the amounts invested in the stock in each period.

The dollar-weighted return is less than the time-weighted return in this example because the stock fared relatively poorly in the second year, when the investor was holding twice as much of it. The greater weight that the dollar-weighted average places on the second-year return results in this case in a lower measure of investment performance. In general, dollar- and time-weighted returns will differ, and the difference can be positive or negative depending on the configuration of period returns and portfolio composition.

Which measure of performance is superior? At first blush, it appears that the dollar-weighted return must be more relevant. After all, the more money you invest in a stock when its performance is superior, the more money you end up with. Certainly your performance measure should reflect this.

Time-weighted returns are more widely used, however, especially in the money management industry. In most cases, a portfolio manager may not directly control the timing or the amount of money invested in securities. Pension fund management is a good example. A pension fund manager faces cash inflows into the fund when pension contributions are made and cash outflows when pension benefits are paid. The amount of money invested at any time can vary for reasons beyond the manager's control. Because dollars invested do not depend on the manager's choice, it is inappropriate to weight returns by dollars invested when measuring the investment ability of the manager. Consequently, the money management industry normally uses time-weighted returns for performance evaluation.

Concept Check

> *Question 1.*   Shares of XYZ Corp. pay a $2 dividend at the end of every year on December 31. An investor buys two shares of the stock January 1 at a price of $20 each, sells one of those shares for $22 a year later the next January 1, and sells the second share an additional year later for $19. Find the time- and dollar-weighted rates of return on the two-year investment.

Arithmetic versus Geometric Averages

Our example takes the arithmetic average of the two annual returns, 10 percent and 5.66 percent, as the time-weighted average, 7.83 percent. Another approach is to take a geometric average, denoted r_G.

The motivation for this calculation comes from the principle of compounding. If dividend proceeds are reinvested, the accumulated value of an investment in the stock will grow by a factor of 1.10 in the first year and by an additional factor of 1.0566 in the second year. The compound average growth rate, r_G, is then calculated as the solution to the following equation.

$$(1 + r_G)^2 = (1.10)(1.0566).$$

This approach would entail computing

$$1 + r_G = [(1.10)(1.0566)]^{1/2} = 1.0781$$

or $r_G = 7.81$ percent.

More generally for an *n*-period investment, the geometric average rate of return is given by:

$$1 + r_G = [(1 + r_1)(1 + r_2) \ldots (1 + r_n)]^{1/n}$$

where r_t is the return in each time period.

The geometric average return in this example, 7.81 percent, is slightly less than the arithmetic average return, 7.83 percent. This is a general property: geometric averages never exceed arithmetic ones. To see the intuition for this result, consider a stock that doubles in price in period 1 ($r_1 = 100$ percent) and halves in price in period 2 ($r_2 = -50$ percent). The arithmetic average is $r_A = [100 + (-50)]/2 = 25$ percent, while the geometric average is $r_G = [(1 + 1)(1 - .5)]^{1/2} - 1 = 0$. The effect of the -50 percent return in period 2 fully offsets the 100 percent return in period 1 in the calculation of the geometric average, resulting in an average return of zero. This is not true of the arithmetic average. In general, the bad returns have a greater influence on the averaging process in the geometric technique. Therefore, geometric averages are lower.

Moreover, the difference in the two averaging techniques will be greater the greater is the variability of period-by-period returns. The general rule is as follows:

$$r_G \approx r_A - 1/2\sigma^2 \qquad \qquad \textbf{11.1}$$

where σ^2 is the variance of returns. Equation 11.1 is exact when returns are normally distributed.

For example, consider Table 11.1, which presents arithmetic and geometric returns over the 1926–1989 period for a variety of investments. The arithmetic averages all exceed the geometric ones, with the difference greatest in the case of stocks of small firms, where annual returns exhibit the greatest standard deviation. The difference between the two averages falls to zero only when there is no variation in yearly returns, although the table indicates that by the time the standard deviation falls to a level characteristic of T-bills, the difference is quite small.

To illustrate Equation 11.1, consider the average returns for large stocks. According to the equation,

$$.103 \approx .124 - 1/2(.209)^2$$
$$.103 \approx .102.$$

As predicted, the arithmetic mean (.124) exceeded the geometric mean (.103) by approximately one half the variance in returns. Clearly, when comparing returns, one never should mix and match the two averaging techniques. Moreover, one should be aware that when comparing average returns from strategies with

Table 11.1 *Average Annual Returns by Investment Class, 1926–1989*

	Arithmetic Average	Geometric Average	Difference	Standard Deviation
Common stocks of small firms*	17.7	12.2	5.5	35.3
Common stocks of large firms	12.4	10.3	2.1	20.9
Long-term Treasury bonds	4.9	4.6	0.3	8.6
U.S. Treasury bills	3.7	3.6	0.1	3.4

*These are firms with relatively low market values of equity. Market capitalization is computed as price per share times shares outstanding.

From *Stocks, Bonds, Bills, and Inflation* (SBBI). Updated in *SBBI 1990 Yearbook*, (Chicago: Ibbotson Associates).

different volatilities, the use of the geometric mean tends to favor the low-variance strategy.

11.2 Risk-Adjusted Returns

Comparison Groups

Calculating average portfolio returns does not mean the task is done. Returns must be adjusted for risk before we can compare them meaningfully.

The fact that common stocks have offered higher average returns than Treasury bonds (as demonstrated in Table 11.1) does not prove that stocks are superior investment vehicles. One must consider the fact that stocks also have been more volatile investments. For the same reason, the fact that a mutual fund outperforms the S&P 500 over a long period is not necessarily evidence of superior stock selection ability. If the mutual fund has a higher beta than the index, it *should* outperform the index (on average) to compensate investors in the fund for the higher nondiversifiable risk they bear. Thus, performance evaluation must involve risk as well as return comparisons.

The simplest and most popular way to adjust returns for portfolio risk is to compare rates of return with those of other investment funds with similar risk characteristics. For example, high-yield bond portfolios are grouped into one "universe," growth stock equity funds are grouped into another universe, and so on. Then the (usually time-weighted) average returns of each fund within the universe are ordered, and each portfolio manager receives a percentile ranking depending on relative performance within the **comparison universe,** the collection of funds to which performance is compared. For example, the manager with the ninth-best performance in a universe of 100 funds would be the 90th percentile manager: her performance was better than 90 percent of all competing funds over the evaluation period.

These relative rankings are usually displayed in a chart like that in Figure 11.1. The chart summarizes performance rankings over four periods: one quarter, one year, three years, and five years. The top and bottom lines of each box are drawn at the rate of return of the 95th and 5th percentile managers. The three dotted lines correspond to the rates of return of the 75th, 50th (median), and 25th percentile managers. The diamond is drawn at the average return of a particular fund, the Markowill Group, and the square is drawn at the return of

Comparison universe *The set of portfolio managers with similar investment styles that is used in assessing the relative performance of an individual portfolio manager.*

Figure 11.1
Universe comparison.
Periods ending
December 31, 1991.

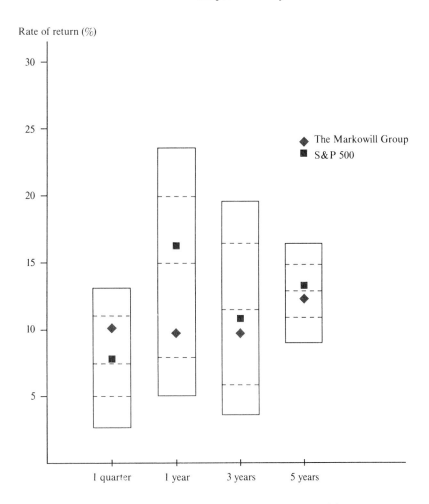

a benchmark index such as the S&P 500. This format provides an easy-to-read representation of the performance of the fund relative to the comparison universe.

This comparison with other managers of similar investment groups is a useful first step in evaluating performance. Such rankings can be misleading even so. Consider that within a particular universe some managers may concentrate on particular subgroups, so that portfolio characteristics are not truly comparable. For example, within the equity universe, one manager may concentrate on high beta stocks. Similarly, within fixed-income universes, interest-rate risk can vary across managers. These considerations show that we need a more precise means for risk adjustment.

Risk Adjustments

Methods of risk-adjusted performance using mean-variance criteria developed simultaneously with the capital asset pricing model. Jack Treynor (1966), William Sharpe (1966), and Michael Jensen (1969) were quick to recognize the implications of the CAPM for rating the performance of managers. Within a short time, academicians were in command of a battery of performance measures, and a bounty of scholarly investigation of mutual fund performance was pouring from the ivory tower. Soon after, agents emerged (A. G. Becker is one example) who were willing to supply rating services to portfolio managers eager for regular feedback. This trend has since lost some of its force.

One explanation for the lagging popularity of risk-adjusted performance measures is the generally negative cast to resulting performance statistics. In nearly efficient markets, it is extremely difficult for analysts to perform well enough to overcome costs of research and transaction costs. We saw in Chapter 10 that most professionally managed equity funds have generally underperformed the S&P 500 index on both risk-adjusted and raw return measures.

Another reason mean-variance criteria may have suffered relates to intrinsic problems in these measures. We will explore some of these problems below.

For now, however, we can catalogue some possible risk-adjusted performance measures and examine the circumstances in which each measure might be most relevant. To illustrate these measures, we will use a hypothetical portfolio for which monthly returns in the past five years resulted in the following statistics. We also present comparable data for the market portfolio for the same period.

	Portfolio	**Market**
Beta	0.8	1.0
Average return	16%	14%
Standard deviation	20%	24%

Finally, suppose the average return on risk-free assets during the five-year period was 6 percent.

Three risk-adjusted performance statistics are the Sharpe measure, the Treynor measure, and the Jensen measure.

$$\text{Sharpe measure:} \frac{\bar{r}_p - \bar{r}_f}{\sigma_p}$$

Sharpe measure
Reward-to-volatility ratio; ratio of portfolio excess return to standard deviation.

The **Sharpe measure** divides average portfolio excess return over the sample period by the standard deviation of returns over that period. The numerator is the incremental return the portfolio earned in comparison with an alternative investment in the risk-free asset, and the denominator is the increment in portfolio volatility compared with the risk-free alternative. Therefore, the ratio measures the reward to (total) volatility trade-off. (The bars over r_p as well as r_f denote the fact that, because the risk-free rate may not be constant over the measurement period, we are taking a sample average of both.) Using our numbers, the Sharpe measure for the portfolio is $(16 - 6)/20 = 0.5$, and for the market $(14 - 6)/24 = .33$.

$$\text{Treynor measure:} \frac{\bar{r}_p - \bar{r}_f}{\beta_p}$$

Treynor measure
Ratio of portfolio excess return to beta.

Like Sharpe's, the **Treynor measure** gives average excess return per unit of risk incurred, but uses systematic risk instead of total risk. The Treynor measure for the portfolio over this period is $(16 - 6)/0.8 = 12.5$, while for the market portfolio it is $(14 - 6)/1.0 = 8$.

Jensen measure: $\alpha_p = \bar{r}_p - [\bar{r}_f + \beta_p(\bar{r}_M - \bar{r}_f)]$.

Jensen measure
The alpha of an
investment.

The **Jensen measure** is the average return on the portfolio over and above that predicted by the CAPM, given the portfolio's beta and the average market return. The Jensen measure is the portfolio's alpha value. Using our numbers, the Jensen measure is $16 - [6 + .8(14 - 6)] = 3.6$ percent.

Each measure has its own appeal. In this instance, all three measures are consistent in revealing that the portfolio outperformed the market benchmark on a risk-adjusted basis. However, this need not be the case. As the next Concept Check illustrates, the three measures do not necessarily provide consistent assessments of relative performance, as the risk measures used to adjust returns differ substantially.

Concept Check

Question 2. Consider the following data for a particular sample period:

	Portfolio P	Market M
Average return	35%	28%
Beta	1.2	1.0
Standard deviation	42%	30%

Calculate the following performance measures for portfolio P and the market: Sharpe, Jensen (alpha), Treynor. The T-bill rate during the period was 6 percent. By which measures did portfolio P outperform the market?

Because different risk adjustment procedures can yield different implications for performance evaluation, it is essential that you choose the appropriate measure for the task. For example, suppose you are a pension fund manager who is selecting potential portfolio managers to oversee investment of the fund's assets. If you envision hiring one investment manager to manage all the fund's assets, then you must be concerned with the total variability of investment performance. Both the systematic and firm-specific risk remaining in the portfolio will affect total risk because the pension fund is not diversified across managers. The manager's portfolio will be the entire portfolio, with no further opportunities for diversification. In this case, the Sharpe measure is the appropriate basis on which to evaluate the portfolio manager. Because that manager is in charge of the entire portfolio, she must be attentive to diversification of firm-specific risk and rightly should be judged on her achievement of return to total portfolio volatility.

In contrast, suppose your pension fund is large, and you envision hiring many managers, giving each a fraction of the total assets of the plan. You hope that hiring a set of managers, each with an investment specialty, will enhance returns. This means the pension plan effectively ends up with a portfolio of portfolio managers. Each manager can pursue his or her specialty without paying much attention to issues of diversification because the plan as a whole will have diversified returns across the several managed portfolios. With assets spread across many portfolio managers, the residual firm-specific risks of each portfolio become irrelevant because of diversification across portfolios. In this case, with managers explicitly free to specialize, only nondiversifiable risk should matter.

Table 11.2 *Portfolio Performance*

	Portfolio P	**Portfolio Q**	**Market**
Beta	.90	1.60	1.0
Excess return, $r - r_f$	11%	19%	10%
Alpha*	2%	3%	0
Treynor measure	12.2	11.9	10

*Alpha = Excess return − (Beta × Market excess return)
$$= (r - r_f) - \beta(r_M - r_f)$$
$$= r - [r_f + \beta(r_M - r_f)]$$

Such circumstances call for the use of a beta-based risk adjustment, and either the Treynor or Jensen measure would be appropriate.

To distinguish between the Treynor and Jensen measures, consider Table 11.2, which details the performance of two portfolios, *P* and *Q*, as well as the market portfolio. Portfolio *P* has the lower alpha, or Jensen's measure, but it also has the lower beta. Its excess risk-adjusted return per unit of systematic risk incurred is actually higher than that of portfolio *Q*. This is reflected in *P*'s higher Treynor measure.

If we were to set a goal of a portfolio beta of 0.9 as an appropriate level of systematic risk, then portfolio *P* would be the better choice. Portfolio *P* offers an excess return of 11 percent with a beta of 0.9. To achieve an overall beta of 0.9 using portfolio *Q* (which has a beta of 1.60), we would need to mix the portfolio with Treasury bills. Weights of 7/16 in bills and 9/16 in portfolio *Q* would result in an overall beta of 0.9, but would reduce excess return to 9/16 × 19 percent = 10 11/16 percent, which is less than portfolio *P*'s excess return.

Figure 11.2 illustrates these differences. Although *Q* has the higher alpha, the line from the origin to *Q*, which represents the achievable combinations of excess return and beta, lies *below* portfolio *P*'s line, meaning it offers less attractive opportunities.

The Treynor measure tells us the ratio of excess return earned per unit of systematic risk incurred. As our comparison of portfolios *P* and *Q* suggests, Treynor would argue that it is appropriate to measure performance as excess return divided by beta because we would want to standardize all portfolios to an appropriate level of systematic risk before choosing among them. Because the ratio of excess return to beta is the slope of the line from the origin to points *P* or *Q* in Figure 11.2, the portfolio with the higher Treynor measure will be the one with the steeper line in the figure.

It is important to use the performance measure that fits the relevant scenario. Evaluating portfolios by different performance measures may yield quite different results.

Risk Adjustments with Changing Portfolio Composition

One potential problem with risk-adjustment techniques is they all assume that portfolio risk, whether it is measured by standard deviation or beta, is constant over the relevant time period. This isn't necessarily so. If a manager attempts to increase portfolio beta when he or she thinks the market is about to go up and to decrease beta when he or she is pessimistic, both the standard deviation

Figure 11.2
Treynor measure.

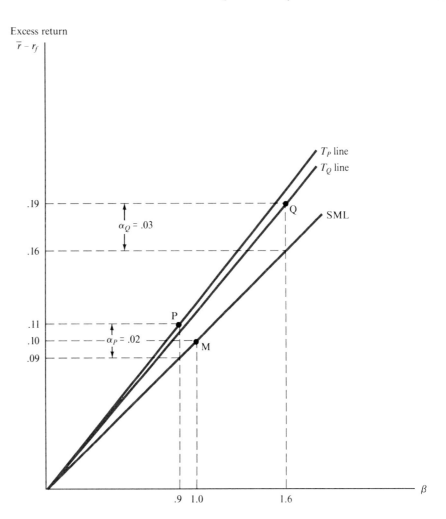

and the beta of the portfolio will change over time, by design. This can wreak havoc with our performance measures. Let's look at an example.

Suppose the Sharpe measure of the passive strategy (investing in a market index fund) is 0.4. A portfolio manager is in search of a better, active strategy. Over an initial period of, say, 52 weeks, he executes a low-risk or defensive strategy with an annualized mean excess return of 1 percent and a standard deviation of 2 percent. This makes for a Sharpe measure of 0.5, which beats the passive strategy.

Over the next period of another 52 weeks, this manager finds that a high-risk or aggressive strategy is optimal, with an annual mean excess return of 9 percent and standard deviation of 18 percent. Here again the Sharpe measure is 0.5. Over the two years, our manager maintains a better-than-passive Sharpe measure.

Figure 11.3 shows a pattern of (annualized) quarterly returns that is consistent with our description of the manager's strategy over two years. In the first four quarters, the excess returns are -1 percent, 3 percent, -1 percent, and 3 percent, making for an average of 1 percent and standard deviation of 2 percent. In the next four quarters, the returns are -9 percent, 27 percent, -9

Figure 11.3
Portfolio returns.

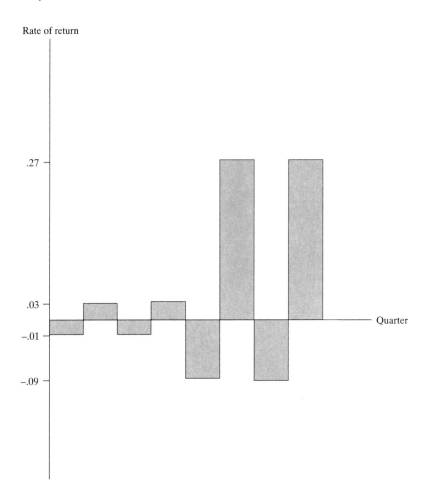

percent, and 27 percent, making for an average of 9 percent and standard deviation of 18 percent. Thus, *each* year undoubtedly exhibits a Sharpe measure of 0.5.

But if we take the eight-quarter sequence as a single measurement period, not two periods, and measure the portfolio's mean and standard deviation over that full period, we get an average excess return of 5 percent and standard deviation of 13.42 percent, making for a Sharpe measure of only 0.37, apparently inferior to the passive strategy!

What happened? Sharpe's measure does not recognize the shift in the mean from the first four quarters to the next as a result of a strategy change. Instead, the difference in mean returns in the two years adds to the *appearance* of volatility in portfolio returns. The change in mean returns across time periods contributed to the variability of returns over the sample period. But in this case, variability per se should not be interpreted as volatility or riskiness in returns. Part of the variability in returns is due to intentional choices that shift the expected or mean return. This part should not be ascribed to uncertainty in returns. Unfortunately, an outside observer might not realize that policy changes within the sample period are the source of some of the return variability. Therefore, the active strategy with shifting means appears riskier than it really is, which biases the estimate of the Sharpe measure downward.

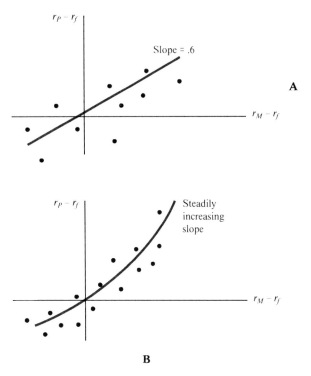

Figure 11.4 **Characteristic lines. A,** no market timing, beta is constant. **B,** market timing, beta increases with expected market excess return.

For actively managed portfolios, therefore, it is crucial to keep track of portfolio composition and changes in portfolio mean return and risk. We will see another example of this problem when we talk about market timing.

11.3 *Market Timing*

In its pure form, market timing involves shifting funds between a market index portfolio and a safe asset, such as T-bills or a money market fund, depending on whether the market as a whole is expected to outperform the safe asset. In practice, most managers do not shift fully between bills and the market. How might we measure partial shifts into the market when it is expected to perform well?

To simplify, suppose the investor holds only the market index portfolio and T-bills. If the weight on the market were constant, say 0.6, then the portfolio beta also would be constant, and the portfolio characteristic line would plot as a straight line with a slope 0.6, as in Figure 11.4A. If, however, the investor could correctly time the market and shift funds into it in periods when the market does well, the characteristic line would plot as in Figure 11.4B. The idea is that if the timer can predict bull and bear markets, more will be shifted into the market when the market is about to go up. The portfolio beta and the slope of the characteristic line will be higher when r_M is higher, resulting in the curved line that appears in B.   .

Treynor and Mazuy (1966) tested to see whether portfolio betas did in fact increase prior to market advances, but they found little evidence of timing ability. A similar test was implemented by Henriksson (1984). His examination of market timing ability for 116 funds in 1968–1980 found that, on average, portfolio betas actually *fell* slightly during market advances, although in most cases the response of portfolio beta to the market was not statistically significant at the conventional 5 percent level. Eleven funds had statistically positive values of market timing, while eight had significantly negative values. Overall, 62 percent of the funds had negative point estimates of timing ability.

In sum, empirical evidence shows little evidence of market timing ability. Perhaps this should be expected; given the tremendous values to be reaped by a successful market timer, it would be surprising in nearly efficient markets to uncover clear-cut evidence of such skills.

11.4   *Performance Attribution Procedures*

Rather than focus on risk-adjusted returns, practitioners often want simply to ascertain which decisions resulted in superior or inferior performance. Superior investment performance depends on an ability to be in the "right" securities at the right time. Such timing and selection ability may be considered broadly, such as being in equities as opposed to fixed-income securities when the stock market is performing well. Or it may be defined at a more detailed level, such as choosing the relatively better-performing stocks within a particular industry.

Portfolio managers constantly make both broad-brush asset market allocation decisions as well as more detailed sector and security allocation decisions within markets. Performance attribution studies attempt to decompose overall performance into discrete components that may be identified with a particular level of the portfolio selection process.

Attribution studies start from the broadest asset allocation choices and progressively focus on ever-finer details of portfolio choice. The difference between a managed portfolio's performance and that of a benchmark portfolio then may be expressed as the sum of the contributions to performance of a series of decisions made at the various levels of the portfolio construction process. For example, one common attribution system decomposes performance into three components: (1) broad asset market allocation choices across equity, fixed-income, and money markets; (2) industry (sector) choice within each market; and (3) security choice within each sector.

To illustrate this method, consider the attribution results for a hypothetical portfolio. The portfolio invests in stocks, bonds, and money market securities. An attribution analysis appears in Tables 11.3 through 11.6. The portfolio return over the month is 5.34 percent.

The first step is to establish a benchmark level of performance against which performance ought to be compared. This benchmark is called the **bogey.** It is designed to measure the returns the portfolio manager would earn if he or she were to follow a completely passive strategy. "Passive" in this context has two attributes. First, it means the allocation of funds across broad asset classes is set in accord with a notion of "usual" or neutral allocation across sectors. This would be considered a passive asset market allocation. Second, it means that

Bogey The return an investment manager is compared to for performance evaluation.

Table 11.3 *Performance of the Managed Portfolio*

Bogey Performance and Excess Return		
Component	Benchmark Weight	Return of Index during Month (Percent)
Equity (S&P 500)	.60	5.81
Bonds (Shearson Lehmann)	.30	1.45
Cash (money market)	.10	0.48

Bogey = (.60 × 5.81) + (.30 × 1.45) + (.10 × 0.48) = 3.97 percent

Return of managed portfolio	5.34 percent
− Return of bogey portfolio	3.97
Excess return of managed portfolio	1.37 percent

within each asset class, the portfolio manager holds an indexed portfolio such as the S&P 500 index for the equity sector. In such a manner, the passive strategy used as a performance benchmark rules out both asset allocation as well as security selection decisions. Any departure of the manager's return from the passive benchmark must be due to either asset allocation bets (departures from the neutral allocation across markets) or security selection bets (departures from the passive index within asset classes.)

While we've already discussed in earlier chapters the justification for indexing within sectors, it is worth briefly explaining the determination of the neutral allocation of funds across the broad asset classes. Weights that are designated as "neutral" will depend on the risk tolerance of the investor and must be determined in consultation with the client. For example, risk-tolerant clients may place a large fraction of their portfolio in the equity market, perhaps directing the fund manager to set neutral weights of 75 percent equity, 15 percent bonds, and 10 percent cash equivalents. Any deviation from these weights must be justified by a belief that one or another market will either over- or underperform its usual risk-return profile. In contrast, more risk-averse clients may set neutral weights of 45 percent/35 percent/20 percent for the three markets. Therefore, their portfolios in normal circumstances will be exposed to less risk than that of the risk-tolerant client. Only intentional bets on market performance will result in departures from this profile.

In Table 11.3, the neutral weights have been set at 60 percent equity, 30 percent fixed-income, and 10 percent cash (money market securities). The bogey portfolio, comprised of investments in each index with the 60/30/10 weights, returned 3.97 percent. The managed portfolio's measure of performance is positive and equal to its actual return less the return of the bogey: 5.34 − 3.97 = 1.37 percent. The next step is to allocate the 1.37 percent excess return to the separate decisions that contributed to it.

Asset Allocation Decisions

Our hypothetical managed portfolio is invested in the equity, fixed-income, and money markets with weights of 70 percent, 7 percent, and 23 percent, respectively. The portfolio's performance could have to do with the departure of this

Table 11.4 *Performance Attribution*

	A. Contribution of Asset Allocation to Performance				
Market	(1) Actual Weight in Market	(2) Benchmark Weight in Market	(3) Excess Weight	(4) Market Return Minus Bogey (Percent)	(5) = (3) × (4) Contribution to Performance (Percent)
Equity	.70	.60	.10	1.84	.1840
Fixed-income	.07	.30	−.23	−2.52	.5796
Cash	.23	.10	.13	−3.49	−.4537
Contribution of asset allocation					.3099

	B. Contribution of Selection to Total Performance				
Market	(1) Portfolio Performance (Percent)	(2) Index Performance (Percent)	(3) Excess Performance (Percent)	(4) Portfolio Weight	(5) = (3) × (4) Contribution (Percent)
Equity	7.28	5.81	1.47	.70	1.03
Fixed-income	1.89	1.45	0.44	.07	.03
Contribution of selection within markets					1.06

weighting scheme from the benchmark 60/30/10 weights and/or to superior or inferior results *within* each of the three broad markets.

To isolate the effect of the manager's asset allocation choice, we measure the performance of a hypothetical portfolio that would have been invested in the indexes for each market with weights 70/7/23. This return measures the effect of the shift away from the benchmark 60/30/10 weights without allowing for any effects attributable to active management of the securities selected within each market.

Superior performance relative to the bogey is achieved by overweighting investments in markets that turn out to perform better than the bogey and by underweighting those in poorly performing markets. The contribution of asset allocation to superior performance equals the sum over all markets of the excess weight in each market times the return of the market index in excess of the bogey.

Table 11.4A demonstrates that asset allocation contributed 31 basis points to the portfolio's overall excess return of 137 basis points. The major factor contributing to superior performance in this month is the heavy weighting of the equity market in a month when the equity market has an excellent return of 5.81 percent.

Sector and Security Selection Decisions

If 0.31 percent of the excess performance can be attributed to advantageous asset allocation across markets, the remaining 1.06 percent then must be attributable to sector selection and security selection within each market. Table 11.4B details the contribution of the managed portfolio's sector and security selection to total performance.

Panel B shows that the equity component of the managed portfolio has a return of 7.28 percent versus a return of 5.81 percent for the S&P 500. The fixed-

Table 11.5   *Sector Selection within the Equity Market*

Sector	(1) Beginning of Month Weights (Percent) Portfolio	(2) S&P 500	(3) Difference in Weights	(4) Sector Return	(5) Sector Over/Under Performance*	(6) = (3) × (5) Sector Allocation Contribution
Basic materials	1.96	8.3	− 6.34	6.4	0.9	− 5.7
Business services	7.84	4.1	3.74	6.5	1.0	3.7
Capital goods	1.87	7.8	− 5.93	3.7	− 1.8	10.7
Consumer cyclical	8.47	12.5	− 4.03	8.4	2.9	− 11.7
Consumer noncyclical	40.37	20.4	19.97	9.4	3.9	77.9
Credit sensitive	24.01	21.8	2.21	4.6	0.9	2.0
Energy	13.53	14.2	− 0.67	2.1	− 3.4	2.3
Technology	1.95	10.9	− 8.95	− 0.1	− 5.6	50.1
Total						129.3

*S&P 500 performance net of dividends was 5.5 percent. Returns were compared net of dividends.

income return is 1.89 percent versus 1.45 percent for the Shearson Lehman Index. The superior performance in both equity and fixed-income markets weighted by the portfolio proportions invested in each market sums to the 1.06 percent contribution to performance attributable to sector and security selection.

Table 11.5 documents the sources of the equity market performance by each sector within the market. The first three columns detail the allocation of funds within the equity market compared to their representation in the S&P 500. Column (4) shows the rate of return of each sector, and column (5) documents the performance of each sector relative to the return of the S&P 500. The contribution of each sector's allocation presented in column (6) equals the product of the difference in the sector weight and the sector's relative performance.

Note that good performance (a positive contribution) derives from overweighting well-performing sectors such as consumer nondurables, as well as underweighting poorly performing sectors such as capital goods. The excess return of the equity component of the portfolio attributable to sector allocation alone is 1.29 percent. As the equity component of the portfolio outperformed the S&P 500 by 1.47 percent, we conclude that the effect of security selection within sectors must have contributed an additional 1.47 − 1.29 or 0.18 percent to the performance of the equity component of the portfolio.

A similar sector analysis can be applied to the fixed-income portion of the portfolio, but we do not show those results here.

Summing Up Component Contributions

In this particular month, all facets of the portfolio selection process were successful. Table 11.6 details the contribution of each aspect of performance. Asset allocation across the major security markets contributes 31 basis points. Sector and security allocation within those markets contributes 106 basis points, for total excess portfolio performance of 137 basis points.

The sector and security allocation of 106 basis points can be partitioned further. Sector allocation within the equity market results in excess performance of 129.3 basis points, and security selection within sectors contributes 18 basis

Table 11.6   *Portfolio Attribution: Summary*

			Contribution (Basis points)
1. Asset allocation			31
2. Selection			
a. Equity excess return			
i. Sector allocation	129		
ii. Security allocation	18		
	147	× .70 (portfolio weight) =	102.9
b. Fixed-income excess return	44	× .07 (portfolio weight) =	3.1
Total excess return of portfolio			137.0

points. (The total equity excess performance of 147 basis points is multiplied by the 70 percent weight in equity to obtain contribution to portfolio performance.) Similar partitioning could be done for the fixed-income sector.

Concept Check

Question 3.
a.   Suppose the benchmark weights had been set at 70 percent equity, 25 percent fixed-income, and 5 percent cash equivalents. What then are the contributions of the manager's asset allocation choices?
b.   Suppose the S&P 500 return is 5 percent. Compute the new value of the manager's security selection choices.

11.5   *Mutual Fund Data*

1. Many observations are needed to draw significant conclusions even when portfolio mean and variance are constant.
2. Shifting parameters when portfolios are actively managed make accurate performance evaluation all the more elusive.

While there is no way to overcome these objective difficulties completely, it is clear that to obtain reasonably reliable performance measures we need to:

1. Maximize the number of observations by taking more frequent return readings.
2. Specify the exact makeup of the portfolio to obtain better estimates of the risk parameters at each observation period.

Traditional academic research uses monthly, weekly, and more recently even daily data. But such research cannot address or examine changes in portfolio composition because the data usually are unavailable. For these reasons, performance evaluation is a slippery concept in both the academic and practitioner communities.

What sort of evaluation occurs in practice? Performance reports for portfolio managers traditionally have been based on quarterly data over 5 to 10 years.

Currently, managers of mutual funds are required to disclose the exact composition of their portfolios only quarterly, however.

Trading activity that immediately precedes the quarterly reporting dates is known as *window dressing*. Window dressing involves changes in portfolio composition to make it look as if the manager chose successful stocks. If IBM performed well over the quarter, for example, a portfolio manager might make sure his or her portfolio includes a lot of IBM on the reporting date, whether or not it did during the quarter and whether or not IBM is expected to perform as well over the next quarter.

In the presence of window dressing, even the reported quarterly composition data can be misleading. Mutual funds publish portfolio values on a daily basis, which means the rate of return for each day is publicly available, but portfolio composition is not.

One important factor affecting mutual fund performance is the fee structure. You should be aware of four general classes of fees.

Front-end load A sales commission that is charged when the shares in a mutual fund are purchased.

Front-End Load   A **front-end load** is a commission or sales charge paid when you purchase the shares. These charges typically fall between 4 percent and 8.5 percent and are used to pay brokers to sell the fund. Low-load funds have loads that range from 1 percent to 3 percent of invested funds. No-load funds have no front-end sales charges. Loads effectively reduce the funds being invested. Each $1,000 invested in a fund with an 8.5 percent load results in a sales charge of $85, and a portfolio that starts at only $915. You need cumulative returns of 9.3 percent of your net investment (85/915 = .093) just to break even.

Back-end load A fee that is charged when the shares in a mutual fund are sold.

Back-End Load   A **back-end load** is a redemption or "exit" fee incurred when you sell your shares. Typically, funds that impose back-end loads start them at 5 percent or 6 percent and reduce them by 1 percentage point for every year the funds are left invested. Thus, an exit fee that starts at 6 percent would fall to 4 percent by the start of your third year.

Operating Expenses   Operating expenses refer to the costs incurred by the mutual fund in operating the portfolio, including administrative expenses and advisory fees paid to the investment manager. These expenses are usually expressed as a percent of total assets under management and may range from 0.2 percent to 2 percent.

12b-1 Charges   The Securities and Exchange Commission allows the manager of 12b-1 funds to use fund assets to pay for distribution costs such as advertising, promotional literature including annual reports and prospectuses, and commissions paid to brokers. These **12b-1 fees** are named after the SEC rule that permits use of these plans. Some funds use 12b-1 charges instead of front-end loads to generate fees with which to pay brokers. 12b-1 charges (if any) must be added to operating expenses to obtain the true annual expense ratio of the fund. The SEC now requires that all funds publish a consolidated expense table that summarizes all relevant fees.

12b-1 fees. Fees to cover a mutual fund's distribution costs and commissions paid to brokers.

You can identify funds with various charges by the following letters placed after the fund name in the listing of mutual funds in the financial pages: r denotes redemption or exit fees (also called a deferred sales charge); p denotes

12b-1 fees; t denotes both redemption and 12b-1 fees. Finally, you can identify front-end fees because two prices will be listed. The offer price is what you must pay for a fund. The net asset value (NAV), which is the value per share of the assets held in the fund, is what you will receive if you sell your shares. The difference is the load. For example, consider Figure 11.5. The highlighted fund at the bottom right corner of Figure 11.5 has an offer price of $10.03 and an NAV of $9.55, implying a front-end load of 5.03 percent. In addition, the p in-

MUTUAL FUND QUOTATIONS

Cont. From Preceding Page

	NAV	Offer Price	NAV Chg.
Munic	13.05	NL	...
USGov	9.44	NL	-.01
St Clair:			
CapGr	15.17	NL	-.18
IntBd	9.73	NL	-.01
TFInt	10.11	NL	...
Salomon Bros:			
Cap	16.84	17.73	-.17
Inves	16.34	17.20	-.17
Opport	24.44	NL	-.13
SalmFI t	10.07	10.49	-.01
SalemG p	16.24	16.92	-.18
SchaferV	30.88	NL	-.08
Schield p	12.10	12.60	-.09
Schrodr	8.77	8.77	-.09
Schrod p	16.70	16.70	+.05
ScotWid	11.99	12.69	+.05
Scudder Funds:			
CalTx	10.47	NL	...
CapGt	18.17	NL	-.14
Devel	28.47	NL	-.20
EqtyIn	11.84	NL	-.06
Globl	19.06	NL	+.05
GNMA	14.77	NL	-.07
Gold	9.76	NL	+.14
GrwIn	14.23	NL	-.06
Incom	13.23	NL	-.02
IntlBd	13.07	NL	+.08
Intl Fd	36.04	NL	+.15
MMB	8.50	NL	...
MA Tx	12.47	NL	-.01
MedTF	10.19	NL	...
NYTax	10.81	NL	-.01
OHTax	12.23	NL	...
PA Tax	12.43	NL	...
ST Bond	11.86	NL	-.02
TxFHI	11.22	NL	-.02
TxFr93	10.67	NL	-.01
TxFr96	11.01	NL	...
Zr1995	11.87	NL	-.02
Zr2000	12.53	NL	-.04
Seafirst IRA:			
AstA f	11.89	NL	+.04
BICh f	14.04	NL	+.11
Bond f	10.48	NL	...
Secural	12.41	13.02	-.10
Security Funds:			
Action	9.68	....	-.08
Bond p	7.39	7.76	-.01
Equty	5.56	5.90	-.07
Invest	7.04	7.47	-.03
OmniFd	2.96	3.14	-.02
Ultra	6.56	6.96	-.03
Selected Funds:			
AmSh p	16.15	NL	-.18
SplSh p	21.50	NL	-.10
USGov	9.19	NL	-.02
Seligman Group:			
CapFd	15.40	16.17	-.10
ColoTx	7.09	7.44	...
CmStk	12.32	12.93	-.13
Comun	12.02	12.62	-.11
FLTax	7.23	7.59	-.01
Growth	5.45	5.72	-.05
Inco	11.43	12.00	-.03
LaTx	8.00	8.40	...
MassTx	7.65	8.03	-.01
MdTx	7.77	8.16	...
MichTx	8.18	8.59	...
MinnTx	7.73	8.12	-.01
MO Tx	7.53	7.91	...
NatlTx	7.72	8.10	-.01
NJTE p	7.34	7.71	...
NY Tax	7.67	8.05	...
OhioTx	7.89	8.28	...
OrTE	7.27	7.63	...
PaTE p	7.56	7.94	...
CaTax	6.36	6.66	...
CaTxQ	6.49	6.80	...
SCTF	7.56	7.94	...

	NAV	Offer Price	NAV Chg.
HYdB p	5.68	5.96	...
MtgSc p	6.57	6.90	-.01
Sentinel Group:			
Balan	13.40	14.64	-.08
Bond f	6.16	6.50	-.01
Com S	26.14	28.57	-.32
GvSecs	9.67	10.21	-.01
Grwth	16.20	17.10	-.20
Sequoia	48.56	NL	-.04
Sentry	14.74	NL	-.13
Shearson Funds:			
Advsr p	21.77	23.04	-.22
AgrGr	19.86	20.91	-.24
Aprec	9.31	9.80	-.10
ATG	8.16	8.59	-.06
ATIn	125.41	125.41	-1.55
AZ Mu	9.63	10.14	+.01
CalMu	15.67	16.49	+.03
FdVal	5.98	6.29	-.08
GlbOp	25.23	26.56	...
HiYld	12.12	12.76	+.01
MgdG	12.13	12.77	-.02
MMun	15.02	15.81	+.02
MAMu	11.94	12.57	+.01
NJMu	12.22	12.86	...
NYMu	16.09	16.94	...
1990s p	9.44	9.94	-.14
PrcM	13.48	14.19	+.26
PrnRt	10.80	NL	-.07
PrinII	7.86	NL	-.04
SmCa	16.23	17.08	-.17
WInc p	7.65	7.89	-.01
WWPr p	1.98	1.98	...
Shearson Ports:			
Convt t	12.21	12.21	...
DirVal t	13.53	13.53	-.15
DvsInc	7.93	7.93	-.01
Europ t	13.34	13.34	+.17
GlbBd t	15.43	15.43	...
GlbEq t	10.81	10.81	+.01
GvSec t	9.12	9.12	-.02
GrOpr t	16.31	16.31	-.13
Gwth t	13.84	13.84	-.12
INVG t	10.76	10.76	-.01
HiInc t	9.63	9.63	+.01
IntGv t	11.48	11.48	-.01
Intl t	17.90	17.90	+.13
MtgSc t	11.06	11.06	-.02
MOPS t	63.87	63.87	-1.75
OptIn t	14.34	14.34	-.06
PrcMt t	11.64	11.64	+.20
Sectr t	12.72	12.72	-.22
ST Gl t	7.82	7.82	-.01
SplEq t	11.74	11.74	-.05
Stratg t	16.85	16.85	-.10
TxEx t	16.83	16.83	...
Util t	13.41	13.41	-.04
ShrmD	7.82	NL	-.02
Sit New Begin:			
Grwth	38.65	NL	-.35
TaxFree	9.58	NL	...
US Gov	10.66	NL	-.02
SkylBal p	10.13	10.54	-.07
SkySpE p	13.36	13.89	-.04
Smith Barney:			
Equty p	15.65	16.60	-.16
IncGro	11.51	12.21	-.10
IncRet	9.36	9.48	-.01
LtdTrm	6.37	6.50	...
MoGvt	12.44	12.96	-.01
MuCal	11.68	12.17	+.01
MunNt	12.52	13.04	+.01
MuNY	11.88	12.38	+.01
USGvt	13.35	13.91	-.02
Utlty	12.14	12.71	-.03
SoGen	17.80	18.49	+.05
SoundSh	13.78	NL	-.09
SAM SC	10.44	NL	-.06
SAM Val	13.11	NL	-.10
SthestG t	16.02	16.02	+.01
Sover In	13.25	13.95	-.11
SpPtStk	27.40	27.40	-.34
State Bond Grp:			

	NAV	Offer Price	NAV Chg.
Divers	8.68	9.11	-.07
Progrs	12.01	12.61	-.11
TaxEx	10.51	11.01	...
USGv p	5.05	5.32	...
St FarmFds:			
Balan	26.04	26.04	-.19
Gwth	19.42	19.42	-.20
Interm	10.24	10.24	-.01
Muni	8.03	8.03	+.01
StStreet Resh:			
Exc	179.91	179.91	-2.63
Gth	101.62	101.62	-1.64
Inv	17.31	18.13	-.29
Steadman Funds:			
Am Ind	1.61	NL	-.01
Assoc	.62	NL	-.01
Invest	1.26	NL	-.02
Ocean	2.51	NL	-.05
Stein Roe Fds:			
Cap Op	19.38	NL	-.18
GvtInc	9.89	NL	-.02
HYMu	11.74	NL	...
Income	9.00	NL	-.01
IntBd	8.55	NL	-.01
IntMu	10.75	NL	...
MgdM	8.84	NL	...
PrimE	11.76	NL	-.10
Specl	18.71	NL	-.06
Stock	20.90	NL	-.23
TotRet	24.87	NL	-.15
Strategic Funds:			
Gold	3.00	3.28	+.07
Invst	2.00	2.19	+.03
Silvr	3.38	3.69	+.11
StratDv	24.88	NL	+.02
Strat Gth	19.29	NL	-.09
Strong Funds:			
Advtg	9.70	NL	...
CmStk	12.54	12.80	-.08
Discov	16.15	16.48	-.12
GovSc	10.14	NL	-.02
Inco	9.02	NL	-.01
Invst	18.15	18.33	-.07
MunBd	9.26	NL	...
Oppty	18.84	19.22	-.12
ST Bd	9.67	NL	...
Total	17.18	17.35	-.11
SunAmerica Fds:			
AgGth p	12.27	13.02	-.03
CapAp t	11.73	11.73	-.06
CvSec p	9.15	9.61	+.04
Grwth p	12.42	13.18	-.13
HiYld p	8.05	8.45	+.01
Home t	10.34	10.34	-.04
IncPl t	6.39	6.39	...
Stripe p	12.31	12.92	...
TotRt p	13.08	13.88	-.06
GvPl p	9.80	10.29	-.03
Templeton Group:			
Forgn	23.12	25.27	+.11
GlbOp	9.70	10.35	-.02
Grwth	15.23	16.64	-.02
Incom	9.88	10.35	+.03
RlEst	10.15	11.09	...
SmalCo	7.58	8.28	-.01
Value	9.86	10.78	-.02
World	14.44	15.78	-.03
Thomson Group:			
CvScB t	9.17	9.17	+.01
GlblB t	10.20	10.20	-.03
GwthB t	18.96	18.96	-.25
IncoB t	x 8.33	8.33	-.08
OporB t	15.90	15.90	-.17
PrcMtB	8.08	8.08	+.14
TExB t	11.32	11.32	+.02
USGvB t	x 9.21	9.21	-.08
Thornburg Fds:			
LtdCal	12.25	12.60	+.01
LtdGv p	12.13	12.41	-.01
LtMu p	12.82	13.18	-.01
Tower Funds:			

	NAV	Offer Price	NAV Chg.
LA Mun	10.34	10.83	+.01
US Gv	10.36	10.85	-.02
Transamerica:			
CA TF p	9.95	10.45	+.02
GvInc p	8.36	8.57	-.01
GvSec p	8.09	8.49	-.02
GrIn p	10.93	11.48	-.15
InvQ fp	8.91	9.35	-.03
Lowry p	9.38	9.85	-.10
Sunblt p	19.07	20.02	-.04
TF Bd	10.04	10.54	+.01
Tech p	13.98	14.68	-.12
TrnsamericaSpcl:			
BlChp t	10.48	10.48	-.14
CvSec t	10.44	10.44	-.06
EmgG t	17.05	17.05	-.14
Globl t	11.59	11.59	-.02
GvInc t	9.68	9.68	-.02
HiYld t	6.97	6.97	+.01
HYTF t	9.02	9.02	+.01
NatRs t	11.91	11.91	+.05
TrinEq	11.54	11.54	-.13
TrnSBd	10.07	10.07	...
20th Century:			
BalInv	13.54	NL	-.13
Gift	10.57	NL	-.12
Grwth	20.06	NL	-.24
HerInv	8.12	NL	-.04
LTBnd	92.04	NL	-.07
Select	38.54	NL	-.54
TxEIn	98.67	NL	+.04
TxELT	99.30	NL	+.08
Ultra	13.11	NL	-.21
USGv	91.83	NL	-.05
Vista	9.55	NL	-.07
USF&G Funds:			
AxeB p	9.44	10.02	-.03
AxeCr p	10.99	11.66	+.04
AxeGr p	8.43	8.94	-.03
AxeInc p	4.90	5.14	...
AxTE p	10.19	10.70	...
ChnFI p	10.10	10.60	-.01
ChnGI p	12.39	13.15	-.13
EurG p	10.38	11.01	+.11
EurE p	11.31	12.00	+.12
OTC S p	15.66	16.62	-.04
USAA Group:			
AgvGt	18.46	NL	-.06
Balan	11.22	NL	-.03
Cornst	18.28	NL	+.01
CA Bd	10.02	NL	...
Gold	6.69	NL	+.10
Grwth	15.63	NL	-.18
Inco	11.65	NL	-.03
IncStk	12.00	NL	-.09
Intl	11.33	NL	+.06
TxEH	13.19	NL	+.01
TxEIt	12.05	NL	...
TxESh	10.37	NL	+.01
VA Bd	10.32	NL	...
UST Master:			
Equity	14.28	14.95	-.10
Intl	9.09	9.52	+.08
IntTE	8.85	9.27	...
LT TE	9.17	9.60	...
MgdIn	9.17	9.60	-.02
NY TE	8.21	8.60	-.01
Unified Mgmnt:			
Gwth	14.66	15.35	-.01
Inco	11.10	11.62	-.06
Indian	8.97	9.39	+.01
Mutl	16.58	17.36	-.18
Union Inv:			
Balan	10.51	NL	-.05
GrEq	11.29	NL	-.12
IntBd	10.19	NL	...
VIMom	10.69	NL	-.07
United Funds:			
Accm	6.82	7.45	-.07
Bond	5.86	6.40	-.02
Con Inc	17.03	18.61	-.13
GldGv	6.75	7.38	+.07

	NAV	Offer Price	NAV Chg.
IntGth	6.36	6.95	+.06
Hi Inc	7.61	8.32	+.02
HiIncII	3.56	3.89	...
Incom	18.80	20.55	-.25
Muni	6.98	7.29	+.01
MunHi	4.95	5.17	...
NCcpt	6.92	7.56	-.04
Retire	6.48	7.08	-.05
ScEng	12.32	13.46	-.17
Vang	5.94	6.49	-.07
Utd Services:			
AllAm	17.22	NL	-.24
Euro	4.63	NL	+.02
GlbRs	5.61	NL	...
GldShr	3.13	NL	+.06
Grwth	7.30	NL	-.09
Inco	11.74	NL	-.07
WldGld	9.55	NL	+.16
RlEst	8.88	NL	-.03
US TF	11.39	NL	+.02
USBosF	....	....	...
USBosG	16.07	16.07	-.19
√alFrg	9.00	NL	-.02
Value Line Fd:			
AggrIn	6.81	NL	+.01
Conv	11.11	NL	-.02
Fund	17.28	NL	-.16
Incom	7.03	NL	-.04
Lev Gt	26.22	NL	-.30
MuBd	10.25	NL	...
NY TE	9.56	NL	-.01
Spl Sit	15.86	NL	-.11
US Gvt	12.07	NL	-.02
Van Eck:			
GldRs p	3.83	4.11	+.06
IntInv	11.26	12.31	+.23
WldIn p	9.71	10.19	+.06
WldTr p	14.41	15.29	+.03
VanKampen Mer:			
CATF p	15.73	16.54	...
Gwth p	17.81	18.73	-.20
HiYld p	9.07	9.54	+.01
InTF p	17.92	18.84	...
MunIn	14.33	15.07	...
PA TF	15.83	16.65	...
ST GI	9.63	9.93	...
TxFH p	15.47	16.27	...
USGv p	15.33	16.12	-.03
Vance Exchange:			
CapE	138.93	NL	-2.04
DBst	72.64	NL	-.89
Divrs	142.25	NL	-2.02
ExFd	207.24	NL	-2.32
EBos	168.92	NL	-2.13
FdEx	125.90	NL	-1.55
ScFid	110.07	NL	-1.50
Vanguard Group:			
AssetA	12.42	NL	-.10
BdMkt	9.48	NL	-.02
Convrt	9.43	NL	-.01
EqInc	11.67	NL	-.16
Explr	33.22	NL	-.12
Morg	12.12	NL	-.12
Prmcp	15.12	NL	-.10
VHYS	10.26	NL	-.05
V Pref	8.60	NL	+.01
V ARP	18.13	NL	...
Quant	15.13	NL	-.18
STAR	12.04	NL	-.09
TC Int	28.75	NL	+.32
TCUsa	25.66	NL	-.33
GNMA	9.87	NL	-.01
HiYBd	6.67	NL	+.01
IGBnd	8.17	NL	-.02
ShrtTr	10.54	NL	-.01
STGvt	10.06	NL	-.01
US Tr	9.74	NL	-.03
Idx 500	35.38	NL	-.48
IdxExt	14.07	NL	-.05
IdxEur	9.84	NL	+.14
IdxPac	9.73	NL	+.01
IdxInst	[illegible]	NL	-.48

	NAV	Offer Price	NAV Chg.
MuHY	10.11	NL	...
MuInt	12.23	NL	...
MunLd	10.36	NL	...
MuLg	10.44	NL	+.01
MInLg	11.62	NL	...
MuShf	15.50	NL	+.01
Cal Ins	10.24	NL	...
NJIns	10.61	NL	-.01
NYIns	9.80	NL	-.01
OhioIn	10.40	NL	...
PennIn	10.25	NL	...
VSPE r	14.24	NL	-.12
VSPG r	9.21	NL	+.11
VSPH r	31.13	NL	-.16
VSPS r	17.45	NL	-.17
VSPT r	14.31	NL	-.10
Wellsl	16.60	NL	-.06
Welltn	17.56	NL	-.15
Wndsr	12.14	NL	-.14
Wnds II	14.62	NL	-.18
WldInt	10.97	NL	+.11
WldUS	12.70	NL	-.16
Venture Advisers:			
IncPl	4.74	4.98	+.01
Muni t	9.21	9.21	...
NY Ven	9.42	9.89	-.08
RPFB t	6.62	6.62	-.01
RPFE t	24.81	NL	-.20
VikEqIn	18.76	NL	-.26
Vista Funds:			
CapGr	17.91	18.75	-.21
GrInc	22.76	23.83	-.20
NY TF	10.80	11.31	+.01
TF Inc	10.80	11.31	+.02
GvInc	11.23	11.76	-.03
Volumet	14.76	NL	-.14
Vonotbl	11.95	12.58	-.05
Voyageur Fds:			
CO TF	10.08	10.49	...
GrStk p	19.81	21.02	-.13
MN Ins	9.65	10.13	...
MNInt	10.38	10.67	...
MNTF	11.71	12.29	...
Weiss Peck Greer:			
Tudor	22.23	NL	-.15
Govt	10.27	NL	-.02
Gwth	124.08	NL	-.47
GrInc	22.41	NL	-.21
WallSt	7.38	7.81	-.07
Wells IRA-401K:			
AstAl	15.32	NL	-.10
CpStk	26.80	NL	-.36
FixInc	13.41	NL	-.03
Westcore:			
STBd	9.82	10.02	...
IntBd	9.74	10.20	...
BdPlu	15.52	16.25	-.02
BasVl	19.29	20.20	-.20
LT Bd	10.17	10.65	-.02
ModVl	12.37	12.95	-.19
Midco	13.31	13.94	-.11
SITE	....	....	...
Westwd	13.83	14.41	-.15
WlmBI	10.24	10.24	-.02
WmPPA	10.35	10.87	...
Wood Struthers:			
Neuw	12.27	NL	-.08
Pine	11.96	NL	-.07
WinG t	10.87	10.87	-.09
Wright Funds:			
GvOb	12.12	NL	-.04
JrBlCh	14.01	NL	-.06
NearB	10.28	NL	-.01
QulCor	12.88	NL	-.12
SlBlCh	15.99	NL	-.15
TotRet	11.75	NL	-.03
YamGlb	8.36	8.78	-.01
Zweig Funds:			
ZS Gv p	9.55	10.03	-.02
Strat	12.05	12.75	-.14
ZS P p	12.19	12.90	-.11
TFLtd	10.39	10.55	+.01

Figure 11.5 Listing of mutual fund quotations.

Table 11.7   *Impact of Costs on Investment Performance*

| | Cumulative Proceeds (All Dividends Reinvested) | | |
	Fund A	Fund B	Fund C
Initial investment*	$10,000	$10,000	$ 9,200
5 years	17,234	16,474	15,225
10 years	29,699	27,141	25,196
15 years	51,183	44,713	41,698
20 years	88,206	73,662	69,006

*After front-end load, if any.

Notes:
1. Fund A is no load with .5% expense ratio.
2. Fund B is no load with 1.5% expense ratio.
3. Fund C has an 8% load on purchase and reinvested dividends with a 1% expense ratio. The dividend yield on fund C is 5%. (Thus, the 8% load on reinvested dividends reduces net returns by .08 × 5% = 0.4%.)
4. Gross return on all funds is 12% per year before expenses.

dicates the presence of 12b-1 fees. Funds with no loads are identified by the abbreviation NL in the offering price column.

Fees can have a big effect on performance. Table 11.7 shows the cumulative value of three funds, all of which start with $10,000 and earn an annual 12 percent return on investment before fees. Fund A has total operating expenses of 0.5 percent, no load, and no 12b-1 charges. This might represent a low-cost producer like Vanguard. Fund B has no load but has 1 percent in management expenses and 0.5 percent in 12b-1 fees. This level of fees is perhaps slightly above average, but not unusual in the industry. Finally, fund C has 1 percent in management expenses, no 12b-1 charges, but assesses an 8 percent front-end load on purchases as well as reinvested dividends. We assume the dividend yield on the fund is 5 percent.

Note the substantial return advantage of low-cost fund A. Moreover, that differential grows over time.

Summary

1. Returns can be measured as dollar- or time-weighted averages. In performance evaluation, time-weighted returns generally are preferred because the manager does not usually have discretion over the net inflow or outflow of funds from the portfolio.

2. The appropriate performance measure depends on the role of the portfolio to be evaluated. The Sharpe measure is most appropriate when the portfolio represents the entire investment fund. The Treynor ratio or Jensen measure is appropriate when the portfolio is to be mixed with several other assets, allowing for diversification of firm-specific risk outside of the portfolio.

3. The shifting mean and variance of actively managed portfolios make it even harder to assess performance. A typical example is in the attempt of portfolio managers to time the market, resulting in ever-changing portfolio betas and standard deviations.

4. Common attribution procedures partition performance improvements to asset allocation, sector selection, and security selection. Performance is assessed by calculating departures of portfolio composition from a benchmark or neutral portfolio.

5. Mutual fund performance is affected by front-end loads, back-end loads, operating expenses, and 12b-1 fees.

Key Terms

back-end load, 313
bogey, 308
comparison
  universe, 300
dollar-weighted rate of
  return, 298

front-end load, 313
Jensen measure, 303
Sharpe measure, 302
time-weighted rate of
  return, 298

Treynor measure, 302
12b-1 fees, 313

Selected Readings

Mutual fund performance is reported regularly in the financial press. Look for issues of Money, Business Week, Financial World, and Forbes.

Performance measurement is the focus of an ICFA publication titled:
Performance Measurement: Setting the Standards, Interpreting the Numbers, 1989. This compilation includes the report of the Financial Analysts Federation on standards for performance presentation.

Problem Sets

Questions 1–8 appeared in past CFA Examinations.

1. A plan sponsor with a portfolio manager who invests in small-capitalization, high-growth stocks should have the plan sponsor's performance measured against which *one* of the following?
  a. S&P 500 index.
  b. Wilshire 5000 index.
  c. Dow Jones Industrial Average.
  d. S&P 400 index.

2. In measuring the comparative performance of different fund managers, the preferred method of calculating rate of return is:
  a. Internal.
  b. Time weighted.
  c. Dollar weighted.
  d. Income.

3. Which *one* of the following is a valid benchmark against which a portfolio's performance can be measured over a given time period?
  a. The portfolio's dollar-weighted rate of return.
  b. The portfolio's time-weighted rate of return.
  c. The portfolio manager's "normal" portfolio.
  d. The average beta of the portfolio.

4. Assume you invested in an asset for two years. The first year you earned a 15 percent return, and the second year you earned a *negative* 10 percent return. What was your annual geometric return?

a. 1.7 percent.
b. 2.5 percent.
c. 3.5 percent.
d. 5.0 percent.

5. Assume you purchased a rental property for $50,000 and sold it one year later for $55,000 (there was no mortgage on the property). At the time of the sale, you paid $2,000 in commissions and $600 in taxes. If you received $6,000 in rental income (all of it received at the end of the year), what annual rate of return did you earn?
   a. 15.3 percent.
   b. 15.9 percent.
   c. 16.8 percent.
   d. 17.1 percent.

6. A portfolio of stocks generates a −9 percent return in 1990, a 23 percent return in 1991, and a 17 percent return in 1992. The annualized return (geometric mean) for the entire period is:
   a. 7.2 percent.
   b. 9.4 percent.
   c. 10.3 percent.
   d. None of the above.

7. A two-year investment of $2,000 results in a return of $150 at the end of the first year and a return of $150 at the end of the second year, in addition to the return of the original investment. The internal rate of return on the investment is:
   a. 6.4 percent.
   b. 7.5 percent.
   c. 15.0 percent.
   d. None of the above.

8. In measuring the performance of a portfolio, the time-weighted rate of return is superior to the dollar-weighted rate of return because:
   a. When the rate of return varies, the time-weighted return is higher.
   b. The dollar-weighted return assumes all portfolio deposits are made on day 1.
   c. The dollar-weighted return can only be estimated.
   d. The time-weighted return is unaffected by the timing of portfolio contributions and withdrawals.

9. Consider the rate of return of stocks ABC and XYZ.

Year	r_{ABC}	r_{XYZ}
1	.20	.30
2	.10	.10
3	.14	.18
4	.05	.00
5	.01	−.08

   a. Calculate the arithmetic average return on these stocks over the sample period.
   b. Which stock has greater dispersion around the mean?
   c. Calculate the geometric average returns of each stock. What do you conclude?

Year	Beginning of Year Price	Dividend Paid at Year-End
1991	$100	$4
1992	$110	$4
1993	$90	$4
1994	$95	$4

An investor buys three shares of XYZ at the beginning of 1991, buys another two shares at the beginning of 1992, sells one share at the beginning of 1993, and sells all four remaining shares at the beginning of 1994.

a. What are the arithmetic and geometric average time-weighted rates of return for the investor?

b. What is the dollar-weighted rate of return. Hint: Carefully prepare a chart of cash flows for the *five* dates corresponding to the turns of the year for January 1, 1991 to December 31, 1994. If your calculator cannot calculate internal rate of return, you will have to use trial and error.

11. Based on current dividend yields and expected capital gains, the expected rates of return on portfolio *A* and *B* are 0.11 and 0.14, respectively. The beta of *A* is 0.8 while that of *B* is 1.5. The T-bill rate is currently 0.06 while the expected rate of return of the S&P 500 index is 0.12. The standard deviation of portfolio *A* is 0.10 annually, while that of *B* is 0.31, and that of the index is .20.

a. If you currently hold a market index portfolio, would you choose to add either of these portfolios to your holdings? Explain.

b. If instead you could invest *only* in bills and *one* of these portfolios, which would you choose?

12. Evaluate the timing and selection abilities of four managers whose performances are plotted in the following four scatter diagrams.

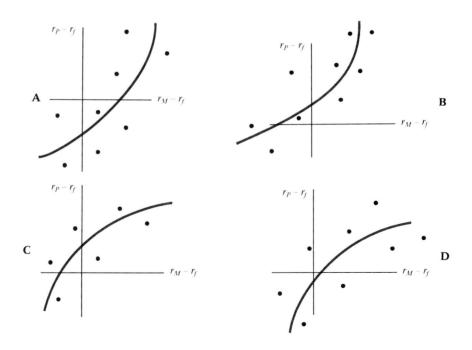

13. Consider the following information regarding the performance of a money manager in a recent month. The table presents the actual return of each sector of the manager's portfolio in column (1), the fraction of the portfolio allocated to each sector in column (2), the benchmark or neutral sector allocations in column (3), and the returns of sector indexes in column (4).

	(1) Actual Return	(2) Actual Weight	(3) Benchmark Weight	(4) Index Return
Equity	.02	.70	.60	.025 (S&P 500)
Bonds	.01	.20	.30	.012 (Salomon Brothers Index)
Cash	.005	.10	.10	.005

a. What was the manager's return in the month. What was her over- or underperformance?

b. What was the contribution of security selection to relative performance?

c. What was the contribution of asset allocation to relative performance? Confirm that the sum of selection and allocation contributions equals her total "excess" return relative to the bogey.

14. Convention wisdom says one should measure a manager's investment performance over an entire market cycle. What arguments support this contention? What arguments contradict it?

15. Does the use of universes of managers with similar investment styles to evaluate relative investment performance overcome the statistical problems associated with instability of beta or total variability?

16. During a particular year, the T-bill rate was 6 percent, the market return was 14 percent, and a portfolio manager with beta of 0.5 realized a return of 10 percent. Evaluate the manager based on the portfolio alpha.

17. The chairman provides you with the following data, covering one year, concerning the portfolios of two of the fund's equity managers (firm *A* and firm *B*). Although the portfolios consist primarily of common stocks, cash reserves are included in the calculation of both portfolio betas and performance. By way of perspective, selected data for the financial markets are included in the following table:

	Total Return	Beta
Firm *A*	24.0%	1.0
Firm *B*	30.0	1.5
S&P 500	21.0	
Lehman, Kuhn Loeb Total Bond Index	31.0	
91-day Treasury bills	12.0	

a. Calculate and compare the risk-adjusted performance of the two firms relative to each other and to the S&P 500.

b. Explain *two* reasons the conclusions drawn from this calculation may be misleading.

18. Carl Karl, a portfolio manager for the Alpine Trust Company, has been responsible since 1985 for the City of Alpine's Employee Retirement Plan, a municipal pension fund. Alpine is a growing community, and city services and employee payrolls have expanded in each of the past 10 years. Contributions to the plan in fiscal 1990 exceeded benefit payments by a three-to-one ratio.

The plan's Board of Trustees directed Karl five years ago to invest for total return over the long term. However, as trustees of this highly visible public fund, they cautioned him that volatile or erratic results could cause them embarrassment. They also noted a state statute that mandated that not more than 25 percent of the plan's assets (at cost) be invested in common stocks.

At the annual meeting of the trustees in November 1990, Karl presented the following portfolio and performance report to the Board:

Alpine Employee Retirement Plan

Asset Mix as of 9/30/90	At Cost (Millions)		At Market (Millions)	
Fixed-income assets:				
Short-term securities	$ 4.5	11.0%	$ 4.5	11.4%
Long-term bonds and mortgages	26.5	64.7	23.5	59.5
Common stocks	10.0	24.3	11.5	29.1
	$41.0	100.0%	$39.5	100.0%

Investment Performance

	Annual Rates of Return for Periods Ending 9/30/80	
	5 Years	1 Year
Total Alpine Fund:		
Time-weighted	8.2%	5.2%
Dollar-weighted (Internal)	7.7%	4.8%
Assumed actuarial return	6.0%	6.0%
U. S. Treasury bills	7.5%	11.3%
Large sample of pension funds (average 60% equities, 40% fixed income)	10.1%	14.3%
Common stocks—Alpine Fund	13.3%	14.3%
Average portfolio beta coefficient	0.90	0.89
Standard & Poor's 500 Stock Index	13.8%	21.1%
Fixed-income securities—Alpine Fund	6.7%	1.0%
Salomon Brothers' Bond Index	4.0%	−11.4%

Karl was proud of his performance and was chagrined when a trustee made the following critical observations:

a. "Our one-year results were terrible, and it's what you've done for us lately that counts most."

b. "Our total fund performance was clearly inferior compared to the large sample of other pension funds for the last five years. What else could this reflect except poor management judgment?"

c. "Our common stock performance was especially poor for the five-year period."

d. "Why bother to compare your returns to the return from Treasury bills and the actuarial assumption rate? What your competition could have earned for us or how we would have fared if invested in a passive index (which doesn't charge a fee) are the only relevant measures of performance."

e. "Who cares about time-weighted return? If it can't pay pensions, what good is it!"

Appraise the merits of each of these statements and give counter arguments that Mr. Karl can use.

Part Three

Fixed-Income Securities

■ ■

Chapter

12

Bond Prices and Yields

In the previous chapters on risk and return relationships, we have treated securities at a high level of abstraction. We have assumed implicitly that a prior, detailed analysis of each security already has been performed, and that its risk and return features have been assessed.

We turn now to specific analyses of particular security markets. We examine valuation principles, determinants of risk and return, and portfolio strategies commonly used within and across the various markets.

Fixed-income security A security such as a bond that pays a specified cash flow over a specific period.

We begin by analyzing **fixed-income securities.** A fixed-income security is a claim on a specified periodic stream of income. Fixed-income securities have the advantage of being relatively easy to understand because much of the risk is absent. The level of payments is fixed in advance, so risk considerations are minimal as long as the issuer of the security is sufficiently creditworthy. That makes these securities a convenient starting point for our analysis of the universe of potential investment vehicles.

The bond is the basic fixed-income security, and this chapter reviews the principles of bond pricing. It shows how bond prices are set in accordance with market interest rates, and why bond prices change with those rates. After examining the Treasury bond market, where default risk may be ignored, we move to the corporate bond sector. Here, we look at the determinants of credit risk and the default premium built into bond yields. We examine the impact of call and convertibility provisions on prices and yields. Finally, we take a look at the yield curve, the relationship between bond maturity and bond yield. After studying this chapter you should be able to:

- Compute a bond's price given its yield to maturity, and compute its yield to maturity given its price.
- Calculate how bond prices will change over time for a given interest-rate projection.

- Identify the determinants of bond safety and rating.
- Analyze how callable, convertible, and sinking fund provisions will affect a bond's equilibrium yield to maturity
- Analyze the factors likely to affect the shape of the yield curve at any time.

12.1   *Bond Prices and Yields*

Bond   *A security that obligates the issuer to make specified payments to the holder over a period of time.*

Coupon rate   *A bond's annual interest payments per dollar of par value.*

Par value   *The face (maturity) value of the bond.*

A **bond** is a simple borrowing arrangement in which the borrower issues (sells) an IOU to the investor. The arrangement obligates the issuer to make specified payments to the bondholder on specified dates. A typical *coupon bond* obligates the issuer to make semiannual payments of interest, called coupon payments, to the bondholder for the life of the bond, and then to repay the original principal, or borrowed money, at a specified maturity date. The **coupon rate** of the bond is the coupon payment divided by the bond's **par value.**

To illustrate, a bond with par value of $1,000 and coupon rate of 8 percent is sold to a buyer for a $1,000 payment. The bondholder is then entitled to a payment of 8 percent of $1,000, or $80 per year, for the stated life of the bond, say 30 years. That $80 payment typically comes in two semiannual installments of $40 each. After the 30-year life of the bond, the borrower (issuer) repays the original $1,000 principal to the lender (the bondholder).

Review of the Present Value Relationship

Because a bond's coupon payments and principal repayment all occur months or years into the future, the price an investor would be willing to pay for a claim to those payments depends on the value of dollars to be received in the future compared to dollars in hand today. The *present value* of a claim to a dollar to be paid in the future is the market price at which that claim would sell if it were traded in the securities market.

We know that the present value of a dollar to be received in the future is less than one dollar. The time spent waiting to receive the dollar imposes an opportunity cost on the investor—if the money is not in hand today, it cannot be invested to start generating income immediately. Denoting the current market interest rate by r, the present value of a dollar to be received n years from now is $1/(1 + r)^n$.

To see why this is so, consider an example in which the interest rate is 5 percent, $r = .05$. According to the present value rule, the value of $1 to be received in 10 years would be $1/(1.05)^{10} = \$.614$. A little over 61 cents is the amount that would be paid in the marketplace for a claim to a payment of $1 in 10 years. This is because a person investing today at the going 5 percent rate of interest realizes that only $.614 needs to be set aside now in order to provide a final value of $1 in 10 years, as $.614 \times 1.05^{10} = \$1.00$. The present value formula tells us exactly how much an investor should be willing to pay for a claim to a future cash flow. This value will be the current price of the claim.

We simplify for now by assuming there is one interest rate that is appropriate for discounting cash flows of any maturity, but we can relax this assumption easily. In practice, there may be different discount rates for cash flows accruing in different periods. For the time being, however, we ignore this refinement.

Bond Pricing

In the example above, we asserted that the 30-year maturity, 8 percent coupon bond could be sold to the public at an issue price of $1,000; that is, we assumed the bond could be sold at its par value. This is a bit of a leap, because we do not yet know whether investors would be willing to pay $1,000 for the 60 semi-annual payments of $40 and the ultimate repayment of the $1,000 in year 30. To arrive at the price they would be willing to pay for the bond, investors need to compute the present value of the cash flows they stand to receive from purchasing the bond.

In our case, the bond would sell at $1,000 if the market interest rate were exactly equal to the 8 percent coupon rate, or more precisely, if the market interest rate were 4 percent per six-month period. In this event, it is easy to confirm that the present value of the bond's 60 semiannual coupon payments of $40 each would equal $904.94, while the $1,000 principal repayment would have a present value of $1,000/(1.04)^{60} = $95.06, for a total bond value of $1,000. You can perform these calculations easily on any financial calculator or use a set of present value tables such as those included in Appendix E at the end of the text.

Symbolically, we write

$$\$1,000 = \sum_{t=1}^{60} \frac{\$40}{(1.04)^t} + \frac{\$1,000}{(1.04)^{60}} \qquad \textbf{12.1}$$

The summation sign in Equation 12.1 directs us to add 60 terms, each of which is $40 divided by 1.04 to a power that ranges from 1 to 60. This first expression gives us the present value of a $40 annuity. For expositional simplicity we can write Equation 12.1 as

$$\$1,000 = \$40 \times PA(4\%, 60) + \$1,000 \times PF(4\%, 60)$$

where PA(4%, 60) represents the present value of an annuity of $1 when the interest rate is 4 percent and the annuity is to last for 60 periods, while PF(4%, 60) similarly represents the present value of a single payment of $1 to be received in 60 periods. In our example, each period is six months.

Of course, if the interest rate were not equal to the bond's coupon rate, the bond would not sell at par value. For example, if the interest rate were to rise to 10 percent (5 percent per six months), the bond's price would fall by $189.29 to $810.71, as follows:

$$\$40 \times PA(5\%, 60) + \$1,000 \times PF(5\%, 60)$$
$$= \$757.17 + \$53.54$$
$$= \$810.71$$

At the higher current interest rate, the present value of the payments to be received by the bondholder is lower. Therefore, the bond price will fall as market interest rates rise. This illustrates a crucial general rule in bond valuation. When interest rates rise, bond prices must fall because the present value of the bond's payments are obtained by discounting at a higher interest rate.

Figure 12.1
The inverse relationship between bond prices and yields.

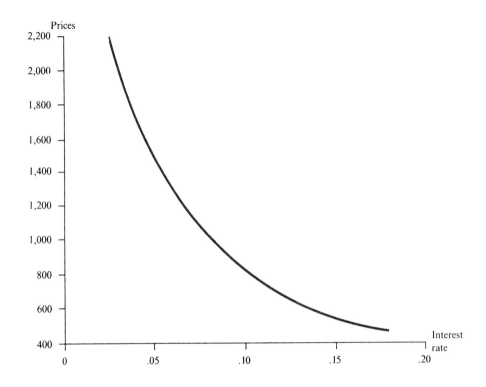

Table 12.1 *Bond Prices at Different Interest Rates* (8% coupon bond, coupons paid semiannually)

	Bond Price at Given Market Interest Rate				
Time to Maturity	**4%**	**6%**	**8%**	**10%**	**12%**
1 year	1,038.83	1,019.13	1,000.00	981.41	963.33
10 years	1,327.03	1,148.77	1,000.00	875.35	770.60
20 years	1,547.11	1,231.15	1,000.00	828.41	699.07
30 years	1,695.22	1,276.76	1,000.00	810.71	676.77

Figure 12.1 shows the price of the 30-year, 8 percent coupon bond for a range of interest rates. The negative slope illustrates the inverse relationship between prices and yields. Note also from the figure (and from Table 12.1) that the shape of the curve implies that an increase in the interest rate results in a price decline that is smaller than the price gain that results from a decrease of equal magnitude in the interest rate. This property of bond prices is called *convexity* because of the convex shape of the bond price curve. This curvature reflects the fact that progressive increases in the interest rate result in progressively smaller reductions in the bond price.[1] Therefore, the price curve becomes flatter at higher interest rates.

---

[1]The progressively smaller impact of interest rate increases results from the fact that at higher rates the bond is worth less. Therefore, an additional increase in rates operates on a smaller initial base, resulting in a smaller price reduction.

Concept Check

> *Question 1.*   Calculate the price of the bond for a market interest rate of 3 percent per half year. Compare the capital gains for the interest rate decline to the losses incurred when the rate increases to 5 percent.

Corporate bonds at issue typically sell at par value. This means the underwriters of the bond issue (the firms that market the bonds to the public for the issuing corporation) must choose a coupon rate that very closely approximates market yields. In a primary issue of bonds, the underwriters attempt to sell the newly issued bonds directly to their customers. If the coupon rate is inadequate, the bonds will not be salable at par value.

After the bonds are issued, bondholders may buy or sell bonds in secondary markets such as the one operated by the New York Stock Exchange or the over-the-counter market, where most bonds trade. In these secondary markets, bond prices move in accordance with market forces. The bond prices fluctuate inversely with the market interest rate.

The inverse relationship between price and yield is a central feature of fixed-income securities. Interest rate fluctuations represent the main source of risk in the fixed-income market, and we devote considerable attention in the next chapter to assessing the sensitivity of bond prices to market yields. For now, however, it is sufficient to highlight one key factor that determines that sensitivity, namely, the maturity of the bond.

A general rule in evaluating bond price risk is that, keeping all other factors the same, the longer the maturity of the bond, the greater the sensitivity of price to fluctuations in the interest rate. For example, consider Table 12.1, which presents the price of an 8 percent coupon bond at different market yields and times to maturity. For any departure of the interest rate from 8 percent (the rate at which the bond sells at par value), the change in the bond price is smaller for shorter times to maturity.

This makes sense. If you buy the bond at par with an 8 percent coupon rate, and market rates subsequently rise, then you suffer a loss: you have tied up your money earning 8 percent when alternative investments offer higher returns. This is reflected in a capital loss on the bond—a fall in its market price. The longer the period for which your money is tied up, the greater the loss, and correspondingly the greater the drop in the bond price. In Table 12.1, the row for one-year maturity bonds shows little price sensitivity—that is, with only one year's earnings at stake, changes in interest rates are not too threatening. But for 30-year maturity bonds, interest rate swings have a large impact on bond prices.

This is why short-term Treasury securities such as T-bills are considered to be the safest. They are free not only of default risk, but also largely of price risk attributable to interest rate volatility.

Yield to Maturity

Yield to maturity (YTM)   *A measure of the average rate of return that will be earned on a bond if held to maturity.*

In practice, an investor considering the purchase of a bond is not quoted a promised rate of return. Instead, the investor must use the bond price, maturity date, and coupon payments to infer the return offered by the bond over its life. The **yield to maturity** (YTM) is a measure of the average rate of return that will be earned on a bond if it is bought now and held until maturity. To calculate the yield to maturity, we solve the bond price equation for the interest rate given the bond's price.

For example, suppose the 8 percent coupon, 30-year bond is selling at $1,276.76. What rate of return would be earned by an investor purchasing the bond at market price? To answer this question, we find the interest rate at which the present value of the remaining bond payments equals the bond price. This is the rate that is consistent with the observed price of the bond. Therefore, we solve for *r* in the following equation:

$$\$1,276.76 = \sum_{t=1}^{60} \frac{\$40}{(1 + r)^t} + \frac{\$1,000}{(1 + r)^{60}}$$

or, equivalently,

$$1,276.76 = 40 \times PA(r, 60) + 1,000 \times PF(r, 60).$$

These equations have only one unknown variable, the interest rate, *r*. You can use a financial calculator to confirm that the solution to the equation is *r* = .03, or 3 percent per half year.[2] This is considered the bond's yield to maturity, as the bond would be fairly priced at $1,276.76 if the fair market rate of return on the bond over its entire life were 3 percent per half year. The bond's yield to maturity would be quoted in the financial press at an annual percentage rate (APR) of 6 percent, despite the fact that its effective annual yield (because of the effect of compound interest) is 6.09 percent ($1.03^2 - 1 = .0609$).

Because yield to maturity is difficult to calculate without a financial calculator, bond market participants sometimes use an approximation. They first determine average income per year by spreading prospective capital gains or losses over the remaining life of the bond. For example, the bond we've been discussing now sells at $1,276.76 and matures at $1,000 in 30 years. Therefore, it will suffer average losses over 30 years of $276.76/30 = $9.23 per year. Therefore, the average annual income it provides is the $80 coupon minus the $9.23 capital loss, or $70.77. The average price of the bond over its remaining life is taken to be the average of its current price and maturity value, in this example, (1,276.76 + 1,000)/2 = 1,138.38. Hence, the YTM would be approximated as average income divided by average price, or 70.77/1,138.38 = .0622, or 6.22 percent. The actual YTM for this bond was shown to be 6 percent, while the approximation is 6.22 percent.

To summarize, the approximate YTM formula is

$$YTM = \frac{Coupon + (Par\ value - Market\ price)/Remaining\ maturity}{(Price + Par\ value)/2}$$

The approximation works best when the bond is selling near par value.

The bond's yield to maturity is the internal rate of return on an investment in the bond. The yield to maturity can be interpreted as the compound rate of return over the life of the bond under the assumption that all bond coupons can be reinvested at an interest rate equal to the bond's yield to maturity. If this is not the case, the yield to maturity will not be the same as the return over the bond's life. Nevertheless, yield to maturity is widely accepted as a proxy for

---

[2]Without a financial calculator, you still could solve the equation, but you would need to use a trial-and-error approach.

average return, because alternative measures require forecasts of future reinvestment rates.

Yield to maturity is different from the *current yield* of a bond, which is the bond's annual coupon payment divided by the bond price. For example, for the 8 percent, 30-year bond currently selling at $1,276.76, the current yield would be $80/$1,276.76 = .0627, or 6.27 percent per year. In contrast, recall that the effective annual yield to maturity is 6.09 percent. For this bond, which is selling at a premium over par value ($1,276 rather than $1,000), the coupon rate (8 percent) exceeds the current yield (6.27 percent), which exceeds the yield to maturity (6.09 percent). The coupon rate exceeds current yield because the coupon rate divides the coupon payments by par value ($1,000) rather than by the bond price ($1,276). In turn, the current yield exceeds yield to maturity because the yield to maturity accounts for the built-in capital loss on the bond: the bond bought today for $1,276 will eventually fall in value to $1,000 at maturity.

Concept Check

Question 2.   What will be the relationship among coupon rate, current yield, and yield to maturity for bonds selling at discounts from par?

 ## 12.2   *Bond Prices over Time*

Although bonds generally promise a fixed flow of income to their owners, that income stream is not riskless unless the investor can be sure the issuer will not default on the obligation. All corporate bonds, for example, entail some risk of default. Even though the prospective cash flows are specified when the bond is purchased, the actual bond payments are uncertain, for they depend to some extent on the ultimate financial status of the firm. U.S. government fixed-income securities, on the other hand, may be treated as virtually free of default risk.

Because these securities are free of default risk, they present fewer complicating issues for analysis. Hence, we will illustrate the properties of bond prices using Treasury securities as our example, deferring until later in the chapter the discussion of riskier nongovernment securities.

Zero-Coupon Bonds

Zero-coupon bond   A bond paying no coupons that sells at a discount and provides only a payment of par value at maturity.

Original issue discount bonds are less common than coupon bonds issued at par. These are bonds that are issued intentionally with low coupon rates that cause the bond to sell at a discount from par value. An extreme example of this type of bond is the **zero-coupon bond,** which carries no coupons and must provide all its return in the form of price appreciation. Zeros provide only one cash flow to their owners, and that is on the maturity date of the bond.

U.S. Treasury bills are examples of short-term zero-coupon instruments. The Treasury issues or sells a bill for some amount less than $10,000, agreeing to repay $10,000 at the bill's maturity. All of the investor's return comes in the form of price appreciation over time.

Longer-term zero-coupon bonds can be created synthetically. Several investment banking firms buy coupon-paying Treasury bonds and sell rights to single payments backed by the bonds. These bonds are said to be *stripped* of coupons.

LYONs and TIGRs, No Bears, Oh, My! LYONs and TIGRs, No . . .

Blame it all on Merrill Lynch & Co.

The firm's TIGRs—Treasury investment growth receipts—were successful enough to spawn a slew of imitators. Salomon Brothers Inc. soon followed with CATS, or certificates of accrual on Treasury securities. Now, more than animals are running amok on Wall Street.

How About a Test Drive?

Salomon is selling securities backed by auto loans called CARs, or certificates of automobile receivables. Drexel Burnham Lambert Inc. calls its version of the same thing FASTBACs, or first automotive short-term bonds and certificates.

One type of securities can be bought, depending on the firm, as STARS, or short-term auction-rate stock; DARTS, or Dutch-auction-rate transferable securities; MAPS, market-auction preferred stock; AMPS, auction-market preferred stock; and CAMPS, cumulative auction-market preferred stock.

Shearson Lehman Brothers Inc. recently tagged a floating-rate mortgage-backed security with one of Wall Street's most popular words: FIRSTS, or floating-interest-rate short-term securities.

Merrill Lynch, knowing no boundaries, added COLTS, or continuously offered long-term securities, and OPOSSMS, options to purchase or sell specific mortgage-backed securities. Salomon bolstered its lineup with HOMES, or homeowner-mortgage Euro securities, and CARDs, certificates for amortizing revolving debts, backed by credit-card receivables.

A Salomon spokeswoman gives one explanation for the practice: "Names without acronyms can be tongue-twisting and hard to remember." A Merrill official offers another: "It's one-upmanship."

Some officials say the trend has gotten out of hand. Wesley Jones, head of product development at First Boston Corp., says if an acronym "sounds like an animal, it won't describe what you've got."

ZCCBs and SLOBs

Likewise, by the time a name has been massaged to produce an acronym, it may tell little of the product. For example, Merrill Lynch offers LYONs, or liquid-yield option notes; these are really zero-coupon convertible bonds, but calling them ZCCBs wouldn't sound nearly as good for these companions of TIGRs.

Of course, the uncontrived names of some securities actually form acronyms, but these rarely make useful marketing tools. First Boston, for instance, once underwrote an offering of secured-lease obligation bonds. It used the full name.

They often have colorful names such as CATS (certificates of accrual on Treasury securities, issued by Salomon Brothers) or TIGRs (Treasury investment growth receipts, issued by Merrill Lynch). The single payments are, in essence, zero-coupon bonds collateralized by the original Treasury securities and so are virtually free of default risk (see the accompanying box).

Treasury bills are issued with initial maturities of less than one year. Thus, if a bill with a six-month maturity is issued at a price of $9,600, we would determine the half-year yield to maturity over the bill's life by solving

$$\$9,600 = \$10,000/(1 + r)$$

to find that $r = .0417$, or 4.17 percent per half year. The effective annual rate would be 8.51 percent ($1.0417^2 = 1.0851$).

Recall, however, that bill yields are quoted using the bank discount method, which is not easily comparable to either the APR or the effective yield. You want to understand principles rather than institutional details, so we will consistently cast our discussion in terms of effective interest rates.

What should happen to T-bill prices as time passes? On their maturity dates, bills must sell for $10,000 because the payment of par value is imminent. Before maturity, however, bills should sell at discounts from par, as the present value of the future $10,000 payment is less than $10,000. As time passes, then, if the interest rate remains constant, the bill's price steadily approaches par value. In fact, if the interest rate is constant over the life of the Treasury bill, the bill's price will increase at exactly the rate of interest.

To see this, consider a Treasury bill with eight months until maturity, and suppose the market interest rate is 1 percent per month. The price of the bill today will be $10,000/1.01^8$, or $9,234.83. Next month, with only seven months until maturity, the bill price will be $10,000/1.01^7$, or $9,327.18, a 1 percent increase over its value the previous month. Because the present value of the bill is now discounted for one fewer month, its price has increased by the one-month discount factor.

Figure 12.2 presents the price path of a 10-year zero-coupon bond until its maturity date for an annual market interest rate of 10 percent. The bond prices rise exponentially, not linearly, until its maturity.

Figure 12.2
The price of a 10-year zero-coupon bond over time. Price equals $1,000/(1.10)^t$, where t is time until maturity.

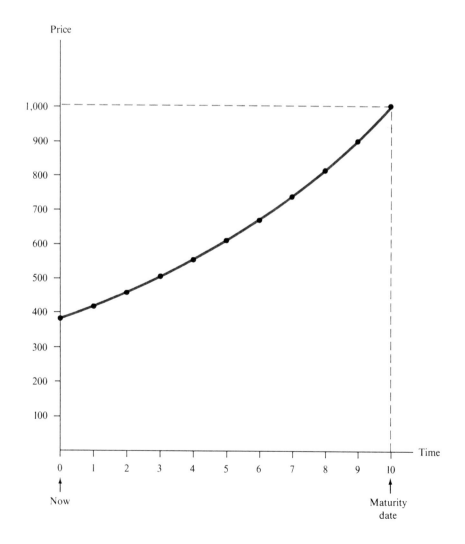

The tax authorities recognize that the "built-in" price appreciation on original issue discount (OID) bonds such as T-bills or other zero-coupon bonds represents an implicit interest payment to the holder of the security. The IRS, therefore, calculates a price appreciation schedule to impute interest income for the portion of the built-in appreciation the investor owes taxes for during the tax year even if the asset is not sold or does not mature until a future year. Any additional gains or losses that arise from changes in market interest rates are treated as capital gains or losses if the OID bond is sold during the tax year.

Coupon Bonds

We can use U.S. Treasury bonds and notes as our prototype default-free coupon bond. Like bills, T-notes and T-bonds pose no default risk. T-note maturities range up to 10 years, while bonds are issued with maturities ranging from 10 to 30 years. Both are issued in denominations of $1,000 or more. Both make semi-annual coupon payments that are set at an initial level that enables the government to sell the securities at or near par value. Aside from their differing maturities at issue date, the only major distinction between T-notes and T-bonds is that in the past, some T-bonds issued by the Treasury were *callable* for a given period, usually during the last five years of the bond's life. The call provision gives the Treasury the right to repurchase the bond at par value anytime during the call period. The Treasury no longer issues callable bonds.

Figure 12.3 is an excerpt from the listing of Treasury issues in *The Wall Street Journal*. The highlighted bond matures in February 2003. Its coupon rate is 10.75 percent. The bid and ask prices are quoted in points plus fractions of 1/32 of a point (the numbers after the colons are the fractions of a point). Although bonds are sold in denominations of $1,000 par value, the prices are quoted as a percent of par value. Therefore, the bid price of the bond is 118:14 = 118 14/32 = 118.4375 percent of par value, or $1,184.375, while the ask price is 118 22/32 percent of par, or $1,186.875.

As we have noted, the reported yield to maturity, 8.26 percent, is calculated by determining the six-month yield and then doubling it, rather than compounding it for two half-year periods. Using this simple interest technique to annualize means the yield is quoted on an APR (annual percentage rate) basis rather than as an effective annual yield. The APR method in this context is also called the bond equivalent yield, which was explained in Chapter 4.

The bonds in the right-most column of Figure 12.3 are stripped U.S. Treasuries, all of which are zero-coupon bonds. Their prices decline steadily as maturity increases.

Figure 12.3 sh   hat the yields on most bonds are fairly similar. Some bonds, however, such as the 3 1/2 Nov 1998 bonds, offer seemingly quite low yields. These bonds, known as *flower bonds,* are special because they may be used to settle federal estate taxes at par value under certain conditions. Because individuals using these bonds for estate tax purposes may sell them to the U.S. government for their full par value, flower bonds sell at close to par value despite their low coupon payments. Flower bonds are no longer issued by the Treasury.

The callable bonds are easily identified in Figure 12.3 because a range of the years in which the bond is callable appears in the maturity date column. Recall that yields on premium bonds (bonds selling above par value) are calculated as the yield to the first call date because those bonds are considered most likely to

Figure 12.3
Listing of Treasury issues.
From *The Wall Street Journal*, March 13, 1991. Reprinted by permission of *THE WALL STREET JOURNAL*, © 1001 Dow Jones & Company, Inc. All Rights Reserved Worldwide.

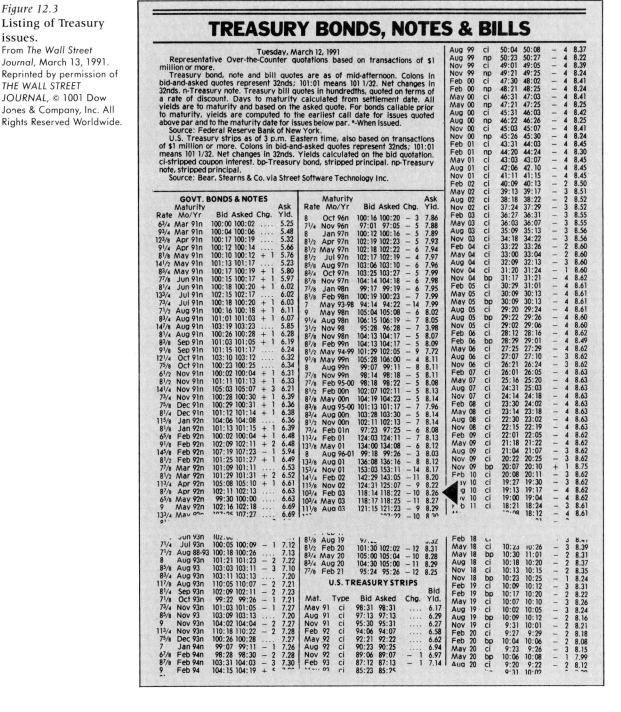

be called, while yields on discount bonds are calculated as the yield to maturity date.

In practice, a bond buyer must pay the ask price for the bond plus any accrued interest. If a bond is purchased between coupon payments, the buyer must pay the seller for the prorated share of the upcoming semiannual coupon. For example, if 40 days have passed since the last coupon payment, and there are 182 days in the semiannual coupon period, the seller is entitled to a payment of accrued interest of 40/182 of the semiannual coupon. The sale, or invoice price, of the bond would equal the stated price plus the accrued interest.

Figure 12.4 illustrates the pattern of bond prices over time. Assume a bond paying annual coupons is issued at par at a coupon rate of 10 percent, and market rates remain at 10 percent. The quoted price of the bond remains at $1,000, while the invoice price follows a ratchet pattern, gradually reaching $1,100 just before a coupon payment and falling back to $1,000 just after the coupon is paid.

This explains why the price of a maturing bond is listed at $1,000 rather than $1,000 plus one coupon payment. A purchaser of an 8 percent coupon bond one day before the bond's maturity would receive $1,040 on the following day and so should be willing to pay a total price of $1,040 for the bond. In fact, $40 of that total payment constitutes the accrued interest for the preceding half-year period, and that is owed to the bond seller. The bond price is quoted net of accrued interest in the financial pages, and thus appears as $1,000.

As we noted earlier, a T-bond will sell at par value when its coupon rate equals the market interest rate. In these circumstances, the investor receives fair compensation for the time value of money in the form of the recurring interest payments. No further capital gain is necessary to provide fair compensation.

If the coupon rate were lower than the market interest rate, the coupon payments alone would not provide investors as high a return as they could earn elsewhere in the market. To receive a fair return on such an investment, then, investors also would need to earn capital gains on their bonds to augment the

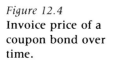

Figure 12.4
Invoice price of a coupon bond over time.

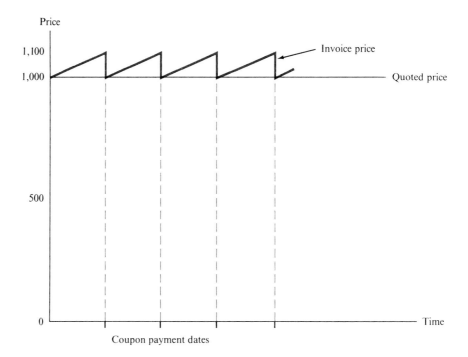

insufficient interest income. The bonds, therefore, would have to sell below par value to provide a "built-in" capital gain on the investment.

To illustrate this point, suppose a bond was issued several years ago when the interest rate was 7 percent. The bond's annual coupon rate was thus set at 7 percent. (We will suppose for simplicity that the bond pays its coupon annually.) Now, with three years left in the bond's life, the interest rate is 8 percent per year. The bond's fair market price is the present value of the remaining annual coupons plus principal repayment. That present value is

$$\$70 \times PA(8\%, 3) + \$1,000 \times PF(8\%, 3) = \$974.23$$

which is less than par value.

In another year, after the next coupon is paid, the bond would sell at

$$\$70 \times PA(8\%, 2) + \$1,000 \times PF(8\%, 2) = \$982.17$$

thereby yielding a capital gain over the year of $7.94. If an investor had purchased the bond at $974.23, the total return over the year would equal the coupon payment plus capital gain, or $70 + $7.94 = $77.94. This represents a rate of return of $77.94/$974.23, or 8 percent, exactly the current rate of return available elsewhere in the market.

Concept Check

Question 3.   What will the bond price be in yet another year, when only one year remains until maturity? What is the rate of return to an investor who purchases the bond at $982.17 and sells it one year hence?

When bond prices are set according to the present value formula, any discount from par value provides an anticipated capital gain that will augment a below-market coupon rate just sufficiently to provide a fair total rate of return. Conversely, if the coupon rate exceeds the market interest rate, then the interest income by itself is greater than that available elsewhere in the market. Investors will bid up the price of these bonds above their par values. As the bonds approach maturity, they will fall in value because fewer of these above-market coupon payments remain. The resulting capital losses offset the large coupon payments so that the bondholder again receives only a fair rate of return.

Question 8 at the end of the chapter asks you to work through the case of the high coupon bond. Figure 12.5 traces out the price paths of high and low coupon bonds (net of accrued interest) as time to maturity approaches. The low coupon bond enjoys capital gains, while the high coupon bond suffers capital losses.

We use these examples to show that each bond offers investors the same total rate of return. Although the capital gain versus income components differ, the price of each bond is set to provide competitive rates, as we should expect in well-functioning capital markets. Security returns all should be comparable on an after-tax risk-adjusted basis. If they are not, investors will try to sell low-return securities, thereby driving down the prices until the total return at the now-lower price is competitive with other securities. Prices should continue to adjust until all securities are fairly priced in that expected returns are appropriate (given necessary risk and tax adjustments).

Figure 12.5
Price paths of coupon bonds.

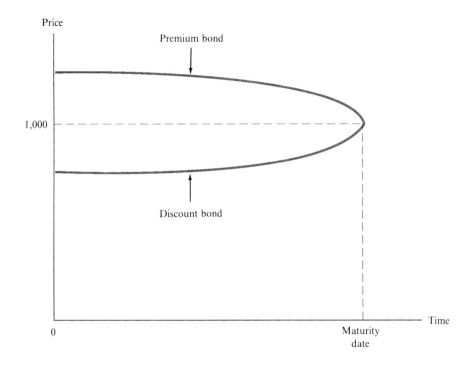

12.3 Corporate Bonds

Like the government, corporations borrow money by issuing bonds. Figure 12.6 is a sample of corporate bond listings in *The Wall Street Journal*. The data presented here differ only slightly from U.S. Treasury bond listings. For example, the IBM 9 3/8 bond pays a coupon rate of 9.375 percent and matures in 2004. Unlike Treasury bonds, corporate bonds trade in increments of 1/8 point. IBM's *current yield* is 9.4 percent, which is simply the annual coupon payment divided by the bond price ($93.75/$992.50). Recall that current yield, unlike yield to maturity, ignores any prospective capital gains or losses based on the bond's price relative to par value. The trading volume column shows that 70 bonds traded on that day. The change from yesterday's closing price is given in the last column. Like government bonds, corporate bonds sell in units of $1,000 par value but are quoted as a percent of par value.

Although the bonds listed in Figure 12.6 trade on a formal exchange, operated by the New York Stock Exchange, most bonds are traded over the counter in a loosely organized network of bond dealers linked by a computer quotation system. (See Chapter 5 for a comparison of exchange versus OTC trading.) In practice, the bond market can be quite "thin," in that there are few investors interested in trading a particular bond at any particular time. Figure 12.6 shows that trading volume of many bonds on the New York exchange is quite low. On any day, it could be difficult to find a buyer or seller for a particular issue, which introduces some "liquidity risk" into the bond market. It may be difficult to sell bond holdings quickly if the need arises.

Bonds issued in the United States today generally are *registered* bonds, meaning the issuing firm keeps records of the owner of the bond and can mail interest

NEW YORK EXCHANGE BONDS

CORPORATION BONDS
Volume, $41,990,000

Bonds	Cur Yld	Vol	Close	Net Chg.
Advst 9s08	cv	14	76	+ 1
AlaP 8⅞s03	9.5	5	93½	+ 1½
AlaP 8¼s03	9.2	8	89⅜	+ ⅜
AlaP 12⅝10	11.9	5	106⅜	+ 1⅛
AlaP 10s18	10.0	5	100	+ 1⅝
AlskAr 6⅞14	cv	10	87½	− ¼
vjAlgl 10¾99f	...	87	39	− ½
vjAlgl 10.4s02f	...	31	26	− ⅜
AlldC zr92	...	15	80	+ ½
AlldC zr2000	...	14	37⅜	...
AlldC zr9	...	5	74¼	+ ¾
AlldC zr99	...	35	42	+ ½
AlldC zr09	...	100	16	− ⅛
Alcoa 9s95	9.1	24	99¼	+ 1⅝
AMAX 14½94	12.8	10	113½	+ ¼
AmBas 14⅞98	16.9	150	88⅛	+ ⅛
vjAmdur 5½93	cv	23	17⅛	+ ⅛
AAirl 4¼92	4.8	15	89⅛	...
AmGnFn zr90s	...	1	93⅝	− 29/32
AmGnFn 12¾94	11.5	8	111	− 6
ATT 3⅞90r	3.9	7	98 27/32	...
ATT 5⅝95	6.5	15	86¼	+ 1⅜
ATT 5½97	6.7	10	81½	+ ¼
ATT 6s00	7.6	35	78½	+ 1
ATT 5⅛01	7.2	2	70⅞	− ⅞
ATT 8¾00	9.0	179	97¾	+ ⅜
ATT 7s01	8.4	135	82⅞	+ ⅜
ATT 7⅛03	8.7	36	82⅛	+ ⅝
ATT 8.80s05	9.2	93	95¼	+ ⅝
ATT 8⅝s07	9.2	28	93⅝	+ ⅜
ATT 8⅝26	9.7	148	89⅛	+ ⅛
vjAmes 10s95f	...	14	31⅛	− 1⅞
vjAmes 7½14f	cv	162	15¼	...
Amoco 6s91	6.3	5	95⅞	+ ⅛
Amoco 9.2s04	9.3	39	99¼	+ 1
Amoco 8⅝16	9.4	20	91⅜	...
AmocoCda 7⅜13	6.3	102	117½	+ 1½
Andarko 5¾12	cv	10	107	+ 1
Anhr 8⅝16	9.8	35	88¼	+ ¼
Anhr 6s92	6.4	10	93⅛	− 1⅜
Anhr 9.20s05	9.2	20	99⅝	+ ⅝
ArizP 10⅝00	10.6	10	100½	+ ¼
Arml 13½94	12.7	5	106	...
Athlne 15⅝91	15.6	25	100¼	...
ARch 10⅜95	9.9	10	104⅜	...
ARch 10⅞[illegible]	[illegible]	9	108⅝	...
ARc[illegible]				⅛
[illegible]ast 11⅛98	11.[illegible]			
ColuG 9s94	9.1	30	[illegible]	...
ColuG 8⅜96	9.0	10	93⅛	+ ⅜
CmlSo 4½91	cv	5	93	+ ⅛
CmwE 8¾05	9.8	6	89	...
CmwE 9⅜04	9.9	22	95	...
CmwE 8⅛07J	9.6	10	84½	+ 1¼
CmwE 8⅛07D	9.5	5	85½	+ 1⅝
CmwE 15⅜00	14.3	5	107¾	+ ½
CmwE 11¾15	10.9	5	107⅝	...
Consec 12½96	13.8	10	90½	+ ⅞
Consec 12¾97	14.1	82	90⅜	− ⅛
ConEd 9⅜00	9.4	1	99¼	− ¾
ConEd 7.9s01	9.0	10	87⅞	− ⅝
ConEd 7¾03	9.0	5	86⅛	+ ⅛
ConEd 8.4s03	9.3	34	90¼	+ ¼
ConEd 9⅛04	9.5	5	95¾	...
ConNG 8¾99	9.1	5	95¾	− 5¼
CnPw 5⅞96	7.3	1	81	+ ¾
CnPw 6⅞98	8.3	5	83	+ ⅞
CnPw 8⅝00	9.7	10	88½	...
CnPw 9¾06	10.1	1	96¼	+ ⅝
CnPw 8⅞07	9.9	4	90	...
vjCtlInf 9s06f	cv	3	[illegible]	⅞

Bonds	Cur Yld	Vol	Close	Net Chg.
CritAc 11⅞14	...	2	101⅛	...
CritAc 13.30s14	13.0	4	102½	− ¼
CritAc 13⅛14	12.9	3	101⅞	...
CritAc 11½15	11.3	2	102	...
CritAc 11¼15	11.0	6	102	+ ⅞
Dana dc5⅞06	cv	75	75	...
DataDes 8½08	cv	1	62	+ 7
Datpnt 8⅞06	cv	30	31	...
DaytH 10¾13	10.5	37	102½	+ ½
DetEd 6.4s98	8.1	1	79¼	+ ¼
DetEd 9s99	9.6	15	94	...
DetEd 9.15s00	9.6	4	95	+ 2
DetEd 8.15s00	9.3	8	87¼	+ ¼
DetEd 8⅛01	9.3	1	87¾	+ 1½
DetEd 7⅜01	9.0	16	81¾	+ ¼
DetEd 10⅝06	10.5	1	101	+ 1
Dow 8⅝08	9.7	64	89	− ¼
duPnt 8.45s04	9.2	8	91⅞	+ ½
duPnt 8½06	9.3	123	91⅝	+ ⅛
duPnt dc6s01	7.9	135	75⅝	+ ⅜
DukeP 7⅜02	8.9	10	83¼	+ ¼
DukeP 8⅛03	9.2	4	88¼	+ 1⅛
DukeP 9½05	9.4	40	101	+ 2
DukeP 8⅛07	9.4	2	86	+ 1¾
DukeP 9⅜08	9.6	22	97¾	...
DukeP 10⅛09	10.0	2	101¾	+ 1¾
ECL 9s89f	...	1	98	...
EKod 8⅝16	10.1	77	85¾	+ ⅜
EmbSuit 10½94	11.1	10	94⅞	− 1⅝
EmbSuit 11s99	11.9	5	92½	+ ⅜
Ens 10s01	cv	37	104¾	+ ¼
EnvSys 6¾11	cv	10	68½	+ ½
Equitc 10s04	cv	10	17	...
Exxon 6s97	7.3	11	82½	...
Exxon 6½98	7.7	35	84	...
Exxon 8¼94	8.5	50	97	+ ¼
FedN zr14s	...	60	11¼	− ⅛
FedN zr19s	...	210	7⅜	− ¼
Fireman 9⅝16	10.1	2	95¼	+ 1⅝
FUnRE 10¼09	cv	26	91¾	− 1¼
FisbM 4¾97	cv	10	36½	+ 1½
FleetFn 8½10	cv	15	108	...
Flemg 6½96	cv	1	92½	− ¼
FlaECs 5s01	7.4	2	67⅛	...
FrdC 7½91	7.7	10	97⅛	− ⅛
FrdC 7½92	7.8	7	96¾	...
FrdC 7½93	7.8	3	95⅝	+ 1⅝
FrdC 7⅞93	8.3	5	95¼	+ ⅛
FrdC 8⅜02	[illegible]		[illegible]	+ ⅜
[illegible]CN 12⅞98	21.5	[illegible]		
IllBel 8¼16	9.4	75	88	+ 1
IlCnt 11¼99	11.5	9	98	− ¼
IllPw 8¼07	10.1	2	81⅝	+ ⅛
IllPw 8⅞08	9.9	4	89⅜	+ 1⅜
IllPw 9⅜16	10.2	40	92	+ ⅜
IndBel 8⅛11	9.2	10	88¾	+ 3⅜
IndBel 10s14	10.0	10	100½	− 1½
IndBel 8s14	9.3	7	86	+ ¼
vjItgRs 13⅛95f	...	234	2⅛	+ ⅛
vjItgRs 10¾96f	...	50	2	...
vjItgRs 12¼98f	...	10	2	...
IBM 9⅜04	9.4	70	99¼	− ⅛
IBM 7⅞04	cv	228	97¾	+ ⅜
IBM 10¼95	9.9	75	103⅜	+ ¼
IBM 9s98	9.0	5	100	− ½
IPap 8.85s95	8.9	15	99¼	+ 1¼
IntRec 9s10	cv	36	75	+ 1⅛
JPInd 7¼13	cv	5	97	...
Jamswy 8s05	cv	8	66¾	− ¼
JCP 9⅝06	9.9	10	97	− 1½
vjJonsLI 6¾94f	...	5	15⅜	+ ⅜
vjJonsLI 6½88f	...	6	16⅛	...

Quotations as of 4 p.m. Eastern Time
Tuesday, May 8, 1990

Volume $42,340,000

	Domestic Tue.	Domestic Mon.	All Issues Tue.	All Issues Mon.
Issues traded	626	588	629	593
Advances	298	255	299	257
Declines	175	208	177	211
Unchanged	153	125	153	125
New highs	5	5	5	5
New lows	29	21	30	21

SALES SINCE JANUARY 1
(000omitted)

1990	1989	1988
$4,012,056	$2,532,136	$2,802,855

Dow Jones Bond Averages

−1989− High	−1989− Low	−1990− High	−1990− Low		−1990− Close	−1990− Chg.	−1990− %Yld	−1989− Close	−1989− Chg.
94.15	87.35	93.04	88.48	20 Bonds	89.11	+0.12	9.91	88.61	+ 0.04
95.26	86.95	94.48	89.23	10 Utilities	89.89	+0.05	9.91	88.50	− 0.01
93.26	87.60	91.60	87.55	10 Industrials	88.33	+0.18	9.91	88.71	+ 0.08

Bonds	Cur Yld	Vol	Close	Net Chg.
vjLTV 11½97f	...	23	15¾	+ ⅝
vjLTV 15s00f	...	5	25⅞	+ 1⅜
LaFrg 7s13	cv	10	98¾	+ 1¼
Leget 6½06	cv	28	100	− ½
Litton flt00	...	1	95¼	...
LoewCp zr04	...	24	37¾	...
vjLomF zr01f	...	2	7⅝	− 1⅝
vjLomF 9s10f	cv	78	24	− 3
vjLomF 7s11f	cv	25	24	− 1¼
vjLomF 10¾93f	...	108	23½	− 3
vjLomF 11⅜95f	...	130	23¼	− 2¾
LomNM 10½93	14.7	5	71¼	− 2¾
LglsLt 12⅝92	12.2	11	103¼	+ 1¼
LglsLt 10⅞99	10.8	13	100¼	+ 1
LglsLt 11⅞15	11.6	22	102¾	+ ½
LglsLt 11.7s93	11.4	50	102½	− 1
LglsLt 11½14	11.5	133	100	+ ½
Loral 7¼10	cv	25	84½	...
Lorilld 6⅝93	7.0	1	95	...
Lorilld 6⅞93	7.5	8	91½	...
LouLE 8½00	cv	20	89	− 1
vjLykes 11s00f				
[illegible]GE 8s2003	9.2			
PGE 7½s04	9.0	20	[illegible]	+ ¾
PGE 8¼08	9.6	25	86¼	+ ⅜
PGE 8½09	9.8	10	87	− ½
PGE 9⅜11	9.9	5	94½	+ ¼
PGE 10⅛12	10.1	100	100	− ½
PcLumb 12s96	14.9	65	80⅜	+ ⅜
PNwT 8⅝10	9.5	11	91	+ ⅞
PNwT 8¾08	9.7	6	90⅜	+ ⅛
PNwT 9s12	9.7	1	93	...
PacTT 8.65s05	9.4	5	92	...
P[illegible] 8¾06	9.4	43	92⅝	+ ⅝
[illegible]s07	9.3	15	84	+ ½
Pa[illegible] 7¼08	9.1	41	80	+ ¾
PacTT 9½11	9.8	21	97⅛	+ ⅛
PacTT 8⅞15	9.7	27	91⅜	+ 1⅞
PacTT 8⅜17	9.6	35	86⅞	+ ⅝
PacTT 9⅝14	9.9	13	97	+ ⅞
PacTT 9s18	9.8	10	91¾	+ ¼
PacTT 9⅝18	9.9	57	96⅞	− ⅛
PacTT 9⅞16	9.9	17	99½	+ ½
PacTT 9¾19	10.0	46	97⅝	...
PAA dc13½03	[illegible]7.4	635	49¼	− ¼

Bonds	Cur Yld	Vol	Close	Net Chg.
PeryDr 8½10	cv	40	75¾	...
Petrie 8s10	cv	11	112	+ 1
PhilEl 9s95	9.3	10	96½	+ ⅜
PhilEl 7½99	8.8	66	85	+ 1¼
PhilEl 8½04	9.6	8	88½	+ 1⅝
PhilEl 11⅝00	11.2	31	104¼	− ⅝
PhilEl 11s00	10.9	5	101⅜	...
PhilEl 9⅛06	9.9	5	91⅞	+ ⅞
PhilEl 14¾05	13.5	21	109⅜	+ ⅜
PhilEl 11¾14	11.0	52	106¾	+ ¾
PhilEl 11s11	11.0	52	100⅜	− ⅛
PhilP 7⅝01	9.2	5	83	...
PhilP 8⅞00	9.6	1	92½	− ½
PhilP 12¼12	11.5	5	106¼	...
PhilP 11¼13	10.9	50	103⅝	...
PhilP 13⅞97	12.0	95	108¾	...
PhilP 14¾00	13.6	89	110	− ⅜
PogoP 8s05	cv	5	74	− ¾
PopeTl 6s12	cv	30	98	+ ½
Potltch 5¾12	cv	15	99¼	+ ¾
PotEl 9½s05	9.5	18	100	− ⅛
[illegible]				1⅜

Figure 12.6 Listing of corporate bonds.

checks to the owner. Registration of bonds is helpful to tax authorities in the enforcement of tax collection. *Bearer bonds* are those traded without any record of ownership. The investor's physical possession of the bond certificate is the only evidence of ownership.

Promised versus Expected Yields

Corporate bonds are subject to potential default of the bond issuer. If the issuer declares bankruptcy, the bondholders will not receive all the payments promised when the bonds were issued. Because of this, we must distinguish between the bond's promised yield to maturity and its expected yield. The promised or stated yield will be realized only if the firm ultimately meets the obligations of the bond issue. Therefore, the stated yield is the maximum possible yield to maturity of the bond. The expected yield to maturity must take into account the possibility of a default.

Default premium
The increment to promised yield that compensates the investor for default risk.

To compensate investors for the possibility of bankruptcy, a corporate bond must offer a **default premium.** The default premium is a differential in promised yield between the corporate bond and an otherwise-identical government bond that is riskless in terms of default. If the corporation remains solvent and pays the investor the promised yield, the investor will realize a higher total yield to maturity than can be realized from the government bond. If, however, the firm goes bankrupt, the corporate bond is likely to provide a lower return than the government bond. The corporate bond has the potential for both better and worse performance than the default-free Treasury bond.

The pattern of default premiums offered on risky bonds is sometimes called the *risk structure of interest rates*. The greater the default risk, the higher the default premium. Such default risk is measured by both Moody's and Standard & Poor's, both of which assign letter grades to the bonds of corporations and municipalities to reflect their assessment of the safety of the bond issue. The top rating is AAA (Standard & Poor's) or Aaa (Moody's). Moody's modifies each rating class with a 1, 2, or 3 suffix (e.g., Aaa1, Aaa2, Aaa3) to provide a finer gradation of ratings. S&P uses a + or − modification.

Investment grade bond   *A bond rated BBB and above by Standard and Poor's, or Baa and above by Moody's.*

Those rated BBB or above (S&P) or Baa and above (Moody's) are considered **investment grade bonds,** while lower-rated bonds are classified as **speculative grade or junk bonds.** Certain regulated institutional investors such as insurance companies have not always been allowed to invest in speculative grade bonds.

Speculative grade or junk bonds   *Bond rated BB or lower by Standard & Poor's, Ba or lower by Moody's, or an unrated bond.*

Figure 12.7 provides the definitions of each bond rating classification. Figure 12.8 shows yields to maturity of bonds of different risk classes since 1953. You can see here clear evidence of the presence of default-risk premiums on promised yields. Although yield spreads vary over time, higher promised yields clearly are associated with lower ratings.

One particular manner in which yield spreads seem to vary over time is related to the business cycle. Yield spreads tend to be wider when the economy is in a recession. Apparently, investors perceive a higher probability of bankruptcy when the economy is faltering, even holding bond ratings constant. They require a commensurately higher default premium. This is sometimes termed a *flight to quality,* meaning investors move their funds into safer bonds unless they can obtain larger premiums on lower-rated securities.

Figure 12.7
Definitions of each
bond rating class.

	Bond Ratings			
	Very High Quality	**High Quality**	**Speculative**	**Very Poor**
Standard & Poor's	AAA AA	A BBB	BB B	CCC D
Moody's	Aaa Aa	A Baa	Ba B	Caa C

At times both Moody's and Standard & Poor's have used adjustments to these ratings.
S&P uses plus and minus signs: A+ is the strongest A rating and A− the weakest.
Moody's uses a 1, 2, or 3 designation—with 1 indicating the strongest.

Moody's	S&P	
Aaa	AAA	Debt rated Aaa and AAA has the highest rating. Capacity to pay interest and principal is extremely strong.
Aa	AA	Debt rated Aa and AA has a very strong capacity to pay interest and repay principal. Together with the highest rating, this group comprises the high-grade bond class.
A	A	Debt rated A has a strong capacity to pay interest and repay principal, although it is somewhat more susceptible to the adverse effects of changes in circumstances and economic conditions than debt in higher rated categories.
Baa	BBB	Debt rated Baa and BBB is regarded as having an adequate capacity to pay interest and repay principal. Whereas it normally exhibits adequate protection parameters, adverse economic conditions or changing circumstances are more likely to lead to a weakened capacity to pay interest and repay principal for debt in this category than in higher rated categories. These bonds are medium grade obligations.
Ba	BB	Debt rated in these categories is regarded, on balance, as predominantly speculative with respect to capacity to pay interest and repay
B	B	
Caa	CCC	principal in accordance with the terms of the obligation. BB and Ba
Ca	CC	indicate the lowest degree of speculation, and CC and Ca the highest degree of speculation. Although such debt will likely have some quality and protective characteristics, these are outweighed by large uncertainties or major risk exposures to adverse conditions. Some issues may be in default.
C	C	This rating is reserved for income bonds on which no interest is being paid.
D	D	Debt rated D is in default, and payment of interest and/or repayment of principal is in arrears.

From Stephen A. Ross and Randolph W. Westerfield, *Corporate Finance* (St. Louis: Times Mirror/Mosby College Publishing, 1988).

Data from various editions of *Standard & Poor's Bond Guide* and *Moody's Bond Guide.*

Junk Bonds

Junk bonds are nothing more than speculative grade (low-rated or unrated) bonds. Before 1977, almost all junk bonds were "fallen angels," that is, bonds issued by firms that originally had investment-grade ratings but that had since been downgraded. In 1977, however, firms began to issue "original-issue junk."

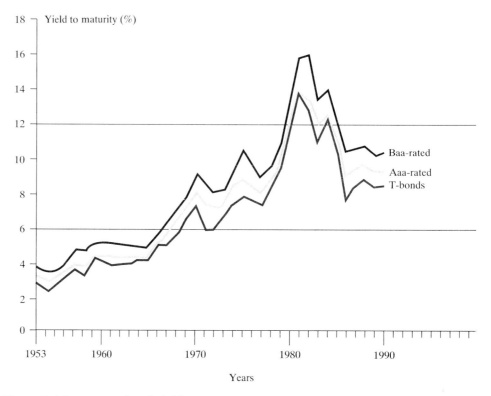

Figure 12.8 Long-term bond yields.

Much of the credit for this innovation is given to Drexel Burnham Lambert, and especially its trader, Michael Milken. Drexel had long enjoyed a niche as a junk bond trader and had established a network of potential investors in junk bonds. Its reasoning for marketing original-issue junk, so-called emerging credits, lay in the belief that default rates on these bonds did not justify the large yield spreads commonly exhibited in the marketplace. Firms not able to muster an investment-grade rating were happy to have Drexel (and other investment bankers) market their bonds directly to the public, as this opened up a new source of financing. Junk issues were a lower-cost financing alternative than borrowing from banks.

Junk bonds gained considerable notoriety in the 1980s when they were used as financing vehicles in leveraged buyouts and hostile takeover attempts. Junk bonds also were extremely popular with investors. Although junk bonds constituted only 3.7 percent of the corporate bond market in 1977, they accounted for 23 percent of the market by 1987 (Perry and Taggart, 1988).

Since then, however, the junk bond market has fallen on hard times. Mergers, acquisitions, and leveraged buyouts financed with junk bonds commonly involved extremely high debt ratios with consequently severe interest-payment burdens. The slowdown in the economy in 1989 raised fears that these interest burdens could not be supported once profit levels fell. Figure 12.9 shows the effect of the debt binge as the economy entered a recession in 1989 and 1990. Interest coverage ratios (the ratio of earnings before interest and taxes to inter-

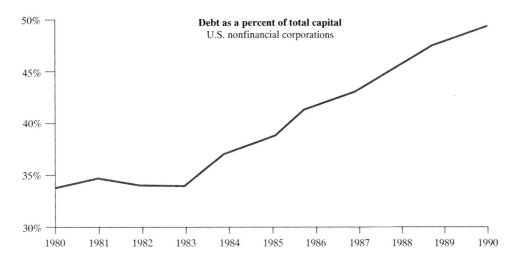

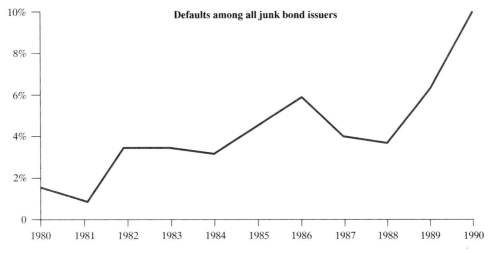

Figure 12.9 Trends in corporate leverage in the 1980s.
From *Fortune*, June 18, 1990, p. 77.

est expense) fell dramatically and default rates rose commensurately. By 1990, the default rate on junk bonds approached 10 percent.

Finally, the legal difficulties of Drexel and Michael Milken in connection with Wall Street's insider trading scandals of the late 1980s tainted the junk bond market. Drexel agreed to pay $650 million in fines and plead guilty to six felony charges to avoid racketeering charges. Milken was indicted on racketeering and security fraud charges, resigned from Drexel, and eventually agreed in a plea bargain to plead guilty to six felony charges and to pay $600 million in fines. Milken was sentenced to 10 years in prison. Moreover, as the junk bond market tumbled in late 1989, Drexel suffered large losses in its own billion-dollar portfolio of junk bonds. In February 1990, Drexel filed for bankruptcy. The speed of its demise is astounding when you consider its 1986 profits, only three years earlier, of about $500 million. The accompanying box presents landmarks in the demise of Drexel.

Junk bond investment performance in this period was extremely poor. While long-term Treasury bonds provided a total return of about 4 percent in the six-month period ending in mid-February 1990 (when Drexel declared bankruptcy), junk bond returns averaged about −9 percent. Prices on junk issues had fallen so severely by this time that junk bond yields exceed Treasury yields by about 7.5 percentage points, the largest margin in history.

Determinants of Bond Safety

Bond rating agencies base their quality ratings largely on an analysis of the level and trend of some of the issuer's financial ratios. The key ratios used to evaluate safety are:

1. *Coverage ratios*—ratios of company earnings to fixed costs. For example, the *times-interest-earned ratio* is the ratio of earnings before interest payments and taxes to interest obligations. The *fixed-charge coverage ratio* adds lease payments and sinking fund payments to interest obligations to arrive at the ratio of earnings to all fixed cash obligations. Low or falling coverage ratios signal possible cash flow difficulties.

2. *Leverage ratio*—debt to equity ratio. A too-high leverage ratio indicates excessive indebtedness, signaling the possibility the firm will be unable to earn enough to satisfy the obligations on its bonds.

3. *Liquidity ratios*. The two common liquidity ratios are the *current ratio* (current assets/current liabilities) and the *quick ratio* (current assets excluding inventories/current liabilities). These ratios measure the firm's ability to pay bills coming due with cash currently being collected.

4. *Profitability ratios*—measures of rates of return on assets or equity. Profitability ratios are indicators of a firm's overall financial health. The *return on assets* (earnings before interest and taxes divided by total assets) is the most popular of these measures. Firms with higher return on assets should be better able to raise money in security markets because they offer prospects for better returns on the firm's investments.

5. *Cash flow to debt ratio*. This is the ratio of total cash flow to outstanding debt.

Standard & Poor's several years ago computed five-year average values of selected ratios for firms in each of the four investment-grade classes, which we

Landmarks in the Drexel-Milken Investigation

May 1986 The SEC and federal prosecutors accuse Drexel's Dennis Levine of making $12.6 million in insider-trading profits while employed at four different firms.

June Mr. Levine pleads guilty to four felony charges and agrees to cooperate with the government. Settling the SEC suit, he agrees to pay $11.6 million.

November Famed arbitrager Ivan F. Boesky agrees to pay a $100 million penalty to settle SEC charges that he traded on inside information supplied by Mr. Levine. Mr. Boesky also agrees to help in the investigation.

February 1987 Mr. Levine is sentenced to two years in prison and is fined $362,000 on the felony counts.

April Mr. Boesky pleads guilty to the criminal charge of conspiring to file false statements with the SEC.

December Mr. Boesky is sentenced to three years in prison.

August 1988 Five officials of an investment partnership called Princeton/Newport LP and Bruce L. Newberg, a former Drexel trader, are indicted on racketeering and other charges.

September The SEC files suit against Drexel, Michael Milken and others, accusing them of insider trading, stock manipulation, fraud and other violations of federal securities laws.

December Drexel agrees to plead guilty to six felony counts relating to securities fraud, settle civil charges brought by the SEC and pay a record $650 million in fines and restitution. Drexel also agrees to cooperate with the government in the case against Mr. Milken.

January 1989 A federal grand jury returns an expanded indictment against the Princeton/Newport defendants.

March Mr. Milken, his brother, Lowell Milken, and Mr. Newberg are charged in a 98-count indictment alleging racketeering and fraud.

April Mr. Milken and his co-defendants enter pleas of innocent. Because of the RICO charges, Mr. Milken must agree to deposit more than $600 million in cash and other assets in accounts to be monitored by the government.

June Judge approves Drexel's SEC settlement that gives federal regulators unprecedented control over Drexel's operations and requires Drexel to exclude Mr. Milken from its business. Mr. Milken resigns from the firm a short time later to start his own financial business, International Capital Access Group.

July The Princeton/Newport defendants are convicted on 63 of 64 counts against them, including racketeering.

November Princeton/Newport defendants are sentenced to prison terms ranging from three to six months.

February 1990 Drexel files for bankruptcy court protection and says it will cease doing business.

April Mr. Milken agrees to plead guilty to six felony counts and pay $600 million in fines and restitution.

From *The Wall Street Journal*, April 23, 1990, p. A4. Reprinted by permission of *THE WALL STREET JOURNAL*, © 1990 Dow Jones & Company, Inc. All Rights Reserved Worldwide.

---

present in Table 12.2. Of course, ratios must be evaluated in the context of industry standards, and analysts differ in the weights they place on particular ratios. Nevertheless, Table 12.2 demonstrates the tendency of ratios to improve along with the firm's rating class.

Bond Indentures

Indenture The document defining the contract between the bond issuer and the bondholder.

A bond is issued with an **indenture,** which is the contract between the issuer and the bondholder. Part of the indenture is a set of restrictions on the firm issuing the bond to protect the rights of the bondholders. Such restrictions include provisions relating to collateral, sinking funds, dividend policy, and allowed further borrowing. The issuing firm agrees to these so-called *protective covenants* in order to market its bonds to investors concerned about the safety of the bond issue.

Table 12.2   *Rating Classes and Median Financial Ratios, 1983–1985*

Rating Category	Fixed-Charge Coverage Ratio	Cash Flow to Long-Term Debt	Return on Capital (%)	Long-Term Debt to Capital (%)
AAA	7.48	3.09	25.60	8.85
AA	4.43	1.18	22.05	18.88
A	2.93	.75	18.03	24.46
BBB	2.30	.46	12.10	31.54
BB	2.04	.27	13.80	42.52
B	1.51	.19	12.01	52.04
CCC	0.75	.15	2.70	69.28

From Standard & Poor's *Debt Rating Guide*, 1986.

Sinking Funds

Bonds call for the repayment of principal at the end of the bond's life. This repayment constitutes a large cash commitment for the issuer. To help ensure the commitment does not create a cash flow crisis, the firm agrees to establish a **sinking fund** to spread the principal repayment burden over several years. The fund may operate in one of two ways:

Sinking fund A bond indenture that calls for the issuer to periodically repurchase some proportion of the outstanding bonds prior to maturity.

1. The firm may repurchase a fraction of the outstanding bonds in the open market each year to reduce the amount to be repaid all at one time in the future.
2. The firm can purchase a fraction of outstanding bonds at a special call price associated with the sinking fund provision. The firm has an option to purchase the bonds at either the market price or the sinking fund price, whichever is lower. To allocate the burden of the sinking fund call fairly among bondholders, the bonds chosen for the call are selected at random based on serial number.[3]

The sinking fund call differs from a conventional bond call in two important ways. First, the firm can repurchase only a limited fraction of the bond issue at the sinking fund call price. At best, some indentures allow firms to use a *doubling option,* which allows repurchase of double the required number of bonds at the sinking fund call price. Second, the sinking fund call price generally is lower than the call price established by other call provisions in the indenture. The sinking fund call price usually is set at the bond's par value.

Although sinking funds ostensibly protect bondholders by making principal repayment more likely, they can hurt the investor. If interest rates fall and bond prices rise, firms will benefit from the sinking fund provision that enables them to repurchase their bonds at below-market prices. In these circumstances, the firm's gain is the bondholder's loss.

One bond issue that does not require a sinking fund is a *serial bond* issue. In a serial bond issue, the firm sells bonds with staggered maturity dates. As bonds mature sequentially, the principal repayment burden for the firm is spread over time just as it is with a sinking fund. Serial bonds do not include call provisions.

---

[3]While it is uncommon, the sinking fund provision also may call for periodic payments to a trustee with the payments invested so that the accumulated sum can be used for retirement of the entire issue at maturity.

Subordination of Further Debt

One of the factors determining bond safety is total outstanding debt of the issuer. If you bought a bond today, you would be understandably distressed to see the firm tripling its outstanding debt tomorrow. Your bond would be of lower quality than it appeared when you bought it. To prevent firms from harming bondholders in this manner, **subordination clauses** restrict the amount of additional borrowing. Additional debt might be required to be subordinated in priority to existing debt; that is, in the event of bankruptcy, *subordinated* or *junior* debtholders will not be paid unless and until the prior senior debt is fully paid off. For this reason, subordination is sometimes called a "me-first rule," meaning the senior (earlier) bondholders are to be paid first in the event of bankruptcy.

Subordination clauses Restrictions on additional firm borrowing that stipulate that senior bondholders will be paid first in the event of bankruptcy.

Dividend Restrictions

Covenants also limit firms in the amount of dividends they are allowed to pay. These limitations protect the bondholders because they force the firm to retain assets rather than paying them out to stockholders. A typical restriction disallows payments of dividends if cumulative dividends paid since the firm's inception exceed cumulative net income plus proceeds from sales of stock.

Collateral

Collateral A specific asset pledged against possible default on a bond.

Some bonds are issued with specific collateral behind them. **Collateral** can take several forms, but it represents a particular asset of the firm that the bondholders receive if the firm defaults on the bond. If the collateral is property, the bond is called a *mortgage bond*. If the collateral takes the form of other securities held by the firm, the bond is a *collateral trust bond*. In the case of equipment, the bond is known as an *equipment obligation bond*. This last form of collateral is used most commonly by firms such as railroads, where the equipment is fairly standard and can be easily sold to another firm should the firm default and the bondholders acquire the collateral.

Debenture A bond not backed by specific collateral.

Because of the specific collateral that backs them, collateralized bonds generally are considered the safest variety of corporate bonds. General **debenture** bonds by contrast do not provide for specific collateral; they are *unsecured* bonds. The bondholder relies solely on the general earning power of the firm for the bond's safety. If the firm defaults, debenture owners become general creditors of the firm. Because they are safer, collateralized bonds generally offer lower yields than general debentures.

Callable and Convertible Bonds

Callable bonds A bond that the issuer may repurchase at a given price in some specified period.

Callable bonds allow the issuer to repurchase the bond at a specified price before maturity. For example, if a company issues a bond with a high coupon rate when market interest rates are high, and then interest rates fall, the firm might like to retire the high-priced debt and issue new bonds at a lower coupon rate, which would reduce interest payments. This is called *refunding*.

In the absence of a call provision, the firm would have to pay fair market prices to buy back the original issue, and those market prices would reflect the increased present value of the bond's scheduled payments. The call provision, which allows the firm to repurchase the bond at the call price, lets the issuer avoid paying the full present value to the bondholders. The firm, rather than the bondholder, benefits from falls in interest rates.

Of course, the firm's benefit is the bondholder's burden. Holders of callable bonds will not reap capital gains from falls in the interest rate if the bonds are called away from them. The firm's option to call the bond at a specified price takes away from the bondholder any upside capital gains potential beyond the call price. To compensate investors for this risk, callable bonds are issued with higher coupons and promised yields to maturity than noncallable bonds.

Figure 12.10 illustrates the risk of call to the bondholder. The red line is the value at various market interest rates of a "straight" (noncallable) bond with par value $1,000, 8 percent coupon, and 30-year time to maturity. The black line is the value of the same bond if it is callable at $1,100. At high interest rates, the risk of call is negligible, and the values of the bonds converge. At lower rates, however, the values of the bonds begin to diverge, with the difference reflecting the value of the firm's option to reclaim the callable bond at $1,100. Finally, at very low interest rates, the bond is called, and its value simply equals $1,100.

The call price of a bond is commonly set at an initial level near par value plus one annual coupon payment. As time passes, the call price falls, gradually approaching par value.

Callable bonds typically come with a period of *call protection,* an initial time during which the bonds are not callable. Such bonds are referred to as *deferred* callable bonds. An implicit form of call protection operates for bonds selling at deep discounts from their call prices. Even if interest rates fall a bit, deep-

Figure 12.10
Bond prices, callable and straight debt.

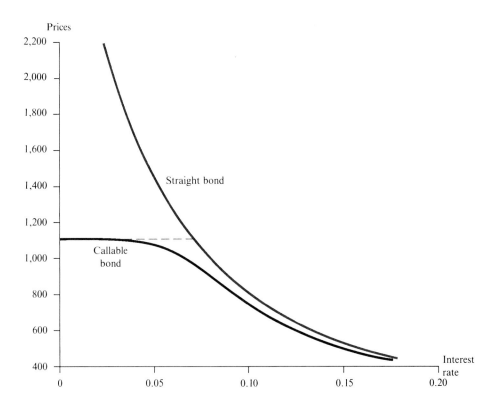

discount bonds still will sell below the call price and thus will not be subject to a call.

Premium bonds that might be selling near their call prices, however, are especially apt to be called if rates fall further. If interest rates fall, a callable premium bond is likely to provide a lower return than could be earned on a discount bond whose potential price appreciation is not limited by the likelihood of a call. Investors in premium bonds often are more interested in the bond's yield to call rather than its yield to maturity as a consequence, for it is possible the bond will be retired at the call date.

Concept Check

Question 4.   The yield to maturity on two 10-year maturity bonds currently is 7 percent. Each bond has a call price of $1,100 and pays coupons once per year. One bond has a coupon rate of 6 percent, the other 8 percent. Assume for simplicity that bonds are called as soon as the present value of their remaining payments exceeds their call price. What will be the capital gain on each bond if the market interest rate falls to 6 percent?

Concept Check

Question 5.   Would you expect a premium bond with the same call price as a discount bond to offer a lower, equal, or higher promised yield to maturity than the discount bond?

Figure 12.11 shows the terms of a callable bond issued by IBM as described in *Moody's Industrial Manual.* The bond was issued in 1979 but was not callable until 1983. After 1983, the call price falls until it eventually reaches par value in 1998. Moreover, the bond was not callable until 1989 if the purpose of the call was to refinance the firm's debt at a lower interest rate. These terms gave bondholders complete call protection until 1983 and partial protection through 1989. *Limited* amounts of the bonds, however, could be called at par value starting in 1985 according to sinking fund provisions.

Put bond *A bond that the holder may choose either to exchange for par value at some date or to extend for a given number of years.*

Convertible bonds *A bond with an option allowing the bondholder to exchange the bond for a specified number of shares of common stock in the firm.*

A relatively new development is the **put bond** or extendable bond. While the callable bond gives the issuer the option to extend or retire the bond at the call date, the put bond gives this option to the bondholder. If the bond's coupon rate exceeds current market yields, for instance, the bondholder will choose to extend the bond's life. If the bond's coupon rate is too low, it will be optimal not to extend; the bondholder instead reclaims principal, which can be invested at current yields.

Convertible bonds give bondholders an option to exchange each convertible bond for a specified number of shares of common stock of the firm. The *conversion ratio* gives the number of shares for which each bond may be exchanged. To see the value of this right, suppose a convertible bond that is issued at par value of $1,000 is convertible into 40 shares of a firm's stock. The current stock price is $20 per share, so the option to convert is not profitable now. Should the stock price later rise to $30, however, each bond may be converted profitably

Figure 12.11
Callable bond issued by IBM.
From Moody's Investors Services, New York. Reprinted by permission.

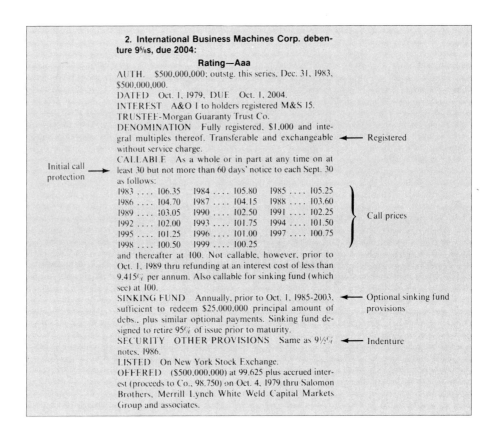

into $1,200 worth of stock. The *market conversion value* is the current value of the shares for which the bonds may be exchanged. At the $20 stock price, for example, the bond's conversion value is $800. The *conversion premium* is the excess of the bond value over its conversion value. If the bond were selling currently for $950, its premium would be $150.

Convertible bonds give their holders the ability to share in price appreciation of the company's stock. Again, this benefit comes at a price; convertible bonds offer lower coupon rates and stated or promised yields to maturity than nonconvertible bonds. At the same time, the actual return on the convertible bond may exceed the stated yield to maturity if the option to convert becomes profitable.

We discuss convertible and callable bonds further in Chapter 18.

Floating-Rate Bonds

Floating-rate bond
A bond whose coupon rate is reset periodically according to a specified market rate.

Floating-rate bonds mimic short-term bonds in the sense that they are designed to minimize the holder's interest rate risk. As with variable-rate mortgages, the interest rate the borrower pays is reset periodically depending on market conditions. For example, the rate paid might be adjusted annually to the current T-bill rate plus 2 percent. At each reset, the bond price should revert to par value, as the bond is now offering the current market yield. The fact that the bond always pays close to current market rates minimizes its price risk. Interest rate risk for floaters is more a function of the length of the reset period than of the bond's maturity.

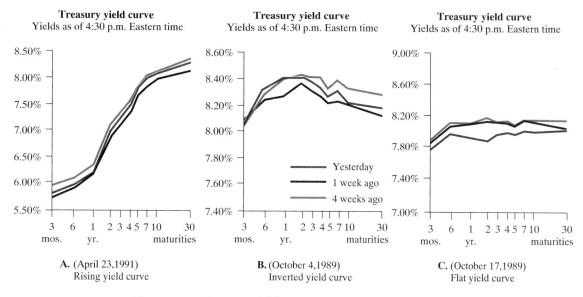

A. (April 23,1991)
Rising yield curve

B. (October 4,1989)
Inverted yield curve

C. (October 17,1989)
Flat yield curve

Figure 12.12 **Treasury yield curves.**
Source: From various editions of *THE WALL STREET JOURNAL*. Reprinted by permission of *THE WALL STREET JOURNAL*. All Rights Reserved Worldwide.

The yield spread on floaters is fixed over the life of the security, which may be many years, in contrast to short-term bonds or money-market instruments. The major risk involved in floaters has to do with changing credit conditions. The financial health of the firm may deteriorate, for example, meaning a greater yield premium is required than is offered by the security. Or the risk premium the market demands for a particular risk category also may change, as in the flight-to-quality phenomenon. If the appropriate yield premium changes, the bond price will not revert to par value on the reset date.

12.4 *The Yield Curve*

Yield curve *A graph of yield to maturity as a function of term to maturity.*

Term structure of interest rates *The relationship between yields to maturity and terms to maturity across bonds.*

Return to Figure 12.3, and you will see that while yields to maturity on bonds of various maturities are reasonably similar, yields do differ. Bonds with shorter maturities generally offer lower yields to maturity than longer-term bonds. The graphical relationship between the yield to maturity and the term to maturity is called the **yield curve.** The relationship is also called the **term structure of interest rates** because it relates yields to maturity to the term (maturity) of each bond. The yield curve is published regularly in *The Wall Street Journal;* three such sets of curves are reproduced in Figure 12.12. The yield curve is said to be "flat" if yields on bonds of different maturities are approximately equal. This is the case in Figure 12.12C. A "rising" yield curve is illustrated in 12.12A where longer-term bonds generally have higher yields. An "inverted" curve is illustrated in 12.12B, where longer term bonds have lower yields (for maturities beyond one year). Rising yield curves are most commonly observed. We will see why momentarily.

Why should bonds of differing maturity offer different yields? The two most plausible possibilities have to do with expectations of future rates and risk premiums. We will consider each of these arguments in turn.

The Expectations Theory

Suppose everyone in the market believes firmly that while the current one-year interest rate is 8 percent, the interest rate on one-year bonds next year will rise to 10 percent. What would this belief imply about the proper yield to maturity on two-year bonds issued today?

Ignoring the effects of compound interest, it is easy to see that an investor who buys the one-year bond and rolls the proceeds into another one-year bond in the following year will earn, on average, 9 percent per year. This value is just the average of the 8 percent earned this year and the 10 percent earned next year.

For investments in two-year bonds to be competitive with the strategy of rolling over one-year bonds, they too must offer an average return of 9 percent over the two-year holding period. Hence, the yield curve will be upward sloping; while one-year bonds offer an 8 percent yield to maturity, two-year bonds must offer a 9 percent yield.

Expectations hypothesis Theory that yields to maturity are determined solely by expectations of future short-term interest rates.

This notion is the essence of the **expectations hypothesis** of the yield curve, which asserts that the slope of the yield curve is attributable to expectations of changes in short-term rates. Relatively high yields on long-term bonds are attributed to expectations of future increases in rates, while relatively low yields on long-term bonds (a downward-sloping or inverted yield curve) are attributed to expectations of falling short-term rates. While many factors can influence expectations of future rates, one of the most important is inflation. Increases in expected inflation, for example, increase expected future nominal interest rates and can result in a rising yield curve. For this reason, some investors view the yield curve as a means to infer the market consensus prognosis for future inflation.

One of the implications of the expectations hypothesis is that expected holding-period returns on bonds of all maturities ought to be about equal. Even if the yield curve is upward sloping (so that two-year bonds offer higher yields to maturity than one-year bonds), this does not necessarily mean investors expect higher rates of return on the two-year bonds. As we've seen, the higher initial yield to maturity on the two-year bond is necessary to compensate investors for the fact that interest rates next year will be even higher. Over the two-year period, and indeed over any holding period, this theory predicts that holding-period returns will be equalized across bonds of all maturities.

Forward rate The inferred short-term rate of interest for a future period that makes the expected total return of a long-term bond equal to that of rolling over short-term bonds.

In fact, advocates of the expectations hypothesis commonly turn the theory on its head to arrive at an estimate of the market's expectation of the future short-term interest rate. For example, if one-year bonds offer an 8 percent return while two-year bonds have a 9 percent yield to maturity, then according to the expectations hypothesis, the market's expectations of next year's one-year rate must be 10 percent. At this level, the sequence of two one-year investments will provide a cumulative return of about 18 percent (8 percent followed by 10 percent) while the two-year investment also will return 18 percent (two years at an average return of 9 percent). The future short rate that makes expected returns to these two investment strategies equal is called the **forward rate** of interest.

The Liquidity Preference Theory

Liquidity preference theory   Theory that investors demand a risk premium on long-term bonds.

We have seen that longer-term bonds are subject to greater interest rate risk than short-term bonds. As a result, investors in long-term bonds might require a risk premium to compensate them for tying up money longer. In this case, the yield curve will be upward sloping even in the absence of any expectations of future increases in rates. The source of the upward slope in the curve is investor demand for higher expected returns on assets perceived as riskier.

This viewpoint is called the **liquidity preference theory** of the term structure. Its name derives from the fact that shorter-term bonds have more "liquidity" than longer-term bonds, in the sense that they offer greater price certainty and trade in more active markets with lower bid-ask spreads. The preference of investors for greater liquidity makes them willing to hold these shorter-term bonds even if they do not offer expected returns as high as those of longer-term bonds.

The risk premium required to hold longer-term bonds is called a **liquidity premium.** It is the extra expected return demanded by investors as compensation for the lower liquidity in longer-term bonds.

Liquidity premium   The extra expected return demanded by investors as compensation for the lower liquidity of longer-term bonds.

Advocates of the liquidity preference theory also note that issuers of bonds seem to prefer to issue long-term bonds. This allows them to lock in an interest rate on their borrowing for long periods. If issuers do prefer to issue long-term bonds, they will be willing to pay higher yields on these issues as a way of shedding interest rate risk. In sum, borrowers demand higher rates on longer-term bonds, and issuers are willing to pay higher rates on longer-term bonds. The conjunction of these two preferences means longer-term bonds typically should offer higher expected rates of return to investors than shorter-term bonds. These expectations will show up in an upward-sloping yield curve.

One application of this principle arises in the practice of *riding the yield curve*. This strategy is used by many investors in the short-term money market. When the yield curve is upward sloping, investors will increase the maturity of their investments, say from one month to two months, in order to earn the liquidity premium. A recent study by Grieves and Marcus (1992) shows that this strategy has proven to be effective.

If the liquidity preference theory is valid, the forward rate of interest is not a good estimate of market expectations of future interest rates. Even if rates are expected to remain unchanged, for example, the yield curve will slope upward because of the liquidity premium. That upward slope would be mistakenly attributed to expectations of rising rates if one were to use the pure expectations hypothesis to interpret the yield curve.

Market Segmentation Theory

Both the liquidity premium and expectations hypothesis theories of the term structure implicitly view bonds of different maturities as some sort of substitute for each other. That is, investors considering holding bonds of one maturity might be attracted instead into holding bonds of another maturity by the prospect of earning a risk premium. In this sense, markets for bonds of all maturities are inextricably linked, and yields on short and long bonds are determined jointly in market equilibrium. Forward rates cannot differ from expected short rates by more than a fair risk premium, or investors will reallocate their fixed-income portfolios to exploit what they perceive as abnormal profit opportunities.

In contrast, the *market segmentation* or *preferred habitat* theory holds that long and short maturity bonds are traded in essentially distinct or segmented markets, each of which finds its own equilibrium independently. The activities of long-term borrowers and lenders determine rates on long-term bonds. Similarly, short-term traders set short rates independently of long-term expectations. The term structure of interest rates, in this view, is determined by the equilibrium rates set in the various maturity markets.

This view of the market is not common today. Both borrowers and lenders seem to compare long and short rates as well as expectations of future rates before deciding whether to borrow or lend long or short term. That they make these comparisons, and are willing to move into a particular maturity if it seems sufficiently profitable to do so, indicates that all-maturity bonds compete with each other for investors' attention, which implies the rate on a bond of any given maturity is determined with an eye toward rates on competing bonds. Markets are not so segmented that an appropriate term premium cannot attract an investor preferring one investment horizon to consider a different one.

A Synthesis

Of course, it is silly to treat theories of the term structure as requiring an either/or choice between expectations and risk premiums. Both of these factors can influence the yield curve, and both should be considered in interpreting the curve.

Figure 12.13 shows two possible yield curves. In Figure 12.13A, rates are expected to rise over time. This fact, together with a liquidity premium, makes the yield curve steeply upward sloping. In Figure 12.13B, rates are expected to fall, which tends to make the yield curve slope downward, even though the liquidity premium lends something of an upward slope. The net effect of these two opposing factors is a "hump-shaped" curve.

These two examples make it clear that the combination of varying expectations and risk or liquidity premiums can result in a wide array of yield-curve profiles. For example, an upward-sloping curve does not in and of itself imply expectations of higher future interest rates because the slope can result either from expectations or from risk premiums. A curve that is more steeply sloped than usual might signal expectations of higher rates, but even this inference is perilous.

Figure 12.14 shows the variability of prices on long-term Treasury bonds over a 10-year period during which interest rate risk fluctuated dramatically. So might we expect risk premiums on various maturity bonds to fluctuate, meaning the slope of the yield curve can vary because of varying risk as well as varying expected future rates.

Figure 12.15 presents yield spreads between short-term and long-term bonds for the 18 years ending in 1990. The figure shows that the yield curve is generally upward sloping in that the longer-term bonds usually offer higher yields to maturity, despite the fact that rates could not have been expected to increase throughout the entire period. This tendency is the empirical basis for the liquidity premium doctrine that at least part of the upward slope in the yield curve must be because of a risk premium.

Figure 12.13
Illustrative yield curves.

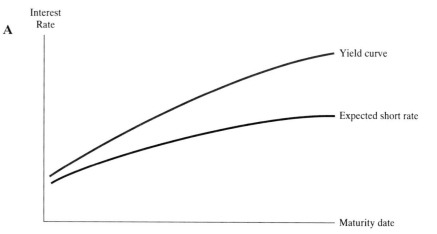

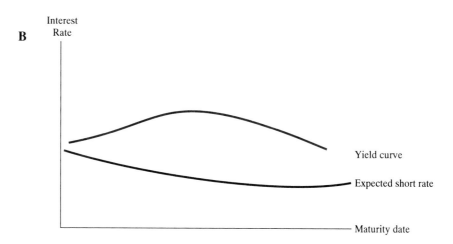

Figure 12.14
Price volatility of a 30-year Treasury bond, January 1977 to December 1987.
Courtesy Fidelity Management Trust Company, Boston.

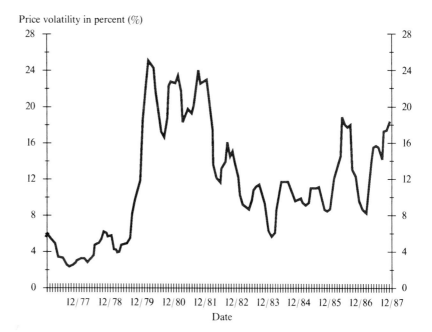

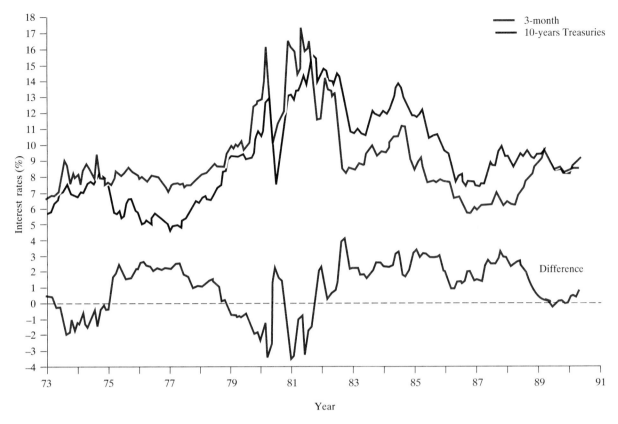

Figure 12.15 **Interest Rates, 1973–1990.**
(3-month versus 10-year Treasuries)

Summary

1.   Fixed-income securities are distinguished by their promise to pay a fixed or specified stream of income to their holders. The coupon bond is a typical fixed-income security.

2.   The yield to maturity is the single interest rate that equates the present value of a security's cash flows to its price. Bond prices and yields are inversely related.

3.   For premium bonds, the coupon rate is greater than the current yield, which is greater than the yield to maturity. The order of these inequalities is reversed for discount bonds.

4.   Treasury bills are U.S. government-issued zero-coupon bonds with original maturities of up to one year. Prices of zero-coupon bonds rise exponentially over time, providing a rate of appreciation equal to the interest rate. The IRS treats this price appreciation as an imputed taxable interest income to the investor.

5.   Treasury notes and bonds have original maturities greater than one year. They are issued at or near par value, with their prices quoted net of accrued interest. T-bonds may be callable during their last five years of life.

6.   When bonds are subject to potential default, the stated yield to maturity is the maximum possible yield to maturity that can be realized by the bondholder. In the event of default, however, that promised yield will not be realized. To compensate bond investors for default risk, bonds must offer default premiums, that is, promised yields in excess of those offered by default-free government securities. If the firm remains healthy, its bonds will provide higher returns than government bonds. Otherwise the returns may be lower.

7. Bond safety is often measured using financial ratio analysis. Bond indentures are another safeguard to protect the claims of bondholders. Common indentures specify sinking fund requirements, collateralization of the loan, dividend restrictions, and subordination of future debt.

8. Callable bonds should offer higher promised yields to maturity to compensate investors for the fact that they will not realize full capital gains should the interest rate fall and the bonds be called away from them at the stipulated call price. Bonds often are issued with a period of call protection. In addition, discount bonds selling significantly below their call price offer implicit call protection.

9. Put bonds give the bondholder rather than the issuer the option to terminate or extend the life of the bond.

10. Convertible bonds may be exchanged, at the bondholder's discretion, for a specified number of shares of stock. Convertible bondholders "pay" for this option by accepting a lower coupon rate on the security.

11. Floating-rate bonds pay a fixed premium over a reference short-term interest rate. Risk is limited because the rate paid is tied to current market conditions.

12. The term structure of interest rates refers to the interest rates for various terms to maturity embedded in the prices of default-free bonds.

13. The expectations hypothesis of the yield curve asserts that differences in yields to maturity in bonds of different maturities are attributable solely to expectations of changes in future short-term rates. The liquidity preference theory asserts that investors prefer shorter-term bonds and will generally accept lower yields on them, giving rise to a usually upward-sloping yield curve.

Key Terms

bond, 326
callable bonds, 347
collateral, 347
convertible bonds, 349
coupon rate, 326
debenture or unsecured
 bond, 347
default premium, 340
expectations
 hypothesis, 352
fixed-income
 securities, 325

floating-rate bonds, 350
forward rate, 352
indenture, 345
investment grade
 bonds, 340
liquidity preference
 theory, 353
liquidity premium, 353
par value, 326
put bond, 349
sinking fund, 346

speculative grade or
 junk bonds, 340
subordination
 clauses, 347
term structure of
 interest rates, 351
yield curve, 351
yield to maturity, 329
zero-coupon bond, 331

Selected Readings

A comprehensive treatment of institutional details and pricing conventions in the fixed-income market can be found in the following reference books:
Stigum, Marcia. *The Money Market*. Homewood, Ill.: Dow Jones-Irwin, 1983.

Stigum, Marcia. *Money Market Calculations: Yields, Break-Evens, and Arbitrage.* Homewood, Ill.: Dow Jones-Irwin, 1981.

Surveys of fixed-income instruments and investment characteristics are contained in:
Stigum, Marcia, and Frank J. Fabozzi. *Bond and Money Market Instruments.* Homewood, Ill.: Dow Jones-Irwin, 1987.
Fabozzi, Frank J., and Irving M. Pollack. *The Handbook of Fixed Income Securities.* Homewood, Ill.: Dow Jones-Irwin, 1987.

A classic presentation of yield curve analytics is contained in:
Homer, Sidney, and Martin Liebowitz. *Inside the Yield Book: New Tools for Bond Market Strategy.* Englewood Cliffs, N.J.: Prentice Hall, 1972.

Problem Sets

1. Which security has a higher *effective* annual interest rate?
   a. A three-month T-bill selling at $97,645.
   b. A coupon bond selling at par and paying a 10 percent coupon semiannually.

2. Treasury bonds paying an 8 percent coupon rate with *semiannual* payments currently sell at par value. What coupon rate would they have to pay in order to sell at par if they paid their coupons *annually*?

3. Two bonds have identical times to maturity and coupon rates. One is callable at 105, the other at 110. Which should have the higher yield to maturity? Why?

4. Consider a bond with a 10 percent coupon and with yield to maturity = 8 percent. If the bond's YTM remains constant, then in one year, will the bond price be higher, lower, or unchanged? Why?

5. Under the **expectations hypothesis,** if the yield curve is upward sloping, the market must expect an increase in short-term interest rates. True/false/uncertain? Why?

6. Under the **liquidity preference theory,** if inflation is expected to be falling over the next few years, long-term interest rates will be higher than short-term rates. True/false/uncertain? Why?

7. The yield curve is upward sloping. Can you conclude that investors expect short-term interest rates to rise? Why or why not?

8. Consider a bond paying a coupon rate of 10 percent per year semiannually when the market interest rate is only 4 percent per half year. The bond has three years until maturity.
   a. Find the bond's price today and six months from now after the next coupon is paid.
   b. What is the total rate of return on the bond?

9. Assume you have a one-year investment horizon and are trying to choose among three bonds. All have the same degree of default risk and mature in 10 years. The first is a zero-coupon bond that pays $1,000 at maturity. The second has an 8 percent coupon rate and pays the $80 coupon once per year. The third has a 10 percent coupon rate and pays the $100 coupon once per year.
   a. If all three bonds are now priced to yield 8 percent to maturity, what are their prices?
   b. If you expect their yields to maturity to be 8 percent at the beginning of next year, what will their prices be then? What is your holding-period return on each bond?

 10. Assume two firms PG and CLX were concurrently to undertake private debt placements with the following contractual details:

	PG	**CLX**
Issue size	$1 billion	$100 million
Issue price	100	100
Maturity	1993*	2003
Coupon	10%	11%
Collateral	First mortgage	Unsecured
First call date	1998	1995
Call price	111	106
Sinking fund—beginning	nil	1993
—amount	nil	$5 million/year

*Extendable at the option of the holder for an additional 10 years (to 2003) with no change in coupon rate.

Ignoring credit quality, identify four features of these issues that might account for the lower coupon on the PG debt. Explain.

A large forest products manufacturer has outstanding two Baa-rated, $150 million par amount, intermediate-term debt issues:

	10.10% Notes	**Floating-Rate Notes**
Maturity	1995	1992
Issue date	6-12-85	9-27-84
Callable (beginning on)	6-15-91	10-01-89
Callable at	100	100
Sinking fund	None	None
Current coupon	10.10%	9.9%
Coupon changes	Fixed	Every 6 months
Rate adjusts to	—	1% above 6-month T-bill rate
Range since issued	—	12.9% - 8.3%
Current price	73 3/8	97
Current yield	13.77%	10.3%
Yield to maturity	15.87%	—
Price range since issue	100–72	102–93

Given these data:

a. State the minimum coupon rate of interest at which the firm could sell a fixed-rate issue at par due in 1995. Assume the same indenture provisions as the 10.10 percent notes, and disregard any tax considerations.

b. Give two reasons why the floating-rate notes are not selling at par (offering price).

c. State and justify whether the risk of call is high, moderate, or low for the fixed-rate issue.

d. Assuming a decline in interest rates is anticipated, identify and justify which issue would be most appropriate for an actively managed bond portfolio where total return is the primary objective.

e. Explain why yield to maturity is not valid for the floating-rate note.

12. You have the following information about a convertible bond issue:

Burroughs Corp.
7¼% Due 8/1/2010

Agency rating (Moody's/S&P)	A3/A−
Conversion ratio	12.882
Market price of convertible	$102.00
Market price of common stock	$ 66.00
Dividend per share—common	$ 2.60
Call price (first call—8/1/1990)	$106.00
Estimated floor price	$ 66.50

Using this information, calculate the following values and show calculations.
a. Market conversion value.
b. Conversion premium per common share.
c. Current yield—convertible.
d. Dividend yield—common.

13. As the portfolio manager for a large pension fund, you are offered the following bonds:

	Coupon	Maturity	Price	Call Price	Yield to Maturity
Edgar Corp. (new issue)	14.00%	2002	$101 3/4	$114	13.75%
Edgar Corp. (new issue)	6.00	2002	48 1/8	103	13.60

Assuming you expect a decline in interest rates over the next three years, identify which of the bonds you would select. Justify your answer.

14. The yield to maturity on one-year zero-coupon bonds is 8 percent. The yield to maturity on two-year zero-coupon bonds is 9 percent.
a. What is the forward rate of interest for the second year?
b. If you believe in the expectations hypothesis, what is your best guess as to the expected value of the short-term interest rate next year?
c. If you believe in the liquidity preference theory, is your best guess as to next year's short-term interest rate higher or lower than in (*b*)?

15. The multiple-choice problems following are based on questions that appeared in past CFA examinations.
a. Which bond probably has the highest credit quality?
   (1) Sumter, South Carolina, Water and Sewer Revenue Bond.
   (2) Riley County, Kansas, General Obligations Bond.
   (3) University of Kansas Medical Center Refunding Revenue Bonds (insured by American Municipal Bond Assurance Corporation).
   (4) Euless, Texas, General Obligation Bond (refunded and secured by the U.S. government in escrow to maturity).
b. The spread between Treasury and BAA corporate bond yields widens when:
   (1) Interest rates are low.
   (2) There is economic uncertainty.
   (3) There is a "flight from quality."
   (4) All of the above.

c. The market risk of an AAA-rated preferred stock relative to an AAA-rated bond is:
   (1) Lower.
   (2) Higher.
   (3) Equal.
   (4) Unknown.

d. A bond with a call feature:
   (1) Is attractive because the immediate receipt of principal plus premium produces a high return.
   (2) Is more apt to be called when interest rates are high, because the interest saving will be greater.
   (3) Will usually have a higher yield than a similar noncallable bond.
   (4) None of the above.

e. The yield to maturity on a bond is:
   (1) Below the coupon rate when the bond sells at a discount, and above the coupon rate when the bond sells at a premium.
   (2) The discount rate that will set the present value of the payments equal to the bond price.
   (3) The current yield plus the average annual capital gain rate.
   (4) Based on the assumption that any payments received are reinvested at the coupon rate.

f. A particular bond has a yield to maturity on an APR basis of 12.00 percent but makes equal quarterly payments. What is the effective annual yield to maturity?
   (1) 11.45 percent.
   (2) 12.00 percent.
   (3) 12.55 percent.
   (4) 37.35 percent.

g. In which *one* of the following cases is the bond selling at a discount?
   (1) Coupon rate is greater than current yield, which is greater than yield to maturity.
   (2) Coupon rate, current yield, and yield to maturity are all the same.
   (3) Coupon rate is less than current yield, which is less than yield to maturity.
   (4) Coupon rate is less than current yield, which is greater than yield to maturity.

h. Consider a five-year bond with a 10 percent coupon that has a present yield to maturity of 8 percent. If interest rates remain constant, one year from now the price of this bond will be:
   (1) Higher.
   (2) Lower.
   (3) The same.
   (4) Par.

i. A revenue bond is distinguished from a general obligation bond in that revenue bonds:
   (1) Are issued by counties, special districts, cities, towns, and state-controlled authorities, whereas general obligation bonds are only issued by the states themselves.
   (2) Are typically secured by limited taxing power, whereas general obligation bonds are secured by unlimited taxing power.
   (3) Are issued to finance specific projects and are secured by the revenues of the project being financed.
   (4) Have first claim to any revenue increase of the tax authority issuing the bonds.

   j. Serial obligation bonds differ from *most* other bonds because:
     (1) They are secured by the assets and taxing power of the issuer.
     (2) Their par value is usually well below $1,000.
     (3) Their term to maturity is usually very long (30 years or more).
     (4) They possess multiple maturity dates.

   k. Which *one* of the following is *not* an advantage of convertible bonds for the investor?
     (1) The yield on the convertible will typically be higher than the yield on the underlying common stock.
     (2) The convertible bond will likely participate in a major upward move in the price of the underlying common stock.
     (3) Convertible bonds are typically secured by specific assets of the issuing company.
     (4) Investors normally may convert to the underlying common stock.

   l. The call feature of a bond means the:
     (1) Investor can call for payment on demand.
     (2) Investor can only call if the firm defaults an interest payment.
     (3) Issuer can call the bond issue before the maturity date.
     (4) Issuer can call the issue during the first three years.

   m. The annual interest paid on a bond relative to its prevailing market price is called its:
     (1) Promised yield.
     (2) Yield to maturity.
     (3) Coupon rate.
     (4) Current yield.

   n. Which of the following statements is *true*?
     (1) The expectations hypothesis indicates a flat yield curve if anticipated future short-term rates exceed current short-term rates.
     (2) The basic conclusion of the expectations hypothesis is that the long-term rate is equal to the anticipated short-term rate.
     (3) The liquidity hypothesis indicates that, all other things being equal, longer maturities will have lower yields.
     (4) The segmentation hypothesis contends that borrowers and lenders are constrained to particular segments of the yield curve.

   o. Which theory explains the shape of the yield curve by considering the relative demands for various maturities?
     (1) Relative strength theory.
     (2) Segmentation theory.
     (3) Unbiased expectations theory.
     (4) Liquidity premium theory.

Chapter

13

Managing Fixed-Income Investments

In this chapter, we turn to various strategies that fixed-income portfolio managers can pursue, making a distinction between passive and active strategies. A *passive investment strategy* takes market prices of securities as fairly set. Rather than attempting to beat the market by exploiting superior information or insight, passive managers act to maintain an appropriate risk-return balance given market opportunities. One special case of passive management is an immunization strategy that attempts to insulate the portfolio from interest rate risk.

An *active investment strategy* attempts to achieve returns more than commensurate with risk borne. In the context of fixed-income management, this style of management can take two forms. Active managers either use interest rate forecasts to predict movements in the entire fixed-income market, or they employ some form of intramarket analysis to identify particular sectors of the fixed-income market (or particular bonds) that are relatively mispriced.

We start our discussion with an analysis of the sensitivity of bond prices to interest rate fluctuations. The concept of duration, which measures interest rate sensitivity, is basic to formulating both active and passive fixed-income strategies. We then turn to passive strategies and show how duration matching strategies can be used to immunize the holding-period return of a fixed-income portfolio from interest rate risk. Finally, we explore a variety of active strategies, including intramarket analysis, interest rate forecasting, and interest rate swaps. After studying this chapter you should be able to:

- Analyze the features of a bond that affect the sensitivity of its price to interest rates.
- Compute the duration of bonds.

- Formulate fixed-income immunization strategies for various investment horizons.
- Analyze the choices to be made in an actively managed fixed-income portfolio.
- Determine how swaps can be used to mitigate interest rate risk.

13.1   Interest Rate Risk

You know already there is an inverse relationship between bond prices and yields and that interest rates can fluctuate substantially. As the box illustrates, bond volatility exceeded stock volatility for much of the 1980s. As interest rates rise and fall, bondholders experience capital losses and gains. It is these gains or losses that make fixed-income investments risky, even if the coupon and principal payments are guaranteed as in the case of Treasury obligations.

Why do bond prices respond to interest rate fluctuations? In a competitive market, all securities must offer investors fair expected rates of return. If a bond is issued with an 8 percent coupon when competitive yields are 8 percent, then it will sell at par value. If the market rate rises to 9 percent, however, who would purchase an 8 percent coupon bond at par value? The bond price must fall until its expected return increases to the competitive level of 9 percent. Conversely, if the market rate falls to 7 percent, the 8 percent coupon on the bond is attractive compared to yields on alternative investments. Investors eager for that return would respond by bidding the bond price above its par value until the total rate of return falls to the market rate.

Interest Rate Sensitivity

It is easy to confirm with numerical examples that long-term bond prices generally are more sensitive to interest rate movements than those of short-term bonds. Consider Table 13.1, which gives bond prices for 8 percent annual coupon bonds at different yields to maturity and times to maturity. (For simplicity, we assume coupons are paid once a year rather than semiannually.)

The shortest-term bond falls in value by less than 1 percent when the interest rate increases from 8 percent to 9 percent. The 10-year bond falls by 6.4 percent and the 20-year bond by more than 9 percent. Longer-term bonds are more

Table 13.1   *Prices of 8% Annual Coupon Bond*

Bond's Yield to Maturity	T = 1 Year	T = 10 Years	T = 20 Years
8%	1,000	1,000	1,000
9%	990.83	935.82	908.71
Percent change in price*	−0.92%	−6.42%	−9.13%

*Equals value of bond at a 9% yield to maturity minus value of bond at (the original) 8% yield, divided by the value at 8% yield.

'Boring' Bonds?
They've Been More Volatile Than Stocks

During the 1980s, the corporate bond market has been more volatile than the stock market. The fluctuation in bonds increased sharply after October 1979, when the Federal Reserve adopted a policy allowing wider moves in short-term interest rates. Since then, returns in the bond market generally have varied more than in the stock market, according to the volatility indexes compiled by Shearson Lehman Economics. The highest peak shows a period when bonds were seven times as volatile as stocks. Bonds settled down considerably in late 1986, and stocks have fluctuated more since last October. But, as fears about the dollar's decline and accelerating inflation permeate the fixed-income markets, the volatility of bonds is picking up again.

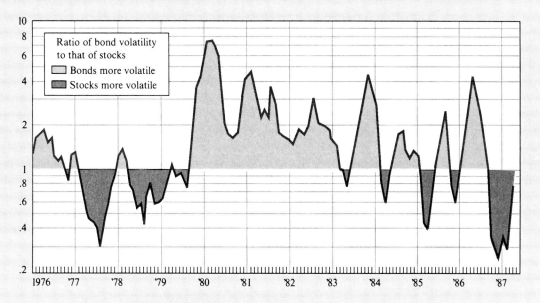

Note: Bond volatility index based on daily yields of triple-A, 20-year corporate bonds and stock volatility index based on daily changes in total return (the change in price and reinvestment of dividends) of the S&P 500-stock index; both are averaged monthly.
Source: Shearson Lehman Brothers Inc.
From *The Wall Street Journal*, May 15, 1987. Reprinted by permission of *THE WALL STREET JOURNAL*. © 1987 Dow Jones & Company, Inc. All Rights Reserved Worldwide.

sensitive to interest rate increases because higher interest rates have a greater impact on more distant future payments. The one-year bond, for example, is so close to maturity that the present value of the remaining payments is hardly affected by the increase in the interest rate. As payments become more and more distant, however, the effect of discounting at a higher rate becomes progressively more telling, which means prices are affected much more by the increase in the interest rate.

Let us now look at a similar example using a zero-coupon bond rather than the 8 percent coupon bond. The results are shown in Table 13.2.

Table 13.2 *Prices of Zero-Coupon Bond*

Bond's Yield to Maturity	T = 1 Year	T = 10 Years	T = 20 Years
8%	925.93	463.19	214.55
9%	917.43	422.41	178.43
Percent change in price*	−0.92%	−8.80%	−16.84%

*Equals value of bond at a 9% yield to maturity minus value of bond at (the original) 8% yield, divided by the value at 8% yield.

For both maturities beyond one year, there is more of a decrease in the price of the zero-coupon bond attributable to the increase in the interest rate than in the case of the 8 percent coupon bond. Given that long-term bonds are more sensitive to interest rate movements than short-term bonds, this observation suggests that in some sense a zero-coupon bond represents a longer-term investment than an equal-time-to-maturity coupon bond. In fact, this insight about effective maturity is a useful one that we can make mathematically precise.

For now let's note simply that the times to maturity of the two bonds in this example are not perfect measures of the long- or short-term nature of the bonds. The 8 percent bond makes many coupon payments, most of which come years before the bond's maturity date. Each payment may be considered to have its own "maturity date," which suggests that the *effective* maturity of the bond should be measured as some sort of average of the maturities of all the cash flows paid out by the bond. The zero-coupon bond by contrast makes only one payment at maturity. Its time to maturity is a well-defined concept.

Duration

To deal with the concept of the "maturity" of a bond that makes many payments, we need a measure of the average maturity of the bond's promised cash flows to serve as a summary statistic of the effective maturity of the bond. This measure should also give us some information on the sensitivity of a bond to interest rate changes because we have noted that price sensitivity tends to increase with time to maturity.

Duration A measure of the effective maturity of a bond, defined as the weighted average of the times until each payment, with weights proportional to the present value of the payment.

Frederick Macaulay (1938) termed this effective maturity concept the **duration** of the bond; he suggested that duration be computed as the weighted average of the times to each coupon or principal payment made by the bond. He recommended further that the weight applied to each time to payment be related to the "importance" of that payment to the value of the bond, specifically, that the weight for each payment time be the proportion of the total value of the bond accounted for by that payment. This proportion is just the present value of the payment divided by the bond price. Macaulay's duration formula for a security providing its owner cash flows at times 1,2,3, . . .,T is given by

$$D = w_1 + 2w_2 + 3w_3 + 4w_4 + \ldots + Tw_T$$

$$\begin{array}{cc} \text{time until} & \text{weight} & \text{time until} & \text{weight of} \\ \text{2nd cash} & \text{of 2nd} & \text{4th CF} & \text{4th CF} \\ \text{flow} & \text{CF} \end{array}$$

(13.1)

Table 13.3 *Calculating the Duration of Two Bonds*

	(1) Time until Payment (In years)	(2) Payment	(3) Payment Discounted at 10 Percent (YTM)	(4) Weight*	(5) Column (1) Times Column (4)
A. 8% bond	1	$ 80	$ 72.727	.0765	.0765
	2	80	66.116	.0690	.1392
	3	1,080	811.420	.8539	2.5617
Sum:			$950.263	1.0000	2.7774
B. Zero-coupon bond	1–2	$ 0	$ 0	0	0
	3	1,000	751.31	1.0	3
Sum:			$751.31	1.0	3

*Weight = Present value of each payment [column (3)] divided by the bond price: $950.26 for bond A and $751.31 for bond B.

where

D is the security's duration.
T is the time until maturity.
y is the bond's yield to maturity.
w_t is the weight applied to the time until payment t, and equals the present value of that cash flow (coupon and/or principal payment) received by the bondholder divided by the total value of the bond.

An analytic way to write the weight applied to each time until payment is

$$w_t = \frac{\text{PV}(\text{CF}_t)}{\text{Price}} = \frac{\text{CF}_t/(1 + y)^t}{\text{Price}}$$

These weights sum to exactly 1.0 because the sum of the cash flows discounted at the yield to maturity equals the bond price.

An example of how to apply Equation 13.1 appears in Table 13.3, where we derive the durations of an 8 percent coupon and zero-coupon bond each with three years to maturity. We assume that the yield to maturity on each bond is 10 percent.

The numbers in column (5) are the products of time to payment and payment weight. Each of these products corresponds to one of the terms in Equation 13.1. According to that equation, we can calculate the duration of each bond by adding the numbers in column (5). The duration of the zero-coupon bond is exactly equal to its time to maturity, three years. This makes sense for, with only one payment, the average time until payment must be the bond's maturity. The three-year coupon bond in contrast has a shorter duration of 2.7774 years.

Duration is a key concept in fixed-income portfolio management for at least three reasons. First, it is a simple summary statistic of the effective average maturity of the portfolio. Second, it turns out to be an essential tool in immunizing portfolios from interest rate risk. We will explore this application in our discussion of passive bond management. Third, duration is a measure of the interest rate sensitivity of a bond portfolio, which we explore here.

We have already noted that long-term bonds are more sensitive to interest rate movements than short-term bonds. The duration measure enables us to quantify this relationship. It turns out that, when interest rates change, the percentage change in a bond's price is proportional to its duration. Specifically, the proportional change in a bond's price can be related to the change in its yield to maturity, *y,* according to the rule:

$$\frac{\Delta P}{P} = -D \times \left[\frac{\Delta(1 + y)}{1 + y} \right] \qquad (13.2)$$

The proportional price change equals the proportional change in (1 plus the bond's yield) times the bond's duration. Therefore, bond price volatility is proportional to the bond's duration, and duration becomes a natural measure of interest rate exposure.[1] This relationship is key to interest rate risk management.

Practitioners commonly use Equation 13.2 in a slightly different form. They define "modified duration" as $D^* = D/(1 + y)$ and rewrite 13.2 as

$$\Delta P/P = -D^* \Delta y \qquad (13.2')$$

The percentage change in bond price is just the product of modified duration and the change in the bond's yield to maturity.

Example: Bond A has maturity of three years, a coupon rate of 8 percent paid annually, and a yield to maturity of 9 percent. Its price is $974.69, and its duration is 2.78 years. Bond B has maturity of 30 years, a coupon rate of 8 percent, and a yield to maturity of 9 percent. Its price is $897.26, and its duration is 11.37 years. What will happen to the price of each bond if market yields increase to 9.1 percent?

Solution: The interest rate has increased by 0.1 percentage points, which in decimal form, means that $\Delta y = .001$. The modified duration of bond A is $D^* = 2.78/1.09 = 2.55$ years. Therefore, Equation 13.2' implies that the fractional change in the bond's price will be $\Delta P/P = -2.55 \times .001 = -.00255$. Therefore, the predicted fall in price is 0.255 percent of the original price, or $.00255 \times \$974.69 = \$2.485$. Similarly, bond B has a modified duration, $D^* = 11.37/1.09 = 10.43$ years. Therefore, $\Delta P/P = -10.43 \times .001 = -.01043$, and the predicted fall in price is $.01043 \times 897.26 = \$9.358$.

The percentage change in the bond price is proportional to modified duration, making modified duration a natural measure of the bond's exposure to interest rate volatility.

To confirm the relationship between duration and the sensitivity of bond price to interest rate changes, let's compare the price sensitivity of the three-year coupon bond in Table 13.3, which has a duration of 2.7774 years, to the sensitivity of a zero-coupon bond with maturity and duration of 2.7774 years. Both should have equal interest rate exposure if duration is a useful measure of price sensitivity.

The three-year bond sells for $950.263 at the initial interest rate of 10 percent. If the bond's yield increases by 1 basis point (1/100 of a percent) to 10.01 percent, its price will fall to $950.0231, a percentage decline of .0252 percent. The zero-coupon bond has a maturity of 2.7774 years. At the initial interest rate of 10 percent, it sells at a price of $767.425 ($1,000/1.10^{2.7774}$). Its price falls to $767.2313 ($1000/1.1001^{2.7774}$) when the interest rate increases, for an identical

---

[1]Actually, Equation 13.2 is only approximately valid for large changes in the bond's yield. The approximation becomes exact as one considers smaller, or localized, changes in yields.

.0252 percent capital loss. We conclude, therefore, that equal-duration assets are equally sensitive to interest rate movements.

Incidentally, this example confirms the validity of Equation 13.2. The equation predicts the proportional price change of the two bonds should have been $-2.7774 \times .0001/1.10 = .000252$, or .0252 percent, just as we found from direct computation.

Concept Check

> **Question 1.**
> *a.* Calculate as in Table 13.3 the price and duration of a two-year maturity, 9 percent coupon bond when the market interest rate is 10 percent.
> *b.* Now suppose the interest rate increases to 10.05 percent. Calculate the new value of the bond, and the percentage change in the bond's price.
> *c.* Calculate the percentage change in the bond's price predicted by the duration formula in Equation 13.2 or 13.2′. Compare this value to your answer for (*b*).

The sensitivity of a bond's price to changes in market interest rates is influenced by three key factors: time to maturity, coupon rate, and yield to maturity. These determinants of price sensitivity are important to fixed-income portfolio management. Therefore, we summarize some of the important relationships in the following five rules. These rules are also illustrated in Figure 13.1, which contains plots of durations of bonds of various coupon rates, yields to maturity, and times to maturity.

We have already established:

Rule 1: The duration of a zero-coupon bond equals its time to maturity.

We have also seen that the three-year coupon bond has a lower duration than the three-year zero because coupons early in the bond's life lower the bond's weighted average time until payments. This illustrates another general property:

Rule 2: Holding time to maturity and yield to maturity constant, a bond's duration and interest rate sensitivity are higher when the coupon rate is lower.

This property is attributable to the impact of early coupons on the average maturity of a bond's payments. The lower these coupons, the less weight these early payments have on the weighted average maturity of all the bond's payments. Compare the plots in Figure 13.1 of the durations of the 3 percent coupon and 15 percent coupon bonds, each with identical yields of 15 percent. The plot of the duration of the 15 percent coupon bond lies below the corresponding plot for the 3 percent coupon bond.

Rule 3: Holding the coupon rate constant, a bond's duration and interest rate sensitivity generally increase with time to maturity. Duration always increases with maturity for bonds selling at par or at a premium to par.

This property of duration is fairly intuitive. What is surprising is that duration need not always increase with time to maturity. For some deep discount bonds, such as the 3 percent coupon bond selling to yield 15 percent in Figure 13.1, duration may eventually fall with increases in maturity. For virtually all traded bonds, however, it is safe to assume that duration increases with maturity.

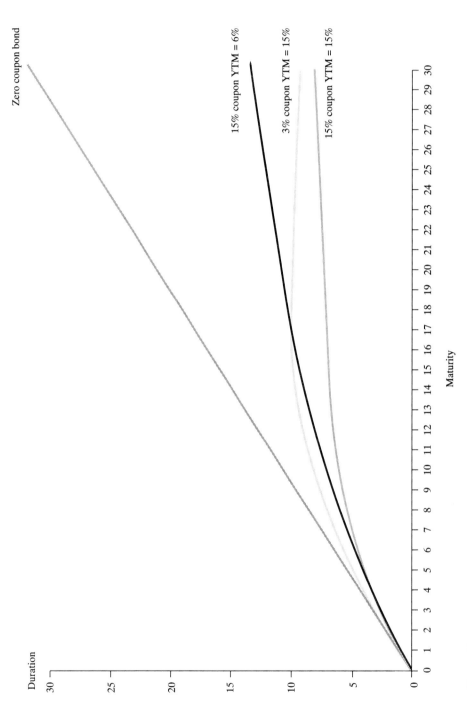

Figure 13.1

Notice in Figure 13.1 that for the zero-coupon bond, maturity and duration are equal. For all the coupon bonds, however, duration increases by less than a year for each year's increase in maturity. The slope of the duration graph is less than one, and duration is always less than maturity for positive-coupon bonds.

While long-maturity bonds generally will be high-duration bonds, duration is a better measure of the long-term nature of the bond because it also accounts for coupon payments. Only when the bond pays no coupons is time to maturity an adequate measure; then maturity and duration are equal.

Notice also in Figure 13.1 that the two 15 percent coupon bonds have different durations when they sell at different yields to maturity. The lower-yield bond has greater duration. This makes sense, because at lower yields the more distant payments due have relatively greater present values, and thereby account for a greater share of the bond's total value. Thus, in the weighted-average calculation of duration, the distant payments receive greater weights, which results in a higher duration measure. This establishes

Rule 4: Holding other factors constant, the duration and interest rate sensitivity of a coupon bond are higher when the bond's yield to maturity is lower.

Rule 4 applies to coupon bonds. For zeros, duration equals time to maturity, regardless of the yield to maturity.

Finally, we present an algebraic rule for the duration of a perpetuity. This rule is derived from and consistent with the formula for duration given in Equation 13.1 but it is far easier to use for infinitely-lived bonds.

Rule 5: The duration of a level perpetuity is $(1 + y)/y$. For example, at a 15 percent yield, the duration of a perpetuity that pays \$100 once a year forever will equal $1.15/.15 = 7.67$ years, while at an 8 percent yield, it will equal $1.08/.08 = 13.5$ years.

Rule 5 makes it obvious that maturity and duration can differ substantially. The maturity of the perpetuity is infinite, while the duration of the instrument at a 15 percent yield is only 7.67 years. The present-value-weighted cash flows early on in the life of the perpetuity dominate the computation of duration. Notice from Figure 13.1 that as their maturities become ever longer, the durations of the two coupon bonds with yields of 15 percent both converge to the duration of the perpetuity with the same yield, 7.67 years.

Concept Check

Question 2. Show that the duration of a perpetuity increases as the interest rate decreases, in accordance with Rule 4.

Durations can vary widely among traded bonds. Table 13.4 presents durations for several bonds all assumed to pay annual coupons and to yield 8 percent per year. Duration decreases as coupon rates increase and generally increases with time to maturity. According to Table 13.4 and Equation 13.2, if the interest rate were to increase from 8 percent to 8.1 percent, the 6 percent coupon, 20-year bond would fall in value by about 1.04 percent ($= 11.231 \times .1\%/1.08$) while the 10 percent coupon, one-year bond would fall by only 0.093 percent ($= 1 \times .1\%/1.08$). Notice also from Table 13.4 that only for the perpetual bond is duration independent of coupon rate.

Table 13.4   *Durations of Annual Coupon Bonds*   *(Initial bond yield = 8%)*

Years to Maturity	Coupon Rates (% per year)			
	6	8	10	12
1	1.000	1.000	1.000	1.000
5	4.439	4.312	4.204	4.110
10	7.615	7.247	6.996	6.744
20	11.231	10.604	10.182	9.880
Infinite (perpetuity)	13.500	13.500	13.500	13.500

13.2   *Passive Bond Management*

Passive managers take bond prices as fairly set and seek to control only the risk of their fixed-income portfolio. Generally, there are two ways of viewing this risk, depending on the investor's circumstances. Some institutions, such as banks, are concerned with protecting the portfolio's current net worth or net market value against interest rate fluctuations. Newly formulated risk-based capital guidelines for commercial banks and thrift institutions require the setting aside of additional capital as a buffer against potential losses in market value incurred from interest rate fluctuations. The amount of capital required is directly related to the losses that may be incurred under various changes in market interest rates. Other investors, such as pension funds, may have an investment goal to be reached after a given number of years. These investors are more concerned with protecting the future values of their portfolios.

Immunization A *strategy to make net worth unaffected by interest rate movements.*

What is common to the bank and pension fund, however, is interest rate risk. The net worth of the firm and its ability to meet future obligations fluctuate with interest rates. If they adjust the maturity structure of their portfolios, these institutions can shed their interest rate risk. **Immunization** and dedication techniques refer to strategies that investors use to shield their portfolios from exposure to interest rate fluctuations.

Net Worth Immunization

Many banks and thrift institutions have a natural mismatch between asset and liability maturity structures. Liabilities are primarily the deposits owed to customers, most of which are short-term in nature and consequently of low duration. Assets are comprised largely of commercial and consumer loans or mortgages. These assets are of longer duration than deposits, which means their values are correspondingly more sensitive than deposits to interest rate fluctuations. When interest rates increase unexpectedly, banks can suffer serious decreases in net worth—their assets fall in value by more than their liabilities.

Flannery and James (1984) have shown that prices of bank stocks do in fact tend to fall when interest rates rise. In another study, Kopcke and Woglom (1979) found that market values of total liabilities exceeded total assets for some savings banks in Connecticut in several years during the 1970s, a period following significant increases in interest rates. Had these banks been required to carry their assets at market value on their balance sheets, they would have been declared insolvent. Clearly, banks are subject to interest rate risk.

The watchword in bank portfolio strategy has become asset and liability management. Techniques called *gap* management limit the disparity between asset and liability durations. Adjustable-rate mortgages are one example. Conventional mortgages fall in value when market interest rates rise, but adjustable-rate mortgages do not because the rates they pay are tied to an index of the current market rate. Even if the indexing is imperfect or entails lags, indexing greatly diminishes a bank's sensitivity to interest rate fluctuations. On the other side of the balance sheet, bank certificates of deposit with fixed terms to maturity lengthen the duration of bank liabilities, also reducing the duration gap.

In this way, banks attempt to protect their overall position by immunizing themselves against interest rate movements. As long as bank assets and liabilities are roughly equal in size, any change in interest rates will affect the value of assets and liabilities equally, if their durations are also equal. Interest rates will not affect net worth, in other words. Therefore, banks, which typically have roughly equal assets and liabilities, can shed interest rate risk by equating the durations of their assets and liabilities.

Target Date Immunization

Pension funds are different from banks. They think more in terms of future commitments than current net worth. Pension funds have an obligation to provide workers with a flow of income on retirement, and they must have sufficient funds available to meet such commitments. As interest rates fluctuate, both the value of the fund's assets and the rate at which those assets generate income fluctuate. The pension fund manager, therefore, may want to protect or "immunize" the fund's future accumulated value at the target date against interest rate movements.

Pension funds are not alone in this concern. Any institution with a future fixed obligation might consider immunization a reasonable risk management policy. Insurance companies, for example, also pursue immunization strategies. The notion of immunization was introduced by F. M. Redington (1952), an actuary for a life insurance company.

The idea behind immunization is that duration-matched assets and liabilities let the asset portfolio meet the firm's obligations despite interest rate movements. A concrete example would be a life insurance company that has issued a GIC obligating it to pay out $14,693.28 in five years. (GIC stands for guaranteed investment contract, which resembles a zero-coupon bond issued by the insurance company. An insurance company commonly issues GICs directly to customers instead of selling zeros in the capital market.)

If the current market interest rate is 8 percent, the present value of a $14,693.28 obligation is $10,000. The insurance company chooses to fund its obligation with $10,000 of 8 percent *annual* coupon bonds, selling at par value, with six years to maturity. As long as the market interest rate stays at 8 percent, the company has fully funded the obligation, as the present value of the obligation exactly equals the value of the bonds.

Table 13.5A shows that if interest rates remain at 8 percent, the accumulated funds from the bond will grow to exactly the $14,693.28 obligation. Over the five-year period, the year-end coupon income of $800 is reinvested at the prevailing 8 percent market interest rate. At the end of the period, the bonds can be sold for $10,000; they still will sell at par value because the coupon rate still equals the market interest rate. Total income after five years from reinvested coupons and the sale of the bond is precisely $14,693.28.

If interest rates change, however, two offsetting influences will affect the ability of the fund to grow to the targeted value of $14,693.28. If interest rates rise, the fund will suffer a capital loss, impairing its ability to satisfy the obligation. The bonds will be worth less in five years than if interest rates had remained at 8 percent. However, at a higher interest rate, reinvested coupons will grow at a faster rate, offsetting the capital loss. In other words, fixed-income investors face two offsetting types of interest rate risk: price risk and reinvestment rate risk. Increases in interest rates cause capital losses but at the same time increase the rate at which reinvested income will grow. If the portfolio duration is chosen appropriately, these two effects will cancel out exactly. When the portfolio duration is set equal to the investor's horizon date, the accumulated value of the investment fund at the horizon date will be unaffected by interest rate fluctuations. For a horizon equal to the portfolio's duration, price risk and reinvestment risk exactly cancel out.

In the example we are discussing, the duration of the six-year maturity bonds used to fund the GIC is five years. You can confirm this following the procedure in Table 13.3. Because the fully funded plan has equal duration for its assets and

Table 13.5   *Terminal Value of a Bond Portfolio after 5 Years*   (All proceeds reinvested)

Payment Number	Years Remaining until Obligation	Accumulated Value of Invested Payment	
A. Rates Remain at 8%			
1	4	$800 \times (1.08)^4 =$	1,088.39
2	3	$800 \times (1.08)^3 =$	1,007.77
3	2	$800 \times (1.08)^2 =$	933.12
4	1	$800 \times (1.08)^1 =$	864.00
5	0	$800 \times (1.08)^0 =$	800.00
Sale of bond	0	$10,800/1.08 =$	10,000.00
			14,693.28
B. Rates Fall to 7%			
1	4	$800 \times (1.07)^4 =$	1,048.64
2	3	$800 \times (1.07)^3 =$	980.03
3	2	$800 \times (1.07)^2 =$	915.92
4	1	$800 \times (1.07)^1 =$	856.00
5	0	$800 \times (1.07)^0 =$	800.00
Sale of bond	0	$10,800/1.07 =$	10,093,46
			14,694.05
C. Rates Increase to 9%			
1	4	$800 \times (1.09)^4 =$	1,129.27
2	3	$800 \times (1.09)^3 =$	1,036.02
3	2	$800 \times (1.09)^2 =$	950.48
4	1	$800 \times (1.09)^1 =$	872.00
5	0	$800 \times (1.09)^0 =$	800.00
Sale of bond	0	$10,800/1.09 =$	9,908.26
			14,696.02

Note: The sale price of the bond portfolio equals the portfolio's final payment ($10,800) divided by $1 + r$, because the time to maturity of the bonds will be one year at the time of sale.

liabilities, the insurance company should be immunized against interest rate fluctuations. To confirm that this is the case, let us now investigate whether the bond can generate enough income to pay off the obligation five years from now regardless of interest rate movements.

Tables 13.5B and C consider two possible interest rate scenarios: rates either fall to 7 percent or increase to 9 percent. In both cases, the annual coupon payments from the bond are reinvested at the new interest rate, which is assumed to change before the first coupon payment, and the bond is sold in year 5 to help satisfy the obligation of the GIC.

Table 13.5B shows that if interest rates fall to 7 percent, the total funds will accumulate to $14,694.05, providing a small surplus of $.77. If rates increase to 9 percent as in Table 13.5C, the fund accumulates to $14,696.02, providing a small surplus of $2.74.

Several points are worth highlighting. First, duration matching balances the difference between the accumulated value of the coupon payments (reinvestment rate risk) and the sale value of the bond (price risk). That is, when interest rates fall, the coupons grow less than in the base case, but the gain on the sale of the bond offsets this. When interest rates rise, the resale value of the bond falls, but the coupons more than make up for this loss because they are reinvested at the higher rate. Figure 13.2 illustrates this case. The solid curve traces out the accumulated value of the bonds if interest rates remain at 8 percent. The dashed curve shows that value if interest rates happen to increase. The initial impact is a capital loss, but this loss eventually is offset by the now-faster growth rate of reinvested funds. At the five-year horizon date, the two effects just cancel, leaving the company able to satisfy its obligation with the accumulated proceeds from the bond.

We can also analyze immunization in terms of present as opposed to future values. Figure 13.3A shows the initial balance sheet for the insurance company's GIC account. Both assets and the obligation have market values of $10,000, so that the plan is just fully funded. Figures 13.3B and C show that whether the interest rate increases or decreases, the value of the bonds funding the GIC and

Figure 13.2
Growth of invested funds. The solid curve represents the growth of portfolio value at the original interest rate. If interest rates increase at time *t** the portfolio value falls but increases thereafter at the faster rate represented by the broken curve. At time *D* (duration) the curves cross.

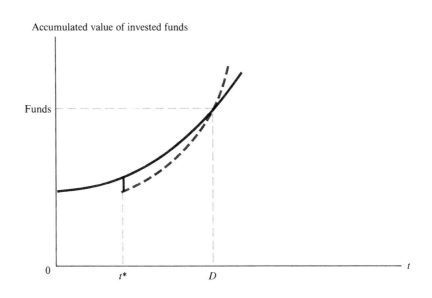

A. Interest Rate = 8%

Assets		Liabilities	
Bonds	$10,000	Obligation	$10,000

B. Interest Rate = 7%

Assets		Liabilities	
Bonds	$10,476.65	Obligation	$10,476.11

C. Interest Rate = 9%

Assets		Liabilities	
Bonds	$9,551.41	Obligation	$9,549.62

Notes:

$$\text{Value of bonds} = 800 \, PA(r, 6) + 10{,}000 \, PF(r,6)$$

$$\text{Value of obligation} = \frac{14{,}693.28}{(1 + r)^6} = 14{,}693.28 \, PF(r, 6)$$

Figure 13.3 **Market value balance sheet.**

the present value of the company's obligation change by virtually identical amounts. Regardless of the interest rate change, the plan remains fully funded, with the surplus in Figures 13.3B and C just about zero. The duration-matching strategy has ensured that both assets and liabilities react equally to interest rate fluctuations.

Figure 13.4 is a graph of the present values of the bond and the single-payment obligation as a function of the interest rate. At the current rate of 8 percent, the values are equal, and the obligation is fully funded by the bond. Moreover, the two present value curves are tangent at $y = 8$ percent. As interest rates change, the change in value of both the asset and the obligation is equal, so the obligation remains fully funded. For greater changes in the interest rate, however, the present value curves diverge. This reflects the fact that the fund actually shows a small surplus at market interest rates other than 8 percent.

Why is there any surplus in the fund? After all, we claimed that a duration-matched asset and liability mix would make the investor indifferent to interest rate shifts. Actually, such a claim is valid only for *small* changes in the interest rate, because as bond yields change, so too does duration. (Recall Rule 4 for duration.) In fact, while the duration of the bond in this example is equal to five years at a yield to maturity of 8 percent, the duration rises to 5.02 years when the bond yield falls to 7 percent and drops to 4.97 years at $y = 9$ percent. That is, the bond and the obligation were not duration-matched *across* the interest rate shift, so that the position was not fully immunized.

Rebalancing
Realigning the proportions of assets in a portfolio as needed.

This example demonstrates the need for **rebalancing** immunized portfolios. As interest rates and asset durations change, managers must rebalance, that is, change the composition of, the portfolio of fixed-income assets continually to realign its duration with the duration of the obligation. Moreover, even if interest rates do not change, asset durations *will* change solely because of the passage of time. Recall from Figure 13.1 that duration generally decreases less rapidly than maturity as time passes, so even if an obligation is immunized at the outset, the durations of the asset and liability will fall at different rates. Without portfolio

Figure 13.4
Immunization.

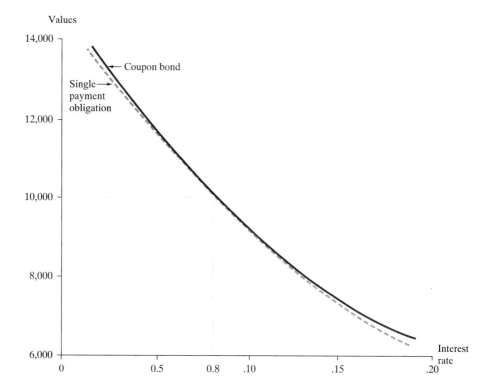

rebalancing, durations will become unmatched and the goals of immunization will not be realized. Therefore, immunization is a passive strategy only in the sense that it does not involve attempts to identify undervalued securities. Immunization managers still actively update and monitor their positions.

Another example should highlight the need for rebalancing. Consider a portfolio manager facing an obligation of $19,487 in seven years. At a market interest rate of 10 percent, the investment has a present value of $10,000. Suppose the manager wishes to immunize the obligation by holding only three-year zero-coupon bonds and perpetuities paying annual coupons. (Our focus on zeros and perpetuities helps to keep the algebra simple.) At current interest rates, the perpetuities have a duration of $1.10/.10 = 11$ years. The duration of the zero is simply three years.

For assets with equal yields, the duration of a portfolio is the weighted average of the durations of the assets making up the portfolio. To achieve the desired portfolio duration of seven years, the manager would have to choose appropriate values for the weights of the zero and the perpetuity in the overall portfolio. Call w the zero's weight and $(1 - w)$ the perpetuity's weight. Then w must be chosen to satisfy the equation

$$w \times 3 \text{ years} + (1 - w) \times 11 \text{ years} = 7 \text{ years}$$

which implies that $w = 1/2$. The manager invests $5,000 in the zero-coupon bond and $5,000 in the perpetuity, providing annual coupon payments of $500 per year indefinitely. The portfolio duration is then seven years, and the position is immunized.

Next year, even if interest rates do not change, rebalancing will be necessary. The present value of the obligation will have grown to $11,000, as it is one year closer to maturity. The manager's funds also have grown to $11,000: the zero-coupon bonds have increased in value from $5,000 to $5,500 with the passage of time, while the perpetuity has paid its annual $500 coupon and remains worth $5,000. The portfolio weights must be changed, however. The zero-coupon bond now will have a duration of two years, while the perpetuity duration remains at 11 years. The obligation is now due in six years. The weights must now satisfy the equation

$$w \times 2 + (1 - w) \times 11 = 6$$

which implies that $w = 5/9$. To rebalance the portfolio and maintain the duration match, the manager now must invest a total of $11,000 \times 5/9 = $6,111.11$ in the zero-coupon bond. This requires that the entire $500 coupon payment be invested in the zero, with an additional $111.11 of the perpetuity sold and invested in the zero-coupon bond to maintain an immunized position.

Concept Check

Question 3. What would be the immunizing weights in the second year if the interest rate falls to 8 percent?

Of course, rebalancing of the portfolio entails transaction costs as assets are bought or sold, so continuous rebalancing is not feasible. In practice, managers strike some compromise between the desire for perfect immunization, which requires continual rebalancing, and the need to control trading costs, which dictates less frequent rebalancing.

Cash Flow Matching and Dedication

Cash flow matching
Matching cash flows
from a fixed-income
portfolio with an
obligation.

Dedication strategy
Refers to multiperiod
cash flow matching.

The problems associated with immunization seem to have a simple solution. Why not simply buy a zero-coupon bond that provides a payment in an amount exactly sufficient to cover the projected cash outlay? This is **cash flow matching,** which automatically immunizes a portfolio from interest rate movements because the cash flow from the bond and the obligation exactly offset each other.

Cash flow matching on a multiperiod basis is referred to as a **dedication strategy.** In this case, the manager selects either zero-coupon or coupon bonds that provide total cash flows in each period that match a series of obligations. In 1985, for example, General Electric purchased $824 million of zero-coupon bonds to finance part of its pension plan. GE is not alone in this strategy. Other major pension plan dedications include American Information Technologies Corp. (for $2.4 billion), Chrysler Corp. (for $1.1 billion), and Bethlehem Steel for $700 million. Unlike GE, these firms used conventional bonds rather than zeros in their dedications.

Cash flow matching is not widely pursued, however, probably because of the constraints it imposes on bond selection. Immunization/dedication strategies would seem to be appealing to firms that do not wish to bet on general movements in interest rates, yet these firms may want to immunize using bonds they believe are undervalued. Cash flow matching places enough constraints on bond selection that it can make it impossible to pursue a dedication strategy using only "underpriced" bonds. Firms looking for underpriced bonds exchange exact and easy dedication for the possibility of achieving superior returns from their bond portfolios.

Concept Check

Question 4. How would an increase in trading costs affect the attractiveness of dedication versus immunization?

Sometimes, cash flow matching is not possible. To cash flow match for a pension fund that is obligated to pay out a perpetual flow of income to current and future retirees, the pension fund would need to purchase fixed-income securities with maturities ranging up to hundreds of years. Such securities do not exist, making exact dedication infeasible. Immunization is easy, however. If the interest rate is 8 percent, for example, the duration of the pension fund obligation is $1.08/.08 = 13.5$ years (see Rule 5 above). Therefore, the fund can immunize its obligation by purchasing zero-coupon bonds with maturity of 13.5 years and a market value equal to that of the pension liabilities.

Concept Check

Question 5.
a. Suppose the pension fund is obligated to pay out $800,000 per year in perpetuity. What should be the face value of the zero-coupon bond it purchases to immunize its obligation?
b. Now suppose the interest rate immediately increases to 8.1 percent. How should the fund rebalance in order to remain immunized against further interest rate shocks? Ignore transaction costs.

13.3 *Active Bond Management*

Sources of Potential Profit

Broadly speaking, there are two sources of potential value in active bond management. The first is interest rate forecasting; that is, anticipating movements across the entire spectrum of the fixed-income market. If interest rate declines are forecast, managers will increase portfolio duration; if increases seem likely, they will shorten duration. The second source of potential profit is identification of relative mispricing within the fixed-income market. An analyst might believe, for example, that the default premium on one bond is unnecessarily large and the bond is underpriced.

These techniques will generate abnormal returns only if the analyst's information or insight is superior to that of the market. There is no way of profiting from knowledge that rates are about to fall if everyone else in the market is on to this. In that case, the anticipated lower future rates are built into bond prices in the sense that long-duration bonds are already selling at higher prices that reflect the anticipated fall in future short rates. If the analyst does not have information before the market does, it will be too late to act on that information—prices will have responded already to the news. You know this from our discussion of market efficiency.

For now we simply repeat that valuable information is differential information. And it is worth noting that interest rate forecasters have a notoriously poor track record.

Homer and Leibowitz have developed a popular taxonomy of active bond portfolio strategies. They characterize portfolio rebalancing activities as one of four types of *bond swaps*. In the first two swaps, the investor typically believes the yield relationship between bonds or sectors is only temporarily out of alignment. Until the aberration is eliminated, gains can be realized on the underpriced bond during a period of realignment called the *workout period*.

Substitution swap Exchange of one bond for a bond with similar attributes but more attractively priced.

1. The **substitution swap** is an exchange of one bond for a nearly identical substitute. The substituted bonds should be of essentially equal coupon, maturity, quality, call features, sinking fund provisions, and so on. A substitution swap would be motivated by a belief that the market has temporarily mispriced the two bonds, with a discrepancy representing a profit opportunity.

Intermarket spread swap Switching from one segment of the bond market to another.

2. The **intermarket spread swap** is an exchange of two bonds from different sectors of the bond market. It is pursued when an investor believes the yield spread between two sectors of the bond market is temporarily out of line. For example, if the current spread between corporate and government bonds is considered too wide and expected to narrow, the investor will shift from government into corporate bonds. If the yield spread does narrow, corporates will outperform governments.

Rate anticipation swap A switch made in response to forecasts of interest rate changes.

3. The **rate anticipation swap** is an exchange of bonds with different maturities. It is pegged to interest rate forecasting. Investors who believe rates will fall will swap into bonds of greater duration. Conversely, when rates are expected to rise, they will swap into low-duration bonds.

Pure yield pickup swap Moving to higher-yield bonds, usually with longer maturies.

4. The **pure yield pickup swap** is an exchange of a shorter-duration bond for a longer-duration bond. This swap is pursued not in response to perceived mispricing but as a means of increasing return by holding higher-yielding, longer-maturity bonds. The investor is willing to bear the interest rate risk this strategy entails. Riding the yield curve, discussed in the previous chapter, is an example of a pure yield pickup strategy.

Tax swap Swapping two similar bonds to receive a tax benefit.

We can add a fifth swap, called a **tax swap** to this list. This simply refers to a swap to exploit some tax advantage. For example, an investor may swap from one bond that has decreased in price to another if realization of capital losses is advantageous for tax purposes.

Investors and analysts commonly use this classification of strategies, if only implicitly. Consider these quotations from the Merrill Lynch "Fixed-Income Strategy" booklet of April 1986.

> Projected returns at alternative settings of the funds rate strongly favor ownership of short-term notes. At almost every [projected] setting of the [federal] funds rate, returns from both 10-year notes and 30-year bonds would be negative. . . . In a rising interest rate environment, where yields rise by 35 basis points for two-year notes and 25 basis points for three-year notes, the two-year is projected to outperform by approximately 50 basis points (page 10).

This analysis has to do with rate anticipation, which follows from Merrill Lynch's overall macroeconomic analysis. Given Merrill Lynch's belief in rising rates, it recommends short asset durations.

Following this general analysis comes a sector-oriented intramarket spread analysis that expresses Merrill Lynch's view that yield relationships across two fixed-income submarkets are temporarily out of line. The history of 1982–1984 leads Merrill Lynch to believe that corporate yields will fall relative to Treasury yields, making corporates attractive relative to Treasuries:

Corporate/Treasury yield ratios are unusually high for both intermediate and long-term securities. These ratios are now [April 1986] almost as high as those that emerged late in 1982, following a sharp drop in bond yields. The respective yield ratios for new-issue long-term AA utilities and AA industrials were 1.17 and 1.13 at the end of this past quarter, compared with 1.22 and 1.15 in December 1982. By mid-1983, these ratios had declined to 1.10 and 1.08, respectively. By July 1984, they had declined further, to 1.08 and 1.05. Yield ratios for intermediate corporates display a similar pattern. This record suggests that corporate/Treasury yield ratios are likely to fall in the months ahead if, as we expect, the Treasury yield curve steepens (page 16).

Finally, we see an example of a yield pickup recommendation:

Although the slope of the corporate yield curve is 30 to 50 basis points steeper than that of the Treasury curve, it has flattened by approximately the same degree. Thus, any steepening in the Treasury curve would probably spark a similar response in corporates, hurting the long corporate market much more than the short and intermediate coupons. Consequently, the 2- to 10-year maturity sector performs far better in the total return simulations [than longer-term issues]. Moreover, since this is the steepest area of the yield curve, it offers investors the opportunity to capture more than 90 percent of the yield on long bonds while owning 10-year rather than 30-year maturities (page 17).

The Merrill Lynch strategy book is devoted to broad sectors of the fixed-income market and so does not include any examples of substitution swaps.

An Example of a Fixed-Income Investment Strategy

To demonstrate a reasonably active fixed-income portfolio strategy, we discuss here the policies of Sanford Bernstein & Co., as explained in a 1985 speech by its manager of fixed-income investments, Francis Trainer. The company believes big bets on general marketwide interest movements are unwise. Instead, it concentrates on exploiting numerous instances of perceived *relative* minor pricing misalignments *within* the fixed-income sector. The firm takes as a risk benchmark the Shearson Lehman Hutton Government/Corporate Bond Index, which includes the vast majority of publicly traded bonds with maturities greater than one year. Any deviation from this passive or neutral position must be justified by active analysis. Bernstein considers a neutral portfolio duration to be equal to that of the index, which was 4.5 years in September 1985, the date of Trainer's speech.

The firm is willing to make only limited bets on interest rate movements. As Francis Trainer puts it in his speech:

If we set duration of our portfolios at a level equal to the index and never allow them to vary, this would imply that we are perpetually neutral on the direction of interest rates. However, as those of you who have followed our economic forecasts are aware, this is rarely the case. We believe the utilization of these forecasts will add value and, therefore, we incorporate our economic forecast into the bond management process by altering the durations of our portfolios.

However, in order to prevent fixed-income performance from being dominated by the accuracy of just a single aspect of our research effort, we limit the degree to which we are willing to alter our interest rate exposure. Under the vast majority of circumstances, we will not permit the duration of our portfolios to differ from that of the Shearson Lehman Index by more than one year.

The company expends most of its effort in exploiting numerous but minor inefficiencies in bond prices that result from lack of attention by its competitors. Its analysts follow about 1,000 securities, attempting to "identify specific securities that are attractive or unattractive as well as identify trends in the richness or cheapness of industries and sectors." These two activities would be characterized as substitution swaps and intermarket spread swaps in the Homer Leibowitz scheme.

Sanford Bernstein & Co. realizes that market opportunities will arise, if at all, only in sectors of the bond market that present the least competition from other analysts. For this reason, it tends to avoid recently issued bonds because "most of the attention that is focused on the bond market is concentrated on those securities that have been recently issued." Similarly, it tends to focus on relatively more complicated bond issues in the belief that extensive research efforts give the firm a comparative advantage in that sector. Finally, the company does not take unnecessary risks. If there do not appear to be enough seemingly attractive bonds, funds are placed in Treasury securities as a "neutral" parking space until new opportunities are identified.

To summarize the key features of this sort of strategy, we can make the following observations:

1. A firm like Bernstein has a respect for market prices. It believes only minor mispricing usually can be detected. It works toward meaningful abnormal returns by combining numerous *small* profit opportunities, not by hoping for success of one big bet.
2. To have value, information cannot be reflected already in market prices. A large research staff must focus on market niches that appear to be neglected by others.
3. Interest rate movements are extremely hard to predict, and attempts to time the market can wipe out all the profits of intramarket analysis.

What are the results of such a philosophy? Figure 13.5 charts Bernstein's performance over various periods ending in 1989. Each rectangle depicts performance in different periods. The left-most rectangle uses the seven-year period 1983–1989, the next uses the six-year period 1984–1989, and so on. The horizontal lines in each rectangle are drawn at the rate of return realized by the 5th, 25th, 50th, 75th, and 95th percentile manager in a sample of fixed-income managers. The diamond is Sanford Bernstein & Co.'s performance, which has tended to be above average over the period. We cannot know whether over the long run the company will continue to be successful in the analysis of security and sector underpricing that its strategy statement calls for. However, its strategy is a reasonable one for those who wish to pursue active bond management.

13.4   *Interest Rate Swaps*

Interest rate swaps Parties trade the cash flows corresponding to different securities without actually exchanging the securities directly.

Interest rate swaps have emerged recently as a major fixed-income tool. An interest rate swap is a contract between two parties to exchange a series of cash flows similar to those that would result if the parties instead were to exchange equal dollar values of different types of bonds. Swaps arose originally as a means of managing interest rate risk. The volume of swaps has increased from virtually zero in 1980 to about $390 billion in the first half of 1989. (Interest rate

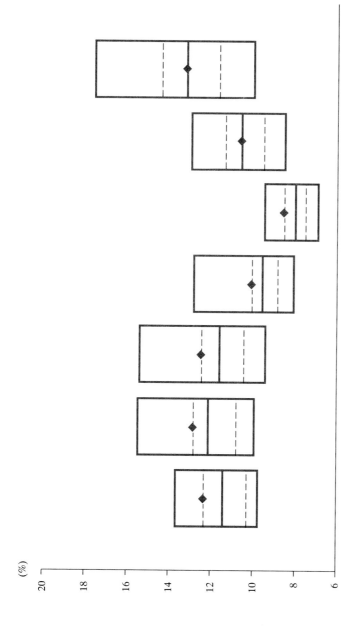

(%)

	1983–89	1984–89	1985–89	1986–89	1987–89	1988–89	1989*
95th percentile	13.6	15.4	15.4	12.2	9.4	12.9	17.5
75th percentile	12.3	12.8	12.4	10.1	8.5	11.3	14.3
Median	11.4	12.1	11.6	9.5	7.9	10.5	13.1
25th percentile	10.3	10.8	10.4	8.8	7.5	9.5	11.6
5th percentile	9.8	9.9	9.3	8.0	6.8	8.4	9.9
Bernstein intermediate-duration accounts	12.4	13.0	12.4	10.1	8.5	10.5	13.3
Percentile ranking	78	81	75	76	76	50	52
Shearson Lehman Hutton Gov't Corp. Bond Index	11.8	12.5	12.0	9.8	7.9	10.9	14.2

*1989 return is preliminary.

Figure 13.5 **Bond funds: total fund annualized rates of return (for periods ending December 31, 1989)**

swaps do not have anything to do with the Homer/Leibowitz bond swap taxonomy set out earlier.)

A typical risk management swap is between two parties exposed to opposite types of interest rate risk. On one side could be a savings and loan institution with short-term variable-rate liabilities (deposits) and long-term fixed-rate assets such as conventional mortgages. This institution will suffer losses if interest rates rise. On the other side of the swap might be a corporation that has issued long-term noncallable fixed-rate bonds and has invested in short-term or variable-rate assets. The corporation will lose if interest rates fall.

A swap would work as follows. The S&L would agree to make fixed-rate payments to the corporation based on some *notional* principal amount and fixed interest rate. For example, with a fixed rate of 10 percent and notional principal of $10 million, the S&L would pay $1 million per year for the period of the swap. On the other side, the corporation pays an agreed-upon short-term interest rate times the notional principal to the S&L. Typically, that short rate is tied to the LIBOR (London Interbank Offered Rate), which is an interest rate at which banks borrow from each other in the Eurodollar market. For example, the corporation may pay LIBOR plus 50 basis points. (A basis point is 1/100 of 1 percent, so 50 basis points is a half-percentage point premium.) If LIBOR is 8 percent, the corporation initially will pay 8.5 percent of the notional principal, or $850,000 per year to the S&L. As LIBOR changes, so too will the corporation's payments.

How does a swap affect the net interest rate exposure of each party? The S&L started with long-term fixed-rate assets and variable-rate liabilities. The swap imposes a long-term fixed-rate liability on the bank, but brings variable-rate inflows from the corporation. It thus reduces or eliminates the S&L's net interest rate exposure. The corporation also has reduced its risk. It can fund its variable-rate obligation under the swap arrangement with its short-term assets and can use the fixed-rate payments received from the swap to make the coupon payments on its long-term debt.

Figure 13.6 depicts the balance sheets of the two parties before and after the swap. While each party is maturity mismatched before the swap, each has both short- and long-term assets and liabilities after the swap, which eliminates the original mismatch.

The swap arrangement does not mean a new loan has been made. The participants have agreed only to exchange a fixed cash flow stream for a variable cash flow stream. In practice, participants in a swap do not deal with each other directly. Instead, each usually trades with a dealer who acts as an intermediary. The dealer makes a market in swaps, entering one side of a swap with one party and the other side with another party. In some cases, swaps are brokered, meaning the two parties are matched up directly instead of each trading with a dealer.

Concept Check

Question 6. A pension fund holds a portfolio of money market securities the analyst believes are providing excellent yields. What type of swap will mitigate the fund's interest rate risk?

Why do firms arrange these swaps? For example, why do they not originally borrow short-term instead of borrowing long and entering a swap? In early years

Bank		Corporations	
Assets	**Liabilities**	**Assets**	**Liabilities**
A. Before the swap			
Long-term loans	Short-term deposits	Variable-rate or short-term assets	Long-term bonds
	Net worth		Net worth
B. After the swap			
Long-term loans	Short-term deposits	Short-term assets	Long-term bonds
Claim to variable-rate cash flows	Obligation to make fixed cash payments	Claim to fixed cash flows	Obligation to make variable-rate payments
	Net worth		Net worth

Figure 13.6 Interest rate swap.

of the swap market, the answer seemed to lie in systematic differences in the perceived credit ratings in different markets. Participants in these markets claimed European banks placed more weight than U.S. banks on a firm's size, name recognition, and product line compared to its credit rating. Thus, it might have paid for a firm that wanted to borrow long term instead to borrow short term in the United States and swap into long-term obligations with a European trading partner. The practice once exploited a type of market inefficiency, specifically, differences in credit assessments across national markets. Now, however, these inefficiencies seem to have been arbitraged away. Swaps simply provide a means to restructure balance sheets and manage risk very quickly with small transaction costs.

Interest rate swaps create an interesting problem for financial statement analysis. Firms are not required to disclose them in corporate financial statements unless the swaps have a "material impact" on the firm, and even then they appear only in the footnotes. This means the firm's true net obligations may be quite different from its apparent or presented debt structure.

Summary

1. Even default-free bonds such as Treasury issues are subject to interest rate risk. Longer-term bonds generally are more sensitive to interest rate shifts than short-term bonds. A measure of the average life of a bond is Macaulay's duration, defined as the weighted average of the times until each payment made by the security, with weights proportional to the present value of the payment.

2. Duration is a direct measure of the sensitivity of a bond's price to a change in its yield. The proportional change in a bond's price equals the negative of duration times the proportional change in $1 + y$.

3. Immunization strategies are characteristic of passive fixed-income portfolio management. Such strategies attempt to render the individual or firm immune from movements in interest rates. This may take the form of immunizing net worth or, instead, immunizing the future accumulated value of a fixed-income portfolio.

4. Immunization of a fully funded plan is accomplished by matching the durations of assets and liabilities. To maintain an immunized position as time passes and interest rates change, the portfolio must be periodically rebalanced.

5. A more direct form of immunization is dedication or cash flow matching. If a portfolio is perfectly matched in cash flow with projected liabilities, rebalancing will be unnecessary.

6. Active bond management can be decomposed into interest rate forecasting techniques and intermarket spread analysis. One popular taxonomy classifies active strategies as substitution swaps, intermarket spread swaps, rate anticipation swaps, or pure yield pickup swaps.

7. Interest rate swaps are major recent developments in the fixed-income market. In these arrangements, parties trade the cash flows of different securities without actually exchanging any securities directly. This is a useful tool to manage the duration of a portfolio. It also has been used by corporations to borrow at advantageous interest rates in foreign credit markets that are viewed as more hospitable than domestic ones.

Key Terms

cash flow matching, 378
dedication, 378
duration, 366
immunization, 372
interest rate swaps, 382

intermarket spread
    swap, 380
pure yield pickup
    swap, 380

rate anticipation
    swap, 380
rebalancing, 376
substitution swap, 380
tax swap, 380

Selected Readings

Duration and immunization are analyzed in an extensive literature. A good treatment is:

Bierwag, G. O. *Duration Analysis.* Cambridge, Mass.: Ballinger Publishing Company, 1987.

Useful general references to techniques of fixed-income portfolio management may be found in:

Fabozzi, Frank, and T. Dessa Fabozzi. *Bond Markets, Analysis and Strategies.* Englewood Cliffs, N.J.: Prentice Hall, 1989.

A classic exposition of active bond management strategies is:

Homer, Sidney, and Martin L. Leibowitz. *Inside the Yield Book: New Tools for Bond Market Strategy.* Englewood Cliffs, N.J.: Prentice Hall, 1972.

Our discussion of interest rate swaps follows an article in Barron's:

Forsyth, Randall W. "The $150 Billion Baby." *Barron's,* August 19, 1985, p. 15.

Problem Sets

1. A nine-year bond has a yield of 10 percent and a duration of 7.194 years. If the market yield changes by 50 basis points, what is the percentage change in the bond's price?

2. Find the duration of a 6 percent coupon bond making *annual* coupon payments if it has three years until maturity and a yield to maturity of 6 percent. What is the duration if the yield to maturity is 10 percent?

3. A pension plan is obligated to make disbursements of $1 million, $2 million, and $1 million at the end of the each of the next three years, respectively. Find the duration of the plan's obligations if the interest rate is 10 percent annually.

4. If the plan in question 3 wants to fully fund and immunize its position, how much of its portfolio should it allocate to one-year zero-coupon bonds and perpetuities, respectively, if these are the only two assets funding the plan?

5. You own a fixed-income asset with a duration of five years. If the level of interest rates, which is currently 8 percent, goes down by 10 basis points, how much do you expect the price of the asset to go up (in percentage terms)?

6. Rank the durations of the following pairs of bonds.
    a. Bond A is an 8 percent coupon bond, with 20-year time to maturity selling at par value.

    Bond B is an 8 percent coupon, 20-year maturity bond selling below par value.

    b. Bond A is a 20-year, noncallable coupon bond with a coupon rate of 8 percent, selling at par.

    Bond B is a 20-year, callable bond with a coupon rate of 9 percent, also selling at par.

7. Rank the following bonds in order of descending duration.

Bond	Coupon	Time to Maturity	Yield to Maturity
A	15%	20 years	10%
B	15	15	10
C	0	20	10
D	8	20	10
E	15	15	15

8. You will be paying $10,000 a year in tuition expenses at the end of the next two years. Bonds currently yield 8 percent.
    a. What is the present value and duration of your obligation?
    b. What maturity zero-coupon bond would immunize your obligation?
    c. Suppose you buy a zero-coupon bond with value and duration equal to your obligation. Now suppose that rates immediately increase to 9 percent. What happens to your net position, that is, to the difference between the value of the bond and that of your tuition obligation? What if rates fall to 7 percent?

9. What type of interest rate swap would be appropriate for a corporation holding long-term assets that it funded with floating-rate bonds?

10. What type of interest rate swap would be appropriate for a speculator who believes interest rates will soon fall?

11. You are managing a portfolio of $1 million. Your target duration is 10 years, and you can choose from two bonds: a zero-coupon bond with maturity 5 years, and a perpetuity, each currently yielding 5 percent.
    a. How much of each bond will you hold in your portfolio?
    b. How will these fractions change *next year* if target duration is now nine years?

12. You manage a pension fund that will provide retired workers with lifetime annuities. You determine that the payouts of the fund are essentially going to resemble level perpetuities of $1 million per year. The interest rate is 10 percent. You plan to fully fund the obligation using 5-year and 20-year maturity zero-coupon bonds.
    a. How much *market value* of each of the zeros will be necessary to fund the plan if you desire an immunized position?
    b. What must be the *face value* of the two zeros to fund the plan?

13. Your client is concerned about the apparent inconsistency between the following two statements.

    ■ Short-term interest rates are more volatile than long-term rates.

- The rates of return of long-term bonds are more volatile than returns on short-term securities.

Discuss why these two statements are not necessarily inconsistent.

14. The following questions appeared in past CFA Examinations.
    (1) Which set of conditions will result in a bond with the greatest volatility?
    - *a.* A high coupon and a short maturity.
    - *b.* A high coupon and a long maturity.
    - *c.* A low coupon and a short maturity.
    - *d.* A low coupon and a long maturity.

    (2) An investor who expects declining interest rates would be likely to purchase a bond that has a _____ coupon and a _____ term to maturity.
    - *a.* Low, long.
    - *b.* High, short.
    - *c.* High, long.
    - *d.* Zero, long.

    (3) With a zero-coupon bond:
    - *a.* Duration equals the weighted average term to maturity.
    - *b.* Term to maturity equals duration.
    - *c.* Weighted average term to maturity equals the term to maturity.
    - *d.* All of the above.

    (4) As compared with bonds selling at par, deep discount bonds will have:
    - *a.* Greater reinvestment risk.
    - *b.* Greater price volatility.
    - *c.* Less call protection.
    - *d.* None of the above.

15. The ability to *immunize* a bond portfolio is very desirable for bond portfolio managers in some instances.
    - *a.* Discuss the components of interest rate risk—that is, assuming a change in interest rates over time, explain the two risks faced by the holder of a bond.
    - *b.* Define immunization and discuss why a bond manager would immunize his or her portfolio.
    - *c.* Explain why a duration-matching strategy is a superior technique to a maturity-matching strategy for the minimization of interest rate risk.
    - *d.* Explain in specific terms how you would use a zero-coupon bond to immunize a bond portfolio. Discuss why a zero-coupon bond is an ideal instrument in this regard.

16. You are the manager for the bond portfolio of a pension fund. The policies of the fund allow for the use of active strategies in managing the bond portfolio.

    It appears that the economic cycle is beginning to mature, inflation is expected to accelerate, and in an effort to contain the economic expansion, central bank policy is moving toward constraint. For each of the situations below, *state* which one of the two bonds you would prefer. *Briefly justify* your answer in each case.
    - *a.* Government of Canada (Canadian pay) 10 percent due in 1984 and priced at 98.75 to yield 10.50 percent to maturity.
      or
      Government of Canada (Canadian pay) 10 percent due in 1995 and priced at 91.75 to yield 11.19 percent to maturity.
    - *b.* Texas Power and Light Co., 7½ due in 2002, rated AAA, and priced at 62 to yield 12.78 percent to maturity
      or
      Arizona Public Service Co. 7.45 due in 2002, rates A −, and priced at 56 to yield 14.05 percent to maturity.
    - *c.* Commonwealth Edison 2¾ due in 1999, rated Baa, and priced at 25 to yield 14.9 percent to maturity
      or

Commonwealth Edison 15⅜ due in 2000, rated Baa, and priced at 102.75 to yield 14.9 percent to maturity.

d. Shell Oil Co. 8½ sinking fund debentures due in 2000, rated AAA, and priced at 69 to yield 12.91 percent to maturity

or

Warner-Lambert 8⅞ sinking fund debentures due in 2000, rated AAA, and priced at 75 to yield 12.31 percent to maturity.

e. Bank of Montreal (Canadian pay) 12 percent certificates of deposit due in 1993, rated AAA, and priced at 100 to yield 12 percent to maturity

or

Bank of Montreal (Canadian pay) floating rate notes due in 1999, rated AAA. Coupon currently set at 10.65 percent and priced at 100 (coupon adjusted semiannually to .5 percent above the three-month Government of Canada Treasury bill rate).

17. The following bond swaps could have been made in recent years as investors attempted to increase the total return on their portfolio.

From the information presented below, identify the reason(s) investors may have made each swap.

Action		Call	Price	YTM (%)
a. Sell	Baa1 Georgia Pwr. 1st mtg. 11⅝% due 2000	108.24	75⅝	15.71
Buy	Baa1 Georgia Pwr. 1st mtg. 7⅜% due 2001	105.20	51⅛	15.39
b. Sell	Aaa Amer. Tel & Tel notes 13¼% due 1991	101.50	96⅛	14.02
Buy	U.S. Treasury notes 14¼% due 1991	NC	102.15	13.83
c. Sell	Aa1 Chase Manhattan zero coupon due 1992	NC	25¼	14.37
Buy	Aa1 Chase Manhattan float rate notes due 2009	103.90	90¼	—
d. Sell	A1 Texas Oil & Gas 1st mtg. 8¼% due 1997	105.75	60	15.09
Buy	U.S. Treasury bond 8¼% due 2005	NC	65.60	12.98
e. Sell	A1 Kmart convertible deb. 6% due 1999	103.90	62¾	10.83
Buy	A2 Lucky Stores S.F. deb. 11¾% due 2005	109.86	73	16.26

Part Four
Security Analysis

■ ■

Chapter

14

Macroeconomic and Industry Analysis

To determine a proper price for a firm's stock, the security analyst must forecast the dividends and earnings that can be expected from the firm. Because the prospects of the firm are tied to those of the broader economy, however, valuation analyses must consider the business environment in which the firm operates. For some firms, macroeconomic circumstances might have a greater influence on profits than the firm's relative performance within its industry.

It often makes sense to do a "top down" analysis of a firm's prospects. One starts with the broad economic environment, examining the state of the aggregate economy and even the international economy. From there, one considers the implications of the outside environment on the industry in which the firm operates. Finally, the firm's position within the industry is examined.

This chapter treats the broad-based aspects of fundamental analysis—macroeconomic and industry analysis. The two chapters following cover firm-specific analysis. We begin with an overview of the significance of the key variables usually used to summarize the state of the macro economy. We then discuss government macroeconomic policy. We conclude the analysis of the macro environment with a discussion of business cycles. Finally, we move to industry analysis, treating issues concerning the sensitivity of the firm to the business cycle, and the typical lifecycle of an industry.

After studying this chapter you should be able to:

- Predict the effect of monetary and fiscal policies on key macroeconomic variables such as GNP, interest rates, and the inflation rate.
- Use leading, coincident, and lagging economic indicators to describe and predict the economy's path through the business cycle.

■ Predict which industries will be more or less sensitive to business cycle fluctuations.

14.1   *The Macro Economy*

An investment analyst must understand the macro economy because it determines the environment in which all firms operate. The ability to forecast the macro economy can translate into spectacular investment performance. But it is not enough to forecast the macro economy well. One must forecast it *better* than your competitors to earn abnormal profits.

In this section, we will review some of the key concepts used to describe the state of the macro economy. In the next section, we will offer a brief introduction to macroeconomic analysis.

Some of the key variables that analysts use to assess the state of the macro economy include:

Gross national product *The market value of goods and services produced over a period of time.*

Gross National Product **Gross national product,** or GNP, is the measure of the economy's total production of goods and services. Rapidly growing GNP indicates an expanding economy with ample opportunity for a firm to increase sales. Another popular measure of the economy's output is *industrial production.* This statistic provides a measure of economic activity more narrowly focused on the manufacturing side of the economy.

Unemployment rate *The ratio of the number of people classified as unemployed to the total labor force.*

Employment The **unemployment rate** is the percentage of the labor force (those who are either working or actively seeking employment) yet to find work. The unemployment rate measures the extent to which the economy is operating at full capacity. The unemployment rate is a factor related to workers only, but further insight into the strength of the economy can be gleaned from the employment rate of other factors of production. Analysts also look at the factory capacity utilization rate, which is the ratio of actual output from factories to potential output.

Inflation *The rate at which the general level of prices for goods and services is rising.*

Inflation **Inflation** is the rate at which the general level of prices is rising. High rates of inflation often are associated with "overheated" economies, that is, economies where the demand for goods and services is outstripping productive capacity, which leads to upward pressure on prices. Most governments walk a fine line in their economic policies. They hope to stimulate their economies enough to maintain nearly full employment, but not so much as to bring on inflationary pressures. The perceived trade-off between inflation and unemployment is at the heart of many macroeconomic policy disputes. There is considerable room for disagreement as to the relative costs of these policies as well as the economy's relative vulnerability to these pressures at any particular time.

Interest Rates High interest rates reduce the present value of future cash flows, thereby reducing the attractiveness of investment opportunities. For this reason, real interest rates are key determinants of business investment expenditures. Demand for housing and high-priced consumer durables such as automobiles, which are commonly financed, also is highly sensitive to interest rates because interest rates affect interest payments.

Budget deficit *The amount by which government spending exceeds government revenues.*

Budget Deficit The **budget deficit** of the federal government is the difference between government spending and revenues. Any budgetary shortfall must be offset by government borrowing. Large amounts of government borrowing can force up interest rates by increasing the total demand for credit in the economy. Economists generally believe excessive government borrowing will "crowd out" private borrowing and investing by forcing up interest rates and choking off business investment.

Exchange rate *The rate at which domestic currency can be converted into foreign currency.*

Exchange Rates The **exchange rate** is the rate at which domestic currency can be converted into foreign currency. For example, on July 2, 1990, it took $1.77 to purchase one British pound. Exchange rate fluctuations affect the international competitiveness of domestically produced goods. If the U.S. dollar appreciates, meaning it can be exchanged for a greater number of British pounds, then British goods priced in pounds become cheaper to U.S. consumers.

For example, an item produced in England and priced at 10 pounds would cost a U.S. consumer $17.70 at the July 2 exchange rate. If the exchange rate appreciates to $1.70 per pound, then the dollar cost of the item will fall to $17.00. (Appreciation means it takes fewer dollars to buy one pound. The exchange rate quoted in dollars per pound falls.)

Conversely, the appreciation of the U.S. dollar means British consumers must lay out more pounds to purchase goods priced in terms of U.S. dollars. Hence, exchange rates can affect the balance between imports and exports. Appreciating currency tends to stimulate imports and discourage exports.

Exchange rates also affect inflation rates. Depreciation of the dollar, for example, increases the U.S. cost of imported goods. The immediate effect is to increase U.S. prices and the U.S. inflation rate.

Current account *The difference between imports and exports, including merchandise, services, and transfers such as foreign aid.*

Trade Balance The **current account** is the difference between imports and exports, including merchandise, services, and transfers such as foreign aid. A current account deficit means a country imports more than it exports. A surplus indicates more exports than imports. We've noted already that appreciation of a currency makes foreign goods cheaper to domestic consumers. Hence, currency appreciation can increase imports. Conversely, currency appreciation can reduce exports by making it more costly for foreigners to purchase domestically produced goods. Thus, the current account is affected by exchange rate movements.

The trade deficit in turn acts on exchange rates. A persistent U.S. deficit implies that the demand for foreign currency by U.S. consumers who are purchasing foreign goods exceeds the demand for dollars by foreigners purchasing U.S. goods. This imbalance places downward pressure on the value of the dollar in terms of other currencies. For this reason, news of an unfavorable trade deficit often causes the dollar to depreciate.

The current account is not the only determinant of exchange rates. The demand for dollars, for example, is determined also by the desire of investors to hold dollar-denominated assets in their portfolios. This demand will be determined in large part by the real interest rate in the United States compared to that in other countries. It also will be influenced by the "safe haven" attribute of U.S. investments (i.e., the attraction of investments in a country with the economic and political stability that the United States provides).

Sentiment   Consumers' and producers' optimism or pessimism concerning the economy are important determinants of economic performance. If consumers have confidence in their future income levels, for example, they will be more willing to spend on big-ticket items. Similarly, businesses will increase production and inventory levels if they anticipate higher demand for their products. In this way, beliefs influence how much consumption and investment will be pursued and affect the aggregate demand for goods and services.

Figure 14.1 presents a graphic overview of the macro economy in June 1990 by the editors of *Financial World*. Notice the organization of the macro economy according to various measures in broad categories of finance, prices, production, employment, and sentiment.

Concept Check

Question 1.   Consider an economy where the dominant industry is automobile production for domestic consumption as well as export. Now suppose the auto market is hurt by an increase in the length of time people use their cars before replacing them. Describe the probable effects of this change on (*a*) GNP, (*b*) unemployment, (*c*) the government budget deficit, (*d*) interest rates, (*e*) the balance of trade, (*f*) the exchange rate.

14.2   *Demand and Supply Shocks*

Demand shock   *An event that affects the demand for goods and services in the economy.*

Supply shock   *An event that influences production capacity and costs in the economy.*

A useful way to organize your analysis of the factors that might influence the macro economy is to classify any impact as a supply or demand shock. A **demand shock** is an event that affects the demand for goods and services in the economy. Examples of positive demand shocks are reductions in tax rates, increases in the money supply, increases in government spending, or increases in foreign export demand. A **supply shock** is an event that influences production capacity and costs. Examples of supply shocks are changes in the price of imported oil, freezes that might destroy large quantities of agricultural crops, changes in the educational level of an economy's work force, or changes in the wage rates at which the labor force is willing to work.

Demand shocks are usually characterized by aggregate output moving in the same direction as interest rates and inflation. For example, a big increase in government spending will tend to stimulate the economy and increase GNP. It also might increase interest rates by increasing the demand for borrowed funds by the government as well as by businesses that might desire to borrow to finance new ventures. Finally, it could increase the inflation rate if the demand for goods and services is raised to a level at or beyond the total productive capacity of the economy.

Supply shocks are usually characterized by aggregate output moving in the opposite direction as inflation and interest rates. For example, a big increase in the price of imported oil will be inflationary because costs of production will rise, which eventually will lead to increases in prices of finished goods. The

Figure 14.1 Overview of the macro economy in June 1990.
Reprinted by permission of *Financial World.*

PRODUCTION

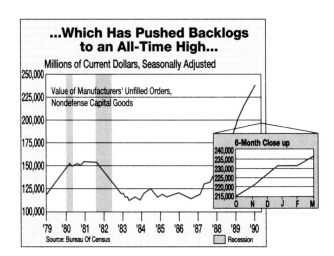

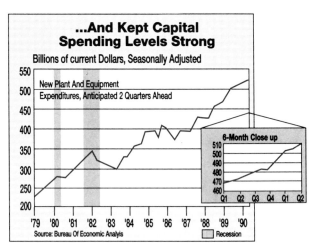

EMPLOYMENT

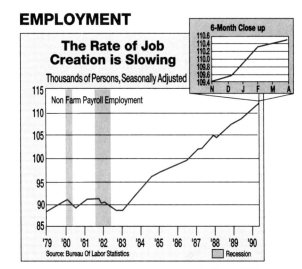

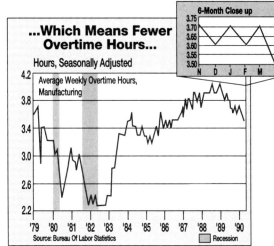

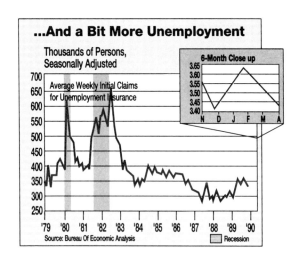

Figure 14.1
(*continued*)

Finance

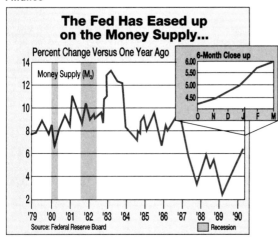

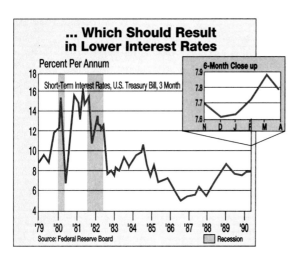

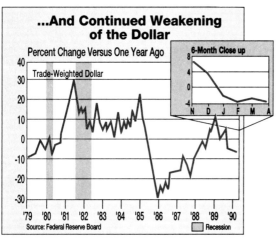

Prices

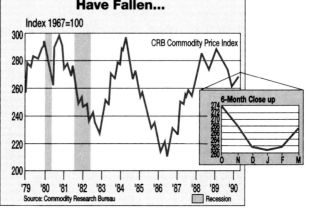

Figure 14.1
(concluded)

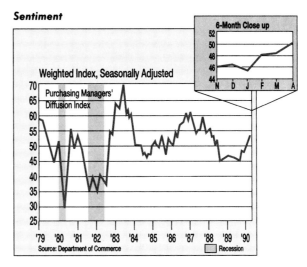

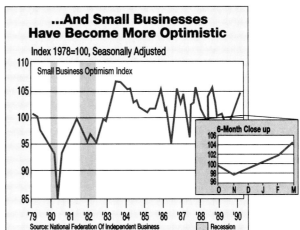

increase in inflation rates over the near term can lead to higher nominal interest rates. Against this background, aggregate output will be falling. With raw materials more expensive, the productive capacity of the economy is reduced, as is the ability of individuals to purchase goods at now-higher prices. GNP, therefore, tends to fall.

How can we relate this framework to investment analysis? You want to identify the industries that will be most helped or hurt in any macroeconomic scenario you envision. For example, if you forecast a tightening of the money supply, you might want to avoid industries such as automobile producers that might be hurt by the likely increase in interest rates. We caution you again that these forecasts are no easy task. Macroeconomic predictions are notoriously unreliable. And again, you must be aware that in all likelihood, your forecast will be made using only publicly available information. Any investment advantage you have will be a result only of better analysis—not better information.

14.3 *Federal Government Policy*

As the previous section would suggest, the government has two broad classes of macroeconomic tools—those that affect the demand for goods and services, and those that affect the supply. For most of postwar history, demand-side policy has been of primary interest. The focus has been on government spending, tax levels, and monetary policy. Since 1981, however, increasing attention has been focused on supply-side economics. Broadly interpreted, supply-side concerns have to do with enhancing the productive capacity of the economy, rather than increasing the demand for the goods and services the economy can produce. In practice, supply-side economists have focused on the appropriateness of the incentives to work, innovate, and take risks that result from our system of taxation. However, issues such as national policies on education, infrastructure (such as communication and transportation systems), and research and development also are properly regarded as part of supply-side macroeconomic policy.

Fiscal Policy

Fiscal policy The use of government spending and taxing for the specific purpose of stabilizing the economy.

Fiscal policy refers to the government's spending and tax actions and is part of "demand-side management." Fiscal policy is probably the most direct way either to stimulate or to slow the economy. Decreases in government spending directly deflate the demand for goods and services. Similarly, increases in tax rates immediately siphon income from consumers and result in fairly rapid decreases in consumption.

Ironically, although fiscal policy has the most immediate impact on the economy, the formulation and implementation of such policy is usually painfully slow and involved. This is because fiscal policy requires enormous amounts of compromise between the executive and legislative branches. Tax and spending policy must be initiated and voted on by Congress, which requires considerable political negotiations, and any legislation passed must be signed by the president, requiring more negotiation. Thus, while the impact of fiscal policy is relatively immediate, its formulation is so cumbersome that fiscal policy cannot in practice be used to fine-tune the economy.

Moreover, much of government spending, such as that for Medicare or social security, is nondiscretionary, meaning that it is determined by formula rather than policy and cannot be changed in response to economic conditions. This places even more rigidity into the formulation of fiscal policy.

A common way to summarize the net impact of government fiscal policy is to look at the government's budget deficit or surplus, which is simply the difference between revenues and expenditures. A large deficit means the government is spending considerably more than it is taking in by way of taxes. The net effect is to increase the demand for goods (via spending) by more than it reduces the demand for goods (via taxes), therefore, stimulating the economy. Figure 14.2 is a graph of government surpluses or deficits since 1960. Notice the huge increase in deficits that resulted from the tax cuts in the early 1980s.

Deficit
(in tens of $ billions)

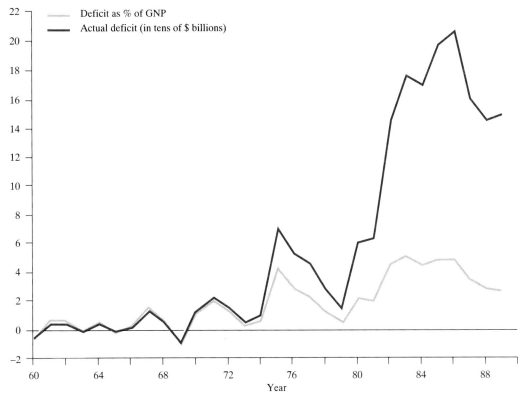

Figure 14.2 **U.S. government deficit.**

Deficits are associated with increased interest rates. As we noted, government borrowing competes for funds with private borrowing. Large deficits force up interest rates as the demand for funds increases. This effect was explained in Chapter 6. Real interest rates (interest rates net of inflation) in the last decade have been quite high by historical standards. Figure 14.3 shows that while real rates in the 20 years before the 1980s were about 1 percent on average, in the 1980s they averaged over 4 percent.

Monetary Policy

Monetary policy
Actions taken by the Board of Governors of the Federal Reserve System to influence the money supply or interest rates.

Monetary policy refers to the manipulation of the money supply to affect the macro economy and is the other main leg of demand-side policy. Monetary policy works largely through its impact on interest rates. Increases in the money supply lower short-term interest rates, ultimately encouraging investment and consumption demand. Over longer periods, however, most economists believe a higher money supply leads only to a higher price level and does not have a permanent effect on economic activity. Thus, the monetary authorities face a difficult balancing act. Expansionary monetary policy probably will lower interest rates and thereby stimulate investment and some consumption demand in the short run, but these circumstances ultimately will lead only to higher prices.

Real rate of interest

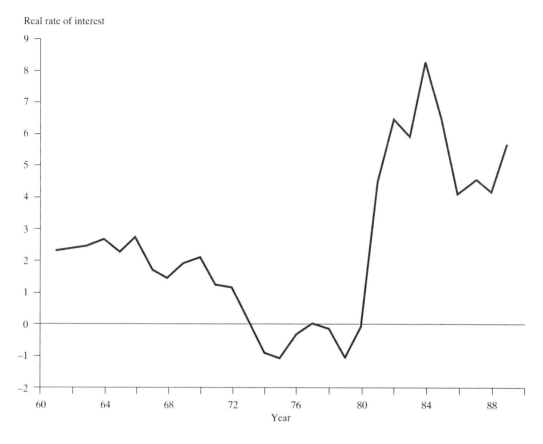

Figure 14.3 **Real interest rates, 1961–1989.**
Real interest rate calculated as yield to maturity on three-year Treasury bond minus the average of the lagging, contemporaneous, and leading annual inflation rate.
From *Economic Report of the President,* 1990.

The stimulation/inflation trade-off is implicit in all debate over proper monetary policy.

Fiscal policy is cumbersome to implement but has a fairly direct impact on the economy, while monetary policy is easily formulated and implemented but has a less direct impact. Monetary policy is determined by the Board of Governors of the Federal Reserve System. Board members are appointed by the president for 14-year terms and are reasonably insulated from political pressure. The board is small enough, and often sufficiently dominated by its chairperson, that policy can be formulated and modulated relatively easily.

Implementation of monetary policy also is quite direct. The most widely used tool is the open market operation, in which the Fed buys or sells bonds for its own account. When the Fed buys securities, it simply "writes a check," thereby increasing the money supply. (Unlike us, the Fed can pay for the securities without drawing down funds at a bank account.) Conversely, when the Fed sells a security, the money paid for it leaves the money supply. Open market operations occur daily, allowing the Fed to fine-tune its monetary policy.

Other tools at the Fed's disposal are the discount rate, which is the interest rate it charges banks on short-term loans, and the reserve requirement, which is the fraction of deposits that banks must hold as cash on hand or as deposits with the Fed. Reductions in the discount rate signal a more expansionary monetary policy. Lowering reserve requirements allows banks to make more loans with each dollar of deposits and stimulates the economy by increasing the effective money supply.

Monetary policy affects the economy in a more roundabout way than fiscal policy. While fiscal policy directly stimulates or dampens the economy, monetary policy works largely through its impact on interest rates. Increases in the money supply lower interest rates, which stimulate investment demand. As the quantity of money in the economy increases, investors will find that their portfolios of assets include too much money. They will rebalance their portfolios by buying securities such as bonds, forcing bond prices up and interest rates down. In the longer run, individuals may increase their holdings of stocks as well and ultimately buy real assets, which stimulates consumption demand directly. The ultimate effect of monetary policy on investment and consumption demand, however, is less immediate than that of fiscal policy.

Concept Check

Question 2.   Suppose the government wants to stimulate the economy without increasing interest rates. What combination of fiscal and monetary policy might accomplish this goal?

Supply-Side Policies

Fiscal and monetary policy are demand-oriented tools that affect the economy by stimulating the total demand for goods and services. The implicit belief is that the economy will not by itself arrive at a full employment equilibrium, and that macroeconomic policy can push the economy toward this goal. In contrast, supply-side policies treat the issue of the productive capacity of the economy. The goal is to create an environment in which workers and owners of capital have the maximum incentive and ability to produce and develop goods.

Supply-side economists also pay considerable attention to tax policy. While demand siders look at the effect of taxes on consumption demand, supply siders focus on incentives and marginal tax rates. They argue that lowering tax rates will elicit more investment and improve incentives to work, thereby enhancing economic growth. Some go so far as to claim that reductions in tax rates can lead to increases in tax revenues because the lower tax rates will cause the economy and the revenue tax base to grow by more than the tax rate is reduced.

The accompanying box gives an exposition of the supply-side philosophy. The author urges a reduction in tax rates to increase tax revenues, observing that federal tax receipts increased in the 1980s despite the sharp reduction in income tax rates. (Note, however, that while income tax rates did fall in the 1980s, social security taxes increased dramatically. While GNP increased by 27 percent [after inflation] between 1981 and 1989, individual income tax receipts rose about 25.5 percent. In contrast, social security tax revenues rose 55 percent. The combined marginal tax rate [from income and social security taxes] certainly fell for upper-income individuals, but not necessarily for the bulk of the population.)

Want More Money, Mr. Bush? Cut Taxes

Those who spent the past week trying to divine the meaning of President Bush's words on taxes focused on one phrase. Early on—the first time the issue came up publicly—the president acknowledged a need for greater "tax revenues." Later, at the week's end, the president said that in his negotiations to solve the budget problem a number of things would be considered "including tax increases." The difference here between "higher tax revenues" and "tax increases" is crucial. The important fact is that, the government's new posture notwithstanding, the two do not usually coincide.

Capital-Gains Advantage

A lower capital-gains tax would increase the pace at which capital gains were realized, raising revenues directly as well as through the increased economic growth arising from more efficient mobility of capital. It would bid up the value of assets subject to the capital-gains tax and thus raise the amount of taxable gain, move more venture capital out of tax-exempt funds into the hands of taxable individuals, raise personal incentives to save and to take longer-term risks and greatly reduce the cost of the S&L bailout by raising the value of the thrifts' real estate and bonds. A lower capital-gains tax could shave tens of billions off the deficit.

As the chart shows, inflation-adjusted federal revenues have expanded at an unprecedented rate since fiscal 1983. Measured in constant 1982 dollars, tax revenues were nearly stagnant during the 1970s, hovering between $500 and $600 billion. Since 1980, real federal revenues have increased by more than one third! Tax collections are about the same percentage of GNP as they were 10 years ago, but, thanks largely to the Reagan tax cuts, the U.S. economy is nearly one third larger—largely because the 1980s were the years of important tax cuts.

If the government in 1980 had instead set out to increase taxes by one third, average federal tax rates would have had to have been increased by one third. It is hard to believe the economy could have grown at all in the 1980s under such an onerous tax increase, much less experienced, as it did, a huge increase in growth.

Even a seemingly modest increase in tax rates on incomes or sales can be self-defeating. In the short run, it can cause a recession. In the long run, it can slow economic growth. Yet the U.S. government's own budgetary accountants' revenue estimates from various increases in tax rates always assume that taxes do no damage whatsoever to the economy.

The Congressional Budget Office predicts, for example, that a one percentage point increase in the corporate tax rate would yield an extra $1.3 billion next year, on the untenable assumption that it would have no effect on corporate investment or employment. But if it really had no effect, then an extra $65 billion could be collected by simply raising the corporate tax rate to 84 percent. A $5 oil import fee is likewise supposed to raise $7.7 billion on the assumption that higher energy prices do no damage. If that made sense, we could raise $65 billion by imposing an oil import fee to raise prices to $60 a barrel.

Raising the top [personal] tax rate to 33 percent could hurt the economy, and therefore the budget, in many different ways. The higher tax rate on interest income and dividends would raise interest rates and sink the stock market by reducing the demand for taxable securities. Those losses in the stock and bond markets would in turn damage the budget (through higher interest expense, lower capital-gains tax receipts, weak taxable sales and profits due to reduced wealth, etc.). The result of such a higher tax rate could easily widen the budget deficit by tens of billions of dollars for many years to come.

The alleged beneficial effect of higher tax rates on savings is another myth arising from static accounting. The whole idea assumes that higher tax

Concept Check

Question 3. The tax cuts in the 1980s were followed by rapid growth in GNP. How would demand-side and supply-side economists differ in their interpretations of this phenomenon?

A Picture Is Worth a Thousand Words

Federal tax receipts, in billions of constant 1982 dollars

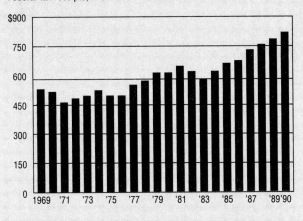

rates would in fact yield higher revenues over time, that higher revenues would actually be devoted to reduced deficits and that increasing the government's revenue at the expense of the private sector would not reduce the private sector's ability or willingness to save. Not one of these assumptions is consistent with experience. Instead, the ability of private households and firms to save would be seriously undermined by higher tax rates on what people earn or buy, and the value of U.S. stocks, bonds, and real estate would also be depressed by the reduction in prospective after-tax returns.

Actually, the United States has had some instructive experience with trying to raise federal revenues by increasing the tax share of GNP, rather than by increasing GNP itself. The first major effort was in mid-1932, when individual income tax rates were roughly tripled. Revenues subsequently fell by 16 percent. The next experiment was the surtax of 1969–70. Interest rates rose sharply for many months after the higher rates were imposed, falling only as the economy was shoved into a recession that did not end until the surtax was removed.

Measuring by the GNP

Then there were the unlegislated tax increases resulting from inflation and "bracket creep" in 1974–75 and 1981–82, when revenues once again declined with the contracting economy. In fact, federal tax receipts have never exceeded the current 19.6 percent of GNP since World War II without tipping the economy into recession. The option of attaining significant and sustained "tax revenue increases" through higher tax rates is a politician's illusion; it has never worked.

Couldn't the contractionary effect of higher tax rates be offset by an easier monetary policy? Not really. Even if higher tax rates generated more real revenue, which they do not, it makes no sense to argue that smaller deficits justify any easier monetary policy than would otherwise be appropriate. This amounts to saying that if the government sold fewer bonds, then it could safely print more money. But bonds and money are not at all the same. Higher tax rates would weaken the supply side of the economy, while an easy money policy merely stimulates spending or "demand." The result of that "policy mix" is always stagflation—witness Britain.

There is actually only one way in which real tax revenues can be significantly increased over the next decade, and that is the same way that real revenues were increased over the past decade—namely, by increases in employment, profits, capital gains, and sales. That is why President Bush's proposed "growth incentives"—lower tax rates on capital gains—are not at all inconsistent with real and sustainable "tax revenue increases." Higher tax rates, on the other hand, are inconsistent with growth incentives, and therefore with the preservation of the past decade's remarkable increase in real revenues.

From Alan Reynolds, "Want More Money, Mr. Bush? Cut Taxes," *The Wall Street Journal*, July 5, 1990, p. A10. Reprinted by permission of *THE WALL STREET JOURNAL*, © 1990 Dow Jones & Company, Inc. All Rights Reserved Worldwide.

14.4   *Business Cycles*

We've looked at the tools the government uses to fine-tune the economy, attempting to maintain low unemployment and low inflation. Despite these efforts, economies repeatedly seem to pass through good and bad times. One determinant of the broad asset allocation decision of many analysts is a forecast of whether the macro economy is improving or deteriorating. A forecast that differs from the market consensus can have a major impact on investment strategy.

The Business Cycle

*Business cycle
Repetitive cycles of
recession and recovery.*

The economy recurrently experiences periods of expansion and contraction, although the length and depth of those cycles can be irregular. This recurring pattern of recession and recovery is called the **business cycle.** Figure 14.4 presents graphs of several measures of production and income for the years 1964–1990. The production series all show clear variation around a generally rising trend. The bottom graph of capacity utilization also evidences a clear cyclical (although irregular) pattern.

*Peak   The transition
from the end of an
expansion to the start
of a contraction.*

*Trough   The transition
point between reces-
sion and recovery.*

The transition points across cycles are called peaks and troughs, labeled P and T at the top of the graph. A **peak** is the transition from the end of an expansion to the start of a contraction. A **trough** occurs at the bottom of a recession just as the economy enters a recovery. The shaded areas in Figure 14.4 all represent periods of recession. The National Bureau of Economic Research (NBER) is the official designator of peak and trough points.

One interesting feature of Figure 14.4 is the duration of the expansion of the economy since 1982. Although the economy finally entered a recession in 1990, the length of this expansion was remarkable.

Economic Indicators

*Leading economic
indicators   Economic
series that tend to
rise or fall in advance
of the rest of the
economy.*

Given the cyclical nature of the business cycle, it is not surprising that the cycle can be predicted. The NBER has developed a set of cyclical indicators to help forecast, measure, and interpret short-term fluctuations in economic activity. **Leading economic indicators** are those economic series that tend to rise or fall in advance of the rest of the economy. Coincident and lagging indicators, as their names suggest, move in tandem with or somewhat after the broad economy.

Eleven series are grouped into a widely followed composite index of leading economic indicators. Similarly, four coincident and seven lagging indicators form separate indexes. The composition of these indexes appears in Table 14.1.

Figure 14.5 graphs these three series over the period 1955–1990. The numbers on the charts near the turning points of each series indicate the length of the lead time or lag time (in months) from the turning point to the designated peak or trough of the corresponding business cycle. While the index of leading indicators consistently turns before the rest of the economy, the lead time is somewhat erratic. Moreover, the lead time for peaks is consistently longer than that for troughs.

The stock market price index is a leading indicator. This is as it should be, as stock prices are forward-looking predictors of future profitability. Unfortunately, this makes the series of leading indicators much less useful for investment policy—by the time the series predicts an upturn, the market has already made its move. While the business cycle may be somewhat predictable, the stock market may not be. This is just one more manifestation of the efficient market hypothesis.

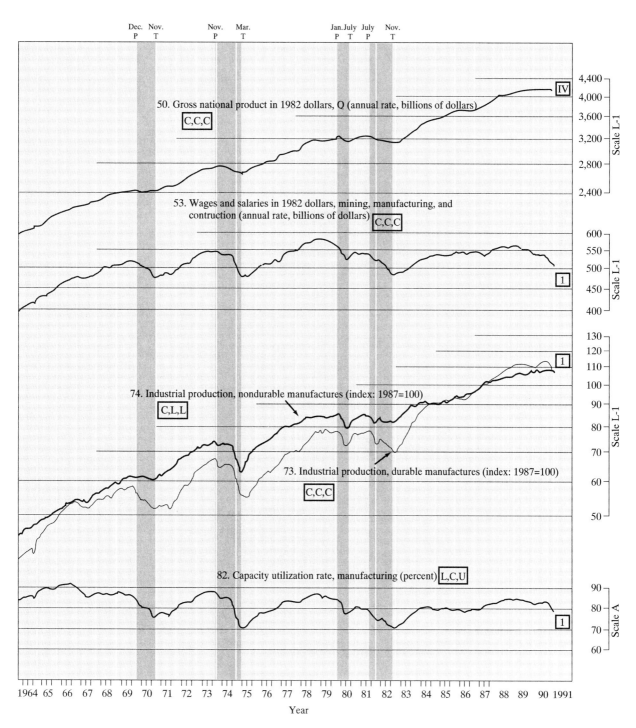

Figure 14.4 **Cyclical indicators, 1964–1990.**
From *Survey of Current Business.*

CYCLICAL INDICATORS

Composite Indexes

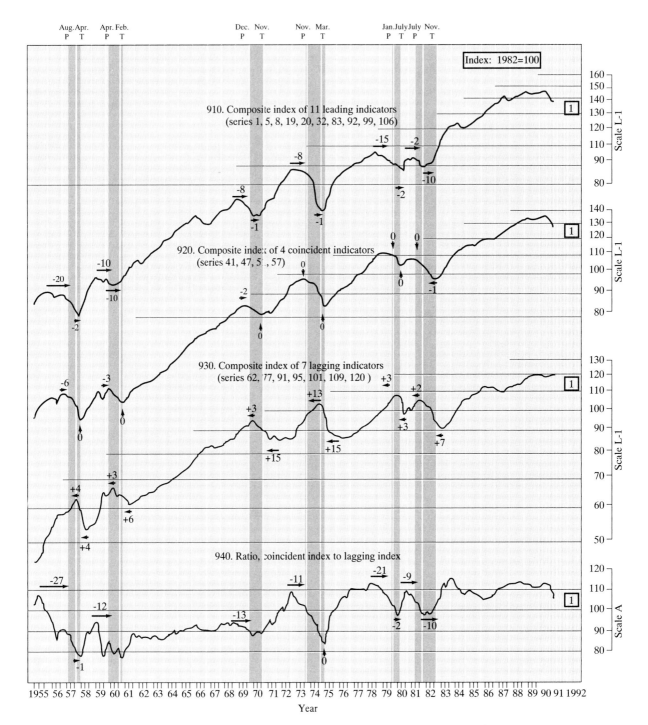

Figure 14.5 **Indexes of leading, coincident, and lagging indicators.**
Note: The numbers and arrows indicate length of leads (−) and lags (+) in months from business cycle turning dates.

Table 14.1 *Indexes of Economic Indicators*

A. Leading Indicators
1. Average weekly hours of production workers (manufacturing)
2. Average weekly initial claims for unemployment insurance
3. Manufacturers new orders (consumer goods and materials industries)
4. Vendor performance—slower deliveries diffusion index
5. Contracts and orders for plant and equipment
6. New private housing units authorized by local building permits
7. Change in manufacturers' unfilled orders (durable goods industries)
8. Change in sensitive materials prices
9. Stock prices, 500 common stocks
10. Money supply (M2)
11. Index of consumer expectations

B. Coincident Indicators
1. Employees on nonagricultural payrolls
2. Personal income less transfer payments
3. Industrial production
4. Manufacturing and trade sales

C. Lagging Indicators
1. Average duration of unemployment
2. Ratio of trade inventories to sales
3. Change in index of labor cost per unit of output
4. Average prime rate charged by banks
5. Commercial and industrial loans outstanding
6. Ratio of consumer installment credit outstanding to personal income
7. Change in consumer price index for services

From *Survey of Current Business*, U.S. Department of Commerce, February 1991.

14.5 *Industry Analysis*

Sensitivity to the Business Cycle

Once the analyst forecasts the state of the macro economy, it is necessary to determine the implication of that forecast for specific industries. Not all industries are equally sensitive to the business cycle. For example, consider Figure 14.6, which is a graph of automobile production and shipments of tobacco products, both scaled so that 1977 has a value of 100.

Clearly the tobacco industry is virtually independent of the business cycle. Demand for tobacco products does not seem affected by the state of the macro economy in any meaningful way. This is not surprising. Tobacco consumption is determined largely by habit and is a small enough part of most budgets that it will not be given up in hard times.

Auto production by contrast is highly volatile. In recessions, consumers can try to prolong the lives of their cars until their income is higher. The two worst years for auto production according to Figure 14.6 were 1975 and 1982. These were also years of deep recession. In 1982, the unemployment rate was 9.5 percent, and in 1975 it was 8.3 percent.

Three factors will determine the sensitivity of a firm's earnings to the business cycle. First is the sensitivity of sales. Necessities will show little sensitivity to business conditions. Examples of industries in this group are food, drugs, and

Figure 14.6
Industry cyclicality.
From *Business Statistics*, 1961–88, U.S. Department of Commerce.

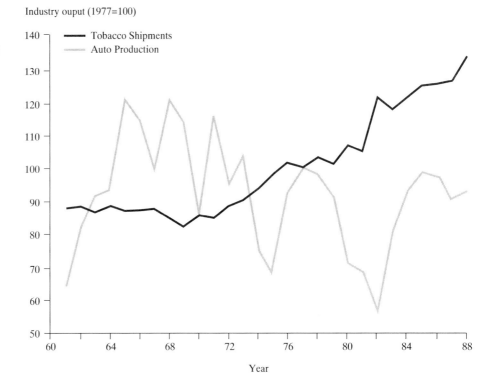

Industry ouput (1977=100)

medical services. Other industries with low sensitivity will be those for which income is not a crucial determinant of demand. As we noted, tobacco products are examples of this type of industry. Another industry in this group is movies, because consumers tend to substitute movies for more expensive sources of entertainment when income levels are low. In contrast, firms in industries such as machine tools, steel, autos, and transportation are highly sensitive to the state of the economy.

The second factor determining business cycle sensitivity is operating leverage, which refers to the division between fixed and variable costs. (Fixed costs are those the firm incurs regardless of its production levels. Variable costs are those that rise or fall as the firm produces more or less product.) Firms with variable as opposed to fixed costs will be less sensitive to business conditions. This is because in economic downturns, these firms can reduce costs as output falls in response to falling sales. Profits for firms with high fixed costs will swing more widely with sales because costs do not move to offset revenue variability. Firms with high fixed costs are said to have high operating leverage, as small swings in business conditions can have large impacts on profitability.

An example might help illustrate this concept. Consider two firms operating in the same industry with identical revenues in all phases of the business cycle: recession, normal, and expansion. Firm A has short-term leases on most of its equipment and can reduce its lease expenditures when production slackens. It has fixed costs of $5 million and variable costs of $1 per unit of output. Firm B has long-term leases on most of its equipment and must make lease payments regardless of economic conditions. Its fixed costs are higher, $8 million, but its variable costs are only $.50 per unit. Table 14.2 shows that firm A will do better

Table 14.2   *Operating Leverage*

Scenario:	Recession		Normal		Expansion	
Firm:	**A**	**B**	**A**	**B**	**A**	**B**
Sales (million units)	5	5	6	6	7	7
Price per unit	$ 2	$ 2	$ 2	$ 2	$ 2	$ 2
Revenue ($ million)	10	10	12	12	14	14
Fixed costs ($ million)	5	8	5	8	5	8
Variable costs ($ million)	5	2.5	6	3	7	3.5
Total costs ($ million)	$10	$10.5	$11	$11	$12	$11.5
Profits	$ 0	$ (0.5)	$ 1	$ 1	$ 2	$ 2.5

in recessions than firm B, but not as well in expansions. A's costs move in conjunction with its revenues to help performance in downturns and impede performance in upturns.

The third factor influencing business cycle sensitivity is financial leverage, which is the use of borrowing. Interest payments on debt must be paid regardless of sales. They are fixed costs that also increase the sensitivity of profits to business conditions. We will have more to say about financial leverage in Chapter 16.

Investors should not always prefer industries with lower sensitivity to the business cycle. Firms in sensitive industries will have high-beta stocks and are riskier. But while they swing lower in downturns, they also swing higher in upturns. As always, the issue you need to address is whether the expected return on the investment is fair compensation for the risks borne.

Concept Check

Question 4. What will be profits in the three scenarios for firm C with fixed costs of $2 million and variable costs of $1.50 per unit? What are your conclusions regarding operating leverage and business risk?

Industry Life Cycles

Examine the biotechnology industry and you will find many firms with high rates of investment, high rates of return on investment, and low dividend payout rates. Do the same for the electric utility industry and you will find lower rates of return, lower investment rates, and higher dividend payout rates. Why should this be?

The biotech industry is still new. Recently available technologies have created opportunities for highly profitable investment of resources. New products are protected by patents, and profit margins are high. With such lucrative investment opportunities, firms find it advantageous to put all profits back into the firm. The companies grow rapidly on average.

Eventually, however, growth must slow. The high profit rates will induce new firms to enter the industry. Increasing competition will hold down prices and profit margins. New technologies become proven and more predictable, risk levels fall, and entry becomes even easier. As internal investment opportunities become less attractive, a lower fraction of profits are reinvested in the firm. Cash dividends increase.

Ultimately, in a mature industry, we observe "cash cows," firms with stable dividends and cash flows and little risk. Growth rates might be similar to that of the overall economy. Industries in early states of their life cycles offer high-risk/high-potential-return investments. Mature industries offer lower-risk, lower-return combinations.

Innovation is usually the driving force behind industries in the early high-growth phase, but other factors might also create such opportunities. For example, the unification of Germany has created great growth opportunities for many West German companies. Ultimately, however, the forces of economic competition cause growth to be self-limiting. The exploitation of profit opportunities brings about new sources of supply that eventually reduce prices, profits, investment returns, and finally growth. The maturing of an industry is an inevitable process.

Summary

1. Macroeconomic policy aims to maintain the economy near full employment without aggravating inflationary pressures. The proper trade-off between these two goals is a source of ongoing debate.

2. The traditional tools of macro policy are government spending and tax collection, which comprise fiscal policy, and manipulation of the money supply via monetary policy. Expansionary fiscal policy can stimulate the economy and increase GNP but tends to increase interest rates. Expansionary monetary policy works by lowering interest rates.

3. The business cycle is the economy's recurring pattern of expansions and recessions. Leading economic indicators can be used to anticipate the evolution of the business cycle because their values tend to change before those of other key economic variables.

4. Industries differ in their sensitivity to the business cycle. More sensitive industries tend to be those producing high-priced goods for which the consumer has considerable discretion as to the timing of purchase. Examples are automobiles or consumer durables. Other sensitive industries are those that produce capital equipment for other firms. Operating leverage and financial leverage increase sensitivity to the business cycle.

Key Terms

budget deficit, 395	gross national product, 394	peak, 406
business cycle, 406		supply shock, 396
current account, 395	inflation, 394	trough, 406
demand shock, 396	leading economic indicators, 406	unemployment rate, 394
exchange rate, 395		
fiscal policy, 400	monetary policy, 401	

Selected Readings

Overviews of the macro economy appear regularly in several business periodicals. Try, for example:
   Business Week, Financial World, Fortune, or Forbes.

More formal evaluations of the economy appear annually in:
   The Economic Report of the President and weekly in the Survey of Current Business.

Problem Sets

1. What monetary and fiscal policies might be prescribed for an economy in a deep recession?

2. Suppose you believe the Fed is going to dramatically loosen monetary policy. What would be your recommendations about investments in the following industries:
   a. Gold mining.
   b. Construction.

3. If you believed the U.S. dollar is about to depreciate, what would be your stance on investments in U.S. auto producers?

4. According to supply-side economists, what will be the long-run impact on prices of a reduction in income tax rates?

5. Consider two firms producing videocassette recorders. One uses a highly automated robotics process, while the other uses human workers on an assembly line and pays overtime when there is heavy production demand.
   a. Which firm will have higher profits in a recession? In a boom?
   b. Which firm's stock will have a higher beta?

6. The following questions appeared on recent CFA Examinations.
   a. Which one of the following statements *best* expresses the central idea of countercyclical fiscal policy?
      (1) Planned government deficits are appropriate during economic booms, and planned surpluses are appropriate during economic recessions.
      (2) The balanced budget approach is the proper criterion for determining annual budget policy.
      (3) Actual deficits should equal actual surpluses during a period of deflation.
      (4) Government deficits are planned during economic recessions, and surpluses are utilized to restrain inflationary booms.
   b. The supply-side view stresses that:
      (1) Aggregate demand is the major determinant of real output and aggregate employment.
      (2) An increase in government expenditures and tax rates will cause real income to rise.
      (3) Tax rates are a major determinant of real output and aggregate employment.
      (4) Expansionary monetary policy will cause real output to expand without causing the rate of inflation to accelerate.
   c. Which *one* of the following propositions would a strong proponent of supply-side economics be *most* likely to stress?
      (1) Higher marginal tax rates will lead to a reduction in the size of the budget deficit and lower interest rates because they expand government revenues.
      (2) Higher marginal tax rates promote economic inefficiency and thereby retard aggregate output because they encourage investors to undertake low productivity projects with substantial tax-shelter benefits.

(3) Income redistribution payments will exert little impact on real aggregate supply because they do not consume resources directly.

(4) A tax reduction will increase the disposable income of households. Thus, the primary impact of a tax reduction on aggregate supply will stem from the influence of the tax change on the size of the budget deficit or surplus.

d. Which one of the following series is *not* included in the index of leading economic indicators?

(1) New building permits; private housing units.

(2) Net business formation.

(3) Stock prices.

(4) Inventories on hand.

e. How would an economist who believes in crowding out complete the following sentence? "The increase in the budget deficit causes real interest rates to rise, and therefore private spending and investment:

(1) Increase."

(2) Stay the same."

(3) Decrease."

(4) Initially increase but eventually will decrease."

f. If the central monetary authorities want to reduce the supply of money to slow the rate of inflation, the central bank should:

(1) Sell government bonds, which will reduce the money supply; this will cause interest rates to rise and aggregate demand to fall.

(2) Buy government bonds, which will reduce the money supply; this will cause interest rates to rise and aggregate demand to fall.

(3) Decrease the discount rate, which will lower the market rate of interest; this will cause both costs and prices to fall.

(4) Increase taxes, which will reduce costs and cause prices to fall.

Chapter

Equity Valuation Models

$\mathbf{Y}$ou saw in our discussion of market efficiency that finding undervalued securities is hardly easy. At the same time, there are enough chinks in the armor of the efficient market hypothesis that the search for such securities should not be dismissed out of hand. Moreover, it is the ongoing search for mispriced securities that maintains a nearly efficient market. Even infrequent discoveries of minor mispricing justify the salary of a stock market analyst.

This chapter describes the ways stock market analysts try to uncover mispriced securities. The models presented are those used by **fundamental analysts,** those analysts who use information concerning the current and prospective profitability of a company to assess its fair market value. Fundamental analysts are different from **technical analysts,** who essentially use trend analysis to uncover trading opportunities. We discuss technical analysis in Chapter 17.

We start with a discussion of alternative measures of the value of a company. From there, we progress to quantitative tools called dividend discount models that security analysts commonly use to measure the value of a firm as an ongoing concern. Next, we turn to price/earnings, or P/E, ratios, explaining why they are of such interest to analysts but also highlighting some of their shortcomings. We explain how P/E ratios are tied to dividend valuation models and, more generally, to the growth prospects of the firm. After studying this chapter you should be able to:

Fundamental analysts
Analysts who compare stock prices to determinants of value such as earnings and dividends prospects.

Technical analysts
Analysts who search for recurrent and predictable stock price patterns.

- Calculate the intrinsic value of a firm using either a constant growth or multistage dividend discount model.
- Calculate the intrinsic value of a stock using a dividend discount model in conjunction with a price/earnings ratio.
- Assess the growth prospects of a firm from its P/E ratio.

15.1   *Balance Sheet Valuation Methods*

Book value *The net worth of common equity according to a firm's balance sheet.*

A common valuation measure is **book value,** which is the net worth of a company as shown on the balance sheet. Table 15.1 gives the balance sheet totals for IBM to illustrate how to calculate book value per share.

Book value of IBM stock on December 31, 1989, was $66.52 per share ($38,509 million divided by 578.9 million shares). On that same date, IBM stock had a market price of $94.13. Would it be fair to say IBM stock was overpriced?

The book value is the result of applying a set of arbitrary accounting rules to spread the acquisition cost of assets over a specified number of years, whereas the market price of a stock takes account of the firm's value as a going concern. In other words, the market price reflects the present value of its expected future cash flows. It would be unusual if the market price of IBM stock were exactly equal to its book value.

Can book value represent a "floor" for the stock's price, below which level the market price can never fall? Although IBM's book value per share on December 31, 1989, was less than its market price, other evidence disproves this notion. On January 16, 1991, Digital Equipment Corp. stock had a book value of $67.59 per share and a market price of $59.38. Clearly, book value cannot always be a floor for the stock's price.

Liquidation value *Net amount that can be realized by selling the assets of a firm and paying off the debt.*

A better measure of a floor for the stock price is the **liquidation value** per share of the firm. This represents the amount of money that could be realized by breaking up the firm, selling its assets, repaying its debt, and distributing the remainder to the shareholders. The reasoning behind this concept is that if the market price of equity drops below the liquidation value of the firm, the firm becomes attractive as a takeover target. A corporate raider would find it profitable to buy enough shares to gain control and then actually to liquidate because the liquidation value exceeds the value of the business as a going concern.

Replacement cost *Cost to replace a firm's assets.*

Another balance sheet concept that is of interest in valuing a firm is the **replacement cost** of its assets less its liabilities. Some analysts believe the market value of the firm cannot get too far above its replacement cost because, if it did, competitors would try to replicate the firm. The competitive pressure of other similar firms entering the same industry would drive down the market value of all firms until they came into equality with replacement cost.

Tobin's q *Ratio of market value of the firm to replacement cost.*

This idea is popular among economists, and the ratio of market price to replacement cost is known as **Tobin's q,** after the Nobel-Prize-winning economist James Tobin. In the long run, according to this view, the ratio of market price to replacement cost will tend toward 1, but the evidence is that this ratio can differ significantly from 1 for very long periods of time.

Although focusing on the balance sheet can give some useful information about a firm's liquidation value or its replacement cost, the analyst must usually

Table 15.1   *IBM Balance Sheet, December 31, 1989 ($ million)*

Assets	Liabilities and Owners' Equity	
$77,734	Liabilities	$39,225
	Common equity	$38,509
	578.9 million shares outstanding	

turn to the expected future cash flows for a better estimate of the firm's value as a going concern. We now examine the quantitative models that analysts use to value common stock in terms of the future earnings and dividends the firm will yield.

15.2 *Intrinsic Value versus Market Price*

The most popular model for assessing the value of a firm as a going concern takes off from the observation that an investor in stock expects a return consisting of cash dividends and capital gains or losses. We begin by assuming a one-year holding period and supposing that ABC stock has an expected dividend per share, $E(D_1)$, of \$4, the current price of a share, P_0, is \$48, and the expected price at the end of a year, $E(P_1)$, is \$52.

The holding-period return the investor expects is $E(D_1)$ plus the expected price appreciation, $E(P_1) - P_0$, all divided by the current price P_0:

$$\begin{aligned}
\text{Expected HPR} &= E(r) \\
&= \frac{E(D_1) + [E(P_1) - P_0]}{P_0} \\
&= \frac{4 + (52 - 48)}{48} \\
&= 0.167 \\
&= 16.7\%
\end{aligned}$$

Note that $E(\ )$ denotes an expected future value. Thus, $E(P_1)$ represents the expectation today of the stock price one year from now. $E(r)$ is referred to as the stock's expected holding period return. It is the sum of the expected dividend yield, $E(D_1)/P_0$, and the expected rate of price appreciation, the capital gains yield, $[E(P_1) - P_0]/P_0$.

But what is the investor's *required* rate of return on the stock? From the CAPM we know that the required rate, k, is equal to $r_f + \beta[E(r_M) - r_f]$. Suppose $r_f = 6$ percent, $\beta = 1.2$, and $E(r_M) - r_f = 5$ percent. Then the value of k is

$$\begin{aligned}
k &= 6\% + 1.2 \times 5\% \\
&= 12\%
\end{aligned}$$

For ABC, the rate of return the investor expects exceeds the required rate based on ABC's risk by a margin of 4.7 percent. Naturally, the investor will want to include more of ABC stock in the portfolio than a passive strategy would dictate.

Intrinsic value The present value of a firm's expected future net cash flows discounted by the required rate of return.

Another way to see this is to compare the intrinsic value of a share of stock to its market price. The **intrinsic value,** denoted V_0, of a share of stock is defined as the present value of all cash payments to the investor in the stock, including dividends as well as the proceeds from the ultimate sale of the stock, discounted at the appropriate risk-adjusted interest rate, k. Whenever the intrinsic value, or the investor's own estimate of what the stock is really worth, exceeds the market price, the stock is considered undervalued and a good investment. In the case of ABC, using a one-year investment horizon and a forecast that the stock can be sold at the end of the year at price $P_1 = \$52$, the intrinsic value is

$$V_0 = \frac{E(D_1) + E(P_1)}{1 + k}$$

$$= \frac{\$4 + \$52}{1.12}$$

$$= \$50$$

Because intrinsic value, $50, exceeds current price, $48, we conclude the stock is undervalued in the market. We again conclude investors will want to buy more ABC than they would following a passive strategy.

If the intrinsic value turns out to be lower than the current market price, investors should buy less of it than under the passive strategy. It might even pay to go short on ABC stock as we discussed in Chapter 5.

Market capitalization rate *The market-consensus estimate of the appropriate discount rate for a firm's cash flows.*

In market equilibrium, the current market price will reflect the intrinsic value estimates of all market participants. This means the individual investor whose V_0 estimate differs from the market price, P_0, in effect must disagree with some or all of the market consensus estimates of $E(D_1)$, $E(P_1)$, or k. A common term for the market consensus value of the required rate of return, k, is the **market capitalization rate,** which we use often throughout this chapter.

Concept Check

> **Question 1.** You expect the price of IBX stock to be $59.77 per share a year from now. Its current market price is $50, and you expect it to pay a dividend one year from now of $2.15 a share.
>
> *a.* What is the stock's expected dividend yield, rate of price appreciation, and holding-period return?
>
> *b.* If the stock has a beta of 1.15, the risk-free rate is 6 percent per year, and the expected rate of return on the market portfolio is 14 percent per year, what is the required rate of return on IBX stock?
>
> *c.* What is the intrinsic value of IBX stock, and how does it compare to the current market price?

15.3 Dividend Discount Models

Consider an investor who buys a share of Steady State Electronics stock, planning to hold it for one year. The intrinsic value of the share is the present value of the dividend to be received at the end of the first year, D_1, and the expected sales price, P_1. We will henceforth use the simpler notation P_1 instead of $E(P_1)$ to avoid clutter. Keep in mind, though, future prices and dividends are unknown, and we are dealing with expected values, not certain values. We've already established

$$V_0 = \frac{D_1 + P_1}{1 + k} \tag{15.1}$$

While dividends are fairly predictable given a company's history, you might ask how we can estimate P_1, the year-end price. According to Equation 15.1, V_1 (the year-end value) will be

$$V_1 = \frac{D_2 + P_2}{1 + k}$$

If we assume the stock will be selling for its intrinsic value next year, then $V_1 = P_1$, and we can substitute this value for P_1 into Equation 15.1 to find

$$V_0 = \frac{D_1}{1+k} + \frac{D_2 + P_2}{(1+k)^2}$$

This equation may be interpreted as the present value of dividends plus sales price for a two-year holding period. Of course, now we need to come up with a forecast of P_2. Continuing in the same way, we can replace P_2 by $(D_3 + P_3)/(1+k)$, which relates P_0 to the value of dividends plus the expected sales price for a three-year holding period.

More generally, for a holding period of H years, we can write the stock value as the present value of dividends over the H years, plus the ultimate sale price, P_H.

$$V_0 = \frac{D_1}{1+k} + \frac{D_2}{(1+k)^2} + \cdots + \frac{D_H + P_H}{(1+k)^H} \qquad \textbf{(15.2)}$$

Note the similarity between this formula and the bond valuation formula developed in Chapter 12. Each relates price to the present value of a stream of payments (coupons in the case of bonds, dividends in the case of stocks) and a final payment (the face value of the bond, or the sales price of the stock). The key differences in the case of stocks are the uncertainty of dividends, the lack of a fixed maturity date, and the unknown sales price at the horizon date. Indeed, one can continue to substitute for price indefinitely to conclude

$$V_0 = \frac{D_1}{1+k} + \frac{D_2}{(1+k)^2} + \frac{D_3}{(1+k)^3} + \cdots \qquad \textbf{(15.3)}$$

Dividend discount model (DDM) *A formula for the intrinsic value of a firm equal to the present value of all expected future dividends.*

Equation 15.2 states the stock price should equal the present value of all expected future dividends into perpetuity. This formula is called the **dividend discount model (DDM)** of stock prices.

It is tempting, but incorrect, to conclude from Equation 15.3 that the DDM focuses exclusively on dividends and ignores capital gains as a motive for investing in stock. Indeed, we assume explicitly in Equation 15.1 that capital gains (as reflected in the expected sales price, P_1) are part of the stock's value. At the same time, the price at which you can sell a stock in the future depends on dividend forecasts at that time.

The reason only dividends appear in Equation 15.3 is not that investors ignore capital gains. It is instead that those capital gains will be determined by dividend forecasts at the time the stock is sold. That is why in Equation 15.2 we can write the stock price as the present value of dividends plus sales price for *any* horizon date. P_H is the present value at time H of all dividends expected to be paid after the horizon date. That value is then discounted back to today, time 0. The DDM asserts that stock prices are determined ultimately by the cash flows accruing to stockholders, and those are dividends.

The Constant Growth DDM

Equation 15.3 as it stands is still not very useful in valuing a stock because it requires dividend forecasts for every year into the indefinite future. For a more structured valuation approach, we need to introduce some simplifying assumptions. A useful first pass at the problem is to assume that Steady State Electronics dividends are trending upward at a stable growth rate that we will call g. Then if $g = .05$, and the most recently paid dividend was $D_0 = 3.81$, expected future dividends are

$$D_1 = D_0(1 + g) = 3.81 \times 1.05 = 4.00$$
$$D_2 = D_0(1 + g)^2 = 3.81 \times (1.05)^2 = 4.20$$
$$D_3 = D_0(1 + g)^3 = 3.81 \times (1.05)^3 = 4.41 \quad \text{etc.}$$

Using these dividend forecasts in Equation 15.3, we solve for intrinsic value as

$$V_0 = \frac{D_0(1 + g)}{1 + k} + \frac{D_0(1 + g)^2}{(1 + k)^2} + \frac{D_0(1 + g)^3}{(1 + k)^3} + \cdots$$

This equation can be simplified to

$$V_0 = \frac{D_0(1 + g)}{k - g} = \frac{D_1}{k - g} \qquad \textbf{(15.4)}$$

Note in Equation 15.4 that we divide D_1 (not D_0) by $k - g$ to calculate intrinsic value. If the market capitalization rate for Steady State is 12 percent, now we can use Equation 15.4 to show that the intrinsic value of a share of Steady State stock is

$$\frac{\$4.00}{.12 - .05} = \$57.14$$

Constant growth DDM *A form of the dividend discount model that assumes dividends will grow at a constant rate.*

Equation 15.4 is called the **constant growth DDM** or the Gordon model, after Myron J. Gordon, who popularized the model. It should remind you of the formula for the present value of a perpetuity. If dividends were expected not to grow, then the dividend stream would be a simple perpetuity, and the valuation formula would be $P_0 = D_1/k$.[1] Equation 15.4 is a generalization of the perpetuity formula to cover the case of a *growing* perpetuity. As g increases, the stock price also rises.

The constant growth DDM is valid only when g is less than k. If dividends were expected to grow forever at a rate faster than k, the value of the stock would be infinite. If an analyst derives an estimate of g that is greater than k, that growth rate must be unsustainable in the long run. The appropriate valuation model to use in this case is a multistage DDM such as that discussed below.

The constant growth DDM is so widely used by stock market analysts that it is worth exploring some of its implications and limitations. The constant growth rate DDM implies that a stock's value will be greater:

1. The larger its expected dividend per share.
2. The lower the market capitalization rate, k.
3. The higher the expected growth rate of dividends.

Another implication of the constant growth model is that the stock price is expected to grow at the same rate as dividends. To see this, suppose Steady

---

[1] Recall from introductory finance that the present value of a $1 per year perpetuity is $1/k$. For example, if $k = 10$ percent, the value of the perpetuity is $\$1/.10 = \$10$. Notice that if $g = 0$ in Equation 15.4, the constant growth DDM formula is the same as the perpetuity formula.

State stock is selling at its intrinsic value of $57.14, so that $V_0 = P_0$. Then,

$$P_0 = \frac{D_1}{k - g}$$

Note that price is proportional to dividends. Therefore, next year, when the dividends paid to Steady State stockholders are expected to be higher by $g = 5$ percent, price also should increase by 5 percent. To confirm this, note

$$D_2 = \$4(1.05) = \$4.20$$
$$P_1 = D_2/(k - g) = \$4.20/(.12 - .05) = \$60.00$$

which is 5 percent higher than the current price of $57.14. To generalize,

$$P_1 = \frac{D_2}{k - g} = \frac{D_1(1 + g)}{k - g} = \frac{D_1}{k - g}(1 + g)$$
$$= P_0(1 + g)$$

Therefore, the DDM implies that in the case of constant growth of dividends, the rate of price appreciation in any year will equal that constant growth rate, g. Note that for a stock whose market price equals its intrinsic value ($V_0 = P_0$) the expected holding-period return will be

$$\begin{aligned} E(r) &= \text{Dividend yield} + \text{Capital gains yield} \\ &= \frac{D_1}{P_0} + \frac{P_1 - P_0}{P_0} \\ &= \frac{D_1}{P_0} + g \end{aligned} \qquad (15.5)$$

This formula offers a means to infer the market capitalization rate of a stock, for if the stock is selling at its intrinsic value, then $E(r) = k$, implying that $k = D_0/P_0 + g$. By observing the dividend yield, D_1/P_0, and estimating the growth rate of dividends, we can compute k. This equation is also known as the *discounted cash flow (DCF) formula*.

This is an approach often used in rate hearings for regulated public utilities. The regulatory agency responsible for approving utility pricing decisions is mandated to allow the firms to charge just enough to cover costs plus a "fair" profit, that is, one that allows a competitive return on the investment the firm has made in its productive capacity. In turn, that return is taken to be the expected return investors require on the stock of the firm. The $D_1/P_0 + g$ formula provides a means to infer that required return.

Concept Check

Question 2.

a. IBX's stock dividend at the end of this year is expected to be $2.15, and it is expected to grow at 11.2 percent per year forever. If the required rate of return on IBX stock is 15.2 percent per year, what is its intrinsic value?

b. If IBX's current market price is equal to this intrinsic value, what is next year's expected price?

c. If an investor were to buy IBX stock now and sell it after receiving the $2.15 dividend a year from now, what is the expected capital gain (i.e., price appreciation) in percentage terms? What is the dividend yield, and what would be the holding-period return?

Stock Prices and Investment Opportunities

Consider two companies, No-Opps and Good-Opps, each with expected earnings in the coming year of $5 per share. Both companies could in principle pay out all of these earnings as dividends, maintaining a perpetual dividend flow of $5 per share. If the market capitalization rate were $k = 12.5$ percent, both companies would then be valued at $D_1/k = \$5/.125 = \$40$ per share. Neither firm would grow in value, because with all earnings paid out as dividends, and no earnings reinvested in the firm, both companies' capital stock and earnings capacity would remain unchanged over time; earnings and dividends would not grow.

Actually, we are referring here to earnings net of the funds necessary to maintain the productivity of the firm's capital, that is, earnings net of "economic depreciation." In other words, the earnings figure should be interpreted as the maximum amount of money the firm could pay out each year in perpetuity without depleting its productive capacity. For this reason, the net earnings number may be quite different from the accounting earnings figure that the firm reports in its financial statements. (We explore this further in the next chapter.)

Dividend payout ratio   Percentage of earnings paid out as dividends.

Plowback ratio or earnings retention ratio   The proportion of the firm's earnings that is reinvested in the business (and not paid out as dividends).

Now suppose one of the firms, Good-Opps, engages in projects that generate a return on investment of 15 percent, which is greater than the required rate of return, $k = 12.5$ percent. It would be foolish for such a company to pay out all of its earnings as dividends. If Good-Opps retains or plows back some of its earnings into its highly profitable projects, it can earn a 15 percent rate of return for its shareholders, while if it pays out all earnings as dividends, it forgoes the projects, leaving shareholders to invest the dividends in other opportunities at a fair market rate of only 12.5 percent. Suppose, therefore, Good-Opps lowers its **dividend payout ratio** (the fraction of earnings paid out as dividends) from 100 percent to 40 percent, maintaining a **plowback ratio** (the fraction of earnings reinvested in the firm) at 60 percent. The plowback ratio is also referred to as the **earnings retention ratio.**

Concept Check

Question 3.   What must be the sum of the payout and plowback ratios?

The dividend of the company, therefore, will be $2 (40 percent of $5 earnings) instead of $5. Will share price fall? No—it will rise! Although dividends initially fall under the earnings reinvestment policy, subsequent growth in the assets of the firm because of reinvested profits will generate growth in future dividends, which will be reflected in today's share price.

How much growth will be generated? Suppose Good-Opps starts with plant and equipment of $100 million and is all equity financed. With a return on investment or equity (ROE) of 15 percent, total earnings are ROE × $100 million $= .15 \times \$100$ million $= \$15$ million. There are 3 million shares of stock outstanding, so earnings per share are $5, as posited above. If 60 percent of the $15 million in this year's earnings is reinvested, then the value of the firm's capital stock will increase by $0.60 \times \$15$ million $= \$9$ million, or by 9 percent. The percentage increase in the capital stock is the rate at which income was generated (ROE) times the plowback ratio (the fraction of earnings reinvested in more capital), which we will denote as b.

Now endowed with 9 percent more capital, the company earns 9 percent more income, and pays out 9 percent higher dividends. The growth rate of the dividends, therefore, is

$$
\begin{aligned}
g &= \text{ROE} \times b \\
&= .15 \times .60 \\
&= .09.
\end{aligned}
$$

If the stock price equals its intrinsic value, it should sell at

$$
P_0 = \frac{D_1}{k - g} = \frac{\$2}{.125 - .09} = \$57.14
$$

When Good-Opps pursued a no-growth policy and paid out all earnings as dividends, the stock price was only $40. When it reduced current dividends and plowed funds back into the company, the growth rate increased enough to cause the stock price to increase.

The difference between the no-growth price of $40 and the actual price of $57.14 can be ascribed to the present value of the company's excellent investment opportunities. One way to think of the company's value is to describe its stock price as the sum of the no-growth value (the value of current earnings per share, E_1, in perpetuity) plus the present value of these growth opportunities, which we will denote as PVGO. In terms of the example we have been following, PVGO = 17.14:

$$
\begin{aligned}
P_0 &= \frac{E_1}{k} + \text{PVGO} \\
57.14 &= 40 + 17.14.
\end{aligned}
$$

(15.6)

It is important to recognize that growth per se is not what investors desire. Growth enhances company value only if it is achieved by investment in projects with attractive profit opportunities (i.e., with ROE > k). To see why, let's now consider Good-Opps' unfortunate sister company, No-Opps. No-Opps' ROE is only 12.5 percent, just equal to the required rate of return, k. The NPV of its investment opportunities is zero. We've seen that following a zero-growth strategy with $b = 0$ and $g = 0$, the value of No-Opps will be $E_1/k = \$5/.125 = \$40$ per share. Now suppose No-Opps chooses a plowback ratio of $b = .60$, the same as Good-Opps' plowback. Then g would be

$$
\begin{aligned}
g &= \text{ROE} \times b \\
&= 0.125 \times 0.60 \\
&= 0.075,
\end{aligned}
$$

and the stock price becomes

$$
P_0 = \frac{D_1}{k - g} = \frac{\$2}{.125 - .075} = \$40
$$

no different from the no-growth strategy.

In the case of No-Opps, the dividend reduction used to free funds for reinvestment in the firm generates only enough growth to maintain the stock price at the current level. This is as it should be: If the firm's projects yield only what investors can earn on their own, shareholders cannot be made better off by a high reinvestment rate policy. This demonstrates that "growth" is not the same as growth opportunities. To justify reinvestment, the firm must engage in projects with better prospective returns than those shareholders can find elsewhere. Notice also that the PVGO of No-Opps is zero: $PVGO = P_0 - E_1/k = 40 - 40 = 0$. With $ROE = k$, there is no advantage to plowing funds back into the firm; this shows up as PVGO of zero.

Concept Check

Question 4.
a. Calculate the price of a firm with a plowback ratio of 0.60 if its ROE is 20 percent. Current earnings, E_1, will be $5 per share, and $k = 12.5$ percent.
b. What if ROE is 10 percent, less than the market capitalization rate? Compare price in this instance to that of a firm with the same ROE and E_1, but a plowback ratio $b = 0$.

Life Cycles and the Constant Growth Model

As useful as the constant growth DDM formula is, you need to remember that it is based on a simplifying assumption, namely, that the dividend growth rate will be constant forever. In fact, firms typically pass through life cycles with very different dividend profiles in different phases. In early years, there are ample opportunities for profitable reinvestment in the company. Payout ratios are low, and growth is correspondingly rapid. In later years, the firm matures, production capacity is sufficient to meet market demand, competitors enter the market, and attractive opportunities for reinvestment may become harder to find. In this mature phase, the firm may choose to increase the dividend payout ratio, rather than retain earnings. The dividend level increases, but thereafter grows at a slower rate because of fewer company growth opportunities.

Table 15.2 demonstrates this profile. It gives 1989 return on assets, dividend payout ratio, and five-year growth rate in earnings per share of a sample of the firms included in Value Line's computer industry versus those in the U.S. central region electric utility group.

The computer firms as a group have had attractive investment opportunities. The average return on assets of these firms is 16.2 percent, and the firms have responded with quite high plowback ratios. Many of these firms pay no dividends at all. The high return on assets and high plowback result in rapid growth. The average five-year growth of earnings per share in this group was 26.3 percent.

In contrast, the electric utilities are more representative of mature firms. Their return on assets is lower, 8.3 percent; dividend payout is higher, 81.3 percent; and average growth has been lower, 2.7 percent.

To value companies with temporarily high growth, analysts use a multistage version of the dividend discount model. Dividends in the early high-growth period are forecast and their combined present value calculated. Then, once the firm is projected to settle down to a steady growth phase, the constant growth DDM is applied to value the remaining stream of dividends.

Table 15.2 *Financial Ratios in Two Industries, 1989*

	Return on Assets	Payout Ratio	Growth Rate 1985–89
Computers			
Amdahl	12.5	7	34.1
Apple	27.3	12	45.2
Compaq	22.8	0	52.6
Cray	12.5	0	17.8
Digital	13.3	0	24.1
IBM	11.3	52	2.9
NCR	19.0	24	10.5
Tandem	11.1	0	23.3
Average	16.2	11.9	26.3
Electric Utilities			
Central PSW	8.2	82	6.5
Central Illinois Public Service	7.6	94	2.5
Commonwealth Edison	6.8	105	−8.6
Detroit Edison	8.7	67	3.8
Interstate Power	8.8	76	1.7
Iowa Resources	7.9	87	2.2
Kansas City Power	8.2	77	1.4
Minnesota Power	7.8	89	6.8
Ohio Edison	8.7	90	1.3
Texas Utilities	8.5	69	4.4
Wisconsin Energy	10.0	58	7.8
Average	8.1	83.6	2.2

We can illustrate this with a real-life example. Figure 15.1 is a Value Line Investment Survey report on Hewlett-Packard, a designer and manufacturer of electronic components. Some of the relevant information in early 1990 is highlighted.

HP's beta appears at the circled A, the recent stock price at the B, the per share dividend payments at the C, the ROE (referred to as percent earned on net worth) at the D, and the dividend payout ratio (referred to as percent of all dividends to net profits) at the E. The rows ending at C, D, and E are historical time series. The bold-faced italicized entries under 1990 are estimates for that year. Similarly, the entries in the far right column (labeled 92–94E) are forecasts for some time between 1992 and 1994, which we will take to be 1993.

Note that while dividends were $.36 per share in 1989, dividends forecast for 1993 are $.75. Hence, Value Line forecasts rapid short-term growth in dividends, approximately 20 percent per year. If we use linear interpolation between 1989 and 1993, we obtain dividend forecasts as follows:

1990	$.45
1991	$.55
1992	$.65
1993	$.75

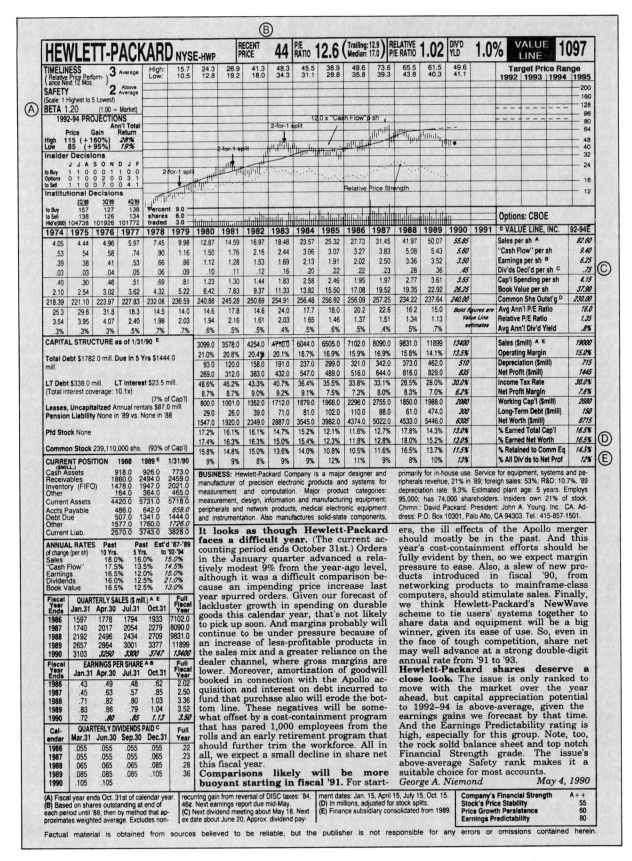

Figure 15.1 Value Line Investment Survey report on Hewlett-Packard.

Now let us assume the dividend growth rate levels off in 1993. What is a good guess for that steady-state growth rate? Value Line forecasts a dividend payout ratio of 0.12 and an ROE of 16.5 percent, implying long-term growth will be

$$g = \text{ROE} \times b = 16.5\% \times (1 - .12) = 14.5\%$$

Our estimate of HP's intrinsic value using an investment horizon of 1993 is, therefore,

$$V_0 = \frac{.45}{1 + k} + \frac{.55}{(1 + k)^2} + \frac{.65}{(1 + k)^3} + \frac{.75 + P_{1993}}{(1 + k)^4}$$

Here, P_{1993} represents the forecasted price at which we can sell our shares of HP at the end of 1993, when dividends enter their constant growth phase. That price, according to the constant growth DDM, should be

$$P_{1993} = \frac{D_{1994}}{k - g} = \frac{D_{1993}(1 + g)}{k - g} = \frac{.75(1.145)}{k - .145}$$

The only variable remaining to be determined in order to calculate intrinsic value is the market capitalization rate, k.

One way to obtain k is from the CAPM. Observe from the Value Line data that HP's beta is 1.20. Suppose the consensus forecast for the expected rate of return on the market portfolio in 1990 was about 14.5 percent. Using this value, and the fact that Treasury bills were yielding about 8 percent at the time, allows us to solve for k as

$$\begin{aligned} k &= r_f + \beta[E(r_M) - r_f] \\ &= 8\% + 1.2[14.5\% - 8\%] \\ &= 15.8\% \end{aligned}$$

Therefore, our guess for the stock price in 1993 is

$$P_{1993} = \frac{.75(1.145)}{.158 - .145} = 66.06$$

and the estimate of intrinsic value is

$$V_0 = \frac{.45}{1.158} + \frac{.55}{1.158^2} + \frac{.65}{1.158^3} + \frac{.75 + 66.06}{1.158^4} = 38.37$$

We know from the Value Line report that HP's actual price was $44 (at the B). Our intrinsic value analysis indicates HP was overpriced. Should we sell our holdings of HP or even sell HP short?

Perhaps. But before betting the farm, stop to consider how firm our estimate is. We've had to guess at dividends in the near future, the ultimate growth rate of those dividends, and the appropriate discount rate. Moreover, we've assumed HP will follow a relatively simple two-stage growth process. In practice, the growth of dividends can follow more complicated patterns. Even small errors in these approximations could upset a conclusion.

For example, suppose we've overestimated either HP's beta or the expected market return, and the actual market capitalization rate should be 15.3 percent instead of 15.8 percent, a change of only a half percentage point. Yet the result is that the intrinsic value of the stock using this market capitalization rate is $62.39, far greater than the $44.00 market price. Our conclusion regarding intrinsic value versus price is turned around completely.

Concept Check

> ***Question 5.***   Confirm that the price of HP using $k = 15.3$ percent is $62.39. Hint: First calculate the stock price in 1993. Then calculate the present value of all interim dividends plus the present value of the 1993 sales price.

This exercise shows that finding bargains is not as easy as it seems. While the DDM is easy to apply, establishing its inputs is more of a challenge. This should not be surprising. In even a moderately efficient market, finding profit opportunities has to be more involved than sitting down with Value Line for a half hour.

Nevertheless, there is evidence that the DDM is of value in identifying good buys. Figure 15.2 presents the results of a study performed by Stockfacts, a division of Salomon Brothers, using a three-stage version of the DDM to estimate the expected return of 250 stocks. Each firm is assigned to one of five portfolios according to expected return. Expected returns were updated each year, and the firms were regrouped into portfolios accordingly. Figure 15.2 shows that the average investment performance of each portfolio conformed to the prediction of the DDM. The best-performing portfolio was the one formed of the highest expected return stocks.

15.4   *Price/Earnings Ratios*

The Price/Earnings Ratio and Growth Opportunities

Price/earnings multiple   The ratio of a stock's price to its earnings per share.

Much of the real-world discussion of stock market valuation concentrates on the firm's **price/earnings multiple,** the ratio of price per share to earnings per share. Our discussion of growth opportunities shows why stock market analysts focus on this multiple, commonly called the P/E ratio. Both companies considered, No-Opps and Good-Opps, had earnings per share, EPS, of $5, but Good-Opps reinvested 60 percent of earnings in prospects with an ROE of 15 percent, while No-Opps paid out all earnings as dividends. No-Opps had a price of $40, giving it a P/E multiple of 40/5 = 8.0, while Good-Opps sold for $57.14, giving it a multiple of 57.14/5 = 11.4. This observation suggests the P/E ratio might serve as a useful indicator of expectations of growth opportunities. We can see this explicitly by rearranging Equation 15.6 to

$$\frac{P_0}{E_1} = \frac{1}{k}\left[1 + \frac{\text{PVGO}}{E/k}\right] \qquad (15.7)$$

When PVGO = 0, Equation 15.7 shows that $P_0 = E_1/k$. The stock is valued like a nongrowing perpetuity of EPS_1. The P/E ratio is just $1/k$. However, as PVGO becomes an increasingly dominant contributor to price, the P/E ratio can rise dramatically. The ratio of PVGO to E/k has a simple interpretation. It is the ratio of the component of firm value due to growth opportunities to the component of value due to assets already in place (i.e., the no-growth value of the firm, E/k). When future growth opportunities dominate the estimate of total value, the firm will command a high price relative to current earnings. Thus, a high P/E multiple appears to indicate a firm is endowed with ample growth opportunities.

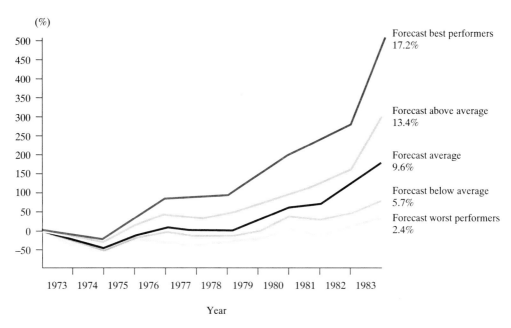

(%)

Forecast best performers
17.2%

Forecast above average
13.4%

Forecast average
9.6%

Forecast below average
5.7%

Forecast worst performers
2.4%

Year

Figure 15.2 **Total return by quintiles; ranking based on implied market
capitalization rate, 1973–1982.**

Let's see if this is so. In 1989, Motorola's P/E ratio was 12.6 while Boston
Edison's was 9.3. These numbers do not necessarily imply Motorola was overpriced compared to Boston Edison. If investors believed at the time that Motorola would grow faster than Boston Edison, the higher P/E multiple would be
justified. That is, an investor might well pay a higher price per dollar of current
earnings if he or she expects that earnings stream to grow rapidly. In fact, Motorola's growth rate has been consistent with its higher P/E multiple. Its earnings per share more than doubled in the 1980s (rising from $1.99 in 1980 to $4.11
in 1989) while Boston Edison earnings grew only 27.7 percent (from $1.37 in
1980 to $1.75 in 1989). Figure 15.4, p. 432, shows the EPS history of the two
companies.

Clearly, it is differences in expected growth opportunities that justify particular differentials in P/E ratios across firms. The P/E ratio actually is a reflection
of the market's optimism concerning a firm's growth prospects. In their use of
a P/E ratio, analysts must decide whether they are more or less optimistic than
the market. If they are more optimistic, they will recommend buying the stock.

There is a way to make these insights more precise. Look again at the constant growth DDM formula, $P_0 = D_1/(k-g)$. Now recall that dividends equal
the earnings that are *not* reinvested in the firm: $D_1 = E_1(1-b)$. Recall also that
$g = \text{ROE} \times b$. Hence, substituting for D_1 and g, we find that

$$P_0 = \frac{E_1(1-b)}{k - \text{ROE} \times b}$$

implying the P/E ratio is

$$\frac{P_0}{E_1} = \frac{1-b}{k - \text{ROE} \times b} \tag{15.8}$$

Table 15.3 *Effect of ROE and Plowback on Growth and the P/E Ratio*

	Plowback Rate(b)			
ROE	**0**	**.25**	**.50**	**.75**
A. Growth Rate, g				
10%	0	2.5%	5.0%	7.5%
12%	0	3.0%	6.0%	9.0%
14%	0	3.5%	7.0%	10.5%
B. P/E Ratio				
10%	8.33	7.89	7.14	5.56
12%	8.33	8.33	8.33	8.33
14%	8.33	8.82	10.00	16.67

Assumption: $k = 12\%$ per year.

It is easy to verify that the P/E ratio increases with ROE. This makes sense, because high ROE projects give the firm good opportunities for growth.[2] We also can verify that the P/E ratio increases for higher b as long as ROE exceeds k. This too makes sense. When a firm has good investment opportunities, the market will reward it with a higher P/E multiple if it exploits those opportunities more aggressively by plowing back more earnings into those opportunities.

Remember we noted, however, that growth is not desirable for its own sake. Examine Table 15.3 where we use Equation 15.8 to compute both growth rates and P/E ratios for different combinations of ROE and b. While growth always increases with the plowback rate (move across the rows in Table 15.3A), the P/E ratio does not (move across the rows in Panel B). In the top row of Table 15.3B, the P/E falls as the plowback rate increases. In the middle row, it is unaffected by plowback. In the third row, it increases.

This pattern has a simple interpretation. When the expected ROE is less than the required return, k, investors prefer that the firm pay out earnings as dividends rather than reinvest earnings in the firm at an inadequate rate of return. That is, for ROE lower than k, the value of the firm falls as plowback increases. Conversely, when ROE exceeds k, the firm offers superior investment opportunities, so the value of the firm is enhanced as those opportunities are more fully exploited by increasing the plowback rate.

Finally, where ROE just equals k, the firm offers "break-even" investment opportunities with a fair rate of return. In this case, investors are indifferent between reinvestment of earnings in the firm or elsewhere at the market capitalization rate, because the rate of return in either case is 12 percent. Therefore, the stock price is unaffected by the plowback rate.

One way to summarize these relationships is to say the higher the plowback rate, the higher the growth rate, but a higher plowback rate does not necessarily mean a higher P/E ratio. A higher plowback rate increases P/E only if investments undertaken by the firm offer an expected rate of return higher than the market capitalization rate. Otherwise, higher plowback hurts investors because it means more money is sunk into prospects with inadequate rates of return.

---

[2]Note that Equation 15.8 is a simple rearrangement of the DDM formula, with ROE $\times b = g$. Because that formula requires that $g<k$, Equation 15.8 is valid only when ROE $\times b < k$.

Concept Check

Question 6.   ABC stock has an expected ROE of 12 percent per year, expected earnings per share of $2, and expected dividends of $1.50 per share. Its market capitalization rate is 10 percent per year.
a. What are its expected growth rate, its price, and its P/E ratio?
b. If the plowback rate were 0.4, what would be the expected dividend per share, the growth rate, price, and the P/E ratio?

Pitfalls in P/E Analysis

No description of P/E analysis is complete without mentioning some of its pitfalls. First, consider that the denominator in the P/E ratio is accounting earnings, which are influenced by somewhat arbitrary accounting rules such as the use of historical cost in depreciation and inventory valuation. In times of high inflation, historic cost depreciation and inventory costs will tend to underrepresent true economic values because the replacement cost of both goods and capital equipment will rise with the general level of prices. As Figure 15.3 demonstrates, P/E ratios have tended to be lower when inflation has been higher.

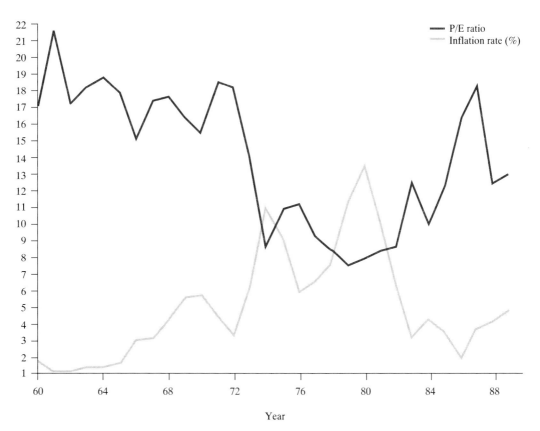

Figure 15.3 **P/E ratios and inflation, 1960–1989.**
From *Economic Report of the President,* 1990.

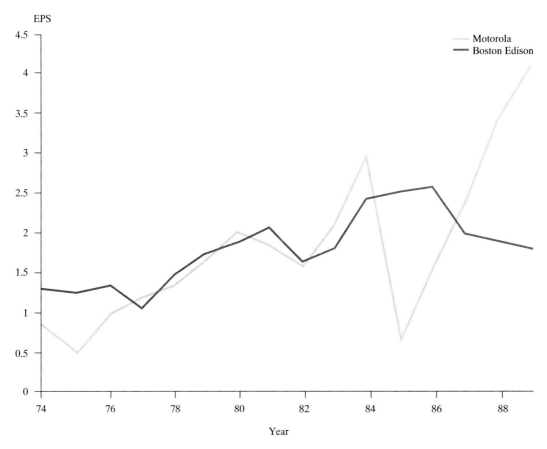

Figure 15.4 **Earnings per share, 1974–1989.**

This reflects the market's assessment that earnings in these periods are of "lower quality," artificially distorted by inflation, and warranting lower P/E ratios.

Another confounding factor in the use of P/E ratios is related to the business cycle. We were careful in deriving the DDM to define earnings as being net of *economic* depreciation, that is, the maximum flow of income that the firm could pay out without depleting its productive capacity. And reported earnings, as we note above, are computed in accordance with generally accepted accounting principles and need not correspond to economic earnings. Beyond this, however, notions of a normal or justified P/E ratio, as in Equations 15.7 or 15.8, assume implicitly that earnings rise at a constant rate, or, put another way, on a smooth trend line. In contrast, reported earnings can fluctuate dramatically around a trend line over the course of the business cycle.

Another way to make this point is to note that the "normal" P/E ratio predicted by Equation 15.8 is the ratio of today's price to the trend value of future earnings, E_1. The P/E ratio reported in the financial pages of the newspaper, by contrast, is the ratio of price to the most recent *past* accounting earnings. Current accounting earnings can differ considerably from future economic earnings. Because ownership of stock conveys the right to future as well as current earnings, the ratio of price to most recent earnings can vary substantially over the business cycle, as accounting earnings and the trend value of economic earnings diverge by greater and lesser amounts.

As an example, Figure 15.4 graphs the earnings per share of Motorola and Boston Edison since 1974. Note that Motorola's EPS fluctuate considerably. This reflects the company's relatively high degree of sensitivity to the business cycle. Value Line estimates its beta at 1.40. Boston Edison, by contrast, shows much less variation in earnings per share around a smoother and flatter trend line. Its beta was only 0.70.

Because the market values the entire stream of future dividends generated by the company, when earnings are temporarily depressed, the P/E ratio should tend to be high—that is, the denominator of the ratio responds more sensitively to the business cycle than the numerator. This pattern is borne out well.

Figure 15.5 graphs the Motorola and Boston Edison P/E ratios. Motorola, with the more volatile earnings profile, also has a more volatile P/E profile. For example, in 1985, when EPS fell to a far-below-trend value of $.61, the P/E rose to 56.3. The market clearly recognized that earnings were depressed only temporarily.

This example shows why analysts must be careful in using P/E ratios. There is no way to say a P/E ratio is overly high or low without referring to the company's long-run growth prospects, as well as to current earnings per share relative to the long-run trend line.

Nevertheless, Figures 15.4 and 15.5 demonstrate a clear relationship between P/E ratios and growth. Despite considerable short-run fluctuations, Motorola's EPS clearly trended upward over the period. Its compound rate of growth between 1974 and 1989 was 11.1 percent. Boston Edison's earnings were nearly flat, with a 15-year average growth rate of 2.0 percent. The growth prospects of Motorola are reflected in its consistently higher P/E multiple.

Combining P/E Analysis and the DDM

Some analysts use P/E ratios in conjunction with earnings forecasts to estimate the price of a stock at an investor's horizon date. The Hewlett-Packard analysis in Figure 15.1 shows Value Line forecasted a P/E ratio for 1993 of 16.0. EPS for 1993 were forecast at $6.25, implying a price in 1993 of 16 × $6.25, or $100. This is considerably higher than the 1993 price of $66.08 that we computed from the dividend discount model using a market capitalization rate of 15.8 percent, but actually a bit lower than the DDM estimate using $k = 15.3$ percent. Given an estimate of $100 for the 1993 sale price, we would compute Hewlett-Packard's intrinsic value as

$$V_0 = \frac{.45}{1.153} + \frac{.55}{1.153^2} + \frac{.65}{1.153^3} + \frac{.75 + 100}{1.153^4} = 57.25$$

which suggests the stock, selling at $44 per share, is undervalued by the market.

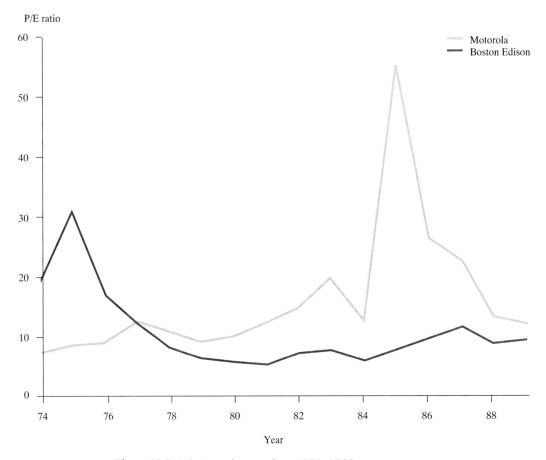

Figure 15.5 Price/earnings ratios, 1974–1989.

15.5 *The Aggregate Stock Market*

The most popular approach to forecasting the overall stock market is the earnings multiplier approach applied at the aggregate level. The first step is to forecast corporate profits for the coming period. Then we derive an estimate of the earnings multiplier, the aggregate P/E ratio, based on a forecast of long-term interest rates. The product of the two forecasts is the estimate of the end-of-period level of the market.

The forecast of the P/E ratio of the market is sometimes derived from a graph similar to that in Figure 15.6, which plots the *earnings yield* (earnings per share divided by price per share, the reciprocal of the P/E ratio) of the S&P 500 and the yield to maturity on 10-year Treasury bonds. The figure shows that both yields rose dramatically in the 1970s. In the case of Treasury bonds, this was because of an increase in the inflationary expectations built into interest rates. The earnings yield on the S&P 500, however, probably rose because of inflationary distortions that artificially increased reported earnings. We have already seen that P/E ratios tend to fall when inflation rates increase. For most of the 1980s, the earnings yield ran about one percentage point below the T-bond rate.

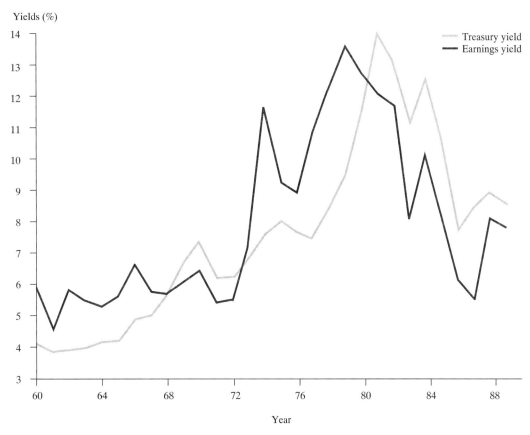

Figure 15.6 Earnings and T-bond yields, 1960–1989.
From *Economic Report of the President*, 1990.

Table 15.4 presents a forecast by Kidder, Peabody of the S&P 500 index. The footnote to the table explains the methodology. Kidder forecasts the earnings yield as the T-bond yield minus 1 percent, which is consistent with the evidence in Figure 15.6. For example, column 1 of Table 15.4 estimates the earnings yield as 9.75 percent − 1 percent = 8.75 percent = E/P. Therefore, P/E is forecast as 1/.0875 = 11.43, approximately the 11.5 value given in the table. This value is multiplied by the estimate of the aggregate EPS of the firms in the S&P 500, $21.50, to obtain a forecast of 247. Other interest rate scenarios appear in the other columns.

Some analysts use an aggregate version of the dividend discounted model rather than an earnings multiplier approach. All of these models, however, rely heavily on forecasts of such macroeconomic variables as GNP, interest rates, and the rate of inflation, which are difficult to predict accurately.

Because stock prices reflect expectations of future dividends, which are tied to the economic fortunes of firms, it is not surprising that the performance of broad-based stock indexes like the S&P 500 is taken as a leading economic indicator, that is, a predictor of the performance of the aggregate economy. Stock prices are viewed as embodying consensus forecasts of economic activity and are assumed to move up or down in anticipation of movements in the economy.

Table 15.4   *S&P 500 Price Targets under Various Scenarios*

	9–12 Month Target	Other Interest Rate Possibilities		"The Bull Scenario"
U.S. T-bond interest rate*	9¾%	9¼%	8¾%	8%
P/E ratio	11.5 × †	12.1 ×	12.9 ×	14.3 ×
EPS (midpoint of 1988 and 1989 est.)	$21.50	$21.50	$21.50	$24.00
S&P price target 1 year out	247	260	277	343

Modified from William J. Gillard. "The Investment Environment and Portfolio Strategy." June 1988, Kidder, Peabody Investment Policy Group.

*Forecast year-end 30-year Treasury bond.

†Assumes an S&P 500 earnings yield 100 basis points below the bond yield. Our reasoning is that, even though the earnings yield exceeded the bond yield for most of the post–World War II era, the earnings yield has been below the bond yield for most of the recent period, beginning with the high-inflation era and extending into the current time. We believe one of the explanations for this current relationship is the abundant liquidity that is buoying the market. In recognition of the market's willingness to accept a lower earnings yield, we assume an 8.7% earnings yield, which implies a P/E of 11.5 ×. Other tests validate this type of number.

The government's index of leading economic indicators, which is taken to predict the progress of the business cycle, is made up in part of recent stock market performance. However, the predictive value of the market is far from perfect. A well-known joke, often attributed to Paul Samuelson, is that the market has forecast eight of the last five recessions.

Summary

1. One approach to firm valuation is to focus on the firm's book value, either as it appears on the balance sheet or as adjusted to reflect current replacement cost of assets or liquidation value. Another approach is to focus on the present value of expected future dividends.

2. The dividend discount model holds that the price of a share of stock should equal the present value of all future dividends per share, discounted at an interest rate commensurate with the risk of the stock.

3. The constant growth version of the DDM asserts that if dividends are expected to grow at a constant rate forever, then the intrinsic value of the stock is determined by the formula

$$V_0 = \frac{D_1}{k - g}$$

This version of the DDM is simplistic in its assumption of a constant value of g. There are more sophisticated multistage versions of the model for more complex environments. When the constant growth assumption is reasonably satisfied, the formula can be inverted to infer the market capitalization rate for the stock:

$$k = \frac{D_1}{P_0} + g$$

4. Stock market analysts devote considerable attention to a company's price-to-earnings ratio. The P/E ratio is a useful measure of the market's assessment of the firm's growth opportunities. Firms with no growth opportunities should have a P/E ratio that is just the reciprocal of the capitalization rate, *k*. As growth opportunities become a progressively more important component of the total value of the firm, the P/E ratio will increase.

5. The models presented in this chapter can be used to explain or to forecast the behavior of the aggregate stock market. The key macroeconomic variables that determine the level of stock prices in the aggregate are interest rates and corporate profits.

Key Terms

book value, 446	fundamental analysts, 415	plowback ratio, 422
constant growth DDM, 420	intrinsic value, 417	price/earnings multiple, 428
discounted dividend model, 419	liquidation value, 416	replacement cost, 416
dividend payout ratio, 422	market capitalization rate, 418	technical analysts, 415
earnings retention ratio, 422		Tobin's *q*, 416

Selected Readings

For the key issues in the recent debate about the link between fundamentals and stock prices see:

Merton, Robert C. "On the Current State of the Stock Market Rationality Hypothesis." In *Macroeconomics and Finance, Essays in Honor of Franco Modigliani,* ed. Rudiger Dornbusch, Stanley Fischer, and John Bossons. Cambridge, Mass.: MIT press, 1986.

Cutler, David M., James M. Poterba, and Lawrence H. Summers. "What Moves Stock Prices?" Cambridge, Mass.: National Bureau of Economic Research, Working Paper No. 2538, March 1988.

West, Kenneth D. "Bubbles, Fads, and Stock Price Volatility Tests: A Partial Evaluation." Cambridge, Mass.: National Bureau of Economic Research, Working Paper No. 2574, May 1988.

Problem Sets

1. *a.* Computer stocks currently provide an expected rate of return of 16 percent. MBI, a large computer company, will pay a year end dividend of $2 per share. If the stock is selling at $50 per share, what must be the market's expectation of the growth rate of MBI dividends?

   b. If dividend growth forecasts for MBI are revised downward to 5 percent per year, what will happen to the price of MBI stock? What will happen to the company's price-earnings ratio?

2. *a.* MF Corp. has an ROE of 16 percent and a plowback ratio of 50 percent. If the coming year's earnings are expected to be $2 per share, at what price will the stock sell? The market capitalization rate is 12 percent.

   b. What price do you expect MF shares to sell for in three years?

3. The constant growth dividend discount model can be used both for the valuation of companies and for the estimation of the long-term total return of a stock.

Assume: $20 = the price of a stock today
           8%   = the expected growth rate of dividends
           $.60 = the annual dividend one year forward

a. Using *only* the above data, compute the expected long-term total return on the stock using the constant growth dividend discount model. Show calculations.

b. Briefly discuss two disadvantages of the constant growth dividend discount model in its application to investment analysis.

c. Identify two alternative methods to the dividend discount model for the valuation of companies.

4. The market consensus is that Analog Electronic Corporation has an ROE = 9 percent, a beta of 1.25, and it plans to maintain indefinitely its traditional plowback ratio of 2/3. This year's earnings were $3 per share. The annual dividend was just paid. The consensus estimate of the coming year's market return is 14 percent, and T-bills currently offer a 6 percent return.

a. Find the price at which Analog stock should sell.

b. Calculate the P/E ratio.

c. Calculate the present value of growth opportunities.

d. Suppose your research convinces you Analog will announce momentarily that it will immediately reduce its plowback ratio to 1/3. Find the intrinsic value of the stock. The market is still unaware of this decision. Explain why V_0 no longer equals P_0 and why V_0 is greater or less than P_0.

5. If the expected rate of return of the market portfolio is 15 percent and a stock with a beta of 1.0 pays a dividend yield of 4 percent, what must the market believe is the expected rate of price appreciation on that stock?

6. The FI Corporation's dividends per share are expected to grow indefinitely by 5 percent per year.

a. If this year's year-end dividend is $8 and the market capitalization rate is 10 percent per year, what must the current stock price be according to the DDM?

b. If the expected earnings per share are $12, what is the implied value of the ROE on future investment opportunities?

c. How much is the market paying per share for growth opportunities (that is, for an ROE on future investments that exceeds the market capitalization rate)?

7. Using the data provided, discuss whether the common stock of United States Tobacco Company is attractively priced based on at least three different valuation approaches. (Hint: use the asset value, DDM, and earnings multiplier approaches.)

	U.S. Tobacco	S&P 500
Recent price	$27.00	$290
Book value per share	$6.42	
Liquidation value per share	$4.90	
Replacement costs of assets per share	$9.15	
Anticipated next year's dividend	$1.20	$8.75
Estimated annual growth in dividends and earnings	10.0%	7.0%
Required return	13.0%	
Estimated next year's EPS	$2.40	$16.50
P/E ratio based on next year's earnings	11.3	17.6
Dividend yield	4.4%	3.0%

8. The risk-free rate of return is 10 percent, the required rate of return on the market is 15 percent, and High-Flyer stock has a beta coefficient of 1.5. If the dividend per share expected during the coming year, D_1, is $2.50 and $g = 5$ percent, at what price should a share sell?

9. Your preliminary analysis of two stocks has yielded the information set forth below. The market capitalization rate for both stock A and stock B is 10 percent per year.

	Stock A	Stock B
Expected return on equity, ROE	14%	12%
Estimated earnings per share, E_1	$2.00	$1.65
Estimated dividends per share, D_1	$1.00	$1.00
Current market price per share, P_0	$27.00	$25.00

   a. What are the expected dividend payout ratios for the two stocks?
   b. What are the expected dividend growth rates of each?
   c. What is the intrinsic value of each stock?
   d. In which, if either, of the two stocks would you choose to invest?

10. The Tennant Company, founded in 1870, has evolved into the leading producer of large-sized floor sweepers and scrubbers, which are ridden by their operators. Some of its financial data are presented in the following table:

Tennant Company
Selected Historic Operating and Balance Sheet Data (000 Omitted)
As of December 31

	1980	1986	1992
Net sales	$47,909	$109,333	$166,924
Cost of goods sold	27,395	62,373	95,015
Gross profits	20,514	46,960	71,909
Selling, general, and administrative expenses	11,895	29,649	54,151
Earnings before interest and taxes	8,619	17,311	17,758
Interest on long-term debt	0	53	248
Pre-tax income	8,619	17,258	17,510
Income taxes	4,190	7,655	7,692
After-tax income	4,429	9,603	9,818
Total assets	$33,848	$ 63,555	$106,098
Total common stockholders' equity	25,722	46,593	69,516
Long-term debt	6	532	2,480
Total common shares outstanding	5,654	5,402	5,320
Earnings per share	$ .78	$ 1.78	$ 1.85
Dividends per share	.28	.72	.96
Book value per share	4.55	8.63	13.07

   a. Based on these data, calculate a value for Tennant common stock by applying the constant growth dividend discount model. Assume an investor's required rate of return is a five percentage point premium over the current risk-free rate of return of 7 percent.

b. To your disappointment, the calculation you completed in part *a* results in a value below the stock's current market price. Consequently, you apply the constant growth DDM using the same required rate of return as in your calculation for part *a,* but using the company's stated goal of earning 20 percent per year on stockholders' equity and maintaining a 35 percent dividend payout ratio. However, you find you are unable to calculate a meaningful answer. Explain why you cannot calculate a meaningful answer, and identify an alternative DDM that may provide a meaningful answer.

11. You are a portfolio manager considering the purchase of Nucor common stock. Nucor is the preeminent "mini-mill" steel producer in the United States. Mini-mills use scrap steel as their raw material and produce a limited number of products, primarily for the construction market. You are provided the following information:

Nucor Corporation	
Stock price (Dec. 30, 1990)	$53.00
1990 Estimated earnings	$ 4.25
1990 Estimated book value	$25.00
Indicated dividend	$ 0.40
Beta	1.10
Risk-free return	7.0%
High grade corporate bond yield	9.0%
Risk premium—stocks over bonds	5.0%

a. Calculate the expected stock market return. Show your calculations.
b. Calculate the implied total return of Nucor stock.
c. Calculate the required return of Nucor stock using the security market line model.
d. Briefly discuss the attractiveness of Nucor based on these data.

12. The stock of Nogro Corporation is currently selling for $10 per share. Earnings per share in the coming year are expected to be $2. The company has a policy of paying out 50 percent of its earnings each year in dividends. The rest is retained and invested in projects that earn a 20 percent rate of return per year. This situation is expected to continue indefinitely.

a. Assuming the current market price of the stock reflects its intrinsic value as computed using the constant growth rate DDM, what rate of return do Nogro's investors require?
b. By how much does its value exceed what it would be if all earnings were paid as dividends and nothing were reinvested?
c. If Nogro were to cut its dividend payout ratio to 25 percent, what would happen to its stock price? What if Nogro eliminated the dividend?

13. The risk-free rate of return is 8 percent, the expected rate of return on the market portfolio is 15 percent, and the stock of Xyrong Corporation has a beta coefficient of 1.2. Xyrong pays out 40 percent of its earnings in dividends, and the latest earnings announced were $10 per share. Dividends were just paid and are expected to be paid annually. You expect that Xyrong will earn an ROE of 20 percent per year on all reinvested earnings forever.

a. What is the intrinsic value of a share of Xyrong stock?
b. If the market price of a share is currently $100, and you expect the market price to be equal to the intrinsic value one year from now, what is your expected one-year holding-period return on Xyrong stock?

Chapter

16

Financial Statement Analysis

In the previous chapter, we explored equity valuation techniques. These techniques take as inputs the firm's dividends and earnings prospects. While the valuation analyst is interested in economic earnings streams, only financial accounting data are readily available. What can we learn from a company's accounting data that can help us estimate the intrinsic value of its common stock?

In this chapter, we show how investors can use financial data as inputs into stock valuation analysis. We start by reviewing the basic sources of such data—the income statement, the balance sheet, and the statement of cash flows. We next discuss the difference between economic and accounting earnings. While economic earnings are more important for issues of valuation, we examine evidence suggesting that, whatever their shortcomings, accounting data still are useful in assessing the economic prospects of the firm. We show how analysts use financial ratios to explore the sources of a firm's profitability and evaluate the "quality" of its earnings in a systematic fashion. We also examine the impact of debt policy on various financial ratios. Finally, we conclude with a discussion of the limitations of financial statement analysis as a tool in uncovering mispriced securities. Some of these limitations are due to differences in firms' accounting procedures. Others arise from inflation induced distortions in accounting numbers. After studying this chapter you should be able to:

- Use a firm's income statement, balance sheet, and statement of cash flows to calculate standard financial ratios.
- Calculate the impact of taxes and leverage on a firm's return on equity using ratio decomposition analysis.
- Measure a firm's operating efficiency using various asset utilization ratios.
- Identify likely sources of biases in conventional accounting data.

16.1   *The Major Financial Statements*

The Income Statement

Income statement   A financial statement showing a firm's revenues and expenses during a specified period.

The **income statement** is a summary of the profitability of the firm over a period of time, such as a year. It presents revenues generated during the operating period, the expenses incurred during that same period, and the company's net earnings or profits, which are simply the difference between revenues and expenses.

It is useful to distinguish four broad classes of expenses: cost of goods sold, which is the direct cost attributable to producing the product sold by the firm; general and administrative expenses, which correspond to overhead expenses, salaries, advertising, and other costs of operating the firm that are not directly attributable to production; interest expense on the firm's debt; and taxes on earnings owed to federal and local governments.

Table 16.1 presents a 1990 income statement for NYNEX, the New York–New England telephone company. At the top are revenues from standard operations. Next come operating expenses, the costs incurred in the course of generating those revenues, including a depreciation allowance. The difference between operating revenues and operating costs is called operating income. Income from other, primarily nonrecurring, sources is then added to obtain earn-

Table 16.1   *Consolidated Statements of Income   (In millions, except per share amounts)*

For the Year Ended December 31	1990	1989	1988
Operating revenues:			
Local service	$ 5,651.0	$ 5,483.3	$ 5,387.0
Long distance	1,365.0	1,410.8	1,415.0
Network access	3,292.3	3,293.4	3,250.5
Other	3,277.0	3,010.0	2,598.0
Total operating revenues	13,585.3	13,197.5	12,650.5
Operating expenses:			
Maintenance and support	3,428.1	3,389.5	3,315.2
Depreciation and amortization	2,337.3	2,319.2	2,186.0
Marketing and customer services	1,316.5	1,198.3	1,228.2
Taxes other than income	1,091.3	993.1	988.3
Selling, general, and administrative	1,695.0	2,288.2	1,723.4
Other	1,701.8	1,252.5	949.4
Total operating expenses	11,570.0	11,440.8	10,390.5
Operating income	2,015.3	1,756.7	2,260.0
Other income—net	2.4	8.2	49.1
Earnings before interest expense and income taxes	2,017.7	1,764.9	2,309.1
Interest expense	700.0	691.4	620.9
Earnings before income taxes	1,317.7	1,073.5	1,688.2
Income taxes	368.3	265.9	373.2
Net income	$ 949.4	$ 807.6	$ 1,315.0
Earnings per share	$ 4.78	$ 4.10	$ 6.63
Weighted average number of shares outstanding	198.7	197.0	198.3

ings before interest and taxes (EBIT), which is what the firm would have earned if not for obligations to its creditors and the tax authorities. EBIT is a measure of the profitability of the firm's operations abstracting from any interest burden attributable to debt financing. The income statement then goes on to subtract net interest expense from EBIT to arrive at taxable income. Finally, the income tax due the government is subtracted to arrive at net income, the "bottom line" of the income statement.

The Balance Sheet

Balance sheet   An accounting statement of a firm's financial position at a specified time.

While the income statement provides a measure of profitability over a period of time, the **balance sheet** provides a "snapshot" of the financial condition of the firm at a particular time. The balance sheet is a list of the firm's assets and liabilities at that moment. The difference in assets and liabilities is the net worth of the firm, also called *stockholders' equity*. Like income statements, balance sheets are reasonably standardized in presentation. Table 16.2 is the balance sheet of NYNEX for year-end 1990.

The first section of the balance sheet gives a listing of the assets of the firm. Current assets are presented first. These are cash and other items such as accounts receivable or inventories that will be converted into cash within one year. Next comes a listing of long-term assets, which generally corresponds to the company's property, plant, and equipment. The sum of current and long-term assets is total assets, the last line of the assets section of the balance sheet.

The liability and stockholders' equity section is arranged similarly. First come short-term or "current" liabilities such as accounts payable, accrued taxes, and debts that are due within one year. Following this is long-term debt and other liabilities due in more than a year. The difference between total assets and total liabilities is stockholders' equity. This is the net worth or book value of the firm. Stockholders' equity is divided into par value of stock, capital surplus (additional paid-in capital), and retained earnings, although this division is usually unimportant. Briefly, par value plus capital surplus represent the proceeds realized from the sale of stock to the public, while retained earnings represent the buildup of equity from profits plowed back into the firm. Even if the firm issues no new equity, book value will increase each year by the retained earnings of the firm.

The Statement of Cash Flows

Statement of cash flows   A financial statement showing a firm's cash receipts and cash payments during a specified period.

The **statement of cash flows** replaces what used to be called the statement of changes in financial position or flow of funds statement. It is a report of the cash flow generated by the firm's operations, investments, and financial activities. This statement has only recently (since 1987) been mandated by the Financial Accounting Standards Board and is sometimes called the FASB Statement No. 95.

While the income statement and balance sheets are based on accrual methods of accounting, which means revenues and expenses are recognized when incurred even if no cash has yet been exchanged, the statement of cash flows recognizes only transactions in which cash changes hands. For example, if goods are sold now, with payment due in 60 days, the income statement will treat the

Table 16.2 *Consolidated Balance Sheet* *(In millions)*

For the Year Ended December 31	1990	1989
Assets		
Current assets:		
Cash and temporary cash investments	$ 121.7	$ 155.0
Receivables (net of allowance of $173.0 and $175.4, respectively)	2,642.1	2,498.5
Inventories	436.7	401.4
Prepaid expenses	326.7	297.3
Deferred charges and other current assets	386.2	316.4
Total current assets	3,913.4	3,668.6
Property, plant, and equipment—net	19,728.9	19,464.5
Deferred charges and other assets	3,008.4	2,775.9
Total assets	$26,650.7	$25,909.0
Liabilities and stockholders' equity		
Current liabilities:		
Accounts payable	$ 2,979.4	$ 2,914.2
Short-term debt	1,467.7	946.3
Other current liabilities	1,044.5	718.1
Total current liabilities	5,491.6	4,578.6
Long-term debt	6,945.4	6,465.0
Deferred income taxes	2,856.0	3,108.5
Unamortized investment tax credits	570.0	644.6
Other long-term liabilities and deferred credits	1,638.0	1,743.2
Total liabilities	17,501.9	16,539.9
Commitments and contingencies		
Stockholders' equity:		
Preferred stock—$1 par value, 70,000,000 shares authorized	—	—
Preferred stock—Series A Junior Participating—$1 par value, 5,000,000 shares authorized	—	—
Common stock—$1 par value, 750,000,000 shares authorized	207.5	204.6
Additional paid-in capital	6,016.7	5,791.9
Retained earnings	3,935.9	3,869.4
Treasury stock—7,375,946 and 7,554,746 shares, respectively, at cost	(572.9)	(496.8)
Deferred compensation—LESOP Trust	(438.4)	—
Total stockholders' equity	9,148.8	9,369.1
Total liabilities and stockholders' equity	$26,650.7	$25,909.0

revenue as generated when the sale occurs, and the balance sheet will be immediately augmented by accounts receivable, but the statement of cash flows will not recognize the transaction until the bill is paid and the cash is in hand.

Table 16.3 is the 1990 statement of cash flows for NYNEX. The first entry listed under cash flows from operations is net income. The next entries modify that figure by components of income that have been recognized but for which cash has not yet changed hands. Increases in accounts receivable, for example, mean income has been claimed on the income statement, but cash has not yet

Table 16.3 *Consolidated Statements of Cash Flows* (In millions)

For the Year Ended December 31	1990	1989	1988
Cash flows from operating activities:			
Net income	$ 949.4	$ 807.6	$1,315.0
Adjustments to reconcile net income to net cash provided by operating activities:			
Depreciation and amortization	2,337.3	2,319.2	2,186.0
Amortization of unearned lease income—net	(47.6)	(32.4)	(21.7)
Deferred income taxes—net	(23.2)	(145.8)	6.5
Deferred tax credits—net	(60.4)	(80.5)	(75.6)
Interest charged construction	(40.6)	(41.8)	(50.8)
Changes in operating assets and liabilities net of acquisition of 1988:			
Receivables	(143.6)	11.9	(224.2)
Inventories	(35.3)	(15.0)	(4.2)
Prepaid expenses	(29.4)	(46.7)	(38.9)
Deferred charges and other current assets	(69.8)	42.3	(14.8)
Accounts payable	51.8	459.6	128.2
Other current liabilities	326.4	66.5	120.3
Other—net	(340.1)	123.9	(139.0)
Total adjustments	1,925.5	2,661.2	1,871.8
Net cash provided by operating activities	2,874.9	3,468.8	3,186.8
Cash flows from investing activities:			
Capital expenditures	(2,493.2)	(2,420.6)	2,783.6
Acquisition—net of cash acquired	—	—	(267.0)
Investment in leased assets	(172.2)	(232.3)	(135.5)
Cash received from leasing activities	65.9	60.4	13.8
Other investing activities—net	(74.3)	(14.1)	(30.1)
Net cash used in investing activities	(2,673.8)	(2,606.6)	(3,202.4)
Cash flows from financing activities:			
Increase (decrease) in commercial paper	594.7	(311.9)	912.8
Issuance of long-term debt	680.5	600.2	88.3
Repayment of long-term debt	(306.6)	(278.1)	(124.9)
Issuance of common stock	89.5	—	—
Purchase of treasury stock	(446.1)	—	(302.4)
Dividends paid	(846.4)	(843.1)	(790.7)
Net cash used in financing activities	(234.4)	(832.9)	(216.9)
Net (decrease) increase in cash and temporary cash investments	(33.3)	29.3	(232.5)
Cash and temporary cash investments at beginning of year	155.0	125.7	358.2
Cash and temporary cash investments at end of year	$ 121.7	$ 155.0	$ 125.7

been collected. Hence, increases in accounts receivable reduce the cash flows realized from operations in this period. Similarly, increases in accounts payable mean expenses have been incurred, but cash has not yet left the firm. Any payment delay increases the company's net cash flows in this period.

Another major difference between the income statement and the statement of cash flows involves depreciation, which is a major addition to income in the adjustment section of the statement of cash flows in Table 16.3. The income statement attempts to "smooth" large capital expenditures over time to reflect a measure of profitability not distorted by large infrequent expenditures. The depreciation expense on the income statement is a way of doing this by recognizing capital expenditures over a period of many years rather than at the specific time of those expenditures.

The statement of cash flows, however, recognizes the cash implication of a capital expenditure when it occurs. It will ignore the depreciation "expense" over time, but will account for the full capital expenditure when it is paid in the second section, entitled cash flows from investing activities.

Rather than smooth or allocate expenses over time, as in the income statement, the statement of cash flows reports cash flows separately for operations, investing, and financing activities. This way, any large cash flows such as those for big investments can be recognized explicitly as nonrecurring without affecting the measure of cash flow generated by operating activities.

The second section of the statement of cash flows is the accounting of cash flows from investing activities. These entries are investments in the capital stock necessary for the firm to maintain or enhance its productive capacity.

Finally, the last section of the statement lists the cash flows realized from financing activities. Issuance of securities will contribute positive cash flows. For example, NYNEX issued $594.7 million more in commercial paper than it retired in 1990, which was a major source of cash flow. In contrast, payments of dividends and repurchase of stock reduced net cash flow. Notice that while dividends paid are included in the cash flows from financing, interest payments on debt are included with operating activities, presumably because unlike dividends, interest payments are not discretionary.

The statement of cash flows provides evidence on the well-being of a firm. If a company cannot pay its dividends and maintain the productivity of its capital stock out of cash flow from operations, for example, and it must resort to borrowing to meet these demands, this is a serious warning that the firm cannot maintain dividend payout at its current level in the long run. The statement of cash flows will reveal this developing problem, when it shows that cash flow from operations is inadequate and that borrowing is being used to maintain dividend payments at unsustainable levels.

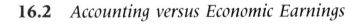

16.2   *Accounting versus Economic Earnings*

Accounting earnings
Earnings of a firm as reported on its income statement.

Economic earnings
The real flow of cash that a firm could pay out forever in the absence of any change in the firm's productive capacity.

We've seen that stock valuation models require a measure of economic earnings or sustainable cash flow that can be paid out to stockholders without impairing the productive capacity of the firm. In contrast, **accounting earnings** are affected by several conventions regarding the valuation of assets such as inventories (e.g., LIFO versus FIFO treatment), and by the way some expenditures such as capital investments are recognized over time (as depreciation expenses). We will discuss problems with some of these accounting conventions in greater detail later in the chapter. In addition to these accounting issues, as the firm makes its way through the business cycle, its earnings will rise above or fall below the trend line that might more accurately reflect sustainable **economic earnings.** This introduces an added complication in interpreting net income figures. One might wonder how closely accounting earnings approximate economic earnings and, correspondingly, how useful accounting data might be to investors attempting to value the firm.

In fact, the net income figure on the firm's income statement does convey considerable information concerning a firm's prospects. We see this in the fact that stock prices tend to increase when firms announce earnings greater than market analysts or investors had anticipated. There are several studies to this effect.

In one study, Niederhoffer and Regan (1972) formed three groups of stock: the 50 stocks with the greatest price increases in 1970, the 50 with the greatest price decreases, and 50 randomly selected stocks. In the worst-performing group, earnings declined by 83 percent (compared with analysts' forecasts of a 15.3 percent *increase*), while in the best-performing group, earnings increased 21.4 percent (the analysts forecast a 7.7 percent increase). The implication is that deviation of actual earnings from projected earnings is the driving force behind abnormal stock returns.

In a more recent study, Foster, Olsen, and Shevlin (1984) used time series of earnings for many firms to forecast the coming quarter's earnings announcement. They estimated an equation for more than 2,000 firms between 1974 and 1981:

$$E_{i,t} = E_{i,t-4} + a_i(E_{i,t-1} - E_{i,t-5}) + g_i$$

where

$$E_{i,t} = \text{Earnings of firm } i \text{ in quarter } t$$
$$a_i = \text{Adjustment factor for firm } i$$
$$g_i = \text{Growth factor for firm } i$$

The rationale is that this quarter's earnings, $E_{i,t}$, will equal last year's earnings for the same quarter, $E_{i,t-4}$, plus a factor representing recent above-trend earnings performance as measured by the difference between last quarter's earnings and the corresponding quarter's earnings a year earlier, plus another factor that represents steady earnings growth over time. Regression techniques are used to estimate a_i and g_i. Given these estimates, the equation is used together with past earnings to forecast future earnings.

Now it is easy to determine earnings surprises. Simply take the difference between actual earnings and forecasted or expected earnings, and see whether earnings surprises correlate with subsequent stock price movements.

Before doing so, however, these researchers introduced an extra refinement (first suggested by Latane and Jones [1979]). Instead of using the earnings forecast error itself as the variable of interest, they first divided the forecast errors for each period by the standard deviation of forecast errors calculated from earlier periods; they effectively deflated the earnings surprise in a particular quarter by a measure of the typical surprise in an average quarter. This discounts forecast errors for firms with historically very unpredictable earnings. A large error for such firms might not be as significant as for a firm with typically very predictable earnings. The resulting "normalized" forecast error commonly is called the "standardized unexpected earnings" (SUE) measure. SUE is the variable that was correlated with stock price movements.

Each earnings announcement was placed in one of 10 deciles ranked by the magnitude of SUE, and the abnormal returns of the stock in each decile were calculated. The abnormal return in a period is the portfolio return after adjusting for both the market return in that period and the portfolio beta. It measures return over and above what would be expected given market conditions in that period. Figure 16.1 is a graph of the cumulative abnormal returns.

The results of this study are dramatic. The correlation between SUE ranking and abnormal returns across deciles is as predicted. There is a large abnormal return (a large increase in cumulative abnormal return) on the earnings announcement day (time 0). The abnormal return is positive for high-SUE and negative for low-SUE (actually negative-SUE) firms.

The more remarkable, and disturbing, result of the study concerns stock price movements *after* the announcement date. The cumulative abnormal returns of high-SUE stocks continue to grow even after the earnings information becomes public, while the low-SUE firms continue to suffer negative abnormal returns. The market appears to adjust to the earnings information only gradually, resulting in a sustained period of abnormal returns.

Evidently, one can earn abnormal profits simply by waiting for earnings announcements and purchasing a stock portfolio of high-SUE companies. These are precisely the types of predictable continuing trends that ought to be impossible in an efficient market.

This finding is not unique. Many earnings announcement studies have found similar results. This phenomenon remains a puzzle for future research.

You might wonder whether security analysts can predict earnings more accurately than mechanical time series equations. After all, analysts have access to these statistical equations and to other qualitative and quantitative data. The evidence seems to be that analysts in fact do outperform such mechanical forecasts.

Figure 16.1
Cumulative abnormal returns in response to earnings announcements.

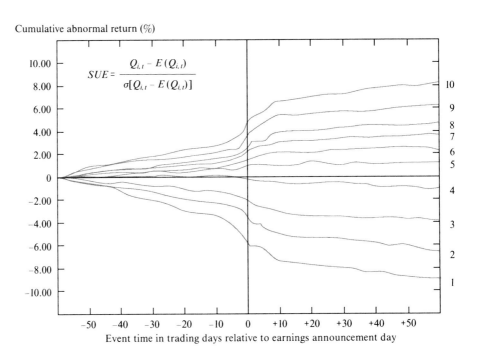

Cumulative abnormal return (%)

$$SUE = \frac{Q_{i,t} - E(Q_{i,t})}{\sigma[Q_{i,t} - E(Q_{i,t})]}$$

Event time in trading days relative to earnings announcement day

Brown and Rozeff (1978) compared earnings forecasts from the *Value Line Investment Survey* with those made using a sophisticated statistical technique called a Box-Jenkins model. The Value Line forecasts generally were more accurate. While 54 percent of the Box-Jenkins forecasts were within 25 percent of the realized values, and 26.5 percent were within 10 percent, 63.5 percent of the Value Line forecasts were within 25 percent and 23 percent were within 10 percent. Apparently, the qualitative data and firm-specific fundamental analysis that analysts bring to bear are of value.

16.3 *Return on Equity*

Past versus Future ROE

Return on equity (ROE) The ratio of net profits to common equity.

We noted in Chapter 15 that **return on equity** (ROE) is one of the two basic factors in determining a firm's growth rate of earnings. There are two sides to using ROE. Sometimes it is reasonable to assume that future ROE will approximate its past value, but a high ROE in the past does not necessarily imply a firm's future ROE will be high.

A declining ROE, on the other hand, is evidence that the firm's new investments have offered a lower ROE than its past investments. The best forecast of future ROE in this case may be lower than the most recent ROE. The vital point for an analyst is not to accept historical values as indicators of future values. Data from the recent past may provide information regarding future performance, but the analyst should always keep an eye on the future. It is expectations of future dividends and earnings that determine the intrinsic value of the company's stock.

Financial Leverage and ROE

An analyst interpreting the past behavior of a firm's ROE or forecasting its future value must pay careful attention to the firm's debt-equity mix and to the interest rate on its debt. An example will show why. Suppose Nodett is a firm that is all-equity financed and has total assets of $100 million. Assume it pays corporate taxes at the rate of 40 percent of taxable earnings.

Table 16.4 shows the behavior of sales, earnings before interest and taxes, and net profits under three scenarios representing phases of the business cycle. It also shows the behavior of two of the most commonly used profitability mea-

Table 16.4 *Nodett's Profitability over the Business Cycle*

Scenario	Sales ($ millions)	EBIT ($ millions)	ROA (% per year)	Net Profit ($ millions)	ROE (% per year)
Bad year	80	5	5	3	3
Normal year	100	10	10	6	6
Good year	120	15	15	9	9

Table 16.5   *Impact of Financial Leverage on ROE*

Scenario	EBIT ($ millions)	Nodett		Somdett	
		Net Profits ($ millions)	ROE (%)	Net Profits* ($ millions)	ROE † (%)
Bad year	5	3	3	1.08	1.8
Normal year	10	6	6	4.08	6.8
Good year	15	9	9	7.08	11.8

*Somdett's after-tax profits are given by .6(EBIT − $3.2 million).

†Somdett's equity is only $60 million.

Return on assets (ROA) Earnings before interest and taxes divided by total assets.

sures: operating **return on assets** (ROA), which equals EBIT/assets, and ROE, which equals net profits/equity.

Somdett is an otherwise identical firm to Nodett, but $40 million of its $100 million of assets are financed with debt bearing an interest rate of 8 percent. It pays annual interest expense of $3.2 million. Table 16.5 shows how Somdett's ROE differs from Nodett's.

Note that annual sales, EBIT, and therefore ROA for both firms are the same in each of the three scenarios, that is, business risk for the two companies is identical. It is their financial risk that differs. Although Nodett and Somdett have the same ROA in each scenario, Somdett's ROE exceeds that of Nodett in normal and good years and is lower in bad years.

We can summarize the exact relationship among ROE, ROA, and leverage in the following equation:[1]

$$\text{ROE} = (1 - \text{Tax rate})\left[\text{ROA} + (\text{ROA} - \text{Interest rate})\frac{\text{Debt}}{\text{Equity}}\right] \quad (16.1)$$

The relationship has the following implications. If there is no debt or if the firm's ROA equals the interest rate on its debt, its ROE will simply equal (1 minus the tax rate) times ROA. If its ROA exceeds the interest rate, then its

[1]The derivation of Equation 16.1 is as follows:

$$\text{ROE} = \frac{\text{Net profit}}{\text{Equity}}$$
$$= \frac{\text{EBIT} - \text{Interest} - \text{Taxes}}{\text{Equity}}$$
$$= \frac{(1 - \text{Tax rate})(\text{EBIT} - \text{Interest})}{\text{Equity}}$$
$$= (1 - \text{Tax rate})\frac{(\text{ROA} \times \text{Assets} - \text{Interest rate} \times \text{Debt})}{\text{Equity}}$$
$$= (1 - \text{Tax rate})\left[\text{ROA} \times \frac{(\text{Equity} + \text{Debt})}{\text{Equity}} - \text{Interest Rate} \times \frac{\text{Debt}}{\text{Equity}}\right]$$
$$= (1 - \text{Tax rate})\left[\text{ROA} + (\text{ROA} - \text{Interest rate})\frac{\text{Debt}}{\text{Equity}}\right]$$

ROE will exceed (1 minus the tax rate) times ROA by an amount that will be greater the higher the debt-to-equity ratio.

This result makes intuitive sense: if ROA exceeds the borrowing rate, the firm earns more on its money that it pays out to creditors. The surplus earnings are available to the firm's owners, the equity holders, which raises ROE. If, on the other hand, ROA is less than the interest rate, then ROE will decline by an amount that depends on the debt-to-equity ratio.

To illustrate the application of Equation 16.1, we can use the numerical example in Table 16.5. In a normal year, Nodett has an ROE of 6 percent, which is .6 (1 minus the tax rate) times its ROA of 10 percent. However, Somdett, which borrows at an interest rate of 8 percent and maintains a debt/equity ratio of ⅔, has an ROE of 6.8 percent. The calculation using Equation 16.1 is

$$ROE = .6[10\% + (10\% - 8\%)^{2}/_{3}]$$
$$= .6[10\% + {}^{4}/_{3}\%]$$
$$= 6.8\%$$

The important point to remember is that increased debt will make a positive contribution to a firm's ROE only if the firm's ROA exceeds the interest rate on the debt.

Note also that financial leverage increases the risk of the equityholder returns. Table 16.5 shows that ROE on Somdett is worse than that of Nodett in bad years. Conversely, in good years, Somdett outperforms Nodett because the excess of ROA over ROE provides additional funds for equity holders. The presence of debt makes Somdett more sensitive to the business cycle than Nodett. Even though the two companies have equal business risk (reflected in their identical EBITs in all three scenarios), Somdett carries greater financial risk than Nodett.

Even if financial leverage increases the expected ROE of Somdett relative to Nodett (as it seems to in Table 16.5), this does not imply the market value of Somdett's equity will be higher. Financial leverage increases the risk of the firm's equity as surely as it raises the expected ROE.

Concept Check

Question 1.   Mordett is a company with the same assets as Nodett and Somdett but a debt-to-equity ratio of 1.0 and an interest rate of 9 percent. What would its net profit and ROE be in a bad year, a normal year, and a good year?

16.4   *Ratio Analysis*

Decomposition of ROE

To understand the factors affecting a firm's ROE, including its trend over time and its performance relative to competitors, analysts often "decompose" ROE into the product of a series of ratios. Each component ratio is in itself meaningful, and the process serves to focus the analyst's attention on the separate factors influencing performance. This kind of decomposition of ROE is often called the Du Pont system.

One useful decomposition of ROE is

$$\text{ROE} = \frac{\text{Net profit}}{\text{Pretax profit}} \times \frac{\text{Pretax profit}}{\text{EBIT}} \times \frac{\text{EBIT}}{\text{Sales}} \times \frac{\text{Sales}}{\text{Assets}} \times \frac{\text{Assets}}{\text{Equity}}$$

$$(1) \quad \times \quad (2) \quad \times (3) \times (4) \times (5)$$

Table 16.6 shows all these ratios for Nodett and Somdett Corporations under the three different economic scenarios.

Let us first focus on factors 3 and 4. Notice that their product, EBIT/Assets, gives us the firm's ROA.

Factor 3 is known as the firm's operating **profit margin** or **return on sales** (ROS). ROS shows operating profit per dollar of sales. In an average year, Nodett's ROS is 0.10, or 10 percent; in a bad year, it is 0.0625, or 6.25 percent, and in a good year, .125, or 12.5 percent.

Return on sales (ROS) or profit margin The ratio of operating profits per dollar of sales (EBIT divided by sales).

Asset turnover (ATO) The annual sales generated by each dollar of assets (sales/assets).

Factor 4, the ratio of sales to assets, is known as **asset turnover** (ATO). It indicates the efficiency of the firm's use of assets in the sense that it measures the annual sales generated by each dollar of assets. In a normal year, Nodett's ATO is 1.0 per year, meaning that sales of $1 per year were generated per dollar of assets. In a bad year, this ratio declines to 0.8 per year, and in a good year, it rises to 1.2 per year.

Comparing Nodett and Somdett, we see that factors 3 and 4 do not depend on a firm's financial leverage. The firms' ratios are equal to each other in all three scenarios.

Similarly, factor 1, the ratio of net income after taxes to pretax profit, is the same for both firms. We call this the tax-burden ratio. Its value reflects both the government's tax code and the policies pursued by the firm in trying to minimize its tax burden. In our example it does not change over the business cycle, remaining a constant .6.

While factors 1, 3, and 4 are not affected by a firm's capital structure, factors 2 and 5 are. Factor 2 is the ratio of pretax profits to EBIT. The firm's pretax

Table 16.6 *Ratio Decomposition Analysis for Nodett and Somdett*

	ROE	(1) Net Profit / Pretax Profit	(2) Pretax Profit / EBIT	(3) EBIT / Sales (ROS)	(4) Sales / Assets (ATO)	(5) Assets / Equity	(6) Compound Leverage Factor (2) × (5)
Bad Year							
Nodett	.030	.6	1.000	.0625	.800	1.000	1.000
Somdett	.018	.6	.360	.0625	.800	1.667	.600
Normal Year							
Nodett	.060	.6	1.000	.100	1.000	1.000	1.000
Somdett	.068	.6	.680	.100	1.000	1.667	1.134
Good Year							
Nodett	.090	.6	1.000	.125	1.200	1.000	1.000
Somdett	.118	.6	.787	.125	1.200	1.667	1.311

profits will be greatest when there are no interest payments to be made to debt-holders. In fact, another way to express this ratio is

$$\frac{\text{Pretax profits}}{\text{EBIT}} = \frac{\text{EBIT} - \text{Interest expense}}{\text{EBIT}}$$

We will call this factor the interest-burden (IB) ratio. It takes on its highest possible value, 1, for Nodett, which has no financial leverage. The higher the degree of financial leverage, the lower the IB ratio. Nodett's IB ratio does not vary over the business cycle. It is fixed at 1.0, reflecting the total absence of interest payments. For Somdett, however, because interest expense is fixed in dollar amount while EBIT varies, the IB ratio varies from a low of 0.36 in a bad year to a high of 0.787 in a good year.

Leverage ratio
Measure of debt to
total capitalization
of a firm.

Factor 5, the ratio of assets to equity, is a measure of the firm's degree of financial leverage. It is called the **leverage ratio** and is equal to 1 plus the debt-to-equity ratio.[2] In our numerical example in Table 16.6, Nodett has a leverage ratio of 1 while Somdett's is 1.667.

From our discussion in Section 16.2, we know that financial leverage helps boost ROE only if ROA is greater than the interest rate on the firm's debt. How is this fact reflected in the ratios of Table 16.6?

The answer is that to measure the full impact of leverage in this framework, the analyst must take the product of the IB and leverage ratios (that is, factors 2 and 5, shown in Table 16.6 as column 6). For Nodett, factor 6, which we call the compound leverage factor, remains a constant 1.0 under all three scenarios. But for Somdett, we see that the compound leverage factor is greater than 1 in normal years (1.134) and in good years (1.311), indicating the positive contribution of financial leverage to ROE. It is less than 1 in bad years, reflecting the fact that when ROA falls below the interest rate, ROE falls with increased use of debt.

We can summarize all of these relationships as follows: ROE = Tax burden × Interest burden × Margin × Turnover × Leverage. Because

$$\text{ROA} = \text{Margin} \times \text{Turnover}$$

and

$$\text{Compound leverage factor} = \text{Interest burden} \times \text{Leverage}$$

we can decompose ROE equivalently as follows:

$$\text{ROE} = \text{Tax burden} \times \text{ROA} \times \text{Compound leverage factor}$$

Table 16.6 compares firms with the same ROS and ATO but different degrees of financial leverage. Comparison of ROS and ATO usually is meaningful only in evaluating firms in the same industry. Cross-industry comparisons of these two ratios are often meaningless and can even be misleading.

For example, let us take two firms with the same ROA of 10 percent per year. The first is a supermarket chain, the second is a gas and electric utility.

---

[2] $\dfrac{\text{Assets}}{\text{Equity}} = \dfrac{\text{Equity} + \text{Debt}}{\text{Equity}} = 1 + \dfrac{\text{Debt}}{\text{Equity}}$

Table 16.7 *Differences between ROS and ATO across Industries*

	ROS	×	**ATO**	=	**ROA**
Supermarket chain	.02		5.0		.10
Utility	.20		0.5		.10

As Table 16.7 shows, the supermarket chain has a "low" ROS of 2 percent and achieves a 10 percent ROA by "turning over" its assets five times per year. The capital-intensive utility, on the other hand, has a "low" ATO of only 0.5 times per year and achieves its 10 percent ROA by having an ROS of 20 percent. The point here is that a "low" ROS or ATO ratio need not indicate a troubled firm. Each ratio must be interpreted in light of industry norms.

Even within an industry, ROS and ATO sometimes can differ markedly among firms pursuing different marketing strategies. In the retailing industry, for example, Neiman-Marcus pursues a high-margin, low-ATO policy compared to Wal-Mart, which pursues a low-margin, high-ATO policy.

Concept Check

Question 2. Do a ratio decomposition analysis for the Mordett corporation of Question 1, preparing a table similar to Table 16.6.

Turnover and Other Asset Utilization Ratios

It is often helpful in understanding a firm's ratio of sales to assets to compute comparable efficiency-of-utilization, or turnover, ratios for subcategories of assets. For example, fixed-asset turnover would be

$$\frac{\text{Sales}}{\text{Fixed assets}}$$

This ratio measures sales per dollar of the firm's money tied up in fixed assets.

To illustrate how you can compute this and other ratios from a firm's financial statements, consider Growth Industries, Inc. (GI). GI's income statement and opening and closing balance sheets for the years 19X1, 19X2, and 19X3 appear in Table 16.8.

GI's total asset turnover in 19X3 was 0.303, which was below the industry average of 0.4. To understand better why GI underperformed, we decide to compute asset utilization ratios separately for fixed assets, inventories, and accounts receivable.

GI's sales in 19X3 were $144 million. Its only fixed assets were plant and equipment, which were $216 million at the beginning of the year and $259.2 million at year's end. Average fixed assets for the year were, therefore, $237.6 million [($216 million + $259.2 million)/2]. GI's fixed asset turnover for 19X3 was $144 million per year/$237.6 million = .606 per year. In other words, for every dollar of fixed assets, there were $.606 in sales during the year 19X3.

Table 16.8   *Growth Industries Financial Statements, 19X1–19X3 ($ thousands)*

	19X0	19X1	19X2	19X3
Income statements				
Sales revenue		$100,000	$120,000	$144,000
Cost of goods sold (including depreciation)		55,000	66,000	79,200
Depreciation		15,000	18,000	21,600
Selling and administrative expenses		15,000	18,000	21,600
Operating income		30,000	36,000	43,200
Interest expense		10,500	19,095	34,391
Taxable income		19,500	16,905	8,809
Income tax (40% rate)		7,800	6,762	3,524
Net income		11,700	10,143	5,285
Balance sheets (end of year)				
Cash and marketable securities	$ 50,000	60,000	72,000	86,400
Accounts receivable	25,000	30,000	36,000	43,200
Inventories	75,000	90,000	108,000	129,600
Net plant and equipment	150,000	180,000	216,000	259,200
Total assets	$300,000	$360,000	$432,000	$518,400
Accounts payable	$ 30,000	$ 36,000	$ 43,200	$ 51,840
Short-term debt	45,000	87,300	141,957	214,432
Long-term debt (8% bonds maturing in 19X7)	75,000	75,000	75,000	75,000
Total liabilities	$150,000	$198,300	$260,157	$341,272
Shareholders' equity (1 million shares outstanding)	$150,000	$161,700	$171,843	$177,128
Other data				
Market price per common share at year-end		$93.60	$61.00	$21.00

Comparable figures for the fixed-asset turnover ratio for 19X1 and 19X2 and the 19X3 industry average are

19X1	19X2	19X3	19X3 Industry average
.606	.606	.606	.700

GI's fixed asset turnover has been stable over time and below the industry average.

Whenever a financial ratio includes one item from the income statement, which covers a period of time, and another from the balance sheet, which is a "snapshot" at a particular time, the practice is to take the average of the beginning and end-of-year balance sheet figures. Thus, in computing the fixed-asset turnover ratio you divide sales (from the income statement) by average fixed assets (from the balance sheet).

Another widely followed turnover ratio is the inventory turnover ratio, which is the ratio of cost of goods sold per dollar of inventory. It is usually expressed as cost of goods sold (instead of sales revenue) divided by average inventory. It measures the speed with which inventory is turned over.

In 19X1, GI's cost of goods sold (less depreciation) was $40 million, and its average inventory was $82.5 million [(75 million + $90 million)/2]. Its inventory turnover was 0.485 per year ($40 million/$82.5 million). In 19X2 and 19X3, inventory turnover remained the same and continued below the industry average of 0.5 per year.

Another measure of efficiency is the ratio of accounts receivable to sales. The accounts receivable ratio usually is computed as average accounts receivable/sales × 365. The result is a number called the **average collection period,** or **days receivables,** which equals the total credit extended to customers per dollar of daily sales. It is the number of days' worth of sales tied up in accounts receivable. You can also think of it as the average lag between the date of sale and the date payment is received.

Average collection period, or day's receivables The ratio of accounts receivable to daily sales, or the total amount of credit extended per dollar of daily sales.

For GI in 19X3 this number was 100.4 days:

$$\frac{(\$36 \text{ million} + \$43.2 \text{ million})/2}{\$144 \text{ million}} \times 365 = 100.4 \text{ days}$$

The industry average was 60 days.

In summary, use of these ratios lets us see that GI's poor total asset turnover relative to the industry is in part caused by lower than average fixed-asset turnover and inventory turnover and higher than average days receivables. This suggests GI may be having problems with excess plant capacity along with poor inventory and receivables management procedures.

Liquidity and Coverage Ratios

Liquidity and interest coverage ratios are of great importance in evaluating the riskiness of a firm's securities. They aid in assessing the financial strength of the firm.

Liquidity ratios include the current ratio, quick ratio, and interest coverage ratio.

Current ratio A ratio representing the ability of the firm to pay off its current liabilities by liquidating current assets (current assets/current liabilities).

1. **Current ratio:** current assets/current liabilities. This ratio measures the ability of the firm to pay off its current liabilities by liquidating its current assets (that is, turning them into cash). It indicates the firm's ability to avoid insolvency in the short run. GI's current ratio in 19X1, for example, was (60 + 30 + 90)/(36 + 87.3) = 1.46. In other years, it was

19X1	19X2	19X3	19X3 Industry Average
1.46	1.17	.97	2.0

This represents an unfavorable time trend and poor standing relative to the industry.

Quick ratio or acid test ratio A measure of liquidity similar to the current ratio except for exclusion of inventories (cash plus receivables divided by current liabilities).

2. **Quick ratio:** (cash + receivables)/current liabilities. This ratio is also called the **acid test ratio.** It has the same denominator as the current ratio, but its numerator includes only cash, cash equivalents, and receivables. The quick ratio is a better measure of liquidity than the current ratio for firms whose inventory is not readily convertible into cash. GI's quick ratio shows the same disturbing trends as its current ratio:

19X1	19X2	19X3	19X3 Industry Average
.73	.58	.49	1.0

Interest coverage ratio, or times interest earned A financial leverage measure arrived at by dividing earnings before interest and taxes by interest expense.

3. **Interest coverage ratio:** EBIT/interest expense. This ratio is often called **times interest earned.** It is closely related to the interest-burden ratio discussed in the previous section. A high coverage ratio tells the firm's shareholders and lenders that the likelihood of bankruptcy is low because annual earnings are significantly greater than annual interest obligations. It is widely used by both lenders and borrowers in determining the firm's debt capacity and is a major determinant of the firm's bond rating.

GI's interest coverage ratios are

19X1	*19X2*	*19X3*	*19X3 Industry Average*
2.86	1.89	1.26	5

GI's interest coverage ratio has fallen dramatically over this three-year period, and by 19X3 it is far below the industry average. Probably its credit rating has been declining as well, and no doubt GI is considered a relatively poor credit risk in 19X3.

Market Price Ratios

There are two market price ratios: the market-to-book-value ratio and the price/earnings ratio.

Market-to-book-value ratio Market price of a share divided by book value per share.

The **market-to-book-value ratio** (P/B) equals the market price of a share of the firm's common stock divided by its *book value,* that is, shareholders' equity per share. Analysts sometimes consider the stock of a firm with a low market-to-book value to be a "safer" investment, seeing the book value as a "floor" supporting the market price.

Analysts presumably view book value as the level below which market price will not fall because the firm always has the option to liquidate, or sell, its assets for their book values. However, this view is questionable. In fact, some firms, such as Digital (see Chapter 15), do sometimes sell for less than book value. Nevertheless, low market-to-book-value ratio is seen by some as providing a "margin of safety," and some analysts will screen out or reject high P/B firms in their stock selection process.

Proponents of the P/B screen would argue that, if all other relevant attributes are the same for two stocks, the one with the lower P/B ratio is safer. Although there may be firms for which this approach has some validity, book value does not necessarily represent liquidation value, which renders the margin of safety notion unreliable.

The theory of equity valuation offers some insight into the significance of the P/B ratio. A high P/B ratio is an indication that investors think a firm has opportunities of earning a rate of return on their investment in excess of the market capitalization rate, k.

To illustrate this point, we can return to the numerical example in Chapter 15, Section 15.5 and its accompanying table. That example assumes the market capitalization rate is 12 percent per year. Now add the assumptions that the book value per share is $8.33, and that the coming year's expected EPS is $1, so that in the case for which the expected ROE on future investments also is 12 percent, the stock will sell at $1/.12 = $8.33, and the P/B ratio will be 1.

Price/earnings
ratio   The ratio of a
stock's price to its
earnings per share.
Also referred to as the
P/E multiple.

Table 16.9 shows the P/B ratio for alternative assumptions about future ROE and plowback ratio.

Reading down any column, you can see how the P/B ratio changes with ROE. The numbers reveal that, for a given plowback ratio, the P/B ratio is higher, the higher the expected ROE. This makes sense, because the greater the expected profitability of the firm's future investment opportunities, the greater its market value as an ongoing enterprise compared with the cost of acquiring its assets.

We've noted that the **price/earnings ratio** that is based on the firm's financial statements and reported in newspaper stock listings is not the same as the price/earnings multiple that emerges from a discounted dividend model. The numerator is the same (the market price of the stock), but the denominator is different. The P/E ratio uses the most recent past accounting earnings, while the P/E multiple predicted by valuation models uses expected future economic earnings.

Many security analysts pay careful attention to the accounting P/E ratio in the belief that among low P/E stocks they are somehow more likely to find bargains than with high P/E stocks. The idea is that you can acquire a claim on a dollar of earnings more cheaply if the P/E ratio is low. For example, if the P/E ratio is 8, you pay $8 per share per $1 of *current* earnings, while if P/E is 12, you must pay $12 for a claim on $1 of current earnings.

Note, however, that current earnings may differ substantially from future earnings. The higher P/E stock still may be a bargain relative to the low P/E stock if its earnings and dividends are expected to grow at a faster rate. Our point is that ownership of the stock conveys the right to future earnings, as well as to current earnings. An exclusive focus on the commonly reported accounting P/E ratio can be shortsighted, because by its nature it ignores future growth in earnings.

An efficient markets adherent will be skeptical of the notion that a strategy of investing in low P/E stocks would result in an expected rate of return greater than that of investing in high or medium P/E stocks having the same risk. The empirical evidence on this question is mixed, but if the strategy had worked in the past, it almost surely would not work in the future because too many investors would be following it. This is the lesson of market efficiency.

Table 16.9   *Effect of ROE and Plowback Ratio on P/B*

	Plowback Ratio (b)			
ROE	**0**	**25%**	**50%**	**75%**
10%	1.00	.95	.86	.67
12%	1.00	1.00	1.00	1.00
14%	1.00	1.06	1.20	2.00

The assumptions and formulas underlying this table are: $E_1 = \$1$; book value per share $= \$8.33$; $k = 12\%$ per year.

$$g = b \times \text{ROE}$$
$$P_0 = \frac{(1 - b)E}{k - g}$$
$$P/B = P_0/\$8.33$$

Before leaving the P/B and P/E ratios, it is worth pointing out the relationship among these ratios and ROE:

$$\text{ROE} = \frac{\text{Earnings}}{\text{Book value}}$$

$$= \frac{\text{Market price}}{\text{Book value}} \div \frac{\text{Market price}}{\text{Earnings}}$$

$$= \text{P/B ratio} \div \text{P/E ratio}$$

Earnings yield *The ratio of earnings to price, E/P.*

By rearranging the terms, we find that a firm's **earnings yield,** the ratio of earnings to price, is equal to its ROE divided by the market-book value ratio:

$$\frac{E}{P} = \frac{\text{ROE}}{\text{P/B}}$$

Thus, a company with a high ROE can have a relatively low earnings yield because its P/B ratio is high. This indicates a high ROE does not in and of itself imply the stock is a good buy: the price of the stock already may be bid up to reflect an attractive ROE. If so, the P/B ratio will be above 1.0, and the earnings yield to stockholders will be below the ROE, as the equation demonstrates. The relationship shows that a strategy of investing in the stock of high ROE firms may produce a lower holding-period return than investing in those with a low ROE.

Clayman (1987) has found that investing in the stocks of 29 "excellent" companies, with mean reported ROE of 19.05 percent during the period 1976 to 1980, produced results much inferior to investing in 39 "unexcellent" companies, those with a mean ROE of 7.09 percent during the period. An investor putting equal dollar amounts in the stocks of the unexcellent companies would have earned a portfolio rate of return over the 1981 to 1985 period that was 11.3 percent higher per year than the rate of return on a comparable portfolio of excellent company stocks.

Concept Check

> ***Question 3.*** What were GI's ROE, P/E, and P/B ratios in the year 19X3? How do they compare to the industry average ratios, which were:
> ROE = 8.64%
> P/E = 8
> P/B = .69
> How does GI's earnings yield in 19X3 compare to the industry average?

16.5 *An Illustration of Financial Statement Analysis*

In her 19X3 annual report to the shareholders of Growth Industries, Inc., the president wrote: "19X3 was another successful year for Growth Industries. As in 19X2, sales, assets, and operating income all continued to grow at a rate of 20%."

Is she right?

We can evaluate her statement by conducting a full-scale ratio analysis of Growth Industries. Our purpose is to assess GI's performance in the recent

Table 16.10   *Key Financial Ratios of Growth Industries, Inc.*

Year	ROE	(1) Net Profit / Pretax Profit	(2) Pretax Profit / EBIT	(3) EBIT / Sales (ROS)	(4) Sales / Assets (ATO)	(5) Assets / Equity	(6) Compound Leverage Factor (2) × (5)	(7) ROA (3) × (4)	P/E	P/B
19X1	7.51%	.6	.650	30%	.303	2.117	1.376	9.09%	8	.58
19X2	6.08	.6	.470	30	.303	2.375	1.116	9.09	6	.35
19X3	3.03	.6	.204	30	.303	2.723	.556	9.09	4	.12
Industry average	8.64%	.6	.800	30%	.400	1.500	1.200	12.00%	8	.69

past, to evaluate its future prospects, and to determine whether its market price reflects its intrinsic value.

Table 16.10 shows the key financial ratios we can compute from GI's financial statements. The president is certainly right about the growth in sales, assets, and operating income. Inspection of GI's key financial ratios, however, contradicts her first sentence: 19X3 was not another successful year for GI—it appears to have been another miserable one.

ROE has been declining steadily from 7.51 percent in 19X1 to 3.03 percent in 19X3. A comparison of GI's 19X3 ROE to the 19X3 industry average of 8.64 percent makes the deteriorating time trend appear especially alarming. The low and falling market-to-book-value ratio and the falling price/earnings ratio indicate investors are less and less optimistic about the firm's future profitability.

The fact that ROA has not been declining, however, tells us that the source of the declining time trend in GI's ROE must be inappropriate use of financial leverage. And we see that, while GI's leverage ratio climbed from 2.117 in 19X1 to 2.723 in 19X3, its interest-burden ratio fell from 0.650 to 0.204—with the net result that the compound leverage factor fell from 1.376 to 0.556.

The rapid increase in short-term debt from year to year and the concurrent increase in interest expense make it clear that, to finance its 20 percent growth rate in sales, GI has incurred sizable amounts of short-term debt at high interest rates. The firm is paying rates of interest greater than the ROA it is earning on the investment financed with the new borrowing. As the firm has expanded, its situation has become ever more precarious.

In 19X3, for example, the average interest rate on short-term debt was 20 percent versus an ROA of 9.09 percent. (We compute the average interest rate on short-term debt by taking the total interest expense of $34,391,000, subtracting the $6 million in interest on the long-term bonds, and dividing by the beginning-of-year short-term debt of $141,957,000.)

GI's problems become clear when we examine its statement of cash flows in Table 16.11. The statement is derived from the income statement and balance sheet in Table 16.8. GI's cash flow from operations is falling steadily, from $12,700,000 in 19X1 to $6,725,000 in 19X3. The firm's investment in plant and equipment, by contrast, has increased greatly. Net plant and equipment (i.e., net of depreciation) rose from $150,000,000 in 19X0 to $259,200,000 in 19X3. This near doubling of the capital assets makes the decrease in cash flow from operations all the more troubling.

The source of the difficulty is GI's enormous amount of short-term borrowing. In a sense, the company is being run as a pyramid scheme. It borrows more

Table 16.11   *Growth Industries Statement of Cash Flows ($ Thousands)*

	19X1	19X2	19X3
Cash Flow from Operating Activities			
Net income	$ 11,700	$ 10,143	$ 5,285
+ Depreciation	15,000	18,000	21,600
+ Decrease (increase) in accounts receivable	(5,000)	(6,000)	(7,200)
+ Decrease (increase) in inventories	(15,000)	(18,000)	(21,600)
+ Increase in accounts payable	6,000	7,200	8,640
	$ 12,700	$ 11,343	$ 6,725
Cash Flow from Investing Activities			
Investment in plant and equipment*	$(45,000)	$(54,000)	$(64,800)
Cash Flow from Financing Activities			
Dividends paid†	$ 0	$ 0	$ 0
Short-term debt issued	$ 42,300	$ 54,657	$ 72,475
Change in cash and marketable securities‡	$ 10,000	$ 12,000	$ 14,400

*Gross investment equals increase in net plant and equipment plus depreciation.

†We can conclude that no dividends are paid because stockholders' equity increases each year by the full amount of net income, implying a plowback ratio of 1.0.

‡Equals cash flow from operations plus cash flow from investment activities plus cash flow from financing activities. Note that this equals the yearly change in cash and marketable securities on the balance sheet.

and more each year to maintain its 20 percent growth rate in assets and income. However, the new assets are not generating enough cash flow to support the extra interest burden of the debt, as the falling cash flow from operations indicates. Eventually, when the firm loses its ability to borrow further, its growth will be at an end.

At this point GI stock might be an attractive investment. Its market price is only 12 percent of its book value, and with a P/E ratio of 4 its earnings yield is 25 percent per year. GI is a likely candidate for a takeover by another firm that might replace GI's management and build shareholder value through a radical change in policy.

Concept Check

Question 4. You have the following information for IBX Corporation for the years 1991 and 1988 (all figures are in $ millions):

	1991	1988
Net income	$ 253.7	$ 239.0
Pretax income	411.9	375.6
EBIT	517.6	403.1
Average assets	4,857.9	3,459.7
Sales	6,679.3	4,537.0
Shareholders' equity	2,233.3	2,347.3

What is the trend in IBX's ROE, and how can you account for it in terms of tax burden, margin, turnover, and financial leverage?

The Many Ways of Figuring Financial Results

An investor in First Boston Corp. might have had a pleasant surprise while reading the investment banking company's 1987 financial statement. Despite taking heavy hits in the volatile bond markets and October's stock crash, First Boston reported earnings of $3.12 per share—down 40 percent from the heights of 1986, but about the same as profits in 1984.

But hold on. Looking through Value Line's *Investment Survey,* the same investor would be dismayed to find that First Boston's earnings for last year were only 59¢ a share. What gives? In this case the explanation is fairly simple. Value Line doesn't take into account the profits First Boston made in selling its Park Avenue headquarters, while the company and other reporting services such as Standard & Poor's do.

This type of discrepancy in reported financial figures is very common (table) and points to a general rule: Where the bottom line falls depends on who's drawing it. S&P's *Stock Report* generally follows the company's accounting in regard to nonrecurring items, but Value Line doesn't. For example, Union Carbide's reserve for Bhopal litigation amounted to 40¢ per share. S&P and Carbide subtracted it from earnings, but Value Line left it in.

The Bottom Line: Take Your Choice

	1987 Earnings per Share	
	S&P	Value Line
Alcoa	$2.52	$4.14
Affiliated Publ.	4.08	0.61
First Boston	3.12	0.59
Merrill Lynch	3.58	1.52
Union Carbide	1.76	2.17

Data from Standard & Poor's Corp., Value Line Inc.

Forecast Tool

With the rash of mergers, acquisitions, and divestitures in recent years, the varying approaches of reporting services can result in enormous differences. In 1985, for example, when Warner-Lambert cut its losses by selling three hospital-supply units, S&P showed the company losing $4.05 per share for the year, while Value Line reported a gain of $3.05 per share.

To try to get a "clear-cut number," Value Line will remove from earnings such items as gains or losses from discontinued operations and other special items, says a senior analyst at the firm. He says such a number is more useful to investors looking at the future earning power of a company. Similarly, *Business Week's* Corporate Scoreboard shows earnings from continuing operations, excluding special, nonrecurring, or extraordinary items. Dan Mayper at S&P says S&P's philosophy is to reflect all the special items in the figures and explain their significance in the narrative of the report.

There are also wide variations when it comes to computing a company's book value. That's basically what's left over when you subtract liabilities from assets. Unlike Value Line, S&P gives no credit to such intangible assets as customer lists, patents, trademarks, or franchises. Companies with many intangibles on their books, such as broadcasters and publishers, are bound to look a lot worse in S&P's calculations. For example, Capital Cities/ABC had a 1986 per-share book value of $120.82, said Value Line, while S&P showed a negative net worth of $24.26 per share.

Value Line analyst Marc Gerstein believes that including the intangibles on the balance sheet gives the best idea of a company's value as an ongoing concern. S&P regards its approach as more conservative, designed to approximate the company's liquidation value.

Reprinted from April 11, 1988, issue of *Business Week* by special permission, copyright © 1988 by McGraw-Hill, Inc.

16.6   *Comparability Problems*

Financial statement analysis gives us a good amount of ammunition for evaluating a company's performance and future prospects. But comparing financial results of different companies is not so simple. There is more than one acceptable way to represent various items of revenue and expense according to generally accepted accounting principles (GAAP). This means two firms may have exactly the same economic income yet very different accounting incomes.

Furthermore, interpreting a single firm's performance over time is complicated when inflation distorts the dollar measuring rod. Comparability problems are especially acute in this case because the impact of inflation on reported results often depends on the particular method the firm adopts to account for inventories and depreciation. The security analyst must adjust the earnings and the financial ratio figures to a uniform standard before attempting to compare financial results across firms and over time.

Comparability problems can arise out of the flexibility of GAAP guidelines in accounting for inventories and depreciation and in adjusting for the effects of inflation. Other important potential sources of noncomparability include the capitalization of leases and other expenses and the treatment of pension costs, but they are beyond the scope of this book. The nearby box illustrates the types of problems an analyst must be aware of in using financial statements to identify bargain stocks.

Inventory Valuation

LIFO *The last-in first-out accounting method of valuing inventories.*

FIFO *The first-in first-out accounting method of inventory valuation.*

There are two commonly used ways to value inventories: **LIFO** (last-in first-out) and **FIFO** (first-in first-out). We can explain the difference using a numerical example.

Suppose Generic Products, Inc., (GPI) has a constant inventory of 1 million units of generic goods. The inventory turns over once per year, meaning the ratio of cost of goods sold to inventory is 1.

The LIFO system calls for valuing the million units used up during the year at the current cost of production, so that the last goods produced are considered the first ones to be sold. They are valued at today's cost.

The FIFO system assumes that the units used up or sold are the ones that were added to inventory first, and goods sold should be valued at original cost.

If the price of generic goods were constant, at the level of $1, say, the book value of inventory and the cost of goods sold would be the same, $1 million under both systems. But suppose the price of generic goods rises by 10 cents per unit during the year as a result of general inflation.

LIFO accounting would result in a cost of goods sold of $1.1 million, while the end-of-year balance sheet value of the 1 million units in inventory remains $1 million. The balance sheet value of inventories is given as the cost of the goods still in inventory. Under LIFO the last goods produced are assumed to be sold at the current cost of $1.10; the goods remaining are the previously produced goods, at a cost of only $1. You can see that, although LIFO accounting accurately measures the cost of goods sold today, it understates the current value of the remaining inventory in an inflationary environment.

In contrast, under FIFO accounting, the cost of goods sold would be $1 million, and the end-of-year balance sheet value of the inventory is $1.1 million. The result is that the LIFO firm has both a lower reported profit and a lower balance sheet value of inventories than the FIFO firm.

LIFO is preferred over FIFO in computing economic earnings (that is, real sustainable cash flow), because it uses up-to-date prices to evaluate the cost of goods sold. A disadvantage is that LIFO accounting induces balance sheet distortions when it values investment in inventories at original cost. This practice results in an upward bias in ROE because the investment base on which return is earned is undervalued.

In computing the gross national product, the U.S. Department of Commerce has to make an inventory valuation adjustment (IVA) to eliminate the effects of FIFO accounting on the cost of goods sold. In effect, it puts all firms in the aggregate onto a LIFO basis.

Depreciation

Another source of problems is the measurement of depreciation, which is a key factor in computing true earnings. The accounting and economic measures of depreciation can differ markedly. According to the *economic* definition, depreciation is the amount of a firm's operating cash flow that must be reinvested in the firm to sustain its real cash flow at the current level.

The *accounting* measurement is quite different. Accounting depreciation is the amount of the original acquisition cost of an asset that is allocated to each accounting period over an arbitrarily specified life of the asset. This is the figure reported in financial statements.

Assume, for example, that a firm buys machines with a useful economic life of 20 years at $100,000 apiece. In its financial statements, however, the firm can depreciate the machines over 10 years using the straight-line method, for $10,000 per year in depreciation. Thus, after 10 years a machine will be fully depreciated on the books, even though it remains a productive asset that will not need replacement for another 10 years.

In computing accounting earnings, this firm will overestimate depreciation in the first 10 years of the machine's economic life and underestimate it in the last 10 years. This will cause reported earnings to be understated compared with economic earnings in the first 10 years and overstated in the last 10 years.

If the management of the firm had a zero plowback policy and distributed as cash dividends only its accounting earnings, it would pay out too little in the first 10 years relative to the sustainable cash flow. Similarly, a security analyst who relied on the (unadjusted) reported earnings figure during the first few years would see understated economic earnings and would underestimate the firm's intrinsic value.

Depreciation comparability problems add one more wrinkle. A firm can use different depreciation methods for tax purposes than for other reporting purposes. Most firms use accelerated depreciation methods for tax purposes and straight-line depreciation in published financial statements. There also are differences across firms in their estimates of the depreciable life of plant, equipment, and other depreciable assets.

The major problem related to depreciation, however, is caused by inflation. Because conventional depreciation is based on historical costs rather than on the current replacement cost of assets, measured depreciation in periods of inflation is understated relative to replacement cost, and *real* economic income (sustainable cash flow) is correspondingly overstated.

The situation is similar to what happens in FIFO inventory accounting. Conventional depreciation and FIFO both result in an inflation-induced overstatement of real income because both use original cost instead of current cost to calculate net income.

For example, suppose Generic Products, Inc., has a machine with a three-year useful life that originally cost $3 million. Annual straight-line depreciation is $1 million, regardless of what happens to the replacement cost of the machine. Suppose inflation in the first year turns out to be 10 percent. Then the true annual depreciation expense is $1.1 million in current terms, while conventionally measured depreciation remains fixed at $1 million per year. Accounting income overstates *real* economic income by the inflation factor, $.1 million.

As it does in the case of inventory valuation, the Commerce Department in its computation of GNP tries to adjust aggregate depreciation. It does this by applying "capital consumption allowances" (CCA), to account for the distorting effects of conventional depreciation techniques.

Inflation and Interest Expense

While inflation can cause distortions in the measurement of a firm's inventory and depreciation costs, it has perhaps an even greater effect on calculation of *real* interest expense. Nominal interest rates include an inflation premium that compensates the lender for inflation-induced erosion in the real value of principal. From the perspective of both lender and borrower, therefore, part of what is conventionally measured as interest expense should be treated more properly as repayment of principal.

For example, suppose Generic Products has debt outstanding with a face value of $10 million at an interest rate of 10 percent per year. Interest expense as conventionally measured is $1 million per year. However, suppose inflation during the year is 6 percent, so that the real interest rate is 4 percent. Then $.6 million of what appears as interest expense on the income statement is really an inflation premium, or compensation for the anticipated reduction in the real value of the $10 million principal; only $.4 million is *real* interest expense. The $.6 million reduction in the purchasing power of the outstanding principal may be thought of as repayment of principal, rather than as an interest expense. Real income of the firm is, therefore, understated by $.6 million.

This mismeasurement of real interest means inflation deflates the statement of real income. The effects of inflation on the reported values of inventories and depreciation that we have discussed work in the opposite direction.

Concept Check

> **Question 5.**   In a period of rapid inflation, companies ABC and XYZ have the same *reported* earnings. ABC uses LIFO inventory accounting, has relatively fewer depreciable assets, and has more debt than XYZ. XYZ uses FIFO inventory accounting. Which company has the higher *real* income and why?

Inflation Accounting

In recognition of the need to adjust for the effects of inflation, the Financial Accounting Standards Board in 1980 issued Rule No. 33 (FASB 33). It required large public corporations to supplement their customary financial statements with data pertaining to the effect of inflation.

A survey reported by Norby (1983), however, indicated that security analysts, by and large, were ignoring the inflation-adjusted data. One possible reason is that analysts believed FASB 33 just added another element of noncomparability. In other words, analysts may have judged the inflation-adjusted earnings to be poorer estimates of real economic earnings than the original unadjusted figures.

In 1987, after a lengthy evaluation of the effects of FASB 33, the FASB decided to discontinue it. Today, analysts interested in adjusting reported financial statements for inflation are on their own.

16.7   *Value Investing: The Graham Technique*

No presentation of fundamental security analysis would be complete without a discussion of the ideas of Benjamin Graham, the greatest of the investment "gurus." Until the evolution of modern portfolio theory in the latter half of this century, Graham was the single most important thinker, writer, and teacher in the field of investment analysis. His influence on investment professionals remains very strong.

Graham's magnum opus is *Security Analysis,* written with Columbia Professor David Dodd in 1934. Its message is similar to the ideas presented in this chapter. Graham believed careful analysis of a firm's financial statements could turn up bargain stocks. Over the years, he developed many different rules for determining the most important financial ratios and the critical values for judging a stock to be undervalued. Through many editions, his book has had a profound influence on investment professionals. It has been so influential and successful, in fact, that widespread adoption of Graham's techniques has led to elimination of the very bargains they are designed to identify.

In a 1976 seminar Graham said:[3]

> I am no longer an advocate of elaborate techniques of security analysis in order to find superior value opportunities. This was a rewarding activity, say, forty years ago, when our textbook "Graham and Dodd" was first published; but the situation has changed a good deal since then. In the old days any well-trained security analyst could do a good professional job of selecting undervalued issues through detailed studies; but in the light of the enormous amount of research now being carried on, I doubt whether in most cases such extensive efforts will generate sufficiently superior selections to justify their cost. To that very limited extent I'm on the side of the "efficient market" school of thought now generally accepted by the professors.

Nonetheless, in that same seminar, Graham suggested a simplified approach to identify bargain stocks:

> My first, more limited, technique confines itself to the purchase of common stocks at less than their working-capital value, or net current-asset value, giving no weight to the plant and other fixed assets, and deducting all liabilities in full from the current assets. We used this approach extensively in managing investment funds, and over a thirty-odd-year period we must have earned an average of some 20 percent per year from this source. For a while, however, after the

---

[3]As cited by John Train in *Money Masters* (New York: Harper & Row, Publishers, Inc., 1987).

mid-1950s, this brand of buying opportunity became very scarce because of the pervasive bull market. But it has returned in quantity since the 1973–1974 decline. In January 1976 we counted over 100 such issues in the Standard & Poor's *Stock Guide*—about 10 percent of the total. I consider it a foolproof method of systematic investment—once again, not on the basis of individual results but in terms of the expectable group outcome.

There are two convenient sources of information for those interested in trying out the Graham technique. Both Standard & Poor's *Outlook* and *The Value Line Investment Survey* carry lists of stocks selling below net working capital value.

Summary

1. The primary focus of the security analyst should be the firm's real economic earnings rather than its reported earnings. Accounting earnings as reported in financial statements can be a biased estimate of real economic earnings, although empirical studies reveal that reported earnings convey considerable information concerning a firm's prospects.

2. A firm's ROE is a key determinant of the growth rate of its earnings. ROE is affected profoundly by the firm's degree of financial leverage. An increase in a firm's debt-to-equity ratio will raise its ROE and hence its growth rate only if the interest rate on the debt is less than the firm's return on assets.

3. It is often helpful to the analyst to decompose a firm's ROE ratio into the product of several accounting ratios and to analyze their separate behavior over time and across companies within an industry. A useful breakdown is

$$\text{ROE} = \frac{\text{Net profits}}{\text{Pretax profits}} \times \frac{\text{Pretax profits}}{\text{EBIT}} \times \frac{\text{EBIT}}{\text{Sales}} \times \frac{\text{Sales}}{\text{Asssets}} \times \frac{\text{Assets}}{\text{Equity}}$$

4. Other accounting ratios that have a bearing on a firm's profitability and/or risk are fixed-asset turnover, inventory turnover, days receivables, and the current, quick, and interest coverage ratios.

5. Two ratios that make use of the market price of the firm's common stock in addition to its financial statements are the ratios of market-to-book value and price-to-earnings. Analysts sometimes take low values for these ratios as a margin of safety or a sign that the stock is a bargain.

6. A strategy of investing in stocks with high reported ROE seems to have produced a lower rate of return to the investor than investing in low ROE stocks. This implies that high reported ROE stocks were overpriced compared with low ROE stocks.

7. A major problem in the use of data obtained from a firm's financial statements is comparability. Firms have a great deal of latitude in how they choose to compute various items of revenue and expense. It is, therefore, necessary for the security analyst to adjust accounting earnings and financial ratios to a uniform standard before attempting to compare financial results across firms.

8. Comparability problems can be acute in a period of inflation. Inflation can create distortions in accounting for inventories, depreciation, and interest expense.

Key Terms

Selected Readings

The classic book on the use of financial statements in equity valuation, now in its fifth edition, is:

Cottle, S.; R. Murray; and F. Block. *Graham and Dodd's Security Analysis.* New York: McGraw-Hill, Inc., 1988.

Problem Sets

1. The Crusty Pie Co., which specializes in apple turnovers, has a return on sales higher than the industry average, yet its ROA is the same as the industry average. How can you explain this?

2. The ABC Corporation has a profit margin on sales below the industry average, yet its ROA is above the industry average. What does this imply about its asset turnover?

3. Firm *A* and firm *B* have the same ROA, yet firm *A*'s ROE is higher. How can you explain this?

   (Questions 4 through 17 are from past CFA Examinations, Level I.)

4. Which of the following *best* explains a ratio of "net sales to average net fixed assets" that *exceeds* the industry average?

   a. The firm added to its plant and equipment in the past few years.

   b. The firm makes less efficient use of its assets than other firms.

   c. The firm has a lot of old plant and equipment.

   d. The firm uses straight-line depreciation.

5. The rate of return on assets is equivalent to:

   a. Profit margin × Total asset turnover

   b. Profit margin × Total asset turnover × Leverage ratio/Interest expense

   c. $\dfrac{\text{Net income} + \text{Interest expense net of income tax} + \text{Minority interest in earnings}}{\text{Average total assets}}$

   d. $\dfrac{\text{Net income} + \text{Minority interest in earnings}}{\text{Average total assets}}$

   1. *a* only

   2. *a* and *c*

   3. *b* only

   4. *b* and *d*

6. The financial statements for Seattle Manufacturing Corporation are to be used to compute the following ratios for 1991 (Tables 16A and 16B).
   a. Return on total assets.
   b. Earnings per share of common stock.
   c. Acid test ratio.
   d. Interest coverage ratio.
   e. Receivables collection period.
   f. Leverage ratio.

Table 16A *Seattle Manufacturing Corp. Consolidated Balance Sheet, as of December 31 ($ millions)*

	1990	1991
Assets		
Current assets:		
Cash	$ 6.2	$ 6.6
Short-term investment in commercial paper	20.8	15.0
Accounts receivable	77.0	93.2
Inventory	251.2	286.0
Prepaid manufacturing expense	1.4	1.8
Total current assets	356.6	402.6
Leased property under capital leases net of accumulated amortization	181.4	215.6
Other	6.2	9.8
Total assets	$544.2	$628.0
Liabilities		
Current liabilities:		
Accounts payable	$143.2	$161.0
Dividends payable	13.0	14.4
Current portion of long-term debt	12.0	16.6
Current portion of obligations under capital leases	18.8	22.6
Estimated taxes on income	10.8	9.8
Total current liabilities	$197.8	$224.4
Long-term debt	86.4	107.0
Obligations under capital leases	140.8	165.8
Total liabilities	$425.0	$497.2
Shareholders' equity		
Common stock, $10 per value 4,000,000 shares authorized, 3,000,000 and 2,680,000 outstanding, respectively	26.8	30.0
Cumulative preferred stock, Series A 8%; $25 par value; 1,000,000 authorized; 600,000 outstanding	15.0	15.0
Additional paid-in capital	26.4	27.0
Retained earnings	51.0	58.8
Total shareholders' equity	119.2	130.8
Total liabilities and shareholders' equity	$544.2	$628.0

Table 16B   *Seattle Manufacturing Corp. Income Statement, Years Ending December 31 ($ millions)*

	1990	1991
Sales	$1,166.6	$1,207.6
Other income, net	12.8	15.6
Total revenues	1,179.4	1,223.2
Cost of sales	$ 912.0	$ 961.2
Amortization of leased property	43.6	48.6
Selling and administrative expense	118.4	128.8
Interest expense	16.2	19.8
Total costs and expenses	1,090.2	1,158.4
Income before income tax	$ 89.2	$ 64.8
Income tax	19.2	10.4
Net income	$ 70.0	$ 54.4

7. The financial statements for Chicago Refrigerator Inc. are to be used to compute the following ratios for 1991 (Tables 16C and 16D).
   a. Quick ratio.
   b. Return on assets.
   c. Return on common shareholders' equity.
   d. Earnings per share of common stock.
   e. Profit margin.
   f. Times interest earned.
   g. Inventory turnover.
   h. Leverage ratio.

8. The financial statements for Atlas Corporation are to be used to compute the following ratios for 1991 (Tables 16E and 16F).
   a. Acid-test ratio.
   b. Inventory turnover.
   c. Earnings per share.
   d. Interest coverage.
   e. Leverage.

9. Just before the onset of inflation, a firm switched from FIFO to LIFO. If nothing else changed, the inventory turnover for the next year would be:
   a. Higher
   b. Lower
   c. Unchanged
   d. Unpredictable from the information given.

10. In an inflationary period, the use of FIFO will make which *one* of the following more realistic than the use of LIFO?
   a. Balance sheet.
   b. Income statement.
   c. Cash flow statement.
   d. None of the above.

11. A company acquires a machine with an estimated 10-year service life. If the company uses the sum-of-the-years-digits depreciation method instead of the straight-line method:
   a. Income will be higher in the 10th year.
   b. Total depreciation expense for the 10 years will be lower.
   c. Depreciation expense will be lower in the first year.
   d. Scrapping the machine after eight years will result in a larger loss.

Table 16C *Chicago Refrigerator Inc. Balance Sheet, as of December 31*
($ thousands)

	1990	1991
Assets		
Current assets:		
Cash	$ 683	$ 325
Accounts receivable	1,490	3,599
Inventories	1,415	2,423
Prepaid expenses	15	13
Total current assets	3,603	6,360
Property, plant, equipment, net	1,066	1,541
Other	123	157
Total assets	$4,792	$8,058
Liabilities		
Current liabilities:		
Notes payable to bank	$ —	$ 875
Current portion of long-term debt	38	116
Accounts payable	485	933
Estimated income tax	588	472
Accrued expenses	576	586
Customer advance payment	34	963
Total current liabilities	1,721	3,945
Long-term debt	122	179
Other liabilities	81	131
Total liabilities	1,924	4,255
Shareholders' equity		
Common stock, $1 par value 1,000,000 shares authorized; 550,000 and 829,000 outstanding, respectively	550	829
Preferred stock, Series A 10%; $25.00 par value; 25,000 authorized; 20,000 and 18,000 outstanding, respectively	500	450
Additional paid-in capital	450	575
Retained earnings	1,368	1,949
Total shareholders' equity	$2,868	$3,803
Total liabilities and shareholders' equity	$4,792	$8,058

Table 16D *Chicago Refrigerator Inc. Income Statement, Years Ending December 31*
($ thousands)

	1990	1991
Net sales	$7,570	$12,065
Other income, net	261	345
Total revenues	7,831	12,410
Cost of goods sold	$4,850	$ 8,048
General administrative and marketing expense	1,531	2,025
Interest expense	22	78
Total costs and expenses	6,403	10,151
Net income before tax	$1,428	$ 2,259
Income tax	628	994
Net income	$ 800	$ 1,265

Table 16E   Atlas Corporation Consolidated Balance Sheet, as of December 31
($ millions)

	1990	1991
Assets		
Current Assets		
Cash	$ 3.1	$ 3.3
Short-term investment in commercial paper	2.9	—
Accounts receivable	38.5	46.6
Inventory	125.6	143.0
Prepaid manufacturing expense	.7	.9
Total current assets	$170.8	$193.8
Leased property under capital leases net of accumulated amortization	$ 90.7	$107.8
Other	3.1	4.9
Total assets	$264.6	$306.5
Liabilities		
Current Liabilities		
Accounts payable	$ 71.6	$ 81.7
Dividends payable	6.5	6.0
Current portion of long-term debt	6.0	8.3
Current portion of obligation under capital leases	9.4	11.3
Estimated taxes on income	5.4	4.9
Total current liabilities	$ 98.9	$112.2
Long-term debt	$ 43.2	$ 53.5
Obligations under capital leases	70.4	82.9
Total liabilities	$212.5	$248.6
Shareholders' equity		
Common stock, $10 par value		
2,000,000 shares authorized; 1,340,000 and 1,500,000 outstanding, respectively	13.4	15.0
Additional paid-in capital	13.2	13.5
Retained earnings	25.5	29.4
Total shareholders' equity	52.1	57.9
Total liabilities and shareholders' equity	$264.6	$306.5

Table 16F   Atlas Corporation Income Statement, Years Ending December 31,
($ millions)

	1990	1991
Sales	$583.3	$603.8
Other income, net	6.4	2.8
Main revenues	589.7	606.6
Cost of sales	456.0	475.6
Amortization of leased property	21.8	24.3
Selling and administrative expense	59.2	64.4
Interest expense	8.1	9.9
Total costs and expenses	545.1	574.2
Income before income tax	44.6	32.4
Income tax	9.6	5.2
Net income	$ 35.0	$ 27.2

[Questions 12–17 appeared on past CFA examinations]

12. Why might a firm's ratio of long-term debt to long-term capital be lower than the industry average, but its ratio of income-before-interest-and-taxes to debt-interest charges be lower than the industry average?
    a. The firm has higher profitability than average.
    b. The firm has more short-term debt than average.
    c. The firm has a high ratio of current assets to current liabilities.
    d. The firm has a high ratio of total cash flow to total long-term debt.

13. Assuming continued inflation, a firm that uses LIFO will tend to have a _____ current ratio than a firm using FIFO, and the difference will tend to _____ as time passes.
    a. Higher, increase.
    b. Higher, decrease.
    c. Lower, decrease.
    d. Lower, increase.

14. In a cash flow statement prepared in accordance with FASB 95, cash flow from investing activities *excludes:*
    a. Cash paid for acquisitions.
    b. Cash received from sale of fixed assets.
    c. Inventory increase due to new (internally developed) product line.
    d. All of the above.

15. Cash flow from operating activities *includes:*
    a. Inventory increases resulting from acquisitions.
    b. Inventory changes due to changing exchange rates.
    c. Interest paid to bondholders.
    d. Dividends paid to stockholders.

16. Cash flow from investing activities *excludes:*
    a. Cash paid for acquisitions.
    b. Cash received from sale of fixed assets.
    c. Inventory increase due to new (internally developed) product line.
    d. All of the above.

17. All other things being equal, what effect will the payment of a cash dividend have on the following ratios?

	Times Interest Earned	**Debt/Equity Ratio**
a.	Increase	Increase
b.	No effect	Increase
c.	No effect	No effect
d.	Decrease	Decrease

18. The Du Pont formula defines the net return on shareholders' equity as a function of the following components:

    - Operating margin.
    - Asset turnover.
    - Interest burden.
    - Financial leverage.
    - Income tax rate.

    Using *only* the data in Table 16G shown on page 474.

a. Calculate each of the five components listed above for 1985 and 1989, and calculate the return on equity (ROE) for 1985 and 1989, using all of the five components.

b. Briefly discuss the impact of the changes in asset turnover and financial leverage on the change in ROE from 1985 to 1989.

Table 16G   *Income Statements and Balance Sheets*

	1985	1989
Income statement data		
Revenues	$542	$979
Operating income	38	76
Depreciation and amortization	3	9
Interest expense	3	0
Pre-tax income	32	67
Income taxes	13	37
Net income after tax	19	30
Balance sheet data		
Fixed assets	$ 41	$ 70
Total assets	245	291
Working capital	123	157
Total debt	16	0
Total shareholders' equity	159	220

Chapter

Technical Analysis

In the three previous chapters, we examined fundamental analysis of equity, considering how the general macroeconomic environment and the specific prospects of the firm or industry might affect the present value of the dividend stream the firm can be expected to generate. In this chapter, we examine technical analysis. Technical analysis focuses more on past price movements of a company than on the underlying fundamental determinants of future profitability. Technicians believe that past price and volume data signal future price movements.

Such a view is diametrically opposed to that of the efficient market hypothesis, which holds that all historical data must be reflected in stock prices already. As we lay out the basics of technical analysis in this chapter, we will point out the contradiction between the assumptions on which these strategies are based and the notion of well-functioning capital markets with rational and informed traders. After studying this chapter you should be able to:

- Use the Dow theory to identify situations that technicians would characterize as buy or sell opportunities.
- Use indicators such as volume, breadth, short interest, or confidence indexes to measure the "technical condition" of the market.
- Explain why most of technical analysis is at odds with an efficiently functioning stock market.

17.1   Technical Analysis

Technical analysis is in most instances an attempt to exploit recurring and predictable patterns in stock prices to generate abnormal trading profits. Technicians do not necessarily deny the value of fundamental information such as we

475

have discussed in the three past chapters. Many technical analysts believe stock prices eventually "close in on" their fundamental values. Technicians believe, nevertheless, that shifts in market fundamentals can be discerned before the impact of those shifts is fully reflected in prices. As the market adjusts to a new equilibrium, astute traders can exploit these price trends.

Technicians also believe that market fundamentals can be perturbed by irrational factors. More or less random fluctuations in price will accompany any underlying trend. If these fluctuations dissipate slowly, they can be taken advantage of for abnormal profits.

These presumptions, of course, clash head-on with those of the efficient market hypothesis (EMH) and with the logic of well-functioning capital markets. According to the EMH, a shift in market fundamentals should be reflected in prices immediately. According to technicians, though, that shift will lead to a gradual price change that can be recognized as a trend. Such easily exploited trends in stock market prices would be damning evidence against the EMH, as they would indicate profit opportunities that market participants had left unexploited.

A more subtle version of technical analysis holds that there are patterns in stock prices that can be exploited, but that once investors identify and attempt to profit from these patterns, their trading activity affects prices, thereby altering price patterns. This means the patterns that characterize market prices will be constantly evolving, and only the best analysts who can identify new patterns earliest will be rewarded. We call this phenomenon *self-destructing* patterns and explore it further later in the chapter.

The notion of evolving patterns is consistent with almost but not-quite efficient markets. It allows for the possibility of temporarily unexploited profit opportunities, but it also views market participants as aggressively exploiting those opportunities once they are uncovered. The market is continually groping toward full efficiency, but it is never quite there.

This is in some ways an appealing middle position in the ongoing debate between technicians and proponents of the EMH. Ultimately, however, it is an untestable hypothesis. Technicians will always be able to identify trading rules that would have worked in the past but need not work any longer. Is this evidence of a once viable trading rule that has now been eliminated by competition? Perhaps. But it is far more likely the trading rule could have been identified only after the fact.

Until technicians can prove rigorous evidence that their trading rules provide *consistent* trading profits, we must doubt the viability of those rules. As you saw in the chapter on the efficient market hypothesis, the evidence on the performance of professionally managed funds does not support the efficacy of technical analysis.

17.2   *Charting*

Technical analysts are sometimes called *chartists* because they study records or charts of past stock prices and trading volume, hoping to find patterns they can exploit to make a profit. In this section, we examine several specific charting strategies.

The Dow Theory

Dow theory *A technique that attempts to discern long- and short-term trends in stock market prices.*

The **Dow theory,** named after its creator Charles Dow (who established *The Wall Street Journal*), is the grandfather of most technical analysis. The aim of the Dow theory is to identify long-term trends in stock market prices. The two indicators used are the Dow Jones Industrial Average (DJIA) and the Dow Jones Transportation Average (DJTA). The DJIA is the key indicator of underlying trends, while the DJTA usually serves as a check to confirm or reject that signal.

The Dow theory posits three forces simultaneously affecting stock prices:

1. The *primary trend* is the long-term movement of prices, lasting from several months to several years.
2. *Secondary or intermediate* trends are caused by short-term deviations of prices from the underlying trend line. These deviations are eliminated via *corrections* when prices revert back to trend values.
3. *Tertiary or minor trends* are daily fluctuations of little importance.

Figure 17.1 represents these three components of stock price movements. In this figure, the primary trend is upward, but intermediate trends result in short-lived market declines lasting a few weeks. The intraday minor trends have no long-run impact on price.

Figure 17.2 depicts the course of the DJIA during 1988. The primary trend is upward, as evidenced by the fact that each market peak is higher than the previous peak (point F versus D versus B). Similarly, each low is higher than the previous low (E versus C versus A). This pattern of upward-moving "tops" and "bottoms" is one of the key ways to identify the underlying primary trend. Notice in Figure 17.2 that, despite the upward primary trend, intermediate trends still can lead to short periods of declining prices (points B through C, or D through E).

Support level *A price level below which it is supposedly unlikely for a stock or stock index to fall.*

Resistance level *A price level above which it is supposedly unlikely for a stock or stock index to rise.*

The Dow theory incorporates notions of support and resistance levels in stock prices. A **support level** is a value below which the market is relatively unlikely to fall. A **resistance level** is a value above which it is difficult to rise. Support and resistance levels are determined by the recent history of prices. In Figure 17.3, the price at point C would be viewed as a resistance level because the recent intermediate-trend high price was unable to rise above C. Hence, piercing the resistance point is a bullish signal. The fact that the transportation index also pierces its resistance level at point D confirms the bull market signal.

Technicians see resistance and support levels as resulting from common psychological investor traits. Consider, for example, stock XYZ, which traded for several months at a price of $72 and then declined to $65. If the stock eventually begins to increase in price, $72 is a natural resistance level because the many investors who bought originally at $72 will be eager to sell their shares as soon as they can break even on their investment. Whenever prices near $72, a wave of selling pressure would develop. Such activity imparts to the market a type of "memory" that allows past price history to influence current stock prospects.

Concept Check

Question 1. Describe how technicians might explain support levels.

Figure 17.1
Dow Theory trends.
From Melanie F. Bowman
and Thom Hartle, "Dow
Theory," *Technical Analysis
of Stocks and Commodities,*
September 1990, p. 690.

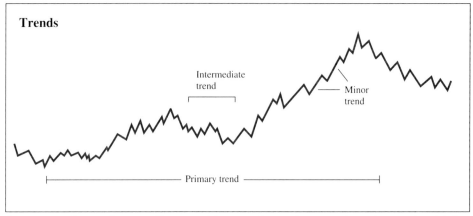

Trends

The primary trend is typically measured in years and the intermediate trend is measured in weeks to months, while the minor trend will last from days to weeks.

Figure 17.2
**Dow Jones Industrial
Average in 1988.**
From Melanie F. Bowman
and Thom Hartle, "Dow
Theory," *Technical Analysis
of Stocks and Commodities,*
September 1990, p. 690.

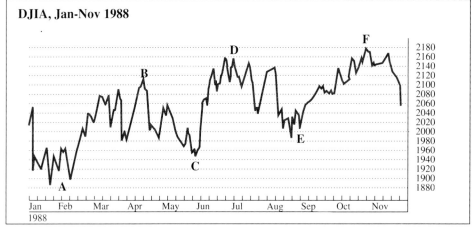

DJIA, Jan-Nov 1988

During 1988 the DJIA was bullish as points B, D and F and points A, C and E were a series of higher highs and higher lows, respectively.

Figure 17.3
Dow Theory signals.
From Melanie F. Bowman
and Thom Hartle, "Dow
Theory," *Technical Analysis
of Stocks and Commodities,*
September 1990, p. 690.

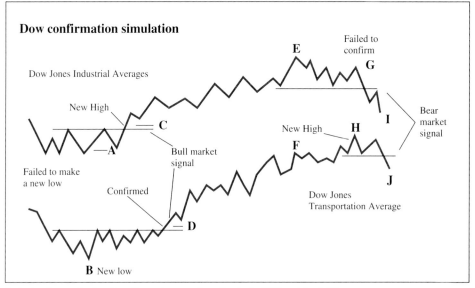

Dow confirmation simulation

A simulated example of confirmation and non-confirmation by the DJIA and the DJTA.

At point G, the DJIA fails to move to a higher high when the DJTA reaches a higher high at point H. This contradictory signal, called a *nonconfirmation,* is a warning sign. At points I and J, both indexes fall below the low points of the previous trading range, which is taken as a signal of the end of the primary bull market.

In evaluating the Dow theory, don't forget the lessons of the efficient market hypothesis. The Dow theory is based on a notion of predictably recurring price patterns. Yet the EMH holds that if any pattern is exploitable, many investors would attempt to profit from such predictability, which would ultimately move stock prices and cause the trading strategy to self-destruct. While Figure 17.2 certainly appears to describe a classic upward primary trend, one always must wonder whether we can see that trend only *after* the fact. Recognizing patterns as they emerge is far more difficult.

A recent variation on the Dow theory is the Elliott wave theory. Like the Dow theory, the idea behind Elliott waves is that stock prices can be described by a set of wave patterns. Long-term and short-term wave cycles are superimposed and result in a complicated pattern of price movements, but by interpreting the cycles, one can, according to the theory, predict broad movements. Robert Prechter is a famous advocate of this technique. The accompanying box reproduces a *Wall Street Journal* profile of Prechter.

Other Charting Techniques

The Dow theory posits a particular, and fairly simple, type of pattern in stock market prices: long-lasting trends with short-run deviations around those trends. Not surprisingly, several more involved patterns have been identified in stock market prices. Figure 17.4 illustrates several of these patterns. If stock prices actually follow any of these patterns, profit opportunities would result. The patterns are reasonably straightforward to discern, meaning future prices could be extrapolated from current prices.

A variant on pure trend analysis is the *point and figure chart* depicted in Figure 17.5. This figure has no time dimension. It simply traces significant upward or downward moves in stock prices without regard to their timing. The data for Figure 17.5 come from Table 17.1

Suppose as in Table 17.1, that a stock's price is currently $40. If the price rises by at least $2, you put an X in the first column at $42 in Figure 17.5. Another increase of at least $2 calls for placement of another X in the first column, this time at the $44 level. If the stock then falls by at least $2, you start a new column and put an O next to $42. Each subsequent $2 price fall results in another O in the second column. When prices reverse yet again and head upward, you begin the third column with an X denoting each consecutive $2 price increase.

The single asterisks in Table 17.1 mark an event resulting in the placement of a new X or O in the chart. The daggers denote price movements that result in the start of a new column of Xs or Os.

Sell signals are generated when the stock price *penetrates* previous lows, and buy signals occur when previous high prices are penetrated. A *congestion area* is a horizontal band of Xs and Os created by several price reversals. These three regions are indicated in Figure 17.6.

Wave Theory Wins Robert Prechter Title of Wall Street Guru

Technical Analyst Is Successor to Granville, Mendelson; Preparing for a Cataclysm

GAINESVILLE, Ga—Outside the window is rural Georgia, a vista of leggy pines surrounding a sprawling lake.

Inside is bedlam.

A brisk round of buying has just sent the Dow Jones Industrial Average up sharply, and Robert R. Prechter and some of his staff are trying to figure out what's going on. A half-dozen phone lines blink impatiently as subscribers to Mr. Prechter's consulting service wait for marching orders. Other employees process newsletter subscriptions and bills on computer terminals. As the day wears on, the noise level in the room rises to a dull roar, not unlike the din heard on Wall Street trading desks more than 800 miles away.

A Market Rosetta Stone

This is the home of the Elliott wave principle, an arcane system of technical analysis that thousands of investors have come to believe is the Rosetta stone of the stock market. Mr. Prechter, 37 years old, is the theory's champion and oracle, and his influence on the market extends far beyond the subscribers to his newsletter, the Elliott Wave Theorist.

Rumors about Mr. Prechter's latest calls galvanize traders across the country. As a result, he is often credited, or blamed, for sudden shifts in the stock market and praised for his prescience. Early last July, Mr. Prechter advised his subscribers to take profits on short-term positions. When the Dow Jones Industrial Average lost more than 79 points the following week, many people held Mr. Prechter responsible. In early September, he issued another warning, and the average dropped more than 120 points a short time later. Monday before last, when the market fell more than 28 points in the first 15 minutes of trading, market watchers noted that Mr. Prechter had told hot-line subscribers the previous Friday night that the market was vulnerable to a correction.

Of course, Mr. Prechter has also made many wrong calls, most notably in the short-term stock market and in bonds. So far, his Wall Street followers have dismissed them as minor flaws in an exceptional record, but the role of market guru is difficult to sustain for long. Wall Street is fickle, and some of Mr. Prechter's predecessors, like Joseph Granville, Henry Kaufman, and John A. Mendelson, know that a few bad calls can turn the public's adulation to derision. "No one can be right 100 percent of the time," says Mr. Granville.

Mr. Prechter's popularity comes at a time when technical analysis, the system of predicting stock prices using past price and volume statistics, has been making a comeback on Wall Street. The technicians' rivals, the fundamentalists, have been unable to explain how the current economic situation justifies a 20 percent gain in the stock market since the beginning of the year. The startling volatility of the market has also undermined the fundamentalists' view that investors behave rationally.

But technical analysis continues to be regarded skeptically by many academicians and money managers. Hundreds of studies of market patterns have failed to find one that can make consistently accurate predictions. Furthermore, critics say, if such a system could be found, it would be neutralized very quickly by the rush of investors using it.

"I tend to classify technical analysis like Tarot," says Stephen Figlewski, a professor of finance at New York University. "The people who use it successfully—if there are such people—bring a lot more to it than just charts."

Some also argue that a record as good as Mr. Prechter's may well be pure chance. "Most people don't understand that with stochastic [random] systems, you can get lucky and have a long string of good calls," says James B. Ramsey, a professor of economics at New York University. "It's a low probability event, but it's not a zero-probability event."

Like other technicians. Mr. Prechter favors one kind of chart but uses others to support or challenge his initial conclusions. His primary system is based on patterns first discerned—or, some would say, fabricated—in the late 1930s by Ralph N. Elliott, an accountant who had lost some of his savings in the 1929 stock–market crash.

The idea behind the Elliott principle is that stock prices are a barometer of the national mood and that the mood moves in predictable waves between optimism and pessimism. The waves, which are based on stock market data, unfold in specific sequences. For example, the waves in a bull market rally will go up, down, up, down, and up, followed by a correction in which waves will go down, up, down. Each wave contains smaller series of waves so that, for example, between January and July of 1984, the market was in a second wave on one scale and a fifth wave on another. A single large wave can last as long as several centuries; one that occurs within other waves can last as short a time as an hour.

In what Elliott and Mr. Prechter call the Grand Supercycle, or the largest scale identified so far, the market is now in a fifth wave, and it won't end until the Dow Jones Industrial Average hits 3686 sometime in 1988. After that, Mr. Prechter says, expect a cataclysm worse than the 1929 crash. Then, if history repeats itself, and Mr. Prechter firmly believes it does, a depression and major war will follow.

Although most people remember only his accurate calls, Mr. Prechter has also had his share of blunders. He himself concedes that beginning in 1985, he consistently called the bond market wrong for more than a year. "I shorted bonds three times on the way up," he says. Other investors contend that his gold forecasts have cost them money.

Mr. Prechter says that his interpretations, not the charts he uses, should be blamed for the bad calls. Furthermore, he says, anyone could take the same charts and, with a certain amount of discipline, do what he does. "Nobody needs me," he says. "All I do is take Elliott's observations and us-ing those patterns and guidelines, I rank the probabilities of the likely paths of the market. It's just a matter of memorizing the patterns and their implications."

Nobody may need him, but Mr. Prechter makes his living from those who think they do. His monthly newsletter, with occasional interim reports, costs $233 a year, and a third or more of his roughly 15,000 subscribers pay an additional $377 a year for his thrice-weekly hot line. Subscribers may also call one of his three assistants for instant advice at the rate of $30 a minute.

To the critics who wonder why a person who is so smart about the market makes his living—albeit a good one—writing a newsletter, Mr. Prechter quotes a friend who also writes a newsletter. "I want other people to know how smart I am," he says.

As certain as Mr. Prechter is of the Elliott wave principle, he also knows that "hot hands" in the market often have short lives. "I'm probably going to be wrong about something in some big way around the top," he says. "Undoubtedly the top will take too long and probably I'll put out caution too early, in which case people will say baloney on this crash stuff."

In the meantime, Mr. Prechter feels that he is a target for all those who dislike technical analysis in general and hot technicians specifically. "There are people who hate the idea that anyone can be successful at predicting the market," he says. "I just try to avoid them. But sometimes you walk out on the dusty street at noon, and there's some guy standing there with his guns."

Abridged from Cynthia Crossen, "Wave Theory Wins Robert Prechter Title of Wall Street Guru," *The Wall Street Journal,* March 18, 1987, p. 1. Reprinted by permission of *THE WALL STREET JOURNAL,* © 1987 Dow Jones & Company, Inc. All Rights Reserved Worldwide.

Figure 17.4
Chart representation of market bottoms and tops.
From Irwin Shishko, "Techniques of Forecasting Commodity Prices," *Commodity Yearbook* (New York: Commodity Research Bureau, 1965), p. 4.

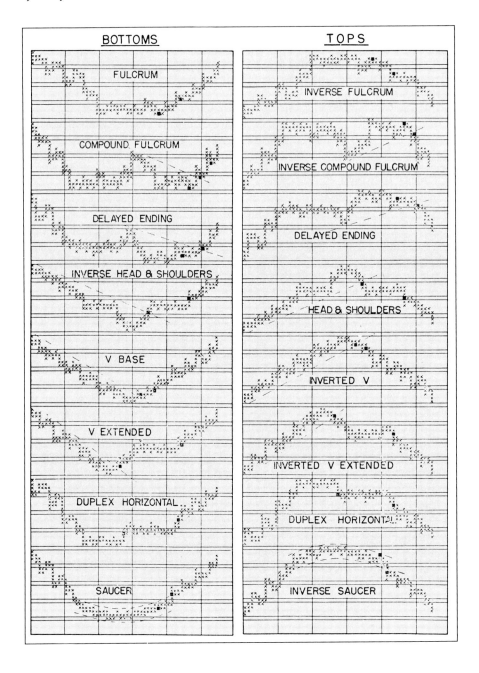

One can devise point and figure charts using price increments other than $2, but it is customary in setting up a chart to require reasonably substantial price changes before marking pluses or minuses.

Concept Check

Question 2. Draw a point and figure chart using the history in Table 17.1 with price increments of $3.

Figure 17.5
Point and figure chart
for Table 17.1

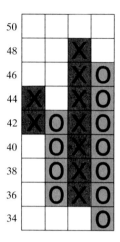

Table 17.1 *Stock Price History*

Date	Price	Date	Price
January 2	40	February 1	40*
January 3	40-1/2	February 2	41
January 4	41	February 5	40-1/2
January 5	42*	February 6	42*
January 8	41-1/2	February 7	45*
January 9	42-1/2	February 8	44-1/2
January 10	43	February 9	46*
January 11	43-3/4	February 12	47
January 12	44*	February 13	48*
January 15	45	February 14	47-1/2
January 16	44	February 15	46†
January 17	41-1/2†	February 16	45
January 18	41	February 19	44*
January 19	40*	February 20	42*
January 22	39	February 21	41
January 23	39-1/2	February 22	40*
January 24	39-3/4	February 23	41
January 25	38*	February 26	40-1/2
January 26	35*	February 27	38*
January 29	36†	February 28	39
January 30	37	March 1	36*
January 31	39*	March 2	34*

A Warning

The search for patterns in stock market prices is nearly irresistible, and the ability of the human eye to discern apparent patterns is remarkable. Unfortunately, it is possible to perceive patterns that really don't exist. Consider Figure 17.7, which presents simulated and actual values of the Dow Jones Industrial Average during 1956 taken from a famous study by Harry Roberts (1959). In Figure 17.7B, it appears as though the market presents a classic head-and-shoulders pattern where the middle hump (the head) is flanked by two shoulders. When the price index "pierces the right shoulder"—a technical trigger point—it

Figure 17.6
Point and figure chart with sell signal, buy signal, and congestion areas.

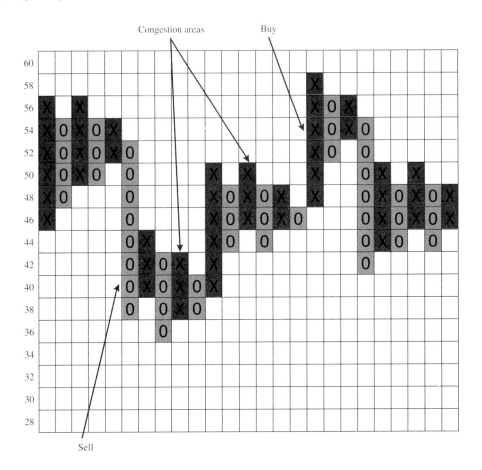

is believed to be heading lower, and it is time to sell your stocks. Figure 17.7A also looks like a "typical" stock market pattern.

Can you tell which of the two graphs is constructed from the real value of the Dow and which from the simulated data? Figure 17.7A is based on the real data. The graph in B was generated using "returns" created by a random number generator. These returns *by construction* were patternless, but the simulated price path that is plotted appears to follow a pattern much like that of A.

Figure 17.8 shows the weekly price changes behind the two panels in Figure 17.7. Here the randomness in both series—the stock price as well as the simulated sequence—is obvious.

A problem related to the tendency to perceive patterns where they don't exist is data mining. After the fact, you can always find patterns and trading rules that would have generated enormous profits. If you test enough rules, some will have worked in the past. Unfortunately, picking a theory that would have worked after the fact carries no guarantee of future success.

In this regard, consider a curious investment rule that has worked with uncanny precision since 1967. In years that an original National Football League team wins the Superbowl (played in January), bet on the stock market rising for the rest of the year. In years that a team from the American Football Conference that was not originally an NFL team wins, bet on a market decline.

Figure 17.7
**Actual and simulated
levels for stock
market prices of 52
weeks.**
From Harry Roberts, "Stock
Market 'Patterns' and
Financial Analysis:
Methodological
Suggestions," *Journal of
Finance,* March 1959,
pp. 5–6.

A

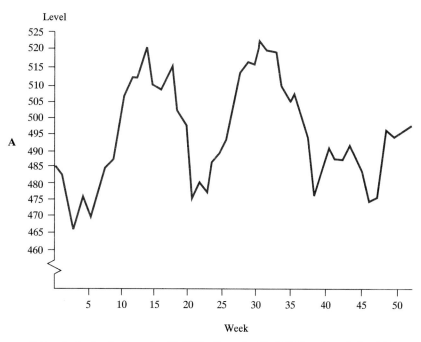

Friday closing levels, December 30, 1955—December 28, 1956, Dow Jones Industrial Average

B

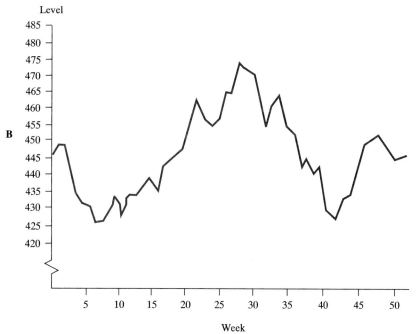

Between 1967 and 1990, the NYSE index rose in the year following the Superbowl 15 of the 17 times that an NFC or original NFL team won. The market fell in six out of seven years that an AFC team won. Despite the overwhelming past success of this rule, would you use it to invest your money? We suspect not.

Figure 17.8
Actual and simulated changes in weekly stock prices for 52 weeks.
From Harry Roberts, "Stock Market 'Patterns' and Financial Analysis: Methodological Suggestions," *Journal of Finance*, March 1959, pp. 5–6.

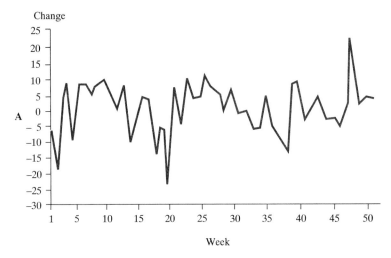

Changes from Friday to Friday (closing) January 6, 1956–December 28, 1956. Dow Jones Industrial Average

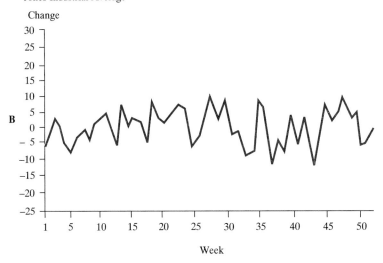

In evaluating trading rules, you should always ask whether the rule would have seemed reasonable *before* you looked at the data. If not, you might be buying into the one arbitrary rule among many that happened to have worked in the recent past. The hard but crucial question is whether there is reason to believe that what worked in the past should continue to work in the future.

17.3   *Technical Indicators*

Technical analysts use technical indicators besides charts to assess prospects for market declines or advances. We will examine some popular indicators in this section.

DIARIES

NYSE	WED	TUES	WK AGO
Issues traded	1,981	1,988	1,990
Advances	659	487	356
Declines	833	1,077	1,200
Unchanged	489	424	434
New highs	6	5	1
New lows	248	276	278
zAdv vol (000)	68,047	29,694	25,874
zDecl vol (000)	74,617	105,139	129,075
zTotal vol (000)	161,260	149,570	167,890
Closing tick[1]	−418	−111	−378
Closing trin[2]	.87	1.60	1.48
zBlock trades	3,503	3,077	3,558

[1]The net difference of the number of stocks closing higher than their previous trade from those closing lower; NYSE trading only.
[2]A comparison of the number of advancing and declining issues with the volume of shares rising and falling. Generally, a trin of less than 1.00 indicates buying demand; above 1.00 indicates selling pressure.
z-NYSE or Amex only.

Market Volume

Market volume is sometimes used to measure the strength of a market rise or fall. Increased investor participation in a market advance or retreat is viewed as a measure of the significance of the movement. Technicians consider market advances to be a more favorable omen of continued price increases when they are associated with increased trading volume. Similarly, market reversals are considered more bearish when associated with higher volume. The *trin statistic* is the ratio of the number of advancing to declining issues divided by the ratio of volume in advancing versus declining issues:

$$\text{Trin} = \frac{\text{Number advancing/Number declining}}{\text{Volume advancing/Volume declining}}$$

This expression can be rearranged as:

$$\text{Trin} = \frac{\text{Volume declining/Number declining}}{\text{Volume advancing/Number advancing}}$$

Therefore, trin is the ratio of average volume in declining issues to average volume in advancing issues. Ratios above 1.0 are considered bearish because the falling stocks would then have higher average volume than the advancing stocks, indicating net selling pressure. *The Wall Street Journal* reports trin every day in the market diary section, as in Figure 17.9.

Note, however, for every buyer, there must be a seller of stock. Rising volume in a rising market should not necessarily indicate a larger imbalance of buyers versus sellers. For example, a trin statistic above 1.0, which is considered bearish, could equally well be interpreted as indicating that there is more *buying* activity in declining issues.

Breadth

The **breadth** of the market is a measure of the extent to which movement in a market index are reflected widely in the price movements of all the stocks in the market. The most common measure of breadth is the spread between the number of stocks that advance and decline in price. If advances outnumber declines by a wide margin, then the market is viewed as being stronger because the rally is widespread. These breadth numbers also are reported daily in *The Wall Street Journal* (see Figure 17.9).

Some analysts cumulate breadth data each day as in Table 17.2. The cumulative breadth for each day is obtained by adding that day's net advances (or declines) to the previous day's total. The direction of the cumulated series is then used to discern broad market trends.

Short Interest

Short interest is the total number of shares of stock currently sold short in the market. Some technicians interpret short interest as bullish, some as bearish. The bullish perspective is that because all short sales must be covered (i.e., short-sellers eventually must purchase shares to return the ones they have borrowed), short interest represents latent future demand for the stocks. As short sales are covered, the demand created by the share purchase will force prices up.

The bearish interpretation of short interest is based on the fact that short-sellers tend to be larger, more sophisticated investors. Accordingly, increased short interest reflects bearish sentiment by those investors "in the know," which would be a negative signal of the market's prospects.

Odd-Lot Trading

Just as short-sellers tend to be larger institutional traders, odd-lot traders are almost always small individual traders. (An odd lot is a transaction of fewer than 100 shares; 100 shares is one round lot.) The **odd-lot theory** holds that these small investors tend to miss key market turning points, typically buying stocks after a bull market has already run its course and selling too late into a bear market. Therefore, the theory suggests that when odd-lot traders are widely buying, you should sell, and vice versa.

Table 17.2   *Breadth*

Day	Advances	Declines	Net Advances	Cumulative Breadth
1	802	748	54	54
2	917	640	277	331
3	703	772	−69	262
4	512	1122	−610	−348
5	633	1004	−371	−719

Note: The sum of advances and declines varies across days because some stock prices are unchanged.

The Wall Street Journal publishes odd-lot trading data every day. You can construct an index of odd-lot trading by computing the ratio of odd-lot purchases to sales. A ratio substantially above 1.0 is bearish because it implies small traders are net buyers.

Confidence Index

Barron's computes a confidence index using data from the bond market. The presumption is that actions of bond traders reveal trends that will emerge soon in the stock market.

Confidence index
Ratio of the yield of top-rated corporate bonds to the yield on intermediate grade bonds.

The **confidence index** is the ratio of the average yield on 10 top-rated corporate bonds divided by the average yield on 10 intermediate-grade corporate bonds. The ratio will always be below 100 percent because higher-rated bonds will offer lower promised yields to maturity. When bond traders are optimistic about the economy, however, they might require smaller default premiums on lower-rated debt. Hence, the yield spread will narrow, and the confidence index will approach 100 percent. Therefore, higher values of the confidence index are bullish signals.

Concept Check

Question 3. Yields on lower-rated debt will rise after fears of recession have spread through the economy. This will reduce the confidence index. Should the stock market now be expected to fall or will it already have fallen?

Relative Strength

Relative strength
Recent performance of a given stock or industry compared to that of a broader market index.

Relative strength measures the extent to which a security has outperformed or underperformed either the market as a whole or its particular industry. Relative strength is computed by calculating the ratio of the price of the security to a price index for the industry. For example, the relative strength of IBM versus the computer industry would be measured by movements in the ratio of Price (IBM) /Price(computer industry index). A rising ratio implies IBM has been outperforming the rest of the industry. If relative strength can be assumed to persist over time, then this would be a signal to buy IBM.

Similarly, the relative strength of an industry relative to the whole market can be computed by tracking the ratio of the industry price index to the market price index.

17.4 *The Value Line System*

The Value Line ranking system may be the most celebrated and well-documented example of successful stock analysis. Value Line is the largest investment advisory service in the world. Besides publishing the *Value Line Investment Survey,* which provides information on investment fundamentals for approximately 1,700 publicly traded companies, Value Line also ranks each of these stocks according to their anticipated price appreciation over the next 12 months. Stocks ranked in group 1 are expected to perform the best, while those in group 5 are expected to perform the worst. Value Line calls this "ranking for timeliness."

Figure 17.10 shows the performance of the Value Line ranking system over the 25 years from 1965 to March 1990. Over the total period, the different groups performed just as the rankings would predict, and the differences were quite large. The total 25-year price appreciation for the group 1 stocks was 3,083 percent (or 14.8 percent per year) compared to 15 percent (or 0.5 percent per year) for group 5.

How does the Value Line ranking system work? As Bernhard (1979) explains it, the ranking procedure has three components: (1) relative earnings momentum, (2) earnings surprise, and (3) a value index. Most (though not all) of the Value Line criteria are technically oriented, relying on either price momentum or relative strength. Points assigned for each factor determine the stock's overall ranking.

The relative earnings momentum factor is calculated as each company's year-to-year change in quarterly earnings divided by the average change for all stocks.

The earnings surprise factor has to do with the difference between actual reported quarterly earnings and Value Line's estimate. The points assigned to each stock increase with the percentage difference between reported and estimated earnings.

The value index is calculated from the following regression equation:

$$V = a + b_1 x_1 + b_2 x_2 + b_3 x_3$$

where

x_1 = A score from 1 to 10 depending on the relative earnings momentum ranking, compared with the company's rank for the last 10 years;

x_2 = A score from 1 to 10 based on the stock's relative price, with ratios calculated in a similar way to the earnings ratio;

x_3 = The ratio of the stock's latest 10-week average relative price (stock price divided by the average price for all stocks) to its 52-week average relative price;

and a, b_1, b_2, and b_3 are the coefficients from the regression estimated on 12 years of data.

Finally, the points for each of the three factors are added, and the stocks are classified into five groups according to the total score.

Investing according to this system does seem to produce superior results on paper, as Figure 17.10 shows. Yet as the accompanying box points out, in practice, things are not so simple—Value Line's own mutual funds have not kept up even with the broad market averages. The box illustrates that even apparently successful trading rules can be difficult to implement in the market.

17.5 Can Technical Analysis Work in Efficient Markets?

Self-Destructing Patterns

It should be abundantly clear from our presentation that most of technical analysis is based on ideas totally at odds with the foundations of the efficient market hypothesis. The EMH follows from the idea that rational profit-seeking investors

Figure 17.10
Record of Value Line ranking for timeliness (without allowing for changes in rank, 1965–1990).
From *Value Line Selection & Opinion*, April 20, 1990.

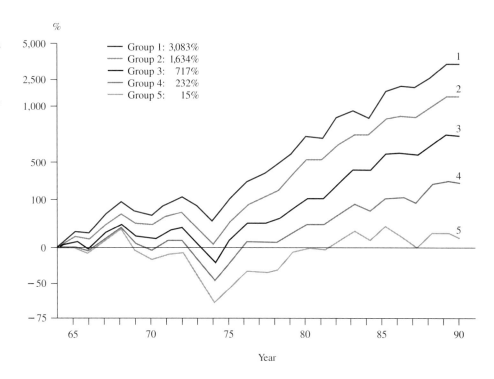

will act on new information so quickly that prices will nearly always reflect all publicly available information. Technical analysis, on the other hand, posits the existence of long-lived trends that play out slowly and predictably. Such patterns, if they exist, would violate the EMH notion of essentially unpredictable stock price changes.

An interesting question is whether a technical rule that seems to work will continue to work in the future once it becomes widely recognized. A clever analyst may occasionally uncover a profitable trading rule, but the real test of efficient markets is whether the rule itself becomes reflected in stock prices once its value is discovered.

Suppose, for example, the Dow theory predicts an upward primary trend. If the theory is widely accepted, it follows that many investors will attempt to buy stocks immediately in anticipation of the price increase; the effect would be to bid up prices sharply and immediately rather than at the gradual, long-lived pace initially expected. The Dow theory's predicted trend would be replaced by a sharp jump in prices. It is in this sense that price patterns ought to be *self-destructing*. Once a useful technical rule (or price pattern) is discovered, it ought to be invalidated once the mass of traders attempt to exploit it.

An instructive example of this phenomenon is the evidence by Jegadeesh (1990) and Lehmann (1990) that stock prices seem to obey a reversal effect; specifically, the best-performing stocks in one week or month tend to fare poorly in the following period, while the worst performers follow up with good performance. Such a phenomenon can be used to form a straightforward technically based trading strategy: buy shares that recently have done poorly and sell shares that recently have done well. Lehmann shows such a strategy would have been extremely profitable in the past.

Paying the Piper

On Paper, Value Line's Performance in Picking Stocks Is Nothing Short of Dazzling . . . for an Investor to Capitalize on That Performance Is a Different Matter

Value Line, Inc., publishes the *Value Line Investment Survey,* that handy review of 1,652 companies. Each week the survey rates stocks from I (best buys) to V (worst). Can you beat the market following these rankings? Value Line tracks the performance of group I from April 1965, when a new ranking formula went into effect. If you bought group I then and updated your list every week, you would have a gain of 15,391 percent by June 30. That means $10,000 would have grown to about $1.5 million, dividends excluded. The market is up only 245 percent since 1965, dividends excluded.

Quite an impressive record. There is only one flaw: It ignores transaction costs. Do transaction costs much matter against a performance like that? What does the investor lose in transaction costs? A percentage point a year? Two percent?

None other than Value Line provides an answer to this question, and the answer is almost as startling as the paper performance. Since late 1983, Value Line has run a mutual fund that attempts to track group I precisely. Its return has averaged a dismal 11 percentage points a year worse than the hypothetical results in group I. The fund hasn't even kept up with the market (*see chart*).

What went wrong? "Inefficiencies and costs of implementation," says Mark Tavel, manager of the fund, Value Line Centurion.

This is not to denigrate Value Line's undeniably impressive stock-picking record. Far from it: One of the funds run for Value Line by Tavel, Leveraged Growth Investors, shines on Forbes' mutual fund honor roll. (Leveraged Growth and the flagship Value Line Fund use the ranking system, but not as closely as Centurion.)

The point here is to illustrate the folly of constant trading. It's a familiar story, but one that investors are prone to forget in the middle of a bull market. It costs money to run the racetrack, and the fellow who steps up to the betting window pays. Wall Street's revenues top $50 billion a year. People who trade pay the bill, and people who try to beat the market with a lot of trading pay dearly.

The Value Line Centurion Fund's turnover is 200 percent a year. That's quite a bit of turnover—al-

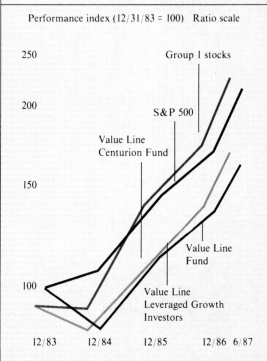

Paper profits

Value Line's hypothetical Group 1 has beaten the market since 1984. But not its funds.

Performance index (12/31/83 = 100)   Ratio scale

though by no means the highest in the business. The turnover is high because in a typical week, 4 of the 100 group I stocks drop down in rank and have to be replaced with new group I stocks. It's not impossible for traders like Centurion to beat the market, but they start out with a handicap.

All of which means that paper performance can be pretty fanciful. "Anytime hypothetical returns are offered as proof of a particular investing style, one should also swallow a large grain of salt," says Cam Schmidt of Potomac Investment Management, a money manager in Bethesda, Md., that brought the Value Line discrepancy to *Forbes'* attention.

What are these inefficiencies and costs? And what do they tell investors about the perils of in-and-out trading?

Fund overhead is not a big item. At the $244 million Centurion, which is available only through variable life and annuity policies sold by Guardian Life, the annual expense ratio averages 0.6 percent. Nor are brokerage commissions large. Funneled at about 5 cents a share mostly to a captive Value Line broker, commissions eat up 0.4 percent of Centurion's assets per year.

So far we have 1 percent. Where's the other 10 percent of the shortfall? Bid-ask spreads, for one. A stock quoted at 39 to sellers might cost a buyer 39½—or even 41 or 42 if the buyer wants a lot of it. With about 95 of the 100 group I stocks at any given time in the Centurion portfolio, Tavel needs to amass an average $2.5 million position in each. Some of these companies have $150 million or less in outstanding shares. The very smallest Tavel doesn't even try to buy.

Timing explains some of the gulf between hypothetical and actual results. The hypothetical performance assumes a purchase at the Wednesday close before publication of the new rankings. Most subscribers get their surveys on Friday morning, however, and buy at the Friday opening—if they are lucky. An internal Value Line rule forbids the funds to act on rank changes before Friday morning.

Why, then, are Wednesday prices used in the performance claims? Because, says Samuel Eisenstadt, Value Line's chief of statistics, until recently that was all Value Line had in its database. Wednesday prices were gathered because it takes nine days to compute, print and mail the results. The hypothetical buy, then, would come a week after the closing prices used to calculate the rankings, and a day and a half before a real buyer could act on the advice. Eisenstadt says a conversion to Friday night scoring is under way and will no doubt depress reported performance.

A day makes all the difference. A 1985 study by Scott Stickel, now an assistant professor at Wharton, showed that almost all of the excess return on a group I stock is concentrated on three days, almost evenly divided: the Friday when subscribers read about the stock's being promoted into group I, the Thursday before and the Monday following. Wait until Tuesday to buy and you might as well not subscribe.

Why are prices moving up on Thursday, the day before publication? Eisenstadt suspects the Postal Service of acting with uncharacteristic efficiency in some parts of the country, giving a few subscribers an early start. Another reason for an uptick: Enough is known about the Value Line formula for smart investors to anticipate a rank change by a few days. The trick is to watch group II (near-top) stocks closely. If a quarterly earnings report comes in far better than the forecast published in *Value Line,* grab the stock. "What happens if you're wrong? You're stuck with a group II stock with terrific earnings," says Eisenstadt.

Come Friday at 9:30 A.M., the throng is at the starting gate. Tavel says he often gets only a small portion of his position established before the price starts to run away from him. How are the individual investors faring? Probably no better. True, a 200-share order is not by itself going to move the market the way Tavel's 20,000-share order will. But if both orders arrive at the opening bell, the small investor is in no position to get a good price. Individuals aren't paying the fund overhead, but then they pay higher commissions than Tavel.

What of the future? Value Line's magic was built on its computer-quick response to favorable earnings reports. Now computers are nothing special. Significantly, they're becoming a lot more common among individual investors, the people who buy the small-cap-stocks where the ranking system has shown its strength. Eisenstadt concedes: "Everyone's playing this earnings surprise game now." But he insists that there's no firm evidence yet that the ranking system is falling apart.

Even if the ranking system loses some of its effectiveness, however, it would be premature to write off Value Line, which trades over the counter near 27. Many of the survey's 120,000 subscribers pay $495 a year just to get the detailed financial histories of the companies in it. Indeed, considering that subscriptions are on the upswing and that it costs maybe $50 to print and mail one, favorable earnings surprises may be in store. If you don't like the horses, buy stock in the track.

Reprinted by permission of *Forbes* magazine, October 19, 1987. © Forbes, Inc. 1987.

The reversal effect is at odds with market efficiency and at the same time consistent with the viability of technical analysis. The real test of the trading rule will come now that the potential of the strategy has been uncovered. Lehmann notes that Rosenberg Institutional Equity Management and the College Retirement Equity Fund now use return reversal strategies in their actively managed portfolios. These activities presumably should eliminate existing profit opportunities by forcing prices to their "correct" levels.

Thus, the market dynamic is one of a continual search for profitable trading rules, followed by destruction by overuse of those rules found to be successful, followed by more search for yet-undiscovered rules.

A New View of Technical Analysis

Two writers offer a rigorous foundation for the potential efficacy of technical analysis (Brown and Jennings, 1990). They envision an economy where many investors have private information regarding the ultimate value of a stock. Moreover, as time passes, each investor acquires additional information. Each investor can infer something of the information possessed by other traders by observing the price at which securities trade. The entire sequence of past prices can turn out to be useful in the inference of the information held by other traders. In this sense, technical analysis can be useful to traders even if all traders rationally use all information available to them.

Most discussions of the EMH envision public information commonly available to all traders and ask only if prices reflect that information. In this sense, the Brown and Jennings framework is more complex. Here, different individuals receive different private signals regarding the value of a firm. As prices unfold, each trader infers the good-news or bad-news nature of the signals received by other traders and updates assessments of the firm accordingly. Prices *reveal* as well as *reflect* information and become useful data to traders. Without addressing specific technical trading rules, the Brown and Jennings model is an interesting and innovative attempt to reconcile technical analysis with the usual assumption of rational traders participating in efficient markets.

Summary

1. Technical analysis is the search for recurring patterns in stock market prices. It is based essentially on the notion that market prices adjust slowly to new information and, thus, is at odds with the efficient market hypothesis.

2. The Dow theory is the earliest chart-based version of technical analysis. The theory posits the existence of primary, intermediate, and minor trends that can be identified on a chart and acted on by an analyst before the trends fully dissipate. Other trend-based theories are based on relative strength and the point and figures chart.

3. Technicians believe high volume and market breadth accompanying market trends add weight to the significance of a trend.

4. Odd-lot traders are viewed as uninformed, which suggests informed traders should pursue trading strategies in opposition to their activity. In contrast, short-sellers are viewed as informed traders, lending credence to their activity.

5. Value Line's ranking system uses technically based data and has shown great ability to discriminate between stocks with good and poor prospects, but the Value Line mutual fund that uses this system most closely has been only a mediocre performer, suggesting that implementation of the Value Line timing system is difficult.

6. New theories of information dissemination in the market suggests there may be a role for the examination of past prices in formulating investment strategies. They do not, however, support the specific charting patterns currently relied on by technical analysts.

Key Terms

breadth, 488	odd-lot theory, 488	short interest, 488
confidence index, 489	relative strength, 489	support level, 477
Dow theory, 477	resistance level, 477	

Problem Sets

1. Consider the graph of stock prices over a two-year period in Figure 17A. Identify likely support and resistance levels.
2. Use the data from *The Wall Street Journal* in Figure 17B to construct the trin ratio for the market. Is the trin ratio bullish or bearish?
3. Calculate market breadth using the same data as in Question 2. Is the signal bullish or bearish?
4. Collect data on the DJIA for a period covering a few months. Try to identify primary trends. Can you tell whether the market currently is in an upward or downward trend?
5. The ratio of put to call options outstanding is viewed by some as a technical indicator. Do you think a high ratio is viewed as bullish or bearish? Should it be?

Figure 17A
Simulated stock price over time.

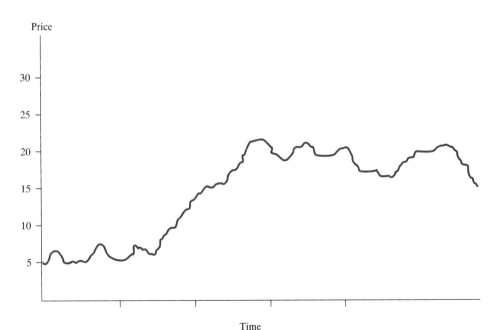

DIARIES

NYSE	TUES	MON	WK AGO
Issues traded	1,988	1,991	1,989
Advances	487	802	288
Declines	1,077	748	1,313
Unchanged	424	441	388
New highs	5	3	0
New lows	276	209	191
zAdv vol (000)	29,694	97,244	14,546
zDecl vol (000)	105,139	53,496	122,450
zTotal vol (000)	149,570	164,980	145,610

6. Using Figure 17C from *The Wall Street Journal,* determine whether market price movements and volume patterns were bullish or bearish around the following dates: May 11; July 6; August 3; August 24. In each instance, compare your prediction to the subsequent behavior of the DJIA in the following few weeks.

Selected Readings

A magazine devoted to technical analysis is Technical Analysis of Stocks and Commodities.
The Value Line method is described in:
  Bernhard, Arnold, *Value Line Methods of Evaluating Common Stocks,* New York: Arnold Bernhard and Co., 1979.

Figure 17C
Dow Jones Industrial Average and market volume.
From *The Wall Street Journal,* October 17, 1990. Reprinted by permission of *THE WALL STREET JOURNAL,* © 1990 Dow Jones & Company, Inc. All Rights Reserved Worldwide.

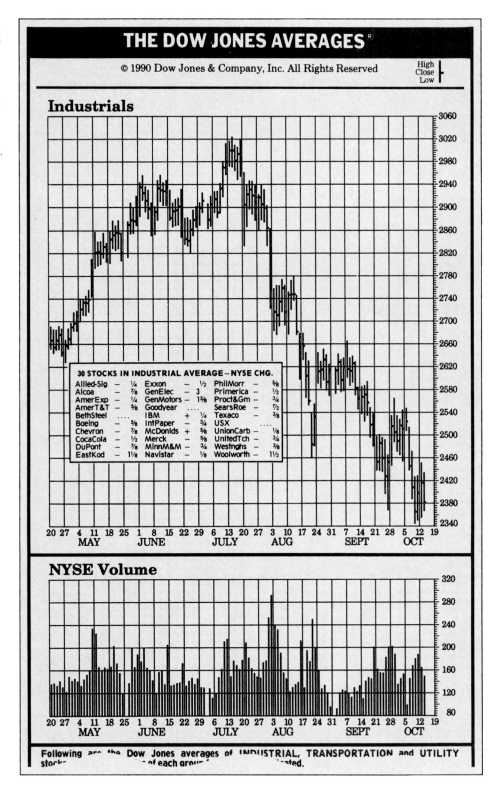

Part Five

Derivative Assets: Options and Futures

■■■■■■■■■■■■■■■■■■■■■■■■■■■■■

Chapter

18

Options Markets: Introduction

T rading of standardized options contracts on a national exchange started in 1973 when the Chicago Board Options Exchange (CBOE) began listing call options. These contracts were almost immediately a great success, crowding out the previously existing over-the-counter trading in stock options. Today, the CBOE is the second-largest securities market in the United States in terms of the value of traded securities. Only the New York Stock Exchange is larger.

Options contracts are traded now on several exchanges. They are written on common stock, stock indexes, foreign exchange, agricultural commodities, precious metals, and interest rate futures. Popular and potent tools in modifying portfolio characteristics, options have become essential tools a portfolio manager must understand.

This chapter is an introduction to options markets. It explains how puts and calls work and examines their investment characteristics. Popular option strategies are considered next. Finally, we examine a range of securities with embedded options such as callable or convertible bonds. After studying this chapter you should be able to:

- Calculate the profit to various option positions as a function of ultimate security prices.
- Formulate option strategies to modify portfolio risk-return attributes.
- Compute the proper relationship between call and put prices.
- Identify embedded options in various securities, and determine how option characteristics affect price attributes of those securities.

18.1 *The Option Contract*

Call option The right
to buy an asset at a
specified exercise price
on or before a speci-
fied expiration date.

*Exercise or strike
price* Price set for
calling (buying) an as-
set or putting (selling)
an asset.

A **call option** gives its holder the right to purchase an asset for a specified price, called the **exercise or strike price,** on or before some specified expiration date. For example, a July call option on IBM stock with exercise price $120 entitles its owner to purchase IBM stock for a price of $120 at any time up to and including the expiration date in July. The holder of the call is not required to exercise the option. Only if the market value of the asset to be purchased exceeds the exercise price will it be profitable for the holder to exercise it. When the market price does exceed the exercise price, the option holder may either sell the option or "call away" the asset for the exercise price and reap a profit. Otherwise, the option may be left unexercised. If it is not exercised before the expiration date of the contract, a call option simply expires and no longer has value.

The purchase price of the option is called the *premium*. It represents the compensation the purchaser of the call must pay for the ability to exercise the option if exercise becomes profitable. Sellers of call options, who are said to *write* calls, receive premium income now as payment against the possibility they will be required at some later date to deliver the asset in return for an exercise price lower than the market value of the asset. If the option is left to expire worthless because the exercise price remains above the market price of the asset, then (aside from transaction costs) the writer of the call clears a profit equal to the premium income derived from the sale of the option.

Put option The right
to sell an asset at a
specified exercise price
on or before a speci-
fied expiration date.

A **put option** gives its holder the right to *sell* an asset for a specified exercise or strike price on or before some expiration date. A July put on IBM with exercise price $120 entitles its owner to sell IBM stock to the put writer at a price of $120 at any time before expiration in July even if the market price of IBM is less than $120. While profits on call options increase when the asset increases in value, profits on put options increase when the asset value falls. A put will be exercised only if the exercise price is greater than the price of the underlying asset, that is, only if its holder can deliver for the exercise price an asset with market value less than the exercise price. (One doesn't need to own the shares of IBM to exercise the IBM put option. Upon exercise, the investor's broker purchases the necessary shares of IBM at the market price and immediately delivers or "puts them" to an option writer for the exercise price. The owner of the put profits by the difference between the exercise price and market price.)

Options and futures contracts are sometimes called *derivative securities*. That is, their values derive from the values of an underlying primary security. The value of an IBM option, for example, depends on the price of IBM stock. Options and futures contracts also are called *contingent claims:* payoff is contingent on prices of other securities.

In the money In the
money describes an
option where exercise
would be profitable.

Out of the money Out
of the money describes
an option where exer-
cise would not be
profitable.

An option is described as **in the money** when its exercise would produce profits for its holder. An option is **out of the money** when exercise would be unprofitable. A call option is in the money when the exercise price is below the asset's value because purchase at the exercise price would be profitable. It is out of the money when the exercise price exceeds the asset value; no one would exercise the right to purchase for the exercise price an asset worth less than that price. Conversely, put options are in the money when the exercise price exceeds the

At the money   The exercise price and asset price are equal.

asset's value, because delivery of the lower-valued asset in exchange for the exercise price is profitable for the holder. Options are **at the money** when the exercise price and asset price are equal.

Options Trading

Some options trade on over-the-counter markets. The OTC market offers the advantage that the terms of the option contract—the exercise price, maturity date, and number of shares committed—can be tailored to the needs of the traders. The costs of establishing an OTC option contract, however, are quite high. Today, virtually all option trading occurs on organized exchanges.

Options contracts traded on exchanges are standardized by allowable maturity dates and exercise prices for each listed option. Each stock option contract provides for the right to buy or sell 100 shares of stock (except when stock splits occur after the contract is listed and the contract is adjusted for the terms of the split).

Standardization of the terms of listed option contracts means all market participants trade in a limited and uniform set of securities. This increases the depth of trading in any particular option, which lowers trading costs and results in a more competitive market. Exchanges, therefore, offer two important benefits: ease of trading, which flows from a central marketplace where buyers and sellers or their representatives congregate, and a liquid secondary market where buyers and sellers of options can transact quickly and cheaply.

Figure 18.1 is a reproduction of listed stock option quotations from *The Wall Street Journal*. The highlighted options are for shares of IBM. The numbers in the column below the company name represent the last recorded price on the New York Stock Exchange for IBM stock, $102 7/8 per share.[1] The first column shows that options are traded on IBM at exercise prices of $90 through $135 in $5 increments. These values are also called the *strike prices*.

The exercise or strike prices bracket the stock price. While exercise prices generally are set at five-point intervals for stocks, larger intervals may be set for stocks selling above $100, and intervals of $2 1/2 will be used for stocks selling below $30. If the stock price moves outside the range of exercise prices of the existing set of options, new options with appropriate exercise prices may be offered. Therefore, at any time, both in-the-money and out-of-the-money options will be listed, as in the IBM example.

Concept Check

Question 1.   Can you tell from the existing set of option contracts in Figure 18.1 whether IBM stock performed well or poorly in the months before this listing?

---

[1]Occasionally, this price may not match the closing price listed for the stock on the stock market page. This is because some NYSE stocks also trade on the Pacific Stock Exchange, which closes after the NYSE, and the stock pages may reflect the more recent Pacific Exchange closing price. The options exchanges, however, close with the NYSE, so the closing NYSE stock price is appropriate for comparison with the closing option price.

Figure 18.1
Listing of stock
option quotations.
From *The Wall Street
Journal,* September 16,
1991. Reprinted by
permission of *THE WALL
STREET JOURNAL,* © 1990
Dow Jones & Company, Inc.
All Rights Reserved
Worldwide.

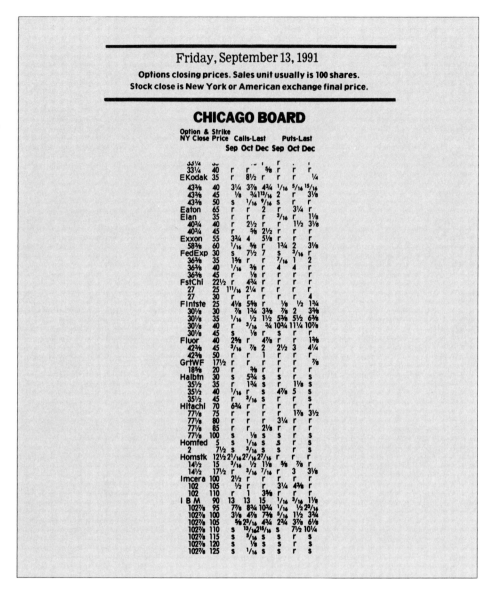

The numbers in the next three columns in Figure 18.1 provide the closing prices of call options on IBM shares with expiration dates of September, October and December. The contracts expire on the Saturday following the third Friday of the month. The prices of IBM call options decrease as one moves down each column toward progressively higher exercise prices. This makes sense, for the right to purchase a share at a given exercise price is worth less as that exercise price increases. At an exercise price of $95, the September IBM call sells for $7 7/8, while the option to purchase for an exercise price of $105 sells for only $5/8. The notation "r" means the option was not traded on that day, while "s" indicates the option with that exercise price and expiration date has not been opened for trading by the exchange.

Throughout Figure 18.1, you will see that many options may go an entire day without trading. Because trading is infrequent, it is not unusual to find option prices that appear out of line with other prices. You might see, for example, two calls with different exercise prices that seem to sell for the same price. This discrepancy arises because the last trades for these options may have occurred at different times during the day. At any moment, the call with the lower exercise price must be worth more than an otherwise-identical call with a higher exercise price.

The last three columns of the IBM entry report prices of put options with various strike prices and times to maturity. In contrast to call options, put prices increase with the exercise price. The right to sell a share of IBM at a price of $90 obviously is less valuable than the right to sell it at $105.

American and European Options

American option Can be exercised on or before its expiration.

European option Can be exercised only at expiration.

An **American option** allows its holder to exercise the right to purchase (if a call) or sell (if a put) the underlying asset on *or before* the expiration date. **European options** allow for exercise of the option only on the expiration date. American options, because they allow more leeway than their European counterparts, generally will be more valuable. Virtually all traded options in this country are American. Foreign currency options and stock index options traded on the Chicago Board Options Exchange are notable exceptions to this rule, however.

The Option Clearing Corporation

The Option Clearing Corporation (OCC), the clearinghouse for options trading, is jointly owned by the exchanges on which stock options are traded. Buyers and sellers of options who agree on a price will strike a deal. At this point, the OCC steps in. The OCC places itself between the two traders, becoming the effective buyer of the option from the writer and the effective writer of the option to the buyer. All individuals, therefore, deal only with the OCC, which effectively guarantees contract performance.

When an option holder exercises an option, the OCC arranges for a member firm with clients who have written that option to make good on the option obligation. The member firm selects from its clients who have written that option to fulfill the contract. The selected client must deliver 100 shares of stock at a price equal to the exercise price for each call option contract written or must purchase 100 shares at the exercise price for each put option contract written.

Because the OCC guarantees contract performance, option writers are required to post margin amounts to guarantee that they can fulfill their contract obligations. The margin required is determined in part by the amount by which the option is in the money, because that value is an indicator of the potential obligation of the option writer upon exercise of the option. When the required margin exceeds the posted margin, the writer will receive a margin call. The holder of the option need not post margin because the holder will exercise the option only if it is profitable to do so. After purchasing the option, no further money is at risk.

Margin requirements are determined in part by the other securities held in the investor's portfolio. For example, a call option writer owning the stock against which the option is written can satisfy the margin requirement simply by allowing a broker to hold that stock in the brokerage account. The stock is then guaranteed to be available for delivery should the call option be exercised.

If the underlying security is not owned, however, the margin requirement is determined by the value of the underlying security as well as by the amount by which the option is in or out of the money. Out-of-the-money options require less margin from the writer, for expected payouts are lower.

Other Listed Options

Options on assets other than stocks are also widely traded. These include options on market indexes and industry indexes, on foreign currency, and even on the futures prices of agricultural products, gold, silver, fixed-income securities, and stock indexes. We will discuss these in turn.

Index Options

An index option is a call or put based on a stock market index such as the S&P 500 or the New York Stock Exchange Index. Index options are traded on several broad-based indexes as well as on a few industry-specific indexes. We discussed many of these indexes in Chapter 4.

The construction of the indexes can vary across contracts or exchanges. For example, the S&P 100 index is a value-weighted average of the 100 stocks in the Standard & Poor's 100 stock group. The weights are proportional to the market value of outstanding equity for each stock. The Major Market Index, by contrast, is a price-weighted average of 20 stocks, most of which are in the Dow Jones Industrial Average group, while the Value Line Index is an equally weighted average of roughly 1,700 stocks.

More recently, options contracts on foreign stock indexes have been introduced. For example, options on the (Japanese) Nikkei 225 stock average trade on the Chicago Mercantile Exchange and options on the Japan Index trade on the American Stock Exchange.

In contrast to stock options, index options do not require that the call writer actually "deliver the index" upon exercise or that the put writer "purchase the index." Instead, a cash settlement procedure is used. The payoff that would accrue upon exercise of the option is calculated, and the option writer simply pays that amount to the option holder. The payoff is equal to the difference between the exercise price of the option and the value of the index. For example, if the S&P index is at $340 when a call option on the index with exercise price $330 is exercised, the holder of the call receives a cash payment of the $10 difference times the contract multiplier of 100, or $1,000 per contract. Figure 18.2 is a sample listing of various index options from *The Wall Street Journal*. These listings are arranged just like those for stock options with the index value taking the place of the stock price. The S&P 100 options contract, often called the OEX after its ticker symbol, is the most actively traded contract on the CBOE, although volume on S&P 500 index contracts has recently grown rapidly. Together, these contracts dominate CBOE volume.

Futures Options

Futures options give their holders the right to buy or sell a specified futures contract, using as a futures price the exercise price of the option. Although the delivery process is slightly complicated, the terms of futures options contracts are designed in effect to allow the option to be written on the futures price itself. The option holder receives upon exercise a net payoff equal to the difference

Figure 18.2
Index options.
From *The Wall Street Journal*, June 12, 1990. Reprinted by permission of *THE WALL STREET JOURNAL*, © 1990 Dow Jones & Company, Inc. All Rights Reserved Worldwide.

Monday, June 11, 1990

OPTIONS

Chicago Board

S&P 100 INDEX

Strike	Calls–Last			Puts–Last		
Price	Jun	Jul	Aug	Jun	Jul	Aug
290	53	....	....	1/16	....	....
295	....	....	....	1/16	5/16	....
300	....	43½	....	1/16	½	1⅛
305	38	....	....	1/16	9/16	1⅜
310	33½	35⅞	35¾	1/16	¾	1⅞
315	29¼	31	30¾	⅛	⅞	2 5/16
320	23⅛	26	26¾	⅛	1⅛	2⅞
325	18¼	21	....	3/16	1⅝	3⅜
330	14	17	20¾	5/16	2¼	4⅜
335	9	13⅛	15	½	3¼	5⅜
340	4¾	9⅝	12⅝	1⅛	4⅝	7¼
345	1¾	6¾	9¼	3⅛	6⅝	9⅜
350	½	4½	7½	7¼	9½	12⅛
355	¼	2 11/16	4⅞	12⅜	13½	15¼
360	⅛	1⅝	3¼	17¼	18⅜	....
365	....	15/16	2¼	....	....	....

Total call volume 125,997 Total call open int. 416,599
Total put volume 146,796 Total put open int. 540,975
The index: High 343.08; Low 339.17; Close 342.90, +3.05

S&P 500 INDEX

Strike	Calls–Last			Puts–Last		
Price	Jun	Jul	Sep	Jun	Jul	Sep
315	....	....	....	....	....	2 1/16
320	....	....	....	....	....	3¼
325	....	....	....	....	¾	....
330	30¾	34	....	1/16	⅝	3⅝
335	25¼	....	....	....	1	4¼
340	20¼	24½	....	⅛	1⅛	5¾
345	15	20¼	....	¼	2	5½
350	12¾	15¼	....	⅜	2⅜	....
355	7⅛	....	18⅛	¾	3⅝	8
360	3¾	9⅛	15	1¾	5	9⅛
365	1¼	5⅝	11¾	5	7⅞	12⅝
370	5/16	3½	9	11¼	11½	13
375	⅛	2¼	7¼	14½	....	16
380	....	1 3/16	....	....	20⅜	....
385	1/16	13/16	....	....	....	....

Total call volume 29,194 Total call open int. 402,951
Total put volume 21,923 Total put open int. 491,095
The index: High 361.63; Low 357.70; Close 361.63, +2.92

American Exchange

MAJOR MARKET INDEX

Strike	Calls–Last			Puts–Last		
Price	Jun	Jul	Aug	Jun	Jul	Aug
485	....	....	....	....	5/16	....
490	....	....	....	....	7/16	....
495	....	....	....	1/16	....	....
500	....	....	....	1/16	11/16	....
515	....	....	....	⅛	....	....
520	....	....	....	⅛	1⅛	....
530	....	....	50⅛	⅛	1 7/16	....
535	42	....	....	3/16	1 11/16	....
540	37½	....	....	¼	2	5¾
545	....	....	....	5/16	3	....
550	....	....	37	5/16	3¼	....
555	23¼	....	....	5/16	4⅞	....
560	18	....	....	½	5⅛	....
565	13½	20⅜	....	¾	5¾	....
570	8½	15⅜	....	1⅜	7	....
575	5	14⅜	....	2½	8¾	....
580	2½	11	16	5	10¾	16⅛
585	1⅛	8⅝	....	8½	13¼	....
590	½	5½	....	13⅛	15⅜	....
595	¼	4½	....	....	....	....

Total call volume 13,106 Total call open int. 73,501
Total put volume 11,232 Total put open int. 66,346
The index: High 576.74; Low 570.63; Close 576.05, +4.42

INTERNATIONAL MARKET INDEX

Strike	Calls–Last			Puts–Last		
Price	Jun	Jul	Aug	Jun	Jul	Aug
315	1⅛	....	....	3½	....	....

Total call volume 5 Total call open int. 432
[illegible] volume 3 [illegible] open int

between the current futures price on the specified asset and the exercise price of the option. Thus, if the futures price is, say, \$37, and the call has an exercise price of \$35, the holder who exercises the call option on the futures gets a payoff of \$2. Many of the foreign exchange options in Figure 18.3 are foreign exchange

West Ger... ...E) 62,500 ... ...ark
Sep .5912 +.0023; Est. vol. 240; Open Int. 509
FINEX—Financial Instrument Exchange, a division of the New York Cotton Exchange. IMM—International Monetary Market at the Chicago Mercantile Exchange. MCE—MidAmerica Commodity Exchange.

FUTURES OPTIONS

JAPANESE YEN (IMM) 12,500,000 yen; cents per 100 yen

Strike	Calls—Settle			Puts—Settle		
Price	Jly-c	Aug-c	Sep-c	Jly-p	Aug-p	Sep-p
63	1.91	....	2.21	0.10	0.27	0.44
64	1.11	1.33	1.55	0.29	0.52	0.75
65	0.51	0.77	1.01	0.69	0.95	1.19
66	0.21	0.41	0.64	1.39	1.57	1.79
67	0.08	0.21	0.38	2.25	....	2.52
68	0.04	0.11	0.22	3.20	....	3.34

Est. vol. 11,519, Fri vol. 4,662 calls, 4,293 puts
Open interest Fri; 46,298 calls, 30,660 puts

W. GERMAN MARK (IMM) 125,000 marks; cents per mark

Strike	Calls—Settle			Puts—Settle		
Price	Jly-c	Aug-c	Sep-c	Jly-p	Aug-p	Sep-p
57	2.19	....	2.50	0.08	0.22	0.41
58	1.32	1.55	1.80	0.21	0.45	0.70
59	0.67	0.95	1.23	0.55	0.83	1.11
60	0.24	0.55	0.81	1.16	1.43	1.66
61	0.11	0.27	0.51	2.00	2.13	2.35
62	0.04	0.14	0.30	2.93	....	3.12

Est. vol. 4,076, Fri vol. 9,765 calls, 10,017 puts
Open interest Fri; 48,137 calls, 54,768 puts

CANADIAN DOLLAR (IMM) 100,000 Can.$, cents per Can.$

Strike	Calls—Settle			Puts—Settle		
Price	Jly-c	Aug-c	Sep-c	Jly-p	Aug-p	Sep-p
835	0.94	1.10	1.28	0.19	0.36	0.53
840	0.61	0.80	0.98	0.36	0.55	0.72
845	0...		0.74	0...	...	0.98

Strike	Calls—Settle			Puts—Settle		
Price	Jly-c	Aug-c	Sep-c	Jly-p	Aug-p	Sep-p
850	0.19	....	0.55	0.93	1.11	1.28
855	0.09	0.23	0.39	....	....	1.61
860	0.05	....	0.28	....	....	1.99

Est. vol. 805, Fri vol. 1,903 calls, 1,823 puts
Open interest Fri; 8,949 calls, 10,116 puts

BRITISH POUND (IMM) 62,500 pounds; cents per pound

Strike	Calls—Settle			Puts—Settle		
Price	Jly-c	Aug-c	Sep-c	Jly-p	Aug-p	Sep-p
1600	5.92	....	6.72	0.16	0.50	1.02
1625	3.68	4.30	4.94	0.40	1.06	1.72
1650	1.92	....	3.50	1.12	1.98	2.70
1675	0.80	1.56	2.36	2.50	....	4.02
1700	0.28	0.86	1.48	4.42	....	5.64
1725	0.12	0.42	0.94	....	....	....

Est. vol. 202, Fri vol. 649 calls, 1,846 puts
Open interest Fri; 10,573 calls, 6,625 puts

SWISS FRANC (IMM) 125,000 francs; cents per franc

Strike	Calls—Settle			Puts—Settle		
Price	Jly-c	Aug-c	Sep-c	Jly-p	Aug-p	Sep-p
67	2.37	....	2.78	0.12	0.33	0.57
68	1.54	....	2.10	0.29	0.58	0.88
69	0.88	1.22	1.54	0.62	0.97	1.29
70	0.44	1.78	1.10	1.17	1.52	1.82
71	0.19	0.46	0.76	1.92	2.19	2.47
72	0.08	0.26	0.50	2.80	....	3.21

Est. vol. 924, Fri vol. 2,623 calls, 3,702 puts
Open interest Fri; 13,534 calls, 21,233 puts

—OTHER CURRENCY FUTURES OPTIONS—

Final or settlement prices of selected contracts. Volume and open interest are totals in all contract months.

Australian Dollar (IMM) $100,000; $ per $

Strike	Jly-c	Aug-c	Sep-c	Jly-p	Aug-p	Sep-p
76			1.41			

Strike		Sep-c			Sep-p	
155	13.50	13.50	....	0.00	1.37	....

Act. vol. Mon. vol. 0. Op. Int. 41.

FINEX—Financial Instrument Exchange, a division of the New York Cotton Exchange. IMM-International Monetary Market at Chicago Mercantile Exchange. LIFFE-London International Financing Futures Exchange.

OPTIONS
PHILADELPHIA EXCHANGE

Option & Underlying	Strike Price	Calls—Last			Puts—Last		
		Jun	Jul	Sep	Jun	Jul	Sep
50,000 Australian Dollars-cents per unit.							
ADollr	...72	r	r	r	r	r	0.25
77.18	...74	r	r	r	0.01	0.10	r
77.18	...75	r	r	r	r	0.18	r
77.18	...76	r	1.28	r	r	r	r
77.18	...77	0.35	r	r	0.13	r	r
77.18	...78	r	0.45	r	r	r	r
50,000 Australian Dollars-European Style.							
77.18	...77	r	r	r	0.15	r	r
31,250 British Pounds-cents per unit.							
BPound	155	13.68	r	r	r	r	r
168.30	157½	r	r	r	r	r	0.75
168.30	.160	r	r	r	r	r	1.10
168.30	162½	6.05	5.90	6.05	r	r	1.80
168.30	.165	r	3.50	r	r	0.82	r
168.30	167½	1.30	1.58	r	0.45	r	r
168.30	.170	0.15	0.75	r	r	r	r
50,000 Canadian Dollars-cents per unit.							
CDollr	.81½	r	r	r	r	r	0.19
85.29	...82	r	r	r	r	0.06	r
85.29	...83	r	r	r	r	0.11	0.40
85.29	.83½	r	r	r	r	0.13	0.59
85.29	...84	r	r	r	0.01	0.24	0.72
85.29	.84½	r	r	r	r	0.35	r
85.29	...85	0.40	0.65	r	0.14	0.64	1.30
85.29	.85½	r	r	r	0.23	0.88	1.71
85.29	...86	0.06	r	r	0.65	r	r
85.29	.86½	r	r	r	r	1.73	r
50,000 Canadian Dollars-European Style.							
CDollar	.81½	3.76	r	r	r	r	r
62,500 West German Marks-cents per unit.							
DMark	.57	r	r	r	r	0.14	r
58.90	...58	1.09	r	r	0.04	0.28	0.75
58.90	.58½	r	r	s	0.10	0.44	s
58.90	...59	0.34	0.74	1.28	0.27	r	s
58.90	.59½	0.13	r	s	r	r	s
58.90	...60	0.06	0.28	r	0.99	r	1.75
58.90	...61	0.01	r	0.53	r	2.00	r
58.90	...62	r	r	0.30	r	r	3.16
62,500 West German Marks-European Style.							
58.90	...54	5.10	r	r	r	r	r
58.90	...57	2.10	r	r	r	r	r
6,250,000 Japanese Yen-100ths of a cent per unit.							
JYen	...61	r	r	r	r	r	0.10
65.03	...63	r	r	r	0.02	0.14	0.49
65.03	...64	r	r	1.70	0.06	0.36	0.79
65.03	.64½	0.42	r	s	0.17	r	s
65.03	...65	0.15	0.55	1.06	0.47	0.77	1.24
65.03	.65½	0.08	r	s	0.80	r	s
65.03	...66	0.02	0.27	0.67	1.30	1.42	r
65.03	.66½	r	0.18	s	r	r	s
65.03	...67	r	0.12	r	r	r	r
65.03	...71	r	r	0.06	r	r	r
6,250,000 Japanese Yen-European Style.							
65.03	...70	r	r	r	r	5.29	r
62,500 Swiss Francs-cents per unit.							
SFranc	.67	r	r	r	r	r	0.65
69.02	...68	r	1.70	r	r	0.33	0.95
69.02	.68½	r	r	s	0.15	r	s
69.02	...69	0.62	1.05	r	r	r	r
69.02	.69½	0.34	0.83	s	r	0.84	s
69.02	...70	0.19	0.58	r	r	r	r
69.02	...71	r	r	0.80	r	r	r
69.02	...72	r	r	0.56	r	r	r
62,500 European Currency Units-cents per unit.							
ECU	122	r	0.97	r	r	1.70	r

Total call vol. 10,750   Call open int. 394,482
Total put vol. 37,062   Put open int. 398,400
r—Not traded.   s—No option offered.
Last is ... ...urchase pric...

Figure 18.3 Foreign exchange options.

futures options; they are written on the futures price of foreign exchange rather than on the actual or spot exchange rate.

Foreign Currency Options

A currency option offers the right to buy or sell a quantity of foreign currency for a specified amount of domestic currency. Foreign currency options have traded on the Philadelphia Stock Exchange since December 1982. Since then, the Chicago Board Options Exchange and the Chicago Mercantile Exchange have listed foreign currency options. Currency option contracts call for purchase or sale of the currency in exchange for a specified number of U.S. dollars. Contracts are quoted in cents or fractions of a cent per unit of foreign currency.

Figure 18.3 shows a *Wall Street Journal* listing of some of these contracts. The size of each option contract is specified for each listing. The call option on the British pound on the Philadelphia exchange, for example, entitles its holder to purchase 31,250 pounds for a specified number of cents per pound on or before the expiration date. The June call option with strike price of 170 cents sells for 0.15 cents, which means each contract costs $\$.0015 \times 31,250 = \$46.875$. The current exchange rate is 168.30 cents per pound. Therefore, the option is out of the money by 1.70 cents, the difference between the current exchange rate (168.30 cents) and the exercise price of 170 cents per pound.

There is an important difference between the options traded on the Philadelphia exchange and the futures options traded on the International Monetary Market (IMM). The former provide payoffs that depend on the difference between the exercise price and the exchange rate at maturity. The latter are foreign exchange futures options that provide payoffs that depend on the difference between the exercise price and the exchange rate *futures price* at maturity. Because exchange rates and exchange rate futures prices generally are not equal, the options and futures-options contracts will have different values, even with identical expiration dates and exercise prices. For example, in Figure 18.3, the call option on the West German mark on the Philadelphia exchange with strike price 59 cents and July maturity is quoted at .74. The corresponding futures option on the IMM with the same strike price and maturity is quoted at .67.

Interest Rate Options

Options on particular U.S. Treasury notes and bonds are listed on the AMEX and the CBOE. Options also are traded on Treasury bills, certificates of deposit, and GNMA pass-through certificates. Options on Treasury bond and Treasury note futures also trade on the Chicago Board of Trade.

18.2 *Values of Options at Expiration*

Call Options

Recall that a call option gives the right to purchase a security at the exercise price. If you hold a call option on IBM stock with an exercise price of $130, and IBM is now selling at $140, you can exercise your option to purchase the stock at $130 and simultaneously sell the shares at the market price of $140, clearing $10 per share. Yet if the shares sell below $130, you can sit on the option and do nothing, realizing no further gain or loss. The value of the call option at expiration equals:

$$\text{Payoff to call holder} = S_T - X \text{ if } S_T > X$$
$$0 \quad \text{if } S_T \leq X.$$

where S_T is the value of the stock at expiration, and X is the exercise price. This formula emphasizes the option property because the payoff cannot be negative. That is, the option is exercised only if S_T exceeds X. If S_T is less than X, exercise does not occur, and the option expires with zero value. The loss to the option holder in this case equals the price originally paid for the right to buy at the exercise price. More generally, the *profit* to the option holder is the payoff to the option minus the original purchase price.

The value at expiration of the call on IBM with exercise price $130 is given by the schedule:

IBM value:	$120	$130	$140	$150	$160
Option value:	0	0	10	20	30

For IBM prices at or below $130, the option is worthless. Above $130, the option is worth the excess of IBM's price over $130. The option's value increases by one dollar for each dollar increase in the IBM stock price. This relationship can be depicted graphically, as in Figure 18.4.

The solid line in Figure 18.4 depicts the value of the call at maturity. The net *profit* to the holder of the call equals the gross payoff less the initial investment

Figure 18.4
Payoff and profit to call option at expiration.

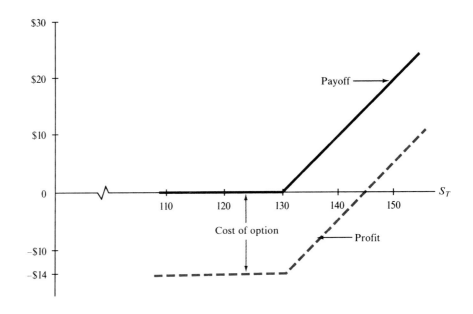

in the call. Suppose the call cost $14. Then the profit to the call holder would be as given in the dashed (bottom) line of Figure 18.4. At option expiration, the investor has suffered a loss of $14 if the stock prices is less than or equal to $130.

Profits do not become positive unless the stock price at expiration exceeds $144. The break-even point is $144, because at that price the payoff to the call, $S_T - X = \$144 - \$130 = \$14$, equals the cost paid to acquire the call. Hence, the call holder shows a profit only if the stock price is higher.

Conversely, the writer of the call incurs losses if the stock price is high. In that scenario, the writer will receive a call and will be obligated to deliver a stock worth S_T for only X dollars:

$$\text{Payoff to call writer} = \begin{array}{ll} -(S_T - X) & \text{if } S_T > X \\ 0 & \text{if } S_T \leq X. \end{array}$$

The call writer, who is exposed to losses if IBM increases in price, is willing to bear this risk in return for the option premium.

Figure 18.5 depicts the payoff and profit diagrams for the call writer. These are the mirror images of the corresponding diagrams for call holders. The break-even point for the option writer also is $144. The (negative) payoff at that point just offsets the premium originally received when the option was written.

Figure 18.5
Payoff and profit to call writers at expiration.

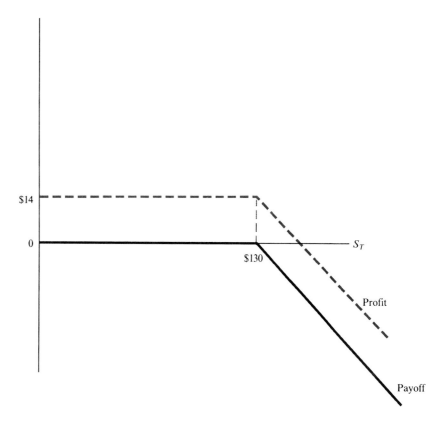

Put Options

A put option conveys the right to sell an asset at the exercise price. In this case, the holder will not exercise the option unless the asset sells for *less* than the exercise price. For example, if IBM shares were to fall to $110, a put option with exercise price $120 could be exercised to give a $10 profit to its holder. The holder would purchase a share of IBM for $110 and simultaneously deliver it to the put option writer for the exercise price of $120.

The value of a put option at expiration is:

$$\text{Payoff to put holder} = 0 \qquad \text{if } S_T \geq X$$
$$X - S_T \qquad \text{if } S_T < X.$$

The solid line in Figure 18.6 illustrates the payoff at maturity to the holder of a put option on IBM stock with an exercise price of $130. If the stock price at option maturity is above $130, the put has no value, as the right to sell the shares at $130 would not be exercised. Below a price of $130, the put value at expiration increases by one dollar for each dollar the stock price falls. The dashed line in Figure 18.6 is a graph of the put option owner's profit at expiration, net of the initial cost of the put.

Concept Check

Question 2. Analyze the strategy of put writing.
a. What is the payoff to a put writer as a function of the stock price?
b. What is the profit?
c. Draw the payoff and profit graphs.
d. When do put writers do well? When do they do poorly?

Writing puts *naked* (i.e., writing a put without an offsetting short position in the stock for hedging purposes) exposes the writer to losses if the market falls. Writing naked out-of-the-money puts was once considered an attractive way to

Figure 18.6
Payoff and profit to put option at expiration.

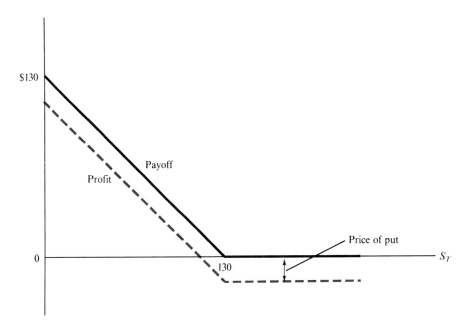

generate income, as it was believed that as long as the market did not fall sharply before the option expiration, the option premium could be collected without the put holder ever exercising the option against the writer. Because only sharp drops in the market could result in losses to the writer of the put, the strategy was not viewed as overly risky. However, the accompanying box notes that in the wake of the market crash of October 1987, such put writers suffered huge losses. Participants now perceive much greater risk to this strategy.

Option versus Stock Investments

Purchasing call options is a bullish strategy; that is, the calls provide profits when stock prices increase. Purchasing puts, in contrast, is a bearish strategy. Symmetrically, writing calls is bearish, while writing puts is bullish. Because option values depend on the price of the underlying stock, purchase of options may be viewed as a substitute for direct purchase or sale of a stock. Why might an option strategy be preferable to direct stock transactions?

For example, why would you purchase a call option rather than buy IBM stock directly? Maybe you have some information that leads you to believe IBM stock will increase in value from its current level, which in our examples we will take to be $140. You know your analysis could be incorrect, and that IBM also could fall in price. Suppose a six-month maturity call option with exercise price $135 currently sells for $14, and the interest rate for the period is 5 percent. Consider these three strategies for investing a sum of money, say, $14,000. For simplicity, suppose IBM will not pay any dividends until after the six-month period.

Strategy A: Purchase 100 shares of IBM stock.
Strategy B: Purchase 1,000 call options on IBM with exercise price $135. (This would require 10 contracts, each for 100 shares.)
Strategy C: Purchase 100 call options for $1,400. Invest the remaining $12,600 in six-month T-bills, to earn 5 percent interest.

Let us trace the possible values of these three portfolios when the options expire in six months as a function of IBM stock price at that time.

	IBM Price				
	$120	**$130**	**$140**	**$150**	**$160**
Value of portfolio A:	$12,000	$13,000	$14,000	$15,000	$16,000
Value of portfolio B:	0	0	5,000	15,000	25,000
Value of portfolio C:	13,230	13,230	13,730	14,730	15,730

Portfolio A will be worth 100 times the share value of IBM. Portfolio B is worthless unless IBM sells for more than the exercise price of the call. Once that point is reached, the portfolio is worth 1,000 times the excess of the stock price over the exercise price. Finally, portfolio C is worth $13,230 from the investment in T-bills ($12,600 × 1.05 = $13,230) plus any profits from the 100 call options. Remember that each of these portfolios involves the same $14,000 initial investment. The rates of return on these three portfolios are as follows:

The Black Hole: How Some Investors Lost All Their Money in the Market Crash

Their Sales of 'Naked Puts' Quickly Come to Grief, Damage Suits Are Filed

When Robert O'Connor got involved in stock-index options, he hoped his trading profits would help put his children through college. His broker, Mr. O'Connor explains, "said we would make about $1,000 a month, and if our losses got to $2,000 to $3,000, he would close out the account."

Instead, Mr. O'Connor, the 46-year-old owner of a small medical X-ray printing concern in Grand Rapids, Mich., got caught in one of the worst investor blowouts in history. In a few minutes on Oct. 19, he lost everything in his account plus an *additional* $91,000—a total loss of 175 percent of his original investment.

"If I had been told what the real risks were, I would never have done this. We're not big rollers," Mr. O'Connor says. "That's my life savings. That's not money to play with."

Scene of Disaster

For Mr. O'Connor and hundreds of other investors, a little-known corner of the Chicago Board Options Exchange was the "black hole" of Black Monday's market crash. In a strategy marketed by brokers nationwide as a sure thing, these customers had sunk hundreds of millions of dollars into "naked puts"—unhedged, highly leveraged bets that the stock market was in no danger of plunging. Most of these naked puts seem to have been options on the Standard & Poor's 100 stock index, which are traded on the CBOE.

Lulled into complacency by the market's long surge, hundreds of brokers marketed naked puts to ill-informed investors ranging from a retired civil servant in Virginia to a quadriplegic woman in Texas. When stocks crashed, many traders with un-hedged positions got margin calls for several times their original investment.

The 'Put' Strategy

The losses were especially sharp in "naked, out-of-the-money puts." A seller of puts agrees to buy stock or stock-index contracts at a set price before the put expires. These contracts are usually sold "out of the money"—priced at a level below current market prices that makes it unprofitable to exercise the option so long as the market rises or stays flat. The seller pockets a small amount per contract.

But if the market plunges, as it did Oct. 19, the option swings into the money. The seller, in effect, has to pay pre-plunge stock prices to make good on his contract—and he takes a big loss.

Moreover, many investors were required to post margin money equal to only 5 percent to 10 percent of the face value of the option contracts—a minuscule amount compared with their exposure to loss. That kind of leverage more resembles Russian roulette than the "risk-free" trading that many customers thought they were doing in naked options, says Robert Gordon, the president of Twenty-First Securities Corp., a New York investment firm.

Brokers across the nation are still smarting as well. In San Francisco, Charles Schwab Corp. said a single trader's activity in stock-index options accounted for $15 million of its $22 million in losses in October. Bear, Stearns & Co. and other big Wall Street houses took heavy hits. Options-related losses sank H. B. Shaine & Co., the Grand Rapids brokerage firm where Mr. O'Connor did business. Some $90 million of losses at First Options of Chicago Inc. may drag its parent company, Continental Illinois Corp., into the red in the fourth quarter. And in London, too, a 23-year-old trainee accountant lost nearly one million pounds (about $1.75

	IBM Price				
	$120	**$130**	**$140**	**$150**	**$160**
A (all stock)	−14.3%	−7.1%	0.0%	7.1%	14.3%
B (all options)	−100	−100	−64.3	7.1	78.6
C (options plus bills)	−5.5	−5.5	−1.9	5.2	12.4

These rates of return are graphed in Figure 18.7.

million) trading options, according to British press reports.

"You have to recognize that there is unlimited potential for disaster" in selling naked options, says Peter Thayer, executive vice president of Gateway Investment Advisors Inc., a Cincinnati-based investment firm that trades options to hedge its stock portfolios. Last September, Gateway bought out-of-the-money put options on the S&P 100 stock index on the CBOE at $2 to $3 a contract as "insurance" against a plunging market. By Oct. 20, the day after the crash, the value of those contracts had soared to $130. Although Gateway profited handsomely, the parties on the other side of the trade were clobbered.

In many cases, brokers played down the risks to attract more customers to a big-commission business. "Brokers were selling these things like annuities," says Elisabeth Richards, a broker and strategic analyst with Heritage Financial Investments Corp. of Falls Church Va.

In Texas, the 56-year-old quadriplegic, who asked not to be named, says she lost her entire $35,000 nest egg trading stock-index options. "It was far too risky for me," she says. She adds that now she is left with only social security.

Firm Sued

Brokers who were pushing naked options assumed that the stock market wouldn't plunge into uncharted territory. Frank VanderHoff, one of the two main brokers who put 50 to 70 H.B. Shaine clients into stock-index options, says he told clients that the strategy's risk was "moderate barring a nuclear attack or a crash like 1929. It wasn't speculative. The market could go up or down, but not *substantially* up or down. If the crash had only been as bad as '29, he adds, "we would have made it." Mr.

VanderHoff says that all his customers read and signed option-trading risk-disclosure documents and that he never promised that accounts would have strictly limited losses.

Nevertheless, Mr. O'Connor and other customers are suing the firm in state court in Grand Rapids. They allege that they weren't fully informed of the risks and that Shaine acted negligently by selling out their options accounts without authority from them. The complaint says that the defendants lost about $100,000 each and that they should be reimbursed that amount, plus $500,000 each in damages.

Similarly, a retired engineer in Niagara Falls, N.Y., who asked that his name be withheld, set up a trust for his daughter and grandson 10 years ago, with himself as trustee. The 76-year-old retiree says he lost nearly $360,000 on Black Monday when he was forced to buy back the stock-index options and the trust account was left about $140,000 in debt to Bear Stearns.

His experience is typical: On Oct. 16, he sold 40 S&P 100 stock-index put options for $1,550 each, or a total of $62,000. In essence, he was betting that after the 108.35 point drop in the Dow Jones Industrial Average that Friday, the market wasn't likely to drop much further and probably would soon rally.

But Black Monday's plunge forced him to buy back the puts to cover his margin calls. Meanwhile, the price of the options had jumped 600 percent to $10,500 a contract—costing him $420,000 for the 40 contracts that he had sold for $62,000 just three days earlier.

Comparing the returns of portfolios B and C to those of the simple investment in IBM stock represented by portfolio A, we see that options offer two interesting features. First, an option offers leverage. Compare the returns of portfolio B and A. When IBM stock falls in price even moderately to $130, the value of portfolio B falls precipitously to zero—a rate of return of negative 100 percent. Conversely, if the stock price increases by 14.3 percent, from $140 to $160, the all-option portfolio jumps in value by a disproportionate 78.6 percent. In this sense, calls are a levered investment on the stock. Their values respond more than proportionately to changes in the stock value.

Figure 18.7 vividly illustrates this point. The slope of the all-option portfolio is far steeper than that for the all-stock portfolio, reflecting its greater proportional sensitivity to the value of the underlying security. The leverage factor is the reason investors (illegally) exploiting inside information commonly choose options as their investment vehicle.

The potential insurance value of options is the second interesting feature, as portfolio C shows. The T-bill plus option portfolio cannot be worth less than $13,230 after six months, as the option can always be left to expire worthless. The worst possible rate of return on portfolio C is −5.5 percent, compared to a (theoretically) worst possible rate of return of IBM stock of − 100 percent if the company were to go bankrupt. Of course, this insurance comes at a price: When IBM does well, portfolio C does not perform quite as well as portfolio A, the all-stock portfolio.

This simple example makes an important point. While options can be used by speculators as effectively leveraged stock positions, as in portfolio B, they

Figure 18.7
Rates of return to three strategies.

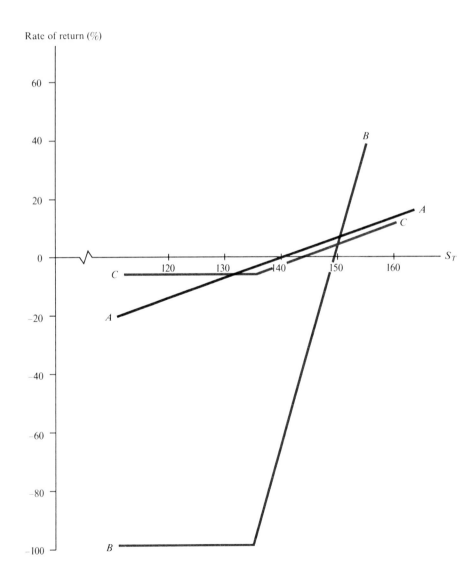

also can be used by investors who desire to tailor their risk exposures in creative ways, as in portfolio C. For example, the call plus T-bills strategy of portfolio C provides a rate of return profile quite unlike that of the stock alone. The absolute limitation on downside risk is a novel and attractive feature of this strategy. We will discuss below several option strategies that provide other novel risk profiles that might be attractive to hedgers and other investors.

The Put-Call Parity Relationship

Say you buy a call option and write a put option, each with the same exercise price, X, and the same expiration date, T. At expiration, the payoff on your investment will equal the payoff to the call, minus the payoff that must be made on the put. The payoff for each option will depend on whether the ultimate stock price, S_T, exceeds the exercise price at contract expiration.

	$S_T \leq X$	$S_T > X$
Payoff of call held	0	$S_T - X$
− Payoff of put written	$-(X - S_T)$	0
Total	$S_T - X$	$S_T - X$

Figure 18.8 illustrates this payoff pattern. Compare the payoff to that of a portfolio made up of the stock plus a borrowing position, where the money to be paid back will grow, with interest, to X dollars at the maturity of the loan. Such a position is a *levered* equity position in which $X/(1 + r_f)^T$ dollars is borrowed today (so that X will be repaid at maturity) and S_0 dollars is invested in the stock. The total payoff of the levered equity position is $S_T - X$, the same as that of the option strategy. Thus, the long call–short put position replicates the levered equity position. Again, we see that option trading provides leverage.

Because the option portfolio has a payoff identical to that of the levered equity position, the costs of establishing them must be equal. The net cash outlay necessary to establish the option position is $C - P$; the call is purchased for C, while the written put generates income of P. Likewise, the levered equity position requires a net cash outlay of $S_0 - X/(1 + r_f)^T$, the cost of the stock less the proceeds from borrowing. Equating these costs, we conclude

$$C - P = S_0 - X/(1 + r_f)^T. \qquad (18.1)$$

Put-call parity theorem   An equation representing the proper relationship between put and call prices.

Equation 18.1 is called the **put-call parity theorem** because it represents the proper relationship between put and call prices. If the parity relation is ever violated, an arbitrage opportunity arises. For example, suppose you confront these data for a certain stock:

Stock price	$110
Call price (six-month maturity, X = $105)	17
Put price (six-month maturity, X = $105)	5
Risk-free interest rate:	10.25% effective annual yield (5% per 6 months)

Figure 18.8
The payoff pattern of a long call–short put position.

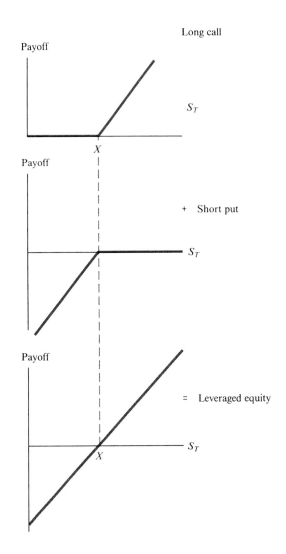

We use these data in the put-call parity theorem to see if parity is violated:

$$C - P \overset{?}{=} S_0 - X(1 + r_f)^T$$
$$17 - 5 \overset{?}{=} 110 - 105/1.05$$
$$12 \overset{?}{=} 10.$$

This result, a violation of parity—12 does not equal 10—indicates mispricing. To exploit the mispricing, you can buy the relatively cheap portfolio (the stock plus borrowing position represented on the right-hand side of the equation) and sell the relatively expensive portfolio (the long call–short put position corresponding to the left-hand side, that is, write a call and buy a put).

Let's examine the payoff to this strategy. In six months, the stock will be worth S_T. The $100 borrowed will be paid back with interest, resulting in a cash flow of $105. The written call will result in a cash outflow of $S_T - \$105$ if S_T exceeds $105. The purchased put pays off $\$105 - S_T$ if the stock price is below $105.

Table 18.1 *Arbitrage Strategy*

| Position | Immediate Cash Flow | Cash Flow in Six Months | |
		$S_T < 105$	$S_T \geq 105$
Buy stock	−110	S_T	S_T
Borrow $X/(1 + r_f)^T = \$100$	+100	−105	−105
Sell call	+17	0	−(S_T − 105)
Buy put	−5	105 − S_T	0
Total	2	0	0

Table 18.1 summarizes the outcome. The immediate cash inflow is $2. In six months, the various positions provide exactly offsetting cash flows: the $2 inflow is realized without any offsetting outflows. This is an arbitrage opportunity investors will pursue on a large scale until buying and selling pressure restores the parity condition expressed in Equation 18.1.

The parity condition actually applies only to options on stocks that pay no dividends before the maturity date of the option. It also applies only to European options, as the cash flow streams from the two portfolios represented by the two sides of Equation 18.1 will match only if each position is held until maturity. If a call and a put may be optimally exercised at different times before their common expiration date, then the equality of payoffs cannot be assured, or even expected, and the portfolios will have different values.

Let's see how well parity works using real data from the IBM options in Figure 18.1. The September call on IBM with exercise price $105 and time to expiration of 5 days cost $.625, while the corresponding put cost $2.75. IBM was selling for $102.875, and the annualized short-term interest rate on this date was 5.3 percent. According to parity, we should find

$$\$.625 - \$2.75 = \$102.875 - \$105/(1.053)^{5/365}$$
$$-\$2.125 = -\$2.051.$$

In this case, parity is violated by less than 8 cents per share, far too small an amount to outweigh the trading costs involved in attempting to exploit the minor mispricing. Moreover, given the infrequent trading of options, this small deviation from parity might be not a real one but attributable to "stale prices."

Option Strategies

An unlimited variety of payoff patterns can be achieved by combining puts and calls with various exercise prices. Below we explain the motivation and structure of some of the more popular ones.

Protective Put

Imagine you would like to invest in a stock, but you are unwilling to bear potential losses beyond some given level. Investing in the stock alone seems risky to you because in principle you could lose all the money you invest. You might consider instead investing in stock and purchasing a put option on the stock. Table 18.2 shows the total value of your portfolio at option expiration:

Table 18.2   *Payoff to Protective Put Strategy*

	$S_T \leq X$	$S_T > X$
Stock	S_T	S_T
Put	$X - S_T$	0
Total	X	S_T

Whatever happens to the stock price, you are guaranteed a payoff equal to the put option's exercise price because the put gives you the right to sell IBM for the exercise price even if the stock price is below that value.

For example, if the strike price is $X = \$115$ and IBM is selling at $112 at option expiration, then the value of your total portfolio is $115: the stock is worth $112 and the value of the expiring put option is

$$X - S_T = \$115 - \$112 = \$3.$$

Another way to look at it is that you are holding the stock and a put contract giving you the right to sell the stock for $115. If the stock price is above $115, say $119, then the right to sell a share at $115 is worthless. You allow the put to expire unexercised, ending up with a share of stock worth $S_T = \$119$.

Protective put
An asset combined with a put option that guarantees minimum proceeds equal to the put's exercise price.

Figure 18.9 illustrates the payoff and profit to this **protective put** strategy. The solid line in Figure 18.9C is the total payoff. The dashed line is displaced downward by the cost of establishing the position, $S_0 + P$. Notice that potential losses are limited.

It is instructive to compare the profit on the protective put strategy with that of the stock investment. For simplicity, consider an at-the-money protective put, so that $X = S_0$. Figure 18.10 compares the profits for the two strategies. The profit on the stock is zero if the stock price remains unchanged, and $S_T = S_0$. It rises or falls by $1 for every dollar swing in the ultimate stock price. The profit on the protective put is negative and equal to the cost of the put if S_T is below S_0. The profit on the protective put increases one for one with increases in the stock price.

Figure 18.10 makes it clear that the protective put offers some insurance against stock price declines in that it limits losses. As we shall see in the next chapter, protective put strategies are the conceptual basis for the portfolio insurance industry. The cost of the protection is that, in the case of stock price increases, your profit is reduced by the cost of the put, which turned out to be unneeded.

Covered Calls

Covered call   Writing a call on an asset together with buying the asset.

A **covered call** position is the purchase of a share of stock with a simultaneous sale of a call on that stock. The position is "covered" because the potential obligation to deliver the stock is covered by the stock held in the portfolio. Writing an option without an offsetting stock position is called by contrast *naked option writing*. The payoff to a covered call, presented in Table 18.3, equals the stock value minus the payoff of the call. The call payoff is subtracted because the covered call position involves issuing a call to another investor who can choose to exercise it to profit at your expense.

Figure 18.9
Value of a protective put position at expiration.

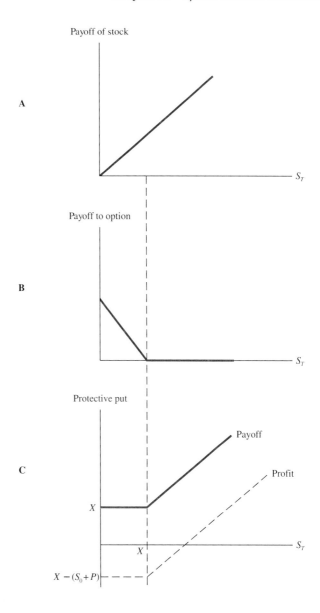

Table 18.3   *Payoff to a Covered Call*

	$S_T \leq X$	$S_T > X$
Payoff of stock	S_T	S_T
$-$ Payoff of call	-0	$-(S_T - X)$
Total	S_T	X

The solid line in Figure 18.11C illustrates the payoff pattern. You see that the total position is worth S_T when the stock price at time T is below X and rises to a maximum of X when S_T exceeds X. In essence, the sale of the call option means the call writer has sold the claim to any stock value above X in return for

Figure 18.10
**Protective put versus
stock investment.**

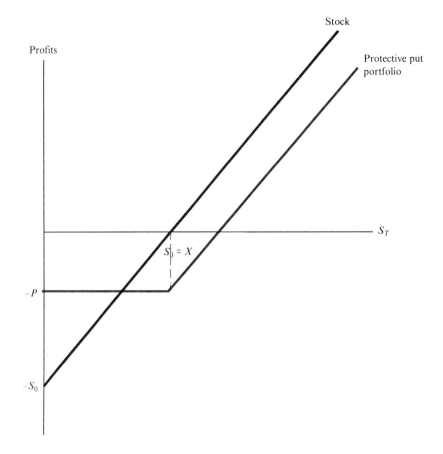

the initial premium (the call price). Therefore, at expiration, the position is worth at most X. The dashed line of Figure 18.11C is the net profit to the covered call.

Writing covered call options has been a popular investment strategy among institutional investors. Consider the managers of a fund invested largely in stocks. They might find it appealing to write calls on some or all of the stock in order to boost income by the premiums collected. Although they thereby forfeit potential capital gains should the stock price rise above the exercise price, if they view X as the price at which they plan to sell the stock anyway, then the call may be viewed as enforcing a kind of "sell discipline." The written call guarantees the stock sale will occur as planned.

For example, assume a pension fund holds 1,000 shares of IBM stock, with a current price of $130 per share. Suppose management intends to sell all 1,000 shares if the share price hits $140, and a call expiring in 90 days with an exercise price of $140 currently sells for $5. By writing 10 IBM call contracts (100 shares each) the fund can pick up $5,000 in extra income. The fund would lose its share of profits from any movement of IBM stock above $140 per share, but given that it would have sold its shares at $140, it would not have realized those profits anyway.

Figure 18.11
Value of a covered call position at expiration.

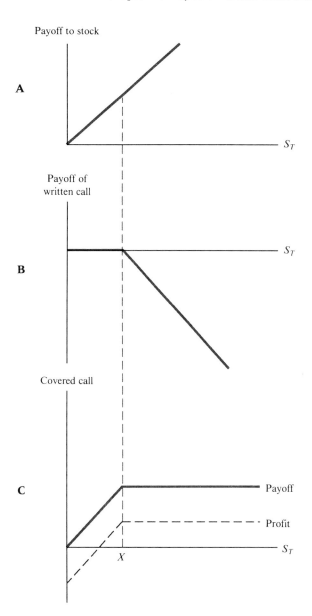

Straddle

Straddle   A combination of a call and a put, each with the same exercise price and expiration date.

A long **straddle** is established by buying both a call and a put on a stock, each with the same exercise price, X, and the same expiration date, T. Straddles are useful strategies for investors who believe a stock will move a lot in price but are uncertain about the direction of the move. For example, suppose you believe an important court case that will make or break a company is about to be settled, and the market is not yet aware of the situation. The stock will either double in value if the case is settled favorably or will drop by half if the settlement goes against the company. The straddle position will do well regardless of

Table 18.4 *Payoff to a Straddle*

	$S_T < X$	$S_T \geq X$
Payoff of call	0	$S_T - X$
+ Payoff of put	$+ (X - S_T)$	$+ \, 0$
Total	$X - S_T$	$S_T - X$

the outcome because its value is highest when the stock price makes extreme upward or downward moves from X.

The kiss of death for a straddle is no movement in the stock price. If S_T equals X, both the call and the put expire worthless, and the investor's outlay for the purchase of the two options is lost. Straddle positions basically are bets on volatility. An investor who establishes a straddle must view the stock as more volatile than the market does. Conversely, investors who *write* straddles—selling both a call and a put—must believe the market is less volatile. They accept the option premiums now, hoping the stock price will not change much before option expiration.

The payoff to a straddle is presented in Table 18.4. The solid line of Figure 18.12C illustrates this payoff. Notice the portfolio payoff is always positive, except at the one point where the portfolio has zero value, $S_T = X$. You might wonder why all investors don't pursue such a no-lose strategy. The straddle requires that both the put and call be purchased. The value of the portfolio at expiration, while never negative, still must exceed the initial cash outlay for a straddle investor to clear a profit.

The dashed line of Figure 18.12 is the profit to the straddle. The profit line lies below the payoff line by the cost of purchasing the straddle, $P + C$. It is clear from the diagram that the straddle position generates a loss unless the stock price deviates substantially from X. The stock price must depart from X by the total amount expended to purchase the call and the put in order for the purchaser of the straddle to clear a profit.

Strips and *straps* are variations of straddles. A strip is two puts and one call on a security with the same exercise price and maturity date. A strap is two calls and one put.

Concept Check

Question 3. Graph the profit and payoff diagrams for strips and straps.

Spreads

Spread A combination of two or more call options or put options on the same asset with differing exercise prices or times to expiration.

A **spread** is a combination of two or more call options (or two or more puts) on the same stock with differing exercise prices or times to maturity. Some options are bought, while others are sold, or written. A *vertical or money spread* involves the purchase of one option and the simultaneous sale of another with a different exercise price. A *horizontal or time spread* refers to the sale and purchase of options with differing expiration dates.

The vertical and horizontal spreads take their names from the way options are listed in the newspaper. Looking vertically down a column of options listings

Figure 18.12
Payoff and profit to a straddle at expiration.

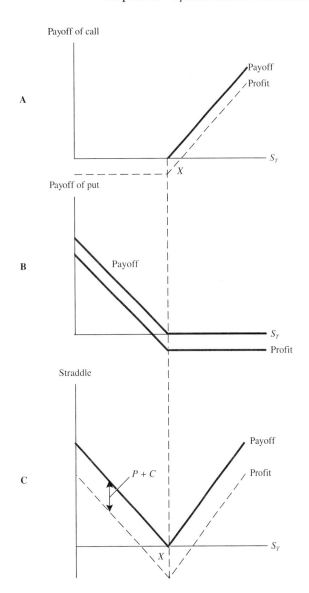

such as in Figure 18.1, you find options with identical maturities but different exercise prices. Moving horizontally across the row are options with identical exercise price but different maturities.

Consider a vertical spread in which one call option is bought at an exercise price X_1, while another call with identical expiration date, but higher exercise price, X_2, is written. The payoff to this position will be the difference in the value of the call held and the value of the call written, as in Table 18.5.

There are now three instead of two outcomes to distinguish: the lowest-price region where S_T is below both exercise prices, a middle region where S_T is between the two exercise prices, and a high-price region where S_T exceeds both exercise prices. Figure 18.13 illustrates the payoff and profit to this strategy, which is called a *bullish spread* because the payoff either increases or is unaffected by stock price increases. Holders of bullish spreads benefit from stock price increases.

Table 18.5 *Payoff to a Bullish Vertical Spread*

	$S_T \leq X_1$	$X_1 < S_T \leq X_2$	$S_T > X_2$
Payoff of call, exercise price = X_1	0	$S_T - X_1$	$S_T - X_1$
$-$ Payoff of call, exercise price = X_2	-0	-0	$-(S_T - X_2)$
Total	0	$S_T - X_1$	$X_2 - X_1$

Figure 18.13
Value of a bullish spread position at expiration.

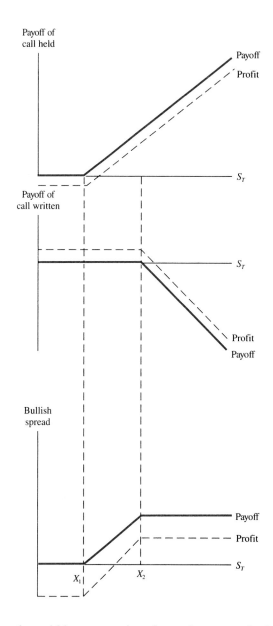

A bullish spread would be appropriate for an investor who has a target wealth goal in mind but is unwilling to risk losses beyond a certain level. If you are contemplating buying a house for $150,000, for example, you might set this figure as your goal. Your current wealth may be $145,000, and you are unwilling to risk losing more than $10,000. A bullish spread on 1,000 shares (10 option contracts) with $X_1 = \$135$ and $X_2 = \$150$ would give you a good chance to realize the $5,000 capital gain without risking a loss of more than $10,000.

Another motivation for a bullish spread might be that the investor thinks one option is overpriced relative to another. For example, an investor who believes the $X = \$135$ call is cheap compared to the $X = \$150$ call might establish the spread, even without a strong desire to take a bullish position in the stock.

18.3 *Option-like Securities*

Suppose you never traded an option directly. Why do you need to appreciate the properties of options in formulating an investment plan? Many financial instruments and agreements have features that convey implicit or explicit options to one or more parties. If you are to value and use these securities correctly, you must understand these embedded option attributes.

Callable Bonds

You know from Chapter 12 that most corporate bonds are issued with call provisions entitling the issuer to buy bonds back from bondholders at some time in the future at a specified call price. A call provision conveys a call option to the issuer, where the exercise price is equal to the price at which the bond can be repurchased. A callable bond arrangement is essentially a sale of a *straight bond* (a bond with no option features such as callability or convertibility) to the investor and the concurrent sale of a call option by the investor to the bond-issuing firm.

There must be some compensation for offering this implicit call option to the firm. If the callable bond were issued with the same coupon rate as a straight bond, we would expect it to sell at a discount to the straight bond equal to the value of the call. To sell callable bonds at par, firms must issue them with coupon rates higher than the coupons on straight debt. The higher coupons are the investor's compensation for the call option retained by the issuer. Coupon rates usually are selected so that the newly issued bond will sell at par value.

Figure 18.14 illustrates this option-like property. The horizontal axis is the value of a straight bond with otherwise identical terms as the callable bond. The dashed 45-degree line represents the value of straight debt. The solid line is the value of the callable bond, and the dotted line is the value of the call option retained by the firm. A callable bond's potential for capital gains is limited by the firm's option to repurchase at the call price.

Concept Check

> *Question 4.* How is a callable bond similar to a covered call strategy on a straight bond?

The option inherent in callable bonds actually is more complex than an ordinary call option because usually it may be exercised only after some initial period of call protection. The price at which the bond is callable may change over time also. Unlike exchange-listed options, these features are defined in the initial

Figure 18.14
**Values of callable
bonds compared with
straight bonds.**

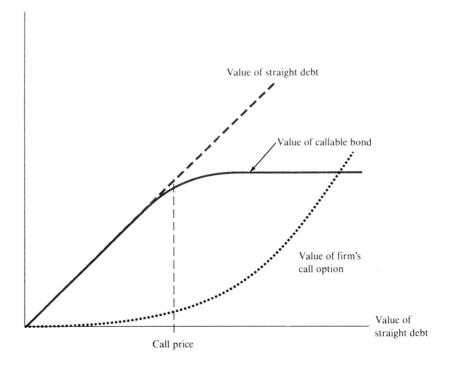

bond covenants and will depend on the needs of the issuing firm and its perception of the market's tastes.

Concept Check

Question 5. Suppose the period of call protection is extended. How will the coupon rate the company needs to offer on its bonds change to enable the issuer to sell the bonds at par value?

Convertible Securities

Convertible bonds and convertible preferred stock convey options to the holder of the security rather than to the issuing firm. A convertible security typically gives its holder the right to exchange each bond or share of preferred stock for a fixed number of shares of common stock, regardless of the market prices of the securities at the time.

Concept Check

Question 6. Should a convertible bond issued at par value have a higher or lower coupon rate than a nonconvertible bond at par?

For example, a bond with a conversion ratio of 10 allows its holder to convert one bond of par value $1,000 into 10 shares of common stock. Alternatively, we say the conversion price in this case is $100: to receive 10 shares of stock, the investor sacrifices bonds with face value $1,000 or $100 of face value per share. If the present value of the bond's scheduled payments is less than 10 times the value of one share of stock, it may pay to convert; that is, the conversion option is in the money. A bond worth $950 with a conversion ratio of 10 could be converted profitably if the stock were selling above $95, as the value of the 10 shares received for each bond surrendered would exceed $950. Most convertible bonds are issued "deep out of the money." That is, the issuer sets the conversion ratio so that conversion will not be profitable unless there is a substantial increase in stock prices and/or decrease in bond prices from the time of issue.

A bond's conversion value equals the value it would have if you converted it into stock immediately. Clearly, a bond must sell for at least its conversion value. If it did not, you could purchase the bond, convert it immediately, and clear a riskless profit. This condition could never persist, for all investors would pursue such a strategy and ultimately would bid up the price of the bond.

The straight bond value or "bond floor" is the value the bond would have if it were not convertible into stock. The bond must sell for more than its straight bond value because a convertible bond has more value; it is in fact a straight bond plus a valuable call option. Therefore, the convertible bond has two lower bounds on its market price: the conversion value and the straight bond value.

Figure 18.15 illustrates the option-like properties of the convertible bond. Figure 18.15A shows the value of the straight debt as a function of the stock price of the issuing firm. For healthy firms, the straight debt value is almost independent of the value of the stock because default risk is small. However, if the firm is close to bankruptcy (stock prices are low), default risk increases, and the straight bond value falls. Panel B shows the conversion value of the bond. Panel C compares the value of the convertible bond to these two lower bonds.

When stock prices are low, the straight bond value is the effective lower bound, and the conversion option is nearly irrelevant. The convertible will trade like straight debt. When stock prices are high, the bond's price is determined by its conversion value. With conversion all but guaranteed, the bond is essentially equity in disguise.

We can illustrate with two examples.

	Bond A	Bond B
Annual coupon	$80	$80
Maturity date	10 years	10 years
Quality rating	Baa	Baa
Conversion ratio	20	25
Stock price	$30	$50
Conversion value	$600	$1250
Market yield on 10-year Baa-rated bonds	8.5%	8.5%
Value as straight debt	$967	$967
Actual bond price	$972	$1255
Reported yield to maturity	8.42%	4.76%

Bond A has a conversion value of only $600. Its value as straight debt, in contrast, is $967. This is the present value of the coupon and principal payments at a market rate for straight debt of 8.5 percent. The bond's price is $972, so the premium over straight bond value is only $5, reflecting the low probability of conversion. Its reported yield to maturity based on scheduled coupon payments and the market price of $972 is 8.42 percent, close to that of straight debt.

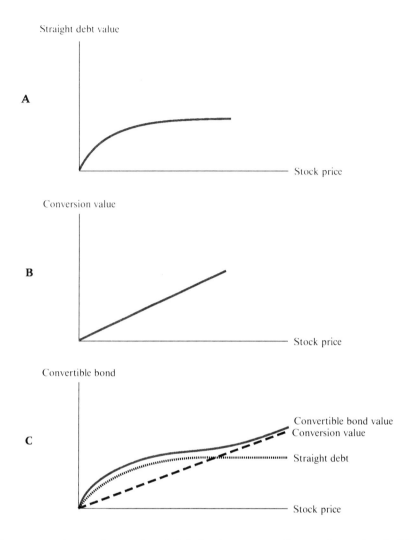

Figure 18.15
Value of a convertible bond as a function of stock price. **A,** Straight debt value, or bond floor. **B,** Conversion value of the bond. **C,** Total value of convertible bond.

The conversion option on bond B is in the money. Conversion value is $1,250, and the bond's price, $1,255, reflects its value as equity (plus $5 for the protection the bond offers against stock price declines). The bond's reported yield is 4.76 percent, far below the comparable yield on straight debt. The big yield sacrifice is attributable to the far greater value of the conversion option.

In theory, we could value convertible bonds by treating them as straight debt plus call options. In practice, however, this approach is often impractical for several reasons:

1. The conversion price frequently increases over time, which means the exercise price for the option changes.
2. Stocks may pay several dividends over the life of the bond, further complicating the option valuation analysis.
3. Most convertibles also are callable at the discretion of the firm. In essence, both the investor and the issuer hold options on each other. If the issuer exercises its call option to repurchase the bond, the bondholders typically have a month during which they still can convert. When issuers use a call

option, knowing bondholders will choose to convert, the issuer is said to have *forced a conversion*. These conditions together mean the actual maturity of the bond is indeterminate.

Warrants

Warrant   An option issued by the firm to purchase shares of the firm's stock.

Warrants are essentially call options issued by a firm. One important difference between calls and warrants is that exercise of a warrant requires the firm to issue a new share of stock to satisfy its obligation—the total number of shares outstanding increases. Exercise of a call option requires only that the writer of the call deliver an already-issued share of stock to discharge the obligation. In this case, the number of shares outstanding remains fixed. Also unlike call options, warrants result in a cash flow to the firm when the warrant holder pays the exercise price. These differences mean warrant values will differ somewhat from the values of call options with identical terms.

Like convertible debt, warrant terms may be tailored to meet the needs of the firm. Also like convertible debt, warrants generally are protected against stock splits and dividends in that the exercise price and the number of warrants held are adjusted to offset the effects of the split.

Warrants are often issued in conjunction with another security. Bonds, for example, may be packaged together with a warrant "sweetener," frequently a warrant that may be sold separately. This is called a *detachable warrant*.

Issue of warrants and convertible securities creates the potential for an increase in outstanding shares of stock if exercise occurs. Exercise obviously would affect financial statistics that are computed on a per share basis, so annual reports must provide earnings per share figures under the assumption that all convertible securities and warrants are exercised. These figures are called *fully diluted earnings per share*.[2]

Collateralized Loans

Most loan arrangements require that the borrower put up collateral to guarantee the loan will be paid back. In the event of default, the lender takes possession of the collateral. A nonrecourse loan gives the lender no recourse beyond the right to the collateral. That is, the lender may not sue the borrower for further payment if the collateral turns out not to be valuable enough to repay the loan.

This arrangement gives an implicit call option to the borrower. Assume the borrower is obligated to pay back L dollars at the maturity of the loan. The collateral will be worth S_T dollars at maturity. (Its value today is S_0.) The borrower has the option to wait until loan maturity and repay the loan only if the collateral is worth more than the L dollars necessary to satisfy the loan. If the collateral is worth less than L, the borrower can default on the loan, discharging the obligation by forfeiting the collateral, which is worth only S_T.

Another way of describing such a loan is to view the borrower as turning over collateral to the lender but retaining the right to reclaim it by paying off the

---

[2]We should note that the exercise of a convertible bond need not reduce EPS. Diluted EPS will be less than undiluted EPS only if interest saved (per share) on the converted bonds is less than the prior EPS.

loan. The transfer of the collateral with the right to reclaim it is equivalent to a payment of S_0 dollars, less a simultaneous recovery of a sum that resembles a call option with exercise price L. Basically, the borrower turns over collateral and keeps an option to "repurchase" it for L dollars at the maturity of the loan if L turns out to be less than S_T. This is a call option.

A third way to look at a collateralized loan is to assume the borrower will repay the L dollars with certainty but also retain the option to sell the collateral to the lender for L dollars, even if S_T is less than L. In this case, the sale of the collateral would generate the cash necessary to satisfy the loan. The ability to "sell" the collateral for a price of L dollars represents a put option, which guarantees the borrower can raise enough money to satisfy the loan simply by turning over the collateral.

It is strange to think we can describe the same loan as involving either a put option or a call option, as the payoffs to calls and puts are so different. Yet the equivalence of the two approaches is nothing more than a reflection of the put-call parity relationship. In our call-option description of the loan, the value of the borrower's liability is $S_0 - C$: the borrower turns over the asset, which is a transfer of S_0 dollars but retains a call that is worth C dollars. In the put-option description, the borrower is obligated to pay L dollars but retains the put, which is worth P: the present value of this net obligation is $L/(1 + r_f)^T - P$. Because these alternative descriptions are equivalent ways of viewing the same loan, the value of the obligations must be equal:

$$S_0 - C = L/(1 + r_f)^T - P. \tag{18.3}$$

Treating L as the exercise price of the option, Equation 18.3 is simply the put-call parity relationship.

Figure 18.16 illustrates this fact. Figure 18.16A is the value of the payment to be received by the lender, which equals the minimum of S_T or L. Panel B shows that this amount can be expressed as S_T minus the payoff of the call implicitly written by the lender and held by the borrower. Panel C shows it also can be viewed as a receipt of L dollars minus the proceeds of a put option.

Levered Equity and Risky Debt

Investors holding stock in incorporated firms are protected by limited liability, which means that if the firm cannot pay its debts, the firm's creditors may attach only the firm's assets, not sue the corporation's equityholders for further payment. In effect, any time the corporation borrows money, the maximum possible collateral for the loan is the total of the firm's assets. If the firm declares bankruptcy, we can interpret this as an admission the assets of the firm are insufficient to satisfy the claims against it. The corporation may discharge its obligations by transferring ownership of the firm's assets to the creditors.

Just as is true for nonrecourse collateralized loans, the required payment to the creditors represents the exercise price of the implicit option, while the value of the firm is the underlying asset. The equityholders have a put option to transfer their ownership claims on the firm to the creditors in return for the face value of the firm's debt.

Alternatively, we may view the equityholders as retaining a call option. They have, in effect, already transferred their ownership claim to the firm to the creditors but have retained the right to reacquire the ownership claim to the firm by

Figure 18.16
Collateralized loan.

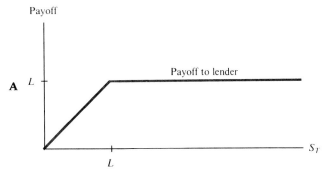

When S_T exceeds L, the loan is repaid and the collateral is reclaimed. Otherwise, the collateral is forfeited and the total loan repayment is worth only S_T.

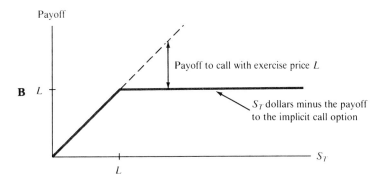

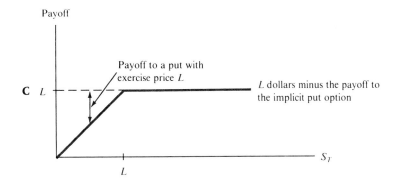

paying off the loan. Hence, the equityholders have the option to "buy back" the firm for a specified price, or they have a call option.

The significance of this observation is that analysts can value corporate bonds using option pricing techniques. The default premium required of risky debt in principle can be estimated using option valuation models. We will consider some of these models in the next chapter.

Summary

1. A call option is the right to buy an asset at an agreed-upon exercise price. A put option is the right to sell an asset at a given exercise price.

2. American options allow exercise on or before the exercise date. European options allow exercise only on the expiration date. Most traded options are American in nature.

3. Options are traded on stocks, stock indexes, foreign currencies, fixed-income securities, and several futures contracts.

4. Options can be used either to lever up an investor's exposure to an asset price or to provide insurance against volatility of asset prices. Popular option strategies include covered calls, protective puts, straddles, and spreads.

5. The put-call parity theorem relates the prices of put and call options. If the relationship is violated, arbitrage opportunities will result. Specifically, the relationship that must be satisfied is

$$C + PV(X) = S_0 + P$$

where X is the exercise price of both the call and the put options, and $PV(X)$ is the present value of a claim to X dollars to be paid at the expiration date of the options.

6. Many commonly traded securities embody option characteristics. Examples of these securities are callable bonds, convertible bonds, and warrants. Other arrangements such as collateralized loans and limited-liability borrowing can be analyzed as conveying implicit options to one or more parties.

Key Terms

American option, 505	in the money, 502	put option, 502
at the money, 503	out of the money, 502	spread, 524
call option, 502	protective put, 520	straddle, 523
covered call, 520	put-call parity	warrant, 531
European option, 505	theorem, 517	
exercise or strike		
price, 502		

Selected Readings

A good treatment of the institutional organization of option markets is in the Chicago Board Options Exchange Reference Manual. The CBOE also publishes a Margin Manual that provides an overview of margin requirements on many option positions.

An excellent discussion of option trading strategies is:
Black, Fischer. "Fact and Fantasy in the Use of Options." *Financial Analysts Journal,* July–August 1975, pp. 3–20.

Problem Sets

1. Suppose you think Wal-Mart stock is going to appreciate substantially in value in the next six months. Say the stock's current price, S_0, is $100, and the call option expiring in six months has an exercise price, X, of $100 and is selling at a price, C, of $10. With $10,000 to invest, you are considering three alternatives.
   a. Invest all $10,000 in the stock, buying 100 shares.
   b. Invest all $10,000 in 1,000 options (10 contracts).
   c. Buy 100 options (one contract) for $1,000, and invest the remaining $9,000 in a money market fund paying 4 percent in interest over six months (8 percent per year).

What is your rate of return for each alternative for four stock prices six months from now? Summarize your results in the table and diagram below.

Rate of Return on Investment

	Price of Stock Six Months from Now			
	80	*100*	*110*	*120*
a. All stocks (100 shares)				
b. All options (1,000 shares)				
c. Bills + 100 options				

2. The common stock of the P.U.T.T. Corporation has been trading in a narrow price range for the past month, and you are convinced it is going to break far out of that range in the next three months. You do not know whether it will go up or down, however. The current price of the stock is $100 per share, and the price of a three-month call option at an exercise price of $100 is $10.

   a. If the risk-free interest rate is 10 percent per year, what must be the price of a three-month put option on P.U.T.T. stock at an exercise price of $100?

   b. What would be a simple options strategy to exploit your conviction about the stock price's future movements? How far would it have to move in either direction for you to make a profit on your initial investment?

3. The common stock of the C.A.L.L. Corporation has been trading in a narrow range around $50 per share for months, and you believe it is going to stay in that range for the next three months. The price of a three-month put option with an exercise price of $50 is $4.

   a. If the risk-free interest rate is 10 percent per year, what must be the price of a three-month call option on C.A.L.L. stock at an exercise price of $50 if it is at the money?

   b. What would be a simple options strategy using a put and a call to exploit your conviction about the stock price's future movement? What is the most money you can make on this position? How far can the stock price move in either direction before you lose money?

   c. How can you create a position involving a put, a call, and riskless lending that would have the same payoff structure as the stock at expiration? What is the net cost of establishing that position now?

 4. On the death of his grandmother several years ago, Bill Melody received as a bequest from her estate 2,000 shares of General Motors common stock. The price of the stock at time of distribution from the estate was $75 a share, and this

became the cost basis of Melody's holding. Late in 1990, Melody agreed to purchase a new condominium for his parents at a total cost of $160,000, payable in full upon its completion in March 1991. Melody planned to sell the General Motors stock in order to raise funds to purchase the condominium.

At year-end 1990, GM's market price was around $75 a share, but it looked to be weakening. This concerned Melody, for if the price of the stock were to drop by a significant amount before he sold, the proceeds would not be sufficient to cover the purchase of the condominium in March 1991.

Melody visited with three investment counseling firms to seek advice in developing a strategy that, at a minimum, would protect the value of his principal at or near $150,000 ($75 a share). Ideally, the strategy would enhance the value to $160,000 so Melody would have the total cost of the condominium. Four alternatives were discussed:

a. Melody's own opinion was to sell the General Motors stock at $75 a share and invest the proceeds in a 10 percent certificate of deposit maturing in three months.

b. Anderson Investment Advisors suggested Melody write a March 1991 call option on his General Motors holding at a strike price of $80. The March 1991 calls were quoted at $2.

c. Cole Capital Management suggested Melody purchase March 1991 at-the-money put contracts on General Motors, now quoted at $2.

d. MBA Associates suggested Melody keep the stock, purchase March 1991 at-the-money put contracts on GM, and finance the purchase by selling March calls with a strike price of $80.

Disregarding transaction costs, dividend income, and margin requirements, rank order the four alternatives in terms of their fulfilling the strategy of at least preserving the value of Melody's principal at $150,000 and preferably increasing the value to $160,000 by March 1991. Support your conclusions by showing the payoff structure of each alternative.

5. *a.* A butterfly spread is the purchase of one call at exercise price X_1, the sale of two calls at exercise price X_2, and the purchase of one call at exercise price X_3. X_1 is less than X_2, and X_2 is less than X_3 by equal amounts, and all calls have the same expiration date. Graph the payoff diagram to this strategy.

   b. A vertical combination is the purchase of a call with exercise price X_2 and a put with exercise price X_1, with X_2 greater than X_1. Graph the payoff to this strategy.

6. A bearish spread is the purchase of a call with exercise price X_2 and the sale of a call with exercise price X_1, with X_2 greater than X_1. Graph the payoff to this strategy and compare it to Figure 18.13.

7. You are attempting to formulate an investment strategy. On the one hand, you think there is great upward potential in the stock market and would like to participate in the upward move if it materializes. However, you are not able to afford substantial stock market losses and so cannot run the risk of a stock market collapse, which you also think is a possibility. Your investment advisor suggests a protective put position: buy both shares in a market index stock fund and put options on those shares with three-month maturity and exercise price of $260. The stock index is currently selling for $300. However, your uncle suggests you instead buy a three-month call option on the index fund with exercise price $280 and buy three-month T-bills with face value $280.

   a. On the same graph, draw the *payoffs* to each of these strategies as a function of the stock fund value in three months. (Hint: Think of the options as being on one "share" of the stock index fund, with the current price of each share of the index equal to $300.)

b. Which portfolio must require a greater initial outlay to establish? (Hint: Does either portfolio provide a final payoff that is always at least as great as the payoff of the other portfolio?)

c. Suppose the market prices of the securities are as follows:

Stock fund	$300
T-bill (face value 280)	$270
Call (exercise price 280)	$ 40
Put (exercise price 260)	$ 2

Make a table of the profits realized for each portfolio for the following values of the stock price in three months: $S_T = \$0, \$260, \$280, \$300, \$320$.

Graph the profits to each portfolio as a function of S_T on a single graph.

d. Which strategy is riskier? Which should have a higher beta?

e. Explain why the data for the securities given in part (*c*) do *not* violate the put-call parity relationship.

8. The agricultural price support system guarantees farmers a minimum price for their output. Describe the program provisions as an option. What is the asset? The exercise price?

9. In what ways is owning a corporate bond similar to writing a put option? A call option?

10. An executive compensation scheme might provide a manager a bonus of $1,000 for every dollar by which the company's stock price exceeds some cutoff level. In what way is this arrangement equivalent to issuing the manager call options on the firm's stock?

11. Consider the following options portfolio. You write a September maturity call option on IBM with exercise price 105. You write a September IBM put option with exercise price 100.

a. Graph the payoff of this portfolio at option expiration as a function of IBM's stock price at that time.

b. What will be the profit/loss on this position if IBM is selling at 102 on the option maturity date? What if IBM is selling at 115? Use *The Wall Street Journal* listing from Figure 18.1 to answer this question.

c. At what two stock prices will you just break even on your investment?

d. What kind of "bet" is this investor making; that is, what must this investor believe about IBM's stock price in order to justify this position?

Chapter

19

Option Valuation

$\mathbf{I}$n the previous chapter, we examined option markets and strategies. We ended by noting that many securities contain embedded options that affect both their values and their risk-return characteristics. In this chapter, we turn our attention to option valuation issues. To understand most option valuation models requires considerable mathematical and statistical background. Still, many of the ideas and insights of these models can be demonstrated in simple examples, and we will concentrate on these.

We start with a discussion of the factors that ought to affect option prices. After this qualitative discussion, we present a simple "two-state" quantitative option valuation model and show how we can generalize it into a useful and accurate pricing tool. Next, we move on to one particular valuation formula, the famous Black-Scholes model, one of the most significant breakthroughs in finance theory in the past two decades.

Finally, we look at some of the more important applications of option pricing theory in portfolio management and control. One of its most controversial applications has been in the provision of portfolio insurance. After studying this chapter, you should be able to:

- Identify the features of an option that affect its market value.
- Compute an option value in a two-scenario model of the economy.
- Compute the Black-Scholes value of an option.
- Compute the hedge ratio of an option.
- Formulate a portfolio insurance plan using option hedge ratios.

538

19.1   *Option Valuation: Introduction*

Intrinsic and Time Values

Intrinsic value   Stock price minus exercise price, or the profit that could be attained by immediate exercise of an in-the-money call option.

Consider a call option that is out of the money at the moment, with the stock price below the exercise price. This does not mean the option is valueless. Even though immediate exercise today would be unprofitable, the call retains a positive value because there is always a chance the stock price will increase sufficiently by the expiration date to allow for profitable exercise. If not, the worst that can happen is that the option will expire with zero value.

The value $S_0 - X$ is sometimes called the **intrinsic value** of in-the-money call options because it gives the payoff that could be obtained by immediate exercise. Intrinsic value is set equal to zero for out-of-the-money or at-the-money options. The difference between the actual call price and the intrinsic value is commonly called the *time value* of the option.

"Time value" is an unfortunate choice of terminology because it may confuse the option's time value with the time value of money. Time value in the options context refers simply to the difference between the option's price and the value the option would have if it were expiring immediately. It is the part of the option's value that may be attributed to the fact that it still has positive time to expiration.

Most of an option's time value typically is a type of "volatility value." As long as the option holder can choose not to exercise, the payoff cannot be worse than zero. Even if a call option is out of the money now, it still will sell for a positive price because it offers the potential for a profit if the stock price increases, while imposing no risk of additional loss should the stock price fall. The volatility value lies in the value of the right not to exercise the option if that action would be unprofitable. The option to exercise, as opposed to the obligation to exercise, provides insurance against poor stock price performance.

As the stock price increases substantially, it becomes more likely the call option will be exercised by expiration. In this case, with exercise all but assured, the volatility value becomes minimal. As the stock price gets ever larger, the option value approaches the "adjusted" intrinsic value, the stock price minus the present value of the exercise price, $S_0 - PV(X)$.

Why should this be? If you *know* the option will be exercised and the stock purchased for X dollars, it is as though you own the stock already. The stock certificate might as well be sitting in your safe-deposit box now, as it will be there in only a few months. You just haven't paid for it yet. The present value of your obligation is the present value of *X*, so the present value of the net payoff of the call option is $S_0 - PV(X)$.[1]

Figure 19.1 illustrates the call option valuation function. The option always increases in value with the stock price. The slope is greatest, however, when the

---

[1]This discussion presumes the stock pays no dividends until after option expiration. If the stock does pay dividends before maturity, then there *is* a reason you would care about getting the stock now rather than at expiration—getting it now entitles you to the interim dividend payments. In this case, the adjusted intrinsic value of the option must subtract the value of the dividends the stock will pay out before the call is exercised. Adjusted intrinsic value would more generally be defined as $S_0 - PV(X) - PV(D)$ where D is the dividend to be paid before option expiration.

Figure 19.1
**Call option value
before expiration.**

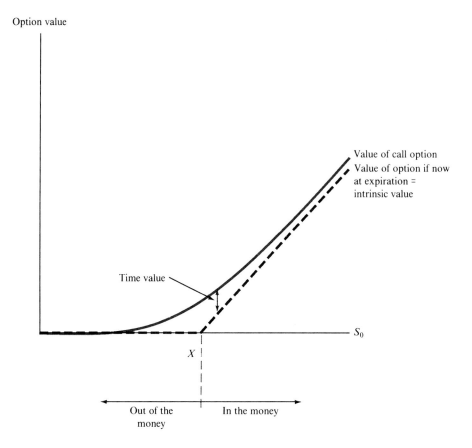

option is deep in the money. In this case, exercise is all but assured, and the option increases in price one for one with the stock price.

Determinants of Option Values

We can identify at least six factors that should affect the value of a call option: the stock price, the exercise price, the volatility of the stock price, the time to expiration, the interest rate, and the dividend rate of the stock. The call option should increase in value with the stock price and decrease in value with the exercise price because the payoff to a call, if exercised, equals $S_T - X$. The magnitude of the expected payoff from the call increases with the difference $S_0 - X$.

Call option value also increases with the volatility of the underlying stock price. To see why, consider circumstances where possible stock prices at expiration may range from $10 to $50 compared to a situation where stock prices may range only from $20 to $40. In both cases, the expected, or average, stock price will be $30. Suppose the exercise price on a call option is also $30. What are the option payoffs?

High-Volatility Scenario

Stock price	$10	$20	$30	$40	$50
Option payoff	0	0	0	10	20

If each outcome is equally likely, with probability 0.2, the expected payoff to the option under high-volatility conditions will be $6.

Low-Volatility Scenario

Stock price	$20	$25	$30	$35	$40
Option payoff	0	0	0	5	10

Again, with equally likely outcomes, the expected payoff to the call option is half as much, only $3.

Despite the fact that the average stock price in each scenario is $30, the average option payoff is greater in the high-volatility scenario. The source of this extra value is the limited loss an option holder can suffer, or the volatility value of the call. No matter how far below $30 the stock price drops, the option holder will get zero. Obviously, extremely poor stock price performance is no worse for the call option holder than moderately poor performance.

In the case of good stock performance, however, the call option will expire in the money, and it will be more profitable the higher the stock price. Thus, extremely good stock outcomes can improve the option payoff without limit, but extremely poor outcomes cannot worsen the payoff below zero. This asymmetry means volatility in the underlying stock price increases the expected payoff to the option, thereby enhancing its value.

Concept Check

> **Question 1.** Should a put option increase in value with the volatility of the stock?

Similarly, longer time to expiration increases the value of a call option. For more distant expiration dates, there is more time for unpredictable future events to affect prices, and the range of likely stock prices increases. This has an effect similar to that of increased volatility. Moreover, as time to expiration lengthens, the present value of the exercise price falls, thereby benefiting the call option holder and increasing the option value. As a corollary to this issue, call option values are higher when interest rates rise (holding the stock price constant) because higher interest rates also reduce the present value of the exercise price.

Finally, the dividend payout policy of the firm affects option values. A high dividend payout policy puts a drag on the rate of growth of the stock price. For any expected total rate of return on the stock, a higher dividend yield must imply a lower expected rate of capital gain. This drag on stock price appreciation decreases the potential payoff from the call option, thereby lowering the call value. Table 19.1 summarizes these relationships.

Concept Check

> **Question 2.** How should the value of a put option respond to the firm's dividend payout policy?

Table 19.1   *Determinants of Call Option Values*

If This Variable Increases,	The Value of a Call Option:
Stock price, S	Increases
Exercise price, X	Decreases
Volatility, σ	Increases
Time to expiration, T	Increases
Interest rate, r_f	Increases
Dividend payouts	Decreases

19.2   *Binomial Option Pricing*

Two-State Option Pricing

A complete understanding of commonly used option valuation formulas is difficult without a substantial mathematics background. Nevertheless, we can develop valuable insight into option valuation by considering a simple special case. Assume a stock price can take only two possible values at option expiration: the stock will either increase to a given higher price or decrease to a given lower price. Although this may seem an extreme simplification, it allows us to come closer to understanding more complicated and realistic models. Moreover, we can extend this approach to describe far more reasonable specifications of stock price behavior. In fact, several major financial firms employ variants of this simple model to value options and securities with option-like features.

Suppose the stock now sells at $100, and the price will either double to $200 or fall in half to $50 by year-end. A call option on the stock might specify an exercise price of $125 and a time to expiration of one year. The interest rate is 8 percent. At year-end, the payoff to the holder of the call option will be either zero, if the stock falls, or $75, if the stock price goes to $200.

These possibilities are illustrated by the following "trees."

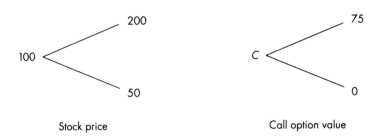

Stock price   Call option value

Compare this payoff to that of a portfolio consisting of one share of the stock and borrowing of $46.30 at the interest rate of 8 percent. The payoff of this portfolio also depends on the stock price at year end:

Value of stock at year end	$50	$200
− Repayment of loan with interest	− 50	− 50
Total	$ 0	$150

We know the cash outlay to establish the portfolio is $53.70: $100 for the stock, less the $46.30 proceeds from borrowing. Therefore, the portfolio's value tree is

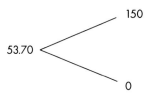

The payoff of this portfolio is exactly twice that of the call option for either value of the stock price. In other words, two call options will exactly replicate the payoff to the portfolio; it follows that two call options should have the same price as the cost of establishing the portfolio. Hence, the two calls should sell for the same price as the "replicating portfolio." Therefore,

$$2C = \$53.70$$

or each call should sell at $C = \$26.85$. Thus, given the stock price, exercise price, interest rate, and volatility of the stock price (as represented by the magnitude of the up or down movements), we can derive the fair value for the call option.

This valuation approach relies heavily on the notion of replication. With only two possible end-of-year values of the stock, the payoffs to the levered stock portfolio replicate the payoffs to two call options and so need to command the same market price. This notion of replication is behind most option pricing formulas. For more complex price distributions for stocks, the replication technique is correspondingly more complex, but the principles remain the same.

One way to view the role of replication is to note that, using the numbers assumed for this example, a portfolio made up of one share of stock and two call options written is perfectly hedged. Its year-end value is independent of the ultimate stock price:

Stock value	$50	$200
− Obligations from 2 calls written	− 0	− 150
Net payoff	$50	$ 50

The investor has formed a riskless portfolio, with a payout of $50. Its value must be the present value of $50, or $50/1.08 = $46.30. The value of the portfolio, which equals $100 from the stock held long, minus 2C from the two calls written, should equal $46.30. Hence, $100 − 2C = $46.30, or C = $26.85.

The ability to create a perfect hedge is the key to this argument. The hedge locks in the end-of-year payout, which can be discounted using the risk-free interest rate. To find the value of the option in terms of the value of the stock, we do not need to know either the option's or the stock's beta or expected rate of return. The perfect hedging, or replication, approach enables us to express the value of the option in terms of the current value of the stock without this information. With a hedged position, the final stock price does not affect the investor's payoff, so the stock's risk and return parameters have no bearing.

The hedge ratio of this example is one share of stock to two calls, or one half. For every call option written, one-half share of stock must be held in the portfolio to hedge away risk. This ratio has an easy interpretation in this context: it is the ratio of the range of the values of the option to those of the stock across the two possible outcomes. The option is worth either zero or $75, for a range of $75. The stock is worth either $50 or $200, for a range of $150. The ratio of ranges, 75/150, is one half, which is the hedge ratio we have established.

The hedge ratio equals the ratio of ranges because the option and stock are perfectly correlated in this two-state example. When the returns of the option and stock are perfectly correlated, a perfect hedge requires that the option and stock be held in a fraction determined only by relative volatility.

We can generalize the hedge ratio for other two-state option problems as

$$H = \frac{C^+ - C^-}{S^+ - S^-}$$

where C^+ or C^- refers to the call option's value when the stock goes up or down, respectively, and S^+ and S^- are the stock prices in the two states. The hedge ratio, H, is the ratio of the swings in the possible end-of-period values of the option and the stock. If the investor writes one option and holds H shares of stock, the value of the portfolio will be unaffected by the stock price. In this case, option pricing is easy: simply set the value of the hedged portfolio equal to the present value of the known payoff.

Using our example, the option pricing technique would proceed as follows:

1. Given the possible end-of-year stock prices, $S^+ = 200$ and $S^- = 50$, and the exercise price of 125, calculate that $C^+ = 75$ and $C^- = 0$. The stock price range is 150, while the option price range is 75.
2. Find that the hedge ratio is $75/150 = .5$.
3. Find that a portfolio made up of 0.5 shares with one written option would have an end-of-year value of $25 with certainty.
4. Show that the present value of $25 with a one-year interest rate of 8 percent is $23.15.
5. Set the value of the hedged position to the present value of the certain payoff:

$$.5S_0 - C_0 = \$23.15$$
$$\$50 - C_0 = \$23.15$$

6. Solve for the call's value, $C_0 = \$26.85$.

What if the option were overpriced, perhaps selling for $30? Then you can make arbitrage profits. Here is how:

	Initial Cash Flow	Cash Flow in 1 Year for Each Possible Stock Price	
		S = 50	S = 200
1. Write 2 options.	$ 60	$ 0	$ −150
2. Purchase 1 share.	−100	50	200
3. Borrow $40 at 8% interest. Repay in 1 year.	40	−43.20	−43.20
Total	$ 0	$ 6.80	$ 6.80

Although the net initial investment is zero, the payoff in one year is positive and riskless. If the option were underpriced, one would simply reverse this arbitrage strategy: buy the option, and sell the stock short to eliminate price risk. Note, by the way, that the present value of the profit to the arbitrage strategy above exactly equals twice the amount by which the option is overpriced. The present value of the risk-free profit of $6.80 at an 8 percent interest rate is $6.30. With two options written in the strategy above, this translates to a profit of $3.15 per option, exactly the amount by which the option was overpriced: $30 versus the "fair value" of $26.85.

Concept Check

Question 3. Suppose the call option had been underpriced, selling at $24. Formulate the arbitrage strategy to exploit the mispricing, and show that it provides a riskless cash flow in one year of $3.08 per option purchased.

Generalizing the Two-State Approach

Although the two-state stock price model seems simplistic, we can generalize it to incorporate more realistic assumptions. To start, suppose we were to break up the year into two six-month segments, and then assert that over each half-year segment the stock price could take on two values. Here we will say it can increase 10 percent or decrease 5 percent. A stock initially selling at 100 could follow these possible paths over the course of the year:

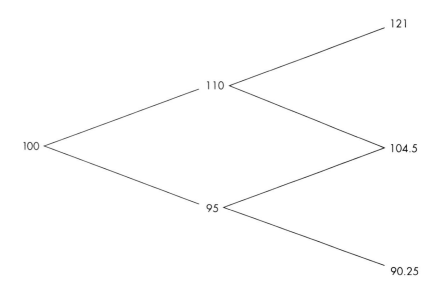

The midrange value of 104.5 can be attained by two paths: an increase of 10 percent followed by a decrease of 5 percent, or a decrease of 5 percent followed by a 10 percent increase.

There are now three possible end-of-year values for the stock and three for the option.

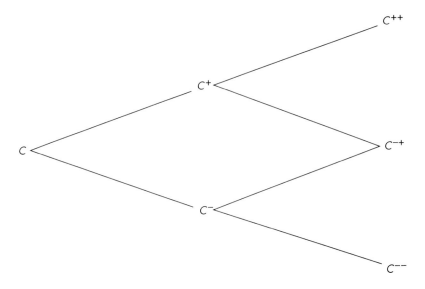

Using methods similar to those we followed above, we could value C^+ from knowledge of C^{++} and C^{+-}, then value C^- from knowledge of C^{-+} and C^{--}, and finally value C from knowledge of C^+ and C^-. And there is no reason to stop at six-month intervals. We could next break the year into four three-month units, or 12 one-month units, or 365 one-day units, each of which would be posited to have a two-state process. Although the calculations become quite numerous and correspondingly tedious, they are easy to program into a computer, and such computer programs are used widely by participants in the options market.

As we break the year into progressively finer subintervals, the range of possible year-end stock prices expands and, in fact, will ultimately take on a familiar bell-shaped distribution. This can be seen from an analysis of the event tree for the stock for a period with three subintervals:

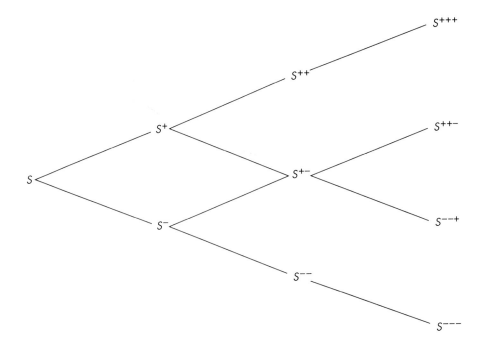

First, notice that as the number of subintervals increases, the number of possible stock prices also increases. Second, notice that extreme events such as S^{+++} or S^{---} are relatively rare, as they require either three consecutive increases or decreases in the three subintervals. More moderate, or midrange, results such as S^{++-} can be arrived at by more than one path—any combination of two price increases and one decrease will result in stock price S^{++-}. Thus, the midrange values will be more likely. The probability of each outcome is described by the binomial distribution, and this multiperiod approach to option pricing is called the **binomial model.**

Binomial model An option valuation model predicated on the assumption that stock prices can move to only two values over any short time period.

For example, using our initial stock price of $100, equal probability of stock price increases or decreases, and three intervals for which the possible price increase is 5 percent and decrease is 3 percent, we can obtain the probability distribution of stock prices from the calculations following. There are eight possible combinations for the stock price movements in the three periods: $+ + +$, $+ + -$, $+ - +$, $- + +$, $+ - -$, $- + -$, $- - +$, $- - -$. Each has probability of 1/8. Therefore, the probability distribution of stock prices at the end of the last interval would be:

Event	*Probability*	*Stock Price*	
3 up movements	1/8	100×1.05^3	$= 115.76$
2 up and 1 down	3/8	$100 \times 1.05^2 \times .97$	$= 106.94$
1 up and 2 down	3/8	$100 \times 1.05 \times .97^2$	$= 98.79$
3 down movements	1/8	$100 \times .97^3$	$= 91.27$

The midrange values are three times as likely to occur as the extreme values. Figure 19.2A is a graph of the frequency distribution for this example. The graph approaches the appearance of the familiar bell-shaped curve. In fact, as the number of intervals increases, as in Figure 19.2B, the frequency distribution progressively approaches the lognormal distribution rather than the normal distribution.[2]

Suppose we were to continue subdividing the interval in which stock prices are posited to move up or down. Eventually, each node of the event tree would correspond to an infinitesimally small time interval. The possible stock price movement within that time interval would be correspondingly small. As those many intervals passed, the end-of-period stock price would more and more closely resemble a lognormal distribution. Thus, the apparent oversimplification of the two-state model can be overcome by progressively subdividing any period into many subperiods.

At any node, one still could set up a portfolio that would be perfectly hedged over the next tiny time interval. Then, at the end of that interval, on reaching the next node, a new hedge ratio could be computed and the portfolio composi-

---

[2]Actually, more complex considerations enter here. The limit of this process is lognormal only if we assume also that stock prices move continuously, by which we mean that over small time intervals only small price movements can occur. This rules out rare events such as sudden, extreme price moves in response to dramatic information (like a takeover attempt). For a treatment of this type of "jump process," see John C. Cox and Stephen A. Ross, "The Valuation of Options for Alternative Stochastic Processes," *Journal of Financial Economics* 3 (January–March 1976), pp. 145–66, or Robert C. Merton, "Option Pricing when Underlying Stock Returns are Discontinuous," *Journal of Financial Economics* 3 (January–March 1976), pp. 125–44.

Figure 19.2
Probability distributions.
A, Possible outcomes and associated probabilities for stock prices after three periods. The stock price starts at $100, and in each period it can increase by 5% or decrease by 3%.
B, Each period is subdivided into two smaller subperiods. Now there are six periods, and in each of these the stock price can increase by 2.5% or fall by 1.5%. As the number of periods increases the stock price distribution approaches the familiar bell-shaped curve.

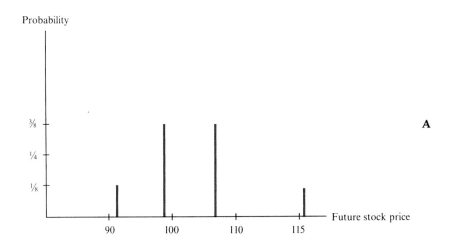

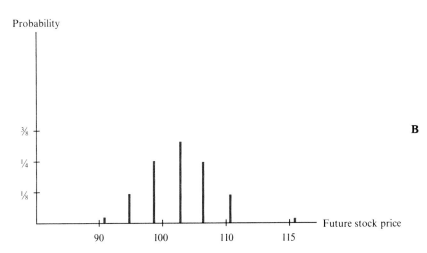

tion could be revised to remain hedged over the coming small interval. By continuously revising the hedge position, the portfolio would remain hedged and would earn a riskless rate of return over each interval. This is called *dynamic hedging,* the continued updating of the hedge ratio as time passes. As the dynamic hedge becomes ever finer, the resulting option valuation procedure becomes more precise.

Concept Check

Question 4. Would you expect the hedge ratio to be higher or lower when the call option is more in the money?

19.3 *Black-Scholes Option Valuation*

While the binomial model we have described is extremely flexible, it requires a computer to be useful in actual trading. An option pricing *formula* would be far easier to use than the involved algorithm involved in the binomial model. It turns out that such a formula can be derived if one is willing to make just two more assumptions: that both the risk-free interest rate and stock price volatility are constant over the life of the option.

The Black-Scholes Formula

Black-Scholes pricing formula An equation to value an option that uses the stock price, the exercise price, the risk-free interest rate, the time to maturity, and the standard deviation of the stock return.

Financial economists searched for years for a workable option pricing model before Black and Scholes (1973) and Merton (1973) derived a formula for the value of a call option. Now widely used by options market participants, the **Black-Scholes pricing formula** for a call option is

$$C_0 = S_0 N(d_1) - X e^{-rT} N(d_2) \tag{19.1}$$

where

$$d_1 = \frac{ln(S_0/X) + (r + \sigma^2/2)T}{\sigma\sqrt{T}}$$
$$d_2 = d_1 - \sigma\sqrt{T}$$

and where

C_0 = Current call option value.
S_0 = Current stock price.
$N(d)$ = The probability that a random draw from a standard normal distribution will be less than d. This equals the area under the normal curve up to d, as in the shaded area of Figure 19.3.
X = Exercise price.
e = 2.71828, the base of the natural log function.
r = Risk-free interest rate (the annualized continuously compounded rate on a safe asset with the same maturity as the expiration of the option, which is to be distinguished from r_f, the discrete period interest rate).
T = Time to maturity of option in years.
ln = Natural logarithm function.
σ = Standard deviation of the annualized continuously compounded rate of return of the stock.

The option value does not depend on the expected rate of return on the stock. In a sense, this information is already built into the formula with inclusion of the stock price, which itself depends on the stock's risk and return characteristics. This version of the Black-Scholes formula is predicted on the assumption that the stock pays no dividends.

Although you may find the Black-Scholes formula intimidating, we can explain it at a somewhat intuitive level. The trick is to view the $N(d)$ terms (loosely) as risk-adjusted probabilities that the call option will expire in the money. First, look at Equation 19.1 assuming both $N(d)$ terms are close to 1.0; that is, when there is a very high probability the option will be exercised. Then the call option value is equal to $S_0 - X e^{-rT}$, which is what we called earlier the adjusted intrinsic value, $S_0 - PV(X)$. This makes sense; if exercise is certain, we have a claim on a stock with current value S_0, and an obligation with present value $PV(X)$, or, with continuous compounding, $X e^{-rT}$.

Figure 19.3
A standard normal curve.

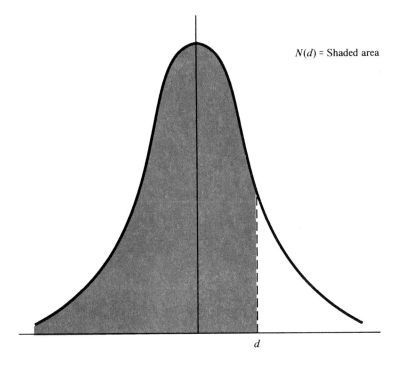

$N(d)$ = Shaded area

d

Now look at Equation 19.1 assuming the $N(d)$ terms are close to zero, meaning the option almost certainly will not be exercised. Then the equation confirms that the call is worth nothing. For middle-range values of $N(d)$ between 0 and 1, Equation 19.1 tells us that the call value can be viewed as the present value of the call's potential payoff adjusting for the probability of in-the-money expiration.

How do the $N(d)$ terms serve as risk-adjusted probabilities? This question quickly leads us into advanced statistics. Notice, however, that d_1 and d_2 both increase as the stock price increases. Therefore, $N(d_1)$ and $N(d_2)$ also increase with higher stock prices. This is the property we would desire of our "probabilities." For higher stock prices relative to exercise prices, future exercise is more likely.

You can use the Black-Scholes formula fairly easily. Suppose you want to value a call option under circumstances as following:

Stock price	S_0 =	100
Exercise price	X =	95
Interest rate	r =	.10
Time to expiration	T =	.25 (one-quarter year)
Standard deviation	σ =	.50

First calculate

$$d_1 = \frac{ln(100/95) + (.10 + .5^2/2).25}{.5\sqrt{.25}} = .43$$
$$d_2 = .43 - .5\sqrt{.25} = .18.$$

Next find $N(d_1)$ and $N(d_2)$. The values of the normal distribution are tabulated and may be found in many statistics textbooks. A table of $N(d)$ is provided here as Table 19.2. The table reveals (using interpolation for .43) that

$$N(.43) = .6664$$
$$N(.18) = .5714.$$

Thus, the value of the call option is

$$C = 100 \times .6664 - 95\, e^{-.10 \times .25} \times .5714$$
$$= 66.64 - 52.94 = \$13.70.$$

Concept Check	**Question 5.** Calculate the call option value if the standard deviation on the stock were 0.6 instead of 0.5. Confirm that the option is worth more using this higher volatility.

What if the option price in our example were \$15 rather than \$13.70? Is the option mispriced? Maybe, but before betting your fortune on that, you may want to reconsider the valuation analysis. First, like all models, the Black-Scholes formula is based on some simplifying abstractions that make the formula only approximately valid.

Some of the important assumptions underlying the formula are the following:

1. The stock will pay no dividends until after the option expiration date.
2. Both the interest rate, r, and variance rate, σ^2, of the stock are constant (or in slightly more general versions of the formula, both are *known* functions of time—any changes are perfectly predictable).
3. Stock prices are continuous, meaning that sudden extreme jumps such as those in the aftermath of an announcement of a takeover attempt are ruled out.

Variants of the Black-Scholes formula have been developed to deal with some of these limitations.

Second, even within the context of the Black-Scholes model, you must be sure of the accuracy of the parameters used in the formula. Four of these—S_0, X, T, and r—are straightforward. The stock price, exercise price, and time to maturity are readily determined. The interest rate used is the money market rate for a maturity equal to that of the option.

The last input, though, the standard deviation of the stock return, is not directly observable. It must be estimated from historical data, from scenario analysis, or from the prices of other options, as we will describe momentarily. Because the standard deviation must be estimated, it is always possible that discrepancies between an option price and its Black-Scholes value are simply artifacts of error in the estimation of the stock's volatility.

In fact, market participants often give the option valuation problem a different twist. Rather than calculating a Black-Scholes option value for a given stock standard deviation, they ask instead: "what standard deviation would be necessary for the option price that I can see to be consistent with the Black-Scholes

Table 19.2 *Cumulative Normal Distribution*

d	N(d)	d	N(d)	d	N(d)
−3.00	.0013	−1.58	.0571	−0.76	.2236
−2.95	.0016	−1.56	.0594	−0.74	.2297
−2.90	.0019	−1.54	.0618	−0.72	.2358
−2.85	.0022	−1.52	.0643	−0.70	.2420
−2.80	.0026	−1.50	.0668	−0.68	.2483
−2.75	.0030	−1.48	.0694	−0.66	.2546
−2.70	.0035	−1.46	.0721	−0.64	.2611
−2.65	.0040	−1.44	.0749	−0.62	.2676
−2.60	.0047	−1.42	.0778	−0.60	.2743
−2.55	.0054	−1.40	.0808	−0.58	.2810
−2.50	.0062	−1.38	.0838	−0.56	.2877
−2.45	.0071	−1.36	.0869	−0.54	.2946
−2.40	.0082	−1.34	.0901	−0.52	.3015
−2.35	.0094	−1.32	.0934	−0.50	.3085
−2.30	.0107	−1.30	.0968	−0.48	.3156
−2.25	.0122	−1.28	.1003	−0.46	.3228
−2.20	.0139	−1.26	.1038	−0.44	.3300
−2.15	.0158	−1.24	.1075	−0.42	.3373
−2.10	.0179	−1.22	.1112	−0.40	.3446
−2.05	.0202	−1.20	.1151	−0.38	.3520
−2.00	.0228	−1.18	.1190	−0.36	.3594
−1.98	.0239	−1.16	.1230	−0.34	.3669
−1.96	.0250	−1.14	.1271	−0.32	.3745
−1.94	.0262	−1.12	.1314	−0.30	.3821
−1.92	.0274	−1.10	.1357	−0.28	.3897
−1.90	.0287	−1.08	.1401	−0.26	.3974
−1.88	.0301	−1.06	.1446	−0.24	.4052
−1.86	.0314	−1.04	.1492	−0.22	.4129
−1.84	.0329	−1.02	.1539	−0.20	.4207
−1.82	.0344	−1.00	.1587	−0.18	.4286
−1.80	.0359	−0.98	.1635	−0.16	.4365
−1.78	.0375	−0.96	.1685	−0.14	.4443
−1.76	.0392	−0.94	.1736	−0.12	.4523
−1.74	.0409	−0.92	.1788	−0.10	.4602
−1.72	.0427	−0.90	.1841	−0.08	.4681
−1.70	.0446	−0.88	.1894	−0.06	.4761
−1.68	.0465	−0.86	.1949	−0.04	.4841
−1.66	.0485	−0.84	.2005	−0.02	.4920
−1.64	.0505	−0.82	.2061	0.00	.5000
−1.62	.0526	−0.80	.2119	0.02	.5080
−1.60	.0548	−0.78	.2177	0.04	.5160

Implied volatility
The standard deviation of stock returns that is consistent with an option's market value.

formula?" This is called the **implied volatility** of the option, the volatility level for the stock that the option price implies. Investors can then judge whether they think the actual stock standard deviation exceeds the implied volatility. If it does, the option is considered a good buy; if actual volatility seems greater than the implied volatility, its fair price would exceed the observed price.

Another variation is to compare two options on the same stock with equal expiration dates but different exercise prices. The option with the higher implied volatility would be considered relatively expensive, because a higher standard

Table 19.2 *Concluded*

d	N(d)	d	N(d)	d	N(d)
0.06	.5239	0.86	.8051	1.66	.9515
0.08	.5319	0.88	.8106	1.68	.9535
0.10	.5398	0.90	.8159	1.70	.9554
0.12	.5478	0.92	.8212	1.72	.9573
0.14	.5557	0.94	.8264	1.74	.9591
0.16	.5636	0.96	.8315	1.76	.9608
0.18	.5714	0.98	.8365	1.78	.9625
0.20	.5793	1.00	.8414	1.80	.9641
0.22	.5871	1.02	.8461	1.82	.9656
0.24	.5948	1.04	.8508	1.84	.9671
0.26	.6026	1.06	.8554	1.86	.9686
0.28	.6103	1.08	.8599	1.88	.9699
0.30	.6179	1.10	.8643	1.90	.9713
0.32	.6255	1.12	.8686	1.92	.9726
0.34	.6331	1.14	.8729	1.94	.9738
0.36	.6406	1.16	.8770	1.96	.9750
0.38	.6480	1.18	.8810	1.98	.9761
0.40	.6554	1.20	.8849	2.00	.9772
0.42	.6628	1.22	.8888	2.05	.9798
0.44	.6700	1.24	.8925	2.10	.9821
0.46	.6773	1.26	.8962	2.15	.9842
0.48	.6844	1.28	.8997	2.20	.9861
0.50	.6915	1.30	.9032	2.25	.9878
0.52	.6985	1.32	.9066	2.30	.9893
0.54	.7054	1.34	.9099	2.35	.9906
0.56	.7123	1.36	.9131	2.40	.9918
0.58	.7191	1.38	.9162	2.45	.9929
0.60	.7258	1.40	.9192	2.50	.9938
0.62	.7324	1.42	.9222	2.55	.9946
0.64	.7389	1.44	.9251	2.60	.9953
0.66	.7454	1.46	.9279	2.65	.9960
0.68	.7518	1.48	.9306	2.70	.9965
0.70	.7580	1.50	.9332	2.75	.9970
0.72	.7642	1.52	.9357	2.80	.9974
0.74	.7704	1.54	.9382	2.85	.9978
0.76	.7764	1.56	.9406	2.90	.9981
0.78	.7823	1.58	.9429	2.95	.9984
0.80	.7882	1.60	.9452	3.00	.9986
0.82	.7939	1.62	.9474	3.05	.9989
0.84	.7996	1.64	.9495		

deviation is required to justify its price. The analyst might consider buying the option with the lower implied volatility and writing the option with the higher implied volatility.

Concept Check

Question 6. Consider the option in the example selling for $15 with Black-Scholes value of $13.70. Is its implied volatility more or less than 0.5?

Put Option Valuation

We have concentrated so far on call option valuation. We can derive Black-Scholes European put option values from call option values using the put-call parity theorem. To value the put option, we simply calculate the value of the corresponding call option in Equation 19.1 from the Black-Scholes formula, and solve for the put option value as

$$P = C + PV(X) - S_0.$$ (19.2)
$$= C + Xe^{-rT} - S_0.$$

We must calculate the present value of the exercise price using continuous compounding to be consistent with the Black-Scholes formula.

Using data from the Black-Scholes call option example ($C = \$13.70$, $X = \$95$, $S = \$100$, $r = .10$, and $T = .25$), we find that a European put option on that stock with identical exercise price and time to maturity is worth

$$P = \$13.70 + \$95e^{-.10 \times .25} - \$100 = \$6.35.$$

As we noted traders can do, we might then compare this formula value to the actual put price as one step in formulating a trading strategy.

Equation 19.2 is valid for European puts on nondividend paying stocks. Listed put options are American options that offer the opportunity of early exercise, however. Because an American option allows its owner to exercise at any time before the expiration date, it must be worth at least as much as the corresponding European option. Therefore, while Equation 19.2 describes only the lower bound on the true value of the American put, in many applications the approximation is very accurate.

19.4   *Using the Black-Scholes Formula*

Hedge Ratios and the Black-Scholes Formula

Hedge ratio or delta   The number of stocks required to hedge against the price risk of holding one option.

In the last chapter, we considered two investments in IBM: 1,000 shares of IBM stock or 10,000 call options on IBM. We saw that the call option position was more sensitive to swings in IBM's stock price than the all-stock position. To analyze the overall exposure to a stock price more precisely, however, it is necessary to quantify these relative sensitivities. A tool that enables us to summarize the overall exposure of portfolios of options with various exercise prices and times to maturity is the hedge ratio. An option's **hedge ratio** is the change in the price of an option for $1 increase in the stock price. A call option, therefore, has a positive hedge ratio and a put option a negative hedge ratio. The hedge ratio is commonly called the option's **delta.**

If you were to graph the option value as a function of the stock value as we have done for a call option in Figure 19.4, the hedge ratio is simply the slope of the value function evaluated at the current stock price. For example, suppose the slope of the curve at $S_0 = \$120$ equals .60. As the stock increases in value by $1, the option increases by approximately $.60, as the figure shows.

For every call option written, 0.60 shares of stock would be needed to hedge the investor's portfolio. For example, if one writes 10 options and holds six

Figure 19.4
Call option value and hedge ratio.

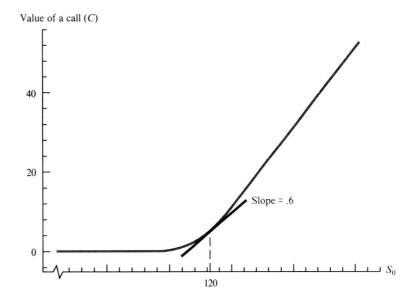

shares of stock, according to the hedge ratio of 0.6, a $1 increase in stock price will result in a gain of $6 on the stock holdings, while the loss on the 10 options written will be 10 × $0.60, an equivalent $6. The stock price movement leaves total wealth unaltered, which is what a hedged position is intended to do. The investor holding the stock and an option in proportions dictated by their relative price movements hedges the portfolio.

Black-Scholes hedge ratios are particularly easy to compute. The hedge ratio for a call is $N(d_1)$, while the hedge ratio for a put is $N(d_1) - 1$. We defined $N(d_1)$ as part of the Black-Scholes formula in Equation 19.1. Recall that $N(d)$ stands for the area under the standard normal curve up to d. Therefore, the call option hedge ratio must be positive and less than 1.0, while the put option hedge ratio is negative and of smaller absolute value than 1.0.

Figure 19.4 verifies the insight that the slope of the call option valuation function is less than 1.0, approaching 1.0 only as the stock price becomes extremely large. This tells us that option values change less than one for one with changes in stock prices. Why should this be? Suppose an option is so far in the money that you are absolutely certain it will be exercised. In that case, every dollar increase in the stock price would increase the option value by one dollar. But if there is a reasonable chance the call option will expire out of the money, even after a moderate stock price gain, a $1 increase in the stock price will not necessarily increase the ultimate payoff to the call; therefore, the call price will not respond by a full dollar.

The fact that hedge ratios are less than 1.0 does not contradict our earlier observation that options offer leverage and are sensitive to stock price movements. Although *dollar* movements in option prices are slighter than dollar movements in the stock price, the *rate of return* volatility of options remains greater than stock return volatility because options sell at smaller prices. In our example, with the stock selling at $120, and a hedge ratio of 0.6, an option with exercise price $120 may sell for $5. If the stock price increases to $121, the call price would be expected to increase by only $.60 to $5.60. The percentage increase in the option value is $.60/$5.00 = 12 percent, however, while the stock

Option elasticity The percentage increase in an option's value given a 1% change in the value of the underlying security.

price increase is only $1/$120 = .83 percent. The ratio of the percent changes is 12%/.83% = 14.4. For every 1 percent increase in the stock price, the option price increases by 14.4 percent. This ratio, the percent change in option price per percent change in stock price, is called the **option elasticity.**

The hedge ratio is an essential tool in portfolio management and control. An example will show why. Consider two portfolios, one holding 750 IBM calls and 200 shares of IBM and the other holding 800 shares of IBM. Which portfolio has greater dollar exposure to IBM price movements? You can answer this question easily using the hedge ratio.

Each option changes in value by H dollars for each dollar change in stock price, where H stands for the hedge ratio. Thus, if H equals 0.6, the 750 options are equivalent to 450 (.6 × 750) shares in terms of the response of their market value to IBM stock price movements. The first portfolio has less dollar sensitivity to stock price change because the 450 share-equivalents of the options plus the 200 shares actually held are less than the 800 shares held in the second portfolio.

This is not to say, however, the first portfolio is less sensitive to the stock's rate of return changes. As we noted in discussing option elasticities, the first portfolio may be of lower total value than the second, so despite its lower sensitivity in terms of total market value, it might have greater rate of return sensitivity. Because a call option has a lower market value than the stock, its price changes more than proportionally with stock price changes, even though its hedge ratio is less than 1.0.

Concept Check

Question 7. What is the elasticity of a put option currently selling for $4 with exercise price $120, and hedge ratio −.4 if the stock price is currently $122?

Portfolio Insurance

Portfolio insurance The practice of using options or dynamic hedge strategies to provide protection against investment losses while maintaining upside potential.

In Chapter 18, we showed that protective put strategies offer a sort of insurance policy on an asset. The protective put has proved to be extremely popular with investors. Even if the asset price falls, the put conveys the right to sell the asset for the exercise price, which is a way to lock in a minimum portfolio value. With an at-the-money put $(X = S_0)$, the maximum loss that can be realized is the cost of the put. The asset can be sold for X, which equals its original value, so even if the asset price falls, the investor's net loss over the period is just the cost of the put. If the asset value increases, however, upside potential is unlimited. Figure 5.19 graphs the profit or loss on a protective put position as a function of the change in the value of the underlying asset.

While the protective put is a simple and convenient way to achieve **portfolio insurance,** that is, to limit the worst-case portfolio rate of return, there are practical difficulties in trying to insure a portfolio of stocks. First, unless the investor's portfolio corresponds to a standard market index for which puts are traded, a put option on the portfolio will not be available for purchase. And if index puts are used to protect a nonindexed portfolio, tracking error can result. For example, if the portfolio falls in value while the market index rises, the put will fail to provide the intended protection. Tracking error limits the investor's

Figure 19.5
**Return characteristics
for a portfolio with a
protective put.**

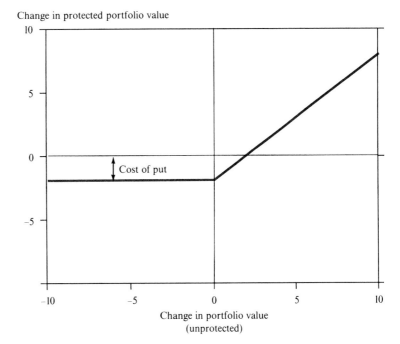

freedom to pursue active stock selection because such error will be greater as the managed portfolio departs more substantially from the market index.

Moreover, the desired horizon of the insurance program must match the maturity of a traded put option in order to establish the appropriate protective put position. While most insurance programs have horizons of several years, actively traded puts are limited to maturities of less than a year. Rolling over a sequence of short-term puts, which might be viewed as a response to this problem, introduces new risks because the prices at which successive puts will be available in the future are not known today.

Providers of portfolio insurance with horizons of several years, therefore, cannot rely on the simple expedient of purchasing protective puts for their clients' portfolios. Instead, they follow trading strategies that replicate the payoffs to the protective put position.

Here is the general idea. Even if a put option on the desired portfolio with the desired expiration date does not exist, a theoretical option pricing model (such as the Black-Scholes model) can be used to determine how that option's price would respond to the portfolio's value if the option did trade. For example, if stock prices were to fall, the put option would increase in value. The option model could quantify this relationship. The net exposure of the (hypothetical) protective put portfolio to swings in stock prices is the sum of the exposures of the two components of the portfolio, the stock and the put. The net exposure of the portfolio equals the equity exposure less the (offsetting) put option exposure.

We can create "synthetic" protective put positions by holding a quantity of stocks with the same net exposure to market swings as the hypothetical protective put position. The key to this strategy is the option delta, or hedge ratio, that is, the change in the price of the protective put option per change in the value of the underlying stock portfolio.

An example will clarify the procedure. Suppose a portfolio is currently valued at $100 million. An at-the-money put option on the portfolio might have a hedge ratio or delta of $-.6$, meaning the option's value swings $.60 for every dollar change in portfolio value, but in an opposite direction. Suppose the stock portfolio falls in value by 2 percent. The profit on a hypothetical protective put position (if the put existed) would be as follows (in millions of dollars):

Loss on stocks	2% of $100	=	$2.00
+ Gain on put:	.6 × $2.00	=	1.20
Net loss			$ .80

We create the synthetic option position by selling a proportion of shares equal to the put option's delta (i.e., selling 60 percent of the shares) and placing the proceeds in risk-free T-bills. The rationale is that the hypothetical put option would have offset 60 percent of any change in the stock portfolio's value, so one must reduce portfolio risk directly by selling 60 percent of the equity and putting the proceeds into a risk-free asset. Total return on a synthetic protective put position with $60 million in risk-free investments such as T-bills and $40 million in equity is

Loss on stocks:	2% of $40	=	$.80
+ Loss on bills:		=	0
Net loss		=	$.80

The synthetic and actual protective put positions have equal returns. We conclude that if you sell a proportion of shares equal to the put option's delta and place the proceeds in cash equivalents, your exposure to the stock market will equal that of the desired protective put position.

The difficulty with this procedure is that deltas constantly change. Figure 19.6 shows that as the stock price falls, the magnitude of the appropriate hedge ratio increases. Therefore, market declines require extra hedging, that is, additional conversion of equity into cash. This constant updating of the hedge ratio is

Dynamic hedging
Constant updating of hedge positions as market conditions change.

called **dynamic hedging.**

Dynamic hedging is one reason portfolio insurance has been said to contribute to market volatility. Market declines trigger additional sales of stock as portfolio insurers strive to increase their hedging. These additional sales are seen as reinforcing or exaggerating market downturns.

In practice, portfolio insurers do not actually buy or sell stocks directly when they update their hedge positions. Instead, they minimize trading costs by buying or selling stock index futures as a substitute for sale of the stocks themselves. As you will see in the next chapter, stock prices and index futures prices

Figure 19.6
Hedge ratios change as the stock price fluctuates.

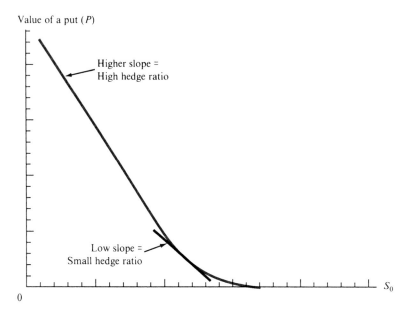

Value of a put (P)

Higher slope = High hedge ratio

Low slope = Small hedge ratio

S_0

0

usually are very tightly linked by cross-market arbitrageurs so that futures transactions can be used as reliable proxies for stock transactions. Instead of selling equities based on the put option's delta, insurers will sell an equivalent number of futures contracts.[3]

Several portfolio insurers suffered great setbacks during the market "crash" of October 19, 1987, when the Dow Jones Industrial Average fell more than 500 points. A description of what happened then should let you appreciate the complexities of applying a seemingly straightforward hedging concept.

1. Market volatility at the crash was much greater than ever encountered before. Put option deltas based on historical experience were too low; insurers underhedged, held too much equity, and suffered excessive losses.

2. Prices moved so fast that insurers could not keep up with the necessary rebalancing. They were "chasing deltas" that kept getting away from them. The futures market saw a "gap" opening, where the opening price was nearly 10 percent below the previous day's close. The price dropped before insurers could update their hedge ratios.

3. Execution problems were severe. First, current market prices were unavailable, with trade execution and the price quotation system hours behind, which made computation of correct hedge ratios impossible. Moreover, trading in stocks and stock futures ceased during some periods. The continuous rebalancing capability that is essential for a viable insurance program vanished during the precipitous market collapse.

4. Futures prices traded at steep discounts to their proper levels compared to reported stock prices, thereby making the sale of futures (as a proxy for equity sales) to increase hedging seem expensive. While you will see in the next

---

[3]Notice, however, that the use of index futures reintroduces the problem of tracking error between the portfolio and the market index.

Figure 19.7
S&P 500 cash-to-futures spread in points at 15-minute intervals.

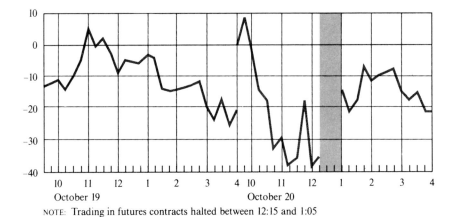

NOTE: Trading in futures contracts halted between 12:15 and 1:05

chapter that stock index futures prices normally exceed the value of the stock index, Figure 19.7 shows that on October 19, futures sold far below the stock index level. The so-called cash-to-futures spread was negative most of the day. When some insurers gambled that the futures price would recover to its usual premium over the stock index, and chose to defer sales, they remained under-hedged. As the market fell farther, their portfolios experienced substantial losses.

Most observers believe the portfolio insurance industry will never recover from the market crash. Participants are now far more sensitive to the practical difficulties in successfully implementing an insurance program. Direct rather than synthetic option strategies now appear more attractive. In this regard, the CBOE has introduced longer-term index options called LEAPS with maturities of a few years.

19.5   *Empirical Evidence*

There have been an enormous number of empirical tests of the Black-Scholes option pricing model. For the most part, the results of the studies have been positive in that the Black-Scholes model generates option values fairly close to the actual prices at which options trade. At the same time, some regular empirical failures of the model have been noted. Geske and Roll (1984) have argued that these empirical results can be attributed to the failure of the Black-Scholes model to account for the possible early exercise of American calls on stocks that pay dividends. They show that the theoretical bias induced by this failure corresponds exactly to the actual "mispricing" observed empirically.

Whaley (1982) examines the performance of the Black-Scholes formula relative to that of more complicated option formulas that allow for early exercise. His findings indicate formulas that allow for the possibility of early exercise do better at pricing than the Black-Scholes formula. The Black-Scholes formula seems to perform worst for options on stocks with high dividend payouts. The true American call option formula, on the other hand, seems to fare equally well in the prediction of option prices on stocks with high or low dividend payouts.

Summary

1. Option values may be viewed as the sum of intrinsic value plus time or "volatility" value. The volatility value is the right to choose not to exercise if the stock price moves against the holder. Thus, option holders cannot lose more than the cost of the option regardless of stock price performance.

2. Call options are more valuable when the exercise price is lower, when the stock price is higher, when the interest rate is higher, when the time to maturity is greater, when the stock's volatility is greater, and when dividends are lower.

3. European put option values can be derived using call option values and the put-call parity theorem.

4. Options may be priced relative to the underlying stock price using a simple two-period, two-state pricing model. As the number of periods increases, the model can approximate more realistic stock price distributions. The Black-Scholes formula may be seen as a limiting case of the binomial option model, as the holding period is divided into progressively smaller subperiods when the interest rate and stock volatility are constant.

5. The hedge ratio is the number of shares of stock required to hedge the price risk involved in writing one option. Hedge ratios are near zero for deep out-of-the-money call options and approach 1.0 for deep in-the-money calls.

6. Although hedge ratios are less than 1.0, call options have elasticities greater than 1.0. The rate of return on a call (as opposed to the dollar return) responds more than one for one with stock price movements.

7. Portfolio insurance can be obtained by purchasing a protective put option on an equity position. When the appropriate put is not traded, portfolio insurance entails a dynamic hedge strategy where a fraction of the equity portfolio equal to the desired put option's delta is sold and placed in risk-free securities.

Key Terms

binomial model, 547
Black-Scholes pricing
    formula, 549
delta, 554

dynamic hedging, 558
hedge ratio, 554
implied volatility, 552

intrinsic value, 539
option elasticity, 556
portfolio insurance, 556

Selected Readings

The breakthrough articles in option pricing are:
    Black, Fischer, and Myron Scholes. "The Pricing of Options and Corporate Liabilities." *Journal of Political Economy* 81 (May–June 1973), pp. 637–59.
    Merton, Robert C. "Theory of Rational Option Pricing." *Bell Journal of Economics and Management Science* 4 (Spring 1973), pp. 141–83.

Good articles on portfolio insurance and replication strategies are:
    Perold, Andre F., and William F. Sharpe. "Dynamic Strategies for Asset Allocation." *Financial Analysts Journal*, January–February 1988, pp. 16–27.
    Rubinstein, Mark, and Hayne Leland. "Replicating Options with Positions in Stock and Cash." *Financial Analysts Journal*, July–August 1981.

The January–February 1988 edition of Financial Analysts Journal *is devoted to issues surrounding portfolio insurance.*

The two-state approach was first suggested in:
 Sharpe, William F. *Investments*. Englewood Cliffs, N.J.: Prentice Hall, 1978.

The approach was developed more fully in:
 Rendelman, Richard J., Jr., and Brit J. Bartter. "Two-State Option Pricing."
 Journal of Finance 34, December 1979, pp. 1093–110.
 Cox, John C., Stephen Ross, and Mark Rubinstein. "Option Pricing: A Simplified
 Approach." *Journal of Financial Economics* 7 (September 1979), pp. 229–63.

Problem Sets

1. We showed in the text that the value of a call option increases with the volatility of the stock. Is this also true of put option values? Use the put-call parity theorem as well as a numerical example to prove your answer.

2. In each of the following questions, you are asked to compare two options with parameters as given. The risk-free interest rate for *all* cases should be assumed to be 6 percent. Assume the stocks on which these options are written pay no dividends.

i.

Put	T	X	σ	Price of Option
A	.5	50	.20	10
B	.5	50	.25	10

Which put option is written on the stock with the lower price?
 a. A.
 b. B.
 c. Not enough information.

ii.

Put	T	S	σ	Price of Option
A	.5	50	.2	10
B	.5	50	.2	12

Which put option must be written on the stock with the lower price?
 a. A.
 b. B.
 c. Not enough information.

iii.

Call	S	X	σ	Price of Option
A	50	50	.20	12
B	55	50	.20	10

Which call option must have the least time to maturity?

a. A.

b. B.

c. Not enough information.

iv.

Call	T	X	S	Price of Option
A	.5	50	55	10
B	.5	50	55	12

Which call option is written on the stock with higher volatility?

a. A.

b. B.

c. Not enough information.

v.

Call	T	X	S	Price of Option
A	.5	50	55	10
B	.5	55	55	7

Which call option is written on the stock with higher volatility?

a. A.

b. B.

c. Not enough information.

3. Reconsider the determination of the hedge ratio in the two-state model (page 544), where we showed that one half share of stock would hedge one option. What is the hedge ratio at the following exercise prices: 115, 100, 75, 50, 25, 10? What do you conclude about the hedge ratio as the option becomes progressively more in the money?

4. Show that Black-Scholes call option hedge ratios also increase as the stock price increases. Consider a one-year option with exercise price $50, on a stock with annual standard deviation 20 percent. The T-bill rate is 8 percent per year. Find $N(d_1)$ for stock prices $45, $50, and $55.

5. We will derive a two-state put option value in this problem. Data: $S_0 = 100$; $X = 110$; $1 + r = 1.1$. The two possibilities for S_T are 130 and 80.

   a. Show that the range of S is 50 while that of P is 30 across the two states. What is the hedge ratio of the put?

   b. Form a portfolio of three shares of stock and five puts. What is the (nonrandom) payoff to this portfolio? What is the present value of the portfolio?

   c. Given that the stock currently is selling at 100, solve for the value of the put. (Answer = 10.91)

6. Calculate the value of the call option on the stock in Question 5 with an exercise price of 110. Verify that the put-call parity theorem is satisfied by your answers to Questions 5 and 6. (Do not use continuous compounding to calculate the present value of X in this example because we are using a two-state model here, not a continuous-time Black-Scholes model.)

7. Use the Black-Scholes formula to find the value of a call option on the following stock:

Time to maturity	=	6 months
Standard deviation	=	50 percent per year
Exercise price	=	50
Stock price	=	50
Interest rate	=	10 percent

8. Recalculate the value of the option in question 7, successively substituting one of the changes below while keeping the other parameters as in question 7:
   a. Time to maturity = 3 months
   b. Standard deviation = 25 percent per year
   c. Exercise price = $55
   d. Stock price = $55
   e. Interest rate = 15 percent
   Consider each scenario independently. Confirm that the option value changes in accordance with the prediction of Table 19.1.

9. Would you expect a $1 increase in a call option's exercise price to lead to a decrease in the option's value of more or less than $1?

10. All else equal, is a put option on a high beta stock worth more than one on a low beta stock?

11. All else equal, is a call option on a stock with a lot of firm-specific risk worth more than one on a stock with little firm-specific risk?

12. All else equal, will a call option with a high exercise price have a higher or lower hedge ratio than one with a low exercise price?

13. Should the rate of return of a call option on a long-term Treasury bond be more or less sensitive to changes in interest rates than is the rate of return of the underlying bond?

14. If the stock price falls and the call price rises, then what has happened to the call option's implied volatility?

15. If the time to maturity falls and the put price rises, then what has happened to the put option's implied volatility?

16. According to the Black-Scholes formula, what will be the value of the hedge ratio of a call option as the stock price becomes infinitely large? Explain briefly.

17. According to the Black-Scholes formula, what will be the value of the hedge ratio of a put option for a very small exercise price?

18. The hedge ratio of an at-the-money call option on IBM is 0.4. The hedge ratio of an at-the-money put option is $-.5$. What is the hedge ratio of an at-the-money straddle position on IBM?

19. These three put options all are written on the same stock. One has a delta of $-.9$, one a delta of $-.5$, and one a delta of $-.1$. Assign deltas to the three puts by filling in this table.

Put	X	Delta
A	10	
B	20	
C	30	

20. You are *very* bullish (optimistic) on stock EFG, much more so than the rest of the market. In each question, choose the portfolio strategy that will give you the

biggest dollar profit if your bullish forecast turns out to be correct. Explain your answer.

a. *Choice A:* $100,000 invested in calls with $X = 50$.

   Choice B: $10,000 invested in EFG stock.

b. *Choice A:* 10 call options contracts (for 100 shares each), with $X = 50$.

   Choice B: 1,000 shares of EFG stock.

21. Imagine you are a provider of portfolio insurance. You are establishing a four-year program. The portfolio you manage is currently worth $100 million, and you hope to provide a minimum return of 0 percent. The equity portfolio has a standard deviation of 25 percent per year, and T-bills pay 5 percent per year. Assume for simplicity that the portfolio pays no dividends (or that all dividends are reinvested).

    a. What fraction of the portfolio should be placed in bills? What fraction in equity?

    b. What should the manager do if the stock portfolio falls by 3 percent on the first day of trading?

22. You would like to be holding a protective put position on the stock of XYZ Co. to lock in a guaranteed minimum value of $100 at year-end. XYZ currently sells for $100. Over the next year, the stock price will increase by 10 percent or decrease by 10 percent. The T-bill rate is 5 percent. Unfortunately, no put options are traded on XYZ Co.

    a. Suppose the desired put option were traded. How much would it cost to purchase?

    b. What would have been the cost of the protective put portfolio?

    c. What portfolio position in stock and T-bills will ensure you a payoff equal to the payoff that would be provided by a protective put with $X = 100$? Show that the payoff to this portfolio and the cost of establishing the portfolio matches that of the desired protective put.

Chapter

20

Futures Markets

$\mathbf{F}$utures and forward contracts are like options in that they specify purchase or sale of some underlying security at some future date. The key difference is that the holder of an option to buy is not compelled to buy and will not do so if the trade is unprofitable. A futures or forward contract, however, carries the obligation to go through with the agreed-upon transaction.

A forward contract is not an investment in the strict sense that funds are paid for an asset. It is only a commitment today to transact in the future. Forward arrangements are part of our study of investments, however, because they offer powerful means to hedge other investments and generally modify portfolio characteristics.

Forward markets for future delivery of various commodities go back at least to ancient Greece. Organized *futures markets,* though, are a relatively modern development, dating only to the 19th century. Futures markets replace informal forward contracts with highly standardized, exchange-traded securities.

This chapter describes the workings of futures markets and the mechanics of trading in these markets. We show how futures contracts are useful investment vehicles for both hedgers and speculators and how the futures price relates to the spot price of an asset. Finally, we take a look at some specific financial futures contracts—those written on stock indexes, foreign exchange, and fixed-income securities. After studying this chapter you should be able to:

- Calculate the profit on futures positions as a function of current and eventual futures prices.
- Formulate futures markets strategies for hedging or speculative purposes.
- Compute the futures price appropriate to a given price on the underlying asset.
- Design arbitrage strategies to exploit futures market mispricing.

20.1   *The Futures Contract*

To see how futures and forwards work and how they might be useful, consider the portfolio diversification problem facing a farmer growing a single crop, let us say wheat. The entire planting season's revenue depends critically on the highly volatile crop price. The farmer can't easily diversify his position because virtually his entire wealth is tied up in the crop.

The miller who must purchase wheat for processing faces a portfolio problem that is the mirror image of the farmer's. He is subject to profit uncertainty because of the unpredictable future cost of the wheat.

Forward contract   An arrangement calling for future delivery of an asset at an agreed-upon price.

Both parties can reduce this source of risk if they enter into a **forward contract** requiring the farmer to deliver the wheat when harvested at a price agreed upon now, regardless of the market price at harvest time. No money need change hands at this time. A forward contract is simply a deferred-delivery sale of some asset with the sales price agreed on now. All that is required is that each party be willing to lock in the ultimate price to be paid or received for delivery of the commodity. A forward contract protects each party from future price fluctuations.

Futures markets formalize and standardize forward contracting. Buyers and sellers do not have to rely on a chance matching of their interests; they can trade in a centralized futures market. The futures exchange also standardizes the types of contracts that may be traded: it establishes contract size, the acceptable grade of commodity, contract delivery dates, and so forth. While standardization eliminates much of the flexibility available in informal forward contracting, it has the offsetting advantage of liquidity because many traders will concentrate on the same small set of contracts. Futures contracts also differ from forward contracts in that they call for a daily settling up of any gains or losses on the contract. In the case of forward contracts, no money changes hands until the delivery date.

In a centralized market, buyers and sellers can trade through brokers without personally searching for trading partners. The standardization of contracts and the depth of trading in each contract allows futures positions to be liquidated easily through a broker rather than personally renegotiated with the other party to the contract. Because the exchange guarantees the performance of each party to the contract, costly credit checks on other traders are not necessary. Instead, each trader simply posts a good faith deposit, called the *margin,* in order to guarantee contract performance.

The Basics of Futures Contracts

Futures price   The agreed-upon price to be paid on a futures contract at maturity.

The futures contract calls for delivery of a commodity at a specified delivery or maturity date, for an agreed-upon price, called the **futures price,** to be paid at contract maturity. The contract specifies precise requirements for the commodity. For agricultural commodities, the exchange sets allowable grades (e.g., No. 2 hard winter wheat or No. 1 soft red wheat). The place or means of delivery of the commodity is specified as well. Delivery of agricultural commodities is made by transfer of warehouse receipts issued by approved warehouses. In the case of financial futures, delivery may be made by wire transfer; in the case of index futures, delivery may be accomplished by a cash settlement procedure such as those for index options. (Although the futures contract technically calls for delivery of an asset, delivery rarely occurs. Instead, parties to the contract much more commonly close out their positions before contract maturity, taking gains or losses in cash.)

Because the futures exchange specifies all the terms of the contract, the traders need bargain only over the futures price. The trader taking the **long position** commits to purchasing the commodity on the delivery date. The trader who takes the **short position** commits to delivering the commodity at contract maturity. The trader in the long position is said to "buy" a contract; the short side trader "sells" a contract. The words *buy* and *sell* are figurative only, because a contract is not really bought or sold like a stock or bond; it is entered into by mutual agreement. At the time the contract is entered into, no money changes hands.

Long position   The trader who commits to purchasing the asset.

Short position   The trader who commits to delivering the asset.

Figure 20.1 shows prices for several agricultural futures contracts as they appear in *The Wall Street Journal*. The boldface heading lists in each case the commodity, the exchange where the futures contract is traded in parentheses, the contract size, and the pricing unit. The first contract listed is for corn, traded on the Chicago Board of Trade (CBT). Each contract calls for delivery of 5,000 bushels, and prices in the entry are quoted in cents per bushel.

The next several rows detail price data for contracts expiring on various dates. The July 1991 maturity corn contract, for example, opened during the day at a futures price of 249 cents per bushel. The highest futures price during the day was 249 1/2, the lowest was 246 1/2, and the settlement price (a representative trading price during the last few minutes of trading) was 246 3/4. The settlement price decreased by 3 cents from the previous trading day. The highest futures price over the contract's life to date was 308 1/4, the lowest 241 1/2 cents. Finally, open interest, or the number of outstanding contracts, was 84,255. Similar information is given for each maturity date.

The trader holding the long position, that is, the person who will purchase the good, profits from price increases. Suppose that when the contract matures in July, the price of corn turns out to be 251 3/4 cents per bushel. The long position trader who entered the contract at the futures price of 246 3/4 cents on May 11 earns a profit of 5 cents per bushel: the eventual price is 5 cents higher than the originally agreed-to futures price. As each contract calls for delivery of 5,000 bushels, (ignoring brokerage fees) the profit to the long position equals 5,000 × \$.05 = \$250 per contract. Conversely, the short position loses 5 cents per bushel. The short position's loss equals the long position's gain.

To summarize, at maturity:

> Profit to long = Spot price at maturity − Original futures price
> Profit to short = Original futures price − Spot price at maturity

where the spot price is the actual market price of the commodity at the time of the delivery.

The futures contract is, therefore, a zero sum game, with losses and gains to all positions netting out to zero. Every long position is offset by a short position. The aggregate profits to futures trading, summing over all investors, also must be zero, as is the net exposure to changes in the commodity price. For this reason, the establishment of a futures market in a commodity should not have a major impact on the spot market for that commodity.

COMMODITY FUTURES PRICES

Figure 20.1 Futures listings.

From *The Wall Street Journal*, June 5, 1991. Reprinted by permission of THE WALL STREET JOURNAL, © 1991 Dow Jones & Company, Inc. All Rights Reserved Worldwide.

Concept Check

> **Question 1.** Graph the profit realized by an investor who enters the long side of a futures contract as a function of the price of the asset on the maturity date. Compare this graph to a graph of the profits realized by the purchaser of the asset itself. Next, try the same exercise for a short futures position and a short sale of the asset.

Existing Contracts

Futures and forward contracts are traded on a wide variety of goods in four broad categories: agricultural commodities, metals and minerals (including energy commodities), foreign currencies, and financial futures (fixed-income securities and stock market indexes). The financial futures contracts are a relatively recent innovation, for which trading was introduced in 1975. Innovation in financial futures has been rapid and is ongoing. Table 20.1 enumerates the various contracts trading in the United States in 1989.

Outside the futures markets, a well-developed network of banks and brokers has established a forward market in foreign exchange. This forward market is not a formal exchange in the sense that the exchange specifies the terms of the traded contract. Instead, participants in a forward contract may negotiate for delivery of any quantity of goods, while in the formal futures markets, contract size is set by the exchange. In forward arrangements, banks and brokers simply negotiate contracts for clients (or themselves) as needed.

Table 20.1 *Futures Contracts, 1989*

Foreign Currencies	*Agricultural*	*Metals and Energy*	*Financial Futures*
British pound	Corn	Copper	Eurodollars
Canadian dollar	Oats	Aluminum	Treasury bonds
Japanese yen	Soybeans	Gold	Treasury bills
Swiss franc	Soybean meal	Platinum	Treasury notes
French franc	Soybean oil	Palladium	Municipal bond index
German mark	Wheat	Silver	30-day interest rate
U.S. dollar index	Barley	Crude oil	LIBOR
European currency unit	Flaxseed	Heating oil	S&P 500 index
Australian dollar	Canola	Gas oil	NYSE index
	Rye	Gasoline	Value Line index
	Cattle (feeder)	Propane	Major market index
	Cattle (live)	CRB index*	OTC index
	Hogs		Short gilt[†]
	Pork bellies		Long gilt[†]
	Cocoa		
	Coffee		
	Cotton		
	Orange juice		
	Sugar		
	Lumber		
	Rice		
	Corn syrup		

*The Commodity Research Bureau's index of futures prices of agricultural as well as metal and energy prices.
[†]Gilts are British government bonds.
From *Commodity Trading Manual*, Chicago Board of Trade, 1989.

20.2   *Mechanics of Trading in Futures Markets*

The Clearinghouse and Open Interest

Trading in futures contracts is more complex than making ordinary stock transactions. If you want to make a stock purchase, your broker simply acts as an intermediary to enable you to buy shares from or sell to another individual through the stock exchange. In futures trading, however, the clearinghouse plays a more active role.

When an investor contacts a broker to establish a futures position, the brokerage firm wires the order to the firm's trader on the floor of the futures exchange. In contrast to stock trading, which involves specialists or market makers in each security, most futures trades in the United States occur among floor traders in the "trading pit" for each contract. Traders use voice or hand signals to signify their desire to buy or sell. Once a trader willing to accept the opposite side of a trade is located, the trade is recorded and the investor is notified.

Clearinghouse   *Established by exchanges to facilitate trading. The clearinghouse interposes itself as a middleman between two traders.*

At this point, just as is true for options contracts, the **clearinghouse** enters the picture. Rather than having the long and short traders hold contracts with each other, the clearinghouse becomes the seller of the contract for the long position and the buyer of the contract for the short position. The clearinghouse is obligated to deliver the commodity to the long position and to pay for delivery from the short; consequently, the clearinghouse's position nets to zero. This arrangement makes the clearinghouse the trading partner of each trader, both long and short. The clearinghouse, bound to perform on its side of each contract, is the only party that can be hurt by the failure of any trader to observe the obligations of the futures contract. This arrangement is necessary because a futures contract calls for future performance, which cannot be as easily guaranteed as an immediate stock transaction.

Figure 20.2 illustrates the role of the clearinghouse. Panel A shows what would happen in the absence of the clearinghouse. The trader in the long position would be obligated to pay the futures price to the short position trader, and

Figure 20.2
A, Trading without the clearinghouse.
B, Trading with a clearinghouse.

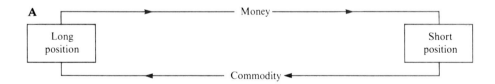

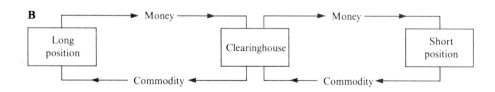

the trader in the short position would be obligated to deliver the commodity. Panel B shows how the clearinghouse becomes an intermediary, acting as the trading partner for each side of the contract. The clearinghouse's position is neutral, as it takes a long and a short position for each transaction.

The clearinghouse makes it possible for traders to liquidate positions easily. If you are currently long in a contract and want to undo your position, you simply instruct your broker to enter the short side of a contract to close out your position. This is called a *reversing trade*. The exchange nets out your long and short positions, reducing your net position to zero. Your zero net position with the clearinghouse eliminates the need to fulfill at maturity either the original long or reversing short position.

The *open interest* on the contract is the number of contracts outstanding. (Long and short positions are not counted separately, meaning that open interest can be defined as either the number of long or short contracts outstanding.) The clearinghouse's position nets out to zero, and so is not counted in the computation of open interest. When contracts begin trading, open interest is zero. As time passes, open interest increases as progressively more contracts are entered. Almost all traders, however, liquidate their positions before the contract maturity date.

Instead of actually taking or making delivery of the commodity, market participants virtually all enter reversing trades to cancel their original positions, thereby realizing the profits or losses on the contract. Actual deliveries and purchases of commodities are then made via regular channels of supply, usually via warehouse receipts. The fraction of contracts that result in actual delivery is estimated to range from less than 1 percent to 3 percent, depending on the commodity and the activity in the contract. The image of a trader awakening one delivery date with a mountain of wheat in the front yard is amusing, but unlikely.

You can see the typical pattern of open interest in Figure 20.1. In the canola contract, for example, the June delivery contract is close to maturity, and open interest is relatively small; most contracts have been reversed already. The next few maturities have significant open interest. Finally, the most distant maturity contracts have little open interest, as they have been available only recently, and few participants have yet traded. For other contracts, where July is the nearest maturity, open interest is typically highest in the July contract.

Marking to Market and the Margin Account

Anyone who saw the film "Trading Places" knows that Eddie Murphy as a trader in orange juice futures had no intention of purchasing or delivering orange juice. Traders simply bet on the futures price of juice. The total profit or loss realized by the long trader who buys a contract at time 0 and closes, or reverses, it at time t is just the change in the futures price over the period, $F_t - F_0$. Symmetrically, the short trader earns $F_0 - F_t$.

Marking to market
The daily settlement of obligations on futures positions.

The process by which profits or losses accrue to traders is called **marking to market.** At initial execution of a trade, each trader establishes a margin account. The margin is a security account consisting of cash or near-cash securities, such as Treasury bills, that ensures the trader is able to satisfy the obligations of the futures contract. Because both parties to a futures contract are exposed to losses, both must post margin. If the initial margin on corn, for example, is 10 percent, then the trader must post $1,234 per contract for the margin account.

(This is 10 percent of the value of the contract ($2.4675 per bushel × 5,000 bushels per contract).

Because the initial margin may be satisfied by posting interest-earning securities, the requirement does not impose a significant opportunity cost of funds on the trader. The initial margin is usually set between 5 percent and 15 percent of the total value of the contract. Contracts written on assets with more volatile prices require higher margins.

On any day that futures contracts trade, futures prices may rise or may fall. Instead of waiting until the maturity date for traders to realize all gains and losses, the clearinghouse requires all positions to recognize profits as they accrue daily. If the futures price of corn rises from 246 3/4 to 248 3/4 cents per bushel, the clearinghouse credits the margin account of the long position for 5,000 bushels times 2 cents per bushel, or $100 per contract. Conversely, for the short position, the clearinghouse takes this amount from the margin account for each contract held. Although the price of corn has changed by only 0.81 percent (2/246.75), the percentage return on the long corn position on that day is 10 times greater: 8.1 percent ($100/$1,234). The 10-to-1 ratio of percentage changes reflects the leverage inherent in the futures position, since the corn contract was established with an initial margin of 1/10th the value of the underlying asset.

This daily settling is called *marking to market*. It means the maturity date of the contract does not govern realization of profit or loss. Marking to market ensures that, as futures prices change, the proceeds accrue to the trader's margin account immediately. We will provide a more detailed example of this process shortly.

Concept Check

Question 2. What must be the net inflow or outlay from marking to market for the clearinghouse?

Maintenance, or variation, margin *An established value below which a trader's margin may not fall. Reaching the maintenance margin triggers a margin call.*

If a trader accrues sustained losses from daily marking to market, the margin account may fall below a critical value called the **maintenance, or variation, margin.** Once the value of the account falls below this value, the trader receives a margin call. For example, if the maintenance margin on corn is 5 percent, then the margin call will go out when the 10 percent margin initially posted has fallen about in half, to $617 per contract. (This requires that the futures price fall only about 13 cents, as each 1 cent drop in the futures price results in a loss of $50 to the long position.) Either new funds must be transferred into the margin account, or the broker will close out enough of the trader's position to meet the required margin for that position. This procedure safeguards the position of the clearinghouse. Positions are closed out before the margin account is exhausted—the trader's losses are covered, and the clearinghouse is not affected.

Marking to market is the major way in which futures and forward contracts differ, besides contract standardization. Futures follow this pay- (or receive-) as-you-go method. Forward contracts are simply held until maturity, and no funds are transferred until that date, although the contracts may be traded.

It is important to note that the futures price on the delivery date will equal the spot price of the commodity on that date. As a maturing contract calls for immediate delivery, the futures price on that day must equal the spot price—the cost of the commodity from the two competing sources is equalized in a competitive market.[1] You may obtain delivery of the commodity either by purchasing it directly in the spot market or by entering the long side of a futures contract.

A commodity available from two sources (spot or futures market) must be priced identically, or else investors will rush to purchase it from the cheap source in order to sell it in the high-priced market. Such arbitrage activity could not persist without prices adjusting to eliminate the arbitrage opportunity. Therefore, the futures price and the spot price must converge at maturity. This is called the **convergence property.**

Convergence property
The convergence of fu-
tures prices and spot
prices at the maturity
of the futures contract.

For an investor who establishes a long position in a contract now (time 0) and holds that position until maturity (time T), the sum of all daily settlements will equal $F_T - F_0$, where F_T stands for the futures price at contract maturity. Because of convergence, however, the futures price at maturity, F_T, equals the spot price, P_T, so total futures profits also may be expressed as $P_T - F_0$. Thus, we see that profits on a futures contract held to maturity perfectly track changes in the value of the underlying asset.

A concrete example can illustrate the time profile of returns to a futures contract. Assume the current futures price for silver for delivery five days from today is $4.10 per ounce. Suppose that over the next five days, the futures price evolves as follows:

Day	Futures Price
0 (today)	$4.10
1	4.20
2	4.25
3	4.18
4	4.18
5 (delivery)	4.21

The spot price of silver on the delivery date is $4.21: the convergence property implies that the price of silver in the spot market must equal the futures price on the delivery day.

The daily mark-to-market settlements for each contract held by the long position will be as follows:

Day	Profit (Loss) per Ounce	× 5,000 Ounces/Contract = Daily Proceeds
1	4.20 − 4.10 = .10	$500
2	4.25 − 4.20 = .05	250
3	4.18 − 4.25 = −.07	−350
4	4.18 − 4.18 = 0	0
5	4.21 − 4.18 = .03	150
		Sum = $550

---

[1]Small differences between the spot and futures price at maturity may persist because of transportation costs, but this is a minor factor.

The profit on day 1 is the increase in the futures price from the previous day, or ($4.20 − $4.10) per ounce. Because each silver contract on the Commodity Exchange calls for purchase and delivery of 5,000 ounces, the total profit per contract is 5,000 times $.10, or $500. On day 3, when the futures price falls, the long position's margin account will be debited by $350. By day 5, the sum of all daily proceeds is $550. This is exactly equal to 5,000 times the difference between the final futures price of $4.21 and original futures price of $4.10. Thus, the sum of all the daily proceeds (per ounce of silver held long) equals $P_T − F_0$.

Cash versus Actual Delivery

Most futures markets call for delivery of an actual commodity such as a particular grade of wheat or a specified amount of foreign currency if the contract is not reversed before maturity. For agricultural commodities, where quality of the delivered good may vary, the exchange sets quality standards as part of the futures contract. In some cases, contracts may be settled with higher- or lower-grade commodities. In these cases, a premium or discount is applied to the delivered commodity to adjust for the quality difference.

Cash delivery The cash value of the underlying asset (rather than the asset itself) is delivered to satisfy the contract.

Some futures contracts call for **cash delivery.** An example is a stock index futures contract where the underlying asset is an index such as the Standard & Poor's 500 or the New York Stock Exchange Index. Delivery of every stock in the index clearly would be impractical. Hence, the contract calls for "delivery" of a cash amount equal to the value that the index attains on the maturity date of the contract. The sum of all the daily settlements from marking to market results in the long position realizing total profits or losses of $S_T − F_0$, where S_T is the value of the stock index on the maturity date T, and F_0 is the original futures price. Cash settlement closely mimics actual delivery, except the cash value of the asset rather than the asset itself is delivered by the short position in exchange for the futures price.

More concretely, the S&P 500 index contract calls for delivery of $500 times the value of the index. At maturity, the index might list at 375, a market value-weighted index of the prices of all 500 stocks in the index. The cash settlement contract calls for delivery of $500 × 375, or $187,500 cash in return for 500 times the futures price. This yields exactly the same profit as would result from directly purchasing 500 units of the index for $187,500 and then delivering it for 500 times the original futures price.

Regulations

Futures markets are regulated by the Commodities Futures Trading Commission, a federal agency. The CFTC sets capital requirements for member firms of the futures exchanges, authorizes trading in new contracts, and oversees maintenance of daily trading records.

The futures exchange may set limits on the amount by which futures prices may change from one day to the next. For example, the price limit on silver contracts traded on the Chicago Board of Trade is $1, which means that if silver futures close today at $4.10 per ounce, trades in silver tomorrow may vary only between $5.10 and $3.10 per ounce. The exchanges may increase or reduce these price limits in response to perceived changes in price volatility of the contract.

Price limits are often eliminated as contracts approach maturity, usually in the last month of trading.

Price limits traditionally are viewed as a means to limit violent price fluctuations. This reasoning seems dubious. Suppose an international monetary crisis overnight drives up the spot price of silver to $8.00. No one would sell silver futures at prices for future delivery as low as $4.10. Instead, the futures price would rise each day by the $1 limit, although the quoted price would represent only an unfilled bid order—no contracts would trade at the low quoted price. After several days of limit moves of $1 per day, the futures price would finally reach its equilibrium level, and trading would occur again. This process means no one could unload a position until the price reached its equilibrium level. This example shows that price limits offer no real protection against fluctuations in equilibrium prices.

Taxation

Because of the mark-to-market procedure, investors do not have control over the tax year in which they realize gains or losses. Instead, price changes are realized gradually, with each daily settlement. Therefore, taxes are paid at year-end on cumulated profits or losses regardless of whether the position has been closed out.

20.3 Futures Markets Strategies

Hedging and Speculation

Hedging and speculating are two polar uses of futures markets. A speculator uses a futures contract to profit from movements in futures prices, a hedger to protect against price movement.

If speculators believe prices will increase, they will take a long position for expected profits. Conversely, they exploit expected price declines by taking a short position. As an example of a speculative strategy, let's consider the use of the T-bond futures contract, the listings for which appear in Figure 20.3. Each T-bond contract on the Chicago Board of Trade (CBT) calls for delivery of $100,000 par value of bonds. The listed futures price of 95–08 (i.e., 95 and 8/32) means the market price of the underlying bonds is 95.25 percent of par, or $95,250. Therefore, for every increase of one point in the T-bond futures price

Figure 20.3
Treasury bond futures.
From *The Wall Street Journal*, May 24, 1991. Reprinted by permission of *THE WALL STREET JOURNAL*, © 1991 Dow Jones & Company, Inc. All Rights Reserved Worldwide.

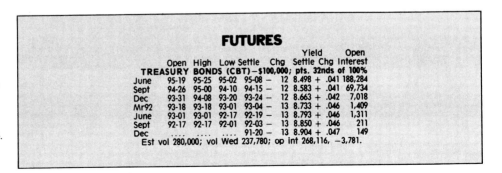

(e.g., to 96–08), the long position gains $1,000, and the short loses that amount. Therefore, if you are bullish on bond prices, you might speculate by buying T-bond futures contracts.

If the T-bond futures price increases by one point to 96–08, then you profit by your speculation by $1,000 per contract. If the forecast is incorrect, and T-bond futures prices decline, you lose $1,000 times the decrease in the futures price for each contract purchased. Speculators bet on the direction of futures price movements.

Why does a speculator buy a T-bond futures contract? Why not buy T-bonds directly? One reason lies in transaction costs, which are far smaller in futures markets.

Another reason is the leverage futures trading provides. Recall that each T-bond contract calls for delivery of $100,000 par value, worth about $95,250 in our example. The initial margin required for this account might be only $10,000. The $1,000 per contract gain translates into a 10 percent ($1,000/$10,000 return on the money put up, despite the fact that the T-bond futures price increases only 1.05 percent (1/95.25). Futures margins, therefore, allow speculators to achieve much greater leverage than is available from direct trading in a commodity.

Hedgers by contrast use futures markets to insulate themselves against price movements. An investor holding a T-bond portfolio, for example, might anticipate a period of interest rate volatility and want to protect the value of the portfolio against price fluctuations. In this case, the investor has no desire to bet on price movements in either direction. To achieve such protection, a hedger takes a short position in T-bond futures, which obligates the hedger to deliver T-bonds at the contract maturity date for the current futures price. This locks in the sales price for the bonds and guarantees that the total value of the bond-plus-futures position at the maturity date is the futures price.[2]

For illustration, suppose as in Figure 20.3 that the futures price for June delivery is $95.25 (per $100 par value), and that the only three possible T-bond prices in June are $94.25, $95.25, and $96.25. If investors currently hold 200 bonds, each with par value $1,000, they would take short positions in two contracts, each for $100,000 par value. Protecting the value of a portfolio with short futures positions is called *short hedging*. Taking the futures position requires no current investment. (The initial margin requirement is small relative to the size of the contract, and because it may be posted in interest-bearing securities, it does not represent a time-value or opportunity cost to the hedger.)

The profits in June from each of the two short futures contracts will be 1,000 times any decrease in the futures price. At maturity, the convergence property ensures that the final futures price will equal the spot price of the T-bonds. Hence, the futures profit will be 2,000 times $(F_0 - P_T)$, where P_T is the price of the bonds on the delivery date, and F_0 is the original futures price, $95.25.

Now consider the hedged portfolio consisting of the bonds and the short futures positions. The portfolio value as a function of the bond price in June can be computed as follows:

---

[2]To keep things simple, we will assume that the T-bond futures contract calls for delivery of a bond with the same coupon and maturity as that in the investor's portfolio. In practice, a variety of bonds may be delivered to satisfy the contract, and a "conversion factor" is used to adjust for the relative values of the eligible delivery bonds. We will ignore this complication.

	T-Bond Price in June		
	$94.25	**$95.25**	**$96.25**
Bond holdings (value = 2,000 P_T)	$188,500	$190,500	$192,500
Futures profits or losses	2,000	0	− 2,000
Total	$190,500	$190,500	$190,500

The total portfolio value is unaffected by the eventual bond price, which is what the hedger wants. The gains or losses on the bond holdings are exactly offset by those on the two contracts held short.

For example, if bond prices fall to $94.25, the losses on the bond portfolio are offset by the $2,000 gain on the futures contracts. That profit equals the difference between the futures price on the maturity date (which equals the spot price on that date of $94.25) and the originally contracted futures price of $95.25. For short contracts, a profit of $1 per $100 par value is realized from the fall in the spot price. Because two contracts call for delivery of $200,000 par value, this results in a $2,000 gain that offsets the decline in the value of the bonds held in portfolio. In contrast to a speculator, a hedger is indifferent to the ultimate price of the asset. The short hedger who has in essence arranged to sell the asset for an agreed-upon price need not be concerned about further developments in the market price.

To generalize this numerical example, you can note that the bond will be worth P_T at maturity, while the profit on the futures contract is $F_0 - P_T$. The sum of the two positions is F_0 dollars, which is independent of the eventual bond price.

A *long hedge* is the analogue to a short hedge for a purchaser of an asset. Consider, for example, a pension fund manager who anticipates a cash inflow in two months that will be invested in fixed-income securities. The manager views T-bonds as very attractively priced now and would like to lock in current prices and yields until the investment actually can be made two months hence. The manager can lock in the effective cost of the purchase by entering the long side of a contract, which commits her to purchasing at the current futures price.

Concept Check

Question 3. Suppose as in our example that T-bonds will be priced at $94.25, $95.25, or $96.25 in two months. Show that the cost in June of purchasing $200,000 par value of T-bonds net of the profit/loss on two long T-bond contracts will be $190,500 regardless of the eventual bond price.

Exact futures hedging may be impossible for some goods because the necessary futures contract is not traded. For example, miners of bauxite, the ore from which aluminum is made, might like to trade in bauxite futures, but they cannot because such contracts are not listed. Because bauxite and aluminum prices are highly correlated, however, a close hedge may be established by shorting aluminum futures. Hedging a position using futures on another commodity is called *cross-hedging*.

Concept Check

Question 4. What are the sources of risk to an investor who uses aluminum futures to hedge an inventory of bauxite?

Basis Risk and Hedging

Basis *The difference between the futures price and the spot price.*

The **basis** is the difference between the futures price and the spot price.[3] As we have noted, on the maturity date of a contract, the basis must be zero: the convergence property implies that $F_T - P_T = 0$. Before maturity, however, the futures price for later delivery may differ substantially from the current spot price.

We discussed the case of a short hedger who holds an asset (T-bonds, in our example) and a short position to deliver that asset in the future. If the asset and futures contract are held until maturity, the hedger bears no risk, as the ultimate value of the portfolio on the delivery date is determined by the current futures price. Risk is eliminated because the futures price and spot price at contract maturity must be equal: gains and losses on the futures and the commodity position will exactly cancel. If the contract and asset are to be liquidated early, before contract maturity, however, the hedger bears **basis risk,** because the futures price and spot price need not move in perfect lockstep at all times before the delivery date. In this case, gains and losses on the contract and the asset need not exactly offset each other.

Basis risk *Risk attributable to uncertain movements in the spread between a futures price and a spot price.*

Some speculators try to profit from movements in the basis. Rather than betting on the direction of the futures or spot prices per se, they bet on the changes in the difference between the two. A long spot-short futures position will profit when the basis narrows. For example, consider an investor holding $100,000 par value of T-bonds, who is short one T-bond futures contract. T-bonds might sell for $94.50, while the futures price for June delivery is $95.25. The basis is 75 cents. Tomorrow, the T-bond spot price might increase to $94.60, while the futures price might increase to $95.31. The basis has narrowed from 75 cents to 71 cents. The investor realizes a capital gain of 10 cents per $100 par value on the T-bond holdings and a loss of 6 cents per $100 par value from the increase in the futures price. The net gain is the decrease in basis, or 4 cents per $100 par value.

Spread (futures) *Taking a long position in a futures contract of one maturity and a short position in a contract of different maturity, both on the same commodity.*

A related strategy is a **spread** position, where the investor takes a long position in a futures contract of one maturity and a short position in a contract on the same commodity, but with a different maturity. Profits accrue if the difference in futures prices between the two contracts changes in the hoped-for direction; that is, if the futures price on the contract held long increases by more (or decreases by less) than the futures price on the contract held short.

Consider an investor who holds a September maturity contract long and a June contract short. If the September futures price increases by 5 cents while

---

[3]Usage of the word *basis* is somewhat loose. It sometimes is used to refer to the futures-spot difference $F - P$, and sometimes to the spot-futures difference $P - F$. We will consistently call the basis $F - P$.

the June futures price increases by 4 cents, the net gain will be 5 cents − 4 cents, or 1 cent. Like basis strategies, spread positions aim to exploit movements in relative price structures rather than to profit from movements in the general level of prices.

20.4   *The Determination of Futures Prices*

The Spot-Futures Parity Theorem

There are at least two ways to obtain an asset at some date in the future. One way is to purchase the asset now and store it until the targeted date. The other way is to take a long futures position that calls for purchase of the asset on the date in question. As each strategy leads to an equivalent result, namely, the ultimate acquisition of the asset, you would expect the market-determined cost of pursuing these strategies to be equal. There should be a predictable relationship between the current price of the asset, including the costs of holding and storing it, and the futures price.

To make this point more obvious, consider a hypothetical futures contract on a stock that pays no dividends.[4] This is a particularly simple example because explicit storage costs for stocks are negligible and because stocks are not subject to seasonal price patterns as most agricultural commodities are. Instead, prices on nondividend-paying stocks are set in market equilibrium at a level such that the expected rate of capital gains equals the fair expected rate of return appropriate to the stock's risk level.

Two strategies that will assure possession of the stock at some future date T are:

Strategy A: Buy the stock at price S_0 now and hold it until time T, when its price will be S_T.

Strategy B: Initiate a long futures position, and invest enough money now in order to pay the futures price when the contract matures.

Strategy B will require an immediate investment of the *present value* of the futures price in a riskless security such as Treasury bills, that is, an investment of $F_0/(1 + r_f)^T$ dollars, where r_f is the rate paid on T-bills. Examine the cash flow streams of these two strategies:

Strategy A:	*Action*	*Initial Cash Flow*	*Cash Flow at Time T*
	Buy stock	$-S_0$	S_T

Strategy B:	*Action*	*Initial Cash Flow*	*Cash Flow at Time T*
	Enter long position	0	$S_T - F_0$
	Invest $F_0/(1 + r_f)^T$ in bills	$-F_0/(1 + r_f)^T$	F_0
	Total for strategy B	$-F_0/(1 + r_f)^T$	S_T

---

[4]In reality, futures contracts on individual stocks do not trade.

The initial cash flow of strategy A is negative, reflecting the cash outflow necessary to purchase the stock at the current price S_0. At time T, the stock will be worth S_T.

Strategy B involves an initial investment equal to the present value of the futures price that will be paid at the maturity of the futures contract. By time T, the investment will grow to F_0. In addition, the profits to the long position at time T will be $S_T - F_0$. The sum of the two components of strategy B will be S_T dollars, exactly enough to purchase the stock at time T regardless of its price at that time.

Each strategy results in an identical value at T: a portfolio value of S_T dollars. Therefore, the cost, or initial cash outflow, required by these strategies also must be equal; it follows that

$$F_0/(1 + r_f)^T = S_0$$

or,

$$F_0 = S_0(1 + r_f)^T \tag{20.1}$$

This gives us a relationship between the current price and the futures price of the stock. The interest rate in this case may be viewed as the "cost of carrying" the stock from the present to time T. The cost in this case represents the time-value-of-money opportunity cost—instead of investing in the stock, you could have invested risklessly in Treasury bills to earn interest income. To quantify the argument, suppose the stock currently sells for $40, and the riskless interest rate is 1 percent per month. The formula indicates the futures price for six-month delivery should be $40 \times (1.01)^6 = \$42.46$.

If Equation 20.1 does not hold, investors could earn arbitrage profits. For example, suppose the futures price is $43 rather than the "appropriate" value of $42.46 that we just derived. An investor could realize arbitrage profits by pursuing a strategy involving a long position in strategy A and a short position in strategy B:

Action	Initial Cash Flow	Cash Flow at Time T (6 Months)
Borrow $40, repay with interest at time T	+40	$-40(1.01)^6 = -42.46$
Buy stock for $40	−40	S_T
Enter short futures position ($F_0 = \$43$)	0	$43 - S_T$
Total	0	$0.54

The net initial investment of this strategy is zero. Moreover, its cash flow at time T is positive and riskless: the total payoff at time T will be $0.54 regardless of the stock price. (The profit is equal to the mispricing of the futures contract, $43 rather than $42.46.) Risk has been eliminated because profits and losses on the futures and stock positions exactly offset each other. The portfolio is perfectly hedged.

Such a strategy produces an arbitrage profit—a riskless profit requiring no initial net investment. If such an opportunity existed, all market participants would rush to take advantage of it. The results? The stock price would be bid up, and/or the futures price offered down until Equation 20.1 is satisfied. A similar analysis applies to the possibility that F_0 is less than \$42.46. In this case, you simply reverse the strategy above to earn riskless profits. We conclude, therefore, that in a well-functioning market in which arbitrage opportunities are competed away, $F_0 = S_0(1 + r_f)^T$.

Concept Check	**Question 5.** Return to the arbitrage strategy just laid out. What would be the three steps of the strategy if F_0 were too low, say \$42? Work out the cash flows of the strategy now and at time T in a table like the one in the text.

The arbitrage strategy can be represented more generally as follows:

Action	Initial Cash Flow	Cash Flow at Time T
1. Borrow S_0	S_0	$-S_0(1 + r_f)^T$
2. Buy stock for S_0	$-S_0$	S_T
3. Enter short futures position	0	$F_0 - S_T$
Total	0	$F_0 - S_0(1 + r_f)^T$

The initial cash flow is zero by construction: the money necessary to purchase the stock in step 1 is borrowed in step 2, and the futures position in step 3, which is used to hedge the value of the stock position, does not require an initial outlay. Moreover, the total cash flow to the strategy at time T is riskless because it involves only terms that are already known when the contract is entered. This situation could not persist, as all investors would try to cash in on the arbitrage opportunity. Ultimately prices would change until the time T cash flow is reduced to zero, at which point F_0 would once again equal $S_0(1 + r_f)^T$. This result is called the **spot-futures parity theorem** or **cost of carry relationship**; it gives the normal or theoretically correct relationship between spot and futures prices.

Spot-futures parity theorem, or cost-of-carry relationship Describes the theoretically correct relationship between spot and futures prices. Violation of the parity relationship gives rise to arbitrage opportunities.

We can easily extend the parity theorem to the case where the stock pays dividends. When the stock provides a dividend yield of d, the net cost of carry is only $r - d$; the time value cost of the wealth that is tied up in the stock is offset by the flow of dividends from the stock. The net opportunity cost of holding the stock is the forgone interest less the dividends received. Therefore, in the dividend-paying case, the spot-futures parity relationship is[5]

$$F_0 = S_0(1 + r_f - d)^T \qquad (20.2)$$

where d is the dividend yield on the stock. Question 5 at the end of the chapter leads you through a more formal demonstration of this result.

The arbitrage strategy just described should convince you that these parity relationships are more than just theoretical results. Any violations of the parity relationship give rise to arbitrage opportunities that can provide large profits to

---

[5]This relationship is only approximate in that it assumes the dividend is paid just before the maturity of the contract.

traders. We will see shortly that index arbitrage in the stock market is a tool to exploit violations of the parity relationship for stock index futures contracts.

Spreads

Just as we can predict the relationship between spot and futures prices, there are similar ways to determine the proper relationships among futures prices for contracts of different maturity dates. Equation 20.2 shows that the futures price is in part determined by time to maturity. If $r_f > d$, as is the case for stock index futures, then the futures price will be higher on longer-maturity contracts. You can easily verify this by examining Figure 20.6, which presents *Wall Street Journal* listings of several stock index futures contracts. For futures on assets like gold, which pay no "dividend yield" we can set $d = 0$ and conclude that F must increase as time to maturity increases.

Equation 20.2 shows that futures prices should all move together. It is not surprising that futures prices for different maturity dates move in unison, for all are linked to the same spot price through the parity relationship. Figure 20.4 plots futures prices on gold for three maturity dates. It is apparent that the prices move in virtual lockstep and that the more distant delivery dates require higher futures prices, as Equation 20.2 predicts.

20.5   *Financial Futures*

Although futures markets have their origins in agricultural commodities, today's market is dominated by contracts on financial assets. Figure 20.5 presents trading volume on the Chicago Board of Trade for various asset categories in the 1980s.

Figure 20.4
Futures prices in January 1986 for kilo gold contracts maturing in February, June, and December 1986.

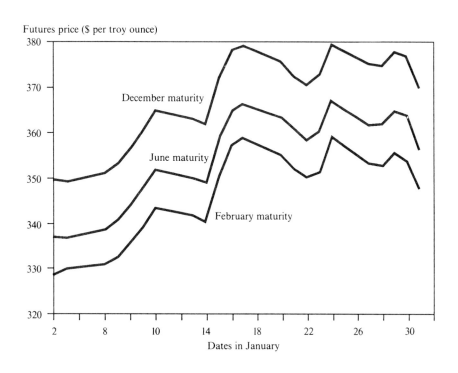

Futures and Futures–Options Trading Volume

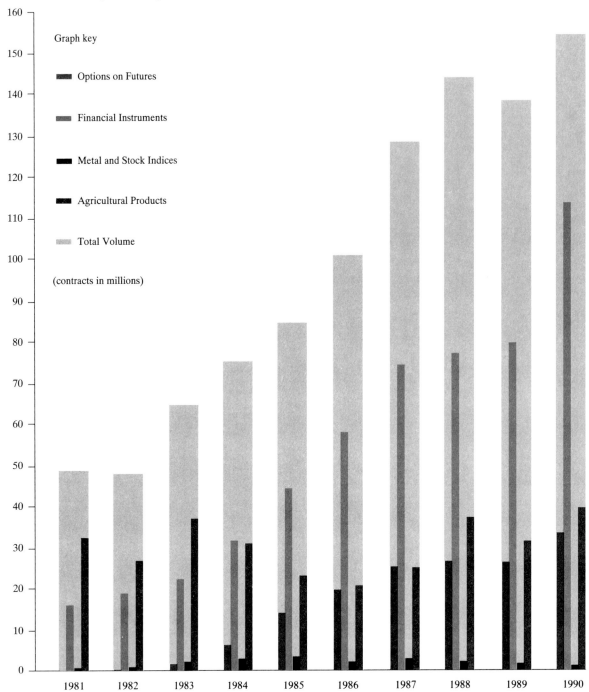

Figure 20.5 **Trading volume in futures contracts.**

Stock Index Futures

We discussed at length above a hypothetical futures contract on a share of stock. In practice, there are no stock futures on individual shares; futures trade instead on stock market indexes such as the Standard & Poor's 500. In contrast to most futures contracts, which call for delivery of a specified commodity, these contracts are settled by a cash amount equal to the value of the stock index in question on the contract maturity date times a multiplier that scales the size of the contract. This cash settlement duplicates the profits that would arise with actual delivery.

There are several stock index futures contracts currently traded. Table 20.2 lists the major ones, showing under contract size the multiplier used to calculate contract settlements. An S&P 500 contract with a futures price of 310 and a final index value of 315, for example, would result in a profit for the long side of $500 \times (315 - 310) = \$2,500$. The S&P contract by far dominates the market in stock index futures.

Most futures contracts such as the S&P 500 or NYSE are written explicitly on a particular stock index. This gives investors the ability to hedge against or speculate on the performance of the given index. The Major Market Index is a bit of an exception. Because the Chicago Board of Trade was not given permission by Dow Jones to create a contract explicitly tied to the Dow Jones Industrial Average, it was forced to create its own index designed to track the DJIA

Table 20.2   *Stock Index Futures*

Contract	Underlying Market Index	Contract Size	Exchange
S&P 500	Standard & Poor's 500 index. A value-weighted arithmetic average of 500 stocks.	$500 times the S&P 500 index	Chicago Mercantile Exchange
Value Line	Value Line Composite Average. An equally weighted arithmetic average of about 1,700 firms.	$500 times the Value Line index	Kansas City Board of Trade
NYSE	NYSE Composite Index. Value-weighted arithmetic average of all stocks listed on the NYSE.	$500 times the NYSE index	New York Futures Exchange
Major Market	Price-weighted arithmetic average of 20 blue-chip stocks. Index is designed to track the Dow Jones Industrial Average.	$250 times the Major Market Index	Chicago Board of Trade
National Over-the-Counter	Value-weighted arithmetic average of 100 of the largest over-the-counter stocks.	$500 times the OTC index	Philadelphia Board of Trade
Nikkei	Nikkei 225 stock average.	$5 times the Nikkei Index	Chicago Mercantile Exchange

as closely as possible. Figure 20.6 is a reproduction of the stock index futures contracts from *The Wall Street Journal*.

The broad-based U.S. stock market indexes are all highly correlated. Table 20.3 presents a correlation matrix for four indexes calculated over the 20-year period ending in 1981. The only index whose correlation with the others is be-

Figure 20.6
Index futures.
From *The Wall Street Journal*, May 24, 1991. Reprinted by permission of *THE WALL STREET JOURNAL*, © 1991 Dow Jones & Company, Inc. All Rights Reserved Worldwide.

INDEX TRADING

FUTURES

S&P 500 INDEX (CME) 500 times index

	Open	High	Low	Settle	Chg	High	Low	Open Interest
June	377.50	379.40	374.00	375.85	– 1.65	393.50	300.90	135,834
Sept	380.50	382.00	376.70	378.55	– 1.65	396.20	304.00	22,823
Dec	380.50	384.65	379.50	381.35	– 1.50	399.30	316.50	2,526

Est vol 51,597; vol Wed 44,742; open int 162,208, +888.
Indx prelim High 378.07; Low 373.55; Close 374.96 –.23

NIKKEI 225 Stock Average (CME)–$5 times NSA

June	25900.	25900.	25770.	25785.	+ 10.0	27800.	21765.	7,061
Sept	26420.	26450.	26365.	26365.	+ 15.0	28350.	23430.	801
Dec	....	....	....	26885.	+ 10.0	28900.	26955.	188

Est vol 1,245; vol Wed 1,102; open int 8,051, –95.
The index: High 25721.27; Low 25350.82; Close 25643.65 +245.99

NYSE COMPOSITE INDEX (NYFE) 500 times index

June	207.00	207.70	204.90	205.80	– 1.00	215.25	165.85	5,523
Sept	208.20	208.90	206.35	207.15	– .95	216.40	173.10	313

Est vol 7,185; vol Wed 5,943; open int 6,181, –19.
The index: High 206.86; Low 204.79; Close 205.45 –.49

MAJOR MKT INDEX (CBT) $250 times index

June	627.00	629.00	621.25	624.00	– 2.80	646.00	607.00	5,885
July	624.00	626.00	623.50	625.60	– 2.80	638.00	610.50	221

Est vol 2,500; vol Wed 1,491; open int 6,136, +164.
The index: High 628.17; Low 620.08; Close 622.57 –2.80

MGMI BASE METAL INDEX (FOX) 100 times index

June	139.70	140.10	139.70	140.00	– .40	186.70	139.70	6,357
July	140.40	140.40	140.20	140.30	– .60	154.20	140.20	1,728
Aug	140.50	140.50	140.30	140.50	– .50	143.00	140.30	353
Sept	140.90	140.90	140.50	140.80	– .40	182.70	141.20	3,713
Dec	....	....	....	141.80	– .20	182.70	141.80	2,353
Mr92	....	....	....	142.10	– .30	160.20	142.50	1,495
June	....	....	....	142.60	....	155.90	142.80	539

Est vol 364; vol Wed 474; open int 16,538, .
The index: High 139.18; Low 138.59; Close 138.73 –.55

–OTHER INDEX FUTURES–

Settlement price of selected contract. Volume and open interest of all contract months.

KC Mini Value Line (KC)–100 times index
Jun 302.00 –1.00; Est. vol. 80; Open int. 207

KC Value Line Index (KC)–500 times index
Jun 301.70 –1.30; Est. vol. 250; Open int. 2,383
The index: High 304.66; Low 302.86; Close 303.55 –.05

CRB Index (NYFE)–250 times index
Jly 216.00 +.45; Est. vol. 79; Open int. 1,562
The index: High 216.40; Low 215.64; Close 216.34 +.56

CBT–Chicago Board of Trade. CME–Chicago Mercantile Exchange. KC–Kansas City Board of Trade. NYFE–New York Futures Exchange, a unit of the New York Stock Exchange.

Table 20.3 *Correlations of Stock Market Indexes*

	Dow Jones	*Value Line*	*S&P 500*	*NYSE*
Dow Jones	1.00	.86	.94	.94
Value Line	.86	1.00	.86	.90
S&P 500	.94	.86	1.00	.98
NYSE	.94	.90	.98	1.00

From David Modest and Mahadevan Sundaresan, "The Relationship between Spot and Futures Prices in Stock Index Futures Markets: Some Preliminary Evidence," *Journal of Futures Markets* 3 (Spring 1983), 15–41.

low 0.90 is the Value Line index. This index uses an equally weighted average of 1,700 firms, as opposed to the NYSE or S&P indexes, which use market-value weights. This means the Value Line contract overweights small firms compared to the other indexes, which may explain the lower observed correlation.

Creating Synthetic Stock Positions

One reason stock index futures are so popular is that they substitute for holdings in the underlying stocks themselves. Index futures let investors participate in broad market movements without actually buying or selling large numbers of stocks.

Because of this, we say futures represent "synthetic" holdings of the market position. Instead of holding the market directly, the investor takes a long futures position in the index. Such a strategy is attractive because the transaction costs involved in establishing and liquidating futures positions are much lower than what would be required to take actual spot positions. Investors who wish to buy and sell market positions frequently find it much cheaper and easier to play the futures market. Market timers who speculate on broad market moves rather than individual securities are large players in stock index futures for this reason.

One means to market time is to shift between Treasury bills and broad-based stock market holdings. Timers attempt to shift from bills into the market before market upturns and to shift back into bills to avoid market downturns, thereby profiting from broad market movements. Market timing of this sort, however, can result in huge trading costs with the frequent purchase and sale of many stocks. An attractive alternative is to invest in Treasury bills and hold varying amounts of market index futures contracts.

The strategy works like this. When timers are bullish, they will establish many long futures positions that they can liquidate quickly and cheaply when expectations turn bearish. Rather than shifting back and forth between T-bills and stocks, traders buy and hold T-bills and adjust only the futures position. (Recall strategies A and B of the preceding section where we showed that a T-bill plus futures position resulted in a payoff equal to the stock price.) This strategy minimizes transaction costs. An advantage of this technique for timing is that investors can implicitly buy or sell the market index in its entirety, where market timing in the spot market would require the simultaneous purchase or sale of all the stocks in the index. This is technically difficult to coordinate and can lead to slippage in execution of a timing strategy.

Index Arbitrage and the Triple-Witching Hour

Index arbitrage A strategy that exploits divergences between actual futures prices and their theoretically correct parity values to make a riskless profit.

Whenever the actual futures price differs from its parity value, there is an opportunity for profit. This is why the parity relationships are so important. One of the most notable developments in trading activity has been the advent of **index arbitrage,** an investment strategy that exploits divergences between the actual futures price on a stock market index and its theoretically correct parity value.

In theory, index arbitrage is simple. If the futures price is too high, short the futures contract and buy the stocks in the index. If it is too low, go long in futures and short the stocks. You can perfectly hedge your position and should earn arbitrage profits equal to the mispricing of the contract.

In practice, however, index arbitrage can be difficult to implement. The problem lies in buying the stocks in the index. Selling or purchasing shares in all 500 stocks in the S&P 500 is difficult for two reasons. The first is transaction costs, which may outweigh any profits to be made from the arbitrage. Second, it is extremely difficult to buy or sell stock of 500 different firms simultaneously. And any lags in the execution of such a strategy can destroy the effectiveness of a plan to exploit short-lived price discrepancies.

Arbitrageurs need to trade an entire portfolio of stocks quickly and simultaneously if they hope to exploit temporary disparities between the futures price and its corresponding stock index. For this they need a coordinated trading program; hence the term **program trading,** which refers to coordinated purchases or sales of entire portfolios of stocks. The response has been the NYSE Super-DOT (designated order turnaround) system, which enables traders to send coordinated buy or sell programs to the floor of the stock exchange over computer lines.

Program trading
Coordinated buy or-
ders and sell orders of
entire portfolios, usu-
ally with the aid of
computers, often to
achieve index arbitrage
objectives.

During the crash of October 1987, there was a considerable amount of program trading and index arbitrage. (Program trading refers generally to coordinated sales or purchases of entire portfolios, while index arbitrage refers specifically to timely exploitation of violations of spot-futures parity.) Although it is not clear that index arbitrage exacerbated the market crash, the New York Stock Exchange has placed limits on the use of Super-DOT after big market price swings, thereby impeding index arbitrage during periods of high volatility. While several firms have announced since that they will forgo such activities, at least for their own accounts, many others continue to engage in the practice, especially for their customers. Figure 20.7 presents estimates of the top volume program traders in early 1990.

In each year, there are four maturing S&P 500 futures contracts. On these four Fridays, which occur simultaneously with the expiration of S&P index options and options on some individual stocks, the market has tended to exhibit above-average volatility. These dates have been dubbed the **triple witching hour** because of the volatility associated with the expirations in the three types of contracts, although it appears that only the futures contract expiration actually affects the market.

Triple-witching
hour   The four times
a year that the S&P
500 futures contract
expires at the same
time as the S&P 100
index option contract
and option contracts
on individual stocks.

Expiration-day volatility can be explained by program trading to exploit arbitrage opportunities. Suppose that some time before a stock index future contract matures, the futures price is a little above its parity value. Arbitrageurs will attempt to lock in superior profits by buying the stocks in the index (the program trading buy order) and taking an offsetting short futures position. If and when the pricing disparity reverses, the position can be unwound at a profit. Alternatively, arbitrageurs can wait until contract maturity day and realize a profit by simultaneously closing out the offsetting stock and futures positions. By waiting until contract maturity, arbitrageurs can be assured that the futures price and stock index price will be aligned—they rely on the convergence property.

Obviously, when many program traders follow such a strategy at contract expiration, a wave of program selling passes over the market. The result? Prices go down. This is the expiration-day effect. If execution of the arbitrage strategy calls for an initial sale (or short sale) of stocks, unwinding on expiration day requires repurchase of the stocks, with the opposite effect: prices will increase.

Figure 20.7
Major program traders.
From *The Wall Street Journal*, August 30, 1990. Reprinted by permission of *THE WALL STREET JOURNAL*, © 1990 Dow Jones & Company, Inc. All Rights Reserved Worldwide.

Top Program Traders

Average weekly program trading volume from July 2 through mid-August for 10 most-active firms, in millions of shares

FIRM	STOCK-INDEX ARBITRAGE	OTHER STRATEGIES	TOTAL
Kidder Peabody	11.7	1.9	13.6
Morgan Stanley	4.1	8.6	12.7
Susquehanna	6.1	0.6	6.7
Goldman Sachs	0.7	5.0	5.7
Merrill Lynch	–	5.1	5.1
Bear Stearns	3.5	1.5	5.0
First Boston	2.0	2.9	4.9
Salomon Brothers	0.7	3.8	4.5
PaineWebber	0.2	3.8	4.0
Shearson Lehman	–	2.7	2.7

Source: New York Stock Exchange

Figure 20.8
Program trading activity.
From *The Wall Street Journal*, May 24, 1991. Reprinted by permission of *THE WALL STREET JOURNAL*, © 1991 Dow Jones & Company, Inc. All Rights Reserved Worldwide.

NYSE PROGRAM TRADING

Volume (in millions of shares) for the week ending May 10, 1991

Top 15 Firms	Index Arbitrage	Other Strategies	Total
Kidder Peabody	11.6	0.7	12.3
Nomura Securities	9.8	0.3	10.1
Morgan Stanley	2.4	6.4	8.8
PaineWebber	1.8	4.7	6.5
First Boston	5.1	0.2	5.3
Merrill Lynch	....	4.9	4.9
Susquehanna	4.2	0.2	4.4
Goldman Sachs	3.9	0.4	4.3
Bear Stearns	2.3	1.7	4.0
LIT America	3.4	....	3.4
Daiwa Securities	2.4	0.2	2.6
Miller Tabak	2.0	....	2.0
Shearson Lehman	....	2.0	2.0
Walsh Greenwood	1.4	....	1.4
Charles Schwab	....	0.8	0.8
OVERALL TOTAL	50.5	23.7	74.2

Source: New York Stock Exchange

The program trading associated with index arbitrage commonly accounts for 5 to 10 percent of NYSE daily volume. *The Wall Street Journal* regularly reports on program trading, both in aggregate and for the largest traders. Figure 20.8 is a reproduction of one such report. An interesting recent development, described in the accompanying box, is the emergence of the Major Market Index as a tool for index arbitrage.

Major Market Index Regains Popularity

But Resurgence Sparks Concern

NEW YORK—Hardly traded after the 1987 crash, the little known Major Market Index is back in favor with big professional stock traders.

But the resurgence of the index, which includes 17 of the 30 stocks on the Dow Jones Industrial Average, is hardly welcome on the floor of the New York Stock Exchange. There, traders in the 30 Dow industrial stocks fear the index will bring a return of the wild pre-crash days of heavy computer-driven program trading.

"If you want to manipulate the market short-term and touch off program buying and selling, the easiest way to do it is with the Major Market Index," said one New York trader.

The Chicago Board of Trade's MMI is often used by program traders because it is cheaper to trade than the Standard & Poor's 500 stock index.

Anyone who wants to buy the stocks underlying the S&P 500 has to buy a basket of 500 stocks: but the MMI has only 20 stocks. Those 20 are among the biggest stocks in America and happen to be the day-to-day favorites of big program traders: stocks such as Merck, International Business Machines, Coca-Cola, Johnson & Johnson and Dow Chemical.

Program traders use computer-driven strategies to profit from small differences between stock index futures and the underlying stocks; they buy whichever is cheaper and sell the more expensive. Be-

cause of the MMI's lower trading volume, the index can be controlled by powerful trading firms, traders say. Consequently, prices of stocks in the index often swing abruptly.

The fear of the MMI by Big Board specialists who make markets in the 30 Dow industrial stocks is easy to understand. Once a month, these Big Board market makers face an explosive hour of trading that forces millions of shares through specialists in an event known as the "double-witching hour."

This is the simultaneous expiration of Standard & Poor's 100-stock index options and MMI futures and options; in the final hour before the big Board closes, futures and options traders unwind trading strategies.

Typically, a blizzard of orders to buy or sell hits the specialists, who are often unable to match the other side of the trade. The result is usually high pressure final-hour search for stock by exchange officials. If the order can't be matched, specialists ultimately must buy or sell the securities, exposing themselves to substantial risk.

"At some time, this thing is going to explode in people's faces," says New York Stock Exchange specialist Brian Hunter of J & B Specialists. "There is no question about it."

With program trading in MMI futures becoming more popular, specialists say the day is coming when

Foreign Exchange Futures

Exchange rates between currencies vary continually and often substantially. This variability can be a source of concern for anyone involved in international business. A U.S. exporter who sells goods in England, for example, will be paid in British pounds, and the dollar value of those pounds depends on the exchange rate at the time payment is made. Until that date, the U.S. exporter is exposed to foreign exchange rate risk. This risk can be hedged through currency futures or forward markets. For example, if you know you will receive £100,000 in 60 days, you can sell those pounds forward today in the forward market and lock in an exchange rate equal to today's forward price.

The forward market in foreign exchange is fairly informal. It is simply a network of banks and brokers that allows customers to enter forward contracts to purchase or sell currency in the future at a currently agreed-upon rate of exchange. The bank market in currencies is among the largest in the world, and most large traders with sufficient creditworthiness execute their trades here rather than in futures markets. Unlike those in futures markets, contracts in

they will be asked to match million-share trades in the one-hour time frame with no one immediately stepping up to supply the stock. Although not impossible technically, it would undoubtedly require a huge financial risk for the floor dealers who would end up buying or selling much of the stock themselves, and bearing the risk over the weekend.

"My job is not to be a block positioner," says R. Peter Sullivan III, partner in the specialist firm Mercator Partners. "I am not here to buy or sell 200,000 or 300,000 shares."

"If there is tremendous imbalance, why should I risk $8 million or $10 million?" says John Geary, partner in Ziebarth, Geary & Co. and the specialist in Merck stock.

Big brokerage firms have helped supply stock during the double-witching hour to ease huge imbalances of buy and sell orders. But there is widespread fear among floor traders that the wrong confluence of events could keep institutions and brokers preoccupied with their portfolios and not trading on the floor.

At the root of the MMI problem, traders say, are unequal rules governing the amount of cash, or margin, needed to trade futures on indexes like the MMI vs. the margin on stocks.

An MMI futures trader can influence $1 million worth of the instrument's underlying stocks with $28,000. Big Board specialist firms need more than ten times that amount—$300,000 for every $1 million of stock—according to exchange rules.

The unequal margin requirements give futures traders a huge advantage over individual investors who own blue-chips like Merck or Johnson & Johnson. With their tremendous margin advantage; a group of futures traders can send individual Dow stocks jumping up or down in price.

The Securities and Exchange Commission is reviewing the double-witching hour, says Richard Ketchum, director of the SEC's division of market regulation. Exchange officials say the SEC may move to force the expiration to Friday morning from Friday afternoon. This would give Big Board specialists a whole day to meet huge buy or sell orders.

But floor traders say that it may take a "mini melt-up or melt-down" in several stocks to force a change in margin guidelines or expiration times.

A change to a morning expiration will undoubtedly cause problems in other markets. It could greatly diminish volume in MMI options, which trade on the American Stock Exchange.

From Craig Torres, "Major Market Index Regains Popularity," *The Wall Street Journal*, August 14, 1989, p. C1. Reprinted by permission of *THE WALL STREET JOURNAL*, © 1989 Dow Jones & Company, Inc. All Rights Reserved Worldwide.

these markets are not standardized in a formal market setting. Instead, each is negotiated separately. Moreover, there is no marking to market as would occur in futures markets. Currency forward contracts call for execution only at the maturity date.

For currency futures, however, there are formal markets established by the Chicago Mercantile Exchange (International Monetary Market), the London International Financial Futures Exchange, and the MidAmerica Commodity Exchange. Here, contracts are standardized by size, and daily marking to market is observed. Moreover, there are standard clearing arrangements that allow traders to enter or reverse positions easily.

Figure 20.9 reproduces a *Wall Street Journal* listing of foreign exchange spot and forward rates. The listing gives the number of U.S. dollars required to purchase some unit of foreign currency and then the amount of foreign currency needed to purchase $1. Figure 20.10 reproduces futures listings, which show the number of dollars needed to purchase a given unit of foreign currency. In Figure 20.9, both spot and forward exchange rates are listed for various delivery dates.

Figure 20.9
Spot and forward prices in foreign exchange.
From *The Wall Street Journal*, June 7, 1991. Reprinted by permission of *THE WALL STREET JOURNAL*, © 1991 Dow Jones & Company, Inc. All Rights Reserved Worldwide.

EXCHANGE RATES

Thursday, June 6, 1991
The New York foreign exchange selling rates below apply to trading among banks in amounts of $1 million and more, as quoted at 3 p.m. Eastern time by Bankers Trust Co. and other sources. Retail transactions provide fewer units of foreign currency per dollar.

Country	U.S. $ equiv. Thurs.	Wed.	Currency per U.S. $ Thurs.	Wed.
Argentina (Austral) ...	.0001008	.0001008	9925.00	9925.00
Australia (Dollar)	.7507	.7593	1.3321	1.3170
Austria (Schilling)	.08110	.08130	12.33	12.30
Bahrain (Dinar)	2.6522	2.6522	.3771	.3771
Belgium (Franc)				
Commercial rate	.02773	.02779	36.06	35.99
Brazil (Cruzeiro)	.00357	.00358	279.89	279.17
Britain (Pound)	1.6870	1.6930	.5928	.5907
30-Day Forward	1.6795	1.6853	.5954	.5934
90-Day Forward	1.6658	1.6714	.6003	.5983
180-Day Forward	1.6494	1.6553	.6063	.6041
Canada (Dollar)	.8722	.8731	1.1465	1.1453
30-Day Forward	.8702	.8711	1.1491	1.1480
90-Day Forward	.8666	.8672	1.1539	1.1532
180-Day Forward	.8615	.8616	1.1608	1.1606
Chile (Peso)	.003007	.003008	332.60	332.50
China (Renmimbi)	.188324	.188324	5.3100	5.3100
Colombia (Peso)	.001750	.001750	571.50	571.35
Denmark (Krone)	.1485	.1488	6.7326	6.7190
Ecuador (Sucre)				
Floating rate	.000966	.000966	1035.00	1035.00
Finland (Markka)	.24155	.24190	4.1400	4.1340
France (Franc)	.16835	.16883	5.9400	5.9230
30-Day Forward	.16786	.16829	5.9575	5.9422
90-Day Forward	.16696	.16739	5.9895	5.9740
180-Day Forward	.16583	.16622	6.0302	6.0160
Germany (Mark)	.5702	.5716	1.7537	1.7495
30-Day Forward	.5689	.5702	1.7579	1.7538
90-Day Forward	.5661	.5674	1.7664	1.7624
180-Day Forward	.5627	.5638	1.7773	1.7737
Greece (Drachma)	.005215	.005215	191.75	191.75
Hong Kong (Dollar) ...	.12922	.12918	7.7390	7.7410
India (Rupee)	.04766	.04766	20.98	20.98
Indonesia (Rupiah)	.0005144	.0005144	1944.00	1944.00
Ireland (Punt)	1.5290	1.5295	.6540	.6538
Israel (Shekel)	.4249	.4230	2.3533	2.3640
Italy (Lira)	.0007698	.0007716	1299.00	1296.01
Japan (Yen)	.007184	.007179	139.20	139.30
30-Day Forward	.007174	.007168	139.40	139.50
90-Day Forward	.007157	.007152	139.73	139.83
180-Day Forward	.007141	.007137	140.04	140.12
Jordan (Dinar)	1.4684	1.4684	.6810	.6810
Kuwait (Dinar)	z	z	z	z
Lebanon (Pound)	.001091	.001091	917.00	917.00
Malaysia (Ringgit)	.3612	.3615	2.7685	2.7665
Malta (Lira)	3.0628	3.0628	.3265	.3265
Mexico (Peso)				
Floating rate	.0003322	.0003322	3010.00	3010.00
Netherland (Guilder) .	.5065	.5072	1.9744	1.9715
New Zealand (Dollar)	.5803	.5825	1.7232	1.7167
Norway (Krone)	.1462	.1467	6.8387	6.8178
Pakistan (Rupee)	.0422	.0422	23.67	23.67
Peru (New Sol)	1.2381	1.2381	.81	.81
Philippines (Peso)	.03697	.03697	27.05	27.05
Portugal (Escudo)	.006610	.006610	151.29	151.29
Saudi Arabia (Riyal) ..	.26663	.26663	3.7505	3.7505
Singapore (Dollar)	.5635	.5647	1.7745	1.7710
South Africa (Rand)				
Commercial rate	.3523	.3535	2.8383	2.8288
Financial rate	.2985	.3003	3.3500	3.3300
South Korea (Won) ...	.0013806	.0013806	724.30	724.30
Spain (Peseta)	.009234	.009251	108.30	108.10
Sweden (Krona)	.1586	.1592	6.3038	6.2816
Switzerland (Franc) ..	.6649	.6680	1.5040	1.4970
30-Day Forward	.6637	.6668	1.5066	1.4998
90-Day Forward	.6617	.6646	1.5112	1.5046
180-Day Forward	.6591	.6619	1.5172	1.5108
Taiwan (Dollar)	.037202	.037189	26.88	26.89
Thailand (Baht)	.03900	.03900	25.64	25.64
Turkey (Lira)	.0002441	.0002446	4097.00	4089.01
United Arab (Dirham) ...	.2724	.2724	3.6715	3.6715
Uruguay (New Peso)				
Financial	.000518	.000518	1930.00	1930.00
Venezuela (Bolivar)				
Floating rate	.01836	.01839	54.47	54.37
SDR	1.33142	1.33105	.75108	.75129
ECU	1.17659	1.17700	.....	.....

Special Drawing Rights (SDR) are based on exchange rates for the U.S., German, British, French and Japanese currencies. Source: International Monetary Fund.
European Currency Unit (ECU) is based on a basket of community currencies. Source: European Community Commission.
z-Not quoted.

FUTURES

	Open	High	Low	Settle	Change	Lifetime High	Low	Open Interest
JAPAN YEN (IMM)—12.5 million yen: $ per yen (.00)								
June		.7171	.7180				.745	43,213

Figure 20.10
Foreign exchange futures.
From *The Wall Street Journal*, June 7, 1991. Reprinted by permission of *THE WALL STREET JOURNAL*, © 1991 Dow Jones & Company, Inc. All Rights Reserved Worldwide.

CURRENCY TRADING

FUTURES

	Open	High	Low	Settle	Change	Lifetime High	Lifetime Low	Open Interest
JAPAN YEN (IMM)—12.5 million yen; $ per yen (.00)								
June	.7184	.7190	.7171	.7180	+ .0006	.8010	.6645	43,213
Sept	.7160	.7163	.7146	.7155	+ .0006	.7995	.7032	9,631
Dec	.7138	.7143	.7138	.7140	+ .0006	.7770	.7038	1,712
Mr92	....	....	.7141	+ .0005		.7540	.7095	1,192
June	....	....		.7143	+ .0006	.7220	.7150	1,470
Est vol 13,545; vol Wed 25,148; open int 57,218, +1,563.								
DEUTSCHEMARK (IMM)—125,000 marks; $ per mark								
June	.5708	.5717	.5689	.5698	— .0013	.6870	.5601	72,017
Sept	.5667	.5676	.5648	.5657	— .0013	.6810	.5561	18,340
Dec	.5634	.5634	.5620	.5621	— .0013	.6670	.5538	469
Est vol 33,764; vol Wed 49,650; open int 90,834, +3,327.								
CANADIAN DOLLAR (IMM)—100,000 dlrs.; $ per Can $								
June	.8720	.8722	.8708	.8715	— .0009	.8733	.7995	27,143
Sept	.8667	.8667	.8655	.8661	— .0009	.8677	.7985	6,211
Dec	.8609	.8617	.8609	.8611	— .0009	.8625	.8175	472
Mr92	....	....	.8568	— .0009		.8578	.8253	987
June	.8530	.8530	.8530	.8527	— .0009	.8533	.8330	173
Est vol 3,766; vol Wed 5,815; open int 35,008, +397.								
BRITISH POUND (IMM)—62,500 pds.; $ per pound								
June	1.6882	1.6920	1.6792	1.6940	—.0064	1.9610	1.6550	24,409
Sept	1.6680	1.6720	1.6582	1.6634	—.0064	1.9360	1.6346	4,803
Dec	1.6460	1.6514	1.6460	1.6472	—.0064	1.7900	1.6200	713
Est vol 13,340; vol Wed 14,971; open int 29,925, +800.								
SWISS FRANC (IMM)—125,000 francs; $ per franc								
June	.6675	.6676	.6635	.6639	— .0038	.8084	.6635	35,761
Sept	.6641	.6643	.6605	.6607	— .0037	.8055	.6605	9,278
Dec	.6600	.6600	.6585	.6583	— .0037	.8090	.6585	162
Est vol 22,587; vol Wed 31,603; open int 45,266, +2,338.								
AUSTRALIAN DOLLAR (IMM)—100,000 dlrs.; $ per A.$								
June	.7510	.7522	.7493	.7494	— .0086	.7815	.7493	1,685
Sept	.7435	.7445	.7415	.7420	— .0085	.7730	.7415	1,076
Est vol 1,433; vol Wed 492; open int 2,761, —154.								
U.S. DOLLAR INDEX (FINEX)—500 times USDX								
June	93.70	94.03	93.60	93.92	+ .25	95.19	81.45	5,339
Sept	94.71	95.00	94.69	94.91	+ .26	96.02	83.17	1,885
Dec	...	....	....	95.71	+ .27	96.62	67.20	492
Est vol 3,740; vol Wed 1,787; open int 7,716, +144.								
The index: High 93.86; Low 93.52; Close 93.75 +.24								

—OTHER CURRENCY FUTURES—

Settlement prices of selected contracts. Volume and open interest of all contract months.

British Pound (MCE) 12,500 pounds; $ per pound
Sep 1.6634 —.0064; Est. vol. 110; Open Int. 239
Japanese Yen (MCE) 6.25 million yen; $ per yen (.00)
Sep .7155 +.0006; Est. vol. 110; Open Int. 226
Swiss Franc (MCE) 62,500 francs; $ per franc
Sep .6607 —.0037; Est. vol. 300; Open Int. 575
Deutschemark (MCE) 62,500 marks; $ per mark
Sep .5657 —.0013; Est. vol. 220; Open Int. 1,140
FINEX—Financial Instrument Exchange, a division of the New York Cotton Exchange. IMM—International Monetary Market at the Chicago Mercantile Exchange. MCE—MidAm... ...y Exchange...

The forward quotations always apply to rolling delivery in 30, 90, or 180 days. Thus, tomorrow's forward listings will apply to a maturity date one day later than today's listing. In contrast, the futures contracts mature at specified dates in March, June, September, and December; these four maturity days are the only dates each year when futures contracts settle.

Interest Rate Futures

The late 1970s and 1980s saw a dramatic increase in the volatility of interest rates, leading to investor desire to hedge returns on fixed-income securities against changes in interest rates. As one example, thrift institutions that had loaned money on home mortgages before 1975 suffered substantial capital losses on those loans when interest rates later increased. An interest rate futures contract could have protected banks against such large swings in yields. The significance of these losses has spurred trading in interest rate futures.

The major interest rate contracts currently traded are on Eurodollars, Treasury bills, Treasury notes, Treasury bonds, and a municipal bond index. The range of these securities provides an opportunity to hedge against a wide spectrum of maturities from very short (T-bills) to long term (T-bonds). In addition, futures contracts tied to interest rates in Germany and the United Kingdom trade on the London International Financial Futures Exchange (LIFFE) and are listed in *The Wall Street Journal*. Figure 20.11 shows listings of some of these contracts in *The Wall Street Journal*.

The Treasury contracts call for delivery of a Treasury bond, bill, or note. Should interest rates rise, the market value of the security at delivery will be less than the original futures price, and the deliverer will profit. Hence, the short position in the interest rate futures contract gains when interest rates rise.

Similarly, Treasury bond futures can be useful hedging vehicles for bond dealers or underwriters. We saw earlier, for example, how the T-bond contract could be used by an investor to hedge the value of a T-bond portfolio or by a pension fund manager who anticipates the purchase of a Treasury bond. The newer contract on the municipal bond index allows for more direct hedging of long-term bonds other than Treasury issues.

An episode that occurred in October 1979 illustrates the potential hedging value offered by T-bond contracts. Salomon Brothers, Merrill Lynch, and other underwriters brought out a $1 billion issue of IBM bonds. As is typical, the underwriting syndicate quoted an interest rate at which it guaranteed the bonds could be sold. (In essence, the syndicate buys the company's bonds at an agreed-upon price and then takes the responsibility of reselling them in the open market. If interest rates increase before the bonds can be sold to the public, the syndicate, not the issuer, bears the capital loss from the fall in the value of the bonds.)

In this case, the syndicate led by Salomon Brothers and Merrill Lynch brought out the IBM debt to sell at yields of 9.62 percent for $500 million of 7-year notes and 9.41 percent for $500 million of 25-year bonds. These yields were only about four basis points above comparable maturity U.S. government bond yields, reflecting IBM's excellent credit rating. The debt issue was brought to market on Thursday, October 4, when the underwriters began placing the bonds with customers. Interest rates, however, rose slightly that Thursday, making the IBM yields less attractive, and only about 70 percent of the issue had been placed by Friday afternoon, leaving the syndicate still holding between $250 million and $300 million of bonds.

Then on Saturday, October 6, the Federal Reserve Board announced a major credit-tightening policy. Interest rates jumped by almost a full percentage point. The underwriting syndicate realized the balance of the IBM bonds could not be placed to its regular customers at the original offering price and decided to sell them in the open bond market. By that time, the bonds had fallen nearly 5 percent in value, so that the underwriter's loss was about $12 million on the unsold bonds. The net loss on the underwriting operation came to about $7 million, after the profit of $5 million that had been realized on the bonds that were placed.

As the major underwriter with the lion's share of the bonds, Salomon lost about $3.5 million on the bond issue. Yet, while most of the other underwriters were vulnerable to the interest rate movement, Salomon had hedged its bond holdings by shorting about $100 million in GNMA and Treasury bond futures.

INTEREST RATE INSTRUMENTS

OPTIONS

Thursday, June 6, 1991
For Notes and Bonds, decimals in closing prices represent 32nds; 1.01 means 1 1/32. For Bills, decimals in closing prices represent basis points; $25 per .01.

Chicago Board Options Exchange

OPTIONS ON LONG-TERM INTEREST RATES

Strike Price	Calls—Last			Puts—Last		
	Jun	Jul	Aug	Jun	Jul	Aug
80	2 9/16	....	....	....	....	....
82½	....	....	....	11/16	....	....

Total call volume 127 Total call open int. 775
Total put volume 20 Total put open int. 1,314
LTX levels: High 82.63; Low 82.05; Close 82.58, +0.40

FUTURES

	Open	High	Low	Settle	Chg	Yield Settle	Chg	Open Interest
TREASURY BONDS (CBT)–$100,000; pts. 32nds of 100%							
June	94-21	94-23	94-05	94-11	− 7	8.597	+ .024	48,899
Sept	93-24	93-29	93-09	93-16	− 7	8.691	+ .024	180,247
Dec	93-00	93-05	92-18	92-25	− 7	8.772	+ .025	4,521
Mr92	92-17	92-20	92-02	92-06	− 7	8.839	+ .025	2,211
June	91-29	91-29	91-17	91-21	− 7	8.900	+ .025	2,120
Sept	....	....	....	91-06	− 7	8.955	+ .026	311
Dec	....	....	....	90-24	− 7	9.006	+ .026	152

Est vol 275,000; vol Wed 383,178; op int 238,461, −7,003.

TREASURY BONDS (MCE)–$50,000; pts. 32nds of 100%							
June	94-22	94-22	94-06	94-09	− 9	8.604	+ .031	1,880
Sept	93-26	93-29	93-09	93-14	− 9	8.698	+ .031	6,658

Est vol 6,000; vol Wed 6,922; open int 8,561, +911.

T–BONDS (CBT)–$100,000; pts of 100%							
June	94-25	94-26	94-16	94-14	− 0-10	97-17	89-28	1,206
Sept	93-29	93-29	93-14	93-18	− 0-10	95-11	93-14	2,251

Est vol 91; vol Wed 2,773; open int 3,457, −24.

GERMAN GOV'T. BOND (LIFFE)							
250,000 marks; $ per mark (.01)							
Sept	85.57	85.69	85.53	85.64	+ .04	86.80	81.33	71,080

Est vol 18,876; vol Wed 25,857; open int 71,082, +2,101.

TREASURY NOTES (CBT)–$100,000; pts 32nds of 100%							
June	98-12	98-14	98-00	98-03	− 8	8.284	+ .038	24,721
Sept	97-22	97-23	97-07	97-12	− 8	8.393	+ .038	52,608
Dec	96-24	96-25	96-19	96-23	− 8	8.493	+ .038	190

Est vol 24,500; vol Wed 28,095; open int 77,519, −370.

5 YR TREAS NOTES (CBT)–$100,000; pts. 32nds of 100%							
June	100-16	100-16	100-08	100-10	− 5.5	7.92	+ .04	17,596
Sept	99-28	99-285	99-19	99-21	− 6.0	8.09	+ .05	49,883

Est vol 14,124; vol Wed 16,673; open int 67,479, −1,935.

2 YR TREAS NOTES (CBT)–$200,000, pts. 32nds of 100%							
June	01-215	101-23	101-17	101-18	− 3	7.148	+ .051	8,758
Sept	01-005	01-005	100-27	100-28	− 4	7.521	+ .068	4,751

Est vol 1,000; vol Wed 1,074; open int 13,489, +261.

30-DAY INTEREST RATE (CBT)-$5 million; pts. of 100%							
June	94.16	94.16	94.15	94.15	+ .01	5.85	− .01	1,475
July	94.14	94.15	94.14	94.14	+ .01	5.86	− .01	1,009
Aug	94.11	94.11	94.09	94.09	....	5.91	....	681
Sept	94.03	94.03	94.02	94.02	....	5.98	....	821
Oct	93.95	93.95	93.94	93.94	− .01	6.06	+ .01	243
Nov	93.85	93.85	93.82	93.82	− .03	6.18	+ .03	115
Dec	....	....	93.60	93.60	− .03	6.40	+ .03	343

Est vol 660; vol Wed 940; open int 4,687, +463.

TREASURY BILLS (IMM)–$1 mil.; pts. of 100%							
	Open	High	Low	Settle	Chg	Discount Settle	Chg	Open Interest
June	94.37	94.39	94.37	94.37	....	5.63	....	15,289
Sept	94.27	94.27	94.23	94.25	....	5.75	....	31,207
Dec	93.85	93.86	93.81	93.82	− .01	6.18	+ .01	6,111
Mr92	....	....	....	93.69	....	6.31	....	238

Est vol 6,192; vol Wed 6,774; open int 52,922, −612.

LIBOR-1 MO. (IMM)–$3,000,000; points of 100%							
June	93.94	93.95	93.89	93.90	....	6.10	....	4,445
July	93.95	93.95	93.88	93.89	+ .01	6.11	− .01	3,313
Aug	93.86	93.89	93.83	93.83	− .01	6.17	+ .01	834
Sept	93.67	93.68	93.67	93.68	− .01	6.32	+ .01	512

Est vol 1,545; vol Wed 1,468; open int 11,172, +580.

| | Open | High | Low | Settle | Chg | High | Low | Open Interest |
| **MUNI BOND INDEX (CBT) — pts. Bond B...** ||||||||

	Open	High	Low	Settle	Chg	High	Low	Open Interest
Sept	90-22	90-23	90-13	90-16	− 5	92-11	87-00	3,175

Est vol 3,500; vol Wed 3,846; open int 7,276, −489.
The index: Close 92-07; Yield 7.32.

EURODOLLAR (IMM)–$1 million; pts of 100%								
	Open	High	Low	Settle	Chg	Yield Settle	Chg	Open Interest
June	93.81	93.82	93.78	93.79	....	6.21	....	179,855
Sept	93.54	93.55	93.49	93.52	....	6.48	....	235,740
Dec	93.03	93.04	92.95	92.98	− .01	7.02	+ .01	143,597
Mr92	92.85	92.86	93.75	92.78	− .02	7.22	+ .02	103,908
June	92.45	92.46	92.34	92.38	− .05	7.62	+ .05	51,841
Sept	92.17	92.18	92.04	92.08	− .07	7.92	+ .07	37,576
Dec	91.89	91.89	91.77	91.89	− .07	8.11	+ .07	32,058
Mr93	91.87	91.88	91.76	91.78	− .07	8.22	+ .07	27,820
June	91.75	91.75	91.63	91.65	− .07	8.35	+ .07	20,311
Sept	91.60	91.60	91.49	91.51	− .06	8.49	+ .06	15,857
Dec	91.38	91.38	91.27	91.29	− .06	8.71	+ .06	10,786
Mr94	91.34	91.34	91.24	91.25	− .06	8.75	+ .06	8,129
June	91.21	91.21	91.11	91.14	− .06	8.86	+ .06	6,286
Sept	91.15	91.15	91.04	91.07	− .07	8.93	+ .07	4,718
Dec	90.97	90.97	90.90	90.93	− .07	9.07	+ .07	4,471
Mr95	90.97	90.97	90.86	90.89	− .07	9.11	+ .07	3,718

Est vol 140,337; vol Wed 132,830; open int 886,671, −1,071.

EURODOLLAR (LIFFE)–$1 million; pts of 100%								
	Open	High	Low	Settle	Change	Lifetime High	Low	Open Interest
June	93.81	93.82	92.78	93.80	....	93.96	90.43	15,602
Sept	93.53	93.55	93.50	93.50	.01	93.77	90.54	12,231
Dec	93.02	93.04	92.96	92.97	....	93.32	90.58	6,066
Mr92	92.85	92.87	92.77	92.78	.02	93.16	90.60	1,909
June	92.47	92.47	92.45	92.39	.04	92.62	90.97	743
Sept	92.16	92.16	92.16	92.11	.03	92.31	90.97	272
Dec	91.88	91.88	91.88	91.83	.03	91.88	91.88	122
Mr93	91.82	91.82	91.82	91.81	.03	91.82	91.82	238

Est vol 3,540; vol Wed 4,487; open int 37,183, +305.

STERLING (LIFFE)–£500,000; pts of 100%								
June	88.78	88.79	88.75	88.76	.01	89.10	85.75	37,167
Sept	89.58	89.62	89.55	89.56	.01	89.69	86.23	38,422
Dec	89.84	89.86	89.81	89.82	.01	89.86	86.52	26,240
Mr92	89.89	89.92	89.88	89.88	.01	89.94	86.68	16,496
June	89.61	89.68	89.61	89.61	.01	89.68	87.45	8,744
Sept	89.38	89.40	89.38	89.40	.03	89.48	87.46	4,384
Dec	89.25	89.25	89.24	89.25	.02	89.50	87.55	2,603
Mr93	89.17	89.17	89.16	89.18	.02	89.54	87.50	1,235
June	89.13	89.13	89.13	89.13	....	89.48	87.58	728
Sept	89.11	89.11	89.11	89.11	....	89.60	88.20	864
Dec	89.09	89.09	89.09	89.09	....	89.43	88.95	990

Est vol 15,683; vol Wed 11,754; open int 137,873, 551.

LONG GILT (LIFFE)–£50,000; 32nds of 100%								
June	89-19	89-28	89-19	89-22	+ 0-03	94-17	84-00	1,042
Sept	89-27	89-28	89-21	89-26	+ 0-03	91-24	89-21	36,384

Est vol 11,963; vol Wed 17,009; open int 37,461, +1,570.

—OTHER INTEREST RATE FUTURES—.

Settlement prices of selected contracts. Volume and open interest of all contract months.

Mortgage-Backed (CBT)–$100,000, pts. & 64ths of 100%
Jly Cpn 8.5 96-20 −6; Est. vol. 5; Open Int. 131

CBT–Chicago Board of Trade. FINEX–Financial Instrument Exchange, a division of the New York Cotton Exchange. IMM–International Monetary Market at Chicago Mercantile Exchange. LIFFE–London International Financial ... Exchange. ...America C...

Figure 20.11 Interest rate futures.
From *The Wall Street Journal*, June 7, 1991. Reprinted by permission of THE WALL STREET JOURNAL, © 1991 Dow Jones & Company, Inc. All Rights Reserved Worldwide.

Holding a short position, Salomon Brothers realized profits on the contract when interest rates increased. The profits on the short futures position resulted because the value of the bonds required to be delivered to satisfy the contract decreased when interest rates rose. Salomon Brothers probably about broke even on the entire transaction, making estimated gains on the futures position of about $3.5 million, which largely offset the capital loss on the bonds it was holding.

How could Salomon Brothers have constructed the proper hedge ratio, that is, the proper number of futures contracts per bond held in its inventory? The T-bond futures contract nominally calls for delivery of an 8 percent coupon, 20-year maturity government bond in return for the futures price. (In practice, other bonds may be substituted for this standard bond to settle the contract, but we will use the 8 percent bond for illustration.) Suppose the market interest rate is 10 percent and Salomon is holding $100 million worth of bonds, with a coupon rate of 10 percent and 20-years to maturity. The bonds currently sell at 100 percent of par value. If the interest rate were to jump to 11 percent, the bonds would fall in value to a market value of $91.98 per $100 of par value, a loss of $8.02 million. (We use semiannual compounding in this calculation.)

To hedge this risk, Salomon would need to short enough futures so that the profits on the futures position would offset the loss on the bonds. The 8 percent, 20-year bond of the futures contract would sell for $82.84 at an interest rate of 10 percent. If the interest rate were to jump to 11 percent, the bond price would fall to $75.93, and the fall in the price of the 8 percent bond, $6.91, would approximately equal the profit on the short futures position per $100 par value.[6] Because each contract calls for delivery of $100,000 par value of bonds, the gain on each short position would equal $6,910. Thus, to offset the $8.02 million loss on the value of the bonds, Salomon theoretically would need to hold $8.02 million/$6,910 = 1,161 contracts short. The total gain on the contracts would offset the loss on the bonds and leave Salomon unaffected by interest rate swings.

The actual hedging problem is more difficult for several reasons: (1) Salomon probably would hold more than one issue of bonds in its inventory; (2) interest rates on government and corporate bonds will not be equal and need not move in lockstep; (3) the T-bond contract may be settled with any of several bonds instead of the 8 percent benchmark bond; and (4) taxes could complicate the picture. Nevertheless, the principles illustrated here underlie all hedging activity.

Summary

1. Forward contracts are arrangements that call for future delivery of an asset at a currently agreed-upon price. The long trader is obligated to purchase the good, and the short trader is obligated to deliver it. If the price at the maturity of the contract exceeds the forward price, the long side benefits by virtue of acquiring the good at the contract price.

---

[6]We say approximately because the exact figure depends on the time to maturity of the contract. We assume here that the maturity date is less than a month away so that the futures price and the bond price move in virtual lockstep.

2. A futures contract is similar to a forward contract, differing most importantly in the aspects of standardization and marking to market, which is the process by which gains and losses on futures contract positions are settled daily. In contrast, forward contracts call for no cash transfers until contract maturity.

3. Futures contracts are traded on organized exchanges that standardize the size of the contract, the grade of the deliverable asset, the delivery date, and the delivery location. Traders negotiate only the contract price. This standardization creates increased liquidity in the marketplace and means buyers and sellers can easily find many traders for a desired purchase or sale.

4. The clearinghouse acts as an intermediary between each pair of traders, acting as the short position for each long, and as the long position for each short, so traders need not be concerned about the performance of the trader on the opposite side of the contract. Traders are required to post margins in order to guarantee their own performance on the contracts.

5. The gain or loss to the long side for a futures contract held between time 0 and t is $F_t - F_0$. Because $F_T = P_T$, the long's profit if the contract is held until maturity is $P_T - F_0$, where P_T is the spot price at time T and F_0 is the original futures price. The gain or loss to the short position is $F_0 - P_T$.

6. Futures contracts may be used for hedging or speculating. Speculators use the contracts to take a stand on the ultimate price of an asset. Short hedgers take short positions in contracts to offset any gains or losses on the value of an asset already held in inventory. Long hedgers take long positions to offset gains or losses in the purchase price of a good.

7. The spot-futures parity relationship states that the equilibrium futures price on an asset providing no services or payments (such as dividends) is $F_0 = P_0(1 + r_f)^T$. If the futures price deviates from this value, then market participants can earn arbitrage profits.

8. If the asset provides services or payments with yield d, the parity relationship becomes $F_0 = P_0(1 + r - d)^T$. This model is also called the cost of carry model, because it states that the futures price must exceed the spot price by the net cost of carrying the asset until maturity date T.

9. Futures contracts calling for cash settlement are traded on various stock market indexes. The contracts may be mixed with Treasury bills to construct artificial equity positions, which makes them potentially valuable tools for market timers. Market index contracts are used also by arbitrageurs who attempt to profit from violations of the parity relationship.

10. Interest rate futures allow for hedging against interest rate fluctuations in several different markets. The most actively traded contract is for Treasury bonds.

Key Terms

basis, 579	forward contract, 567	program trading, 588
basis risk, 579	futures price, 567	short position, 568
cash delivery, 575	index arbitrage, 587	spot-futures parity
clearinghouse, 571	long position, 568	theorem, 582
convergence	maintenance, or	spread, 579
property, 574	variation,	triple-witching
cost of carry	margin, 573	hour, 588
relationship, 582	marking to market, 572	

Selected Readings

The use of futures contracts in risk management is treated extensively in:
Smith, Clifford W., Jr.; Charles W. Simthson; and D. Sykes Wilford. *Managing Financial Risk.* New York: Harper & Row, 1990.

The magazine Futures *provides ongoing analysis of futures and options markets and strategies.*

Problem Sets

1. *a.* Using the accompanying figure, compute the dollar value of the stocks traded on one contract on the Standard & Poor's 500 index. The closing spot price of the S&P 500 index is given in the last line of the figure. If the margin requirement is 10 percent of the futures price times the multiplier of 500, how much must you deposit with your broker to trade the June contract?

   b. If the June futures price were to increase to $390, what rate of return would you earn on your net investment if you entered the long side of the contract at the price shown in the figure?

   c. If the June futures price falls by 1 percent, what is your rate of return?

2. Why is there no futures market in cement?

3. Why might individuals purchase futures contracts rather than the underlying asset?

4. What is the difference in cash flow between short-selling an asset and entering a short futures position?

5. Consider a stock that will pay a dividend of D dollars in one year, which is when a futures contract matures. Consider the following strategy: Buy the stock, short a futures contract on the stock, and borrow S_0 dollars, where S_0 is the current price of the stock.

   a. What are the cash flows now and in one year? (Remember the dividend the stock will pay.)

Figure for problem 1
From *The Wall Street Journal,* June 7, 1991. Reprinted by permission of *THE WALL STREET JOURNAL,* © 1991 Dow Jones & Company, Inc. All Rights Reserved Worldwide.

UTILITIES INDEX

Strike	Calls—Last			Puts—Last		
Price	Jun	Jul	Aug	Jun	Jul	Aug
225	1¼	2 1/16	....	....	....	....

Total call volume 13   Total call open int. 1,401
Total put volume 0   Total put open int. 10,493
The index: High 222.99; Low 221.63; Close 222.03, −0.85

FUTURES

S&P 500 INDEX (CME) 500 times index

	Open	High	Low	Settle	Chg	High	Low	Open Interest
June	386.30	387.10	383.60	384.35	− 1.55	393.50	300.90	108,838
Sept	389.10	389.80	386.35	387.15	− 1.50	396.20	304.00	44,601
Dec	391.80	392.80	389.60	390.20	− 1.55	399.30	316.50	3,715

Est vol 51,511; vol Wed 53,812; open int 157,195, −1,732.
Indx prelim High 385.85; Low 383.13; Close 383.63 −1.47

NIKKEI 225 Stock Average (CME)—$5 times NSA

	Open	High	Low	Settle	Chg	High	Low	Open Interest
June	25220.	25250.	25150.	25230.	− 70.0	27800.	21765.	4,726
Sept	25780	25825.	25780.	25820.	− 75.0	28350.	23430.	3,749
Dec	....	....	....	26355.	− 75.0	28900.	26955.	291

Est vol 891; vol Wed 1,904; open int 8,766, +490.
The index: High 25299.24; Low 24912.12; Close 24984.12−305.45

NYSE COMPOSITE INDEX (NYFE) 500 times index

	Open	High	Low	Settle	Chg	High	Low	Open Interest
June	211.40	211.90	210.00	210.45	− .70	215.25	165.85	5,156
Sept	212.90	213.25	211.40	211.90	− .75	216.40	173.10	961

Est vol 6,359; vol Wed 7,320; open int 6,193, +259.
The index: High 211.29; Low 210.05; Close 210.24 −.64

MAJOR MKT INDEX (CBT) $250 times index
June   422.90 424.40   .90   7.000

   b. Show that the equilibrium futures price must be $F_0 = S_0(1 + r) - D$ to avoid arbitrage.

   c. Call the dividend yield $d = D/S_0$, and conclude that $F_0 = S_0(1 + r - d)$.

6. *a.* A hypothetical futures contract on a nondividend-paying stock with current price \$150 has a maturity of one year. If the T-bill rate is 8 percent, what should the futures price be?

   b. What should the futures price be if the maturity of the contract is three years?

   c. What if the interest rate is 12 percent and the maturity of the contract is three years?

7. Your analysis leads you to believe the stock market is about to rise substantially. The market is unaware of this situation. What should you do?

8. In each of the following cases, discuss how you, as a portfolio manager, could use financial futures to protect a portfolio.

   a. You own a large position in a relatively illiquid bond that you want to sell.

   b. You have a large gain on one of your long Treasuries and want to sell it, but you would like to defer the gain until the next accounting period, which begins in four weeks.

   c. You will receive a large contribution next month that you hope to invest in long-term corporate bonds on a yield basis as favorable as is now available.

9. Suppose the value of the S&P 500 stock index is currently 350. If the one-year T-bill rate is 8 percent and the expected dividend yield on the S&P 500 is 5 percent, what should the one-year maturity futures price be?

10. It is now January. The current interest rate is 8 percent. The June futures price for gold is \$346.30, while the December futures price is \$360.00. Is there an arbitrage opportunity here? If so, how would you exploit it?

11. The Chicago Board of Trade has just introduced a new futures contract on Brandex stock, a company that currently pays no dividends. Each contract calls for delivery of 1,000 shares of stock in one year. The T-bill rate is 6 percent per year.

   a. If Brandex stock now sells at \$120 per share, what should the futures price be?

   b. If the Brandex stock price drops by 3 percent, what will be the change in the futures price and the change in the investor's margin account?

   c. If the margin on the contract is \$12,000, what is the percentage return on the investor's position?

12. Your client, for whom you are underwriting a \$400 million bond issue, is concerned that market conditions will change before the issue is brought to market. He has heard it may be possible to reduce the risk exposure by hedging in the Government National Mortgage Association (GNMA) futures market. Specifically, he asks you to:

   a. Briefly explain how the hedge works.

   b. Describe *four* practical problems that would limit the effectiveness of the hedge.

13. Futures contracts and options on a futures contract can be used to modify risk. Identify the fundamental distinction between a futures contract and an option on a futures contract, and briefly explain the difference in the manner that futures and options modify *portfolio* risk.

14. The S&P portfolio pays a dividend yield of 4 percent annually. Its current value is 350. The T-bill rate is 7 percent. Suppose the S&P futures price for delivery in one year is 370. Construct an arbitrage strategy to exploit the mispricing and show that your profits one year hence will equal the mispricing in the futures market.

15. *a.* How should the parity condition (Equation 20.2) for stocks be modified for futures contracts on Treasury bonds? What should play the role of the dividend yield in that equation?

    b. In an environment with an upward-sloping yield curve, should T-bond futures prices on more distant contracts be higher or lower than those on near-term contracts?

    c. Confirm your intuition by examining Figure 20.3.

Part Six

International Diversification and Active Management

■ ■

Chapter

21

International and Extended Diversification

$\mathbf{A}$lthough we in the United States customarily treat the S&P 500 as the market index portfolio, the practice is increasingly inappropriate. Equities represent less than 25 percent of total U.S. wealth and a much smaller proportion than that of world wealth. In this chapter, we look beyond domestic markets to survey issues of extended diversification.

First, we show how international diversification can improve portfolio performance. Next, we examine exchange rate risk, and how such risk can be mitigated using foreign exchange futures and forward contracts. Then we look at investment strategies in an international context and show how performance attribution studies may be adapted to an international setting. Then we turn to "nontraditional" asset groups such as real estate and precious metals, which can play important roles in investor portfolios. After studying this chapter you should be able to:

- Demonstrate the advantages of international diversification.
- Formulate hedge strategies to offset the currency risk involved in international investments.
- Decompose investment returns into contributing factors such as country, currency, and stock selection.
- Show why investments in precious metals and real estate have been useful additions to traditional portfolios in the last two decades.
- Assess the advantages and disadvantages of adding nontraditional assets such as art or rare coins to portfolios comprised of more traditional investment vehicles.

21.1 *International Investments*

The World Market Portfolio

World investable wealth The part of world wealth that is traded and therefore accessible to investors.

To appreciate the myopia of an exclusive investment focus on U.S. stocks and bonds, consider in Figure 21.1 the components of **world investable wealth.** The pie chart shows the investable part of world wealth, that is, the part of world wealth that is traded and is accessible to investors. According to these estimates, U.S. equity makes up only 13.7 percent of the world portfolio, while U.S. stocks and bonds together comprise 37.8 percent of the world capital market. The figure excludes direct investment in durables and foreign real estate.

Figure 21.2 shows another view of the relative share of the U.S. in the world economy. Here, the breakdown is by gross national product rather than the size of the capital market, but the message is the same: the United States does not comprise the majority of the world economy. International diversification is worth exploring.

Figure 21.1
Total investable capital market: $22.2 trillion as of December 31, 1988.
Gary P. Brinson, "Global Market Risk Premia," in *Quantifying the Market Risk Premium Phenomenon for Investment Decision Making,* ed. William F. Sharpe and Katrina F. Sheppard (Institute of Chartered Financial Analysts, 1990).

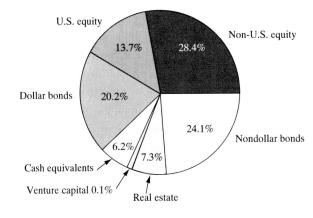

Figure 21.2
Estimates of the GNPs of major economies (December 31, 1988).
From: John A. Morrell, "Introduction to International Equity Diversification," in *International Investing for U.S. Pension Funds* (London/ Venice: Institute for Fiduciary Education, May 6–13, 1989).

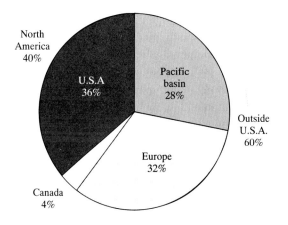

This is clear evidence that "traditional" U.S. assets—stocks, bonds, and bills—are but a small fraction of the potential universe of investments. Table 21.1 further highlights the potential of international diversification per se, even ignoring diversification into real assets such as metals or real estate. The table shows that U.S. equities in 1990 represented only a 47.76 percent share of some of the world's major equity markets. If you confine a portfolio exclusively to U.S. asset classes, clearly you will pass up important opportunities for diversification.

International Diversification

From the discussion of diversification in Chapter 8, you know that adding to a portfolio assets that are not perfectly correlated will enhance the reward-to-volatility ratio. Increasing globalization lets us take advantage of foreign securities as a feasible way to extend diversification.

The evidence in Figure 21.3 is clear. The figure presents the standard deviation of equally weighted portfolios of various sizes as a percent of the average standard deviation of a one-stock portfolio. That is, a value of 20 means the diversified portfolio has only 20 percent the standard deviation of a typical stock.

There is a marked reduction in risk for a portfolio that includes foreign as well as U.S. stocks, so rational investors should invest across borders. Adding international to national investments enhances the power of portfolio diversification.

Table 21.2 presents results from a study of equity returns showing that although the correlation coefficients between the U.S. stock index and stock index portfolios of other large industrialized economies are typically positive, they are much smaller than 1.0. Most correlations are below 0.5. In contrast, correlation coefficients between diversified U.S. portfolios, say, with 40 to 50 securities, typically exceed 0.9. This imperfect correlation across national boundaries allows for the improvement in diversification potential that shows up in Figure 21.3

Table 21.1   *Major Equity Markets, June 1990*

	Value* (Millions)	Percent of Sample
United States	$2,941.3	47.76%
Japan	1,632.9	26.51
United Kingdom	849.8	13.80
France	265.4	4.31
Germany	235.8	3.83
Canada	233.5	3.79
Total	$6,158.7	100

*Market values exclude intercorporate cross-holdings.

From Kenneth R. French and James M. Poterba, "Investor Diversification and International Equity Markets," NBER Working Paper, No. 3609, January 1991.

Figure 21.3
International diversification.
Modified from B. Solnik, "Why Not Diversify Internationally Rather Than Domestically," *Financial Analysts Journal*, July–August 1974.

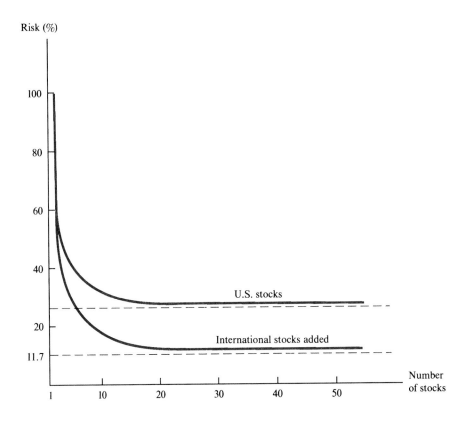

Risk (%)

U.S. stocks

International stocks added

Number of stocks

Concept Check

Question 1.   What would Figure 21.3 look like if we allowed the possibility of diversifying into real estate investments in addition to foreign equity?

Figure 21.4 gives yet a different perspective on opportunities for international diversification. It shows risk-return opportunities offered by several asset classes, alone and combined into portfolios. (All returns here are calculated in terms of U.S. dollars.) The efficient frontiers generated from the full set of assets including foreign stocks and bonds offer the best possible risk-return pairs; they are vastly superior to the risk-return profile of U.S. stocks alone.

Evidence that investors are increasingly aware of the importance of the international sector shows up in the international investments of pension plans. These are summarized in Figure 21.5.

Individuals, too, can now easily invest internationally. Many mutual funds cater to the demand for international diversification. For example, Fidelity offers funds with investments concentrated overseas generally, in Europe, in the Pacific basin, and in developing economies in an emerging opportunities fund. Vanguard, consistent with its indexing philosophy, offers separate index funds for Europe and the Pacific basin. In addition, several firms sponsor single country mutual funds. In 1991, for example, there were funds for these (and other) countries: Austria, Australia, Brazil, Chile, Germany, India, Indonesia, Ireland, Italy, Japan, Korea, Malaysia, Mexico, the Philippines, Portugal, Singapore, Spain, Switzerland, Taiwan, Thailand, Turkey, and the United Kingdom.

Table 21.2 *Correlation Coefficients of Monthly Percentage Changes in Major Stock Market Indexes (Local currencies, June 1981 to September 1987)*

	Australia	Austria	Belgium	Canada	Denmark	France	Germany	Hong Kong	Ireland	Italy	Japan	Malaysia	Mexico	Netherlands	New Zealand	Norway	Singapore	South Africa	Spain	Sweden	Switzerland	United Kingdom
Austria	.219																					
Belgium	.190	.222																				
Canada	.568	.250	.215																			
Denmark	.217	-.062	.219	.301																		
France	.180	.263	.355	.351	.241																	
Germany	.145	.406	.315	.194	.215	.327																
Hong Kong	.321	.174	.129	.236	.120	.201	.304															
Ireland	.349	.202	.361	.490	.387	.374	.067	.320														
Italy	.209	.224	.307	.321	.150	.459	.257	.216	.275													
Japan	.182	-.025	.223	.294	.186	.361	.147	.137	.183	.241												
Malaysia	.329	-.013	.096	.274	.151	-.134	-.020	.159	.082	-.119	.109											
Mexico	.220	.018	.104	.114	-.174	-.009	.002	.149	.113	.114	-.021	.231										
Netherlands	.294	.232	.344	.545	.341	.344	.511	.395	.373	.344	.333	.151	.038									
New Zealand	.389	.290	.275	.230	.148	.247	.318	.352	.314	.142	-.111	.136	.231	.239								
Norway	.355	.009	.233	.381	.324	.231	.173	.356	.306	.042	.156	.262	.050	.405	.201							
Singapore	.374	.030	.133	.320	.133	-.085	.037	.219	.102	-.038	.066	.891	.202	.196	.212	.280						
South Africa	.279	.159	.143	.385	-.113	.267	.007	-.095	.024	.093	.225	-.013	.260	.058	.038	.156	-.056					
Spain	.147	.018	.050	.190	.019	.255	.147	.193	.175	.290	.248	-.071	.059	.170	.095	.075	.056	-.088				
Sweden	.327	.161	.158	.376	.131	.159	.227	.196	.122	.330	.115	.103	.000	.324	.136	.237	.180	.070	.181			
Switzerland	.334	.401	.276	.551	.283	.307	.675	.379	.290	.287	.130	.099	.026	.570	.397	.331	.157	.112	.192	.334		
United Kingdom	.377	.073	.381	.590	.218	.332	.263	.431	.467	.328	.354	.193	.068	.534	.014	.313	.250	.168	.209	.339	.435	
United States	.328	.138	.250	.720	.351	.390	.209	.114	.380	.224	.326	.347	.063	.473	.083	.356	.377	.218	.214	.279	.500	.513

Modified from Richard Roll, "The International Crash of October 1987," *Financial Analysts Journal*, September–October 1988.

Figure 21.4
Efficient frontier with U.S. and unhedged foreign assets *(Based on historical data: January 1978–December 1988).*
From Philippe Jorion, *Journal of Portfolio Management,* Summer 1989, pp. 49–54.

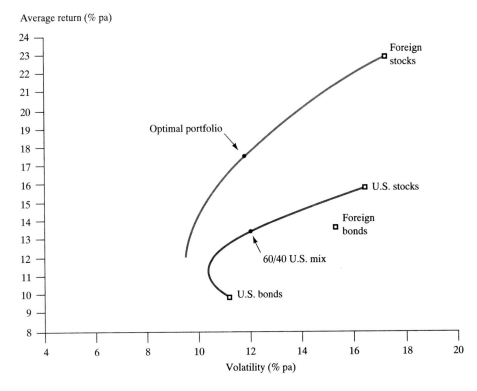

Figure 21.5
Percent of assets invested abroad by private pension funds.
From John A. Morrell, "Introduction to International Equity Diversification," in *International Investing for U.S. Pension Funds* (London/Venice: Institute for Fiduciary Education, May 6–13, 1989).

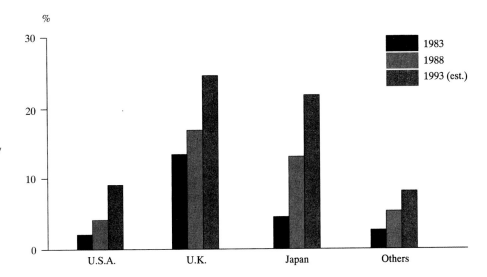

Exchange Rate Risk

International investing poses unique challenges and a variety of new risks for U.S. investors. Information in foreign markets may be less timely and more difficult to come by. In smaller economies with correspondingly smaller securities markets, there may be higher transaction costs and liquidity problems. Investment advisors need special expertise concerning **political risk,** by which we mean the possibility of the expropriation of assets, changes in tax policy, the institution of restrictions on the exchange of foreign currency for domestic currency, or other changes in the business climate of a country. A good example of political risk surrounds the Gulf War in early 1991, when investors in Kuwait saw their investments destroyed by the war.

Beyond these risks, international investing entails **exchange rate risk.** The dollar return from a foreign investment depends not only on the returns in the foreign currency, but also on the exchange rate between the dollar and that currency.

To see this, consider an investment in England in risk-free British government bills paying 10 percent annual interest in British pounds. While these U.K. bills would be the risk-free asset to a British investor, this is not the case for a U.S. investor. Suppose, for example, the current exchange rate is $2 per pound, and the U.S. investor starts with $20,000. That amount can be exchanged for £10,000 and invested at a riskless 10 percent rate in the United Kingdom to provide £11,000 in one year.

What happens if the dollar-pound exchange rate varies over the year? Say that during the year, the pound depreciates relative to the dollar, so that by year-end only $1.80 is required to purchase £1. The £11,000 can be exchanged at the year-end exchange rate for only $19,800 (£11,000 × $1.80/£), resulting in a loss of $200 relative to the initial $20,000 investment. Despite the positive 10 percent pound-denominated return, the dollar-denominated return is a negative 1 percent.

We can generalize from these results. The $20,000 is exchanged for $20,000/$E_0$ pounds, where E_0 denotes the original exchange rate ($2/£). The U.K. investment grows to $(20,000/E_0)[1 + r_f(UK)]$ British pounds, where $r_f(UK)$ is the risk-free rate in the United Kingdom. The pound proceeds ultimately are converted back to dollars at the subsequent exchange rate E_1, for total dollar proceeds of $20,000(E_1/E_0)[1 + r_f(UK)]$. The dollar-denominated return on the investment in British bills, therefore, is

$$1 + r(US) = [1 + r_f(UK)] E_1/E_0. \qquad (21.1)$$

We see in Equation 21.1 that the dollar-denominated return for a U.S. investor equals the pound-denominated return times the exchange rate "return." For a U.S. investor, the investment in the British bill is a combination of a safe investment in the United Kingdom and a risky investment in the performance of the pound relative to the dollar. Here, the pound fared poorly, falling from a value of $2.00 to only $1.80. The loss on the pound more than offsets the earnings on the British bill.

Figure 21.6 illustrates this point. It presents rates of returns on stock and bond market indexes in six countries for a three-month period in 1990. The light boxes depict returns in local currencies, while the dark boxes depict returns in dollars, adjusting for exchange rate movements. It's clear that exchange rate fluctuations over this period had large effects on dollar-denominated returns.

Concept Check

Question 2. Calculate the rate of return in dollars to a U.S. investor holding the British bill if the year-end exchange rate is: *(a)* E_1 = $2.00/£; *(b)* E_1 = $2.20/£.

Figure 21.6
Returns denominated
in local currencies
versus returns
denominated in
dollars.

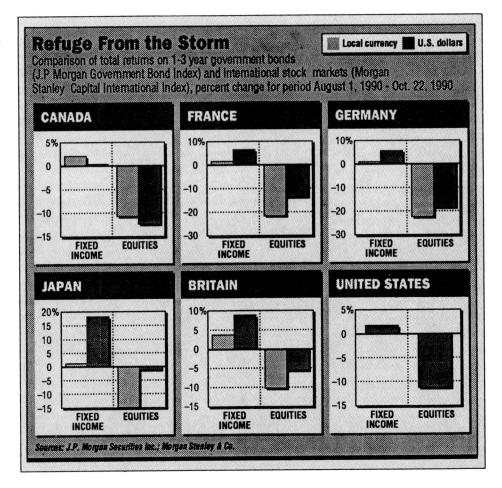

The investor in our example could have hedged the exchange rate risk using a forward or futures contract in foreign exchange. Recall that a forward or futures contract on foreign exchange calls for delivery or acceptance of one currency for another at a stipulated exchange rate. Here, the U.S. investor would agree to deliver pounds for dollars at a fixed exchange rate, thereby eliminating the future risk involved with conversion of the pound investment back into dollars.

If the futures exchange rate had been $F_0 = \$1.93/\pounds$ when the investment was made, the U.S. investor could have assured a riskless dollar-denominated return by locking in the year-end exchange rate at $1.93/£. In this case, the riskless U.S. return would have been 6.15 percent:

$$[1 + r_f(\text{UK})]F_0/E_0$$
$$= (1.10)\, 1.93/2.00$$
$$= 1.0615.$$

Here are the steps to take to lock in the dollar-denominated returns. The futures contract entered in the second step exactly offsets the exchange rate risk incurred in step 1.

Initial Transaction	End of Year Proceeds in Dollars
Exchange $20,000 for £10,000 and invest at 10% in the United Kingdom.	£11,000 × E_1
Enter a contract to deliver £11,000 for dollars at the (forward) exchange rate $1.93/£.	£11,000$(1.93 - E_1)$
Total	£11,000 × $1.93/£ = $21,320

You may recall that this is the same type of hedging strategy at the heart of the spot-futures parity relationship discussed in Chapter 20, where futures markets are used to eliminate the risk of holding another asset. The U.S. investor can lock in a riskless dollar-denominated return either by investing in the United Kingdom and hedging exchange rate risk or by investing in riskless U.S. assets. Because the returns on two riskless strategies must provide equal returns, we conclude

$$1 + r_f(\text{UK}) \frac{F_0}{E_0} = 1 + r_f(\text{US}).$$

Rearranging,

$$\frac{F_0}{E_0} = \frac{1 + r_f(\text{US})}{1 + r_f(\text{UK})}. \tag{21.2}$$

Interest rate parity relationship, or covered interest arbitrage relationship The spot-futures exchange rate relationship that precludes arbitrage opportunities.

This relationship is called the **interest rate parity relationship** or **covered interest arbitrage relationship.**

Consider the intuition behind this result. If $r_f(\text{US})$ is greater than $r_f(\text{UK})$, money invested in the United States will grow at a faster rate than money invested in the United Kingdom. If this is so, why wouldn't all investors decide to invest their money in the United States? One important reason is that the dollar may be depreciating relative to the pound. Although dollar investments in the United States grow faster than pound investments in the United Kingdom, each dollar is worth progressively fewer pounds as time passes. Such an effect will exactly offset the advantage of the higher U.S. interest rate.

To complete the argument, we need only determine how a depreciating dollar will affect Equation 21.1. If the dollar is depreciating, meaning that progressively more dollars are required to purchase each pound, then the forward exchange rate F_0 (which equals the dollars required to purchase one pound for delivery in one year) must exceed E_0, the current exchange rate.

That is exactly what Equation 21.2 tells us: when $r_f(\text{US})$ exceeds $r_f(\text{UK})$, F_0 must exceed E_0. The depreciation of the dollar embodied in the ratio of F_0 to E_0 exactly compensates for the difference in interest rates available in the two countries. Of course, the argument also works in reverse; if $r_f(\text{US})$ is less than $r_f(\text{UK})$, then F_0 will be less than E_0.

What if the interest rate parity relationship were violated? For example, suppose r_f is 6.15 percent, but the futures price is $1.90/£ instead of $1.93/£. You could adopt a strategy to reap arbitrage profits. In this example, let E_1 denote the exchange rate that will prevail in one year. E_1 is, of course, a random variable from the perspective of today's investors.

Action	Initial Cash flow in $	Cash Flow in One Year in $
1. Borrow 1 UK pound in London. Repay in one year.	2.00	$-E_1(1.10)$
2. Convert the pound to $2 and lend in the United States.	-2.00	$2.00(1.0615)$
3. Enter a contract to purchase 1.10 pounds at a (futures) price of $F_0 = \$1.90$	0	$1.10(E_1 - 1.90)$
Total	0	$.033

In step 1, you borrow one pound in the United Kingdom (worth $2 at the current exchange rate) and after one year, repay the pound borrowed with interest. Because the loan is made in the United Kingdom at the U.K. interest rate, you would repay 1.10 pounds, which would be worth $E_1(1.10)$ dollars. The U.S. loan in step 2 is made at the U.S. interest rate of 6.15 percent. The futures position in step 3 results in receipt of 1.10 pounds, for which you would first pay F_0 dollars each and then trade into dollars at rate E_1.

The exchange rate risk here is exactly offset between the pound obligation in step 1 and the futures position in step 3. The profit from the strategy is, therefore, riskless and requires no net investment. This is an arbitrage opportunity.

Concept Check

Question 3. What are the arbitrage strategy and associated profits if the initial futures price is $F_0 = \$1.95$/pound?

Ample empirical evidence bears out this theoretical relationship. For example, on July 17, 1990, the two-month interest rate on dollar-denominated loans in the Euro market was 8.125 percent, while the two-month rate on pound-denominated loans was 15 percent. The exchange rate was $1.8165/£. Substituting these values into Equation 21.2 gives $F_0 = 1.8165 \times (1.08125/1.15)^{2/12} = \$1.7979/£$. The actual forward price at that time for two-month delivery was $1.7966/£, so close to the parity value that transaction costs would prevent arbitrageurs from profiting from the discrepancy.

Unfortunately, such perfect exchange rate hedging is usually not so easy. In our example, we knew exactly how many pounds to sell in the forward or futures market because the pound-denominated proceeds in the United Kingdom were riskless. If the U.K. investment had not been in bills, but instead had been in risky U.K. equity, we would know neither the ultimate value in pounds of our U.K. investment nor how many pounds to sell forward. That is, the hedging opportunity offered by foreign exchange forward contracts would be imperfect.

To summarize, the generalization of Equation 21.1 is that

$$1 + r(US) = [1 + r(foreign)] E_1/E_0 \tag{21.3}$$

where r(foreign) is the possibly-risky return earned in the currency of the foreign investment. You can set up a perfect hedge only in the special case that *r*(foreign) is itself a known number. In that case, you know you must sell in the forward or futures market an amount of foreign currency equal to $[1 + r(foreign)]$ for each unit of that currency you purchase today.

Concept Check

> **Question 4.** How many pounds would need to be sold forward to hedge exchange rate risk in the above example if: *(a)* r(UK) = 20 percent, *(b)* r(UK) = 30 percent?

Passive and Active International Investing

European, Australian, Far East (EAFE) index A widely used index of non-U.S. stocks computed by Morgan Stanley.

When we discussed investment strategies in the purely domestic context, we used a market index portfolio like the S&P 500 as a benchmark passive equity investment. This suggests a world market index might be a useful starting point for a passive international strategy.

One widely used index of non-U.S. stocks is the **Europe, Australia, Far East (EAFE) index** computed by Morgan Stanley. Additional indexes of world equity performance are published by Capital International Indices, Salomon Brothers, First Boston, and Goldman, Sachs. Portfolios designed to mirror or even replicate the country, currency, and company representation of these indexes would be the obvious generalization of the purely domestic passive equity strategy.

Active portfolio management in an international context may be viewed similarly as an extension of active domestic management. In principle, one would form an efficient frontier from the full menu of world securities and determine the optimal risky portfolio. In the context of international investing, however, we more often take a broader asset-allocation perspective toward active management. We focus mainly on potential sources of abnormal returns: currency selection, country selection, stock selection within countries, and cash-bond selection within countries.

We can measure the contribution of each of these factors following a manner similar to the performance attribution techniques introduced in Chapter 11.

Currency selection Asset allocation in which the investor chooses among investments denominated in different currencies.

1. *Currency selection* measures the contribution to total portfolio performance attributable to exchange rate fluctuations relative to the investor's benchmark currency, which we will take to be the U.S. dollar. We might use a benchmark like the EAFE index to compare a portfolio's currency selection for a particular period to a passive benchmark. EAFE currency selection would be computed as the weighted average of E_1/E_0 of the currencies represented in the EAFE portfolio using as weights the fraction of the EAFE portfolio invested in each currency.

Country selection Asset allocation in which the investor chooses among investments in different countries.

2. *Country selection* measures the contribution to performance attributable to investing in the better-performing stock markets of the world. It can be measured as the weighted average of the equity *index* returns of each country using as weights the share of the manager's portfolio in each country. We use index returns to abstract from the effect of security selection within countries. To measure a manager's contribution relative to a passive strategy, we might compare country selection to the weighted average across countries of equity index returns using as weights the share of the EAFE portfolio in each country.

Table 21.3 *Example of Performance Attribution: International*

	EAFE Weight	Return on Equity Index	E_1/E_0	Manager's Weight	Manager's Return
Europe	.30	.10	1.10	.35	.08
Australia	.10	.05	.90	.10	.07
Far East	.60	.15	1.30	.55	.18

Currency Selection

EAFE: $(.30 \times 1.10) + (.10 \times .90) + (.60 \times 1.30) = 1.20$ (20% appreciation)
Manager: $(.35 \times 1.10) + (.10 \times .90) + (.55 \times 1.30) = 1.19$
Loss of 1% relative to EAFE.

Country Selection

EAFE: $(.30 \times .10) + (.10 \times .05) + (.60 \times .15) = .125$
Manager: $(.35 \times .10) + (.10 \times .05) + (.55 \times .15) = .1225$
Loss of .25% relative to EAFE.

Stock Selection

$(.08 - .10).35 + (.07 - .05).10 + (.18 - .15).55 = .0115$
Contribution of 1.15% relative to EAFE.

---

3. *Stock selection* ability may, as in Chapter 11, be measured as the weighted average of equity returns *in excess of the equity index* in each country. Here, we would use local currency returns and use as weights the investments in each country.

4. *Cash/bond selection* may be measured as the excess return derived from weighting bonds and bills differently from some benchmark weights.

Table 21.3 gives an example of how to measure the contribution of the decisions an international portfolio manager might make.

Concept Check

Question 5. Using the data in Table 21.3, compute the manager's country and currency selection if portfolio weights had been 40 percent in Europe, 20 percent in Australia, and 40 percent in the Far East.

Factor Models and International Investing

International investing presents a good opportunity to demonstrate an application of multifactor models of security returns such as those considered in connection with the arbitrage pricing model. Natural factors might include:

1. A world stock index.
2. A national (domestic) stock index.
3. Industrial-sector indexes.
4. Currency movements.

Solnik and de Freitas (1988) use such a framework, and Table 21.4 shows some of their results for several countries. The first four columns of numbers present the *R*-square of various one-factor regressions. Recall that the *R*-square, or R^2, measures the percentage of return volatility of a company's stock that can be explained by the particular factor treated as the independent or explanatory

Table 21.4 *Relative Importance of World, Industrial, Currency, and Domestic Factors in Explaining Return of a Stock*

	Average R-SQR of Regression on Factors				
	Single-Factor Tests				Joint Test
Locality	World	Industrial	Currency	Domestic	All Four Factors
Switzerland	0.18	0.17	0.00	0.38	0.39
West Germany	0.08	0.10	0.00	0.41	0.42
Australia	0.24	0.26	0.01	0.72	0.72
Belgium	0.07	0.08	0.00	0.42	0.43
Canada	0.27	0.24	0.07	0.45	0.48
Spain	0.22	0.03	0.00	0.45	0.45
United States	0.26	0.47	0.01	0.35	0.55
France	0.13	0.08	0.01	0.45	0.60
United Kingdom	0.20	0.17	0.01	0.53	0.55
Hong Kong	0.06	0.25	0.17	0.79	0.81
Italy	0.05	0.03	0.00	0.35	0.35
Japan	0.09	0.16	0.01	0.26	0.33
Norway	0.17	0.28	0.00	0.84	0.85
Netherlands	0.12	0.07	0.01	0.34	0.31
Singapore	0.16	0.15	0.02	0.32	0.33
Sweden	0.19	0.06	0.01	0.42	0.43
All countries	0.18	0.23	0.01	0.42	0.46

Modified from Bruno Solnik, *International Investments*, © 1988, Addison-Wesley Publishing Co., Inc., Reading, Massachusetts. Tables 2 and 7. Reprinted with permission.

variable. Solnik and de Freitas estimate the factor regressions for many firms in a given country and report the average R-square across the firms in that country.

In this case, the table reveals that the domestic factor seems to be the dominant influence on stock returns. While the domestic index alone generates an average R-square of 0.42 across all countries, adding the three additional factors (in the last column of the table) increases average R-square only to 0.46. This is consistent with the low cross-country correlation coefficients in Table 21.2.

At the same time, there is clear evidence of a world market factor in results of the market crash of October 1987. Even though we have said equity returns across borders show only moderate correlation, a study by Richard Roll (1988) shows negative October 1987 equity index returns in all 23 countries considered. Figure 21.7, reproduced from Roll's study, shows the values he found for regional equity indexes during that month. The obvious correlation among returns suggests some underlying world factor common to all economies. Roll found that the beta of a country's equity index on a world index (estimated through September 1987) was the best predictor of that index's response to the October 1987 crash, which lends further support to the presence of a world factor.

Equilibrium in International Capital Markets

We can use the CAPM or the APT to predict expected rates of return in an international capital market equilibrium, just as we can for domestic assets. The models need some adaptation for international use, however.

Figure 21.7
Regional indexes around the crash, October 14–October 26, 1987.
From Richard Roll, "The International Crash of October 1987," *Financial Analysts Journal,* September–October 1988.

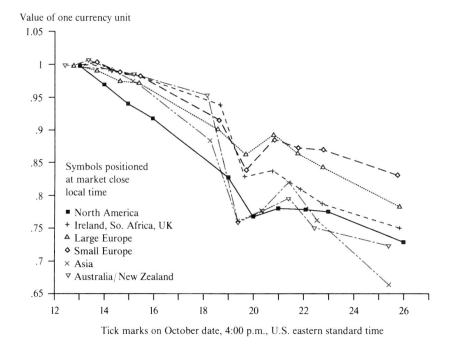

Value of one currency unit

Symbols positioned
at market close
local time

■ North America
+ Ireland, So. Africa, UK
△ Large Europe
◇ Small Europe
× Asia
▽ Australia/New Zealand

Tick marks on October date, 4:00 p.m., U.S. eastern standard time

For example, one might expect that a world CAPM would result simply by replacing a narrow domestic market portfolio with a broad world market portfolio and measuring betas relative to the world portfolio. This approach was pursued in part of a paper by Ibbotson, Carr, and Robinson (1982), who calculated betas of equity indexes of several countries against a world equity index. Their results appear in Table 21.5. The betas for different countries show surprising variability.

While such a straightforward generalization of the simple CAPM seems like a reasonable first step, it is subject to some problems:

1. Taxes, transaction costs, and capital barriers across countries make it difficult and not always attractive for investors to hold a world index portfolio. Some assets are simply unavailable to foreign investors.
2. Investors in different countries view exchange rate risk from the perspective of their different domestic currencies. Thus, they will not agree on the risk characteristics of various securities and, therefore, will not derive identical efficient frontiers.
3. Investors in different countries tend to consume different baskets of goods, either because of differing tastes or because of tariffs, transportation costs, or taxes. If relative prices of goods vary over time, the inflation risk perceived by investors in different countries also will differ.

These problems suggest that the simple CAPM will not work as well in an international context as it would if all markets were fully integrated. Some evidence suggests assets that are less accessible to foreign investors carry higher risk premiums than a simple CAPM would predict (Errunza and Losq, 1985).

The APT seems better designed for use in an international context than the CAPM, as the special risk factors that arise in international investing can be

Table 21.5 *Equity Returns, 1960–1980*

	Average Return	Standard Deviation of Return	Beta	Alpha
Australia	12.20	22.80	1.02	1.52
Austria	10.30	16.90	.01	4.86
Belgium	10.10	13.80	.45	2.44
Canada	12.10	17.50	.77	2.75
Denmark	11.40	24.20	.60	2.91
France	8.10	21.40	.50	.17
Germany	10.10	19.90	.45	2.41
Italy	5.60	27.20	.41	−1.92
Japan	19.00	31.40	.81	9.49
Netherlands	10.70	17.80	.90	.65
Norway	17.40	49.00	−.27	13.39
Spain	10.40	19.80	.04	4.73
Sweden	9.70	16.70	.51	1.69
Switzerland	12.50	22.90	.87	2.66
United Kingdom	14.70	33.60	1.47	1.76
United States	10.20	17.70	1.08	−.69

From Roger G. Ibbotson, Richard C. Carr, and Anthony W. Robinson, "International Equity and Bond Returns," *Financial Analysts Journal*, July–August 1982.

treated much like any other risk factor. World economic activity and currency movements might simply be included in a list of factors already used in a domestic APT model.

21.2   Real Estate

Like international investments, real estate can play an important role in diversified portfolios. Over the period ending in 1985, for example, real estate investments exhibited a risk-return profile far superior to that of the traditional stock/bonds/bills assets classes. As panel A of Table 21.6 shows, real estate (according to appraisal data) had an average return higher than that of stocks (as represented by the S&P 500), with a standard deviation of returns only one quarter as large. (Appraisal data are often used instead of true transaction prices in analysis of real estate returns because most real estate trades only infrequently.)

However, these standard deviations understate the volatility of real estate returns. There is considerable evidence that appraised values respond sluggishly to movements in actual market values (Firstenberg, Ross, Zisler, 1988). Given that appraised values move slowly, they result in artificially low standard deviations of returns. The scale of the numbers, though, still suggests attractive performance, at least through the mid- to late 1980s.

Unfortunately, the recent performance of real estate has been far less impressive. Much of the S&L debacle can be traced to falling real estate values that led to loan defaults and bank insolvencies. Table 21.7 shows estimates of real estate returns for several periods ending in early 1991. The more recent investment experience has been quite poor.

Table 21.6   *Performance of Investments in Real Estate*

A. Average Returns and Volatility

Index	Average Return	Standard Deviation	Series Begins
FRC Index*	13.87	4.37	June 1978
REIT Index†	22.26	19.71	March 1974
S&P 500	9.71	15.35	March 1969
Government bonds	7.91	11.50	March 1969
T-bills	7.51	0.82	March 1969

B. Correlation Matrix

	FRC Index	REITs	S&P 500	Bonds	Bills
FRC Index	1.00	−0.14	−0.26	−0.38	0.30
REIT Index	−0.14	1.00	0.78	0.36	−0.23
S&P 500	−0.26	0.78	1.00	0.49	−0.43
Government bonds	−0.38	0.36	0.49	1.00	−0.09
T-bills	0.30	−0.23	−0.43	−0.09	1.00

*The Frank Russell Company index of real estate values, based on approximately 1,000 properties owned by real estate funds.

†An equally weighted index of 33 REITs holding more than 80% of assets in real estate properties.

From Paul M. Firstenberg, Stephen A. Ross, and Randall C. Zisler, "Real Estate: The Whole Story," *Journal of Portfolio Management,* Spring 1988.

Actual returns of REITs, which are investment trusts that invest in real estate, are an alternative to appraised values for computing real estate investment returns. REITs are publicly traded, so we can measure their returns directly and thereby infer the market valuation of the underlying real estate investments. REIT results in Table 21.6 indicate much higher total return than the appraisal data, but also much higher volatility, if only slightly higher standard deviation than for stocks. These data end before the recent slump, however, so they still paint a too rosy picture of real estate returns.

Historically, real estate has provided outstanding diversification qualities. Panel B of Table 21.6 shows negative correlation of returns on real estate investments (measured from appraisal data) with those of stocks, bonds, and bills, indicating enhanced opportunity for portfolio risk reduction. The REIT data indicate less impressive opportunities for diversification, with a correlation between real estate and stocks of 0.78, and between real estate and bonds of 0.36. Still, even these values show the considerable potential of adding real estate to a traditional portfolio.

Another view of some attractive characteristics of real estate investments emerges from a study by Ibbotson, Siegel, and Love (1985). Index model regressions for several asset classes over 1959–1984 show that U.S. real estate had a beta of only 0.31 when regressed on the world market portfolio and an annual alpha (abnormal risk-adjusted return) of 2.52 percent. This indicates low risk and high return, at least for this historical period. Regression of U.S. real estate returns on the U.S. inflation rate yields a slope coefficient of 0.80, confirming the effectiveness of real estate as an effective inflation hedge. When the rate of inflation rose faster than expected, so did the nominal return on real estate investments.

Table 21.7 *Rates of Return on Real Estate*

Unhappy Returns

Total annual returns on real estate investments based on when the investment was made, in percent

First quarter 1991	−0.2%
One year ago	0.0
Two years ago	2.7
Three years ago	4.1
Four years ago	4.4
Five years ago	4.8
Six years ago	5.6
Seven years ago	6.5
Eight years ago	7.5
Nine years ago	7.6
Ten years ago	8.4
Eleven years ago	9.0
Twelve years ago	10.1

Source: *Russell-NCREIF Property Index*

From *The Wall Street Journal,* June 10, 1991. Reprinted by permission of *THE WALL STREET JOURNAL,* © 1991 Dow Jones & Company, Inc. All Rights Reserved Worldwide.

Table 21.8 *Precious Metal Returns, 1971–1987*

	Average Return (Arithmetic mean)	Standard Deviation of Annual Return
Gold	18.7	27.3
Silver	18.1	40.1
Equity (U.S.)	12.7	15.6

From Jeffrey F. Jaffee, "Gold and Gold Stocks as Investments for Institutional Portfolios," *Financial Analysts Journal* 45 (March–April 1989), pp. 53–59.

21.3 *Precious Metals*

Precious metals have been excellent investments in the past, at least until the last few years. Table 21.8 from a study by Jaffee (1989) documents the performance of gold and silver relative to U.S. equities in the 1971–1987 period. While metals clearly were more volatile, their average returns also outran those of equity. However, since 1987, gold and silver have been poor investments. The rates of return on gold in 1988 and 1989 were 3.1 percent and −20.5 percent, respectively; the returns for silver in these two years were −7.4 percent and −23.2 percent.

One feature often attributed to metals is an ability to serve as an inflation hedge. Jaffee (1989) found that a regression of gold returns on U.S. inflation produced a slope coefficient of 2.95, indicating that a 1 percent increase in inflation was associated with an increased nominal return to metals of almost 3 percent. He warns, however, that the relationship is quite noisy, meaning the hedging value of gold can be unreliable.

An open issue concerns the best way to invest in metals. That is, should one buy metals, futures contracts on metals, or stock in companies that mine and refine metals? Although there is no single correct answer to this question, each approach has certain advantages as well as drawbacks. Buying metals (in the form of gold or silver coins, for example) offers the advantage of small-scale transactions but might entail relatively large storage or insurance costs. Futures contracts offer a low-cost way to bet on prices of traded metals but require a large minimum investment. Futures also allow no opportunity for tax timing because of the mark-to-market provision, and they require frequent monitoring as contracts mature and must be rolled over. Finally, investments in stocks of particular companies that mine or refine metals involve issues of firm-specific risk, quality of management, and particular dividend policies that might have beneficial or deleterious tax or cash flow implications for the investor.

21.4 Other Nontraditional Assets

Figure 21.8 presents returns on a wide range of assets for various periods ending in 1989. We see here that over the 20 years ending in June 1989, nontraditional assets such as coins, Chinese ceramics, or old masters actually outperformed stocks, bonds, and bills. A few words of warning are warranted, however. First, these data do not rank risk along with return, and investment risk in these nontraditionals can be considerable. In the year between May 1990 and May 1991, the best-performing asset in Figure 21.8, coins, turned in a rate of return of −43 percent[1] wiping out nearly half the gains of the previous two decades. Similarly, 1991 has been a very poor year for investments in works of art. In addition, these assets do not trade in liquid markets. If you try to sell an old master, for example, you will need to pay either an auction fee or a bid-ask spread to an art dealer. These costs of buying and selling mean frequent transactions can swiftly wipe out any capital appreciation. Finally, these assets are difficult for amateurs to evaluate in terms of quality and can be expensive to store safely or to insure. While they may have valid places in well-diversified portfolios, they are hardly a free lunch.

Summary

1. U.S. assets are only a small fraction of the world wealth portfolio. International capital markets offer important opportunities for portfolio diversification with enhanced risk-return characteristics.

---

[1]This is according to an index compiled by *Numismatic News* and reported in *USA Today*, May 30, 1991, p. B1.

Van Gogh takes on Wall Street

Compound annual returns on selected investments

Type	20 years	Rank	10 years	Rank	5 years	Rank	1988	Rank	1989	Rank
Coins	16.6%	1	12.9%	2	14.5%	4	14.0%	2	30.2%	3
Chinese ceramics	13.3	2	8.7	6	12.2	5	10.5	4	40.3	2
Gold	11.5	3	2.8	10	−1.6	11	3.1	9	−20.5	13
Old masters	10.9	4	9.6	5	18.4	2	13.4	3	50.7	1
Diamonds	10.4	5	8.3	7	10.7	6	24.9	1	15.5	5
Stocks	10.3	6	17.0	1	20.1	1	−4.9	12	24.5	4
Bonds	8.6	7	10.9	3	17.6	3	6.2	6	11.2	6
Treasury Bills	8.6	7	10.0	4	7.2	7	6.0	7	7.8	7
Oil	8.3	9	1.2	11	−10.7	13	−9.4	14	3.2	11
Housing	7.6	10	5.5	9	5.1	9	1.5	11	6.6	8
Inflation (CPI)	**6.3**	**11**	**5.7**	**8**	**3.5**	**10**	**3.8**	**8**	**5.2**	**10**
U.S. farmland	6.0	12	−0.5	13	−5.3	12	3.1	9	5.9	9
Silver	5.5	13	−4.6	14	−11.2	14	−7.4	13	−23.2	14
Foreign exchange	4.0	14	0.9	12	7.1	8	8.6	5	−13.3	12

Notes: Data on Chinese ceramics and old masters from Sotheby's; diamond information is from the Diamond Registry. Returns on stock assume quarterly reinvestment of dividends; bond returns assume monthly reinvestment. All returns are for the period that ended last June 1.

Figure 21.8 Returns on nontraditional asset classes.
From the *Baltimore Sun*, January 21, 1990, p. 30.

2. Exchange rate risk imparts an extra source of uncertainty to investments denominated in foreign currencies. Much of that risk can be hedged in foreign exchange futures or forward markets, but a perfect hedge is not feasible unless the foreign currency rate of return is known.

3. Several world market indexes can form a basis for passive international investing. Active international management can be partitioned into currency selection, country selection, stock selection, and cash/bond selection.

4. A factor model applied to international investing would include a world factor as well as the usual domestic factors. While some evidence suggests domestic factors dominate stock returns, effects of the October 1987 crash demonstrate existence of an important international factor.

5. Real estate and precious metals also offer attractive diversification attributes. Moreover, both of these asset classes historically have been inflation hedges. Recent performance, however, has been poor.

Key Terms

country selection, 613
covered interest
  arbitrage
   relationship, 611
currency selection, 613

European, Australian,
  Far East (EAFE)
  index, 613
exchange rate risk, 609

interest rate parity
  relationship, 611
political risk, 609
world investable
  wealth, 604

Selected Readings

Forbes magazine published a special section on international investing in the July 23, 1990, issue.

The March–April 1989 issue of Financial Analysts Journal is devoted to issues in international investing.

Problem Sets

1. Suppose a U.S. investor wishes to invest in a British firm currently selling for £40 per share. The investor has $10,000 to invest, and the current exchange rate is $2/£.

   a. How many shares can the investor purchase?

   b. Fill in the table below for rates of return after one year in each of the nine scenarios (three possible prices per share in pounds times three possible exchange rates.)

Price per Share (£)	Pound-Denominated Return (%)	Dollar Denominated Return for Year-End Exchange Rate		
		$1.80/£	$2/£	$2.20/£
£35				
£40				
£45				

   c. When is the dollar-denominated return equal to the pound-denominated return?

2. If each of the nine outcomes in question 1 is equally likely, find the standard deviation of both the pound- and dollar-denominated rates of return.

3. Now suppose the investor in question 1 also sells forward £5,000 at a forward exchange rate of $2.10/£

   a. Recalculate the dollar-denominated returns for each scenario.

   b. What happens to the standard deviation of the dollar-denominated return? Compare it both to its old value and the standard deviation of the pound-denominated return.

4. Calculate the contribution to total performance from currency, country, and stock selection for the manager in the example below:

	EAFE Weight	Return on Equity Index	E_1/E_0	Manager's Weight	Manager's Return
Europe	.30	.20	.9	.35	.18
Australia	.10	.15	1.0	.15	.20
Far East	.60	.25	1.1	.50	.20

5. If the current exchange rate is $1.75/£, the one-year forward exchange rate is $1.85/£, and the interest rate on British government bills is 8 percent per year, what risk-free dollar-denominated return can be locked in by investing in the British bills?

6. If you were to invest $10,000 in the British bills of question 5, how would you lock in the dollar-denominated return?

7. Use the data in Table 21.6 to fill in the following table. What do you conclude?

Portfolio	Average Return	Standard Deviation
All T-bonds		
All real estate (REITs)		
50% bonds/50% REITs		

8. Suppose that the spot price of the Swiss franc is currently 40 cents. The 1-year futures price is 44 cents. Is the interest rate higher in the United States or Switzerland?

9. *a.* The spot price of the British pound is currently $1.50. If the risk-free interest rate on 1-year government bonds is 10 percent in the United States and 15 percent in the United Kingdom, what must the forward price of the pound be for delivery 1 year from now?

   b. How could an investor make risk-free arbitrage profits if the forward price were higher than the price you gave in answer to (*a*)? Give a numerical example.

10. Consider the following information:

$$r_{US} = 15\%$$
$$r_{UK} = 17\%$$
$$E_0 = 2.0 \text{ dollars per pound}$$
$$F_0 = 1.97 \text{ (1-year delivery)}$$

where the interest rates are annual yields on U.S. or U.K. bills. Given this information:

   a. Where would you lend?

   b. Where would you borrow?

   c. How could you arbitrage?

11. John Irish, CFA, is an independent investment advisor who is assisting Alfred Darwin, the head of the Investment Committee of General Technology Corporation, to establish a new pension fund. Darwin asks Irish about international equities and whether the Investment Committee should consider them as an additional asset for the pension fund.

   a. Explain the rationale for including international equities in General's equity portfolio. Identify and describe *three* relevant considerations in formulating your answer.

   b. List *three* possible arguments against international equity investment and briefly discuss the significance of each.

   c. To illustrate several aspects of the performance of international securities over time, Irish shows Darwin the accompanying graph (on the following page) of investment results experienced by a U.S. pension fund in the 1970–83 period. Compare the performance of the U.S. dollar and non-U.S. dollar equity and fixed-income asset categories, and explain the significance of the result of the Account Performance Index relative to the results of the four individual asset class indexes.

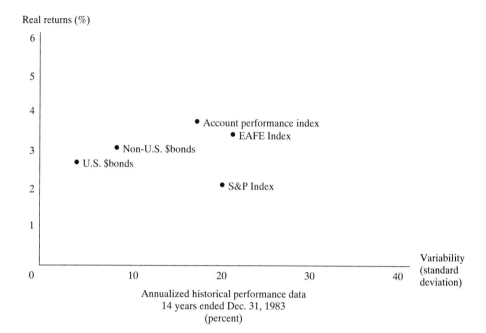

Real returns (%)

Annualized historical performance data
14 years ended Dec. 31, 1983
(percent)

Chapter

22

Active Portfolio Management

So far, we have alluded to active portfolio management in only three contexts: determining the optimal risky portfolio (Chapters 7 and 8); security analysis that generates input to the optimization (Part Four); and fixed-income portfolio management (Part Three). In this chapter, we go further in applying portfolio principles to security analysis.

Anyone who studies the principles of modern finance must wonder about what seems like a contradiction between equilibrium analysis (Part Three)—in particular the theory of efficient markets—and the real-world environment where we all know that profit-seeking investment managers use active strategies to exploit perceived market inefficiencies.

Even if you accept the efficient market hypothesis, there are reasons to believe active management can be effective, and we discuss these at the outset. Next, we consider the objectives of active portfolio management. We analyze two forms of active management: market timing, which is based solely on macroeconomic factors, and security selection, which includes microeconomic forecasting. At the end of the chapter, we show how multifactor models are used in active portfolio management. After studying this chapter you should be able to:

- Value market timing ability.
- Use the Treynor-Black model of efficient security analysis.
- Perform security analysis in multifactor security markets.

22.1 *The Lure of Active Management*

How can a theory of active portfolio management make sense if we accept the notion that markets are in equilibrium? Chapter 10 on market efficiency gives a thorough analysis of efficient market theory; here we can summarize how the theory fits with active management strategy.

Market efficiency prevails when many investors are willing to depart from a passive strategy of efficient diversification, so that they can add mispriced securities to their portfolio. Their objective is to realize "abnormal" returns.

The competition for such returns ensures that prices will be near their "fair" values. This means most managers will not beat the passive strategy *if we take risk into account with reward.* Exceptional managers, however, might beat the average forecasts that are built into market prices and consequently construct portfolios that will earn abnormal returns.

How can this happen? There is economic logic behind the result, as well as some empirical evidence indicating that exceptional portfolio managers can beat the average forecast. First, the economic logic. We must assume that if no analyst can beat the passive strategy, investors will be smart enough not to pay for expensive analysis; they will adopt less-expensive passive strategies. In that case, funds under active management will dry up, and prices will no longer reflect sophisticated forecasts. The resulting profit opportunities will lure back active managers who once again will become successful.[1] The critical assumption here is that investors make wise decisions on how to manage their money. Direct evidence on that has yet to be produced.

As for empirical evidence, consider the following: (1) some portfolio managers experience streaks of abnormal returns that are hard to label as lucky outcomes, (2) the "noise" in realized rates of return is enough that we cannot reject outright the hypothesis that some investment managers can beat the passive strategy by a statistically small, yet economically significant, margin, and (3) some anomalies in realized returns—such as the turn of the year effects—have been sufficiently persistent to suggest that managers who identified them, and acted on them in a timely fashion, could have beaten the passive strategy over prolonged periods.

These observations are enough to convince us that there is a role for active portfolio management. Active management offers an inevitable lure, even if investors agree that security markets are nearly efficient.

At the extreme, suppose capital markets are perfectly efficient, an easily accessible market index portfolio is available, and this portfolio is the efficient risky portfolio. In this case, security selection would be futile. You would do best following a passive strategy of allocating funds to a money market fund (the safe asset) and the market index portfolio. Under these simplifying assumptions, the optimal investment strategy seems to require no effort or know-how.

But this is too hasty a conclusion. To allocate investment funds to the risk-free and risky portfolios requires some analysis. You need to decide the fraction, y, to be invested in the risky market portfolio, M, so you use the formula

$$y = \frac{E(r_M) - r_f}{A\sigma_M^2}$$

[1]This point is worked out fully in Sanford J. Grossman and Joseph E. Stiglitz, "On the Impossibility of Informationally Efficient Markets," *American Economic Review* 70 (June 1980), pp. 393–408.

where $E(r_M) - r_f$ is the risk premium on M, σ_M^2 the variance of M, and A the investor's coefficient of risk aversion. To make a rational allocation of funds requires an estimate of σ_M and $E(r_M)$, so even a passive investor needs to do some forecasting.

Forecasting $E(r_M)$ and σ_M is complicated further because security classes are affected by different environmental factors. Long-term bond returns, for example, are driven largely by changes in the term structure of interest rates, while returns on equity depend on changes in the broader economic environment, including macroeconomic factors besides interest rates. Once you begin considering how economic conditions influence separate sorts of investments, you might as well use a sophisticated asset allocation program to determine the proper mix for the portfolio. It is easy to see how investors get lured away from a purely passive strategy.

Even the definition of a "pure" passive strategy is not very clear-cut, as simple strategies involving only the market index portfolio and risk-free assets now seem to call for market analysis. Our strict definition of a pure passive strategy is one that invests only in index funds and weights those funds by fixed proportions that do not change in response to market conditions. A portfolio strategy that always places 60 percent in a stock-market index fund, 30 percent in a bond index fund, and 10 percent in a money-market fund, regardless of what happens in the market, is a pure passive strategy.

Active management is attractive because the potential profit is enormous, even though competition among managers is bound to drive market prices to near-efficient levels. For prices to remain efficient to some degree, decent profits to diligent analysts must be the rule rather than the exception, although large profits may be difficult to earn. Absence of profits would drive people out of the investment management industry, resulting in prices moving away from informationally efficient levels.

22.2   *Objectives of Active Portfolios*

What does an investor expect from a professional portfolio manager, and how does this expectation affect the manager's response? If all clients were risk neutral (indifferent to risk), the answer would be straightforward: the investment manager should construct a portfolio with the highest possible expected rate of return, and the manager should then be judged by the realized *average* rate of return.

When the client is risk averse, the answer is more difficult. Lacking standards to proceed by, the manager would have to consult with each client before making any portfolio decision in order to ascertain that the prospective reward (average return) matched the client's attitude toward risk. Massive, continuous client input would be needed, and the economic value of professional management would be questionable.

Fortunately, the theory of mean-variance efficiency allows us to separate the "product decision," which is how to construct a mean-variance efficient risky portfolio, from the "consumption decision," which describes the investor's allocation of funds between the efficient risky portfolio and the safe asset. You

How J. P. Morgan Investment
sponsors in international

International fixed income securities account for nearly half the world's $5.4 trillion bond market—and offer plan sponsors increasingly attractive opportunities. J.P. Morgan Investment, the leader in this field, manages more than $3 billion of international fixed income securities. We believe you should consider including international bonds in your pension portfolio.

Estimated market value $5.4 trillion
(publicly issued securities)

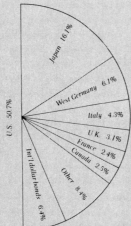

U.S. 50.7%

Japan 16.1%

West Germany 6.1%

Italy 4.3%

U.K. 3.1%

France 2.4%

Canada 2.5%

Other 8.4%

Int'l dollar bonds 6.4%

Shown at J.P. Morgan Investment's London headquarters are international fixed income team members (left to right) Anthony G. Bird, Hans K.-E. Danielsson, Bernard A. Wagenmann, and Adrian F. Lee

finds opportunities for plan fixed income markets

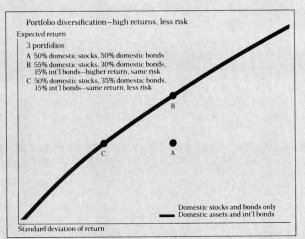

have learned already that construction of the optimal risky portfolio is purely a technical problem and that there is a single optimal risky portfolio appropriate for all investors. Investors differ only in how they apportion investment between that risky portfolio and the safe asset.

The theory of efficient frontiers is not without practitioner adherents. See the accompanying box, which presents an advertisement by J.P. Morgan Investment.

The mean-variance theory also speaks to performance in offering a criterion for judging managers on their choice of risky portfolios. In Chapter 8, we established that the optimal risky portfolio is the one that maximizes the reward-to-variability ratio, that is, the expected excess return divided by the standard deviation. A manager who maximizes this ratio will satisfy all clients regardless of risk aversion.

Clients can evaluate managers using statistical methods to draw inferences from realized rates of return about prospective, or ex ante, reward-to-variability ratios. The Sharpe measure, as this ratio is called, is now an acceptable way to track performance of professionally managed portfolios:

$$S_P = \frac{E(r_P) - r_f}{\sigma_P}.$$

The most able manager will be the one who consistently obtains the highest Sharpe measure, implying the manager has real forecasting ability. A client's judgment of a manager's ability will affect the fraction of investment funds allocated to this manager; the client can invest the remainder with competing managers and in a safe fund.

If managers' Sharpe measures were reasonably constant over time, and clients could reliably estimate them, allocating funds to managers would be an easy decision.

22.3 *Market Timing*

Consider the results of two different investment strategies:

1. Investor X who put $1,000 in 30-day commercial paper on January 1, 1927, and rolled over all proceeds into 30-day paper (or into 30-day T-bills after they were introduced) would have ended on December 31, 1978, 52 years later, with $3,600.
2. Investor Y who put $1,000 in the NYSE index on January 1, 1927, and reinvested all dividends in that portfolio, would have ended on December 31, 1978, with $67,500.

Market timing Asset allocation in which the investment in the market is increased if one forecasts that the market will outperform T-bills.

Suppose we define perfect **market timing** as the ability to tell (with certainty) at the beginning of each month whether the NYSE will outperform 30-day commercial paper. The perfect market timer would shift all funds at the beginning of each month into either cash equivalents (30-day paper) or equities (the NYSE portfolio), whichever is predicted to do better. Beginning with $1,000 on the same date, how would the perfect timer have ended up 52 years later?

This is how Professor Robert Merton began a seminar with finance professors several years ago. The boldest guess of the responses was a few million dollars. The actual result: $5.36 billion.

Concept Check

Question 1. What are the monthly and annually compounded rates of return for the *X, Y,* and perfect-timing strategies over the period 1927–1978?

These results have some lessons for us. The first has to do with the power of compounding. Its effect is particularly important as more and more of the funds under management represent pension savings. The horizons of pension investments may not be as long as 52 years, but they are measured in decades, making compounding a significant factor.

The second is the huge difference between the end value of the all-safe asset strategy ($3,600) and of the all-equity strategy ($67,500). Why would anyone invest in safe assets given this historical record? If you have absorbed all the lessons of this book, you know the reason: risk. The averages of the annualized monthly rates of return and the standard deviations on the all-bills and all-equity strategies are:

	Arithmetic Mean	Standard Deviation
Bills	2.55	2.10
Equities	10.70	22.14

The significantly higher standard deviation of the rate of return on the equity portfolio is commensurate with its significantly higher average return. The higher average return reflects the risk premium.

Is the return premium on the perfect-timing strategy a risk premium? Because the perfect timer never does worse than either bills or the market, the extra return cannot be compensation for the possibility of poor returns; instead it is attributable to superior analysis. The value of superior information is reflected in the tremendous ending value of the portfolio. This value does not reflect compensation for risk.

The monthly results for the all-equity and the perfect-timing portfolios are:

Portfolio: Monthly Statistics	(1) All Equity	(2) Perfect Timer Who Does Not Charge	(3) Perfect Timer Who Imposes a Fair Charge
Average rate of return	.85	2.58	.55
Average excess return	.64	2.37	.34
Standard deviation	5.89	3.82	3.55
Highest return	38.55	38.55	30.14
Lowest return	−29.12	.06	−7.06
Coefficient of skewness	.42	4.28	2.84

Ignore for the moment column 3. The first two rows of results are self-explanatory. The third line, "standard deviation," requires some discussion. The standard deviation of the rate of return earned by the perfect market timer (who does not charge) was 3.82 percent, far higher than the volatility of T-bills. This does not imply that perfect timing is a riskier strategy than bills. Here, standard deviation is a misleading measure of risk.

To see why, consider how you might choose between two hypothetical strategies. Strategy 1 offers a sure rate of return of 5 percent; strategy 2 offers an uncertain return that is given by 5 percent *plus* a random number that is zero with a probability of 0.5 and 5 percent with a probability of 0.5. The results for each strategy are:

	Strategy 1 (%)	Strategy 2 (%)
Expected return	5	7.5
Standard deviation	0	2.5
Highest return	5	10
Lowest return	5	5

Clearly, strategy 2 dominates strategy 1, as its rate of return is *at least* equal to that of strategy 1 and sometimes greater. No matter how risk averse you are, you will always prefer strategy 2 to strategy 1, even though strategy 2 has a significant standard deviation. Compared to strategy 1, strategy 2 provides only good surprises, so the standard deviation in this case cannot be a measure of risk.

You can look at these strategies as analogous to the case of the perfect timer compared with an all-equity or all-bills strategy. In every period, the perfect timer obtains at least as good a return, in some cases better. Therefore, the timer's standard deviation is a misleading measure of risk when you compare perfect timing to an all-equity or all-bills strategy.

Returning to the empirical results, you can see that the highest rate of return is identical for the all-equity and the timing–no charge strategies, while the lowest rate of return is positive for the same perfect timer and disastrous for the all-equity portfolio. Another reflection of this is seen in the coefficient of skewness, which measures the asymmetry of the distribution of returns. Because the equity portfolio is almost (but not exactly) normally distributed, its coefficient of skewness is very low at 0.42. In contrast, the perfect-timing strategy effectively eliminates the negative tail of the distribution of portfolio returns (the part below the risk-free rate). Its returns are "skewed to the right," and its coefficient of skewness is quite large, 4.28.

The third column is perhaps the most interesting of the three. If you were a perfect timer, you would charge clients for your valuable service (saintly benevolence not being one of your other-worldly characteristics). Subtracting a fair fee from the monthly rate of return of the timer's portfolio makes the average rate of return lower than that of the passive, all-equity strategy.

Yet because the fee is set to be fair, the two portfolios (the all-equity and the market-timing-with-fee portfolios) must be equally attractive after risk adjustment. Here again, the standard deviation of the market timing strategy (with fee) is of no help in adjusting for risk because the coefficient of skewness remains high, 2.84. In other words, standard mean-variance analysis presents complications when we use it for valuing market timing. We need an alternative approach.

Valuing Market Timing as an Option

The key to analyzing the pattern of returns to the perfect market timer is to compare the returns of a perfect foresight investor with those of another investor who holds a call option on the equity portfolio. Investing 100 percent in bills plus holding a call option on the equity portfolio will yield returns identical to those of the portfolio of the perfect timer who invests 100 percent in either the safe asset or the equity portfolio, whichever will yield the higher return. The perfect timer's return is shown in Figure 22.1. The rate of return is bounded from below by the risk-free rate, r_f.

To see how the value of information can be treated as an option, suppose the market index currently is at S_0, and a call option on the index has exercise price of $X = S_0(1 + r_f)$. If the market outperforms bills over the coming period, S_T will exceed X; it will be less than X otherwise. Now look at the payoff to a portfolio consisting of this option and S_0 dollars invested in bills.

	Payoff to Portfolio	
Outcome:	$S_T \leq X$	$S_T > X$
Bills	$S_0(1 + r_f)$	$S_0(1 + r_f)$
Option	0	$S_T - X$
Total	$S_0(1 + r_f)$	S_T

The portfolio pays the risk-free return when the market is bearish (that is, the market return is less than the risk-free rate) and pays the market return when the market is bullish and beats bills. This represents perfect market timing. Consequently, the value of perfect timing ability is equivalent to the

Figure 22.1
Rate of return of a
perfect market timer.

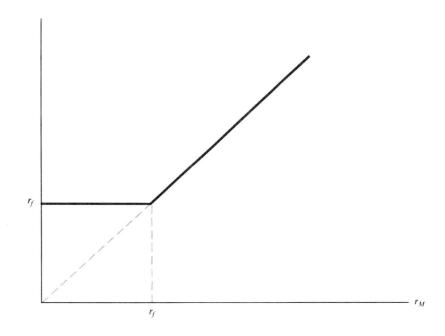

value of the call option, for a call enables the investor to earn the market return only when it exceeds r_f.

This insight let Robert Merton (1981) value timing ability according to the theory of option valuation; it also allows calculation of a fair charge for timing which is subtracted in column 3.

The Value of Imperfect Forecasting

But managers are not perfect forecasters. While managers who are right most of the time presumably do very well; "right most of the time" does not mean merely the *percentage* of the time a manager is right. For example, a Tucson, Arizona, weather forecaster who *always* predicts "no rain" may be right 90 percent of the time, but this "stopped clock" strategy does not require any forecasting ability.

Neither is the overall proportion of correct forecasts an appropriate measure of market forecasting ability. If the market is up two days out of three, and a forecaster always predicts a market advance, the two-thirds success rate is not a measure of forecasting ability. We need to examine the proportion of bull markets ($r_M > r_f$) correctly forecast *and* the proportion of bear markets ($r_M < r_f$) correctly forecast.

If we call P_1 the proportion of the correct forecasts of bull markets and P_2 the proportion for bear markets, then $P_1 + P_1 - 1$ is the correct measure of timing ability. For example, a forecaster who always guesses correctly will have $P_1 = P_2 = 1$ and will show ability of 1 (100 percent). An analyst who always bets on a bear market will mispredict all bull markets ($P_1 = 0$) will correctly "predict" all bear markets ($P_1 = 1$), and will end up with timing ability of $P_1 + P_2 - 1 = 0$. If C denotes the (call option) value of a perfect market timer, then $(P_1 + P_2 - 1)C$ measures the value of imperfect forecasting ability.

Concept Check

Question 2.   What is the market timing score of someone who flips a fair coin to predict the market?

22.4   *Security Selection: The Treynor-Black Model*

Overview of the Treynor-Black Model

Security analysis is the other dimension of active investment management besides timing the overall market and asset allocation. Suppose you are an analyst studying individual securities. Quite likely, you will turn up several securities that appear to be mispriced and offer positive alphas. But how do you exploit your analysis? Concentrating a portfolio on these securities entails a cost, namely, the firm-specific risk you could shed by more fully diversifying. As an active manager, you must strike a balance between aggressive exploitation of security mispricing and diversification aims that recommend against concentrating a portfolio in a few stocks.

Jack Treynor and Fischer Black (1973) have developed a portfolio construction model for managers who use security analysis. It assumes security markets are nearly efficient. The essence of the model is this:

1. Security analysts in an active investment management organization can analyze in depth only a relatively small number of stocks out of the entire universe of securities. The securities not analyzed are assumed to be fairly priced.

2. For the purpose of efficient diversification, the market index portfolio is the baseline portfolio, which the model treats as the passive portfolio.

3. The macro forecasting unit of the investment management firm provides forecasts of the expected rate of return and variance of the passive (market index) portfolio.

4. The objective of security analysis is to form an active portfolio of a necessarily limited number of securities. Perceived mispricing of the analyzed securities is the determining principle in the composition of this active portfolio.

5. Analysts follow several steps to make up the active portfolio and forecast its performance:

a. Estimate the characteristic line of each analyzed security and obtain its beta and residual variance. From the beta and the macro forecast, $E(r_M) - r_f$, determine the *required* rate of return of the security.

b. Determine the expected return. Subtracting the required return yields the expected *abnormal* return (alpha) of the security.

c. Use the estimates for the values of alpha, beta, and residual risk to determine the optimal weight of each security in the active portfolio.

d. Estimate the alpha, beta, and residual variance for the active portfolio according to the weights of the securities in the portfolio.

6. The macroeconomic forecasts for the passive index portfolio and the composite forecast for the active portfolio are used to determine the optimal risky portfolio, which will be a combination of the passive and active portfolios.

Although some sophisticated investment managers use the **Treynor-Black model,** it has not taken the industry by storm. This is unfortunate for several reasons:

1. Just as even imperfect market–timing ability has enormous value, security analysis of the sort Treynor and Black propose has similar potential value. Even with far from perfect security analysis, active management can add value.

2. The Treynor-Black model is easy to implement. Moreover, it is useful even relaxing some of its simplifying assumptions.

3. The model lends itself to use with decentralized decision making, which is essential to efficiency in complex organizations.

Treynor-Black model
An optimizing model for portfolio managers who use security analysis in a nearly efficient market.

Portfolio Construction

Assuming all securities are fairly priced and using the index model as a guideline for the rate of return on securities, the rate of return on security i is given by

$$r_i = r_f + \beta_i(r_M - r_f) + e_i \qquad (22.1)$$

where e_i is the zero mean, firm-specific (nonsystematic) component.

Absent security analysis, Treynor and Black take Equation 22.1 to represent the rate of return on all securities and assume the index portfolio (M) is efficient. For simplicity, they also assume the nonsystematic components of returns, e_i, are independent across securities. Market timing is incorporated in the terms r_M and σ_M, representing index portfolio forecasts. The overall investment in the risky portfolio will be affected by the optimism or pessimism reflected in these numbers.

Assume a team of security analysts investigates a subset of the universe of available securities, with the objective of forming an active portfolio. That portfolio will then be mixed with the index portfolio to improve diversification. For each security, k, that is researched, we write the rate of return as

$$r_k = r_f + \beta_k(r_M - r_f) + e_k + \alpha_k \tag{22.2}$$

where α_k represents the extra (abnormal) expected return attributable to the mispricing of the security. Thus, for each security analyzed, the research team estimates the parameters

$$\alpha_k, \beta_k, \sigma^2(e_k).$$

If all the α_k turn out to be zero, there would be no reason to depart from the passive strategy, and the index portfolio would remain the manager's choice. But this is a remote possibility. In general, there will be a significant number of nonzero α values, some positive and some negative.

Consider first how you would use the active portfolio once you found it. Suppose the **active portfolio** (A) has been constructed somehow and has the parameters

Active portfolio In the context of the Treynor-Black model, the portfolio formed by mixing analyzed stocks of perceived nonzero alpha values. This portfolio is ultimately mixed with the passive market index portfolio.

$$\alpha_A, \beta_A, \sigma^2(e_A).$$

The total variance of the active portfolio is the sum of its systematic variance, $\beta_A^2\sigma_M^2$, plus the nonsystematic variance $\sigma^2(e_A)$. These three paramaters, plus the mean and variance of the index portfolio, are sufficient to identify the opportunity set generated by the active and passive portfolios.

Figure 22.2 shows the optimization process with active and passive portfolios. The dashed efficient frontier line represents the universe of all securities, assuming they are all fairly priced, that is, that all alphas are zero. By definition, the market index (M) is on this efficient frontier and is tangent to the (dashed) capital market line (CML). In practice, our analysts do not need to (indeed cannot) know this frontier, but they need to forecast the index portfolio and construct the optimal risky portfolio using the index and active (A) portfolios. The optimal portfolio (P) will lie on the capital allocation line (CAL) that lies above the CML.

From the viewpoint of an investor with superior analysis, the index portfolio will be inefficient; that is, the active portfolio (A) constructed from mispriced securities will lie above the CML and support an observable efficient frontier.

The optimal combination of the active portfolio with the passive portfolio takes off from the construction of an optimal risky portfolio from two risky assets that we first encountered in Chapter 8. As the active portfolio is not perfectly correlated with the index, further diversification—that is, mixing it with the index—is likely to be beneficial.

We can judge the success of the active management, and the contribution of the active portfolio (A), by the Sharpe measure (ratio of reward to variability) of the resultant risky portfolio (P), compared with that of the index portfolio (M).

Figure 22.2
The optimization process with active and passive portfolios.

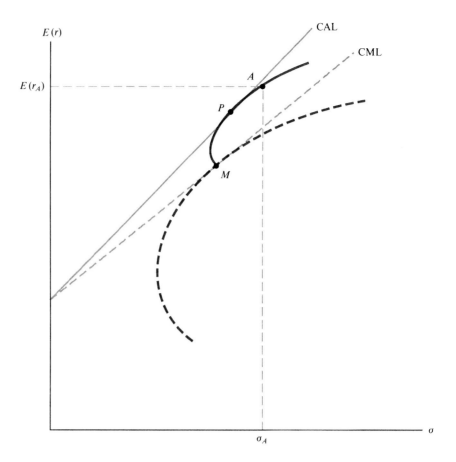

The mathematics of the efficient frontier reveals that the Sharpe measure of the risky portfolio is:

$$S(P) = [S^2(M) + \alpha_A^2/\sigma^2(e_A)]^{1/2}.$$

Thus, the critical variable in determining the success of the active portfolio is its ratio of alpha to nonsystematic risk, $\alpha_A/\sigma(e_A)$.

The intuition here is straightforward. You mix the active portfolio with the index for the benefit of diversification. The position to take in the active portfolio relative to the market portfolio depends on the strength of the active portfolio's abnormal return, α_A, relative to its weakness given by its diversifiable risk, $\sigma^2(e_A)$, sometimes referred to as the *adjusted alpha*.

The contribution of individual securities (say, k) to the active portfolio (A) is analogous to that of the active portfolio to the risky portfolio (P). It is measured by the adjusted alpha, $\alpha_k/\sigma(e_k)$.

22.5 *Multifactor Models and Active Portfolio Management*

Sophisticated investment management organizations often prefer a multifactor versus a single-factor structure of security returns. Yet so far, our analytical framework for active portfolio management seems to rest on the validity of the index model, that is, on a single-factor security model.

To move from a single-factor to a multifactor structure we begin with the *residuals* (nonsystematic components) of the rate of return of the multifactor model. We continue to form the active portfolio by calculating each security's alpha relative to its fair return (given its betas on *all* factors), and then we combine the active portfolio with the portfolio that would be formed in the absence of security analysis. The multifactor framework does, however, raise the issue of the configuration of an efficient passive portfolio from candidate factor portfolios.

To simplify, let us consider a two-factor world, and let the two factor portfolios be called *M* and *H*. Then we generalize the index model to

$$r_i - r_f = \beta_{iM}(r_M - r_f) + \beta_{iH}(r_H - r_f) + \alpha_i + e_i \qquad (22.3)$$
$$= r_\beta + \alpha_i + e_i.$$

β_{iM} and β_{iH} are the betas of the security relative to portfolios *M* and *H*. Given return forecasts on the factor portfolios, r_M and r_H, the fair excess return on a security is denoted r_β and its abnormal return is α_i.

How can we use Equation 22.3 to form an optimal passive portfolio—that is, a portfolio that does not require security analysis? Absent security analysis (assuming all alphas to be zero), we would use the asset allocation program discussed in Chapter 8 to construct the optimal index portfolio. In the two-factor case, as in Equation 22.3, asset allocation is reduced to a universe of two risky assets and a risk-free asset.

Adding security analysis for an active management strategy, we can apply the Treynor-Black model. We proceed as follows.

1. For each security, we estimate the betas (two in this case) and the residual variance.
2. The alpha is determined from security analysis.
3. An active portfolio is constructed on the basis of the ratio of alpha to residual variance.
4. The active portfolio (*A*) betas and residual variance are computed.
5. We apply the asset allocation program to the three portfolios (*M, H,* and *A*) and obtain the optimal risky portfolio.

The only departure from the single-factor case is in step 5. The estimation of two or more betas in step 1 simply implies that a multiple regression has to be used instead of a single-variable one.

It is possible, however, that the factor structure of the market has hedging implications. This means certain clients prefer certain correlation of their portfolios with one or more of the factors. These investors may be willing to accept an inferior Sharpe measure in order to maintain a risky portfolio that has the desired hedge qualities. Portfolio optimization for these investors is more complicated, requiring specific information on client preferences. The portfolio manager will not be able to satisfy diverse clients with one portfolio.

Summary

1. Active portfolio managers attempt to construct a risky portfolio that improves on the reward-to-variability (Sharpe) ratio of a passive strategy.

2. Active management has two components: market timing (or, in a multifactor market, asset allocation) and security analysis.

3. The value of perfect market timing ability is enormous. The rate of return to a perfect market timer will be uncertain, but its risk cannot be measured by standard deviation because perfect timing dominates a passive strategy, providing only "good" surprises.

4. Perfect-timing ability is equivalent to having a call option on the market portfolio. The value of the option can be determined using valuation techniques such as the Black-Scholes formula.

5. The value of *imperfect* timing, such as whether stocks will outperform bills, is given by the sum of the probabilities of the true outcome conditional on the forecast: $P_1 + P_2 - 1$. If perfect timing is equivalent to call option C, then imperfect timing can be valued by: $(P_1 + P_2 - 1)C$.

6. The Treynor-Black model is based on an index model that takes market-timing forecasts as given. The investment manager uses security analysis and statistics to construct an active portfolio. The active portfolio is mixed with the index portfolio to maximize the Sharpe measure of the optimal risky portfolio.

7. In the Treynor-Black model, the weight of each analyzed security is proportional to the ratio of its alpha to its residual variance.

Key Terms

market timing, 630   Treynor-Black   active portfolio, 636
                            model, 635

Selected Readings

The valuation of market timing ability using an option pricing framework is developed in:

Merton, Robert C. "On Market Timing and Investment Performance: An Equilibrium Theory of Value for Market Forecasts." *Journal of Business*, July 1981.

The Treynor-Black model is laid out in:

Treynor, Jack, and Fischer Black. "How to Use Security Analysis to Improve Portfolio Selection." *Journal of Business*, January 1973.

Problem Sets

1. Historical data suggest the standard deviation of an all-equity strategy is about 5.5 percent per month. Suppose the risk-free rate is now 1 percent per month and market volatility is at its historical level. What would be a fair monthly fee to a perfect market timer, according to the Black-Scholes formula?

2. A fund manager scrutinizing the record of two market timers comes up with this information:

Number of months that $r_M > r_f$		135
Correctly predicted by timer A	78	
Correctly predicted by timer B	86	
Number of months that $r_M < r_f$		92
Correctly predicted by timer A	57	
Correctly predicted by timer B	50	

a. What are the conditional probabilities, P_1 and P_2, and the total ability parameters for timers A and B?

b. Using the historical data of question 1, what is a fair monthly fee for the two timers?

Appendixes

■ ■

Appendix

Sources of Financial and Economic Information

I nformation is crucial in successful investing. In many cases, however, the biggest challenge facing investors is not a scarcity of information. For most investors, processing and interpreting the vast amount of information available is an even more daunting task than uncovering information. In this appendix, we provide a guided tour of some of the more important sources of information. We will progress from coverage of more general to more specific topics.

General Interest Publications

The Wall Street Journal is the most widely read source of financial and economic news. It has the highest circulation of any daily newspaper. The *Journal* reports on international, national, industry, and firm-specific news. It provides an extensive daily listing of security prices and interest rates, and it reports firms' earnings and dividend announcements as they are made.

Barron's is a weekly publication with even more extensive reporting of financial market prices, especially foreign security listings. It also contains regular features on various aspects of the securities market.

Investor's Daily began in 1984 in competition with *The Wall Street Journal*. It provides more price data than *The Wall Street Journal* but contains less descriptive reporting.

Business Week is oriented toward ongoing and complete business news reporting. In contrast, *Forbes* and *Fortune* are both biweekly publications and are more oriented toward more lengthy feature stories on particular companies, individuals, or issues. *Forbes* is known in part for its annual report on American industry, where it reports performance of several industries for the past five years. It also assesses performance of mutual funds annually.

Other financial and business-oriented general periodicals are *Dun's Review* and *Financial World*. Two good publications with an institutional focus are *Institutional Investor* and *Pensions and Investments Age*.

Macroeconomic Data

The U.S. government offers an extensive set of publications.

The *Federal Reserve Bulletin* is published monthly by the Board of Governors of the Federal Reserve System. It provides extensive data on the banking system and the money supply. The *Bulletin* is the primary source for most information on the monetary system. It also contains other macroeconomic data such as figures on GNP, interest rates, corporate profits, and employment. Another useful publication is the Federal Reserve *Historical Chart Book* with graphical representation of many useful data series.

The *Survey of Current Business* is published monthly by the U.S. Commerce Department. It provides detailed data on national income and production accounts, which are essentially breakdowns of GNP. The survey also provides considerable data on the labor market. It also provides production data for individual industries as well as employment, interest rates, prices, and foreign economic data.

Business Conditions Digest also has been published by the Commerce Department. This is the source of the economic indicator series (leading, lagging, and coincident indicators) discussed in Chapter 14. However, the *Digest* was discontinued in 1990, and a scaled-down presentation of its contents has been added to the *Survey of Current Business*.

The *Economic Report of the President* is an annual publication with over 100 tables on national income and expenditure, employment and wages, business activity, consumer and producer prices, government finance and budgets, corporate profits, interest rates, and international statistics.

The *Statistical Abstract of the United States* is prepared annually by the U.S. Bureau of the Census. It includes statistics on the social, demographic, economic, and political makeup of the United States in its approximately 1,000 pages of tables.

Industry Data

As noted, the *Survey of Current Business* contains considerable industry data. Other government publications from the Census Bureau are the *Censuses of: Manufacturers; Retail Trade; Service Industries;* and *Wholesale Trade*. The Census Bureau also publishes an *Annual Survey of Manufacturers* and *Current Industrial Reports*.

Private companies also publish industry data and outlooks. Among these are *Moody's Investor Services,* which publishes *Industry Review* and Standard & Poor's Corporation, which publishes *Industry Survey*. S&P covers about 70 industries, providing current and historical information as well as prospects for each. Value Line also provides industry analysis in its weekly *Investment Survey*. Each week a different industry is highlighted. Sample excerpts from these publications appear below with the discussion of company data.

Company Data

The original sources for most company data are annual reports, which are published every year by publicly held corporations. The annual report contains financial statements for the current and recent years and management's assessment of the company's past and future performance. Most firms also issue quarterly financial reports with more sketchy information. More detailed information is provided in the Form 10-K and Form 10-Q all firms with publicly traded securities must file with the Securities and Exchange Commission. Company prospectuses also contain considerable information. The prospectus, which is prepared for investors when the company issues new securities, contains financial statements, as well as considerable data on the company's operations and management. The data in the prospectus are more detailed than in the annual report.

Value Line publishes a wealth of data on about 1,700 firms in its *Investment Survey*. A sample page from the survey appears in Figure A.1. The page contains 15 years of historical and forecast balance sheet and income statement data, stock price history, dividend data, capital structure information, a short description of the company's line of business and prospects, stock beta, and projected stock performance. Value Line's performance forecast, called timeliness, was discussed in Chapter 17. The *Survey* is published weekly. Each week, 6 to 10 industries are analyzed. Over the year, all 1,700 firms are evaluated once.

Moody's Manuals also provide a wealth of company data. Moody's contains recent and historical balance sheets and income statements, information on outstanding securities issued by the firm, and useful descriptive material on the company. Moody's Manuals are arranged as follows: *Bank and Finance; Industrial; International; Municipal & Government; OTC Industrials; OTC Unlisted; Public Utility; Transportation.* Moody's also publishes the monthly *Bond Record* with data on thousands of bonds, the weekly *Bond Survey* of new offerings and current conditions, *Dividend Record, International Bond Review,* and *Handbook of Common Stocks* with financial data on hundreds of firms. The *Handbook* contains brief sketches on each firm with limited financial data, earnings and dividend information, and short descriptions of the firm and its prospects (see Figure A.2).

Standard & Poor's *Corporation Records* are similar to Moody's *Manuals.* They provide data on publicly traded securities. Each volume is updated throughout the year. In addition, S&P's *Stock Reports* provide current and historical financial data on firms traded on the NYSE, AMEX, and NASDAQ markets. These short reports also contain a description of the firm, its current outlook, and important developments. S&P's *Stock Guide* contains short sketches of thousands of companies including: principal business, historic stock price ranges, recent dividend and earnings data, and capital structure data. The *Bond Guide* lists the S&P quality rating for thousands of bonds as well as some key financial ratios pertaining to bond safety. Both guides are published monthly. Sample pages from the *Stock Guide* appear in Figure A.3. S&P also publishes *Dividend Record, Earnings Forecaster,* the weekly *Outlook* with advice on industries and specific securities, as well as several other periodicals.

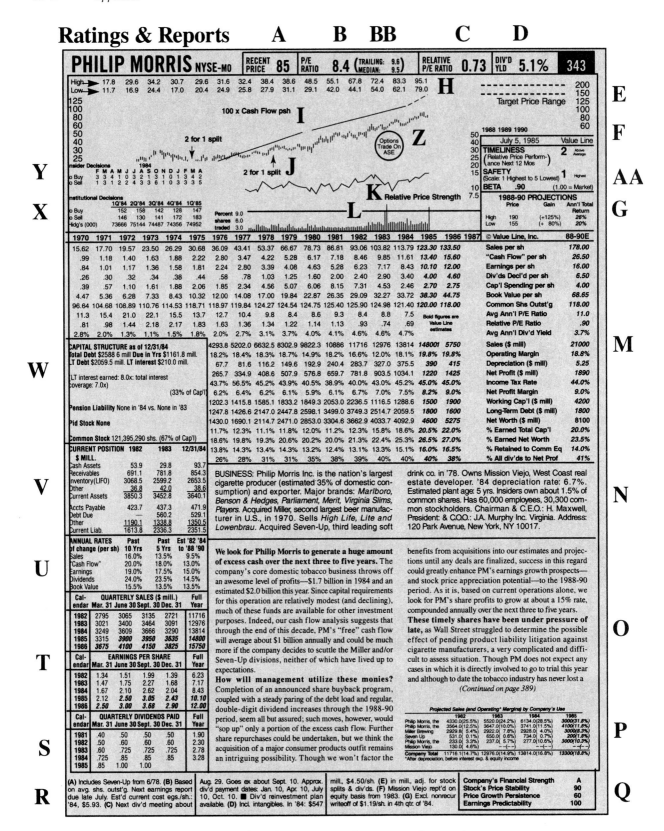

Figure A.1 **Value Line** *Investment Survey,* sample report.

SAMPLE VALUE LINE REPORT

A Recent price—nine days prior to delivery date.

AA Here is the core of Value Line's advice—the rank for Timeliness; the rank for Safety; Beta—the stock's sensitivity to fluctuations of the market as a whole.

B P/E ratio—the most recent price divided by the latest six months' earnings per share plus earnings estimated for the next six months.

BB P/E Median—a rounded average of four middle values of the range of average annual price-earnings ratios over the past 10 years.

C Relative P/E Ratio—the stock's current P/E divided by the median P/E for all stocks under Value Line review.

D Dividend Yield—cash dividends *estimated to be declared in the next 12 months* divided by the recent price.

E The 3-5 year target price range, estimated. The range is placed in proper position on the price chart, and is shown numerically in the "1988-90 Projections" box in the lower right-hand corner of the price chart.

F The date of delivery to the subscribers. The survey is mailed on a schedule that aims for delivery to every subscriber on Friday afternoon.

G Annual Total Return—the estimated future average annual growth plus current dividend yield—plus possible annualized change in the trend of the price-earnings ratio.

H The stock's **highest and lowest price** of the year.

I The Value Line—reported earnings plus depreciation ("cash flow") multiplied by a number selected to correlate the stock's 3- to 5-year projected target price with "cash flow" projected out to 1988-90.

J Monthly price ranges of the stock—plotted on a ratio (logarithmic) grid to show percentage changes in true proportion. For example, a ratio chart equalizes the move of a $10 stock that rises to $11 with a $100 stock that rises to $110. Both have advanced 10% and over the same space on a ratio grid.

K Relative price strength—describes the stock's past price performance relative to the Value Line Composite Average of 1700 stocks. The Timeliness Rank usually predicts the future direction of this line.

L The number of shares traded monthly as a percentage of the total outstanding.

M Statistical milestones that reveal significant long-term trends. The statistics are presented in two ways: 1) The upper series records results on a per-share basis; 2) the lower records results on a company basis. On pages 30 to 33, you will find conclusions that might be drawn from an inspection of these milestones. Note that the statistics for the year 1985 are estimated, as are the figures for the average of the years 1988-90. The estimates would be revised, if necessary, should future evidence require. The weekly *Summary & Index* would promptly call attention to such revisions.

N A condensed summary of the **business.**

O A 400-word report on **recent developments and prospects**—issued once every three months on a preset schedule.

P Most large corporations engage in several lines of business. Hence sales and profit margins are shown by **lines of business.**

Q Value Line indexes of **financial strength, price stability, price growth persistence, and earnings predictability.**

R Footnotes explain a number of things, such as the way earnings are reported, whether "fully diluted," on a "primary" basis, or on an "average shares outstanding" basis.

S Quarterly dividends paid are actual payments. The total of dividends paid in four quarters may not equal the figure shown in the annual series on dividends declared. (Sometimes a dividend declared at the end of the year will be paid in the first quarter of the following year.)

T Quarterly earnings are shown on a **per share** basis (estimates in bold type). Quarterly sales on a gross basis.

U Annual rates of change (on a per share basis). Actual past, estimated future.

V Current position—current assets, current liabilities, and other components of working capital.

W The capital structure as of recent date showing the percentage of capital in long-term debt (33%), and in common stock (67%); the number of times that total interest charges were earned (7.0 in 1984).

X A record of **the decisions taken by the biggest institutions** (over $70 million in equity holdings)—including banks, insurance companies, mutual funds, investment advisers, internally managed endowments, and pension funds—to buy or sell during the past five quarters and how many shares were involved, and the total number of shares they hold.

Y The record of insider decisions—decisions by officers and directors to buy or sell as reported to the SEC a month or more after execution.

Z Options patch—indicates listed options are available on the stock, and on what exchange they are most actively traded.

Figure A.1 (concluded)

INTERNATIONAL BUSINESS MACHINES CORPORATION

LISTED	SYM.	LTPS♦	STPS♦	IND. DIV.	REC. PRICE	RANGE (52 -WEEKS)	YLD
NYSE	IBM	71.4	83.5	$4.84*	101	140 –96	4.8%

HIGH GRADE. WEAK DOMESTIC DEMAND WILL PRESSURE RESULTS DESPITE STRONG OPERATING MARGINS.

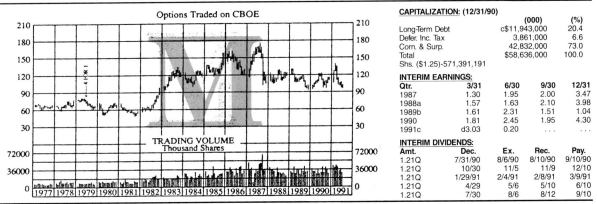

CAPITALIZATION: (12/31/90)

	(000)	(%)
Long-Term Debt	c$11,943,000	20.4
Defer. Inc. Tax	3,861,000	6.6
Com. & Surp.	42,832,000	73.0
Total	$58,636,000	100.0

Shs. ($1.25)-571,391,191

INTERIM EARNINGS:

Qtr.	3/31	6/30	9/30	12/31
1987	1.30	1.95	2.00	3.47
1988a	1.57	1.63	2.10	3.98
1989b	1.61	2.31	1.51	1.04
1990	1.81	2.45	1.95	4.30
1991c	d3.03	0.20	. . .	. . .

INTERIM DIVIDENDS:

Amt.	Dec.	Ex.	Rec.	Pay.
1.21Q	7/31/90	8/6/90	8/10/90	9/10/90
1.21Q	10/30	11/5	11/9	12/10
1.21Q	1/29/91	2/4/91	2/8/91	3/9/91
1.21Q	4/29	5/6	5/10	6/10
1.21Q	7/30	8/6	8/12	9/10

BACKGROUND:

IBM is the largest manufacturer of information processing equipment and systems. IBM applies advanced information technology to solve the problems in business, government, science, space, defense, education, medicine and other areas. IBM offers customers solutions that incorporate information processing systems, software, communication systems and other products and services to address specific needs. While most products are sold or leased through IBM worldwide marketing organization. IBM utilizes external distribution channels through IBM Business Partners. In 1990, revenues were derived: sales, 64%; support, 16%; software, 14% and rentals & financing, 6%.

RECENT DEVELOPMENTS:

IBM announced a strategic alliance with Apple Computer to develop a new operating system that makes computing more user-friendly. For the quarter ended 6/30/91, net income plunged 92% to $114 million compared with $1.41 billion a year ago. Revenues fell 11% to $14.73 billion. Poor results were attributed to the drop in sales of computer equipment, unfavorable foreign currency exchange rates and higher charges related to severance packages. However, demand for workstations and midrange mainframes improved and sales form support services rose 16%.

PROSPECTS:

Intense discount pricing within the computer industry accompanied by lower demand from both domestic and European markets clouds the near-term outlook. Meanwhile, long-term prospects are brightened by IBM's new comprehensive product offerings which include the System/390 ES 9000 line of mainframes, entry level models of the AS/400 minicomputers, two high-end models of the PS/2 computer and the PS/1 home computer. In addition, IBM's alliance with Apple to design an operating system centered around an object oriented software bode well for long-term growth. Brisk demand, competitively-priced workstations and the laptop computer will boost sales.

STATISTICS:

YEAR	GROSS REVS. ($mill.)	OPER. PROFIT MARGIN %	RET. ON EQUITY %	NET INCOME ($mill.)	WORK CAP ($mill.)	SENIOR CAPITAL ($mill.)	SHARES (000)	EARN. PER SH.$	DIV. PER SH.$	DIV PAY %	PRICE RANGE	P/E RATIO	AVG. YIELD %
81	29,070	20.7	18.2	3,308	2,983	2,669	592,294	5.63	3.44	61	71¹/₂– 48³/₈	10.7	6.0
82	34,364	23.4	22.1	4,409	4,805	2,851	602,406	7.39	3.44	47	98 – 55⁵/₈	10.4	4.5
83	40,180	23.9	23.6	5,485	7,763	2,674	610,725	9.04	3.71	41	134¹/₄– 92¹/₄	12.5	3.3
84	45,937	24.5	24.8	6,582	10,735	3,269	612,686	10.77	4.10	38	128¹/₂– 99	10.6	3.6
85	50,056	22.4	20.5	6,555	14,637	3,955	615,418	10.67	4.40	41	158¹/₂–117³/₈	12.9	3.2
86	51,250	15.3	13.9	4,789	15,006	4,169	605,923	7.81	4.40	56	161⁷/₈–119¹/₄	18.0	3.1
87	54,217	14.3	13.7	5,258	17,643	3,858	597,052	8.72	4.40	50	175⁷/₈–102	15.9	3.2
88	59,681	14.7	13.9	a5,491	17,956	8,518	589,741	a9.27	4.40	47	129¹/₂–104¹/₂	12.6	3.8
89	62,710	11.0	9.8	b3,758	14,175	10,825	574,700	b6.47	4.73	73	130⁷/₈– 93³/₈	17.3	4.2
90	**69,018**	**16.0**	**14.1**	**6,020**	**13,644**	**11,943**	**571,391**	**10.51**	**4.84**	**46**	**123¹/₈– 94¹/₂**	**10.4**	**4.4**

♦Long-Term Price Score—Short-Term Price Score: See page 4a. STATISTICS ARE AS ORIGINALLY REPORTED.a-Excludes $315 million ($0.53 per share) credit for an accounting change. b-Includes $2.4 billion ($4.16 a share) charge for restructuring. c-Includes debentures convertible into common stock. e-Includes a net charge of $2.3 billion ($3.96 a sh.) related to changes in accounting for post-retirement benefits.

INCORPORATED: June 16, 1911—NY	**TRANSFER AGENT(S):** First Chicago Trust Co. of N.Y. New York, NY	**OFFICERS:** Chairman & C.E.O. J. F. Akers
PRINCIPAL OFFICE: Old Orchard Road Armonk, NY 10504 Tel.:(914) 765-7777	**REGISTRAR(S):** First Chicago Trust Company of N.Y. New York, NY	President J. D. Kuehler S.V.P. & C.F.O. F. A. Metz, Jr.
ANNUAL MEETING: Last Mon. in April	**INSTITUTIONAL HOLDINGS:** No. of Institutions: 1,441 Shares Held: 302,584,660	Treasurer R. Ripp Secretary J. E. Hickey
NUMBER OF STOCKHOLDERS: 789,046		

Figure A.2 Moody's Handbook of Common Stocks, **sample report.**   (Moody's Investors Service, 1990).

Int'l Business Machines   1210

NYSE Symbol IBM Options on CBOE (Jan–Apr–Jul–Oct) In S&P 500

Price	Range	P–E Ratio	Dividend	Yield	S&P Ranking	Beta
Nov. 26'90	1990					
113 7/8	123⅛–94½	16	4.84	4.3%	A	0.74

Summary

IBM is the world's dominant manufacturer of mainframe computers and is also a major supplier of minicomputers, computer peripheral equipment, personal computers, networking products, and system software. The earnings recovery begun in 1990 should continue into 1991, aided by initial sales of a new generation of mainframe computers. In August, 1990 the company announced that it would put its domestic typewriter and small printer products businesses into a new unit to be majority owned by Clayton & Dubiller, Inc.

Current Outlook

Earnings for 1991 are projected at $10.70 a share, compared with the $10.00 estimated for 1990.
The $1.21 quarterly dividend is the minimum expectation.
Gross income for 1991 should advance at a somewhat slower pace than the almost 8% gain expected for 1990. Progress would be limited by slower worldwide economic growth, despite revenues gains from the introduction of new mainframe and work station lines. Profit margins should improve, with benefits from the domestic cost containment program more than offsetting pricing pressures in the mainframe and minicomputer markets.

Revenues (Billion $)

Quarter	1991	1990	1989	1988
Mar	....	14.19	12.73	12.06
Jun	....	16.50	15.21	13.91
Sep	....	15.28	14.31	13.71
Dec	....	....	20.46	20.00
			62.71	59.66

Revenues for the first nine months of 1990 advanced 8.8%, year to year, aided by increased demand for high end files, AS 400 minicomputers and PS/2 personal computers, software and support services, and higher leasing revenues. Profit margins benefited from the greater volume and initial gains from the cost reduction program. Net income increased 12%, to $6.21 a share (on 1.6% fewer shares) from $5.43.

Capital Share Earnings ($)

Quarter	1991	1990	1989	1988
Mar	E1.85	1.81	1.61	1.57
Jun	E2.55	2.45	2.31	1.63
Sep	E2.00	1.95	1.51	2.10
Dec	E4.30	E3.79	1.04	3.97
	E10.70	E10.00	6.47	9.27

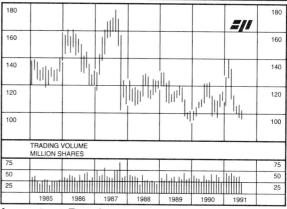

Important Developments

Sep. '90–The company introduced a new generation of mainframe computers, the System/390 line.

Aug. '90–IBM announced that it will consolidate its domestic typewriter, keyboard, personal printers and supplies business into a new unit to be majority owned by Clayton & Dubilier, Inc.

Feb. '90–A new line of high performance technical workstations was introduced.

Jan. '90–The company restructured its domestic operations, resulting in a $2.4 billion pretax charge in the fourth quarter of 1989, equal to $2.58 a share after taxes. Savings from expected capacity reductions and technology investment writedowns could add $1.00 to share earnings by 1991.

Next earnings report expected in mid–January.

Per Share Data ($)

Yr. End Dec. 31	1989	[1]1988	1987	1986	1985	1984	1983	1982	1981	1980
Tangible Bk. Val.	66.33	65.78	62.81	55.40	50.60	41.79	38.02	33.13	30.66	28.18
Cash Flow	13.76	15.80	14.57	13.23	15.64	16.02	15.02	13.36	11.29	10.83
Earnings[2]	6.47	9.27	8.72	7.81	10.67	10.77	9.04	7.39	5.63	6.10
Dividends	4.73	4.40	4.40	4.40	4.40	4.10	3.71	3.44	3.44	3.44
Payout Ratio	72%	47%	50%	56%	41%	38%	41%	47%	62%	56%
Prices–High	130⅞	129½	175⅞	161⅞	158¾	128½	134¼	98	71½	72¾
Low	93⅜	104¼	102	119¼	117⅜	99	92¼	55⅜	48⅜	50⅜
P/E Ratio	20–14	14–11	20–12	21–15	15–11	12–9	15–10	13–8	13–9	12–8

Data as orig. reptd. 1.Reflects acctg. change. 2.Bef. spec. item(s) of +0.53 in 1988. E–Estimated

Standard NYSE Stock Reports
Vol. 57/No. 233/Sec. 13

Standard & Poor's Corp.
25 Broadway, NY, NY 10004

Figure A.3 **Standard & Poor's Stock Guide,** sample report.

1210   International Business Machines Corporation

Income Data (Millions $)

Year Ended Dec. 31	Revs.	Oper. Inc.	% Oper. Inc. of Revs.	Cap Exp.	Depr.	Int. Exp.	[2]Net Bef. Taxes	Eff. Tax Rate	[2]Net Inc.	% Net Inc. of Revs.	Cash Flow
1989	62,710	13,553	21.6	6,414	4,240	1,118	6,645	43.4%	3,758	6.0	7,998
[1]1988	59,681	12,617	21.1	5,431	3,871	802	9,033	39.2%	5,491	9.2	9,362
1987	54,217	11,269	20.8	4,304	3,527	619	8,609	38.9%	5,258	9.7	8,785
1986	51,250	11,175	21.8	4,620	3,316	604	8,389	42.9%	4,789	9.3	8,105
1985	50,056	14,281	28.5	6,430	3,051	443	11,619	43.6%	6,555	13.1	9,606
1984	45,937	14,446	31.4	5,473	3,215	408	11,623	43.4%	6,582	14.3	9,797
1983	40,180	13,216	32.9	4,930	3,627	390	9,940	44.8%	5,485	13.7	9,112
1982	34,364	11,618	33.6	6,685	3,562	514	7,930	44.4%	[1]4,409	12.8	7,971
1981	29,070	9,356	32.2	6,845	3,329	480	5,988	44.8%	3,308	11.4	6,637
1980	26,213	8,499	32.4	6,592	2,759	[1]325	5,897	39.6%	3,562	13.6	6,321

Balance Sheet Data (Million $)

Dec. 31	Cash	Curr. Assets	Curr. Liab.	Ratio	Total Assets	Ret. On Assets	Long Term Debt	Common Equity	Total Inv. Capital	% LT Debt of Cap.	Ret. On Equity
1989	4,961	35,875	21,700	1.7	77,734	5.0%	10,825	38,509	52,614	20.6	9.8%
1988	6,123	35,343	17,387	2.0	73,037	8.1%	8,518	39,509	52,650	16.2	14.2%
1987	6,967	31,020	13,377	2.3	63,688	8.7%	3,858	38,263	47,271	8.2	14.6%
1986	7,257	27,749	12,743	2.2	57,814	8.7%	4,169	34,374	43,067	9.7	14.5%
1985	5,622	26,070	11,433	2.3	52,634	13.7%	3.955	31,990	39,595	10.0	22.4%
1984	4,362	20,375	9,640	2.1	42,808	16.4%	3,269	26,489	31,815	10.3	26.4%
1983	5,536	17,270	9,507	1.8	37,243	15.6%	2,674	23,219	26,606	10.1	25.2%
1982	3,300	13,014	8,209	1.6	32,541	14.1%	2,851	19,960	23,134	12.3	22.9%
1981	2,029	10,303	7,320	1.4	29,586	11.7%	2,669	18,161	21,082	12.7	19.0%
1980	2,112	9,925	6,526	1.5	26,703	13.9%	2,099	16,453	18,734	11.2	22.7%

Data as orig. reptd.; finance subs. consol aft.1987. 1. Reflects acctg. change. 2. Incl. equity in earns. of nonconsol. subs.
3. Bef. spec. Item in 1988.

Business Summary

IBM is the largest manufacturer of data processing equipment and systems. Industry segment contributions to revenues in recent years:

	1989	1988
Processors/peripherals	43%	44%
Workstations	20%	19%
Programs/maint./other	34%	34%
Federal systems	3%	3%

Hardware sales provided 66% of revenues in 1989, software and services 29%, and rentals 5%. Foreign operations contributed 59% of revenues in 1989 and $4.1 billion of net profits.

Processors manipulate data through the operation of a stored program. Peripherals include printers, storage and tele-communication devices. Workstations include small business computers, intelligent workstations and typewriters. Program products include applications and systems software. Maintenance represents separately billed maintenance services. Other revenues are derived from financing revenue, supplies and miscellaneous support services. The Federal systems group serves the U.S. government's defense, space and other agencies.

Dividend Data

Dividends have been paid since 1916. A dividend reinvestment plan is available.

Amt of Divd. $	Date Decl.	Ex-divd. Date	Stock of Record	Payment Date
1.21	Jan. 30	Feb. 5	Feb. 9	Mar. 10'0
1.21	Apr. 30	May 4	May 10	Jun. 9'90
1.21	Jul 31	Aug. 6	Aug. 10	Sep. 10'90
1.21	Oct. 30	Nov. 5	Nov. 9	Dec. 10'90

Next dividend meeting: late Jan.'91.

Finances

Research, development and engineering expense totaled $6.8 billion (11% of gross income) in 1989, versus $5.9 billion (9.9%) in 1988.

Capitalization

Long Term Debt: $11,167,000,000, incl. $1.25 billion of 7⅞% debs. conv. into com. at $153.66 a sh.

Capital Sock: 571,052,736 shs. ($1.25 par).
Institutions hold approximately 51%.
Shareholders of record: 815,580.

Office—Armonk, New York 10504. Tel—(914) 765-1900. Stockholder Relations Dept—690 Madison Ave., NYC 10022. Tel—(212) 735-7000. Chrmn—J. F Akers. Secy—J. E. Hickey. Treas—D. A. Finley. Investor Contact—H, Park. Dirs—J. F Akers, S. D. Bechtel, Jr., H. Brown, J. E. Burke, F. T. Cary, W. T. Coleman, Jr., T. F Frist, Jr., F Gerber N. deB. Katzenbach, N. O. Keohane. J. D. Kuehler, R. W. Lyman, J. R. Monro, T. S. Murphy, J. R. Opel, H. Sihiler, J. B. Slaughter, E. S. Woolard, Jr. Transfer Agent & Registrar—Morgan Shareholder Services Trust Co., NYC. incorporated in New York in 1911. Empl—383.

Figure A.3 (*concluded*)

Dun and Bradstreet's *Industry Norms and Key Business Ratios* is a useful source for evaluating a company's financial strength. This publication offers average financial ratios for 125 industries that can be used as benchmarks for firms in that industry.

In addition to these standard sources, you should be aware that data on firms are available through brokerage reports and investment letters, most of which come with buy or sell recommendations.

Security Markets

Extensive daily listings are available in *The Wall Street Journal, Investor's Daily, New York Times,* and several other newspapers. S&P's *Daily Stock Price Record,* which is published each quarter, contains daily price data for that entire quarter. The *Record* has separate volumes for NYSE, AMEX, and NASDAQ firms. Security prices are also available from computerized data bases. (See discussion below.)

Historical data on price indexes for several asset classes are available from an annual series of publications by Ibbotson Associates titled *Stocks, Bonds, Bills and Inflation. The Wall Street Journal Index* provides historical data on the Dow Jones averages.

Data on the financial marketplace—the stock exchanges, for example—are published annually in the New York Stock Exchange *Fact Book* and American Stock Exchange *Databook*. These publications contain information on trading activity, membership, and investor characteristics.

The Securities and Exchange Commission publishes a monthly *Statistical Bulletin* with data on the security industry. The data provided include trading volume on all exchanges, prices, volatility, and information on new issues. The SEC also publishes an *Annual Report* with a discussion of the year's events, a summary of much of the data that appeared in the *Statistical Bulletin,* and some annual data series.

Computer Data Bases

It is almost impossible to keep up with the rapidly growing collection of computerized data bases. Here is a list of some of the more popular and useful sources.

The *Dow Jones News/Retrieval* is an industry leader for computerized investor services. It is an on-line data base containing current economic, corporate, industry, financial news, reports, and statistics for the United States. Information provided includes news for the current day as well as some historical information. The data base also covers world news, as well as financial and corporate information for Japan, Europe, and Canada. Table A.1 summarizes the data available from the service.

S&P's *Compustat* is another financial data base with annual and quarterly balance sheet and income statement data on companies listed on the NYSE, AMEX, and OTC, regional, and Canadian stock exchanges. The historical data usually are available for up to 20 years (annual tape) or 48 quarters (quarterly tape).

The *CRSP* (Center for Research in Security Prices) tape from the University of Chicago contains daily and monthly price series on NYSE, AMEX, and NASDAQ traded stocks. The center also maintains a government bond tape.

Table A.1   *Dow Jones News/Retrieval Contents*

A. News
    1. Press releases
    2. Credit market news
    3. Business and financial news from *The Wall Street Journal,* Dow Jones News Service
        and other industry publications, including text search capability
    4. National and world news
    5. News alerts
B. Company Profits and Reports
    1. Comprehensive company reports
    2. Company and industry tracking service
C. Company and Industry Statistics and Forecasts
    1. Dun and Bradstreet reports on 750,000 companies
    2. SEC filing extracts
    3. Canadian news
    4. Earnings forecasts
    5. Insider trading reports
    6. Analysts' reports on companies and industries
D. Quotes and Market Averages
    1. Current quotes on stocks, bonds, futures, and indexes
    2. Historical security prices and index levels
    3. Historical Dow Jones Averages
E. Services
    1. On-line brokerage service (Fidelity)
    2. Travel services
    3. *Wall Street Week* transcripts
    4. Shopping
    5. Sports and weather
    6. Book and movie reviews

The Berkeley *Options Data Base* contains records of option quotes on the Chicago Board Options Exchange from 1976.

The *Disclosure Database* contains financial and textual data extracted from Securities and Exchange Commission filings (in particular, the 10-K) and provides information on over 10,000 American and foreign public companies. More than 200 individual fields, categorized into company résumé, financial information, and textual or management information sections, can be searched and displayed. Information sources include the 10-K, 10-Q, and 8-K reports, as well as annual reports to stockholders.

More general economic data bases are:

Citibase (put out by Citicorp) contains 5,000 time series from more than 100 government and private sources.

The International Monetary Fund's *International Financial Statistics* tape contains data on domestic and international finance such as exchange rates, international trade, prices, production, interest rates, and government finance.

The *Flow of Funds Accounts* compiled by the Board of Governors of the Federal Reserve System are available on tape and contain both flows and year-end assets and liabilities of the following sectors: households; businesses; governments; banking; and nonbank finance.

Appendix

Solutions to Concept Checks

1. *a.* Policy, asset allocation
   b. Constraint, regulation
   c. Objective, return requirement
   d. Constraint, horizon
   e. Policy, market timing
   f. Constraint, taxes
   g. Objectives, risk tolerance
   h. Constraint, liquidity

2. Identify the elements that are life-cycle driven in the two schemes of objectives and constraints.

3. A convenient and effective way to organize the answer to this question is to cast it in the context of the investment policy statement framework.

Objectives

Risk: Endowment funds have no "safety nets" such as pension funds enjoy in the event of difficulty, either in the form of corporate assets to fall back on or a call on public (PBGC) assistance. Moreover, endowment fund cash flows may be highly erratic due to the uncertain timing of income from gifts and/or bequests, while pension fund cash flows tend to be very predictable and steady. These differences suggest the typical endowment fund will adopt a more conservative risk-bearing posture than will the typical pension fund, both as to asset class exposures and to the type of security content of such exposures.

Return: Because investment-related spending is usually limited to "yield," endowment funds typically focus their return goals on the matter of current spendable income; pension funds, on the other hand, tend to adopt total return approaches, at least until a plan matures. Although inflation protection is of great importance to both types of funds, endowment funds appear to be less concerned with real return production than are pension funds, perhaps because of their frequent emphasis on " income now" in setting return goals.

Constraints

Time horizon: Although, theoretically, an endowment fund is a perpetuity while a pension fund may well have a finite life span and, therefore, an endowment fund should operate with a very long-term view of investment, such funds in practice tend to adopt shorter horizons than are typical of pension funds (just as they typically assume less risk). Their tendency to emphasize income production in the near term is the probable reason for this common occurrence.

Liquidity: Endowment funds, particularly those that use gifts and bequests to supplement their investment income, often have fairly large liquidity reserves—both to protect against fluctuations in their cash flows and reflecting their generally conservative outlooks—while, except for very mature plans, pension funds tend to require minimum liquidity reserves. Endowment funds also frequently maintain substantial liquid holdings to provide for known future cash payout requirements, such as for new buildings.

Taxes: Here, although differing in detail, the situation of the two forms of institutions are very much the same. In the United States, tax considerations are normally of minimal importance to either.

Regulatory/legal: Endowment fund investment is carried on under state governance, while pension fund investment, in the United States, is carried under federal law, specifically under ERISA. The difference is significant. Endowment funds operate under the prudent man rule, where each investment must be judged on its own merits apart from any other portfolio holdings, while pension plans operate under a broader context for investment—each security being judged in terms of the portfolio as a whole—and an ERISA-mandated diversification requirement that often leads to wider asset-class exposures. In a pragmatic sense, the prudent man rule is aimed at risk *reduction* while the prudent expert provision of ERISA is aimed at risk *management*.

Unique circumstances: Endowment funds often are faced with unique situations that infrequently affect pension fund management, including the scrutiny of such special-interest groups as trustees, alumni, faculty, student organizations, local community pressure groups, etc., each with separate and often incompatible complaints and goals that may need to be accommodated in policy setting and/or in investment content. Similarly, endowment funds are often subjected to severe "social pressures" that, as in the case of South Africa divestment, can have an important investment impact by restricting the available universe of investment securities, mandating participation or nonparticipation in certain industries, sectors, or countries, or otherwise changing investment action from what it would ideally have been. In pension fund investment, ERISA requires that no other interests be put ahead of the interests of the beneficiaries in determining investment actions.

While the above distinctions and differences are accurate *in general,* they are not iron-clad. A growing number of endowment funds are now following in the innovative footsteps of such endowment leaders as The Common Fund and Harvard and Stanford universities by adopting much less conservative approaches and policies in endowment investing than have traditionally been the case. In particular, this affects:

1. Return objective: Reduced emphasis on "income now," increased emphasis on long-term income growth and inflation protection, often including plowing back a portion of current income to augment future income via a larger capital base.
2. Risk objective: Reduced risk aversion is reflected in more aggressive investment strategies, including the use of alternative (to normal stocks, bonds, and cash) instruments and asset categories. Risk control is seen to be enhanced by broader diversification across the investment spectrum and by a broader view of the flexibility of the prudent man rule in an endowment investment context.
3. Constraints:
   a. Time horizon: The concept of perpetuity as the endowment fund's life span has lengthened the investment horizon to at least a pension-fund par and re-

sulted in a greater tolerance for intermediate asset value fluctuation. Policies and strategies are increasingly being formulated in very long-term strategic form, followed by review and updates on a three- to five-year cycle.

b. Liquidity: Not much impact here, except that cash (liquidity) reserves are deliberately kept as small as possible and are intensively managed to maximize their contribution to current income production.

c. Taxes: No change.

d. Regulatory/legal: While the prudent man rule is unchanged, attitudes toward what it requires/permits are changing toward a less restrictive, more facilitative view. In turn, this has encouraged a fuller use of the instruments available to endowment policy makers and investment managers.

e. Unique circumstances: While, for the most part, policies have been adjusted to deal with a wide variety of special interest and social concerns, these aspects of endowment policy making and investment management continue as significant challenges.

Chapter 2

1. The scenario analysis for the two strategies is:

Strategy	Portfolio Return When the Index Fund Returns:	
	24%	**0**
I. Fully invested in the index fund	24%	0%
II. Only half invested in the index fund	$(1/2) \times 7 + (1/2) \times 24 = 15.5\%$	$(1/2) \times 7 + (1/2) \times 0 = 3.5\%$

The expected returns for the two strategies are:

$$E(r_\text{I}) = (2/3)24 + (1/30)0 = 16\%$$
$$E(r_\text{II}) = (2/3)15.5 + (1/3)3.5 = 11.5\%$$

The standard deviations are:

$$\sigma_\text{I} = [(2/3)(24-16)^2 + (1/3)(0-16)^2]^{1/2} = 11.31\%$$
$$\sigma_\text{II} = [(2/3)(15.5-11.5)^2 + (1/3)(3.5-11.5)^2]^{1/2} = 5.66\%$$

Thus, shifting half of the portfolio to the risk-free asset has reduced the standard deviation (risk) from 11.31 percent to 5.66 percent, at the price of reducing the expected rate of return from 16 percent to 11.5 percent. By further shifting the entire portfolio to the risk-free asset, the investor would get the standard deviation down to zero and the expected return to 7 percent.

2. a. With a perfect forecast you would keep the entire portfolio in the index fund when the return is 24 percent (2/3 of the time) and shift the entire portfolio to T-bills when the stock market returns zero (1/3 of the time). In this way, your expected return is: $(2/3)24 + (1/3)7 = 18.33\%$. The standard deviation is not relevant here because while your return will vary over time, you will always anticipate it. So no surprises—no risk.

b. If the forecaster is less than perfect, the answer has to be revised. The actual calculation is tricky. Setting up the meaning of being correct half the time in both high and low markets, the frequency of the realizations (actual rates of return) and forecasts can be summarized by the following table:

Realization	Frequency	Forecast	Frequency	Accuracy	Overall Frequency
Index 24%	2/3	Index 24%	1/2	Correct	(2/3)(1/2) = 2/6
		Index 0%	1/2	Wrong	(2/3)(1/2) = 2/6
Index 0%	1/3	Index 24%	1/2	Wrong	(1/3)(1/2) = 1/6
		Index 0%	1/2	Correct	(1/3)(1/2) = 1/6

Verify from the columns that the forecaster is correct half the time in each type of market and half the time overall. The portfolio position in each case and the rate of return are given by the following table:

Forecast	Position	Realization	Frequency	Portfolio Rate of Return
Index 24%	Index	Index 24%	2/6	24%
Index 24%	Index	Index 0%	1/6	0%
Index 0%	T-bills	Index 24%	2/6	7%
Index 0%	T-bills	Index 0%	1/6	7%

We can now compute the expected return:

$$E(r) = (2/6)24 + (1/6)0 + (2/6)7 + (1/6)7 = 11.5\%$$

The standard deviation is not a valid measure of risk. Half the time, when the forecast is bad, the entire portfolio will be in T-bills with zero risk. The other times, it will be in the index fund. You can check that when the forecast is good, there is still a probability of 2/3 for a good market and 1/3 for a zero market, same as without a forecast. Thus, the standard deviation is 11.31 percent (as computed earlier). Half that standard deviation equals that of keeping half of the portfolio in the index fund all the time. All in all, the forecaster is of no value.

3. The pie chart of the final portfolio can be filled by multiplying the proportions from Table 2.2 as shown below:

Asset	Proportion in Universe	Proportion in Asset Class	Proportion in Country	Proportion in Portfolio
U.S. bills	1.00	.15	.75	.112500
U.S. 30-year bond	.60	.40	.75	.180000
AT&T coupon bond	.40	.40	.75	.120000
IBM stock	.45	.45	.75	.151875
GM stock	.35	.45	.75	.118125
Exxon stock	.20	.45	.75	.067500
Bank of Japan note	1.00	.60	.25	.150000
Sumitomo stock	.50	.40	.25	.050000
Mitsubishi Chem. stock	.50	.40	.25	.050000
				1.000000

4. Using the data in Table 2.2 and the U.S. country portfolio proportions of Table 2.1, the rates of return by scenario are given by:

State of the Economy	Probability	U.S. Country Portfolio Rate of Return	
Boom with low inflation	.1	$74 \times .45 + 4 \times .40 + 6 \times .15 =$	35.8%
Boom with high inflation	.2	$20 \times .45 + (-10).40 + 6 \times .15 =$	5.9
Normal growth	.4	$14 \times .45 + 9 \times .40 + 6 \times .15 =$	10.8
Recession with low inflation	.2	$0 \times .45 + 35 \times .40 + 6 \times .15 =$	14.9
Recession with high inflation	.1	$-(30) \times .45 + 0 \times .40 + 6 \times .15 =$	−12.6

The expected return is: $(.1 \times 35.8) + (.2 \times 5.9) + (.4 \times 10.8) + (.2 \times 14.9) + [.1 \times (-12.6) = 10.8\%]$

5. *a.* Without any tax sheltering, the terminal value of the $10,000 savings will be:

$$\$10,000 \times [1 + (1 - .33).10]^{20} = \$36,583.76.$$

When the contribution itself is not sheltered, but income on it is tax-deferred, the before-tax terminal value will be as before:

$$\$10,000 \times (1 + .10)^{20} = \$67,275.00$$

of which all but $10,000 is taxable at 33 percent. The after-tax terminal value in this case will be: $\$67,275 - .33(67,275 - 10,000) = \$48,374.25$. The value of tax deferral of income is: $\$48,374.25 - 36,583.76 = \$11,790.49$.

When the contribution tax is deferred, the before-tax contribution with an after-tax value of $10,000 (the grossed up value) is $\$10,000/.67 = \$14,925.37$. The terminal value will be:

$$\$14,925.37(1 + .10)^{20} (1 - .33) = \$67,275.00$$

and the value of the tax deferral of the contribution is: $\$67,275.00 - 48,374.25 = \$18,900.75$

b. When retiring in 10 years, the unsheltered terminal value is $19,126.88. When income is sheltered (tax deferred), the after-tax terminal value is $20,678.07. When contribution is sheltered, too, the after-tax terminal value will be $25,937.42.

c. If the bonds are sheltered and stocks pay no cash dividends, then the after-tax terminal value will be:

$$\$200,000(1.1)^{10} - .28[200,000(1.1)^{10} - 200,000] = \$429,498.91.$$

When half the unsheltered account is in bonds, the after-tax terminal value will be:

$$\$429,498.91(150,000/200,000) + 50,000[1 + (1 - .28).1]^{10} = \$422,335.75$$

for a loss of $7,163.16.

Chapter 3

1. *a.* Real;
b. Financial;
c. Real;
d. Real;
e. Financial.

2. No. While Tracy is providing a financial management service, no financial asset is being created.

3. *a.* Derivative, 5,000 barrels of West Texas Crude is the underlying asset;
    b. Primitive;
    c. Primitive;
    d. Composite of primitive (bond) and call option, digital stock is the underlying asset;
    e. Primitive;
    f. Derivative, B-767 jet is the underlying asset;
    g. Primitive.

4. The uninsured bank has to pay a higher rate, the differential depending on how risky depositors perceive the bank to be.

5. As before, the insurer puts up $200,000 ($198,000 + 1,300), which now earns 10 percent. The expected end-of-year value of the account will be $1.10 \times 200,000 - 1,000 = \$219,000$, so the expected rate of return is: $(219,000 - 198,700)/198,700 = 10.22$ percent, a risk premium of 22 basis points. If the policy holder dies within the year, the rate of return will be: $(1.10 \times 200,000 - 200,000 - 198,700) = -89.93\%$. With no benefits paid out, the rate of return will be 10.72 percent. The standard deviation of the rate of return is $[.005(-89.93 - 10.22)^2 + .995(10.72 - 10.22)^2]^{1/2} = 7.10\%$.

    The standard deviation does not change because the risk of the policy has not changed, but the expected return goes up by 2 basis points. Therefore, increases in the risk-free rate, through competitive pressures, will tend to reduce the price of insurance policies.

6. *a.* Used cars trade in dealer markets (used-car lots or at auto dealerships) and in direct search markets when individuals advertise in local newspapers;
    b. paintings trade in broker markets when clients commission brokers to buy or sell art for them, in dealer markets at art galleries, and in auction markets;
    c. rare coins trade mostly in dealer markets in coin shops, but they also trade in auctions and in direct search markets when individuals advertise they want to buy or sell coins.

7. Creative unbundling can separate interest or dividend from capital gains income. Dual funds do just this. In tax regimes where capital gains are taxed at lower rates than other income, or where gains can be deferred, such unbundling may be a way to attract different tax clienteles to a security.

Chapter 4

1. The discount yield at bid is 5.35 percent, so its bid price must be

    $$P = 10,000[1 - .0535 \times (28/360)] = \$9,958.39$$

    compared with the ask price of $9,958.70.

2. In Figure 4.4 (from early April) find the 7⅝ (coupon rate) bond that is listed as: Feb 02–07, that is, maturity date of February 2007, and first call date of February 2002. The ask price is 95⁴/₃₂. The semiannual coupon is 3¹³/₁₆, and there are approximately 32 semiannual periods to maturity and 22 to the first call date. Inputting this data (if you have an advanced calculator you can use the exact data) we obtain:

	To Maturity	To First Call
APR YTM	8.18	8.31
Effective YTM	8.34	8.48

Since the bond is a discount bond (YTM above coupon rate), *The Wall Street Journal* reports the yield to maturity rather than the yield to first call.

3. In Figure 4.5, find the Tennessee Valley Authority 7:00 coupon bond maturing at 1–97. See that its YTM is 8.11 percent. In Figure 4.4, the 8:00 T-bond maturing in Jan 97 has a YTM of 7.82 percent. The significant differential of 29 basis points can be attributed mostly to the difference in risk.

4. Tax rates were reduced substantially in the 1980s. The reduction in these rates would be expected to reduce the tax advantage of municipal bonds. As a result, munis would need to offer higher yields relative to taxable bonds, and the yield ratio would be expected to rise.

5. *a.* You are entitled to a prorated share of IBM's dividend payments and to vote in any of IBM's stockholder meetings.
   b. Your potential gain is unlimited because IBM's stock price has no upper bound.
   c. Your outlay was $50 × 100 = $5,000. Because of limited liability, this is the most you can lose.

6. The price-weighted index increases from 62.5 [(100 + 25)/2] to 65 [(110 + 20)/2], a gain of 4 percent. An investment of one share in each company requires an outlay of $125 that would increase in value to $130, for a return of 4 percent (5/125), which equals the return to the price-weighted index.

7. The market value-weighted index return is calculated by computing the increase in value of the stock portfolio. The portfolio of the two stocks starts with an initial value of $100 million + $500 million = $600 million and falls in value to $110 million + $400 million = $510 million, a loss of 90/600 = .15, or 15 percent. The index portfolio return is a weighted average of the returns on each stock with weights of 1/6 on XYZ and 5/6 in ABC (weights proportional to relative investments). Because the return on XYZ is 10 percent, while that on ABC is −20 percent, the index portfolio return is (1/6)10 + (5/6) (−20) = −15%, equal to the return on the market value-weighted index.

8. The payoff to the call option is $8. The call cost $4.375. The profit is $3.625 per share. The put will pay off zero—it expires worthless since the stock price exceeds the exercise price. The loss is the cost of the put, $2.75.

Chapter 5

1. Limited time-shelf registration was introduced because of its favorable trade-off of saving issue cost against mandated disclosure. Allowing unlimited shelf registration would circumvent "blue sky" laws that ensure proper disclosure.

2. Solving:

$$\frac{100P - \$4,000}{100P} = .4$$

yields $P = \$66.67$ per share.

3. The investor will purchase 150 shares, with a rate of return as follows:

Year-End Change in Price	Year-End Value of Shares	Repayment of Principal and Interest	Investor's Rate of Return
30%	$19,500	$5,450	40.5%
No change	15,000	5,450	−4.5
−30%	10,500	5,450	−49.5

4. *a.* Once Xerox stock goes up to $110, your balance sheet will be:

Assets		Liabilities and Owners' Equity	
Cash	$100,000	Short position in Xerox	$110,000
T-bills	50,000	Equity	40,000

b. Solving:

$$\frac{\$150,000 - 1,000P}{1,000P} = .4$$

yields $P = \$107.14$ per share.

Chapter 6

1. *a.* Solving:

$$1 + R = (1 + r)(1 + i) = (1.03)(1.08) = 1.1124$$
$$r = 11.24\%.$$

b. Solving:

$$1 + R = (1.03)(1.10) = 1.133$$
$$R = 13.3\%.$$

2. The mean excess return for the period 1926–1934 is 4.5 percent (below the historical average), and the standard deviation (dividing by $n-1$) is 30.79 (above the historical average). These results reflect the severe downturn of the great crash and the unusually high volatility of stock returns in this period.

3. $r = (.12 - .13)/.13 = -.00885$ or $-.885\%$.

When the inflation rate exceeds the nominal interest rate, the real rate of return is negative.

Chapter 7

1. The expected rate of return on the risky portfolio is $22,000/100,000 = .22$, or 22 percent. The T-bill rate is 5 percent. The risk premium, therefore, is 22 percent $- 5 = 17$ percent. The standard deviation is $34,292.86/100,000 = .3429$, or 34.29 percent. It does not change when we subtract the T-bill rate from both possible rates of return.

2. The U.S. investor is taking on exchange rate risk by investing in a pound-denominated asset. If the exchange rate moves in the investor's favor, more will be earned from the U.K. bill than the U.S. bill. For example, if both the U.S. and U.K. interest rates are 5 percent, and the current exchange rate is $1.50 per pound, a $1.50 investment today can buy one pound, which can be invested in England at a risk-free rate of 5 percent, for a year-end value of 1.05 pounds. If the year-end exchange rate is $1.60 per pound, the 1.05 pounds can be exchanged for $1.05 \times \$1.6 = \$1.696$ for a rate of return in dollars of $1 + r = \$1.696/\$1.50 = 1.13$, or 13 percent, more than is available from U.S. bills. Therefore, investors will be speculating (rather than gambling) in a foreign-exchange $=$ denominated bill if either the rate is sufficiently higher on the foreign-exchange instrument, or if they *expect* the exchange to move in their favor, or if they have a foreign-exchange-denominated liability, which thereby will be hedged.

3. For the $A = 4$ investor, the utility of the risky portfolio is

$$U = .20 - 1/2 \times 4 \times .2^2 = .12$$

while the utility of bills is

$$U = .07 - 1/2 \times 4 \times 0 = .07.$$

   The investor will prefer the risky portfolio to bills. Of course, a mixture of bills and the risky portfolio might be even better, but that is not a choice here.
   The level of risk aversion for which the utility is the same as that from T-bills (.07) is given by

$$U = .07 = .20 - 1/2 \times A \times .2^2.$$

   Solving for A, we obtain 6.5, which is sufficiently risk averse so that the lower rate of the T-bill is equivalent to the higher expected, but riskier, rate of return on the portfolio.

4. *a.* The less risk-averse investor has a shallower indifference curve. An increase in risk requires less increase in expected return to restore utility to the original level.

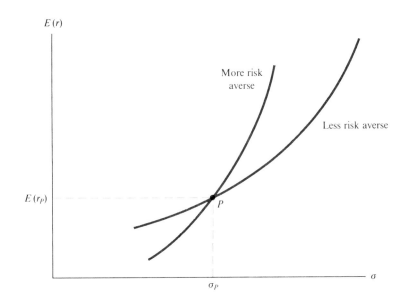

5. Holding 50 percent of your invested capital in ready assets means your investment proportion in the risky portfolio is reduced from 70 percent to 50 percent.

    Your risky portfolio is constructed to invest 54 percent in Vanguard and 46 percent in Shearson. Thus, the proportion of Vanguard in your overall portfolio is $.5 \times .54 = 27$ percent, and the dollar value of your position in Vanguard is $300,000 \times .27 = \$81,000$.

6. In the expected return–standard deviation plane, all portfolios that are constructed from the same risky and risk-free funds (with various proportions) lie on a line from the risk-free rate through the risky fund. The slope of this capital allocation line (CAL) is the same everywhere; hence, the reward-to-variability ratio is the same for all of these portfolios. Formally, if you invest a proportion (y) in a risky fund with expected return $E(r_p)$ and standard deviation σ_p, and the remainder $(1-y)$ in a risk-free asset with a sure rate (r_f), then the portfolio's expected return and standard deviation are:

$$E(r_C) = r_f + y[E(r_P) - r_f]$$
$$\sigma_C = y\sigma_P$$

and the reward-to-variability ratio of this portfolio is

$$S_C = \frac{E(r_C) - r_f}{\sigma_C} = \frac{y[E(r_P) - r_f]}{y\sigma_P} = \frac{E(r_P) - r_f}{\sigma_P}$$

which is independent of the y.

7. The lending and borrowing rates are unchanged at $r_f = 7$ percent and $r_B = 9$ percent. The standard deviation of the risky portfolio is still 22 percent, but its expected rate of return shifts from 15 to 17 percent. The slope of the kinked CAL is

$$\frac{E(r_P) - r_f}{\sigma_P} \qquad \text{for the lending range}$$

$$\frac{E(r_P) - r_f^B}{\sigma_P} \qquad \text{for the borrowing range.}$$

Thus, in both cases, the slope increases: from 8/22 to 10/22 for the lending range, and from 6/22 to 8/22 for the borrowing range.

8. *a.* The parameters are $r_f = .07$, $E(r_p) = .15$, $\sigma_p = .22$. With these parameters, an investor will choose a proportion (y) in the risky portfolio of

$$y = \frac{E(r_P) - r_f}{A\sigma_P^2}.$$

With $A = 3$, we find that

$$y = \frac{.15 - .07}{3 \times .0484} = .55.$$

When the degree of risk aversion decreases from the original value of 4 to the new value of 3, investment in the risky portfolio increases from 41 percent to 55 percent. Accordingly, the expected return and standard deviation of the optimal portfolio increases.

$$E(r_C) = .07 + .55 \times .08 = .114. \text{ (before: .1028)}$$
$$\sigma_C = .5 \times .22 = .121. \quad \text{(before: .0902)}$$

b. All investors whose degree or risk aversion is such that they would hold the risky portfolio in a proportion equal to 100 percent or less ($y<1.0$) are lending and so are unaffected by the borrowing rate. The least risk averse of these investors hold 100 percent in the risky portfolio ($y=1$). We can solve for the degree of risk aversion of investors who would become borrowers from the parameters of the investment opportunities:

$$y = 1.00 = \frac{E(r_P) - r_f}{A\sigma_P^2} = \frac{.08}{.0484A}$$

which implies

$$A = \frac{.08}{.0484} = 1.65.$$

Any investor who is more risk tolerant ($A < 1.65$) would borrow if the borrowing rate were 7 percent. For borrowers,

$$y = \frac{E(r_P) - r_B}{A\sigma_P^2}.$$

Take, for example an investor with $A = 1.1$. When $r_f = r_B = 7$ percent, this investor chooses to invest in the risky portfolio.

$$y = \frac{.08}{1.1 \times .0484} = 1.50$$

which means the investor will borrow 50 percent of the total investment capital. Raise the borrowing rate, in this case to $r_B = 9$ percent, and the investor will invest less in the risky asset. In that case,

$$y = \frac{.06}{1.1 \times .0484} = 1.13$$

and only 13 percent of the investment capital will be borrowed.

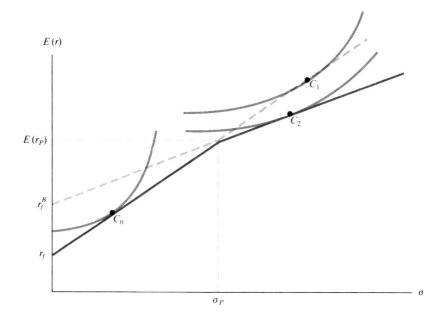

9. If all the investment parameters remain unchanged, the only reason an investor would decrease the proportion invested in the risky asset is because of an increase in the degree of risk aversion. If you think this is unlikely, then you have to reconsider your faith in your assumptions. Perhaps the S&P 500 is not a good proxy for the optimal risky portfolio. Perhaps investors expect a higher real rate on T-bills (inflation is ignored in this model).

Chapter 8

1. *i.* Beta, the slope coefficient of the security on the factor: securities $R_1 - R_6$ have a positive beta. These securities move, on average, in the same direction as the market (R_M). R_1, R_2, R_6 have large betas, so they are "aggressive" in that they carry more systematic risk than R_3, R_4, R_5 that are "defensive." R_7 and R_8 have a negative beta. These are hedge assets that carry negative systematic risk.

ii. Intercept, the expected return when the market is neutral: the estimates show that R_1, R_4, R_8 have a positive intercept, while R_2, R_3, R_5, R_6, R_7 have negative intercepts. To the extent that one believes these intercepts will persist, then a positive value is preferred.

iii. Residual variance, the nonsystematic risk: R_2, R_3, R_7 have a relatively low residual variance. With diversification, this risk will eventually be eliminated, and hence, the difference in the residual variance is of little economic significance.

iv. Total variance, the sum of systematic and nonsystematic risk: R_3 has a low beta and low residual variance, so its total variance will be low. R_1, R_6 have high betas and high residual variance, so their total variance will be high. But R_4 has a low beta and high residual variance, while R_2 has a high beta with a low residual variance. In sum, total variance will often misrepresent systematic risk, which is the part that counts.

2. *a.* Using Equation 8.8 with the data: $\sigma_B = .12$; $\sigma_S = .25$; $w_B = .5$; and $w_S = 1 - w_B = .5$, we obtain the equation:

$$\sigma_P^2 = .15^2 = (w_B\sigma_B)^2 + (w_S\sigma_S)^2 + 2(w_B\sigma_B)(w_S\sigma_S)\rho_{BS}$$
$$= (.5 \times .12)^2 + (.5 \times .25)^2 + 2(.5 \times .12)(.5 \times .25)\rho_{BS}$$

which yields $\rho = .2183$.

b. Using Equation 8.7 and the additional data: $E(r_B) = .10$; $E(r_S) = .17$, we obtain:

$$E(r_P) = w_BE(r_B) + w_SE(r_S) = (.5 \times .10) + (.5 \times .17) = .135, \text{ or } 13.5 \text{ percent.}$$

c. The question is really whether the portfolio on the opportunity set with $\rho_{BS} = .2$ (shown in Table 8.2 and Figure 8.6) that yields an expected return of 13.5 percent has a standard deviation lower than 15 percent. The answer is affirmative because the standard deviation of 15 percent was obtained with the same input, except a higher correlation coefficient of 0.22. With a lower correlation, other things equal, we have a smaller standard deviation. Moreover, without restriction, we can choose investment proportions with different risk-return combinations. Being unrestricted always has a non-negative value.

3. *a.* Using Equations 8.7 and 8.8, we generate the following table:

Table B8.3

Data	X	S	T-Bills
Mean	0.25	0.12	0.05
Standard deviation	0.60	0.30	0.00
Correlation coefficient	0.50		

Portfolio Opportunity Set

Weight in X	Weight in S	Portfolio Mean	Portfolio Standard
−1.00	2.00	−0.01000	0.60000
−0.90	1.90	0.00300	0.55561
−0.80	1.80	0.01600	0.51264
−0.70	1.70	0.02900	0.47149
−0.60	1.60	0.04200	0.43267
−0.50	1.50	0.05500	0.39686
−0.40	1.40	0.06800	0.36497
−0.30	1.30	0.08100	0.33808
−0.20	1.20	0.09400	0.31749
−0.10	1.10	0.10700	0.30447
0.00	1.00	0.12000	0.30000
0.10	1.90	0.13300	0.30447
0.20	0.80	0.14600	0.31749
0.30	0.70	0.15900	0.33808
0.40	0.60	0.17200	0.36497
0.50	0.50	0.18500	0.39686
0.60	0.40	0.19800	0.43267
0.70	0.30	0.21100	0.47149
0.80	0.20	0.22400	0.51264
0.90	0.10	0.23700	0.55561
1.00	0.00	0.25000	0.60000
1.10	−0.10	0.26300	0.64552
1.20	−0.20	0.27600	0.69195
1.30	−0.30	0.28900	0.73912
1.40	−0.40	0.30200	0.78689

(continued)

Table B8.3   *(concluded)*

Portfolio Opportunity Set			
	Weight in X	**Weight in S**	**Portfolio Mean**	**Portfolio Standard**
	1.50	−0.50	0.31500	0.83516
	1.60	−0.60	0.32800	0.88386
	1.70	−0.70	0.34100	0.93290
	1.80	−0.80	0.35400	0.98224
	1.90	−0.90	0.36700	1.03184
	2.00	−1.00	0.38000	1.08167
Optimal portfolio	0.6190	0.3810	0.20048	0.43985
Individual portfolio		A = 3.5		y = 0.2222
Slope of CAL	0.3421			

b. From the above table, we can draw the opportunity set of risky assets as in the following diagram:

Figure B8.3
Opportunity Set for X and S.

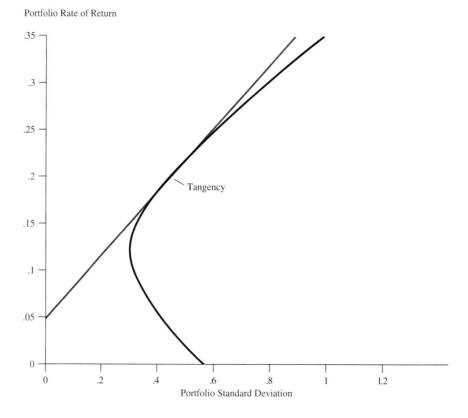

If you draw a ray from the T-bill rate (on the vertical axis) that is tangent to the opportunity set, the point of tangency (portfolio *O*) is approximately at the mean of 20 percent and standard deviation of 45 percent, close to the portfolio with 60 percent in stock *X* and 40 percent in the index fund. Using the formula in footnote 4, you can compute the exact proportion of *O* in *X* as 61.90 percent and 38.10 percent in the index fund. Using the formulas for mean and standard deviation again, we find that the mean of *O* is 20.48 percent and its standard deviation 43.99 percent.

    c. The slope of the CAL (its reward-to-variability ratio) is computed by: $S_O = [E(r_O) - r_f]/s_O = .3421$.

    d. Using Equation 7.6 (from Chapter 7) we compute the optimal position in portfolio O for an investor with $A = 3.5$ as $y = 22.22$ percent. This investor will hold 77.78 percent in T-bills, $.2222 \times .6190 = 13.75$ percent in X, and $.2222 \times .3810 = 8.47$ percent in the index fund.

4. Efficient frontiers derived by portfolio managers depend on forecasts of the rates of return on various securities and estimates of risk, that is, standard deviations and correlation coefficients. The forecasts themselves do not control outcomes. Thus, to prefer a manager with a rosier forecast (northwesterly frontier) is tantamount to rewarding the bearers of good news and punishing the bearers of bad news. What the investor wants is to reward bearers of *accurate* news. Investors should monitor forecasts of portfolio managers on a regular basis to develop the track record of their forecasting accuracy. Portfolio choices of the more accurate forecasters will, in the long run, outperform the field.

Chapter 9

1. The CML would still represent efficient investments. We can characterize the entire population by two representative investors. One is the "uninformed" investor, who does not engage in security analysis and holds the market portfolio, while the other optimizes using the Markowitz algorithm with input from security analysis. The uninformed investor does not know what input the informed investor uses to make portfolio purchases. The uninformed investor knows, however, that if the other investor is informed, the market portfolio proportions will be optimal. Therefore, to depart from these proportions would constitute an uninformed bet, which will, on average, reduce the efficiency of diversification with no compensating improvement in expected returns.

2. Substituting the historical mean and standard deviation in Equation 9.1 yields a coefficient of risk aversion of

$$A^* = \frac{E(r_M) - r_f}{\sigma_M^2} = 1.9.$$

    This relationship also tells us that for the historical standard deviation and a coefficient of risk aversion of 3.5 the risk premium would be:

$$E(r_M) - r_f = A^*\sigma_M^2 = 3.5 \times .21^2 = .154\ (15.4\%).$$

3. $\beta_{Ford} = 1.25$, $\beta_{GM} = 1.15$. Therefore, given the investment proportions, the portfolio beta is

$$\beta_P = w_{Ford}\beta_{Ford} + w_{GM}\beta_{GM} = (.75 \times 1.25) + (.25 \times 1.15) = 1.225$$

and the risk premium of the portfolio will be

$$E(r_P) - r_f = \beta_P[E(r_M) - r_f] = 1.225 \times .08 = .098.$$

4. *a.* The alpha of a stock is its expected return in excess of that required by the CAPM.

$$\alpha = E(r) - [r_f + \beta[E(r_M) - r_f]]$$
$$\alpha_{XYZ} = .12 - [.05 + 1.0(.11 - .05)] = .01$$
$$\alpha_{ABC} = .13 - [.05 + 1.5(.11 - .05)] = -.01$$

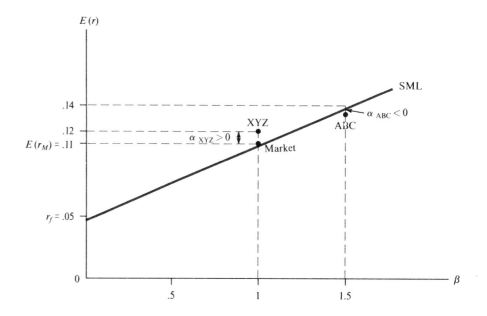

b. The project-specific required rate of return is determined by the project beta coupled with the market risk premium and the risk-free rate. The CAPM tells us an acceptable expected rate of return for the project is

$$E(r_f) + b[E(r_M) - r_f] = 8 + [1.3(16 - 8)] = 18.4\%$$

which becomes the project's hurdle rate. If the IRR of the project is 19 percent, then it is desirable. Any project (of similar beta) with an IRR equal to or less than 18.4 percent should be rejected.

5. The least profitable scenario currently yields a profit of $10,000 and gross proceeds from the equally weighted portfolio of $700,000. As the price of Dreck falls, less of the equally weighted portfolio can be purchased from the proceeds of the short sale. When Dreck's price falls by more than a factor of 10,000/700,000, arbitrage no longer will be feasible, because the profits in the worst state will be driven below zero.

To see this, suppose Dreck's price falls to $10 \times (1 - 1/70)$. The short sale of 300,000 shares now yields $2,957,142, which allows dollar investments of only $985,714 in each of the other shares. In the high real interest rate, low inflation scenario, profits will be driven to zero:

Stock	Dollar Investment	Rate of Return	Dollar Return
Apex	$ 985,714	.20	$ 197,143
Bull	985,714	.70	690,000
Crush	985,714	−.20	− 197,143
Dreck	− 2,957,142	.23	− 690,000
Total	0		0

At any price for Dreck stock below $10 \times (1 - 1/70) = \$9.857$, profits will be negative, which means the arbitrage opportunity is eliminated. Note: $9.857 is not the equilibrium price of Dreck. It is simply the upper bound on Dreck's price that rules out the simple arbitrage opportunity.

6. A portfolio composed of 2/3 of portfolio *A* and 1/3 of the risk-free asset will have the same beta as portfolio *E*, but an expected return of $(1/3 \times 4 + 2/3 \times 10) = 8$ percent, less than that of portfolio *E*. Therefore, one can earn arbitrage profits by shorting the combination of portfolio *A* and the safe asset and buying portfolio *E*.

7. Using Equation 9.11, the expected return is

$$.04 + (.2 \times .06) + (1.4 \times .08) = .164.$$

Chapter 10

1. The information sets that pertain to the weak, semistrong, and strong form of the EMH can be described by:

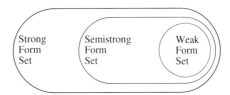

The weak-form information set includes only the history of prices and volumes. The semistrong-form set includes the weak-form set *plus* all publicly available information. In turn, the strong-form set includes the semistrong set *plus* insiders' information. The direction of *valid* implication is

Strong-form EMH⇒semistrong-form EMH⇒weak-form EMH

The reverse direction implication is *not* valid. For example, stock prices may reflect all past price data (weak-form efficiency) but may not reflect relevant fundamental data (semistrong-form inefficiency).

2. If *everyone* follows a passive strategy, sooner or later prices will fail to reflect new information. At this point, there are profit opportunities for active investors who uncover mispriced securities. As they buy and sell these assets, prices again will be driven to fair levels.

3. The answer depends on your prior beliefs about market efficiency., Magellan's record has been incredibly strong. On the other hand, with so many funds in existence, it is less surprising that *some* fund would appear to be consistently superior after the fact. In fact, Magellan's record was so good that even accounting for its selection, after the fact, as the "winner" of an investment "contest," it still appears to be too good to be attributed to chance. For further analysis and discussion of Magellan's performance, refer to the articles listed in the Suggested Readings by Marcus and Samuelson.

4. If profit opportunities can be made, one would expect mutual funds specializing in small stocks to spring into existence. Moreover, one wonders why buyers of small stocks don't compete for those stocks in December and bid up their prices before the January rise.

5. Concern over the deficit was an ongoing issue in 1987. No significant *new* information concerning the deficit was released October 19. Hence, this explanation for the crash is not consistent with the EMH.

Chapter 11

1.

Time	Action	Cash Flow
0	Buy two shares.	−40
1	Collect dividends; then sell one of the shares.	4 + 22
2	Collect dividend on remaining share. Then sell it.	2 + 19

   a. Dollar-weighted return.

$$-40 + \frac{26}{1 + r} + \frac{21}{(1 + r)^2} = 0$$

   $r = .1191 = 11.91$ percent.

   b. Time-weighted return.
   The rates of return on the stock in the two years were:

$$r_1 = \frac{2 + (22 - 20)}{20} = .20$$

$$r_2 = \frac{2 + (19 - 22)}{22} = -.045$$

   $(r_1 + r_2)/2 = 0.77$, or 7.7 percent.

2. Sharpe: $(\bar{r} - \bar{r}_f)/\sigma$
   $S_P = (35 - 6)/42 = .69$
   $S_M = (28 - 6)/30 = .733$
   Jensen: $\bar{r} - [\bar{r}_f + \beta(\bar{r}_M - \bar{r}_f)]$
   $\alpha_P = 35 - [6 + 1.2(28 - 6)] = 2.6\%$
   $\alpha_M = 0$
   Treynor: $(\bar{r} - \bar{r}_f)/\beta$
   $T_P = (35 - 6)/1.2 = 24.2$
   $T_M = (28 - 6)/1.0 = 22$

3. Performance Attribution
   First compute the new bogey performance as
   $(.70 \times 5.81) + (.25 \times 1.45) + (.05 \times .48) = 4.45$.
   a. Contribution of Asset Allocation to Performance

Market	(1) Actual Weight in Market	(2) Benchmark Weight in Market	(3) Excess Weight	(4) Market Return Minus Bogey (Percent)	(5) = (3) × (4) Contribution to Performance (Percent)
Equity	.70	.70	.00	1.36	.00
Fixed-income	.07	.25	−.18	−3.00	.54
Cash	.23	.05	.18	−3.97	−.71
Contribution of asset allocation					−.17

b. Contribution of Selection to Total Performance

Market	(1) Portfolio Performance (Percent)	(2) Index Performance (Percent)	(3) Excess Performance (Percent)	(4) Portfolio Weight	(5) = (3) × (4) Contribution (Percent)
Equity	7.28	5.00	2.28	.70	1.60
Fixed-income	1.89	1.45	0.44	.07	.03
Contribution of selection within markets					1.63

Chapter 12

1. At a semiannual interest rate of 3 percent, the bond is worth $40 \times$ PA(3%, 60) + $1,000 \times$ PF(3%, 60) = $1,276.75, which results in a capital gain of $276.75. This exceeds the capital loss of $189.29 ($1,000 − $810.71) when the interest rate increased to 5 percent.

2. Yield to maturity exceeds current yield, which exceeds coupon rate. Take as an example the 8 percent coupon bond with a yield to maturity of 10 percent per year (5 percent per half year). Its price is $810.71, and therefore its current yield is 80/810.77 = .0987, or 9.87 percent, which is higher than the coupon rate but lower than the yield to maturity.

3. Price = $70 \times$ PA(8%, 4) + $1000 \times$ PF(8%, 4) = $990.74

$$\text{Rate of return to investor} = \frac{\$70 + (\$990.74 - \$982.17)}{\$982.17} = .080$$
$$= 8 \text{ percent}$$

4. The bond with the 6 percent coupon rate currently sells for $60 \times$ PA(7%, 10) + 1,000 $\times$ PF(7%, 10) = $929.76. If the interest rate immediately drops to 6 percent, the bond price will rise to $1,000, for a capital gain of $70.24, or 7.55 percent. The 8 percent coupon bond currently sells for $1,070.24. If the interest rate falls to 6 percent, the present value of the *scheduled* payments increases to $1,147.20. However, the bond will be called at $1,100, for a capital gain of only $29.76, or 2.78 percent.

5. The premium bond should offer a higher promised yield in compensation for its greater susceptibility to being called.

Chapter 13

1. *a.*

(1) Time until Payment	(2) Payment	(3) Payment Discounted at 10%	(4) Weight	(5) Column (1) × Column (4)
1	$ 90	$ 81.8182	.0833	.0833
2	1,090	900.8264	.9167	1.8334
		$982.6446	1.0	1.9167

Duration is 1.1967 years. Price is $982.6446.

b. At an interest rate of 10.05 percent, the bond's price is

$$90 \times PA(10.05\%, 2) + 1,000 \, PF(10.05\%, 2) = 981.7891.$$

The percentage change in price is $-.087$ percent.

c. The duration formula would predict a price change of

$$-\frac{1.9167}{1.10} \times .0005 = -.00087 = -.087\%,$$

which is the same answer that we obtained from direct computation in (*b*).

2. The duration of a level perpetuity is $(1 + y)/y$ or $1 + 1/y$, which clearly falls as y increases. Tabulating duration as a function of y we get:

y	D
.01 (i.e., 1%)	101 years
.02	51
.05	21
.10	11
.20	6
.25	5
.40	3.5

3. The perpetuity's duration now would be $1.08/.08 = 13.5$. We need to solve the following equation for w:

$$w \times 2 + (1 - w) \times 13.5 = 6.$$

Therefore, $w = .6522$.

4. Dedication would be more attractive. Cash flow matching eliminates the need for rebalancing and, thus, saves transaction costs.

5. *a.* The present value of the fund's obligation is $\$800,000/.08 = \$10$ million. The duration is 13.5 years. Therefore, the fund should invest $\$10$ million in zeros with a 13.5 year maturity. The face value of the zeros will be $\$10,000,000 \times 1.08^{13.5} = \$28,263,159$.

   b. When the interest rate increases to 8.1 percent, the present value of the fund's obligation drops to $800,000/.081 = \$9,876,543$ dollars. The value of the zero-coupon bond falls by roughly the same amount, to $\$28,263,159/1.081^{13.5} = \$9,875,835$. The duration of the perpetual obligation falls to $1.081/.081 = 13.346$ years. The fund should sell the zero it currently holds and purchase $\$9,876,543$ in zero-coupon bonds with maturity of 13.346 years.

6. The fund has long-term liabilities and short-term assets. If interest rates fall, it will suffer because the value of the liabilities will rise by more than the value of the assets. To offset this duration mismatch, the fund should swap an obligation to make variable-rate payments in return for receipt of fixed cash flows. The swap gives the fund a long-term asset and a short-term liability.

Chapter 14

1. The downturn in the auto industry will reduce the demand for the product of this economy. The economy will, at least in the short term, enter a recession. This would suggest that:
   a. GNP will fall.
   b. The unemployment rate will rise.
   c. Inflation will fall.
   d. The government deficit will increase. Income tax receipts will fall, and government expenditures on social welfare programs probably will increase.
   e. Interest rates should fall. The contraction in the economy will reduce the demand for credit. Moreover, the lower inflation rate will reduce nominal interest rates.
   f. The balance of trade will deteriorate. Exports will fall as the auto industry declines.
   g. The exchange rate will depreciate in response to the deterioration in the balance of trade.

2. Expansionary fiscal policy coupled with expansionary monetary policy will stimulate the economy, with the loose monetary policy keeping down interest rates.

3. A traditional demand-side interpretation of the tax cuts is that the resulting increase in after-tax income increased consumption demand and stimulated the economy. A supply-side interpretation is that the reduction in marginal tax rates made it more attractive for businesses to invest and for individuals to work, thereby increasing economic output.

4. Firm C has the lowest fixed cost and highest variable costs. It should be least sensitive to the business cycle. In fact, it is. Its profits are highest of the three firms in recessions but lowest in expansions.

	Recession	*Normal*	*Expansion*
Revenue	$10	$12	$14
Fixed cost	2	2	2
Variable cost	7.5	9	10.5
Profits	$ 0.5	$ 1	$ 1.5

Chapter 15

1. *a.* Dividend yield = $2.15/$50 = 4.3%
   Capital gains yield = (59.77 − 50)/50 = 19.54%
   Total return = 4.3% + 19.54% = 23.84%
   b. $k = 6\% + 1.15(14\% - 6\%) = 15.2\%$
   c. $V_0 = (\$2.15 + \$59.77)/1.152 = \$53.75$, which exceeds the market price. This would indicate a "buy" opportunity.

2. *a.* $D_1/(k-g) = \$2.15/(.152-.112) = \$53.75$
   b. $P_1 = P_0(1 + g) = \$53.75(1.112) = \$59.77$

c. The expected capital gain equals $59.77 − $53.75 = $6.02, for a percentage gain of 11.2 percent. The dividend yield is D_1/P_0 = 2.15/53.75 = 4%, for a holding-period return of 4% + 11.2% = 15.2%.

3. The plowback and dividend payout rates must sum to 1.0. Because all earnings are either retained or paid out, the two rates must combine to 100 percent of all earnings.

4. a. g = ROE × b = .20 × .60 = .12
   P_0 = 2/(.125 − .12) = 400
   b. When the firm invests in projects with ROE less than k, its stock price falls. If b = .60, then
   g = .10 × .60 = .06 and
   P_0 = $2/(.125 − .06) = $30.77.
   In contrast, if b = 0, then
   P_0 = $5/.125 = $40.

5. If k = 15.3 percent, then $P_{1993} = \dfrac{.75(1.145)}{.153 − .145}$ = 107.34. Therefore,

$$V_0 = \frac{.45}{1.153} + \frac{.55}{1.153^2} + \frac{.65}{1.153^3} + \frac{.75 + 107.34}{1.153^4} = 62.39.$$

6. a. ROE = 12%
   b = $.50/$2.00 = .25
   g = ROE × b = 12% × .25 = 3%
   P_0 = $D_1/(k − g)$ = $1.50/(.10 − .03) = $21.43
   P_0/E_1 = $21.43/$2.00 = $10.71
   b. If b = .4, then .4 × $2 = $.80 would be reinvested and the remainder of earnings, or $1.20, would be paid as dividends
   g = 12% × .4 = 4.8%
   P_0 = $D_1/(k − g)$ = $1.20/(.10 − .048) = $23.08
   P_0/E_1 = $23.08/$2.00 = 11.54

Chapter 16

1. A debt/equity ratio of 1 implies that Mordett will have $50 million of debt and $50 million of equity. Interest expense will be .09 × $50 million, or $4.5 million per year. Mordett's net profits and ROE over the business cycle will therefore be

		Nodett		**Mordett**	
Scenario	*EBIT*	*Net profits*	*ROE*	*Net profits*[a]	*ROE*[b]
Bad year	$ 5M	$3 million	3%	$.3 million	.6%
Normal year	10M	6	6	3.3	6.6
Good year	15M	9	9	6.3	12.6

[a]Mordett's after-tax profits are given by: .6(EBIT—$4.5 million).
[b]Mordett's equity is only $50 million.

2.

Ratio Decomposition Analysis for Mordett Corporation

	ROE	(1) Net Profit Pretax Profit	(2) Pretax Profit EBIT	(3) EBIT Sales (ROS)	(4) Sales Assets (ATO)	(5) Assets Equity	(6) Combined Leverage Factor (2) × (5)
a. Bad year							
Nodett	.030	.6	1.000	.0625	.800	1.000	1.000
Somdett	.018	.6	.360	.0625	.800	1.667	.600
Mordett	.006	.6	.100	.0625	.800	2.000	.200
b. Normal year							
Nodett	.060	.6	1.000	.100	1.000	1.000	1.000
Somdett	.068	.6	.680	.100	1.000	1.667	1.134
Mordett	.066	.6	.550	.100	1.000	2.000	1.100
c. Good year							
Nodett	.090	.6	1.000	.125	1.200	1.000	1.000
Somdett	.118	.6	.787	.125	1.200	1.667	1.311
Mordett	.126	.6	.700	.125	1.200	2.000	1.400

3. GI's ROE in 19X3 was 3.03% computed as follows:

$$ROE = \frac{\$5,285}{.5(\$171,843 + 177,128)} = .303, \text{ or } 3.03\%$$

Its P/E ratio was $4 = \dfrac{\$21}{\$5.285}$

and its P/B ratio was $.12 = \dfrac{\$21}{\$177}$

Its earnings yield was 25% compared with an industry average of 12.5%.

Note that in our calculations the earnings yield will not equal ROE/(P/B) because we have computed ROE with average shareholders' equity in the denominator and P/B with end-of-year shareholders' equity in the denominator.

4.

IBX Ratio Analysis

Year	ROE	(1) Net Profit Pretax Profit	(2) Pretax Profit EBIT	(3) EBIT Sales (ROS)	(4) Sales Assets (ATO)	(5) Assets Equity	(6) Combined Leverage Factor (2) × (5)	(7) ROA (3) × (4)
1987	11.4%	.616	.796	7.75%	1.375	2.175	1.731	10.65%
1984	10.2%	.636	.932	8.88%	1.311	1.474	1.374	11.65%

ROE went up despite a decline in operating margin and a decline in the tax burden ratio because of increased leverage and turnover. Note that ROA declined from 11.65% in 1984 to 10.65% in 1987.

5. LIFO accounting results in lower reported earnings than does FIFO. Fewer assets to depreciate results in lower reported earnings because there is less bias associated with the use of historic cost. More debt results in lower reported earnings because the inflation premium in the interest rate is treated as part of interest expense and not as repayment of principal. If ABC has the same reported earnings as XYZ despite these three sources of downward bias, its real earnings must be greater.

Chapter 17

1. Suppose a stock had been selling in a narrow trading range around $50 for a substantial period and later increased in price. Now the stock falls back to a price near $50. Potential buyers might recall the price history of the stock and remember the last time the stock fell so low, they missed an opportunity for large gains when it later advanced. They might then view $50 as a good opportunity to buy. Therefore, buying pressure will materialize as the stock price falls to $50, which will create a support level.

2.

49					
46			X	O	
43	X	O	X	O	
40		O	X	O	
37				O	
34				O	

3. By the time the news of the recession affects bond yields, it also ought to affect stock prices. The market should fall *before* the confidence index signals that the time is ripe to sell.

Chapter 18

1. IBM's stock price apparently fell substantially in the months before September 1991. The existence of options with strike prices as high as $125 suggests the stock must have been trading in this range in the recent past. (In fact, IBM was trading above $130 per share during February of 1991.) As the stock price fell, new options with lower exercise prices must have been introduced so that the set of options would continue to bracket the stock price.

2. *a.* Payoff to put writer $= 0 \qquad \text{if } S_T \geq X$
    $$-(X - S_T) \quad \text{if } S_T < X$$
    b. Profit $=$ Initial premium realized $+$ Ultimate payoff
    $$= P \qquad\qquad \text{if } S_T \geq X$$
    $$P - (X - S_T) \quad \text{if } S_T < X$$

c. Put written

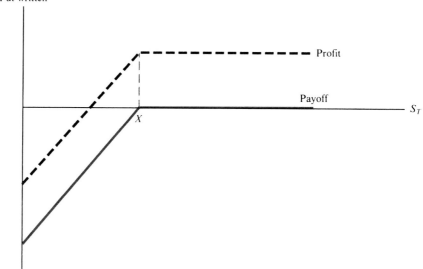

d. Put writers do well when the stock price increases and poorly when it falls.

3.

Payoff to a Strip

	$S_T \leq X$	$S_T > X$
2 Puts	$2(X - S_T)$	0
1 Call	0	$S_T - X$

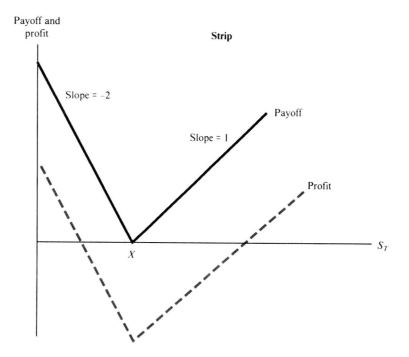

Payoff to a Strap

	$S_T \leq X$	$S_T > X$
1 Put	$X - S_T$	0
2 Calls	0	$2(S_T - X)$

Strap

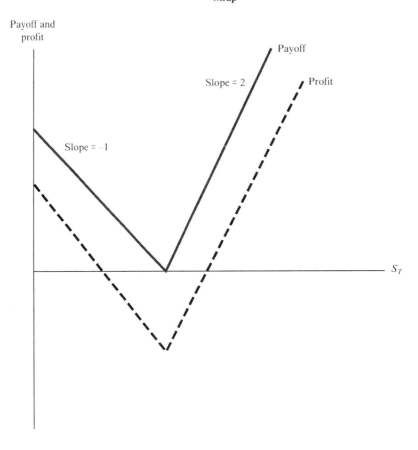

4. The covered call strategy would consist of a straight bond with a call written on the bond. The value of the strategy at option expiration as a function of the value of the straight bond is given in the figure following, which is virtually identical to Figure 18.11.

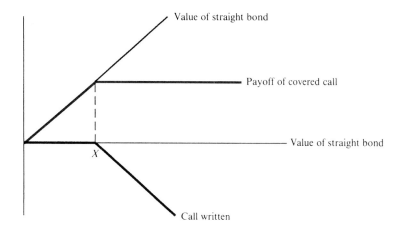

5. The call option is worth less as call protection is expanded. Therefore, the coupon rate need not be as high.

6. Lower. Investors will accept a lower coupon rate in return for the conversion option.

Chapter 19

1. Yes. Consider the same scenarios as for the call

Stock price	$10	$20	$30	$40	$50
Put payoff	$20	$10	$ 0	$ 0	$ 0
Stock price	$20	$25	$30	$35	$40
Put payoff	$10	$ 5	$ 0	$ 0	$ 0

The low volatility scenario yields a lower expected payoff.

2. Puts should be more valuable for higher dividend payout policies. These policies reduce future stock prices, which will increase the expected payout from the put.

3. Because the option now is underpriced, we want to reserve our previous strategy.

	Initial Cash Flow	Cash Flow in 1 Year for Each Possible Stock Price	
		S = 50	S = 200
Buy 2 options	−48	0	150
Short-sell 1 share	100	−50	−200
Lend $52 at 8% interest rate	52	56.16	56.16
Total	0	6.16	6.16

4. Higher. For deep out-of-the-money options, an increase in the stock price still leaves the option unlikely to be exercised. Its value increases only fractionally.

For deep in-the-money options, exercise is likely, and option holders benefit by a full dollar for each dollar increase in the stock, as though they already own the stock.

5. Because $\sigma = .6$, $\sigma^2 = .36$.

$$d_1 = \frac{ln(100/95) + (.10 + .36/2)\ .25}{.6\sqrt{.25}} = .4043$$
$$d_2 = d_1 - .6\sqrt{.25} = .1043$$

Using Table 19.2 and interpolation,

$N(d_1) = .6570$
$N(d_2) = .5415$
$\quad C = 100 \times .6570 - 95\ e^{-.10 \times .25} \times .5415$
$\quad\quad = 15.53$

6. Implied volatility exceeds 0.5. Given a standard deviation of 0.5, the option value is $13.70. A higher volatility is needed to justify the actual $15 price.

7. A $1 increase in stock price is a percentage increase of $1/122 = .82$ percent. The put option will fall by $(.4 \times \$1) = \$.40$, a percentage decrease of $\$.40/\$4 = 10$ percent. Elasticity is $-10/.82 = -12.2$.

Chapter 20

1.

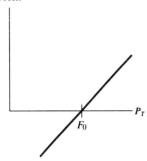

Short futures profit $= F_0 - P_T$

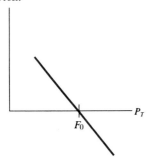

Long futures profit $= P_T - F_0$

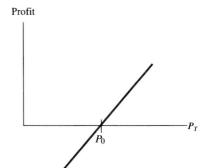

Asset profit $= P_T - P_0$

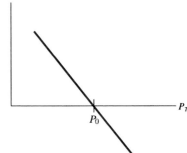

Short sale profit $= P_0 - P_T$

2. The clearinghouse has a zero net position in all contracts. Its long and short positions are offsetting, so that net cash flow from marking to market must be zero.

3.

	T-Bond Price in June		
	$94.25	**$95.25**	**$96.25**
Cash flow to purchase bonds ($= -2{,}000\,P_T$)	−$188,500	−$190,500	−$192,500
Profits on long futures position	−2,000	$0	2,000
Total cash flow	−$190,500	−$190,500	−$190,500

4. The risk would be that aluminum and bauxite prices do not move perfectly together. Thus, basis risk involving the spread between the futures price and bauxite spot prices could persist even if the aluminum futures price were set perfectly relative to aluminum itself.

5.

Action	Initial Cash Flow	Time-T Cash Flow
Lend S_0	−40	$40(1.01)^6 = \$42.46$
Short stock	+40	$-S_T$
Long futures	0	$S_T - \$42$
Total	0	$.46 risklessly

Chapter 21

1. The graph would asymptote to a lower level, as shown in the figure below, reflecting the improved opportunities for diversification. There still would be a positive level of nondiversifiable risk.

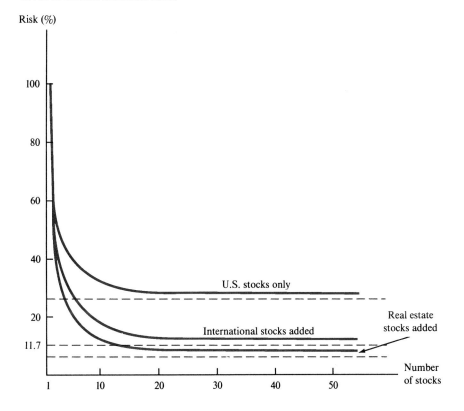

2. $1 + r(\text{US}) = [(1 + r_f(\text{UK})] \times (E_1/E_0)$
    a. $1 + r(\text{US}) = 1.1 \times 1.0 = 1.10$. Therefore, $r(\text{US}) = 10$ percent.
    b. $1 + r(\text{US}) = 1.1 \times 1.1 = 1.21$. Therefore, $r(\text{US}) = 21$ percent.

3. According to interest rate parity, F_0 should be $1.93. As the futures price is too high, we should reverse the arbitrage strategy just considered.

Action	Cash Flow Now ($)	Cash Flow in One Year ($)
Borrow $2 in the United States	2.00	$-2.00(1.0615)$
Convert the borrowed dollars to pounds, and lend in the United Kingdom at a 10% interest rate.	-2.00	$1.10E_1$
Enter a contract to sell 1.10 pounds at a futures price of $1.95/£.	0.00	$1.10(1.95 - E_1)$
Total	0.00	0.022

4. You must sell forward the number of pounds you will end up with at the end of the year. This value cannot be known with certainty, however, unless the rate of return of the pound-denominated investment is known.
    a. $10,000 \times 1.20 = 12,000$ pounds.
    b. $10,000 \times 1.30 = 13,000$ pounds.

5. *Country selection:*

$$(.40 \times .10) + (.20 \times .05) + (.40 \times .15) = .11$$

This is a loss of .015 (1.5 percent) relative to the EAFE passive benchmark.
Currency selection:

$$(.40 \times 1.10) + (.20 \times .9) + (.40 \times 1.30) = 1.14$$

This is a loss of 6 percent relative to the EAFE benchmark.

Chapter 22

1. We show the answer for the annual compounded rate of return for each strategy and leave you to compute the monthly rate:

Beginning-of-period fund: $F_0 = \$1,000$
End-of-period fund for each strategy:

$$F_1 = \begin{cases} 3,600 & \text{strategy = bills only} \\ 67,500 & \text{strategy = market only} \\ 5,360,000,000 & \text{strategy = perfect timing} \end{cases}$$

Number of periods: $N = 52$ years
Annual compounded rate:

$$[1 + r_A]^N = \frac{F_1}{F_0}$$

$$r_A = \left(\frac{F_1}{F_0}\right)^{1/N} - 1$$

$$r_A = \begin{cases} 2.49\% & \text{strategy} = \text{bills only} \\ 8.44\% & \text{strategy} = \text{market only} \\ 34.71\% & \text{strategy} = \text{perfect timing} \end{cases}$$

2. The timer will guess bear or bull markets randomly. One half of all bull markets will be preceded by a correct forecast, and similarly for bear markets. Hence, $P_1 + P_2 - 1 = 1/2 - 1 = 0$.

Appendix

C

Solutions to Selected Problems

Chapter 1   The Investment Process: Objectives and Constraints
1. *c*. Liquidity.
2. *b*. Employees.
3. *b*. Organizing the management process itself.

Chapter 2   The Investment Process: Strategies and Policies
2. *d*. High-income bond fund.
6. *d*. All investors.
7. *b*. The level of the market.

Chapter 3   The Financial System and Institutions
1. *a*. Cash is a financial asset. It is a liability of the government.
   b. No.
   c. Yes.
   d. The taxpayers as a group will make good on the liability.
4. *a*. Primary.
   b. Primitive.
6. *a*. No. It increases exposure to GM.

Chapter 4   Financial Markets and Instruments
2. *a*. 8.45 percent.
3. Ask = $9,886.50.
   Bid = $9,885.00.
4. BEY = 6.98 percent.
5. *i*. EAY = 10 percent. Discount yield = 9.34 percent.
   ii. EAY = 9.9 percent. Discount yield = 9.12 percent.
6. 9.4 percent.
7. *a*. 4.167 percent.
   b. Divisor must be reset to 2.34.
   c. 0.

8. *a.* 3.85 percent.
   b. 1.85 percent.
   c. 1.48 percent.
9. 6.48 percent.

Chapter 5 How Securities Are Traded

1. *a.* $70,000 plus implicit underpricing of $3 per share: $370,000.
2. *a.* Potentially unlimited.
   b. $8 per share.
6. *a.* $50.25.
   b. $51.50.
   c. Increase.
8. *a.* 12 percent.
   b. $35.71.
9. *a.* $2,500.
   b. $57.69.

Chapter 6 Risk and Return: The Basics

4. $E(r)$ = 14 percent.
   σ = 23.24 percent.

5.

Economy	Probability	Price	HPR
Boom	.25	75.93	−15.07%
Normal	.50	100.00	9.00%
Recession	.25	117.54	26.54%

6. The average risk premium for 1926–1990 is 8.40% per year. Adding to a risk-free rate of 8% gives 16.40% per year.
8. *a.* 5.88 percent.
   b. Approximation = 10 percent.
9. *a.* $E(r)$ = − 50 percent.
   b. σ = 1,580 percent.

13.

Economy	Probability	Stock Price	Stock HPR	Put Value	Put HPR	Stock Plus Put Value	Stock Plus Put HPR
Boom	.25	140	44%	0	−100%	144	28.6%
Normal	.50	110	14	0	−100	114	1.8
Recession	.25	80	−16	30	+150	114	1.8

Chapter 7 Capital Allocation to Risky Assets

1. *a.* $86,957.
   b. 15 percent.
   c. $83,333.
2. $A < 1.778$.
6. $A < 0$
7.

W_{bills}	$E(r)$	σ^2	$U(A = 3)$	$U(A = 5)$
0	.145	.0441	.07885	.03475
.4	.111	.0159	.08719	.07131
.8	.077	.00176	.07435	.07259

8. *a.* $E(r)$ = 14%.
   σ = 18.9%.

Stock A	18.9
Stock B	23.1
Stock C	28.0
Total	70.0%

    c. = .3704.

9. *a*. *y* = .8.

   b.

Stock A	21.6%
Stock B	26.4
Stock C	32.0
Bills	20.0
Total	100.0%

   c. σ = .216 (21.6 percent).

10. *a*. 74.07 percent in risky portfolio.

    b. $E(r)$ = 14.4 percent.

11. *a*. *y* = 39.19 percent in risky portfolio.

    b. $E(r)$ = .1092 (10.92 percent).

       σ = .1058.

15. *a*. .464.

    b. .278.

Chapter 8 Efficient Diversification

3. .422.

4. *a*. 14.22 percent.

    b.

T-bills	.4213
Stocks	.4094
Bonds	.1693

5.

Stocks	.2222
Bonds	.7778
Standard deviation	.202

6.

Stocks	1.78 (178 percent)
Bonds	−.78 (short position = 78 percent of wealth)

8. No. Combine *A* and *B* to form a riskless portfolio; show that the "synthetic" risk-free rate is below 10 percent.

11. 68.74 percent.

Chapter 9 Capital Asset Pricing and Arbitrage Pricing Theory

1. 1.5.

2. $27.37.

3. NPV = 15.64.

4. Highest beta is 4.055.

    a. F.

    b. F.

    c. F.

5. *a*. Aggressive beta, β_A = 2.0.

       Defensive beta, β_D = 0.7.

    b. $E(r_A)$ = .17.

       $E(r_D)$ = .0875.

6. Not possible.

8. Not possible.

10. Not possible.

12. Possible.

13. $171.

15. $\beta = -.2$.
17. *a.* 15 percent.
    b. 6 percent.
    c. Underpriced.
18. Yes. *E* offers too high a return.
20. $r_f = 6$ percent.
22. *a.* $\sigma_A^2 = .0756$; $\sigma_B^2 = .05$; $\sigma_C^2 = .1576$.
    b. $\sigma_A^2 = .0256$; $\sigma_B^2 = .04$; $\sigma_C^2 = .0576$.
25. 15.4 percent.
26. $E(r_P) = .07 + .0447\beta_{M1} + .1188\beta_{M2}$.

Chapter 10   The Efficient Markets Hypothesis

1. Zero.
6. No.
7. No.
12. Buy.
14. Small firm in January and weekend anomalies.
15. *a.* Consistent.
    c. Consistent.
    e. Inconsistent.

Chapter 11   Performance Evaluation

9. *a.* $\bar{r}_{ABC} = .10$ $\bar{r}_{XYZ} = .10$
    b. XYZ.
    c. ABC: 9.80 percent.
       XYZ: 9.19 percent.
10. *a.* Arithmetic = 3.15 percent.
       Geometric = 2.33 percent.
    b. IRR = $-.1661$ percent.
13. *a.* Actual = .0165.
       Bogey = .0191.
       Underperformance = .0026 (.26 percent).
    b. $-.0039$.
    c. $+.0013$.
16. $\alpha = 0$.

Chapter 12   Bond Prices and Yields

1. Bills: 10 percent.
    Bond: 10.25 percent.
2. 8.16 percent.
4. Lower.
6. Uncertain.
8. *a.* $P_0 = 1,052.42$ $P_1 = 1,044.52$.
    b. $r = 4$ percent per six months.
9.

	Zero	*8% coupon*	*10% coupon*
P_0	463.19	1,000	1,134.20
P_1	500.25	1,000	1,124.94
HPR	8%	8%	8%

11. *a.* 15.87 percent.
    c. Low.
    d. Fixed rate.

12. *a.* 850.21.
    b. $13.18.
    c. 7.11 percent.
    d. 3.94 percent.
13. 6 percent coupon bond.
14. *a.* 10 percent.
    b. 10 percent.
    c. Lower.

Chapter 13   Managing Fixed-Income Investments

1. 3.27 percent decline.
2. 2.833 years.   2.824 years.
3. 1.9523 years.
4. 90.48 percent of portfolio, or $2.9979 million is placed in zeros; $.3154 million in perpetuities.
5. 0.463 percent.
7. C, D, A, B, E in descending order.
8. *a.* $PV = \$17,832.65$.
      $D = 1.4808$ years.
   b. 1.4808 years.
11. *a.* Place 11/16 of portfolio in the zeros and 5/16 in the perpetuity.
    b. 12/17 in zeros; 5/17 in perpetuities.
12. *a.* 5-year zeros: $6 million.
       20-year zeros: $4 million.
    b. 5-year zeros: $9.66 million.
       20-year zeros: $26.91 million.
16. Rates will increase. Choose the low duration bond.
    a. Choose the 1984 maturity bond.
    c. Choose the 15⅜ percent coupon bond.
    e. Choose the floating-rate bond.

Chapter 14   Macroeconomic and Industry Analysis

1. Loose monetary policy. Expansionary fiscal policy—e.g., lower taxes.
2. Buy gold stocks in anticipation of inflationary pressures.
   Buy construction stocks in anticipation of lower interest rates.
4. Lower equilibrium wages, and lower prices.
5. *a.* Recession is harder on high fixed-cost robotics firm.
   b. Robotics will have higher beta.

Chapter 15   Equity Valuation Models

3. *a.* 11 percent.
4. *a.* $P_0 = \$10.60$.
   b. $P_0/E_1 = 3.33$.
      $P_0/E_0 = 3.53$.
   c. PVGO $= \$-8.15$.
   d. $P_0 = \$15.85$.
5. $g = 11$ percent.
6. *a.* $P_0 = \$160$.
   b. 15 percent.
   c. $40.
8. $20.

10. *a.* $V_0 = \$19.64$.
12. *a.* $k = 20$ percent.
    b. Zero.
    c. Nothing.
    d. Nothing.
13. *a.* $V_0 = 101.82$.
    b. 18.52 percent.

Chapter 16   Financial Statement Analysis

1. Lower ATO.
2. Above industry average.
6. ROA = 14.4 percent (Net income before taxes plus interest/Average assets).
   EPS = \$18.73.
   Acid-test ratio = .51.
   Interest coverage ratio = 4.3.
   Receivables collection period = 25.7 days.
   Leverage (Average assets/Average equity) = 5.33.
7. *a.* Quick ratio = .99.
   b. ROA = 36.4 percent.
   c. ROE = 42.7 percent.
   f. Times interest earned = 30.
   g. Inventory turnover = 4.19.
   h. Leverage = 2.2.

18.

	1985	*1989*
Operating margin	.065	.068
× Asset turnover	2.21	3.36
× Interest burden	.914	1
× Financial leverage	1.54	1.32
× (1 − Tax rate)	(1 − .4063)	(1 − .5522)
= ROE	.12	.135

Chapter 17   Technical Analysis

1. Support: B, D.
   Resistance: A, C.
2. Trin = 1.60.
3. Breadth = − 590.

Chapter 18   Options Markets: Introduction

1.

	Stock Price			
	80	*100*	*110*	*120*
All stocks	− 20	0	10	20
All options	− 100	− 100	0	100
Bills + options	− 6.4	− 6.4	3.6	13.6

2. *a.* $P = \$7.645$.
   b. Buy straddle. Stock price must move by \$17.645 to earn a profit.
3. $C = \$5.18$.
11. *b.* If IBM = \$102, profit = \$.9375.
    If IBM = \$115, profit, \$.9375 − \$10 = − \$9.0625
    c. Break even at either \$105.9375 or \$99.0625.
    d. Low volatility.

Chapter 19 Option Valuation

2. *i.* a.

iii. b.

v. c.

3.

Stock Price	Hedge Ratio
115	.567
100	.667
75	.883
50	1.0
25	1.0
10	1.0

4.

Stock Price	d_1	$N(d_1)$
45	−.0268	.4893
50	.5000	.6915
55	.9766	.8356

7. $C = \$8.13$.

8. *a.* $5.55.

b. $4.79.

c. $6.08.

d. $11.51.

e. $8.72.

9. Less.

11. More.

13. More.

15. Increases.

17. Zero.

21. *a.* 25.8 percent in bills.

74.2 percent in equity.

b. Sell $1.176 million of equity.

22. *a.* $P = \$2.38$.

b. $102.38.

Chapter 20 Futures Markets

1. *a.* $191,815.

b. 14.7 percent.

c. −10 percent.

6. *a.* 162.

b. 188.96.

c. 210.74.

9. 360.50.

10. Given the June futures price, the December futures should be 359.89 ($346.30 \times 1.08^{1/2}$).

11. *a.* 127.20.

b. *F* drops to 123.384.

c. Percent loss is 31.8 percent.

14. *F* is too high by $9.50.

15. *b.* Lower.

Chapter 21 International and Extended Diversification

1. *a.* 125.

   b.

Price per Share	£-Denominated Return	$-Denominated Return		
		$1.80/£	**$2/£**	**$2.20/£**
35	−12.5	−21.25	−12.5	−3.75
40	0	−10	0	10
45	12.5	1.25	12.5	23.75

2. £ return: $\sigma = 10.2$ percent (using 3 degrees of freedom).

   $ return: $\sigma = 13.1$ percent (using 9 degrees of freedom).

3.

Price per Share	$-Denominated Return		
	$1.80/£	**$2/£**	**$2.20/£**
35	−6.25	−7.50	−8.75
40	5	5	5
45	16.25	17.50	18.75

   $ return: $\sigma = 10.2$ percent.

4. Currency: −1.5 percent.

   Country: −.75 percent.

   Stock: −2.45 percent.

5. 14.17 percent.

7.

	Average Return	Standard Deviation
All REITs	22.26%	19.71%
All T-bonds	7.91%	11.50%
50% REITs/50% bonds	15.09%	13.08%

Chapter 22 Active Portfolio Management

2. 2.2% per month.

3. *a.* Timer A is the better forecaster.

   b. Timer B's value is greater by 4 basis points per month.

Appendix

References

Alexander, Sidney. "Price Movements in Speculative Markets: Trends or Random Walks. No. 2." In *The Random Character of Stock Market Prices*. Paul Cootner, ed. Cambridge, Mass.: MIT Press, 1964.

Arbel, Avner. "Generic Stocks: An Old Product in a New Package." *Journal of Portfolio Management,* Summer 1985, pp. 4–13.

Arbel, Avner, and Paul J. Strebel. "Pay Attention to Neglected Firms." *Journal of Portfolio Management* (Winter 1983), pp. 37–42.

Banz, Rolf. "The Relationship between Return and Market Value of Common Stocks." *Journal of Financial Economics* 9 (March 1981), pp. 3–18.

Basu, Sanjoy. "The Investment Performance of Common Stocks in Relation to their Price-Earnings Ratios: A Test of the Efficient Market Hypothesis." *Journal of Finance* 32 (June 1977), pp. 663–82.

———. "The Relationship between Earnings Yield, Market Value, and Return for NYSE Common Stocks: Further Evidence." *Journal of Financial Economics* 12 (June 1983), pp. 129–56.

Bernhard, Arnold. *Value Line Methods of Evaluating Common Stocks*. New York: Arnold Bernhard and Co., 1979.

Black, Fischer. "Yes, Virginia, There is Hope: Tests of the Value Line Ranking System." Graduate School of Business, University of Chicago, 1971.

Black, Fischer, and Myron Scholes. "The Pricing of Options and Corporate Liabilities." *Journal of Political Economy* 81 (May–June 1973), pp. 637–59.

Blume, Marshall E., and Robert F. Stambaugh. "Biases in Computed Returns: An Application to the Size Effect." *Journal of Finance Economics,* 1983, pp. 387–404.

Bogle, John C. "Investing in the 1990s: Remembrance of Things Past, and Things Yet to Come." *Journal of Portfolio Management* (Spring 1991), pp. 5–14.

Brinson, Hood, and Bibower. "Components of Portfolio Performance." *Financial Analysts Journal,* July–August 1986.

Brown, David, and Robert H. Jennings. "On Technical Analysis." *Review of Financial Studies* 2 (1989), pp. 527–52.

Brown, Lawrence D., and Michael Rozeff. "The Superiority of Analysts' Forecasts as Measures of Expectations: Evidence from Earnings." *Journal of Finance,* March 1978.

Clayman, Michelle. "In Search of Excellence: The Investor's Viewpoint." *Financial Analysts Journal,* May–June 1987.

Connolly, Robert. "An Examination of the Robustness of the Weekend Effect." *Journal of Financial and Quantitative Analysis* 24 (June 1989), pp. 133–69.

Copeland, Thomas E., and David Mayers. "The Value Line Enigma (1965–1978): A Case Study of Performance Evaluation Issues." *Journal of Financial Economics* November 1982.

DeBondt, Werner F. M., and Richard Thaler. "Does the Stock Market Overreact?" *Journal of Finance* 40 (1985), pp. 793–805.

Dunn, Patricia, and Rolf D. Theisen. "How Consistently Do Active Managers Win?" *Journal of Portfolio Management* 9 (Summer 1983), pp. 47–53.

Errunza, Vihang, and Etienne Losq. "International Asset Pricing under Mild Segmentation: Theory and Test." *Journal of Finance* 40 (March 1985), pp. 105–124.

Fama, Eugene. "The Behavior of Stock Market Prices." *Journal of Business* 38 (January 1965), pp. 34–105.

Fama, Eugene, and Marshall Blume. "Filter Rules and Stock Market Trading Profits." *Journal of Business* 39 (Supplement, January 1966), pp. 226–41.

Fama, Eugene, and Kenneth R. French. "Permanent and Temporary Components of Stock Prices." *Journal of Political Economy* 96 (1987), pp. 246–73.

Fisher, Irving. *The Theory of Interest: As Determined by Impatience to Spend Income and Opportunity to Invest It.* New York: Augustus M. Kelley, Publishers, 1965, originally published in 1930.

Flannery, Mark J., and Christopher M. James. "The Effect of Interest Rate Changes on the Common Stock Returns of Financial Institutions." *Journal of Finance* 39 (September 1984), pp. 1141–54.

Foster, George; Chris Olsen; and Terry Shevlin. "Earnings Releases, Anomalies, and the Behavior of Security Returns," *The Accounting Review* 59 (October 1984).

French, Kenneth. "Stock Returns and the Weekend Effect." *Journal of Financial Economics* 8 (March 1980), pp. 55–69.

Geske, Robert, and Richard Roll. "On Valuing American Call Options with the Black-Scholes European Formula." *Journal of Finance* 39 (June 1984), pp. 443–56.

Gibbons, Michael, and Patrick Hess. "Day of the Week Effects and Asset Returns." *Journal of Business* 54 (October 1981), pp. 579–98.

Givoly, Dan, and Dan Palmon. "Insider Trading and Exploitation of Inside Information: Some Empirical Evidence." *Journal of Business* 58 (1985), pp. 69–87.

Grieves, Robin, and Alan J. Marcus. "Riding the Yield Curve: Reprise." *Journal of Portfolio Management,* Winter 1992.

Grossman, Sanford J., and Joseph E. Stiglitz. "On the Impossibility of Informationally Efficient Markets." *American Economic Review* 70 (June 1980), pp. 393–408.

Henriksson, Roy D. "Market Timing and Mutual Fund Performance: An Empirical Investigation." *Journal of Business* 57 (January 1984).

Homer, Sidney, and Martin L. Leibowitz. *Inside the Yield Book: New Tools for Bond Market Strategy.* Englewood Cliffs, N.J.: Prentice Hall, 1972.

Ibbotson, Roger G. "Price Performance of Common Stock New Issues," *Journal of Financial Economics* 2 (September 1975).

Ibbotson, Roger; Richard C. Carr; and Anthony W. Robinson. "International Equity and Bond Returns." *Financial Analysts Journal,* (July–August 1982).

Ibbotson, R. C., and L. B. Siegel. "The World Market Wealth Portfolio." *Journal of Portfolio Management,* Winter 1983.

Ibbotson, R. C.; L. B. Siegel; and K. Love. "World Wealth: Market Values and Returns." *Journal of Portfolio Management,* Fall 1985.

Jaffee, Jeffrey F. "Special Information and Insider Trading." *Journal of Business* 47 (July 1974), pp. 410–28.

———. "Gold and Gold Stocks as Investments for Institutional Portfolios." *Financial Analysts Journal* 45 (March–April 1989), pp. 53–59.

Jegadeesh, Narasimhan. "Evidence of Predictable Behavior of Security Returns." *Journal of Finance* 45 (September 1990), pp. 881–98.

Jensen, Michael C. "The Performance of Mutual Funds in the Period 1945–1964." *Journal of Finance,* May 1968.

———. "Risk, the Pricing of Capital Assets, and the Evaluation of Investment Portfolios." *Journal of Business* 42 (April 1969), pp. 167–247.

Keim, Donald B. "Size Related Anomalies and Stock Return Seasonality: Further Empirical Evidence." *Journal of Financial Economics* 12 (June 1983), pp. 13–32.

Kendall, Maurice. "The Analysis of Economic Time Series, Part I: Prices." *Journal of the Royal Statistical Society* 96 (1953), pp. 11–25.

Kopcke, Richard W., and Geoffrey R. H. Woglom. "Regulation Q and Savings Bank Solvency—The Connecticut Experience." In *The Regulation of Financial Institutions,* Federal Reserve Bank of Boston Conference Series, No. 21, 1979.

Latane, H. A., and C. P. Jones. "Standardized Unexpected Earnings—1971–1977," *Journal of Finance,* June 1979.

Lehman, Bruce. "Fads, Martingales and Market Efficiency." *Quarterly Journal of Economics* 105 (February 1990), pp. 1–28.

Levy, Robert A. "The Predictive Significance of Five-Point Chart Patterns." *Journal of Business* 44 (July 1971), pp. 316–23.

Lo, Andrew W., and Craig MacKinlay. "Stock Market Prices Do Not Follow Random Walks: Evidence from a Simple Specification Test." *Review of Financial Studies* 1 (Spring 1988), pp. 41–66.

Loeb, T. F. "Trading Cost: The Critical Link between Investment Information and Results," *Financial Analysts Journal,* May–June 1983.

Macaulay, Frederick. *Some Theoretical Problems Suggested by the Movements of Interest Rates, Bond Yields, and Stock Prices in the United States Since 1856.* New York: National Bureau of Economic Research, 1938.

Marcus, Alan J. "The Magellan Fund and Market Efficiency." *Journal of Portfolio Management* 17 (Fall 1990), pp. 85–88.

Merton, Robert C. "Theory of Rational Option Pricing." *Bell Journal of Economics and Management Science* 4 (Spring 1973), pp. 141–83.

———. "On Market Timing and Investment Performance: An Equilibrium Theory of Value for Market Forecasts." *Journal of Business* 54 (July 1981).

Morrell, John A. "Introduction to International Equity Diversification." In *International Investing for U.S. Pension Funds,* Institute for Fiduciary Education, London/Venice, May 6–13, 1989.

Niederhoffer, Victor, and Patrick Regan. "Earnings Changes, Analysts' Forecasts, and Stock Prices," *Financial Analysts' Journal,* May to June 1972.

Norby, W. C. "Applications of Inflation-Adjusted Accounting Data." *Financial Analysts Journal,* March–April 1983.

Perry, Kevin, and Robert A. Taggart. "The Growing Role of Junk Bonds in Corporate Finance." *Continental Bank Journal of Applied Corporate Finance* 1 (Spring 1988).

Poterba, James M., and Lawrence Summers. "Mean Reversion in Stock Market Prices: Evidence and Implications." *Journal of Financial Economics* 22 (1987), pp. 27–59.

Redington, F. M. "Review of the Principle of Life-Office Valuations." *Journal of the Institute of Actuaries* 78 (1952), pp. 286–340.

Reinganum, Marc R. "The Anomalous Stock Market Behavior of Small Firms in January: Empirical Tests for Tax-Loss Effects." *Journal of Financial Economics* 12 (June 1983), pp. 89–104.

Ritter, Jay R. "The Buying and Selling Behavior of Individual Investors at the Turn of the Year." *Journal of Finance* 43 (July 1988), pp. 701–17.

Roberts, Harry. "Stock Market 'Patterns' and Financial Analysis: Methodological Suggestions." *Journal of Finance* 14 (March 1959), pp. 11–25.

Roll, Richard. "The International Crash of October 1987." *Financial Analysts Journal,* September–October 1988.

Ross, Stephen A. "Return, Risk and Arbitrage." In *Risk and Return in Finance,* I. Friend and J. Bicksler, eds. Cambridge, Mass.: Ballinger, 1976.

Samuelson, Paul. "The Judgment of Economic Science on Rational Portfolio Management." *Journal of Portfolio Management* 16 (Fall 1989), pp. 4–12.

Seyhun, H. Nejat. "Insiders' Profits, Costs of Trading and Market Efficiency." *Journal of Financial Economics* 16 (1986), pp. 189–212.

Sharpe, William F. "Mutual Fund Performance." *Journal of Business* 39 (January 1966).

Sharpe, William S. "A Simplified Model for Portfolio Analysis," *Management Science* IX (January 1963), pp. 277–93.

Shiller, Robert. "Do Stock Prices Move Too Much to Be Justified by Subsequent Changes in Dividends?" *American Economic Review* 71 (June 1981).

Solnik, Bruno, and A. de Freitas. "International Factors of Stock Price Behavior." CESA Working Paper, February 1986, cited in Bruno Solnik. *International Investments*. Reading, Mass.: Addison Wesley Publishing Co., 1988.

Stickel, Scott E. "The Effect of Value Line Investment Survey Rank Changes on Common Stock Prices." *Journal of Financial Economics* 14 (1985), pp. 121–44.

Tobin, James. "Liquidity Preference as Behavior toward Risk." *Review of Economic Studies* XXVI (February 1958), pp. 65–86.

Treynor, Jack L. "How to Rate Management Investment Funds." *Harvard Business Review* 43 (January–February 1966).

Treynor, Jack L., and Kay Mazuy. "Can Mutual Funds Outguess the Market?" *Harvard Business Review* 43 (July–August 1966).

Treynor, Jack, and Fischer Black. "How to Use Security Analysis to Improve Portfolio Selection." *Journal of Business* 46 (January 1973).

Whaley, Robert E. "Valuation of American Call Options on Dividend-Paying Stocks: Empirical Tests." *Journal of Financial Economics* 10 (1982), pp. 29–58.

Appendix

Mathematical Tables

Table E.1 *Future Value of $1 at the End of t Periods = $(1 + r)^t$*

Period	\begin{tabular}{c}Interest rate\end{tabular} 1%	2%	3%	4%	5%	6%	7%	8%	9%
1	1.0100	1.0200	1.0300	1.0400	1.0500	1.0600	1.0700	1.0800	1.0900
2	1.0201	1.0404	1.0609	1.0816	1.1025	1.1236	1.1449	1.1664	1.1881
3	1.0303	1.0612	1.0927	1.1249	1.1576	1.1910	1.2250	1.2597	1.2950
4	1.0406	1.0824	1.1255	1.1699	1.2155	1.2625	1.3108	1.3605	1.4116
5	1.0510	1.1041	1.1593	1.2167	1.2763	1.3382	1.4026	1.4693	1.5386
6	1.0615	1.1262	1.1941	1.2653	1.3401	1.4185	1.5007	1.5869	1.6771
7	1.0721	1.1487	1.2299	1.3159	1.4071	1.5036	1.6058	1.7138	1.8280
8	1.0829	1.1717	1.2668	1.3686	1.4775	1.5938	1.7182	1.8509	1.9926
9	1.0937	1.1951	1.3048	1.4233	1.5513	1.6895	1.8385	1.9990	2.1719
10	1.1046	1.2190	1.3439	1.4802	1.6289	1.7908	1.9672	2.1589	2.3674
11	1.1157	1.2434	1.3842	1.5395	1.7103	1.8983	2.1049	2.3316	2.5804
12	1.1268	1.2682	1.4258	1.6010	1.7959	2.0122	2.2522	2.5182	2.8127
13	1.1381	1.2936	1.4685	1.6651	1.8856	2.1329	2.4098	2.7196	3.0658
14	1.1495	1.3195	1.5126	1.7317	1.9799	2.2609	2.5785	2.9372	3.3417
15	1.1610	1.3459	1.5580	1.8009	2.0789	2.3966	2.7590	3.1722	3.6425
16	1.1726	1.3728	1.6047	1.8730	2.1829	2.5404	2.9522	3.4259	3.9703
17	1.1843	1.4002	1.6528	1.9479	2.2920	2.6928	3.1588	3.7000	4.3276
18	1.1961	1.4282	1.7024	2.0258	2.4066	2.8543	3.3799	3.9960	4.7171
19	1.2081	1.4568	1.7535	2.1068	2.5270	3.0256	3.6165	4.3157	5.1417
20	1.2202	1.4859	1.8061	2.1911	2.6533	3.2071	3.8697	4.6610	5.6044
21	1.2324	1.5157	1.8603	2.2788	2.7860	3.3996	4.1406	5.0338	6.1088
22	1.2447	1.5460	1.9161	2.3699	2.9253	3.6035	4.4304	5.4365	6.6586
23	1.2572	1.5769	1.9736	2.4647	3.0715	3.8197	4.7405	5.8715	7.2579
24	1.2697	1.6084	2.0328	2.5633	3.2251	4.0489	5.0724	6.3412	7.9111
25	1.2824	1.6406	2.0938	2.6658	3.3864	4.2919	5.4274	6.8485	8.6231
30	1.3478	1.8114	2.4273	3.2434	4.3219	5.7435	7.6123	10.063	13.268
40	1.4889	2.2080	3.2620	4.8010	7.0400	10.286	14.974	21.725	31.409
50	1.6446	2.6916	4.3839	7.1067	11.467	18.420	29.457	46.902	74.358
60	1.8167	3.2810	5.8916	10.520	18.679	32.988	57.946	101.26	176.03

Table E.1 (*concluded*)

					Interest rate					
10%	12%	14%	15%	16%	18%	20%	24%	28%	32%	36%
1.1000	1.1200	1.1400	1.1500	1.1600	1.1800	1.2000	1.2400	1.2800	1.3200	1.3600
1.2100	1.2544	1.2996	1.3225	1.3456	1.3924	1.4400	1.5376	1.6384	1.7424	1.8496
1.3310	1.4049	1.4815	1.5209	1.5609	1.6430	1.7280	1.9066	2.0972	2.3000	2.5155
1.4641	1.5735	1.6890	1.7490	1.8106	1.9388	2.0736	2.3642	2.6844	3.0360	3.4210
1.6105	1.7623	1.9254	2.0114	2.1003	2.2878	2.4883	2.9316	3.4360	4.0075	4.6526
1.7716	1.9738	2.1950	2.3131	2.4364	2.6996	2.9860	3.6352	4.3980	5.2899	6.3275
1.9487	2.2107	2.5023	2.6600	2.8262	3.1855	3.5832	4.5077	5.6295	6.9826	8.6054
2.1436	2.4760	2.8526	3.0590	3.2784	3.7589	4.2998	5.5895	7.2058	9.2170	11.703
2.3579	2.7731	3.2519	3.5179	3.8030	4.4355	5.1598	6.9310	9.2234	12.166	15.917
2.5937	3.1058	3.7072	4.0456	4.4114	5.2338	6.1917	8.5944	11.806	16.060	21.647
2.8531	3.4785	4.2262	4.6524	5.1173	6.1759	7.4301	10.657	15.112	21.199	29.439
3.1384	3.8960	4.8179	5.3503	5.9360	7.2876	8.9161	13.215	19.343	27.983	40.037
3.4523	4.3635	5.4924	6.1528	6.8858	8.5994	10.699	16.386	24.759	36.937	54.451
3.7975	4.8871	6.2613	7.0757	7.9875	10.147	12.839	20.319	31.691	48.757	74.053
4.1772	5.4736	7.1379	8.1371	9.2655	11.974	15.407	25.196	40.565	64.359	100.71
4.5950	6.1304	8.1372	9.3576	10.748	14.129	18.488	31.243	51.923	84.954	136.97
5.0545	6.8660	9.2765	10.761	12.468	16.672	22.186	38.741	66.461	112.14	186.28
5.5599	7.6900	10.575	12.375	14.463	19.673	26.623	48.039	85.071	148.02	253.34
6.1159	8.6128	12.056	14.232	16.777	23.214	31.948	59.568	108.89	195.39	344.54
6.7275	9.6463	13.743	16.367	19.461	27.393	38.338	73.864	139.38	257.92	468.57
7.4002	10.804	15.668	18.822	22.574	32.324	46.005	91.592	178.41	340.45	637.26
8.1403	12.100	17.861	21.645	26.186	38.142	55.206	113.57	228.36	449.39	866.67
8.9543	13.552	20.362	24.891	30.376	45.008	66.247	140.83	292.30	593.20	1178.7
9.8497	15.179	23.212	28.625	35.236	53.109	79.497	174.63	374.14	783.02	1603.0
10.835	17.000	26.462	32.919	40.874	62.669	95.396	216.54	478.90	1033.6	2180.1
17.449	29.960	50.950	66.212	85.850	143.37	237.38	634.82	1645.5	4142.1	10143.
45.259	93.051	188.88	267.86	378.72	750.38	1469.8	5455.9	19427.	66521.	*
117.39	289.00	700.23	1083.7	1670.7	3927.4	9100.4	46890.	*	*	*
304.48	897.60	2595.9	4384.0	7370.2	20555.	56348.	*	*	*	*

*FVIF > 99,999.

Table E.2 *Present Value of $1 to Be Received after t Periods $= 1/(1 + r)^t$*

				Interest rate					
Period	1%	2%	3%	4%	5%	6%	7%	8%	9%
1	0.9901	0.9804	0.9709	0.9615	0.9524	0.9434	0.9346	0.9259	0.9174
2	0.9803	0.9612	0.9426	0.9246	0.9070	0.8900	0.8734	0.8573	0.8417
3	0.9706	0.9423	0.9151	0.8890	0.8638	0.8396	0.8163	0.7938	0.7722
4	0.9610	0.9238	0.8885	0.8548	0.8227	0.7921	0.7629	0.7350	0.7084
5	0.9515	0.9057	0.8626	0.8219	0.7835	0.7473	0.7130	0.6806	0.6499
6	0.9420	0.8880	0.8375	0.7903	0.7462	0.7050	0.6663	0.6302	0.5963
7	0.9327	0.8706	0.8131	0.7599	0.7107	0.6651	0.6227	0.5835	0.5470
8	0.9235	0.8535	0.7894	0.7307	0.6768	0.6274	0.5820	0.5403	0.5019
9	0.9143	0.8368	0.7664	0.7026	0.6446	0.5919	0.5439	0.5002	0.4604
10	0.9053	0.8203	0.7441	0.6756	0.6139	0.5584	0.5083	0.4632	0.4224
11	0.8963	0.8043	0.7224	0.6496	0.5847	0.5268	0.4751	0.4289	0.3875
12	0.8874	0.7885	0.7014	0.6246	0.5568	0.4970	0.4440	0.3971	0.3555
13	0.8787	0.7730	0.6810	0.6006	0.5303	0.4688	0.4150	0.3677	0.3262
14	0.8700	0.7579	0.6611	0.5775	0.5051	0.4423	0.3878	0.3405	0.2992
15	0.8613	0.7430	0.6419	0.5553	0.4810	0.4173	0.3624	0.3152	0.2745
16	0.8528	0.7284	0.6232	0.5339	0.4581	0.3936	0.3387	0.2919	0.2519
17	0.8444	0.7142	0.6050	0.5134	0.4363	0.3714	0.3166	0.2703	0.2311
18	0.8360	0.7002	0.5874	0.4936	0.4155	0.3503	0.2959	0.2502	0.2120
19	0.8277	0.6864	0.5703	0.4746	0.3957	0.3305	0.2765	0.2317	0.1945
20	0.8195	0.6730	0.5537	0.4564	0.3769	0.3118	0.2584	0.2145	0.1784
21	0.8114	0.6598	0.5375	0.4388	0.3589	0.2942	0.2415	0.1987	0.1637
22	0.8034	0.6468	0.5219	0.4220	0.3418	0.2775	0.2257	0.1839	0.1502
23	0.7954	0.6342	0.5067	0.4057	0.3256	0.2618	0.2109	0.1703	0.1378
24	0.7876	0.6217	0.4919	0.3901	0.3101	0.2470	0.1971	0.1577	0.1264
25	0.7798	0.6095	0.4776	0.3751	0.2953	0.2330	0.1842	0.1460	0.1160
30	0.7419	0.5521	0.4120	0.3083	0.2314	0.1741	0.1314	0.0994	0.0754
40	0.6717	0.4529	0.3066	0.2083	0.1420	0.0972	0.0668	0.0460	0.0318
50	0.6080	0.3715	0.2281	0.1407	0.0872	0.0543	0.0339	0.0213	0.0134

Table E.2   *(concluded)*

					Interest rate					
10%	12%	14%	15%	16%	18%	20%	24%	28%	32%	36%
0.9091	0.8929	0.8772	0.8696	0.8621	0.8475	0.8333	0.8065	0.7813	0.7576	0.7353
0.8264	0.7972	0.7695	0.7561	0.7432	0.7182	0.6944	0.6504	0.6104	0.5739	0.5407
0.7513	0.7118	0.6750	0.6575	0.6407	0.6086	0.5787	0.5245	0.4768	0.4348	0.3975
0.6830	0.6355	0.5921	0.5718	0.5523	0.5158	0.4823	0.4230	0.3725	0.3294	0.2923
0.6209	0.5674	0.5194	0.4972	0.4761	0.4371	0.4019	0.3411	0.2910	0.2495	0.2149
0.5645	0.5066	0.4556	0.4323	0.4104	0.3704	0.3349	0.2751	0.2274	0.1890	0.1580
0.5132	0.4523	0.3996	0.3759	0.3538	0.3139	0.2791	0.2218	0.1776	0.1432	0.1162
0.4665	0.4039	0.3506	0.3269	0.3050	0.2660	0.2326	0.1789	0.1388	0.1085	0.0854
0.4241	0.3606	0.3075	0.2843	0.2630	0.2255	0.1938	0.1443	0.1084	0.0822	0.0628
0.3855	0.3220	0.2697	0.2472	0.2267	0.1911	0.1615	0.1164	0.0847	0.0623	0.0462
0.3505	0.2875	0.2366	0.2149	0.1954	0.1619	0.1346	0.0938	0.0662	0.0472	0.0340
0.3186	0.2567	0.2076	0.1869	0.1685	0.1372	0.1122	0.0757	0.0517	0.0357	0.0250
0.2897	0.2292	0.1821	0.1625	0.1452	0.1163	0.0935	0.0610	0.0404	0.0271	0.0184
0.2633	0.2046	0.1597	0.1413	0.1252	0.0985	0.0779	0.0492	0.0316	0.0205	0.0135
0.2394	0.1827	0.1401	0.1229	0.1079	0.0835	0.0649	0.0397	0.0247	0.0155	0.0099
0.2176	0.1631	0.1229	0.1069	0.0930	0.0708	0.0541	0.0320	0.0193	0.0118	0.0073
0.1978	0.1456	0.1078	0.0929	0.0802	0.0600	0.0451	0.0258	0.0150	0.0089	0.0054
0.1799	0.1300	0.0946	0.0808	0.0691	0.0508	0.0376	0.0208	0.0118	0.0068	0.0039
0.1635	0.1161	0.0829	0.0703	0.0596	0.0431	0.0313	0.0168	0.0092	0.0051	0.0029
0.1486	0.1037	0.0728	0.0611	0.0514	0.0365	0.0261	0.0135	0.0072	0.0039	0.0021
0.1351	0.0926	0.0638	0.0531	0.0443	0.0309	0.0217	0.0109	0.0056	0.0029	0.0016
0.1228	0.0826	0.0560	0.0462	0.0382	0.0262	0.0181	0.0088	0.0044	0.0022	0.0012
0.1117	0.0738	0.0491	0.0402	0.0329	0.0222	0.0151	0.0071	0.0034	0.0017	0.0008
0.1015	0.0659	0.0431	0.0349	0.0284	0.0188	0.0126	0.0057	0.0027	0.0013	0.0006
0.0923	0.0588	0.0378	0.0304	0.0245	0.0160	0.0105	0.0046	0.0021	0.0010	0.0005
0.0573	0.0334	0.0196	0.0151	0.0116	0.0070	0.0042	0.0016	0.0006	0.0002	0.0001
0.0221	0.0107	0.0053	0.0037	0.0026	0.0013	0.0007	0.0002	0.0001	*	*
0.0085	0.0035	0.0014	0.0009	0.0006	0.0003	0.0001	*	*	*	*

*The factor is zero to four decimal places.

Table E.3 *Present Value of an Annuity of $1 per Period for t Periods* $= [1 - 1/(1 + r)^t]/r$

Number of periods					Interest rate				
	1%	2%	3%	4%	5%	6%	7%	8%	9%
1	0.9901	0.9804	0.9709	0.9615	0.9524	0.9434	0.9346	0.9259	0.9174
2	1.9704	1.9416	1.9135	1.8861	1.8594	1.8334	1.8080	1.7833	1.7591
3	2.9410	2.8839	2.8286	2.7751	2.7232	2.6730	2.6243	2.5771	2.5313
4	3.9020	3.8077	3.7171	3.6299	3.5460	3.4651	3.3872	3.3121	3.2397
5	4.8534	4.7135	4.5797	4.4518	4.3295	4.2124	4.1002	3.9927	3.8897
6	5.7955	5.6014	5.4172	5.2421	5.0757	4.9173	4.7665	4.6229	4.4859
7	6.7282	6.4720	6.2303	6.0021	5.7864	5.5824	5.3893	5.2064	5.0330
8	7.6517	7.3255	7.0197	6.7327	6.4632	6.2098	5.9713	5.7466	5.5348
9	8.5660	8.1622	7.7861	7.4353	7.1078	6.8017	6.5152	6.2469	5.9952
10	9.4713	8.9826	8.5302	8.1109	7.7217	7.3601	7.0236	6.7101	6.4177
11	10.3676	9.7868	9.2526	8.7605	8.3064	7.8869	7.4987	7.1390	6.8052
12	11.2551	10.5753	9.9540	9.3851	8.8633	8.3838	7.9427	7.5361	7.1607
13	12.1337	11.3484	10.6350	9.9856	9.3936	8.8527	8.3577	7.9038	7.4869
14	13.0037	12.1062	11.2961	10.5631	9.8986	9.2950	8.7455	8.2442	7.7862
15	13.8651	12.8493	11.9379	11.1184	10.3797	9.7122	9.1079	8.5595	8.0607
16	14.7179	13.5777	12.5611	11.6523	10.8378	10.1059	9.4466	8.8514	8.3126
17	15.5623	14.2919	13.1661	12.1657	11.2741	10.4773	9.7632	9.1216	8.5436
18	16.3983	14.9920	13.7535	12.6593	11.6896	10.8276	10.0591	9.3719	8.7556
19	17.2260	15.6785	14.3238	13.1339	12.0853	11.1581	10.3356	9.6036	8.9501
20	18.0456	16.3514	14.8775	13.5903	12.4622	11.4699	10.5940	9.8181	9.1285
21	18.8570	17.0112	15.4150	14.0292	12.8212	11.7641	10.8355	10.0168	9.2922
22	19.6604	17.6580	15.9369	14.4511	13.1630	12.0416	11.0612	10.2007	9.4424
23	20.4558	18.2922	16.4436	14.8568	13.4886	12.3034	11.2722	10.3741	9.5802
24	21.2434	18.9139	16.9355	15.2470	13.7986	12.5504	11.4693	10.5288	9.7066
25	22.0232	19.5235	17.4131	15.6221	14.0939	12.7834	11.6536	10.6748	9.8226
30	25.8077	22.3965	19.6004	17.2920	15.3725	13.7648	12.4090	11.2578	10.2737
40	32.8347	27.3555	23.1148	19.7928	17.1591	15.0463	13.3317	11.9246	10.7574
50	39.1961	31.4236	25.7298	21.4822	18.2559	15.7619	13.8007	12.2335	10.9617

Table E.3 *(concluded)*

					Interest rate				
10%	12%	14%	15%	16%	18%	20%	24%	28%	32%
0.9091	0.8929	0.8772	0.8696	0.8621	0.8475	0.8333	0.8065	0.7813	0.7576
1.7355	1.6901	1.6467	1.6257	1.6052	1.5656	1.5278	1.4568	1.3916	1.3315
2.4869	2.4018	2.3216	2.2832	2.2459	2.1743	2.1065	1.9813	1.8684	1.7663
3.1699	3.0373	2.9137	2.8550	2.7982	2.6901	2.5887	2.4043	2.2410	2.0957
3.7908	3.6048	3.4331	3.3522	3.2743	3.1272	2.9906	2.7454	2.5320	2.3452
4.3553	4.1114	3.8887	3.7845	3.6847	3.4976	3.3255	3.0205	2.7594	2.5342
4.8684	4.5638	4.2883	4.1604	4.0386	3.8115	3.6046	3.2423	2.9370	2.6775
5.3349	4.9676	4.6389	4.4873	4.3436	4.0776	3.8372	3.4212	3.0758	2.7860
5.7590	5.3282	4.9464	4.7716	4.6065	4.3030	4.0310	3.5655	3.1842	2.8681
6.1446	5.6502	5.2161	5.0188	4.8332	4.4941	4.1925	3.6819	3.2689	2.9304
6.4951	5.9377	5.4527	5.2337	5.0286	4.6560	4.3271	3.7757	3.3351	2.9776
6.8137	6.1944	5.6603	5.4206	5.1971	4.7932	4.4392	3.8514	3.3868	3.0133
7.1034	6.4235	5.8424	5.5831	5.3423	4.9095	4.5327	3.9124	3.4272	3.0404
7.3667	6.6282	6.0021	5.7245	5.4675	5.0081	4.6106	3.9616	3.4587	3.0609
7.6061	6.8109	6.1422	5.8474	5.5755	5.0916	4.6755	4.0013	3.4834	3.0764
7.8237	6.9740	6.2651	5.9542	5.6685	5.1624	4.7296	4.0333	3.5026	3.0882
8.0216	7.1196	6.3729	6.0472	5.7487	5.2223	4.7746	4.0591	3.5177	3.0971
8.2014	7.2497	6.4674	6.1280	5.8178	5.2732	4.8122	4.0799	3.5294	3.1039
8.3649	7.3658	6.5504	6.1982	5.8775	5.3162	4.8435	4.0967	3.5386	3.1090
8.5136	7.4694	6.6231	6.2593	5.9288	5.3527	4.8696	4.1103	3.5458	3.1129
8.6487	7.5620	6.6870	6.3125	5.9731	5.3837	4.8913	4.1212	3.5514	3.1158
8.7715	7.6446	6.7429	6.3587	6.0113	5.4099	4.9094	4.1300	3.5558	3.1180
8.8832	7.7184	6.7921	6.3988	6.0442	5.4321	4.9245	4.1371	3.5592	3.1197
8.9847	7.7843	6.8351	6.4338	6.0726	5.4509	4.9371	4.1428	3.5619	3.1210
9.0770	7.8431	6.8729	6.4641	6.0971	5.4669	4.9476	4.1474	3.5640	3.1220
9.4269	8.0552	7.0027	6.5660	6.1772	5.5168	4.9789	4.1601	3.5693	3.1242
9.7791	8.2438	7.1050	6.6418	6.2335	5.5482	4.9966	4.1659	3.5712	3.1250
9.9148	8.3045	7.1327	6.6605	6.2463	5.5541	4.9995	4.1666	3.5714	3.1250

Table E.4 *Future Value of an Annuity of $1 per Period for t Periods* $= [(1 + r)^t - 1]/r$

Number of periods	1%	2%	3%	4%	5%	6%	7%	8%	9%
					Interest rate				
1	1.0000	1.0000	1.0000	1.0000	1.0000	1.0000	1.0000	1.0000	1.0000
2	2.0100	2.0200	2.0300	2.0400	2.0500	2.0600	2.0700	2.0800	2.0900
3	3.0301	3.0604	3.0909	3.1216	3.1525	3.1836	3.2149	3.2464	3.2781
4	4.0604	4.1216	4.1836	4.2465	4.3101	4.3746	4.4399	4.5061	4.5731
5	5.1010	5.2040	5.3091	5.4163	5.5256	5.6371	5.7507	5.8666	5.9847
6	6.1520	6.3081	6.4684	6.6330	6.8019	6.9753	7.1533	7.3359	7.5233
7	7.2135	7.4343	7.6625	7.8983	8.1420	8.3938	8.6540	8.9228	9.2004
8	8.2857	8.5830	8.8932	9.2142	9.5491	9.8975	10.260	10.637	11.028
9	9.3685	9.7546	10.159	10.583	11.027	11.491	11.978	12.488	13.021
10	10.462	10.950	11.464	12.006	12.578	13.181	13.816	14.487	15.193
11	11.567	12.169	12.808	13.486	14.207	14.972	15.784	16.645	17.560
12	12.683	13.412	14.192	15.026	15.917	16.870	17.888	18.977	20.141
13	13.809	14.680	15.618	16.627	17.713	18.882	20.141	21.495	22.953
14	14.947	15.974	17.086	18.292	19.599	21.015	22.550	24.215	26.019
15	16.097	17.293	18.599	20.024	21.579	23.276	25.129	27.152	29.361
16	17.258	18.639	20.157	21.825	23.657	25.673	27.888	30.324	33.003
17	18.430	20.012	21.762	23.698	25.840	28.213	30.840	33.750	36.974
18	19.615	21.412	23.414	25.645	28.132	30.906	33.999	37.450	41.301
19	20.811	22.841	25.117	27.671	30.539	33.760	37.379	41.446	46.018
20	22.019	24.297	26.870	29.778	33.066	36.786	40.995	45.762	51.160
21	23.239	25.783	28.676	31.969	35.719	39.993	44.865	50.423	56.765
22	24.472	27.299	30.537	34.248	38.505	43.392	49.006	55.457	62.873
23	25.716	28.845	32.453	36.618	41.430	46.996	53.436	60.893	69.532
24	26.973	30.422	34.426	39.083	44.502	50.816	58.177	66.765	76.790
25	28.243	32.030	36.459	41.646	47.727	54.865	63.249	73.106	84.701
30	34.785	40.568	47.575	56.085	66.439	79.058	94.461	113.28	136.31
40	48.886	60.402	75.401	95.026	120.80	154.76	199.64	259.06	337.88
50	64.463	84.579	112.80	152.67	209.35	290.34	406.53	573.77	815.08
60	81.670	114.05	163.05	237.99	353.58	533.13	813.52	1253.2	1944.8

Table E.4 (concluded)

| | | | | | Interest rate | | | | | |
10%	12%	14%	15%	16%	18%	20%	24%	28%	32%	36%
1.0000	1.0000	1.0000	1.0000	1.0000	1.0000	1.0000	1.0000	1.0000	1.0000	1.0000
2.1000	2.1200	2.1400	2.1500	2.1600	2.1800	2.2000	2.2400	2.2800	2.3200	2.3600
3.3100	3.3744	3.4396	3.4725	3.5056	3.5724	3.6400	3.7776	3.9184	4.0624	4.2096
4.6410	4.7793	4.9211	4.9934	5.0665	5.2154	5.3680	5.6842	6.0156	6.3624	6.7251
6.1051	6.3528	6.6101	6.7424	6.8771	7.1542	7.4416	8.0484	8.6999	9.3983	10.146
7.7156	8.1152	8.5355	8.7537	8.9775	9.4420	9.9299	10.980	12.136	13.406	14.799
9.4872	10.089	10.730	11.067	11.414	12.142	12.916	14.615	16.534	18.696	21.126
11.436	12.300	13.233	13.727	14.240	15.327	16.499	19.123	22.163	25.678	29.732
13.579	14.776	16.085	16.786	17.519	19.086	20.799	24.712	29.369	34.895	41.435
15.937	17.549	19.337	20.304	21.321	23.521	25.959	31.643	38.593	47.062	57.352
18.531	20.655	23.045	24.349	25.733	28.755	32.150	40.238	50.398	63.122	78.998
21.384	24.133	27.271	29.002	30.850	34.931	39.581	50.895	65.510	84.320	108.44
24.523	28.029	32.089	34.352	36.786	42.219	48.497	64.110	84.853	112.30	148.47
27.975	32.393	37.581	40.505	43.672	50.818	59.196	80.496	109.61	149.24	202.93
31.772	37.280	43.842	47.580	51.660	60.965	72.035	100.82	141.30	198.00	276.98
35.950	42.753	50.980	55.717	60.925	72.939	87.442	126.01	181.87	262.36	377.69
40.545	48.884	59.118	65.075	71.673	87.068	105.93	157.25	233.79	347.31	514.66
45.599	55.750	68.394	75.836	84.141	103.74	128.12	195.99	300.25	459.45	700.94
51.159	63.440	78.969	88.212	98.603	123.41	154.74	244.03	385.32	607.47	954.28
57.275	72.052	91.025	102.44	115.38	146.63	186.69	303.60	494.21	802.86	1298.8
64.002	81.699	104.77	118.81	134.84	174.02	225.03	377.46	633.59	1060.8	1767.4
71.403	92.503	120.44	137.63	157.41	206.34	271.03	469.06	812.00	1401.2	2404.7
79.543	104.60	138.30	159.28	183.60	244.49	326.24	582.63	1040.4	1850.6	3271.3
88.497	118.16	158.66	184.17	213.98	289.49	392.48	723.46	1332.7	2443.8	4450.0
98.347	133.33	181.87	212.79	249.21	342.60	471.98	898.09	1706.8	3226.8	6053.0
164.49	241.33	356.79	434.75	530.31	790.95	1181.9	2640.9	5873.2	12941.	28172.3
442.59	767.09	1342.0	1779.1	2360.8	4163.2	7343.9	22729.	69377.	*	*
1163.9	2400.0	4994.5	7217.7	10436.	21813.	45497.	*	*	*	*
3034.8	7471.6	18535.	29220.	46058.	*	*	*	*	*	*

*FVIFA > 99,999.

Name Index

Subject Index

C